Catharina Day

IRELAND

Cadogan Books plc
London House, Parkgate Road, London SW11 4NQ, UK
Distributed in North America by
The Globe Pequot Press
6 Business Park Road, PO Box 833, Old Saybrook,
Connecticut 06475–0833

Book and cover design by Animage
Cover illustrations by Povl Webb
Maps © Cadogan Guides, drawn by Map Creation Ltd

Series Editors: Rachel Fielding and Vicki Ingle

Editing: Polly Phillimore and Linda McQueen
Updating: Jennifer Keegan
Proofreading: Teresa Greally
Indexing: Judith Wardman
Production: Rupert Wheeler Book Production Services

A catalogue record for this book is available from the British Library
ISBN 0–94–7754–64–4

US Library of Congress Cataloging-in-Publication-Data
Day, Catharina. 1957–
    Ireland/Catharina Day -- 3rd ed.
    p. cm. --- (Cadogan guides)
    Includes bibliographical references (p.) and index
    ISBN 0–947754–64–4
1. Ireland--Guidebooks.   I. Title   II. Series
DA980.D39   1995
914.1505'824--dc20   95–2699 CIP

Output by Bookworm Ltd, Manchester
Printed and bound in Finland by Werner Söderström Oy
on Kymexcote

To My Mother

Acknowledgements

Numerous people have helped me compile this book, and to them I wish to say many thanks. It would take many pages to mention all but a few by name for through my researches on the guide I have met lots of delightful people who have given me an insight into their locality. In particular I would like to thank Bord Fáilte and the Northern Ireland Tourist Board who have always been extremely generous with information, advice and good-will. My family have over the years been very supportive and a great help. My mother has been an enthusiastic gatherer of information and her wide general knowledge has been invaluable. My sister Angelique has been a great help, especially with Ulster, as has my sister Georgina with Co. Laois and Co. Offaly. My husband Simon has helped me in countless ways, acting as my agent, and trying out hotels and restaurants on his business trips to Dublin. I am indebted to the late Araminta Swiney who advised me on what to leave out, Flora Armstrong for her initial help with South Ulster and Co. Armagh, Emily Sheard for her work on the maps, John Colclough who recommended eating out and places to stay, Victoria Ingle who helped reshape the 2nd edition and edited it, Rochelle Guillard and Dawn Harvey who coped with my infant twins and my three-year-old, as well as the typing on the 2nd edition. Many thanks to Polly Phillimore who has edited this latest edition, and to Jennifer Keegan who has been a great help updating the practical information. Finally thanks to Paula Levy who first gave me the opportunity to explore and write about this lovely country.

About the Author

Catharina Day comes from a long-established Irish family. She was born in Kenya but moved to County Donegal as a small child. She attended Derry High School before travelling to a convent boarding school, and then University in England. She was married in County Donegal and visits frequently with her husband and four children from her home in Scotland. She has compiled an anthology of Irish literature.

About the Updater

Jennifer Keegan was born in Dublin of a French mother and Irish father. She studied languages at Trinity College and after spending a year in Madrid, went to work for Vogue in London. In addition to writing film and travel pieces, she was responsible for the revision of the Cadogan Guide to New York. She currently lives in Ireland and is a presenter on a fashion programme for Irish television.

Updater's Acknowledgements

Many thanks to my parents for their tolerance and all those who helped with my travels and research—especially Justine Keane, Hilary Finlay, Gary Coyle, Kenneth Deale, Colm McGee, Norma and Brien Boyd—and also to project editor Polly Phillimore for all her patience and her cheerfulness.

Contents

Travel   1–16

Practical A–Z   17–62

Topics   63–80

Introduction

Ireland is the perfect place to take a holiday. This lovely island has physical and spiritual qualities that are seldom found in the Western World. The pace of life is relaxing; the scenery is beautiful and varied, with the sea never far from sight. Dublin, the capital, is cultural, attractive and easy to explore. The people of the country are easy to meet and invariably courteous and friendly. The climate is good and damp, and the sunshine, when it comes, intensifies the already beautiful colours of the landscape. Forget the sun culture and all its paraphernalia; travel with stout shoes and a warm jersey. There is no such thing as a tiresome, hot journey in Ireland. The roads are usually empty and traffic jams are still an exception. Some visitors bent on 'doing' Ireland get from one end of the country to the other within a day's drive, but this is not the way to travel at all; if you rush, the charm of the country and the people will pass you by. The Irish do not approve of rushing.

Whichever direction you decide to go, it is possible to stay in tranquil country houses where the proportions and the furnishings of the rooms are redolent of a more gracious age. Not only is the food delicious, and made from the freshest seafood, local meat, game and vegetables, you also can get well-chosen wines and, of course, decent whiskey and beer. You will find the owners and staff of these places keen to help with any request you have, whether it's finding the origins of your great-granny, or directing you to the best fishing, golf, beaches, crafts, and sites of historical interest.

It is so easy to travel in a country where you can explain your needs in English, and find yourself understood. Those dry archaeological and historical facts suddenly become much more fascinating when you can ask for the local version of events, and hear for yourself the wonderful stories which make up history. The way that the Irish speak is another pleasure in store for you. You will find a race who can express themselves with great character, humour and exactness.

When you are in Ireland, it is certain that the irritations and annoyances which accompany one through everyday life will disappear, and the desire for a good day's tramp in the mountains, a spot of fishing, or a good read before a warm fire will become realities. However, it is important not to stick rigidly to a scheme, and become irritated when it has to be delayed for a while, for nothing in Ireland can be planned right down to the last detail. Information can sometimes only be found out on the spot; and opening times, timetables and other schedules are more subject to change than in many other countries.

Ireland is not a rich island, and is still largely agricultural. It has small areas of industrial development, and it does not have huge motorways, endless suburbia, belching factories, marching powerlines, and too many of the ugly side-effects of industry. Its population is small—about five million, and the Six Counties which form part of the United Kingdom make up around 1,556,000 of that total. The differences between the Six Counties, which are colloquially referred to as 'the North', and the Republic of Ireland, 'the South', are explored in the **History** section later in the guide, and will become apparent as you read the chapter on each county. Until the recent ceasefire (holding at the time of writing) it was a commonly held misconception that it was dangerous to travel in the North. Violence was confined to very small areas and no tourist has ever been harmed by the 'Troubles'. Sensible, unprejudiced travellers will soon discover that, with the exception of a few well-known areas, the North is a quiet, unspoilt and attractive region. If your sympathy for the ordinary people of the province and your admiration for their courage and forbearance has been stirred by their problems, one of the most positive things you can do is visit the province itself. It helps the tourist trade and the confidence of the people.

Both North and South share a fascinating past, as Yeats wrote: 'Behind all Irish history hangs a great tapestry, even Christianity had to accept, and be itself pictured there.' The Irish as a race have a long memory, and a poetic imagination which gives each hill, lough and pile of stones a background or story. The history of Ireland has been turbulent, and its telling fraught with prejudice and misunderstandings. But a fascinating thing to do is to approach it through its excellent literary tradition. Ireland had its Golden Age of learning roughly between the 6th and 11th centuries. Frank O'Connor described it as the civilization of 'the little monasteries'. The monks wrote down the Celtic oral culture, wrote poetry and honoured God during the Dark Ages, when the rest of the Continent was in the hands of the Barbarians. Ireland also had a strict bardic tradition in which members of the poets' guild studied for up to 12 years before they were qualified. From that disciplined environment came mature poetry as evocative and delicate as a Chinese poem: stirring epics such as *The Tain*, which chronicles the wars of a heroic race, and moving love laments. Most of us can only read these poems in translation from the Gaelic; luckily the translations by present-day Irish poets bring them close to us. The voice of the Gaelic poet comments and bemoans the destruction of the Gaelic ways from the 16th century onwards. From the 18th century, the ability of the Irish to express themselves in the language of the Saxon is apparent from the works of Jonathan Swift through to W. B. Yeats and the marvellous poets of today, such as Seamus Heaney. Poetry, the novel and theatre have continued to thrive since the heady days of cultural renaissance and the uprising against the British in 1916. It is wonderful to go to the Abbey Theatre in Dublin or the Druid Theatre in Galway to see a play by Sean O'Casey or Brian Friel. Arts and music festivals flourish throughout the country, as do local historical societies.

Modern Ireland still conjures up a romantic idyll of whitewashed cottages set against a mountain landscape. Yet its highly educated young population has attracted many technological companies who wish to take advantage of their skills. New buildings are constantly appearing to swell the towns, some of them terribly ugly, and there are even such things as roundabouts! As a traveller, you will be able to enjoy all the conveniences of modern-day Europe, but also lose yourself in wilderness and beauty.

By the end of your holiday you may feel tuned in to this country and its people to the point where that famous saying can be aired yet again: that (the English) are more Irish than the Irish themselves: *Ipsis Hibernis hiberniores.*

Guide to the Guide

After a brief introduction to this island and its people, and a selection of the Best of Ireland, there is a comprehensive **Travel** section, followed by the **Practical A–Z** packed with information that will help you get the best from your visit, including advice on where to stay and eat, sports and leisure activities, and even on how to trace your ancestors. The next section, **Topics**, gives brief insights into notable features of Ireland and Irish life which includes some fascinating pieces on the Fairy People and Sacred Trees as well as Historic Houses and Gardens. The short and simple **History** section from pagan times to the present day, outlines the main events and problems that constitute the complex Ireland of today; this is followed by a brief résumé of the religious background and a selection of the country's most famous saints.

The 32 counties are divided into the provinces of **Munster, Connacht, Ulster** and **Leinster**, with Belfast and Dublin featuring separately from the rest of the counties. This constitutes a gazetteer of the whole country with lots of local history and anecdotal knowledge together with descriptions and details of the places of interest. Full, practical lists of transport facilities, tourist information centres and festivals are given at the beginnings of each county section, with shopping and leisure activities, places to stay and eat and entertainment possibilities at the end of each county.

At the end of the book there are features on the **Old Gods and Heroes**, ancient sites and early architecture (with a glossary of terms); an essay on **Language**; a **Chronology**; a recommended **Further Reading** list; and a comprehensive index.

Essential Geography

When I was a child, the shape of Ireland reminded me of a lamb on its side without its tail, its curves and indentations adding up to something rather comforting. Now I know also what beautiful inlets and fine scenery its shape of 32,524 square miles (84,236sq km) traces out, especially if you follow its 2000 miles (3200km) of curving coastline all the way round. Ireland is 303 miles (486km) long, and just 189 miles (303km) across at its widest point. Most of the hills and mountains rise up around the coast forming a rim, whilst the middle of the country is a great limestone plain, gently rolling and flat in parts, scattered with lakes and areas of bog. It is drained by the coiling River Shannon which nearly divides the country in two, finally entering the sea in the southwest between County Clare and County Kerry.

The Counties of Ireland

Imagine for a moment that Ireland is shaped rather like a saucer, with mountains around the rim and flat land in the middle. Most of the coastline is dramatic: ancient rock cliffs alternate with sandy bays, whilst the large central plain of limestone is dotted with low hills called drumlins. Blanket bog has covered a good deal of the lowland where the surface water has collected and been prevented from draining to the sea by the mountains. But where the surface rises above the water table the land is covered in a rich, light soil, which grows the grass that ultimately produces all that delicious Irish butter.

There are many pretty rivers but, after the great Shannon, the other big ones are the Bann in the north; and the Suir, Nore and Barrow in the southeast. Amongst the most scenic are the Blackwater (in County Cork), the Boyne, the Slaney, the Bonet, the Bann and the Suir; they also have the additional bonus of being good salmon rivers. The highest mountain in Ireland is the Carrantuohill (3414ft, 1041m), part of the Macgillicuddy's Reeks in County Kerry. Other beautiful mountain ranges are the Blue Stacks and the Derryveagh Mountains in County Donegal; the Twelve Bens and Maamturk Range in County Galway, and the Mourne Mountains in County Down. Impressive cliffs and golden beaches are commonplace along the west coast, the highest cliffs being those at Slieve League in County Donegal, which rise nearly 2000ft (656m) from the sea. The many hundreds of lovely lakes, large and small, are scattered throughout the countryside. The largest, but not the most beautiful, is Lough Neagh in the north, which covers more than 150 square miles (388sq km). Other large and lovely loughs are the Corrib, Mask and Conn in the west; and, of course, the Loughs Allen, Derg and Ree through which the River Shannon flows, forming a huge waterway through the middle of Ireland.

Ireland can most conveniently be divided into the provinces of Munster, Connacht, Ulster and Leinster; these are ancient divisions dating from the time when pre-Christian kings fought and jostled to increase their lands. The four modern provinces are no longer of political significance; indeed, Ulster is split between the Republic and the British State. But historically, socially and culturally they are very important, and the 32 counties of Ireland are shared out between them in the following way:

Munster covers 29.3 per cent of Ireland and consists of the Counties of Limerick, Kerry, Cork, Waterford, Tipperary and Clare.

Connacht covers 21 per cent of Ireland and consists of the Counties of Galway, Mayo, Roscommon, Sligo and Leitrim.

Ulster covers 26.3 per cent of Ireland and consists of the Counties of Donegal, Monaghan and Cavan, which are in the Republic; and Fermanagh, Tyrone, Londonderry ('Derry', in the Republic), Antrim, Down and Armagh, which are in Northern Ireland.

Leinster covers 23.4 per cent of Ireland and consists of the Counties of Meath, Louth, Longford, Westmeath, Offaly (formerly King's County), Laois (formerly Queen's County), Kildare, Dublin, Wicklow, Wexford, Carlow and Kilkenny.

The four modern provinces correspond roughly to very ancient divisions of Ireland derived from the Fir Bolg invaders. They are used as general geographical indicators: thus, Ulster for North, Munster for South, Leinster for East and Connacht for West. The provincial boundaries have administrative uses for matters such as the Irish language, but more important is the cultural character of the division. As one ancient authority has it: Ulster represents Battle (*Cath*); Munster, Music (*Seis*); Leinster, Prosperity (*Blath*); Connacht, Learning (*Fis*). Perhaps this is too much of a generalization, but you may find it an interesting pastime to recognize the subtle characteristics that set off the different quarters of Ireland.

The Gaeltacht

This is the name given to several areas in Ireland where (Irish) Gaelic is spoken as the everyday language. These areas are mainly in the West, in Counties Donegal, Mayo, Galway and Kerry. You can expect all the signposts to be in Irish. Government grants have encouraged people to stay in the Irish-speaking areas, which are usually very beautiful but poor and isolated. So the tourist industry is important. These areas are relatively unspoiled, with few big hotels; you can B&B in local homes, have some magnificent sport with the fish and the sea, and enjoy the excellent traditional music and dancing which goes on in the bars and in the *Teach Siamsa* (House of Musical Entertainment). Crafts have been encouraged in the Gaeltacht and you will be able to buy hand-woven tweeds and pottery.

The Best of Ireland

Ruined friaries and churches: Cong, Co. Mayo; Killaloe, Co. Clare; Dysert O Dea, Co. Clare; Clonfert Cathedral, Co. Galway; Moyne, Co. Mayo.

Round towers: Glendalough, Co. Wicklow; Devenish Island, Co. Fermanagh; Ardmore, Co. Waterford.

Carved high crosses: Moone, Co. Kildare; Cardonagh, Co. Donegal.

Castles: Carrickfergus and Dunluce Castles, Co. Antrim; Parke's Castle, Co. Leitrim; Cahir Castle, Co. Tipperary.

Fine houses: Castletown, Co. Kildare; Bantry Bay House, Co. Cork; Castle Coole, Co. Fermanagh.

Gardens: Birr Castle, Co. Offaly; Mountstewart, Co. Down; Annestown, Co. Cork; Glenveagh, Co. Donegal.

Folk park: Cultra Park, Co. Down; Bunratty, Co. Clare.

Beaches: There are many beautiful, unspoilt strands; in particular, Portsalon, Co. Donegal; Magilligan, Co. Londonderry; Keel, Achill Island, Co. Mayo; Inch, Co. Kerry; Streedagh, Co. Sligo; Ballyconneely, Co. Galway; White Strand and Spanish Point, Co. Clare; White Park Bay, Co. Antrim.

Golf courses: Bundoran; the Royal County Down, Newcastle; Royal Portrush; Portmarnock; Lahinch; Ballybunion; Killarney; Galway City; Rosses Point; Portsalon, Co. Donegal.

Landscapes: Most of the coastal and mountain stretches of Connacht, especially between Westport and Clifden; views from the top of Croagh Patrick; and Achill Island. Wild bog betwen Mulrany and Bangor Erris; coastal and mountain stretches in Co. Donegal, especially from Lough Salt and from the top of Muckish Mountain. The Antrim Coast, the Burren, Bantry Bay, Knockmealdown Mountains, the Ring of Kerry, the Sperrin Mountains.

Art galleries: The Glebe Gallery, Co. Donegal; the National Gallery, Dublin; the Crawford Gallery, Cork; Chester Beatty, Dublin.

Museums: Ulster; National Museum, Dublin.

Craftshops: Ballycasey Workshops, Co. Tipperary; Nicholas Mosse Pottery, Bennetsbridge, Co. Kilkenny; Craft Park, Roundstone, Co. Galway.

Pubs: Dick Macks, Dingle; Mary Anne's, Castletownshend; Crown Liquor Saloon, Belfast; The Stag's Head, Dublin; Rita's, Portsalon; Moran's on the Weir, Clarinbridge.

Festivals: Wexford Opera Festival; Kilkenny Arts Week; Galway Film Festival; Galway Oyster Festival; Belfast Arts Festival; Dublin Drama Festival; *Feis na nGleann*, Co. Antrim; Music Festival in Great Irish Houses.

Horse events: Dublin Horse Show; Ulster Harp National; Galway Races.

Unusual activity: Seaweed bath, Enniscrone; point-to-points anywhere; Tuam Races; Sham Fight, Scarva, on 13 July; hurling match anywhere in Ireland; Donegal Motor Rally; Puck Fair, Killorgin; Lammas Fair, Ballycastle; visit to Doon Well, Co. Donegal; any Georgian Society tour; Lough Derg Gourmet Ride; farm visit to Leslie Hill, Ballymoney.

A Note on Names

The reader will find that there are occasions when place names vary in spelling from those in this guide book. This is because different translations from the Gaelic exist; there is no completely standardized map to follow. Bartholomews, Ordnance Survey, the RAC and the AA produce very good and detailed maps.

Travel

By Air to the Republic of Ireland

From Europe

British Airways, British Midland, Crossair, Air France, Ryanair, Intermanx, City Jet, TAP Air Portugal, Sabena, Swiss Air, SAS (Scandinavian Airlines), **Lufthansa** and **Iberia** run regular scheduled flights from European capitals and major cities. The Irish national airline, **Aer Lingus,** also handles an enormous number of flights from European destinations, and, if you are going to immerse yourself in all things Irish, you might as well start with this airline, with its air hostesses dressed in green. For flight reservations and information in London, call ✆ (0181) 569 5555.

There are direct flights to Dublin, Cork and Shannon from the four main **London** airports (Heathrow, Gatwick, Luton and Stansted). But there are also numerous additional flights to Irish cities from British regional airports. **Ryanair,** for example, has regular flights connecting Dublin to Cardiff, Coventry, Liverpool and London; Knock to Birmingham, Coventry, Leeds/Bradford and Manchester; Waterford to Liverpool; and also from London (Luton) to Cork, Dublin, Donegal, Galway, Kerry, Shannon and Sligo. For Ryanair in London, ✆ (0171) 435 7101.

Prices are always in a state of flux but are reasonable by European standards. There is a bewildering array of price structures. To give some guideline, SuperApex prices for return flights from London to Dublin cost around £60 to £90.

The major airlines also offer a wide variety of holiday-break fares, where the price of the flight depends on how long you stay and when you travel. You can save a lot of money on these, so it is worth checking out the possibilities.

From the USA and Canada

The main airports for transatlantic flights are **Dublin** and **Shannon,** which are served by direct scheduled flights from Atlanta, Boston, Chicago, Montreal and New York. The main transatlantic carriers flying direct to Ireland are **Delta Air Lines, Aer Lingus** and **Tower Air** who now fly two scheduled flights per week via Newark, but of course many others fly to European destinations, where you can pick up connecting flights.

Since **prices** are constantly changing and there are numerous kinds of deals on offer, the first thing to do is find yourself a travel agent who is capable of laying the current options before you. The time of year you choose can make a great difference to the price and availability of tickets. Expect to pay more and to have to book earlier if you want to travel between June and August. Apex and SuperApex are the most reliable and flexible of the cheap fares. New York to Shannon or Dublin return on an Apex fare ranges from about US$480 in the winter, to US$580 in the shoulder seasons, and US$695 in mid-summer. A number of companies offer cheaper charter flights to Ireland—look in the Sunday travel section of *The New York Times.* Remember to read all the small print as there are often catches, such as big cancellation penalties, restrictions about changing the dates of your flights; and sometimes charter contracts include provisions that allow charter companies to cancel your flight, change the dates of travel and add fuel surcharges after you have paid your fare. If you are considering travelling on to other destinations by air (e.g. London–Dublin–Cork–London or Dublin–Cork–Dublin), it is cheaper to buy a ticket which includes the additional flights with the transatlantic flight, rather than pay for the excursions separately.

Shannon Airport, by the way, is a free-port offering a huge variety of duty-free goods plus a selection of Irish specialities: cut crystal glass, Connemara rugs and marble, Donegal tweed, etcetera. If you do not want to get burdened with lots of presents and packages during your stay in Ireland, you can get everything here at the last minute. Goods bought in the duty-free area just before take-off will be taken on the plane without any extra weight charges. Information on transport and accommodation is available at the **tourist offices** at all the major airports, open all the year round.

transport from the airports

Buses and trains run between the main airports and city centres. They are comfortable, frequent and economic; taxi drivers, by contrast, tend to ask a dramatically high price for a ride into the city. Dublin Bus runs a service between Dublin Airport and the Central Bus Station every 20 minutes; the fare is IR£2.50 one way. Irish Bus runs similar services from Cork Airport to Cork (IR£1.75), and from Shannon Airport to Limerick, the nearest city, 15 miles (25km) away (IR£3.30).

By Air to Northern Ireland

From Europe

British Airways, British Midland, Loganair, Manx Airlines, Air City, Jersey European Airways, KLM run regular flights to Northern Ireland from the UK, Paris and Amsterdam.

The main airport is **Belfast International** (Belfast Aldergrove), but Belfast also has another, smaller airport called Belfast Harbour (also referred to as Belfast City). There are also flights to **Londonderry/Derry** (Eglinton Airport) and **Enniskillen**.

Belfast International serves connections from Birmingham, Bristol, Cardiff, East Midlands, Edinburgh, Glasgow, Leeds/Bradford, Manchester and Newcastle-upon-Tyne. Belfast Harbour Airport serves flights from Birmingham, Blackpool, Edinburgh, Exeter, Glasgow, the Isle of Man, Leeds/Bradford, London (Luton), Manchester, Newcastle-upon-Tyne and Teeside. Eglinton is served by direct flights from Glasgow and Manchester.

A full-price British Midlands return from Belfast to London costs £216. However prices range from £75 to £216. The £75 price offer is if you fly to London and back over a weekend.

There are still no direct flights from **Dublin to Belfast**, mainly because the road and rail links fulfil this need.

From the USA and Canada

There are **no major airlines** operating direct scheduled flights between North America and Northern Ireland. This means that transatlantic travellers to Northern Ireland have to take a direct charter flight, or travel to Great Britain or another European destination, and then take an onward flight to Belfast from there. For charter companies that operate flights to Belfast from New York, Florida and Toronto, look for the advertisements in the travel pages of the major newspapers.

transport from the airports

There is a regular **Airbus** service into Belfast from Belfast International (£3.50 single), and a regular **train** service from Belfast Harbour/City Airport to Belfast Central Station. For Derry from Belfast International Airport it is quickest to take a **taxi** to Antrim railway station (six trains to Derry per day). The 10-minute drive costs an exorbitant £6 or so, but you can spread the cost by sharing the taxi with other travellers.

By Boat

Gone are the days when you could cross the Atlantic by **liner**. The only regular, scheduled sea-crossings to Ireland these days come from Great Britain and continental Europe. The one exception is Cunard Line's *QE2*, which occasionally stops off to pick up travellers at Cork (Cobh) on its way from Southampton to New York, but not on its way back. This has style, but at a price: Cork to New York costs a minimum of £1095 per passenger.

The **ferries** from the British west coast tend to cross the Irish Sea in the shortest distance possible: from the points along the coasts of Wales and Scotland which stretch out furthest towards the east coast of Ireland. Which port and crossing you choose will depend on where you are starting from, and where you wish to go in Ireland—which is not quite such an obvious statement as it may seem. The main crossings are as follows: Fishguard and Pembroke in South Wales serve Rosslare Harbour (near Wexford) and southeast Ireland. Holyhead, off Anglesey in North Wales, takes passengers to Dublin and the neighbouring port of Dun Laoghaire, in the centre of the east coast. Since early 1994 this route is also served by a high-speed **catamaran** which crosses the Irish Sea in one hour and 50 minutes. Northern Ireland has two main ports: Belfast and nearby Larne, which are served by ferries and the sea cat taking the short crossing from Cairnryan and neighbouring Stranraer in southwest Scotland, and by ferries taking the much longer journey from Liverpool.

A service now connects Swansea, in South Wales, to Cork, serving the south of the Republic. Cork also has ferry services to Le Havre and Roscoff in northern France, and there is a service between Rosslare and Le Havre. Lastly, there is a seasonal service to the Isle of Man from Dublin. All the ferry ports are well connected to bus and rail transport (*see* pp.6–7), and all the ferry services have drive-on/drive-off facilities for car drivers.

Prices depend very much on the time of year and the length of the crossing. Price structures also relate to how long you intend to stay in Ireland and, if you are taking your car, the number of passengers in the car, the length of the car, and so forth. To give you some idea of costs, here are a few examples. Figures quoted are for 1 adult, 2 adults and a car or

4 adults and a car. The upper and lower estimates are for high and low season respectively. With P&O, crossing from Cairnryan to Larne in Northern Ireland, passengers pay £20 to £22 each way; cars cost from £137 to £170 each way including 2 adults; but there are also special 60hr and 120hr excursion fares. On Sealink's service between Fishguard and Rosslare in the Republic, passengers pay £17 to £23 each way; cars cost £74 to £175 each way, but this price includes up to four people travelling with the car. The Sealink Catamaran costs approximately £5 more for passengers and £18 more for a car. Cars, including up to four passengers, on the Swansea/Cork ferry cost between £80 and £159. Passenger fares for children are approximately half the adult fare.

Crossings from France are rather more expensive. Le Havre to Rosslare with Irish Ferries costs IR£57–IR£82 for one adult, IR£215–£490 for two adults and a car, and IR£266–£375 for four adults and a car. These prices are one-way.

ferry services

To the Republic from Great Britain

B&I Line, Dublin, ✆ (01) 661 0511; London, ✆ (0171) 499 5744; Liverpool, ✆ (0151) 2273131):

Holyhead–Dublin, 2 sailings daily, all year, 3¼hrs, ✆ (0171) 734 4681.

Pembroke–Rosslare, 2 sailings daily, 21 May–1 Oct; 1 sailing daily rest of year, 4¼hrs.

Sealink British Ferries Ashford, Kent, ✆ (01233) 647022; Dublin, ✆ (01) 280 0338/280 8844:

Holyhead–Dun Laoghaire, 4 sailings daily, all year (excluding 25–26 Dec), 3½hrs, plus 2 catamaran sailings.

Fishguard–Rosslare, 2 sailings daily, 3½hrs (excluding 25–26 Dec).

Isle of Man Steam Packet Company, Douglas, ✆ (0624) 661661:

Isle of Man–Dublin, mid-May–mid-Sept, 4½hrs (contact operators for schedule); Sea Cat, 2hrs 40mins.

Isle of Man–Belfast, mid-May–mid-Sept, 5hrs; Sea Cat, 2hrs 40mins.

Swansea Cork Ferries, Swansea, ✆ (01792) 456116; Cork ✆ (021) 271166:

Swansea–Cork, 1 sailing every other day in each direction 10hrs (overnight crossing from Swansea).

To Northern Ireland from Great Britain

Sealink British Ferries, Ashford, Kent, ✆ (01233) 647022):

Stranraer–Larne, 9–10 sailings daily, all year (excluding 25–26 Dec and 1 Jan), 2hrs 20mins.

P & O European Ferries, Cairnryan, ✆ (01581) 200276; London, ✆ (0181) 575 8555; Larne (01574) 274321:

Cairnryan–Larne, 6 sailings daily, all year, 2¼hrs.

Norse Irish Ferries, Belfast, ✆ (080232) 779090:

Liverpool–Belfast, 1 sailing every other evening, all year, 11hrs.

Seacat, Dublin, ✆ (01) 661 1731 (from mid-Feb '95):

Belfast–Stranraer, 4 sailings daily, all year, 1½hrs.

Note that at some peak times of the year—Easter, Christmas and around the April and October bank holidays—and on all sailings from Liverpool, the number of passengers on certain crossings is controlled. All non-motorist passengers must have a 'sailing control ticket' to board the ship at these times. These can be obtained when you book your crossing, or if you change your booking or have an open ticket, from the ferry offices. It is worth checking whether you need a control ticket before you start your journey.

To the Republic from France

Irish Ferries, Dublin, ✆ (01) 661 0511; Le Havre, ✆ (35) 22 50 28; Cherbourg, ✆ (33) 44 28 96:

Le Havre–Rosslare, 2 to 3 sailings per week, all year, 21hrs.
Cherbourg–Rosslare, 1 to 2 sailings per week, all year, 18hrs.
Le Havre–Cork, 1 sailing per week, summer only, 21½hrs.
Roscoff–Cork, 1 to 3 sailings per week during summer months, 16hrs.
Roscoff–Rosslare, 1 to 3 sailings per week during summer months, 16hrs.

Britanny Ferries, Cork ✆ (021) 277801; Roscoff ✆ (98) 29 28 00:

Roscoff–Cork, 1 sailing per week, Mar–Oct only, 14hrs.

By Train

All the car ferries crossing back and forth between England and Ireland are scheduled to link up with the **British Rail InterCity trains** which go frequently and speedily from London to Fishguard, Liverpool, Holyhead and Stranraer. You can buy your **ticket** at any British Rail station or booking office; credit card bookings can be made on the telephone, on London (0171) 387 7070. There are free **seat reservations** on all direct train services to and from the ports. You can get couchettes on the night trains, but when it is not crowded it is possible to have a comfortable snooze by stretching out along the seats.

London (Euston) to Dublin via Liverpool/Dublin and Holyhead/Dun Laoghaire Port takes 11hrs; London (Paddington) to Wexford via Fishguard and Rosslare takes about 12½hrs; London (Euston) to Belfast via Liverpool about 16hrs; and London (Euston) to Belfast via Stranraer and Larne takes about 13hrs. Of course there are numerous other train routes connecting with the ferry ports.

Adult single **fares** for London–Dublin are between £39 and £49 each way; London–Belfast, £68 to £81.

By Bus

Travelling by bus/ferry to Ireland is quite an endurance test because the journey seems endless, with lots of stops through England and Ireland to pick up other travellers. The main advantage is that it is cheap and gets you straight to destinations in the provinces, so that you do not have to get other buses, trains and taxis on arrival in Ireland. The small coaches to-ing and fro-ing across the Irish Sea are very flourishing private enterprises in the hands of local individuals. They leave all parts of Ireland for the chief cities of England, Scotland and Wales, full to the brim with Irish returning to work or coming home on leave. You will not find details of the smaller companies at your travel agent; look instead at the back of Irish newspapers which you can buy fairly easily in Britain.

Of the major bus companies, **Irish Bus** and **National Express** (Supabus) run regular services between all parts Ireland and Great Britain. National Express buses leave London from the Victoria Coach Station, ✆ (0171) 730 0202. Bus Eireann can be contacted at the headquarters in Dublin, ✆ (01) 830 2222. **Slattery's**, a major private bus company based in Tralee, can be contacted in Dublin, ✆ (01) 661 1366; and also at their coach terminal in London, ✆ (0171) 730 0202.

In **Northern Ireland** the major bus companies are National Express (as above), and Ulsterbus in Belfast, ✆ (01232) 333000.

London to Dublin via Holyhead takes about 12 hours and costs around £16 single, £29 return at off-peak times for day sailings; £36 single, £55 return at peak periods. London to Belfast takes 13 hours, travelling overnight via Stranraer, and costs £39 single, £59 return.

Student and Youth Fares

If you can produce an **International Student Identity Card**, you can expect to get discounts of at least 25% on standard passenger rates for travel. For air travellers, there are student/youth rates for flights between Britain and Ireland, and similar concessions for transatlantic flights. In London, contact Campus Travel, ✆ (0171) 730 3402; or STA Travel Ltd, ✆ (0171) 581 1022.

With an ISIC, you can also buy a **Travelsave Stamp** for £7, which gets you some big savings: 50% off single adult tickets on B&I Line ferry crossings between Britain and Ireland, a discount off mainline rail fares in Ireland, 50% off single adult CIE provincial bus journeys and 50% off the return fare to the Aran Islands by boat. The Stamp is available from **Campus Travel** (*see* above); and also from the **USIT** (The Union of Students International Travel) 19 Aston Quay, Dublin 2, ✆ (01) 679 8833; or in Limerick at Central Buildings, O'Connell St, ✆ (661) 415064, or from any student travel offices at Irish universities.

Within Ireland, the **Education Travel Concession Ticket** entitles a student to greatly reduced travel on all buses listed in the Dublin District Bus and Train Timetable, and for all the suburban train services between Balbriggan and Greystones. You must be able to produce a passport or identity card and the name of the school or college you are attending. Apply to the Group and Educational Dept, Dublin Tourism, 14 Upper O'Connell Street, Dublin 1, ☎ (01) 284 4768.

Tour Operators

There are literally hundreds of tour companies offering all manner of enticing holidays in Ireland. Both Bord Fáilte and the Northern Ireland Tourist Board have lists of the main operators, which are published in their brochures. Alternatively, contact your travel agent.

Special-interest Holidays

Travellers who want holidays with a special focus—ancestor-hunting, angling, bird-watching, farm and country, gastronomy, gardens, golf, horse-riding, sailing, a mixture of these or none of them—are particularly well catered for in Ireland. The main specialist holiday companies are listed in the tourist board brochures. Bord Fáilte also has a *Learning for Leisure* brochure which gives details of organizations offering holidays 'designed to enable participants to acquire new leisure skills—sports, gardening, cookery, arts and crafts, etcetera in a relaxed and green environment'. We can also recommend the following specialist organizations, based in Ireland.

Irish **Cycling** Safaris Ltd (7 Dartry Park, Dublin 6, or UCD Belfield Campus, ☎ (01) 260 0749) offer leisurely one-week cycling holidays covering the Cork/Kerry or the Connemara regions.

Irish **Country** Holidays is a grouping of local communities which offer the visitor a chance to live as part of a rural community. You can spend your week in Ballyhoura, County Limerick; the Barrow/Nore area, Lough Corrib country, West Cork or County Roscommon. Each community has something special to offer in the way of landscape, customs and amenities. Contact Bord Fáilte, PO Box 273, Dublin 8; or the Ballyhoura Fáilte Society, Kilfinane, Co. Limerick, ☎ (063) 91300 or Plunkett House, 84 Merrion Square, Dublin 2, ☎ (01) 676 5796.

Oldeas Gael, Glencolmbkille, Co. Donegal, offer a workshop-type course in **Irish culture and language**, which includes folklore, singing, storytelling, set dancing and local history. Contact Liam O Cuinneagam, 25 Brompton Gardens, Dublin 15, ☎ (01) 821 3566.

Holidays based around courses in **arts and crafts** (weaving, patchwork and painting) can be organized through the Ardress Craft Centre, Kesh, Co. Fermanagh, ☎ (03656) 31267.

Connemara Contour Holidays, Island House, Market Street, Clifden, Co. Galway, ☎ (095) 21379/34682, offer week-long **walking** holidays along the coast or in the mountains led by enthusiastic specialists in archaeology and the environment.

Celtic Nature Expeditions, Michael & Becky O'Connor, The Old Stone House, Dingle, Co. Kerry, ☎ (066) 59882. **Sailing and walking** holidays.

Lastly, John Nicholas Colclough runs fascinating, informative **tours** anywhere in Ireland. He will tailor an itinerary to suit you, organize a car with a guide/driver, and superb accommodation ranging from the traditional farmhouse to the grandest castle. His tours can take in gardens, genealogy, ghosts, gourmet meals, and sites of historical importance. He will act as guide himself—and you cannot find anyone more engaging and informative. He is prepared to investigate any obscure angle on Ireland that you may wish to pursue. Contact Colclough Tours, 71 Waterloo Road, Dublin 4, ✆ (01) 668 6463.

See also the 'Summer Schools' section in **Practical A–Z**, pp.50–2.

Entry Formalities

Passports and Visas

British citizens travelling from Britain do not require a **passport** to enter the **Republic**. All the same, it can be useful to take a passport or some form of identification with you for completing formalities, such as hiring a car. **Citizens of the USA and Canada** must have a valid passport to enter the Republic, but no visa is required.

For **Northern Ireland**, entry formalities are exactly as they are for entry to the United Kingdom. US and Canadian citizens require a passport, but no visa; UK citizens do not need any form of identity documents, but it is as well to carry some, since, if you are stopped in a security check, quick identification will speed the process.

Citizens of **European Union** (EU) countries need a full passport for entry into both the Republic and Northern Ireland.

Passports and visas may be required for visitors of countries not included in the above. Check with your nearest Bord Fáilte office, or the Northern Ireland Tourist Board (*see* pp.52–5), or with the visa departments of the Irish or British embassies. In any case, entry regulations are liable to change, so if you are in any doubt, check before you leave.

Customs

As usual, there are restrictions on the quantities of certain goods you are allowed to bring into the Republic and take across the border to Northern Ireland. These apply to cigarettes and other tobacco products, alcoholic drinks, perfume and gifts and other new goods. The regulations are labyrinthine, since they differ according to whether or not you are resident in the EU, and whether or not the goods were bought in EU countries. Furthermore, EU residents have to take into account two separate structures, one for goods bought in duty-free shops in the EU, and another for goods bought, tax-paid, in an EU country.

To ensure that you have up-to-date information, it is better that you refer to to the tourist offices, airlines and ferry services. However, the **customs regulations** are standard, and, provided that you are seventeen years old or more, you can be sure of being allowed to import at least two hundred cigarettes, 50 cigars, one litre of spirits or two litres of wine and 50 grams of perfume; depending on where you live and where you bought your goods, you may be able to import rather more than this. Note also that in the Republic you are only meant to import other dutiable goods (such as watches and cameras) to a value of IR£34 (goods bought in EU countries, tax-paid, IR£302). If you are carrying used goods that look brand new, it is as well to bring receipts.

Dog- and cat-owners may like to know that they can bring their pet to Ireland, provided that it comes directly from Britain, the Channel Islands or the Isle of Man, and it has lived there for at least six months.

For residents of Britain and other EU countries, the usual EU regulations apply regarding what you can bring into your home country. Again, this depends on whether the goods have been bought in Ireland itself, tax-paid, or in a duty-free shop. Note that you cannot bring fresh meat, vegetables or plants into the UK.

Residents of the USA may each take home US$400-worth of foreign goods without attracting duty, including the tobacco and alcohol allowance. Canadians can bring home $300-worth of goods in a year, plus their tobacco and alcohol allowances.

You can claim back the **Value Added Tax** (VAT) on goods purchased in Ireland and exported by you, provided that you export them within two months of purchase and that their total value exceeds IR£50 (or IR£102 if you are resident in another EU country). The VAT rate is approx 21% since March 1993. You will need a **Cashback voucher** stamped by the shop; this must be stamped by customs before you leave Ireland. You can present the stamped vouchers at the Cashback desk at Shannon or Dublin airports and obtain a refund there and then, or you can claim the refund by post after your return.

Getting Around

By Air

It is quite possible to fly from one city to another in Ireland; but this is a small island and the main destinations are adequately covered by rail and bus, so internal air travel is mainly for the traveller under pressure. **Aer Lingus** and **Ryanair** run flights from Dublin to Cork, Shannon, Galway, Connacht Regional (Knock), Sligo and Waterford.

By Train

In the Republic, domestic train routes are operated by the Irish Rail arm of **CIE** (*Coras Iopair Eireann*), the national transport company which also runs a bus network to most parts of the Republic. The train routes radiate out from Dublin and take you through sleepy little country stations and green countryside. The system is rather like the British system of 40 years ago, with the old signal boxes which still need humans to operate them and keep an eye on things. People are always friendly on trains and the ticket inspectors are far from officious. Services are reliable, and the fares are reasonable. It is much cheaper to buy a return ticket than two singles. Dublin to Cork, for example costs IR£32 single, and a weekend return, Fri–Tues IR£29 return. Best value of all, however, are the special rail cards, allowing unlimited travel over a given period of time (*see* below).

For **information about Irish Rail services,** ✆ Dublin (01) 836 6222. There is a CIE office in Croydon, UK, ✆ (0181) 680 3226; and also in New Jersey, USA, ✆ (201) 292 3899.

Rail travel in Northern Ireland is run by **Northern Ireland Railways** (NIR), with services connecting Belfast to Coleraine and Derry and the ports. This system is fully integrated with the CIE services of the Republic, and lines between Belfast and Dublin are operated jointly by CIE and NIR. It takes two hours to reach Dublin on the Belfast–Dublin non-stop express, and there are six trains a day (three on Sundays). The cost down to Dublin and up to Belfast is £13 day return and £20 for two days or more. For further information about rail travel in Northern Ireland, contact the InterCity Travel Centre, Belfast, ✆ (01232) 230671; or the Travel and Information Centre, Central Station, Belfast, ✆ (01232) 230310.

Special Rail Tickets

There are a number of ways to make good advantage of Ireland's public transport systems through specially priced rail cards. For student fares, *see* p.7.

Irish Explorer for Rail and Bus—which allows you to travel 8 days out of 15. This ticket costs £90.

Irish Explorer for Rail Only—5 days' travel over 15 days. This ticket costs £60.

Irish Rover—An all-Ireland ticket which allows you up to 5 days' travel over 15 days costing £75.

Emerald Card—15 days' travel over 30 days on Bus/Rail for IR£180. There is also an 8-day version which allows 8 days' travel out of 15. This costs IR£105. Children's tickets are all half-price.

Ireland is now part of the **Eurail Pass** network which allows unlimited rail travel on European railways including the Republic of Ireland, but excluding the UK and Northern Ireland. To obtain a pass you must be a resident of a non-European country and buy your pass outside Europe. Prices in Irish punts for under 26/over 26 are as follows: 15 days travel IR£321–IR£402, 21 days IR£522, 1 month IR£466–IR£643, 2 months IR£619–IR£885. There are also special youth rates for anyone up to 26 years old. With a Eurail Pass you can also go from France to Ireland free on the ferry, provided you do not pass through Britain.

For anyone who is a **steam train enthusiast** there are plenty of places in Ireland where you can travel on one as more and more narrow gauge line is opened up. The Northern Irish Tourist Board publish a comprehensive guide to steam trains and railways which covers the whole of Ireland.

By Bus

The **bus service** throughout Ireland is efficient and goes to the most remote places. The main companies are **Irish Bus** (or *Bus Eireann*), run by CIE, in the Republic; and **Ulsterbus** in Northern Ireland. Freelance operators also run many tours. Prices are reasonable. For example, Dublin–Cork, IR£16; Dublin-Galway, IR£10; Dublin–Limerick, IR£13.

In the Republic the main routes are covered by **Expressway** bus services. Dublin is served by **Dublin Bus** (or *Bus Atha Cliath*). CIE also operates a variety of chatty one-day and half-day tours throughout the Republic from various city depots. For details get in touch with Dublin Bus at 59 Upper O'Connell Street, Dublin 1, ✆ (01) 873 4222; CIE, 35 Lower Abbey St, Dublin 1, ✆ (01) 677 1871; or Bus Eireann, Dublin, ✆ (01) 836 6111.

There are also many other smaller independent bus companies that span Ireland such as **Nestor Bus** which does a Galway to Dublin service for IR£9 return and IR£6 single,

✆ (01) 832 0094. The following services run where CIE does not operate: **Suirway Bus Service**, Waterford, ✆ (051) 382209. You can pick up a Provincial Bus and Expressway Timetable at CIE or tourist offices and at some newspaper stands. Note that, in the Republic, bus destinations posted on the front of the bus are often given in Irish; Dublin, for example, may be seen as *Atha Cliath*. If in doubt, ask.

Ulsterbus runs frequent services to all parts of Northern Ireland. You can pick up timetables at any Ulster bus station, or the tourist office in Belfast. The Ulsterbus head office is at the Great Victoria Street Bus Station, ✆ (01232) 320011; the other main bus station is in Oxford Street, ✆ (01232) 232356. The Citybus service operates in Belfast only, ✆ (01232) 246485.

Special Bus Tickets

For concessionary tickets applying to both bus and rail, *see* the 'Special Rail Tickets' section, above.

Ulsterbus operates **Freedom of Northern Ireland Tickets**: one-day ticket UK£9, under-16s UK£4.50; seven-day tickets, UK£28. For further details of special fares and bus excursions, see *On the Move*, published by the Northern Ireland Tourist Office.

Travelsave Stamps can also be used for certain bus services (*see* p.7).

By Car

To explore Ireland with minimum effort and maximum freedom, bring a car. If you fill it up with people who share the ferry and petrol costs, it won't be too expensive. Buy a detailed **road map** and, if you have time, choose a minor road and just meander. It is along these little lanes that the secret life of Ireland continues undisturbed. The black and red cows still chew by the wayside whilst the herdsman, usually an old man or a child, salutes you with an upward nod. Nearby is the farmstead cluttered with bits of old machinery and a cheerful sense of makeshift, where everything is kept to be used again: an old front door will stop a gap in the hedge; old baths serve as cattle troughs; clucking hens roost on the old haycart—next year it might be bought by the tinkers, who will varnish it up to adorn some suburban garden. You will come upon castles, and the ruins of the small, circular buildings called *clochans*, still breathing with memories, tumbled even further by the local farmer in search of stone; and there are views of those many hills which have never reached the pages of any guidebook. One of the best things about driving in Ireland is the lack of other cars and the absence of ugly, if efficient motorways with their obligatory motor inns and petrol stations. There are some big roads with all that sort of thing, but very few. In Northern Ireland the roads manage to be very good but still countrified, and after the bumps and wavy roads of the Republic you feel as though you are gliding along.

Beware of the country driver who tends to drive right in the middle of the road, never looks in his mirror to see if anyone is behind, and is unlikely to indicate if he suddenly decides to turn left or right. Beware of drivers wearing an old tweed cap—they are usually the worst offenders. Then you get the other extreme with crazy speeds on narrow roads. Cars frequently pull out of a side-road in front of you and, just as you are getting up enough steam to pass, suddenly decide to turn off down another side-road again. Don't be alarmed by the sheepdogs which appear from every cottage door to chase your car—they are well skilled at avoiding you.

If your car **breaks down** in any part of Ireland you will always be able to find a mechanic to give you a hand; whether it's late at night or on a Sunday, just ask someone. He or she will sweep you up in a wave of sympathy and send messengers off in all directions to find you someone with a reputation for mechanical genius. If it is some small and common part that has let you down, he will either have it or do something that will get you by until you come to a proper garage. One thing you will notice is that the Irish have a completely different attitude to machinery from most nationalities. In England, if you break down, it is an occasion for embarrassment; everybody rushes by hardly noticing you or pretending not to. In Ireland, if your car has broken down the next passing car will probably stop, and the problem will be readily taken on and discussed with great enjoyment. The Irish can laugh at the occasional failure of material affairs.

Facts and Formalities for Car Drivers

In Ireland you **drive on the left** (when you are not driving in the middle of the road). **Petrol stations** stay open until around eight in the evenings, and the village ones are open after Mass on Sundays. If you are desperate for petrol and every station seems closed, you can usually knock on the door and ask somebody to start the pumps for you. Petrol in the Republic is 60p per litre. The **speed limit** in the Republic is 62mph (99kph) on all roads and 30mph or 40mph (48 kph or 64 kph) through the villages and towns. In the North the speed limit is 70 mph (112 kph) on dual carriageways, 60 mph (96 kph) on country roads, 40 mph (64 kph) in built-up areas and 30 mph (48 kph) in towns.

Drivers and front-seat passengers must always wear a **seat belt**—it is illegal not to. Children under 12 should travel in the back. There are strict drink-driving laws in the Republic as in the North, and the police will use a breathalyzer test if they suspect that you are driving under the influence of alcohol.

There are some excellent **motoring maps**: Bartholomew's ¼-inch, obtainable from the AA and Bord Fáilte, gives good details of minor roads. The principal roads in Northern Ireland are marked A; in the Republic the old system of T (trunk) and L (link) routes is currently being altered to N (national) and R (regional), and you are liable to encounter both systems for a while yet. Scenic routes are signposted and marked on the Bord Fáilte map. Place names on signposts in the Republic are usually given in English and in Irish; in the places where Irish only is used a good map will be useful. The old white signposts give distances in miles; the new green ones give distances in kilometres. All other traffic signs are more or less the same as the standard European ones.

Residents of the Republic of Ireland, Northern Ireland and Great Britain using private cars and motorcycles may cross the borders with very little formality. A **full, up-to-date licence** is all you need. Under EU regulations, private motor insurers will provide the minimum legal cover required in all EU countries, although they may need to be told before you travel. Always carry the **vehicle registration book**. If you have hired a car, be sure to tell the rental company that you intend to cross borders, and that you have all the necessary papers; the rental company should also deal with all the insurance headaches.

Because of the ceasefire, the rules governing border crossings and approved roads are changing. You should use an approved road otherwise you may be liable to penalties. As at January 1995 these are the approved roads:

Moville–Londonderry/Derry R238–A2

Buncrana–Londonderry/Derry R238–A2

Letterkenny–Londonderry/Derry N13–A2; R237–B193

Raphoe–Londonderry/Derry R236–A40

Letterkenny–Strabane N14–A38

Castlefinn–Castlederg R235–C675A

Donegal–Enniskillen, via Pettigoe R232–A35

Ballyshannon–Enniskillen, via Belleek R230–A46

Manorhamilton–Enniskillen, via Belcoo N16–A4

Swanlinbar–Enniskillen R202–A32

Clones–Newtownbutler R183–A34

Monaghan–Rosslea R187–B36

Monaghan–Armagh N12–A3

Carrickmoss–Newry, via Crossmaglen R179–B30

Dundalk-Newry N1–A1

The army checkpoints have decreased considerably but it is as well to carry your licence or some means of identification. **AA** (Automobile Association) offices will usually give you all the details of necessary formalities if you are not clear about anything. Their main office in the Republic is at 23 Rockhill, Blackrock, ✆ (01) 283 3555 and their breakdown service is at 23 Suffolk St, ✆ (01) 677 9481; emergency number in Dublin, ✆ 1800 667788. The AA's Scotland and Northern Ireland Regional Headquarters is at Fanum House, Erskine Harbour, Erskine, Renfrewshire PA8 6AT, ✆ (0141) 812 0144, UK emergency number (0800) 887766. The central London information and travel office is at 30–31 Haymarket, London SW1Y 4EX, ✆ (0171) 9309559.

Parking meters are used to control **car parking** in the central zones of Dublin. The meters are in operation during specific hours from Mondays to Fridays, when street parking other than at meters is prohibited. Yellow lines along the kerbside or edge of the roadway indicate waiting restrictions. In Cork a disc system is used to control parking in the centre. Parking discs can be bought, usually in books of ten, at shops and garages near the car parks. Unexpired time on a parking disc can be used at another parking place.

In Belfast it's best to head for a car park; in Northern Ireland, for security reasons, parking is not permitted in central city areas marked off as 'Control Zones', which are indicated by yellow signs saying 'Control Zone. No Unattended Parking'.

Car Hire Operators

These are only some of the big ones who will meet you at the airports and the ferry ports of the Republic:

Avis Rent-A-Car Ltd, 1 Hanover St East, Dublin 2, ✆ (01) 677 4010.

Budget Rent-A-Car, Dublin Airport, ✆ (01) 844 5919.

Flynn Brothers Self-Drive, Ballygar, Co. Galway, ✆ (0903) 24668.

Hertz Rent-A-Car, Dublin Airport, ✆ (01) 844 5466.

Murray's Europcar, Baggot Street Bridge, Dublin 4, ✆ (01) 668 1777.

For further details contact the **Car Rental Council**, 5 Upper Pembroke St, Dublin 2, ✆ (01) 676 1690.

In Northern Ireland **Avis, Hertz** and **Godfrey Davis (Europcar)** all operate from both Belfast's airports but it's much less expensive to hire a car from their city centre branches. Local firms (see phone book) can offer even better deals. That said, renting a car in Ireland is never cheap. You might be able to bargain slightly if business is slack. Prices start at around IR£185 per week, or UK£165 in Northern Ireland for the smallest car. Look out also for fly-drive, or rail-sail-drive packages offered by some of the airlines and ferry companies: these usually represent major savings. Note that to hire a car you should normally be over 23, and should in possession of a licence which you have held for at least two years without endorsement. The car hire company will organize insurance, but do check this. If you do not take extra collision-damage waiver insurance you can be liable to damage up to IR£1350.

By Bicycle

Ireland is one of the pleasantest places to cycle in. The roads are uncrowded, there are still lots of birds and animals that live around the hedgerows, and there is no pollution to spoil the illusion of rural Ireland. In between the delicious whiffs of gorse or honeysuckle will come strong manure smells! You can bring your bicycle free on the ferry, or you can rent one. In the Republic there is a **Raleigh Rent-A-Bike** network, with some 70 centres throughout the country. Prices begin at about IR£7 per day, IR£30 per week, with a deposit of at least IR£40. Tandems, racing bikes, and ordinary touring bikes are available. For full details get the *Cycling Ireland* leaflet from the nearest Bord Fáilte office; this gives details of the main hire companies, lists Irish cycling holiday specialists, and also describes 23 suggested routes. Alternatively, contact Raleigh Rent-A-Bike Division, Raleigh Ireland Limited, Raleigh House, Kylemore Road, Dublin 10, ✆ (01) 626 1333, ✆ (01) 626 1770. Another Rent-a-Bike store, which has outlets throughout Ireland is the Bike Shop on 58 Lower Gardner St, Dublin 1, ✆ (01) 872 5431 or ✆ (01) 872 5399.

The Northern Ireland Tourist Board produces a leaflet on cycling (*Information Bulletin 3*), which lists tours, routes, and events for cyclists, plus a number of cycle hire companies. Rental rates are comparable to those in the Republic. You can also hire bikes at some youth hostels in the North; contact **YHANI**, ✆ Belfast (01232) 321 4733. Note that bicycles hired in the Republic cannot be taken into Northern Ireland, and vice versa.

Irish Cycling Safaris run well organised and enjoyable holidays bicycling through scenic parts of the country. Contact them at 7 Dartry Park, Dublin 6, ✆ (01) 260 0749.

On Foot

From all accounts hitch-hiking seems to be a safe but rather slow method of transport round the South. You will see more cows and sheep wandering along the minor roads than cars. In the North you might find that people will not pick you up because years of the 'Troubles' have made them cautious. It would be unwise to hitch around border areas; there are plenty of buses that will take you through. On major roads write your destination on a bit of cardboard and hold it up. You will find you have to compete with local people who hitch regularly from town to town.

Getting to the Aran Islands

The Aran Islands to the west of Galway are probably the most famous of islands lying off the west coast of Ireland, but there are many others, each with its own charms. You can reach most of these by boat services from the nearest mainland port. Ask Bord Fáilte for details. A regular boat service to the Aran Islands runs from Galway (3 hours) and Rossaveal (1½ hours). The cost is about the same: IR£15 return from Galway; IR£12 from Rossaveal. Alternatively, you can fly in about half an hour with Aer Arann, taking one of the several daily flights from Galway (Connemara Airport at Caislean Inverin); the return flight costs about IR£45. There is also a regular ferry to Tory Island, Co. Donegal. Bord Fáilte publish a free leaflet listing transport to the islands.

Practical A-Z

Calendar of Events

Calendars of events, available from the tourist offices, present you with a dazzling array of international festivals and small town extravaganzas, where everyone has a ball: jolly music pours into the street, farmers and tradesmen parade their goods and machinery, and there are endless bouncing baby competitions, discos and drinking bouts. Here are the major festivals; other, more local ones are listed in the 'Festivals' sections at the beginning of each county chapter. If you want to plan your holiday around one, check with the tourist office, as some events change every year.

February   **Dublin Film Festival** of new Irish cinema; for information call ✆ (01) 679 2937, ✉ (01) 679 2939.

March   **St Patrick's Week**. Events centre around St Patrick's Day (17 March), with parades, music, dance and theatre, especially in Dublin (festival of traditional Irish music, and classical music festival or *Feis Ceoil*) and Cork, Galway and Limerick, ✆ (091) 63536.

April   **World Irish Dancing Championships**, contact Mr Seamus MacConuladh, ✆ (01) 475 2220.

May   **Fleadh Nua**, Ennis, Co. Clare. Traditional music, song and dance. Further information: Comhaltas Ceoltóirí Eirean, Belgrave Square, Monkstown, Co. Dublin, ✆ (01) 280 0295.

June/July   **AIB Music Festival in Great Irish Houses**, mostly located within a short distance of Dublin. International soloists and orchestras perform in some of Ireland's most beautiful historic houses. Early booking advisable; spaces very limited. Further information: Crawford Tipping, Festival Administrator, 1st Floor Blackrock Post Office, Blackrock, Co. Dublin, ✆ (01) 278 1528, ✉ (01) 278 1529.

Castlebar International Four Days' Walk (late June/July). Walks and music in the evening, pop, traditional and classical. Further information, ✆ (094) 24102.

Galway Arts Festival. One of Ireland's biggest most popular festivals. Theatre, art and music etc., ✆ (091) 583800.

August   **Kilkenny Arts Week**. Classical music recitals, poetry, art exhibitions. Further information: Kilkenny Arts Week, Design Theatre, The Parade, Kilkenny, Co. Kilkenny, ✆ (056) 63663.

Puck Fair, Killorglin. Lots of drink and wildness revolving around a captured goat, ✆ (066) 61595.

Fleadh Cheoil Nah Eireann, Buncrana (changes venues). Sometimes up to 5000 traditional musicians congregate to play impromptu sessions.

While you are there take to the hills and explore the Inishowen Peninsula. Further information: Comhaltas Ceoltoírí Eireann, Belgrave Square, Monkstown, Co. Dublin, ✆ (01) 280 0295.

Rose of Tralee International Festival. Girls of Irish birth and parentage come from all over the world to compete for the title; there are carnival parades, street dancing, fireworks, music, and the Tralee races. Further information: Rose of Tralee Office, 5 Lower Castle St, Tralee, Co. Kerry, ✆ (066) 21322/23227.

Letterkenny International Folk Festival. Music and dance performed by folk groups; also memorable for the surrounding countryside, ✆ (074) 21754.

September   **International Festival of Light Opera**. A dozen light operas, one after the other, performed in the lovely old Theatre Royal. Further information: the Hon. Executive Secretary, Waterford Light Opera Festival Office, 7 Barker Street, Waterford.

Galway International Oyster Festival, Oyster-tasting and music, ✆ (091) 27282/ 22066.

Matchmaking Festival, Lisdoonvarna, Co. Clare. A festival for local bachelors, and Americans in search of a husband, accompanied by a lot of drinking, noise and crowds.

Dublin Theatre Festival (late September/October). Dublin has produced so many brilliant writers: Sheridan, Goldsmith, Shaw, Wilde, Yeats, Synge, O'Casey, Beckett and Behan—to name only the most famous—so it is not surprising that this festival holds a special place in the world theatre scene. You can see work by Irish writers, interspersed with productions by well-known companies from America and Europe. Further information: Festival Director, 47 Nassau Street, Dublin 2, ✆ (01) 677 8439/671 2860.

October   **Wexford Opera Festival** (October/November). Claimed by many to be one of the finest of its kind in Europe. Rare operatic masterpieces are performed in the Theatre Royal, with supporting events of orchestral concerts, chamber music, recitals, films, fringe shows. Further information: Box Office, Wexford Festival Opera, Theatre Royal, Wexford, ✆ (053) 22144, ✉ (053) 24289.

Ballinasloe Horse Fair, one of the oldest horse fairs in Europe. Can get wild. ✆ (0905) 43453.

November   **Belfast International Festival**. Concerts, films, opera, theatre—further information: Festival Office, ✆ (01232) 665577; Box Office ✆ (01232) 667687; adm.

Horse-racing and Other Equestrian Events

April: Irish Grand National (Fairyhouse, Co. Meath)
June: Irish Derby (The Curragh)
July: Irish Oaks (The Curragh)
August: Dublin Horse Show
August: Connemara Pony Show

Children

If you are travelling with children you will find that bed and breakfast establishments will welcome them. Many have family rooms with four or five beds, and charge a reduced price for children. Most supply cots and high chairs, and offer a baby-sitting service, but always check beforehand. Some farm and country houses keep a donkey or pony, and have swings and a play area set up for children.

Irish people love children, and are very tolerant of seeing and hearing them in bars and eating places during the daytime. They will offer children's menus at a cheaper price and generally be helpful, but they will not be so tolerant if you turn up with them for dinner at night. If you are contemplating staying in some of the smart country-house hotels which are full of precious antiques, etcetera, please check that it is a suitable place for children beforehand. The many national monuments, heritage centres, Gardens and parks usually charge much less for children or offer a family ticket which is cheaper.

Climate

Ireland lies on the path of the North Atlantic cyclones, which makes the climate mild, equable and moist. Rainfall is heaviest in the high western coastal areas, where it averages over 80 inches (203cm) a year. On the east coast and over the central plain, rainfall averages between 30 and 40 inches (76 and 101cm). Rain is Ireland's blessing, yet from the reputation it has in its own country and abroad, you might imagine it was a curse. It keeps the fields and trees that famous lush green, and the high level of water vapour in the air gives it a sleepy quality and softens the colours of the landscape. The winds from the east increase the haziness and mute the colours, but these are nearly always followed by winds from the northwest which bring clearer air and sunshine. So the clouds begin to drift and shafts of changing light touch the land. Nearly every drizzly day has this gleam of sunshine, which is why the Irish are always very optimistic about the weather. The Gulf Stream in the Atlantic means that there are never extremes of cold or hot.

Snow is not common, and is seldom severe. The spring tends to be relatively dry, especially after the blustery winds of March, and the crisp colours and freshness of autumn only degenerates into the cold and damp of winter in late December. You can hope for at least six hours of sunshine a day over most of the country during May, June, July and August.

Average Temperatures

January	4°C (39°F)—7°C (45°F)
July/August	14°C (57°F)—24°C (75°F)

Disabled Travellers

Both Bord Fáilte (the Irish Tourist Board) and the Northern Ireland Tourist Board show that Ireland has made considerable efforts to help handicapped travellers, and both of these tourist boards have produced useful booklets containing advice. Particularly commended is *The Disabled Tourist in Northern Ireland*, published by the NITB and distributed free. It lists hotels, guesthouses and restaurants, what to see and where to shop, based on suggestions by individual disabled people. It also gives telephone numbers, so that you can check facilities beforehand.

Bord Fáilte has a similar publication, updated annually, called *Accommodations for the Disabled*. In Dublin the National Rehabilitation Board, 25 Clyde Road, Ballsbridge, Dublin 4, ✆ (01) 668 4181, can supply keys needed for access to special toilets; and the Irish Wheelchair Association, 24 Blackheath Drive, Dublin 3, ✆ (01) 833 8241, can supply wheelchairs for the disabled.

In Britain, RADAR (Royal Association for Disability and Rehabilitation), Unit 12 City Forum, 250 City Road, London EC1V 8AF, ✆ (0171) 250 3222, is an excellent source of advice, and publishes its own fact sheets on holiday planning, accommodation and so forth, and fuller guides for the disabled traveller for the UK and abroad. The Holiday Care Service, 2 Old Bank Chambers, Station Road, Horley, Surrey RH6 9HW, ✆ (01293) 774535 offers advice for all travellers with special needs, and publishes a short information sheet on the Irish Republic.

Electricity

The current is 220 volts AC, so you should bring an adaptor if you have any American appliances. Wall sockets take the standard British-style three-pin (flat) fused plugs, or two-pin (round) plugs. If you are worried, there are good travellers' adaptors on the market which can usually cope with most socket-and-plug combinations that you are liable to encounter abroad.

Embassies and Consulates

British Embassy, 31 Merrion Road, Dublin 4, ✆ (01) 269 5211.

US Embassy (Dublin), 43 Elgin Road, Dublin 4, ✆ (01) 668 8777.

US Consulate (Belfast), 14 Queen's Street, Belfast BT1 6EG, ✆ (01232) 328239.

USTAA, American Embassy, Grosvenor Square, London W1A 1AE, ✆ (0891) 616000.

Canadian Embassy, 65 St Stephen's Green, Dublin 2, ✆ (01) 4781988.

Canadian High Commission, 38 Grosvenor Street, London W1, ℡ (0171) 629 9492.

Australian Embassy, Fitzwilton House, Wilton Terrace, Dublin 2, ℡ (01) 676 1517.

Australian High Commission, Australia House, Strand, London, WC2 B4L, ℡ (0171) 379 4334.

New Zealand High Commission, New Zealand House, 80 Haymarket, London SW1Y 4TQ, ℡ (0171) 930 8422.

Fishing

We are most grateful to Antony Luke for the following personal account. Antony has been returning on holiday to Ireland since 1963. He acts as a consultant on fishing matters to the corporate entertainment company Country & Highland, gives fly-fishing instruction, and organises salmon-fishing parties. He has a cottage on one of the northern isles of Orkney where he keeps a lobster boat, and from where he runs a successful business exporting fish and shellfish.

Whatever the catch, one always returns from Ireland with a story and happy memories. The sport is excellent, and all visitors are treated with great hospitality and charm. Tackle shops are very helpful, and The Irish Tourist Board issues a wealth of information, including dates of angling competitions, and an excellent brochure entitled *Angling in Ireland.*

In general, fishing in Ireland is more available to the general public and less restrictive than in Scotland. Notably, fishing on Sunday is permitted. Unlike the UK, there is no closed season for coarse fishing. Seasons for other types of fishing vary according to region and sometimes specific rivers. Costs are also comparatively low. With few exceptions, a day's permit is unlikely to cost more than IR£25. Government licences are not hefty, but they are required for salmon and sea trout fishing.

For the purposes of licensing, fishing in the Republic can be divided into four categories: game, for salmon and sea trout (migratory); trout (non-migratory); coarse, for perch, roach, rudd, bream, tench, etcetera, and pike; and sea-fishing. Visitors require a licence for the first. A general licence covering all salmon and sea trout costs IR£10 for 21 days, or IR£25 for a season, or IR£3 a day. It is possible to purchase individual or composite licences from Bord Fáilte offices in your country of residence. In the Republic, they can be bought from any Tourist or Fisheries Board office, from all government-run fisheries, and many tackle shops.

One of the finest aspects of the sport in Ireland is the variety of different fishing techniques that are to be found in quite small areas. It is possible to fish a lake system—either dapping or wet-fly—and a river, on the same day. In the UK, this is only possible in a few places on the west coast of Scotland, and to some extent in the Hebrides. The great Irish limestone lakes such as Carra, Conn, Mask and Corrib offer some of the best trout-fishing in the world, especially at the time of the mayfly (mid-May to early June). On Corrib there is also salmon. A ghillied boat is necessary if you wish to fish these beautiful lakes scattered with many hundreds of small islands. Irish ghillies have a great knowledge of the shoals and bays where fish lie. They are also highly entertaining.

Coarse fishing is immensely popular in the Republic, particularly with visitors from the UK, where there is a closed season from mid-March to mid-June. Vast expanses of water throughout the centre of the country are open to visitors, and pike-fishing here is amongst the best in Europe.

It would take a book longer than this one to list all the rivers and loughs for visiting game-fishers. On the whole, salmon-fishing is privately owned, but good association water is available for the general public. On the east coast,the Boyne, Liffey and Slaney rivers have early runs of salmon, and grilse run later—from mid-June. On the south coast, the Nore, Suir, Barrow and the Blackwater, also have early runs of salmon, and grilse later. On the southwest coast, there are a number of rivers and lake systems, notably Lough Currane at Waterville, and the Maine and Laune including the Killarney Lakes. In the mid-west the list is endless, numbering such famous places as Ballynahinch, the Newport, which drains Lough Beltra; Delphi, the Moy and the mighty Shannon. Fishing on the Shannon was adversely affected by the introduction of the hydro-electric scheme in 1929, but the Castleconnel beats are still worth a visit. The Corrib River drains the Corrib system and the famous Galway Weir. Thousands apply every year for a permit to fish here (IR£20 a day), but it is possible to be lucky in the ballot for selection. If not, you can join the crowds at the Galway Salmon Weir Bridge and watch the ranks of salmon stream past.

Also in the mid-west, one of my favourite spots is the River Erriff, administered by the Central Fisheries Board. Running through a glacial vally in the heart of Connemara, it has a wild beauty, culminating in a cascade over the Aasleagh Falls and into the sea at Killary Harbour. Beats are on both banks and generous. Given good conditions, the Erriff can be as prolific as some of the most famous rivers. Visitors can either take a cottage or stay in the Aasleagh Lodge, which offers both dinner and B&B. Book early through the Manager, Erriff Fishery, Aasleagh Lodge, Leenane, County Galway.

Sea trout have been in sad decline over the past five years, especially on the west coast, and a number of well-known sea-trout fisheries have suffered badly due to 'Sea Lice' (which many claim is due to salmon farming). Considerable research is now being done by the Salmon Research Trust at Newport and things have shown a slight improvement. By contrast, runs of salmon and grilse have held up well in recent years.

Sea-angling is becoming increasingly popular with the more hardy fisherman. The Central Fisheries Board issues a comprehensive booklet. More boats are available for hire than ever before, although they can be expensive for the individual; it is best to organise a group of four or more. Kinsale is one of the main centres for sea-angling. Here, when the sea warms a degree or so, odd species of tropical fish arrive. Out of Kinsale there is also good shark-fishing, and many other species such as conger, skate and, for the less selec-tive, huge bags of large pollack can be caught. On the west coast, Cleggan is another small port where boats can be hired. The surrounding area of Connemara is startlingly beautiful, and many self-catering cottages are available to rent.

Other main sea-fishing stations are Rosslare and Dungarvan in Co. Waterford; Youghal, Ballycotton, and Baltimore in Co. Cork; Cahirciveen and the Dingle Peninsula in Co. Kerry; Westport, Achill Island, Newport and Belmullet in Co. Mayo; and Moville in Co. Donegal. As a rule, all stations will be able to supply boats for hire, rods, tackle, etcetera.

Fishing in Northern Ireland

Northern Ireland has a wealth of lakes, rivers and tributaries, and fine sport can be had in all areas. Seasons vary, as they do in the South, and costs are not high.

Lough Erne is well known for quality in all types of fishing. The upper water is mostly for coarse fish, while the lower holds salmon or trout as well. The River Foyle and its tributaries, some running into Lough Foyle, have good runs of salmon and sea trout. The River Bann divides into two; the lower drains Lough Neagh and is famous for its salmon-fishing, but the lower beats are expensive. The Upper Bann rises in the Mountains of Mourne and fish run later. The popularity of sea-fishing has grown immensely in recent years. Twenty-four species of sea-fish are caught regularly. The main centres where boats can be hired are Portrush, Glenarm, Larne and Whitehead in Co. Antrim; and Bangor and Donaghadee in Co. Down.

Rod licences, which are issued by the Fisheries Conservancy Board (FCB) or the Foyle Fisheries Commission (FFC), cost £11.50 for 14 days. Permission to fish from the owner of the water—often the Department of Agriculture, which is the ultimate authority for fisheries in the North—takes the form of a permit and costs £13 for 15 days, or £5 per day. Angling clubs which own waters not held by the Department issue daily tickets costing £2–4. Ghillies charge about £45 per day. All permits and licences for fishing in Northern Ireland, and a lot more information, are available from the Northern Ireland Tourist Office, 48 High Street, Belfast, ✆ (01232) 246609. Alternatively, the Lakeland Visitors' Centre, Enniskillen, ✆ (01365) 23110, is very helpful. Tackle shops throughout the Province issue permits and tickets for, or information on, angling clubs. Thanks to Peter O'Reilly for his help with the updating of this section.

Food and Drink

Eating Out

Eating out in Ireland can be a memorable experience, if the the chef gets it right. The basic ingredients are the best in the world: succulent beef, lamb, salmon, seafood, ham, butter, cream, eggs and wonderful **bread**—which is often homemade, and varies from crumbly nutty-tasting wheaten bread to moist white soda bread, crispy scones, potato bread and barm brack, a rich fruity loaf which is traditionally eaten at Hallowe'en. Irish **potatoes** are light and floury and best when just off the stalk, and crispy carrots and cabbages are sold in every grocery shop, often bought in from the local farms. If you stay in a country-house hotel, the walled garden will probably produce rare and exotic vegetables and fruit.

The history of Ireland has quite a lot to do with the down-side of cooking: overcooked food, few vegetables, and too many synthetic cakes. The landless peasants had little to survive off except potatoes, milk and the occasional bit of bacon, so there is little traditional 'cuisine'. **Fish** was until recently regarded as 'penance food', to be eaten only on Fridays. Local people talk with amusement of those who eat oysters or mussels, and most of the fine seafood harvested from the seaweed-fringed loughs and the open sea goes straight to France, where it appears on the starched linen table-cloths of the best restaurants. But do not despair if you love fat oysters or fresh salmon, because they can always be got, either in the bars, the new-style restaurants which are really excellent, or straight from the fisherman. Remember, everything in Ireland works on a personal basis. Start your enquiries for any sort of local delicacy at the local post office, grocer or butcher, or in the pub.

Having got over the trauma of the famine, and since the relative prosperity of the 1960s, many people in Ireland like to eat **meat**: you cannot fail to notice the number of butchers or 'fleshers' in every town. Steak appears on every menu, and if you are staying in a simple Irish farmhouse, huge lamb chops with a minty sauce, Irish stew made from the best end of mutton neck, onions and potatoes, and bacon and cabbage casserole baked in the oven are delicious possibilities; fish, however, is becoming more and more readily available.

The standard of **restaurants** in Ireland is getting much better. This is especially true of those that are run by people from the Continent, many of whom set up here because of the beauty of the country and the raw ingredients. There are Irish cooks, too, who combine the local specialities and traditional recipes with ingredients and cooking methods from other cultures. Ballymaloe House in County Cork and Drimcong Restaurant in County Galway spring im...ediately to mind. Still, eating out can be a massive disappointment, and it is wise to go to only those establishments which have been recommended. Too many restaurants still serve up musty and watery vegetables, overcooked meat, frozen fish, and salads of the limp lettuce and coleslaw variety. Also, eating out is not cheap, unless you have a pub lunch. Some restaurants offer a tourist menu, but on the whole these establishments offer good value rather than good cooking.

To get around the serious problem of eating cheaply in Ireland, fill up on the huge breakfasts provided by the bed and breakfast places. If the lady of the house also cooks high tea or supper for her guests, take advantage of that as well. The food she produces is usually delicious and very good value. Irish people love their food, and are generous with it: huge portions are normal in the home and often in restaurants. It is a sign of inhospitality to give a poor meal. (They say, 'It was but a daisy in a bull's mouth'.) Bakeries usually sell tea, coffee and soft drinks along with fresh apple pie, doughnuts, cakes and sausage rolls. Roadside cafés serve the usual menu of hamburgers, chicken 'n' chips, etcetera. In the North they do a tearing trade in take-away foods. Many of the big towns have Chinese restaurants, pizza places and fish and chips. Vegetarians will find an increasing number of restaurants in Dublin and the larger towns that cater specifically for their needs. Certainly, vegetarians will find that even where no special menu exists, people are generally keen to provide suitable fare. If you are staying in a country house, you should telephone in advance to let them know you are vegetarian. You can sample the many delicious cheeses of Ireland by finding a good deli or wholefood shop, buying some bread and salad and taking yourself off to eat a picnic in some wonderfully scenic place. If it is drizzling, warm yourself up afterwards with a glass of Irish coffee in the local pub.

You will normally find the service in Ireland friendly and helpful. A variety of good eating places are listed at the end of each county chapter. In the various culinary deserts which exist, those listed are the best of an indifferent lot! The establishments are categorized in the following cost brackets. Do bear in mind that proprietors and places change, so it is always best to phone before you arrive.

luxury

Cost no object. These restaurants include creative and delicious cooking from fine ingredients. They are often in the dining-rooms of rather stately country houses or castles, where the silver and crystal sparkle and you are surrounded by fine pictures and furniture. Or they may be smart, fashionable places in the cities.

expensive

Over IR£20 a head, excluding wine. Restaurants in this category are similar to those in the luxury bracket, with an emphasis on well-cooked vegetables and traditional ingredients. Again, many country-house hotels come under this category, as do seafood restaurants around the coast and city establishments. Lunch in expensive places is often a very reasonably priced set meal, so ask about it if you do not want to fork out for dinner.

moderate

IR£10–20 a head excluding wine. The quality of the food may be as good as the more expensive places, but the atmosphere is informal and, perhaps, a little less stylish.

inexpensive

Under IR£10 a head excluding wine. This category includes bar food, lunchtime places and cafés. You can usually be sure of good homemade soup and one, simple course.

Most restaurants do lunch and dinner but do check before you go. A few do only dinner and Sunday lunches. Some country places only open for the weekend during the winter months. Cafés and snack places are not usually open in the evening for meals. Service is usually included in the bill at all restaurants. In the country towns and sometimes even in Dublin, you may find it difficult to pay by credit card. Check this out before you order your meal! If there is no liquor licence of any sort, the manager is usually quite happy to let you bring in your own wine or beer, if you ask. (The publicans have a monopoly on licences and many restaurants cannot get them without having to fulfil ludicrous requirements for space-planning).

Literature

Bord Fáilte's booklet *Dining in Ireland* (IR£2) tends to be conservative in whom it lists, but it gives you some idea of the sort of food served and the price. The Irish Country Houses and Restaurants Association issues a booklet every year which includes some of the best restaurants in Ireland, and they are not necessarily all that expensive. It is called *The Blue Book*, and can be found in tourist offices throughout the country. Possibly the best publication is Bridgestones *Irish Food Guide*, which lists a directory of sources—smoked salmon, cheese, organic vegetables and good restaurants. Compiled by Sally and John McKenna, price IR£12.95; their Bridgestone's guides to eating in Dublin and around Ireland is also worth a look. The Saturday eating column in *The Irish Times* is another good source of restaurants. Vegetarians will find Walker's *Where Can I Eat in Ireland?* as well as a small book written by Sally McKenna and published by Bridgestone very useful. The Northern Ireland Tourist Board issues a booklet entitled *Let's Eat Out in Northern Ireland*, which lists every eating place, from fish and chip shops to the most expensive and pretentious.

Drink

'The only cure for drinking is to drink more', so goes the Irish proverb. Organizations such as the Pioneers exist to wean the masses off 'the drink'—alcohol costs an arm and a leg, what with the taxes and the publican's cut; yet, nevertheless, an Irish bar can be one of the most convivial places in the world. The delicious liquor, the cosy snugs and the general hubbub of excited conversation, which in the evening might easily spark into a piece of impromptu singing, makes the business of taking a drink very pleasant. Pubs can also be as quiet as a grave, especially in the late afternoon when a few men nod over their pint, and an air of contemplation pervades. Murphy's, Smithwick's ale and Harp lager are three very good legal brews made in Ireland.

Guinness

You are bound to have been lured into trying Guinness by the persuasive advertisements you see all over Europe, for the export trade is thriving; but the place to get a real taste of the creamy dark liquor is in an Irish bar. It is at its most delicious when it is draught and drunk in a bar around Dublin, where it is made. Guinness does not travel well, especially on Irish roads. It is said to get its special flavour from the murky waters of the River Liffey, and you can go and find out for yourself if this is so by visiting the Brewery at St James Gate. The quality of taste once it has left the brewery depends on how well the publican looks after it and cleans the pipe from the barrel, so it varies greatly from bar to bar.

If it's obvious that you are a tourist, your Guinness will be decorated with a shamrock drawn on its frothy head! They've finally managed to get Guinness into a can—by all accounts it's very good but it's apparently important that it's drunk chilled (bottled draught no longer exists). If you are feeling adventurous, try something called black velvet—a mixture of Guinness and champagne.

whiskey

Whiskey has been drunk in Ireland for more than five hundred years and the word itself is derived from *uisge beatha*, the Irish for water of life. It is made from malted barley with a small proportion of wheat, oats and occasionally a pinch of rye. There are several brands, but Jameson's and Paddy are the best made in the south, and Bushmills in the North.

Irish coffee

Irish coffee is a wonderful combination of contrasts: hot and cold, black and white, and very intoxicating. It was first dreamed up in County Limerick earlier this century. It's made with a double measure of Irish whiskey, one tablespoon of double cream, one cup of strong, hot black coffee, and a heaped tablespoon of sugar. To make it, first warm a stemmed whiskey glass. Put in the sugar and enough hot coffee to dissolve the sugar. Stir well. Add the Irish whiskey and fill the glass and pour the cream slowly over a spoon. Do not stir the cream into the coffee; it should float on top. The hot whiskey-laced coffee is drunk through the cold cream.

poteen

Poteen (pronounced 'pot-cheen') is illicit whiskey, traditionally made from potatoes, although nowadays it is often made from grain. Tucked away in the countryside are stills which no longer bubble away over a turf fire, but on a Calor gas stove. Poteen is pretty disgusting stuff unless you get a very good brew, and it probably kills off a lot of braincells, so it's much better to stick to the legal liquid.

wine

If you happen to stay in that wonderful country house, Longueville, near Mallow, you must order a bottle of dry fruity white wine from Ireland's only vineyard. It is delicious, and rare because of the fierceness of the frost and uncertainty of the sunshine.

Bars and Licensing Hours

The old-fashioned serious drinking bar with high counter and engraved glass window, frosted so that the outside world couldn't intrude, is gradually disappearing. It used to be a male preserve. Farmers on a trip into town can be heard bewailing the weather or recounting the latest in cattle, land prices or gossip. What the inns have lost in character they compensate for, to a degree, with comfort. The bar of the local hotel is the place to find the priest when he is off-duty. My favourite drinking establishment is the grocery shop which is also a bar, where you ask for a taxi/plumber/undertaker, only to find that the publican or his brother combine all these talents with great panache!

In the Republic, public houses are open Mon–Sat 10am–11.30pm (unofficially, they may stay open into the early hours of the morning). In winter they close half an hour earlier. On Sundays and St Patrick's Day they open from 12.30am–10pm. There is no service on Christmas Day or Good Friday. In Northern Ireland, public houses are open Mon–Sat 11.30am–11pm, and they are closed on Sundays. You can always get a drink on Sundays at a hotel, though you are supposed to justify it by having a meal as well if you are not staying there. In the Republic, children are often allowed to sit in the lounge bar with packets of crisps and fizzy orange to keep them happy.

If you do get into a conversation in a bar, a certain etiquette is followed: men always buy everybody in your group a drink, taking it in turn to buy a round; women will find they are seldom allowed to! Both sexes offer their cigarettes around when having one. If there are ten in your group you will find yourself drunk from social necessity and out of pocket as well! The price in the Republic of wine, whiskey and beer is much higher than in the UK.

A bottle of whiskey is about IR£14. If you are bringing a car from France or the UK, it might be as well to bring some booze in with you, or stock up in Northern Ireland. The customs allowance is 1½ litres of distilled beverages or spirits, 12 litres of beer and (if the alcohol is bought duty-paid) 4 litres of wine per person. If you are a resident, you have to have been out of the Republic for 48 hours; this is to stop local people from nipping back and forth across the border to buy drink! At the time of writing, the European Court has ruled against this rule, but the judicial process may not be over.

Golf

We are most grateful to Bruce Critchley for this expert guide to Ireland's golf courses. Bruce is one of television's golf commentators, following a successful amateur international career in the 1960s. Now a consultant to golf-course developers, he also, in association with his wife's company, Critchley Pursuits, arranges tours of British, Irish and Continental courses for both English and American enthusiasts.

With the possible exception of Scotland, Ireland can boast more courses per head of population than any other country in the world. As with Scotland, quality is in no way diminished by quantity and, in common with the rest of the British Isles, the greatest courses are situated at the seaside. As host to the British Open Championship, names like St Andrews, Muirfield and Royal Birkdale are famous around the world. The likes of Portmarnock, Mount Juliet and Royal Portrush suffer nothing by comparison. But they are just the tip of Ireland's golfing iceberg, and no discerning golfer's experience is complete without a taste or two of what's littered around the shores.

The East of Ireland

Starting with Dublin, **Portmarnock** is the jewel of the Republic's crown and is situated less that 30 minutes' drive north of the city centre. The road out to Portmarnock passes **Royal Dublin**, and these two courses have for many years shared the honour of hosting the Irish Open Championship. Recently opened and already gaining a remarkable reputation for the quality of its greens and beautiful landscaping is **Luttrelstown** course: only about 15 minutes from the city centre west of Phoenix Park.

From Portmarnock and looking southeast, the only high ground is the Hill of **Howth**, and the course clinging precipitously to its southern slopes is well worth a visit—both for the quality of the golf and the spectacular views around. Just a few miles north and on a peninsula across the water from Malahide, lies the **Island Golf Course**, set amongst rolling dunes where it is hard to believe that Dublin airport is just 15 minutes away—by car. At Newtown House, St Margaret's, adjacent to the airport, only 7 miles to the city centre is the new **Open Golf Centre**. It is unusual in being open to visitors on a pay and play basis seven days a week; as well as offering 27 holes there is a driving range with 4 pros available for lessons. Further north still, next to Drogheda and at the mouth of the Boyne, lies the **County Louth Golf Course**, more widely known as **Baltray**. The home of the East of Ireland Championships, Baltray is reputed to have the finest greens in Ireland.

To the south of Dublin, **Delgany** is regarded as one of the nurseries of Irish golf, having produced several famous players including Harry Bradshaw and Eamon D'Arcy. Further on, both **Woodenbridge** and **Courtown** are two courses not far from the sea and well worth a visit.

Inland from Dublin and to the southwest, **Mount Juliet**, which has hosted the Murphy's Irish Open several years running, is regarded as probably the best inland course in Ireland; **Carlow** is also an exceptional course and **Mullingar** some 50 miles due west has been the scene of several international tournaments in recent years.

The North of Ireland

South of Belfast and close to the border with the Republic, closer to Dublin a few miles west of Phoenix Park, **Luttrelstown**, opened in 1993, is a beautifully landscaped course.

Royal County Down Golf Course at Newcastle is quite possibly the best links course in the world. Scenically stunning and lying right at the base of the Mountains of Mourne, literally where 'they sweep down to the sea', Newcastle is at its visual best in summer when the broom, so dangerous for the errant golfer, is in full bloom.

Up on the northern coast and within a short distance of the Giant's Causeway is **Royal Portrush**, the only Irish course ever to have hosted the Open Championship. Lacking perhaps Newcastle's visual charm, it is nevertheless a great test and only the most competent should tackle it on anything other than a calm day.

While there, don't ignore the **Valley Course**, which partially lies between Portrush and the sea. In fact, an entertaining few days can be spent in the Portrush and Portstewart area, for there are no less than five courses within a mile (1.6km) or so of one another.

Across Loch Foyle to the West, **Ballyliffin Golf Club** is well worth a visit. Set amid daunting sand hills and surrounded by the Atlantic on three sides, the course is nevertheless inland in character. Continuing westward across Lough Swilly, **Portsalon** and **Rosapenna** are a pair of courses from the last century that still test the games and equipment of the modern giants. That, allied to the stunning views of the rugged Donegal coastline, makes for a very special golfing treat.

The West of Ireland

The relatively new linksland, **Donegal Golf Course** at Murvagh, is a splendid challenge, measuring over 7000 yards (6400m) off the back. It was a real test for the ladies in their Irish Championships back in 1979. A gentler proposition is the delightful cliff-top course at the **Bundoran Golf Club** a few miles to the south.

The prince of courses in this part of the world is **Rosses Point**. Situated just outside the town of Sligo and within the shadow of Benbullen, Rosses Point is one of Ireland's great championship courses and has hosted most of the country's major events at one time or another. Close by, and not to be missed, are the seaside courses of **Strandhill** and **Inniscrone**.

Southwards and westwards brings the itinerant golfer to the testing **Westport Golf Course**, set on the shores of Clew Bay. This is another one to tackle on a calm day, as is the new **Ballyconneely Golf Club**, set on the western reaches of Connemara.

Round into the relative calm of Galway Bay, the **Galway Club** offers a more gentle test before moving on to that other great Irish links on the west coast—**Lahinch**. Traditionally the home of the South of Ireland Championships, it is yet another course with nothing but the Atlantic between it and Boston!

The Southwest of Ireland

Should the visitor be anxious to get going after flying into Shannon, he could almost walk to the **Shannon Golf Club** from the airport terminal building. A modern course, inland in character, there is good use of water and lovely views down to the River Shannon. But the real treasures lie on the other side. **Ballybunnion** has long stood beside the very best, and recently a second 18 has been added of almost equal quality. Some 20 miles (32km) to the south, Arnold Palmer has laid out an outstanding course on Kerry's coastline at **Tralee**.

The Ring of Kerry offers two widely differing courses, the **Dooks at Glenbeigh** and the mighty links of **Waterville**. Glenbeigh, only 5750 yards (5260m) in length, is supposedly the third-oldest course in the country and follows the naturally undulating dunes, as courses only could in the last century. Waterville is of much more recent construction and, with the ocean on three sides, the wind is an ever-present factor.

Just inland are a pair of courses on the shores of **Killarney**. Can there be any more beautiful setting for golf anywhere in the world? Perhaps the courses don't quite match up to the view, but then very few would. Nevertheless, it is a joy to play here.

Finally, and even though a little off the beaten track, no trip to this neck of the woods should miss the little nine-hole gem at **Bantry**, overlooking the famous bay with its stunning views.

The South of Ireland

Away from the pounding of the Atlantic Ocean, the courses in the south don't have the sand dunes out of which links courses are traditionally carved. Nonetheless, the natural beauty of the countryside lends a great backdrop wherever courses are constructed. And on the scenic front, the little nine-holer at **Doneraile** should not be passed up.

Cork has a couple of courses of which **Little Island** is the most spectacular. Holes alternate between the edge of the massive quarry on one side and views over the estuary on the other. Southwest of the city, **Bandon Golf Course**, set in the grounds of Castlebernard Castle, is well worth a visit, as is **Midleton** to the east.

To the north, **Clonmel** with its spectacular views over the plains of Tipperary and **Thurles**, where fine old oaks and elms command respect in its parkland setting, are another pair to be taken in as the golfing road leads back to Dublin.

So wherever you go in Ireland, golf courses abound, and whatever your standard you'll find something to enjoy. With facilities getting ever more crowded around the major cities of the world, Ireland offers golf as it used to be—the ability to get on a course in the hours of daylight, and green fees that are not going to break the bank.

A couple of words of advice. If you are thinking of a golfing holiday, some of the courses do get busy in summer and it is always advisable to check with clubs in advance and, where necessary, get a confirmed tee time. Also, every travelling golfer should carry a handicap certificate as proof of competence. Trolleys will be for hire at most clubs and quite a few will be able to lay on caddies if ordered in advance. Golf carts are not yet a feature of Irish golf and are not encouraged. One or two courses will permit their use with a medical certificate, but you will have to provide the cart!

Bord Fàilte publishes a couple of good guides on golfing and recently there have been quite a few books written on golf in Ireland.

Guides

The Irish love for their country and their famous facility with words can make touring with a guide an unforgettable pleasure. The local tourist office (*see* pp.52–5) should be able to put you in touch with a guide. Expect to pay around IR£60 a day, or IR£10 per hour; similar rates apply in the North. In the Republic you can contact Beatrice Healy, a freelance guide, at © (01) 454 5943.

Hazards and Emergencies

midges

Toads and adders are said to have fled from Ireland at the sound of St Patrick's bell tolling from the top of Croagh Patrick mountain; unfortunately, the voracious midges of the west coast did not take their cue! They are very persistent on warm summer evenings, so remember to arm yourself with insect repellent of some sort. There is plenty of choice in the Irish chemists if you forget. Wasps, hornets and horseflies also emerge in summer to irritate.

beasts

If you decide to have a picnic in some inviting green field, just check that there is not a bull in it first. High-spirited bullocks can be just as alarming; they come rushing up to have a good look and playfully knock you over in the process!

sea

A major hazard can be strong currents in the sea. One beach may be perfectly safe for bathing, and the one beside it positively dangerous. Always check with locals before you swim. There are lifeguards on most of the resort beaches.

walkers

Walkers who intend to go through bog and mountainous country be warned that, even though it looks dry enough on the road, once into the heather and moss you will soon sink into waterlogged ground. Wear stout boots (brogues) and bring at least an extra jersey. Sudden mists and rain can descend, and you can get very cold. You should not rely on mountain rescue teams to find you; if you do disappear into a mountain range, leave word locally as to where you plan to go, or a put a note on your car. During the shooting season (grouse and snipe from August to 3 January, duck from September to 31 January, and pheasant from 1 November to 1 January), be careful of wandering into stray shot on the hilly slopes or in marshy places.

motorists

Motorists in Dublin should always lock their cars, and leave them in authorized car parks. Many cars are stolen and taken for 'joy rides' by very young boys. Do not leave luggage or valuables in the car.

the fairies

There is just one last possible hazard which you might only have dreamt about: the mischievous fairies might put a spell on you so that you never want to return to your own country. It's not a joke, for Ireland is an enchanting country and difficult to leave. As a rule it is no use enquiring about charms against this enchantment, or any other; the answer is always the same: 'There used to be a lot of them in the old days but the priests put them down.' You get that answer about poteen too! Underneath, there is a sort of sneaking belief in fairies; for why, in a perfectly modern housing estate outside Sligo, is there a ragged mound which escaped the bulldozer and cement? Perhaps because it is a fairy rath? One last word on fairies: have you ever heard how they came about? Padraic Colum found out from a blind man whom he met in the west, who believed in them as firmly as in the Gospels. When the Angel Lucifer rebelled against God, Hell was made in a minute, and down to it God swept Lucifer and thousands of his followers, until the Angel Gabriel said, 'O God Almighty, Heaven will be swept clean.' God agreed and compromised, saying, 'Them that are in Heaven let them remain so, them that are in Hell, let them remain in Hell; and them that are between Heaven and Hell, let them remain in the air.' And the angels that remained between Heaven and Hell are the fairies.

emergencies

As mentioned above, if you do find yourself in trouble in Ireland, you will find no shortage of sympathetic help. If you fall ill, have an accident, or are the victim of some crime, people will rush to your aid. Whether they bring quite the help you need is another matter. If in doubt, get the advice of your hotel, the local tourist office, or the police. In serious cases (medical or legal), contact your embassy or consulate (*see* p.21). Try to keep your head: in the case of medical treatment, take your insurance documents, inform the people treating you of your insurance cover, and make sure you keep all receipts (or at least get someone reliable to do this for you).

The emergency telephone number (to call any of the emergency services) in both the Republic and the North is 999.

Heritage and Interpretative Centres

In the last ten years there has been a huge increase in these centres all over Ireland. The larger ones incorporate local history, flora and fauna, using audio visuals as an aid, or life-size models and actors dressed in period costume, producing 'an experience to remember'. The Office of Public Works have purpose built a few Interpretative Centres in places of great natural beauty and fragile ecology. Controversy has been provoked by the siting of one such centre in the middle of the Burren. Inevitably such places destroy some of the beauty and peace with huge carparks, WCs, craft centres etc., however sympathetic the architecture and landscaping may be. Many of the small heritage centres double as geneological centres and are situated in fine old buildings (mainly in towns), which have been restored by the efforts and enthusiasm of the local people.

Insurance

general

The best advice is, always insure your holiday, and do so as soon as you book your ticket. Standard travel insurance packages issued by the major insurance companies cover a broad range of risks, including cancellation due to unforeseen circumstances, transport delays caused by strikes or foul weather, loss or theft of baggage, medical insurance and compensation for injury or death. The cost of insurance may seem substantial, but it is negligible when compared to almost any claim, should misfortune befall you.

That said, it is worth checking to see whether any of your existing insurance schemes cover travel risks: certain British household insurance schemes, for example, include limited travel cover.

medical

Do remember that if you need medical or dental treatment you will be expected to pay for the treatment yourself, and then claim back the costs from your insurance company. This, of course, may not be something you can discuss on the operating table. *In extremis* the international emergency services offered by companies such as Europ Assistance or Travel Assistance International, which are often incorporated into travel insurance packages, demonstrate their blessings. For all kinds of medical care, citizens of EU countries can benefit from the mutual agreements that exist between EU member countries. British citizens travelling to the Republic can make use of any GP who has an agreement with the Health Board, but to benefit from this you should take Form E111 with you, obtainable from a Social Security Office in the UK in advance of your departure (you need to allow several weeks for your application to be processed). The same scheme also applies to dentists and to hospitals.

claims

Remember that to make a claim for loss or theft of baggage, you will need evidence that you have reported the loss to the police. Check your insurance details for the documentation required of you by the insurance company in such circumstances. It is, by the way, useful to have more than one copy of your insurance policy—if your baggage is stolen, the document may go with it.

Money

Since the Republic joined the European Monetary System, the Irish pound (IR£) and the English pound (UK£) are no longer worth the same. The difference fluctuates, usually to the detriment of the Irish pound or punt (pronounced 'poont'), although at the time of writing the two currencies stand at about the same level give or take 3–4 pence.

Shopkeepers in the Republic generally accept sterling, but in the North they will not touch your punt, except perhaps in a border town.

Both currencies use the pound as the basic unit, divided into 100 pence. There are coins for the pence in both currencies; and £1 and IR£1 coins. There are notes of £5, £10, £20, £50 in both currencies, and a IR£100 note.

You may bring in any amount of foreign or Irish currency to Ireland, but you must not leave with more than IR£100 cash, in denominations of IR£20 or less, although any uncashed traveller's cheques may be taken out. There are various *bureaux de change* where you can change money, and most major hotels also provide this service, but these are unlikely to offer as good a rate of exchange as the banks. There are exchange counters at the main airports for international flights. Opening times: Dublin: summer 6.45am–10pm, winter 7.30am–8.30pm; Shannon: open to service all flights; Cork: 10am–3pm (Mon–Fri); Knock: open to service all scheduled flights; Belfast International Airport, 7am–8pm.

traveller's cheques

Traveller's cheques and Eurocheques are accepted throughout Ireland. Leading credit and charge cards (MasterCard/Access, Visa, American Express and Diner's Club) are widely accepted in major hotels and restaurants, but do check this beforehand. If the banks are closed, hotels and many large shops will take traveller's cheques.

banks

All small towns have at least one bank. The banks are open Mon–Fri, 10–12.30 and 1.30–4 in the Republic and open until 5:30pm on Thursdays; in the North they close at 4, and in Belfast and Londonderry they do not close for lunch. In the Republic, banks in the larger towns will usually have one day each week—normally market day—when they will stay open until 5pm. In Dublin, banks stay open until 5pm on Thursdays and large branches don't close for lunch.

The bank usually occupies the grandest house in town—the various banking groups seem to have some sort of conscience about historical buildings, which is very rare in Ireland. The moving of money is accompanied by massive security, which looks very out of keeping with the happy-go-lucky attitude in Ireland, but is necessary because bank raids have become so common.

the cost of living

Prices in Ireland are generally on a par with other European countries. What will influence the visitor's view of the general level of costs is more likely to be the current rate of exchange than the local price structure.

Here are a few guidelines for the visitor. An expensive hotel will cost about IR£120 per night for two people in a double room; bed-and-breakfast accommodation (guesthouses), around IR£20 for two. A meal in a restaurant will cost anything from IR£15 to IR£25 and more per head, although tourist menus at hotels can often offer a set meal at around IR£6. A pint of beer costs around IR£2.00; a litre of milk 62p; a pack of 20 cigarettes IR£2.50; a loaf of bread 86p; butter per lb IR£1.40; a kilo of potatoes 30p.

tipping

Tipping is not really a general habit in Ireland, except in taxis and in eating places where there is table service. Taxi-drivers will expect to be tipped at a rate of about 10 per cent of the fare; porters and doormen 50p or so. There is no tipping in pubs, but in hotel bars where you are served by a waiter it is usual to leave a small tip. A service charge of 12 per cent, sometimes 15 per cent, is usually raised automatically on hotel and restaurant bills. Where this is not the case, a tip of this magnitude would be in order, if the service merits it.

Museums and Galleries

Most museums and galleries etc. are either free or charge a small admission price of between IR£1.75 and IR£3. This is indicated throughout the book by '*adm*'; any museum whose admission charge is above IR£4 is indicated as '*adm exp*'. Specific opening hours are given with each museum.

Newspapers

The best newspaper to read whilst in Ireland is the *Irish Times*, followed closely by the *Irish Independent* and the *Cork Examiner*. In Northern Ireland the most widely read morning newspaper is the *Belfast Newsletter*, which has a Unionist slant.

The only evening paper, the *Belfast Telegraph*, is middle-of-the-road. The *Irish Times* on Saturdays lists 'What is on'—exhibitions, festivals, concerts, etcetera around the country. *Image* is a glossy magazine on the lines of *Harpers & Queen*, and has information on fashion, interior decoration and restaurants. *Phoenix* is the Irish equivalent of *Private Eye*.

Packing

Whatever you do, come to Ireland expecting rain—gumboots, umbrellas, raincoats, etcetera are essential, unless you want to stay inside reading a book all day. Once you get out into the rain it is never as bad as it looks, and the clouds begin to clear as you appear. Bring warm jerseys, trousers, woollen socks, and gloves for autumn, winter and early spring. The best thing to do is to expect the cold and wet and then get a pleasant surprise when it's sunny and hot—so do not forget to sneak in a few T-shirts just in case. Sometimes the sun shines furiously in March and April and you end up with a very convincing tan.

If you like walking, bring a pair of fairly stout shoes—trainers end up bedraggled and let the water in. Fishing rods and swimsuits are worth packing, if you think you may have cause to regret leaving them behind. Bring a sleeping bag if you plan to stay at youth hostels. If you plan to stay in bed-and-breakfast accommodation, take your own towels, as those traditionally supplied tend to be on the mean side.

You will be amazed at what the village shop sells, anything from pots and pans to the finest French wines, and maybe some fresh salmon trout if you are lucky. In the Republic you can be sure of finding a shop open until 10 o'clock in the evening and on Sundays as well. The chemists are also well stocked so that headache pills, camera films, contraceptives etcetera are easily obtainable.

Post Offices

Letterboxes are green in the Republic and red in the North. As you would expect, you have to put British stamps on letters posted in the North.

If you do not have a fixed address in Ireland, letters can be sent Poste Restante to any post office and picked up when you produce proof of your identity. If after three months they are gathering dust in the corner of the post office, they will be sent back to the sender. There is a post office in every village which is usually the telephone exchange as well and a hive of activity. You can send telemessages from the post office but you need to book in advance.

The post office should be open 9–5 in weekdays, 9–1 on Saturdays, and closed on Sundays and public holidays. Sub-post offices close on one day a week at 1. The GPO in O'Connell Street, Dublin, is open 8–11 and in the mornings on Sundays and bank holidays.

Public Holidays

New Year's Day	1 January
St Patrick's Day	Republic only, 17 March
Good Friday	(widely observed as a holiday, but not an official one);
Easter Monday	
May Day	1st May/early May N. Ireland
Spring Holiday	N. Ireland only, end May
June Holiday	Republic only, first Monday in June
July 12	N. Ireland only
August Holiday	Republic only, first Monday in August
Summer Holiday	N. Ireland only, end August
October Holiday	Republic only, last Monday in October
Christmas Day	25 December
Boxing Day/St Stephen's Day	26 December

Shopping in Ireland is the most relaxing pastime because nobody ever makes you feel that you have to buy anything, so you can browse to your heart's content. Good design and high-quality craftsmanship make for goods which will last you for a lifetime, and delight the senses. I would choose to take home Irish linen, handloomed tweed, Aran sweaters, pottery, glass and modern Irish silver. These you can find easily in the craft centres which have been set up all over the country. The Craft Council of Ireland, Powerscourt Townhouse, South William St, Dublin 2, ✆ (01) 679 7383, a relatively new body, has given a great boost to the many talented craft workers, and helped them to market their wares and join forces in studios and workshops, usually in IDA (Industrial Development Authority) parks, ✆ (01) 668 6633. If you are in the Dublin area, look out for Marlay Park, Rathfarnham, and The Tower, IDA Enterprise, Pearse Street, Dublin. Another excellent centre is in Roundstone, Co. Galway. If you see something you like at any of the craft shops and centres, buy it then and there because you are not likely to see it again in another shop. These craft items are not cheap because of the artistry and labour involved, but you can find bargains at china, crystal and linen factory shops if you are prepared to seek them out.

The main goodies to take home with you are described in detail below. More fleeting pleasures, which you can share with your friends back home, are smoked salmon, cheese, wheaten bread, home-cured bacon, and whiskey. These are available at Shannon and Dublin Airport shops. Grinning leprechauns, colleen dolls, Guinness slogan T-shirts and shamrock mugs are stacked high in most gift shops if you want something cheerful and cheap, but do not ignore the real products from Ireland.

opening hours

Irish shops are open 9.30–5.30, Mon–Sat. Craft shops in scenic areas are usually open on Sundays as well, especially if they combine as tea shops. In some towns there is an early-closing day when businesses close at one. This is normally a Wednesday, although it may be a different day in some areas. You can be sure that if one town has shut down, its neighbour will be busy, and open for business. Large shopping centres which operate on the outskirts of town are unaffected by early closing. Dunnes Stores can usually be found in these shopping centres. It is the equivalent of the British Marks & Spencer, and sells cheap clothing.

Irish Specialities

Irish lace is one of the lightest and most precious of all the specialities you can pack in your suitcase and you find it in Carrickmacross, County Monaghan, in Kenmare, County Kerry, and in Limerick City. Some smart shops, such as Brown Thomas in Dublin, also stock it, but it is fun if you can go around the convents and co-operatives where the lace is made. In Carrickmacross the nuns design lawn appliqué on a background of net. In Limerick the lace is worked completely in thread on the finest Brussels net.

Carrickmacross lace: from the Lace Cooperative, Carrickmacross, ✆ (042) 62085. Limerick lace: the Good Shepherd Convent, Clare Street, Limerick, ✆ (061) 45183/45178. Available Mon–Fri in the shop attached.

Kenmare lace: Kenmare Lace and Design Centre, Kenmare, ✆ (064) 41679. Shop open Mon–Fri.

Tweed is a wonderful fabric. Not only does it keep you warm in winter, but it also lets your skin 'breathe' and it is useful most of the year round if you live in northern climes and are not addicted to central heating. It is hand-woven from sheep's wool, and the Irish have got not only the texture and tension of the cloth right, but also the speckled, natural colours of the countryside. Donegal tweed is particularly attractive, and in every subtle shade under the sun. It is available all over County Donegal but a particularly wide selection is available from Magees, The Diamond, Donegal Town, ✆ (073) 21100; and McNutts, The Harbour, Downings, ✆ (074) 55324. Both shops also stock sports jackets and wonderfully stylish coats for women. If you explore around Ardara you will still find thick, naturally dyed tweed. Avoca Hand-Weavers, in Co. Wicklow, make fine tweed in brilliant colours. You can also find **bainin** (pronounced 'bawneen'), an undyed tweed which is often used for upholstery. To find this gorgeous stuff in Dublin try the Kilkenny Design Centre and the Blarney Woollen Mills in Nassau Street, ✆ (01) 677 7066; Cleo's, Kildare Street, ✆ (01) 676 1421 and the Powerscourt Centre, between William Street and Clarendon Street.

Hand-knitted sweaters. Make sure you buy one which has the hand-knitted label on it; it makes the whole difference when you are buying an Aran. These are made out of tough wool, lightly coated in animal oils, so they are water-resistant and keep you as warm as toast. You can get them in natural white or various colours, and the pattern differs quite a bit. In the past the wives of the fishermen used to have a family pattern so that they could identify anyone who had drowned. These knits come in a variety of styles; they stretch after being worn a while and last for years. It is possible to buy original and attractive hand-knitted clothing in craft shops all over Ireland, although Connacht, Donegal and the coastal stretches of Munster have the greatest variety. Of course, Dublin has endless boutiques selling such items. Elegant stoles and generous shawls, woven bedspreads and car rugs are other excellent buys. For sale in Connemara, in the Clifden/Leenane region, are soft, striped wool rugs and cured sheepskins which make good bedside rugs.

Linen. Ulster is still famous for its linen, although the blue fields of rippling flax flowers are no more. You can buy excellent linen tea cloths and fine linen sheets in Belfast. Hand-embroidered handkerchiefs and tablecloths in Co. Donegal. Brown Thomas in Grafton Street, Dublin, ✆ (01) 679 5666, sell the most beautiful linen, including double-damask table linen.

Glass. Waterford Crystal is world-famous for its quality and design. All imperfect pieces are smashed, so you cannot buy cheap seconds! County Waterford Glass Ltd, Kilbarry, Waterford, ✆ (051) 73311. You can tour the factory to see it being hand-blown and hand-engraved, and it is sold all over Ireland in good quality stores. It is possible to buy it as you are leaving the country at the Dublin and Shannon Airports' duty-free shops, but the selection is small. All the stores will pack and mail glass overseas for you. It is still possible to buy old Waterford glass, which has a blackish tint to it, in antique shops—but it is very costly. Attractive crystal glass can be bought in Cavan, Tyrone, Sligo and Cork, at the factories there. To my mind, the hand-blown glass designed by the Jerpoint Glassworks in Co. Kilkenny, ✆ (056) 24350, is worth collecting. The inspiration for their thick-lipped and satisfyingly shaped wine goblets and whiskey glasses came from Simon Pearse, who used to make glass in Ireland, but has moved his enterprise to the USA. You can get Jerpoint Glass in the Kilkenny Design Centre and in discerning craft shops. As you travel through Ireland you may well discover other original glass-blowers, as small craft industries are flourishing all over the country.

Pottery and china. Talented potters work in rural communities all over Ireland, and one of the best places to find their work for sale is at IDA centres. Craft shops also usually carry the local potters' work. One of my particular favourites is Roundstone ceramics at the IDA Roundstone Park, Connemara. Seamus Laffan and Rose O'Toole create beautifully shaped and coloured pieces with designs inspired by mythology, such as serpents and fish.

Belleek pottery in Fermanagh produces another very individual type of china. The pottery has been established since the 18th century and the pieces are typically of a lustrous creamy glaze decorated with shamrocks and flowers. Contact the Factory Shop, Belleek, ✆ (036 565) 501. Arklow pottery in Co. Wicklow produces quite pretty stuff, and the factory shop has cheap seconds. Contact The Factory, Arklow; ✆ (0402) 32401. Very attractive kitchen china is produced by Nicholas Mosse, who 'rediscovered' the traditional spongeware decorations, so common until the 1940s. You can buy his work in the Kilkenny Design Centre.

Connemara Marble is a natural green stone found in the west which ranges from bright field-green through to jade and oak-leaf colour, sometimes with stripes of brown in it. Many of the craft shops in the area work the marble into jewellery fashioned in Celtic designs, and sell it with other locally made things such as paperweights or chess sets.

Jewellery, silver and antiques. Amongst all the other trinkets and souvenirs available, *claddagh rings* still remain the nicest of all love tokens and are very evocative of the west of Ireland. For pretty and original jewellery, try the Irish Design Yard in Temple Bar or Emma Stewart-Liberty in the Powerscourt Centre, Dublin, ✆ (01) 791603. Here too you can find good antique shops selling Irish silver and Victorian jewellery. Irish antiques are now very highly prized and expensive. Gone are the great country-house auctions of the 1960s where fine furniture was going for a song. If you are in Dublin during July, try to go to the Antiques Fair at Mansion House. Auctions are held in Adam's Auction House, St Stephen's Green. Look in the *Irish Times* on Saturday for details of auctions and house-contents sales.

Woven baskets. All over Ireland you can buy baskets made of willow or rush in different shapes and sizes: bread baskets, turfholders, place mats and St Brigid Crosses—charms against evil.

Traditional musical instruments. A wonderful present for a musical friend. For *bodhrams* (a type of drum) try Danvel Musical Instruments, Marlay Park Craft Courtyard, Dublin, ✆ (01) 942741. Or Malachy Kearns, Roundstone Musical Instruments, Michael

Killeen Park, Roundstone, Co. Galway, ✆ (095) 35875. He also makes flutes and harps. For *uillean* pipes, contact Eugene Lambe, Fanore, Co. Clare, ✆ (065) 76122; and Charles Roberts, Creagadoo, Glencar, Co. Sligo. For fiddles/violins, contact Peadar O'Loughlin, Clare Business Centre, Ennis, Co. Clare, ✆ (065) 88083.

Unusual and historical gifts can be bought through the Irish Georgian Society, 74 Merrion Square, Dublin 2, ✆ (01) 676 7053. You can buy exotic tablemats depicting foreign and domestic birds by the 18th-century Dublin artist Samuel Dixon; or reproductions of Mrs Delaney's (1700–88) flower collages; maps; jewellery; Castletown Print Rooms sheets, with which you can recreate an 18th-century print room, and the Charlemont fabric, an 18th-century volunteer scene reproduced in 100% cotton.

Food and drink. Soda, wheaten and potato bread are found all over Ireland. When you are leaving the country, McCambridge's brown bread is available at airport shops. If leaving from Ulster, buy some Sheelin Bakery wheaten mix or the freshly made loaves, which are delicious. Smoked salmon is sold all over Ireland, and at the airport shops. If in Co. Galway it is worth seeking the wild salmon smoked by a French couple: contact Salt Lake Manor, Clifden, ✆ (095) 21278. Farmhouse cheese in every shape, size and texture is available from the producer and from wholefood shops and delicatessens. If in Dublin, choose from the excellent selection at Magills on Clarendon St, Dublin 2. Irish whiskey (note the 'e', which is the Irish way of spelling it), is slightly sweeter than Scotch. Try Bushmills, Paddy's, Powers and Jamesons. All these brands are available in off-licences throughout the country. Cork gin is considered to have a delicious tang of juniper, far superior to the English brand of Gordon's. Popular liqueurs are Irish Mist, which contains whiskey and honey; Tullamore Dew; and Bailey's Irish Cream. Definitely worth trying if you like sweet and tasty things, Black Bush is a liqueur whiskey.

Weights and Measures

1 kilogram = 2.205 lb

1 litre = 1.76 Imperial pints = 2.11 US pints

1 centimetre = 0.39 inches

1 metre = 39.37 inches = 3.28 feet

1 kilometre = 0.621 miles

1 hectare = 2.47 acres

1 lb = 0.45 kilograms

1 Imperial pint = 0.56 litres

1 US pint = 0.47 litres

1 Imperial gallon = 4.54 litres

1 US gallon = 3.78 litres

1 foot = 0.305 metres

1 mile = 1.609 kilometres

1 acre = 0.404 hectares

Adventure Sports

The Association for Adventure Sports (AFAS) can give you information and contact telephone numbers and addresses for hand-gliding, mountaineering, canoeing, sub-aqua, board-sailing, surfing—in fact, almost any sport that you can think of! Contact the Association for Adventure Sport (AFAS), House of Sport, Longmile Road, Dublin 12, ✆ (01) 450 9845.

In Northern Ireland, the Sports Council can give you contact numbers and addresses for any sporting activity in the state. Contact the Sports Council for Northern Ireland House of Sport, Upper Malone Road, Belfast, BT9 5LA, ✆ (01232) 381222.

Beagling

This is an athletic sport in which you follow the hounds on foot until they pick up the scent of a hare, then you usually have to start running. The hare is always a good match for the hounds when it is on home ground. You do not need any special clothes or skill and visitors are welcome. They meet in the winter, and often on Sundays. The Irish Tourist Board (Bord Fáilte and NITB) have a list of beagle hunt clubs, or you can write to The Hon. Secretary, Irish Masters of Beagles Assoc., Tipper Road, Naas, Co. Kildare, ✆ (01) 774 301 (office), or (045) 76251 (home).

Bird-watching

You can still hear the corncrake amongst the fields of Rathlin Island, or the choughs calling from the rocky headlands. Walking along the coastal mudflats in winter, whether you are in Co. Down or Co. Wexford, you will very likely see whooper swans. Ireland has more thant 60 bird sanctuaries. For details write to the Wildlife Service, Office of Public Works, 51 St Stephen's Green, Dublin 2, ✆ (01) 661 3111. Field trips are organized by local branches of the Irish Wild Bird Conservancy, and there are details in the quarterly newsletter. Write to the Irish Wild Bird Conservancy, Ruttledge House, 8 Longford Place, Monkstown, Co. Dublin, ✆ (01) 2804322. Or RSPB, Belvoir Park Forest, Belfast 8; ✆ (01232) 491547. Or to the National Trust (NI), Rowallane, Saintfield, Co. Down, BT24 7LH, ✆ (0232) 510721.

Canoeing

This is an exciting and compelling way to tour Ireland via the Liffey and the Barrow Rivers, with their smooth-flowing stretches, rapids and weirs. The other principal rivers are the Nore, Boyne, Slaney, Lee, Shannon, Suir and Blackwater. You can always camp by the waterside as long as you get permission from the owner.

For details of the many rivers and waterways, sea canoeing and tuition, write to: AFAS, House of Sport, Longmile Road, Dublin 12, ✆ (01) 450 9845. Nearly everything a canoeist could require can be bought at the Great Outdoors, Chatham St, Dublin 2, ✆ (01) 6794293. For canoeing in the North, contact the Sports Council, The House of Sport, Upper Malone Road, Belfast, BT9 5LA, ✆ (0232) 381222.

Caving

This activity has become more organised recently with the establishment of the Speleological Union of Ireland .The caving possibilities in the Cavan/Fermanagh area and in Co. Sligo are numerous. For information, contact: AFAS (address above) or Dave Miller of the Irish Speleological Association, 22 Abbey Park, Blackrock, Co Dublin.

Cruising the Inland Waterways

This is an unforgettable and exciting way to travel around Ireland. The main areas are the River Shannon, which is navigable from Lough Key to Killaloe; the River Erne, which has two huge island-studded lakes and is navigable for more than 50 miles (80km) from Belturbet to the little village of Belleek (which makes exquisite china). The two are now linked due to the recent restoration and opening of the Shannon-Erne Waterway; and the Grand Canal and the River Barrow (the canal links Dublin with the Shannon and the Barrow). Along the waterways you pass tumbledown castles, abbeys, beautiful flowers, birds and peaceful, lush scenery. In the evening you can moor up your boat for a meal and a jar and listen to some good traditional music. There are festivals and boat rallies, but they only happen for a couple of days a year, so if it's peace and quiet you want, don't worry.

The **Erne waterway** is beautifully wooded with nature reserves and little islands amongst which to meander. In all, Lough Erne covers 300 square miles (777 sq km) of water. Cruiser hire companies operate around the lakes. Contact the Erne Charter Boat Association through Fermanagh Tourism, Enniskillen, ✆ (01365) 323110. An exciting new development has been the opening of the Shannon Erne waterway which links the North and South and makes it possible to navigate 300km of waterways. It is possible to get a one-way rental. Contact Erincurrach Cruising, Blaney, Enniskillen ✆ (01365) 641507/641737.

On the **Shannon** there are several companies offering luxury cabin cruisers for self-drive hire, ranging from two to eight berths. All are fitted with fridges, gas cookers, hot water and showers; most have central heating. A dinghy, charts, binoculars and safety equipment are included on the river and lough routes. Groceries and stores can be ordered in advance and collected when you arrive. You have to be over 21 to be skipper, and the controls must be understood by at least two people, but no licence is necessary. You get an hour of tuition, or more if you need it. The average price for a six-berth cruiser for one week ranges from IR£550 in April to about IR£1000 in July/August. Ask for details from your travel agent, or the nearest Irish tourist office, or contact the following companies direct:

Emerald Star Line Ltd, ✆ (01) 679 8166 (Dublin office), or ✆ (01509) 41120 (Portumna), or ✆ (078) 20234 (Carrick-on-Shannon).

Ballykeeran Cruisers, Athlone, Co. Westmeath, ✆ (0902) 85163.

Derg Line Cruisers, Killaloe, Co. Clare, ✆ (061) 376364.

Celtic Canal Cruisers Ltd, Tullamore, Co. Offaly, ✆ (0506) 21861.

Shannon Sailing Ltd, Nenagh, Co. Tipperary, ✆ (067) 24295.

Athlone Cruisers Ltd, Athlone, ✆ (0902) 72892.

Day trips and pleasure cruises are also available on the Shannon. Contact the **Jolly Mariner Marina**, Athlone, Co. Westmeath, ✆ (0902) 72892/72113. Some of the companies listed above also operate river cruises. It is possible to take the **Killarney Waterbus** through the famous lakes for a trip of 1½ hours, ✆ (064) 32806.

Other cruiser possibilities include exploring Lough Corrib. Contact: **Corrib Cruisers**, Cong, Co. Mayo, ✆ (092) 46029. Galley cruises, with meals, which go from New Ross up the River Barrow or River Nore. Contact: Dick Fletcher, **Galley Cruising Restaurant**, Bridge Quay, New Ross, Co. Wexford, ✆ (051) 21723.

You will find that there are excellent **pubs and restaurants** catering for the needs of the cruisers; ask at the local tourist office. Good pubs along the Shannon include Hughes Pub, Northgate Street, Athlone; Conlins, Church Street, Athlone; Garry Kennedy's, Portrow; Hough's Pub and Killeen's in Shannonbridge; the Sail Inn, Scarriff; the Jolly Mariner, Sean's Bar and the Green Olive, Athlone; the Crew's Inn in Roosky.

Useful reading: *The Shell Guide to the Shannon, The Guide to the Grand Canal,* and the *Guide to the River Barrow.* Available from Eason and Son Ltd, 40 Lower O'Connell Street, Dublin 1.

Hang-gliding

Ireland is a hang-glider's paradise: shaped like a saucer with a mountainous rim. The wind blows from the sea or from the flat central plains. Most of the hills are bare of power-lines and trees, and the famous turf provides soft landings. Flying in the 26 counties is controlled by the Irish Hang-Gliding Association. Contact: AFAS House of Sport, Longmile Rd, Dublin 12, ✆ (01) 450 9845. In Northern Ireland, contact the Northern Ireland Hang-gliding Club, Hon. Secretary, Tom Purvis, 43 Ransevyn Park, Whitehead, BT38 9LY, Co. Antrim, ✆ (019603) 73439. Also contact AFAS and the Sports Council for Northern Ireland (*see* p.42).

Horse-racing

Irish people are wild about horses; they breed very good ones, and they race them brilliantly. You can go and watch them being exercised on the Curragh in Co. Kildare, a nursery of some of the finest racehorses in the world. Classic flat races which take place on the Curragh are the Airlie/Coolmore Irish 2000 Guineas, and Goffs Irish 1000 Guineas in May, the Budweiser Irish Derby in June, far and away the premier International flat race of the year; the Kildangan Stud Irish Oaks in July, and in September the Jefferson Smurfit Memorial Irish St Leger. Close to the Curragh is the Irish National Stud with its magnificent and authentic Japanese Garden. The flat racing season begins in March and ends in November with occasional Sunday meetings; other important flat racing takes place at the modern Leopardstown course on the south side of Dublin.

The main National Hunt (steeplechasing and jumping courses) are at Leopardstown, Punchestown, Navan, Gowran, Galway and, of course, Fairyhouse, where you can watch the exciting Irish Grand National on Easter Monday. The provincial courses are Ballinrobe, Bellewstown, Dundalk, Clonmel, Downpatrick, Down Royal (also known as The Maze), Kilbeggan, Limerick, Mallow, Roscommon, Sligo, Thurles, Tipperary, and Wexford; other courses where holiday meetings are held include Killarney (mid-July), Galway (end of July), Tramore (mid-August), Laytown (August), Tralee (end of August), and Listowel (late September).

The most fashionable event is the 3-day meeting held at Punchestown near Naas, Co. Kildare during the last week of April. Admission charges for all courses vary between approx IR£5 and IR£10 per adult. A good-value annual badge is available at about IR£75. Most hunts organise Point-to-point meetings—3-mile (4.8km) chases over fences for amateur riders—between January and May. Car park charges are approximately IR£5. Irish point-to-points are usually freezing cold but great fun; the background and form of each horse is known and discussed with great enthusiasm.

A speciality of Irish National Hunt racing are 'Bumpers' which are 2-mile (3.2km) flat races confined to amateur riders, riding novice jumpers. The greatest fun of all are the horse races held on the strands at Laytown at the end of July or beginning of August. The weekly *Irish Field* and daily *Racing Post* and *Sporting Life* publish form, venues and times of all race meetings and point-to-points. The Irish Tourist Board (Bord Fáilte) *Calendar of Events* lists racing fixtures at the back.

Hunting

This is another popular sport in Ireland. Any visitors are welcomed by the various hunts, and it is not very expensive. Ask the Irish Tourist Board (Bord Fáilte) for a list, or the local riding centre for details. Altogether there are 85 recognized packs, and although some are stag hounds and harriers, in the main they are foxhounds. The famous **Galway Blazers** hunt over stone walls in the west. There are double banks in the south, and ditches and streams in the east. The hunting **season** starts in October and ends in March, with meets starting in the mid-morning. Stables for the hire of a horse for the day's hunting can usually be found through the local hunt secretary (although you must be experienced), and costs about IR£60. The cap fee varies from IR£30 to IR£70 per day.

The **Dublin Horse Show**, which is a principal sporting and social event in Ireland, includes showjumping competitions for the Aga Khan Trophy, the Nations Cup and the Grand Prix.

For details on the Scarteen Hunt and the Black and Tans, *see* pp.71–2.

Hurling

This is to the Irish what cricket is to the English. Fifteen men with hurleys thrash away at a leather ball and combine neat footwork in perfect combination with the stick-work. Hurling and Gaelic football are promoted by the **Gaelic Athletic Association** and played with an exhilarating and unbelievably deft skill. When it is played well it can be beautiful to watch and occasionally extremely dangerous. Money earned is put back into national programmes; the GAA is still closely connected with Nationalist objectives. Look in local newspapers for details of matches. The All Ireland Hurling final is usually held at the beginning of September at Croke Park, Dublin.

Mountaineering and Hill-walking

The Irish mountains and hill areas are not high (few peaks are over 3000ft/915m), but they are rugged, varied, beautiful and unspoilt. There are quartz peaks, ridges of sandstone, bog-covered domes, and cliff-edged limestone plateaux. Excellent walking trails have been or are in the process of being developed at the moment. General advice, information and a list of hill-walking and rock-climbing clubs can be obtained from the Mountaineering Council of Ireland, Association for Adventure Sports (AFAS), House of Sport, Long Mile Road, Dublin 12, ✆ (01) 450 9845. They can also send you a full list of guides. Bord Fáilte offices throughout Ireland also stock hill-walking information sheets for individual areas.

The Ordnance Survey ½-inch-to-1-mile maps and a compass are essentials for serious walkers. Please remember there are very few tracks on Irish mountains, and always let your hotel know where you are climbing or walking, or leave a note in your car, just in case you have an accident. Mountain rescue in the Republic is co-ordinated by the Gardai (Police) and in the six counties by the Royal Ulster Constabulary. There are mountain rescue teams in the main mountain areas.

Details of organized courses and holidays can be obtained from Tiglin Adventure Centre, Ashford, Co. Wicklow, ✆ (0404) 40169; and the Youth Hostel Association, *An Oige*, 6 Mountjoy Street, Dublin 1, ✆ (01) 830 4555. For climbing in the Mourne Mountains, contact the Tullymore Mountain Centre, Bryansford, Nr Newcastle, Co. Down, ✆ (013967) 22158. Or House of Sport, Upper Malone Road, Belfast, ✆ (01232) 381222, which will book courses for you.

Connemara Contours, Island House, Market Street, Clifden, Co. Galway, ✆ (095) 21379 offer walking holidays in the west of Ireland.

Polo

You can go to the only residential polo school in Europe. Contact Major Hugh Dawnay, MFH, Whitefield Court Polo School, Waterford, ✆ (051) 884216. Or you can watch it (much cheaper) in Phoenix Park, Dublin. The All Ireland Polo Club in Phoenix Park is one of the oldest clubs in the world. Matches take place Wednesday evenings, Saturday and Sunday afternoons, from May to the middle of September. For more details ring the Club Pavilion, ✆ (01) 677 6248.

Riding Holidays

Ireland is really opening up for horse riders, with many new residential schools and companies offering pony-trekking holidays. The Irish are putting their natural love of horses to good use, and the areas of beauty where you can ride include empty beaches that stretch for miles, heathery valleys, forests, empty country roads and loughside tracks. Accommodation and food are arranged for you. Full details from Bord Fáilte, PO Box 273, Dublin 8, ✆ (01) 284 4768; and the Northern Ireland Tourist Board (NITB), St Anne's Court, 59 North Street, Belfast BT1 1NB, ✆ (01232) 246609.

horse-drawn caravans

You get a trustworthy and solid horse, a barrel-shaped caravan which sleeps four, and you can travel at a relaxing pace, usually about 9 miles (15kms) a day. Cost per week is from IR£200 low-season to IR£500 in July and August. Write for the relevant Fact Sheet, No. IS16C, to Bord Fáilte, PO Box 273, Dublin 8, or contact Mr David Slattery, Slattery's Horse-drawn Caravans, 1 Russell Street, Tralee, Co. Kerry, ✆ (066) 21722; and Dieter and Mary Clissmann, Dieter Clissmann Horse-drawn Caravans, Carrigmore Farm, Wicklow, Co. Wicklow, ✆ (0404) 48188, ✆ (0404) 48288. Kilvahan Horse Drawn Caravans, Cullenagh, Portlaoise, Co. Laois, ✆ (0502) 27048, ✆ (0502) 27225.

Sailing

The Irish coastline is uniquely beautiful, with diverse conditions and landscapes. The waters are never crowded, and the shoreline is completely unspoilt. On one of those sublimely beautiful evenings when the light touches each hill and field with an exquisite clarity, you will think yourself amongst the most privileged in the world. And if you want a bit of a 'crack', there are many splendid bars and restaurants to be visited in the sheltered harbours. But the peace and calm of the sky, the land and the sea in the many inlets is deceptive, for the open seas in the northwest can be rough and treacherous—exposed as they are to the North Atlantic. So a journey around the whole coastline should only be attempted by experienced sailors. If you do not have your own yacht, it is possible to charter a variety of craft; whilst if it is your ambition to learn to sail, there are several small and friendly schools.

Ireland has a long sailing tradition, with more than 125 yacht and sailing clubs around the country. The Royal Cork Yacht Club at Crosshaven is the oldest in the world, and was founded in 1720 as the Water Club of the Harbour of Cork. Many of these clubs preserve their original clubhouses, and emanate a feeling of tradition and comfort. Visitors are made very welcome, and are encouraged to use the club facilities. Those who wish to eat on board can buy wonderful bread, cheese and other high-quality groceries from the local shops. Seafood can be brought from the trawlers fishing the waters around you. And it is possible to find good food and entertainment in local bars and restaurants, especially in the Cork and Kerry area.

where to sail

The Southwest

Ireland's southwest coastline bordering the counties of Cork and Kerry is a favourite with Irish sailors, and it has a good selection of charter companies, sailing schools and board-sailing (wind-surfing) facilities. The harbours are charming, and the peninsulas and islands around which you can sail are magnificent. In the southwest you will also find many sites of historical interest close to the harbours of Crosshaven, Kinsale, Rosscarbery, Glendore, Schull, Rosbrin, Castletownbere, Kenmare, Caherdaniel, Dingle and Tralee.

The West

Further west, in County Galway and County Mayo, there is exciting sailing around the Aran Islands, Clifden, Renville and Clew Bay, and the many deserted islands with hauntingly beautiful names such as Inishglora and Inishkea.

The North

In the north is the glorious coastline of Sligo and Donegal. You need to be an experienced sailor to sail in these waters, for the charts are outdated and inaccurate, whilst the currents and shallows are sometimes treacherous, and there are few facilities for sailors.

The East

More wonderful sailing can be had on Strangford and Carlingford Loughs in County Down, and around the Antrim Coast. Just north of Dublin there are several excellent sailing centres which still retain the charm of fishing villages. Inland is the huge freshwater expanse of Lough Derg in the River Shannon system, where you can anchor in a sheltered bay or in one of the charming canal harbours.

Galway hookers

The most traditional form of sailing boat is the Galway hooker, with its black sails. Galway hookers used to be a familiar sight, transporting turf and other goods between the islands, but by the 1970s they had almost disappeared. Happily, a few sailors discovered what great sport can be had with hooker-racing—you can see these races at summer regattas in the west of Ireland—and the craft of making the hooker is slowly reviving. (Contact address below.)

bringing your own yacht

There is no tax or duty if you bring in your own yacht for a holiday; a special sticker is issued by customs officials on arrival. Mariners should apply to the harbour master of all ports in which they wish to anchor. On arrival at the first port of entry, the flag 'Q' should be shown. Contact should then be made with the local customs official or with a *garda* (civil guard) who will be pleased to assist. Fees are very reasonable in marinas and harbours. It is illegal to land any animals without a special licence from the Department of Agriculture, but this does not apply to pet dogs which come from Great Britain.

yacht charter

The main centres for charter are the southwest coastline, Clifden and Lough Derg. Private charter can be arranged at leading sailing centres elsewhere. Bare-boat and crewed charters are available on boats ranging from four- to seven-berth. The average cost of chartering a four-berth yacht ranges from IR£100 per person per week in the low season to IR£130 per person per week in the high season.

For a complete list of yacht charter companies, contact Bord Fáilte, PO Box 273, Dublin 8, ✆ (01) 284 4768. One of the biggest charter companies in the Cork area is Sail Ireland Charters, ✆ (021) 772927.

sailing holidays

The Celtic Nature Sailing Holidays, Michael & Becky O'Connor, the Old Stone House, Cliddaun, Dingle, ✆/✆ (066) 59882. Expeditions off Dingle and Iveragh Peninsulas on a 13-metre cutter sail boat, with particular emphasis on the natural and cultural history of the area.

sailing schools

Most of the schools are residential and located in areas of scenic beauty. Many offer other outdoor sports such as boardsailing (wind-surfing), canoeing and sub-aqua. A full list of schools is available from Bord Fáilte in Dublin and from the Irish Association for Sail Training, Confederation House, 84–86 Lower Baggot Street, Dublin 2, ✆ (01) 660 1011.

sailing in Northern Ireland

In Ulster, information on yachting facilities, sailing schools and charter companies can be had from the House of Sport, Upper Malone Road, Belfast, ✆ (01232) 381222.

sailing organisations

Irish Sailing Association, 3 Park Road, Dun Laoghaire, County Dublin, ✆ (01) 280 0239. Cormac P. McHenry, the Hon. Secretary, Irish Cruising Club (ICC), 8 Heidelberg, Ardilea, Dublin 14, ✆ (01) 288 4733.

useful media

The Irish Cruising Club (address above) publishes *Sailing Directions* which covers the entire coast of Ireland, and includes details of the coast, sketch plans of harbours, tidal information and information about port facilities. The *Directions* come in two volumes— one for the south and west at IR£30, and one for the north and east, price IR£27. Available from most Irish booksellers, and from Mrs Fox-Mills, The Tansey, Baily, County Dublin, ✆ (01) 832 2823. Also recommended: *Sailing Around Ireland* by Wallace Clark (Batsford), and *Islands of Ireland* by D. McCormick (Osprey, 1977). The BBC issues gale warnings and shipping forecasts on Radio 4.

Sub-aqua

Ireland's oceans are surprisingly warm and clear because they are right in the path of the Gulf Stream, so it would be very difficult to find a better place for underwater swimming or diving. The underwater flora and fauna is vast and varied, and you are always bumping into shoals of fish. *Subsea* is the official journal of the Irish Underwater Council, which publishes information about the affiliated clubs, articles on diving, etcetera. Write to the Hon. Secretary, Irish Underwater Council, Haigh Terrace, Dun Laoghaire, ✆ (01) 284 4601. Centres for experienced divers and equipment hire are in Co. Mayo, Co. Donegal, Co. Galway, Co. Kerry, Co. Clare, Co. Wexford, Co. Down. Ask for the relevant fact sheet in any tourist office.

By the way, it is illegal to take shellfish from the sea.

Surfing

Due to the geographical position of Ireland great swells endlessly pound the west coast, producing waves comparable to those in California. Thus the entire coastline of Ireland is ideal for surfing when the beach, tide and wind conditions are right. Many of the beaches in Counties Donegal, Sligo, Kerry, Waterford and Clare are considered first-rate for breakers. As hire centres are not numerous, it is best to bring your own board and wetsuit; although you can occasionally hire them from hotels and adventure sports centres.

All those interested in the huge Atlantic swell should contact Mr Roc Allan, Chairman of the Irish Surfing Association at 1, Ardeelan Dale, Rossnowlagh, Co. Donegal, ✆ (072) 52522, ✉ (072) 52523 and Mrs M. O'Brien-Moran, Hon. Secretary, 7 Marine Terrace, Tramore, Co. Waterford, ✆ (051) 386582. They will send out details of beaches and surfing centres.

Swimming and Beaches

There are lovely beaches (also called strands) wherever the sea meets the land in Ireland—north, south, east or west. If you wish to go sea-bathing (it can be surprisingly warm because of the Gulf Stream), bear in mind that swimming is not a regulated sport, and that there are lifeguards only on the most popular beaches, if at all. Be aware of the possibility of a strong undertow or current, and ask locally about the safety of beaches.

Summer Schools

The phrase 'Ireland, land of saints and scholars' is delightfully apt when it comes to the tradition of learning. You can study and learn some fascinating subjects in a beautiful environment, and still feel as if you are on holiday. The Irish Tourist Board will send you a free up-to-date list of programmes and prices if you write and ask for the *Live and Learn* booklet, from the **Group and Education Department**, Bord Fáilte, PO Box 273, Dublin 8. The courses range from the seriously intellectual to activity holidays. You can study for a month, two weeks, a few days, the variety is tremendous. Some are run by Ireland's own universities which offer courses on literature, politics, history, Gaelic, and archaeology. Private companies run arts and crafts courses, landscape painting, and English language courses. There are courses in environmental studies in beautiful places such as the Burren, and classes in traditional music and dancing.

Activity holidays include wind-surfing, hill-walking, riding, canoeing, fishing, cycling, golfing and dinghy-sailing. Some cater for all ages from toddlers upwards; in particular the adventure centres which are mainly on the west coast. USIT organize adventure sports, cycling and water sports holidays. For details, contact: 19 Aston Quay, Dublin 2, ✆ (01) 679 8833. One of the most enjoyable summer schools is the **Yeats International Summer School** because it is well run and set in wonderful countryside. The tuition fee of around IR£280 covers lectures, seminars, readings and tours over two weeks. The theme is not only Yeats, his poetry, plays and prose, but also the historical and social background to Irish literature, the Abbey Theatre, Yeats' contemporaries and also Celtic myth and legend.

Enjoyable courses are run by the **Irish Georgian Society**. Contact the Society at 74 Merrion Square, Dublin 2, ✆ (01) 676 7053, ✉ (01) 662 0290.

Here is a selection of those on offer:

literature

Brian Merriman Summer School, 6 Aravon Court, Bray, Co. Wicklow; ✆ (01) 286 9305.

Kiltartan Hedge School, Gort, Co. Galway. Studies in the Coole & Ballylee poetry of W. B. Yeats and Kiltartan writings of Lady Gregory. Contact Dr Louis Muinzer, 33 Jameson Street, Belfast BT7 2GU; ✆ (01232) 649010.

Yeats International Summer School, Yeats Memorial Building, Douglas Hyde Bridge, Sligo; ✆ (071) 42693. Lectures and seminars; *see* above.

John Hewitt International Summer School at St MacNissi's College, Carron Tower, Carnlough, Co. Antrim, ✆ (01266) 44247, July/August. The school explores various literary themes and is named in honour of John Hewitt, an Ulster poet who died recently. You can enjoy lectures, music, poetry readings and plays for a week, or just a day or so.

music

South Sligo Summer School of traditional music and dance, July; ✆ (071) 85010.

Joe Mooney Summer School, Drumshanbo, Co. Leitrim. Irish music and set dancing, mid-July; ✆ (078) 41213.

art/painting

Kerry summer painting school: call Cahirciveen tourist office has details; ✆ (066) 72589.

Burren Landscape Painting Course, Lisdoonvarna, Co. Clare; ✆ (065) 74208.

Photography/painting/sculpture workshop, Burren College of Art, Ballyvaughan, Co. Clare; ✆ (065) 77200.

Painting course in Portaferry, Co. Down. Contact James Watson, Portaferry Hotel; ✆ (02477) 28231.

Crawford School of Art and Gallery, Emmett Place, Cork; ✆ (021) 966777.

crafts

Clare Craft Summer School. Courses in pottery, basket-weaving etc., July; ✆ (065) 41605.

Learn to weave at Ardress Craft Centre, Kesh, Co. Fermanagh; ✆ (013656) 31267.

languages

Devenesh Language School, Corralea, Belcoo, Co. Fermanagh, BT93 5DZ, ✆ (01365) 386668. French courses.

Irish Language Courses for two weeks in Glenties and Glencolumbkille, Co.Donegal. Contact: 2 Isle Harlech, Dublin 14, ✆ (01) 984774/213566 and Donegal Udaras na Gaeltachta, ✆ (075) 31479.

Irish studies

Folklore School, Lahinch, Co. Clare, April/May; ✆ (065) 84365/(065) 81079.

Irish Studies, University College, Cork; ✆ (021) 276871.

Sailing courses in Galway Bay, Contact Galway Bay Sailing Centre, 8 Father Griffin Road, Galway; ℂ (091) 63522.

Telephones

To call the Irish Republic from the UK dial **010 353** followed by the area code minus the first 0. For Northern Ireland codes are as in mainland UK dialling.

It is more expensive to telephone during working hours than outside them. For example, at the time of writing a call to Britain from the Republic costs 36p per minute, but after 6pm and at weekends and on public holidays the charge is 28p per minute. For direct-dial transatlantic calls the standard rate is about 83p per minute with reduced rates after 6pm of 71p and economy rates of 64p a minute.

Note that if you telephone from your hotel you are liable to be charged much more than the standard rate.

Ireland shares the same time zone as Great Britain, and follows the same pattern of seasonal adjustment in the summer (i.e. Greenwich Mean Time plus one hour, from the end of March to the end of October). This is in review at the time of writing in both the UK and Ireland.

Toilets

Loos—public ones, labelled in Irish: *Fir* (men) and *Mna* (women)—are usually in a pretty bad way. Nobody minds if you slip into a lounge bar or hotel to go to the loo, though it's a good excuse to stop for a drink as well.

Tourist Boards

Ireland is served by two separate tourist boards: **Bord Fáilte** (or the Irish Tourist Board) in the Republic, and the **Northern Ireland Tourist Board**.

Bord Fáilte

The people who work for Bord Fáilte would get you to the moon if they could—should you ask for it. They will do literally anything to help and organise whatever is practicable; and if they do not know the answer to something, they can always refer you to someone who does. They can supply you with a wealth of beautifully presented information; most of this is free, although they also publish fuller booklets on, for example, accommodation, for which there are modest charges. They can also book your hotel or B&B, helping you to find one which is in your price range. The Head Office in Dublin is at Baggot Street Bridge, Dublin 2, ℂ (01) 676 5871, ✉ (01) 602 4100. For general postal enquiries write to Bord Fáilte, PO Box 273, Dublin 8. The Head Office is mainly the administration centre; when in Dublin a more useful office to visit is the one at 14 Upper O'Connell Street, Dublin 1, ℂ (01) 284 4768, ✉ (01) 284 1751.

There are some 70 tourist information offices scattered around the Republic, most of which open only during the summer season. The following, however, are open throughout the year. (A full list of tourist information offices can be obtained from Bord Fáilte.)

The Republic of Ireland

Clonmel, ✆ (052) 22960.

Cork City, ✆ (021) 273251, ✉ (021) 273504.

Dublin Airport, ✆ (01) 284 4768, ✉ (01) 284 1751.

Dundalk, ✆ (042) 35484, ✉ (042) 38070.

Dun Laoghaire, ✆ (01) 284 4768/5/6, ✉ (01) 284 1751.

Ennis, ✆ (065) 28366.

Galway, ✆ (091) 63081, ✉ (091) 65201.

Kilkenny, ✆: (056) 51500, ✉ (056) 63955.

Killarney, ✆ (064) 31633, ✉ (064) 34506.

Letterkenny, ✆ (074) 21160, ✉ (074) 25180.

Limerick City, ✆ (061) 317522, ✉ (061) 317939.

Mullingar, ✆ (044) 48650, ✉ (044) 40413.

Oughterard, ✆ (091) 82808.

Rosslare terminal, ✆ (052) 33622, ✉ (053) 33421

Shannon Airport, ✆ (061) 471664.

Skibbereen, ✆ (028) 21766, ✉ (028) 21351.

Sligo, ✆ (071) 61201, ✉ (071) 60360.

Tipperary, ✆ (062) 51457.

Tralee, ✆ (066) 21288.

Waterford, ✆ (051) 75788, ✉ (051) 77388.

Westport, ✆ (098) 25711, ✉ (098) 26709.

Wexford, ✆ (053) 23111; ✉(053) 41743.

Wicklow, ✆ (0404) 69117.

Northern Ireland

Belfast, 53 Castle St, Belfast BT1 1GH, ✆ (01232) 327888, ✉ (01232) 240201.

Derry, 8 Bishop's St, Derry BT48 6PW, ✆ (01504) 369501, ✉ (01504) 369501.

Great Britain

London, 150 New Bond Street, London W1Y 0AQ, ✆ (071) 493 3201, ✉ (0171) 493 9065.

Europe

France, 33 rue de Miromesnil, 75008 Paris, ✆ (1) 47 42 03 36, (1) 47 42 01 64.

The Netherlands, Spuistraat 104, 1012VA Amsterdam, ✆ (020) 622 3101, ✉ (020) 620 8089.

West Germany, Untermainanlage 7, 60329 Frankfurt am Main, ✆ (069) 236492.

Belgium (telephone and written enquiries), Avenue de Beaulieu 25, 1160 Brussels, ✆ (02) 673 9940, ✉ (02) 672 1066.

Denmark (telephone and written enquiries), Klostergarden, Amagertorv 29/3, 1160 Copenhagen K, ✆ (33) 15 80 45, ✉ (33) 93 63 90.

Italy, Via S. Maria Segreta 6, 20123 Milan, ✆ (02) 869 0541, ✉ (02) 869 0396.

North America

USA, 345 Park Avenue, New York, NY 10017, ✆ (212) 418 0800, ✉ (212) 371 9059.

Canada (written and telephone enquiries), 160 Bloor Street East, Suite 1150, Toronto, Ontario, M4W 1BN, ✆ (416) 929 2777, ✉ (416) 929 6783.

Australia

MLC Centre, 38th Level, Martin Place, Sydney, NSW 2000, ✆ (02) 232 7177.

New Zealand

2nd Floor, Dingwall Building, 87 Queen St, PO Box 279, Auckland 1, ✆ (9) 379 3708 and 377 0374.

The Northern Ireland Tourist Board

Like their counterparts in Bord Fáilte, the people who work for the Northern Ireland Tourist Board (NITB) are friendly, helpful and humorous and very proud of their bit of Ireland. The Head Office of the Northern Ireland Tourist Board (NITB) is at River House, 48 High St, Belfast, BT1 2DS, ✆ (01232) 231221, ✉ (01232) 240960; for tourist information, ✆ (01232) 246609.

There are over 30 local tourist offices in Northern Ireland. All of them will give you details of what is on in the province: sports festivals, arts, bus tours, accommodation, etcetera. Many of them are open only during the tourist season, but the following are open all year. (For a full list, contact the NITB Head Office.)

Northern Ireland

Antrim, ✆ (018494) 63113.

Armagh, ✆ (01861) 527808.

Ballycastle, ✆ (0126 57) 62024.

Ballymena, ✆ (01266) 44111.

Banbridge, ✆ (013206) 23322.

Bangor, ✆ (01247) 270069.

Carnlough, ✆ (01574) 885210.

Carrickfergus, ✆ (0196 03) 66455.

Cookstown, ✆ (016487) 66727.

Derry, ✆ (01504) 267284.
Downpatrick, ✆ (01396) 612233.
Enniskillen, ✆ (01365) 323110.
Fivemiletown, ✆ (0136 55) 21409.
Giant's Causeway, ✆ (012657) 31855.
Kilkeel, ✆ (016937) 62525.
Larne, ✆ (01574) 260088.
Larne Harbour, ✆ (01574) 270517.
Limavady, ✆ (015047) 22226.
Magherafelt, ✆ (01648) 32151.
Newcastle, ✆ (013967) 22222.
Omagh, ✆ (01662) 247831.
Portrush, ✆ (01265) 823333.

The Republic

Tourist Information Office, 16 Nassau Street, Dublin 2, ✆ (01) 679 1977, ✆ (01) 679 1863.

Great Britain

London, NITB, 11 Berkeley Street, W1X 5AD, ✆ (0171) 355 5040, ✆ (0171) 409 0487.

North America

USA, NITB, 551 5th Avenue, NY 10176/0799, ✆ (212) 922 0101, ✆ (212) 922 0099.

Europe

West Germany, NITB, 60329 Frankfurt am Main, Taunusstrasse 52–60, West Germany ✆ (069) 23 45 04, ✆ (069) 238 07 17.

Elsewhere in the World

Northern Ireland Tourist Board publications are distributed overseas by the British Tourist Authority, which maintains offices in many countries. Consult the telephone directory.

Where to Stay

Whether you are a traveller with plenty of loot to spend, or one who is intent on lodging as cheaply as possible, Ireland offers plenty of choice. Places to stay range from romantic castles, graceful country mansions, cosy farmhouses, smart city hotels and hostels which, although spartan, are clean and well-run. Many of these hostels have double or family rooms; are independently owned and require no membership cards. They welcome young and old!

At the end of each county chapter there is a list of recommended accommodation, divided into price categories which are explained below. With this list as a guide, it is possible to avoid the many modern and ugly hotels where bland comfort is doled out for huge prices, and to avoid the shabby motels and the musty bed-and-breakfast establishments which are very uncomfortable. Some counties are favoured with many desirable hotels and B&Bs, whilst a few are meagrely served. If that is the case where you are, your best bet for a pleasant stay is to stick to the farmhouse accommodation, which is usually very adequate.

One thing you can be sure of is that the Irish are amongst the friendliest people in Europe, and when they open their doors to visitors they give a great welcome. The many unexpected kindnesses and the personal service that you will experience will contribute immeasurably to your visit. The countryside is beautiful, and there are many sights to see, but what adds enjoyment and richness, above all, to a tour of Ireland is the pleasant conversation and humour of the people.

Prices

Bord Fáilte and the Northern Ireland Tourist Board register and grade hotels and guest houses, and they divide the many B&B businesses into Farm, Town and Country Houses. All of this is very useful, but apart from indicating the variety of services available and the cost, you really do not get much idea of the atmosphere and style of the place. The establishments listed in this book are described and categorized according to price, and include a variety of lodgings ranging from a luxurious castle to a simple farmhouse—all have something very special to offer a visitor. This may be the architecture, the garden, the food, the atmosphere and the chat, or simply the beauty of the surrounding countryside. The most expensive offer high standards of luxury, and the cheapest ones are clean and comfortable. Most are family-owned, with a few bedrooms, and none fits into a uniform classification, but they are all welcoming and unique places to stay. The price categories are of necessity quite loosely based, and some of the more expensive establishments do weekend deals which are very good value. Please, always check prices and terms when making a booking. Rates in the Republic are quoted in Irish punts—the value of which at the time of writing is on a parity with sterling. Sterling is the currency used in Northern Ireland.

luxury

Cost no object. B&B from IR£90 per person. You can expect top-quality lodgings with style and opulence. Furnishings will include priceless antiques, whilst the facilities and service provide every modern convenience you could wish for. Many of the Grade A* hotels in Dublin fall into this category, but there are also delightful castles and mansions set in exquisite grounds.

expensive

From IR£60 B&B per person. All the bedrooms have their own bathroom, direct-dial telephone, central heating, TV and the other paraphernalia of modern living, but they have something else as well—charm, eccentricity, and a feeling of mellow comfort. They are places where you might sleep in a graceful four-poster hung with rich cloth, and wake up to the sort of hospitality where the smell of coffee is just a prelude to a delicious cooked breakfast, and the sharp sweet taste of homemade jam on Irish wheaten bread.

moderate

From IR£30 to IR£60 B&B per person. Although not as luxurious, most of these places have private bathrooms and an extremely high standard of cooking and service. Again, they have a wonderful atmosphere combined with attractive décor which is sometimes more atmospheric for its touch of age.

inexpensive

From IR£10 to IR£20 B&B per person. Pretty whitewashed farmhouses, Georgian manses, rectories, old manor houses, modern bungalows and fine town houses come under this heading. They are very good value, good 'crack', and you will get marvellous plain cooking. Only some of the bedrooms will have en suite facilities, and some will not have central heating, but there will be perfectly good bathrooms close by and washbasins in the room. And if you are travelling in the late spring/summer, you do not need heating anyway!

Reservations

Bord Fáilte and the Northern Ireland Tourist Board can be of immense help when you are making a reservation or trying to decide where to stay. You can make a reservation direct with the premises, or use the Irish Tourist Board offices in Great Britain and Northern Ireland who operate an enquiry and booking service. Offices in other countries operate an enquiry service only. Bord Fáilte and Northern Irish Tourist offices throughout the country will make you a reservation for the price of a telephone call. They will only book you into registered and approved lodgings, and a 10 per cent deposit is payable.

Make sure that you book early for the peak months of June, July and August. At other times of the year it is usually quite all right to book on the morning of the day you wish to stay; this gives you great flexibility. However, the excellent lodgings soon get known by word of mouth, so they are always more likely to be booked up in advance.

Literature

The Bord Fáilte Tourist Offices keep plenty of booklets on various types of accommodation: there is one comprehensive list called *Accommodation Guide*, price IR£4.00; an *Illustrated Hotels and Guesthouses Guide*, price IR£1; an *Illustrated Farmhouse Guide*, an *Illustrated Town and Country Guide*, and a *Caravan and Camping Guide*, all priced at IR£1.50. Other useful publications are the *Self-catering Guide*, *The Blue Book*, which lists Irish country houses and restaurants, *The Hidden Ireland Guide*, *Friendly Homes of Ireland*, and *Elegant Ireland*. All these are available from the tourist offices (the addresses are listed on pp.52–5) or from the various associations that publish them. The Northern Ireland Tourist Board stocks similar publications including a comprehensive list of accommodation called *Where to Stay*, price £2.50.

Bord Fáilte and the Northern Ireland Tourist Board (NITB) register and grade hotels into five categories: **A*** stands for the most luxuriously equipped bedrooms and public rooms with night service, a very high standard of food and plenty of choice. Most bedrooms have their own bath and suites are available—the sort of place where delicious snacks are automatically served with your cocktails. This grading includes baronial mansions set in exquisite grounds or the rather plush anonymity of some Dublin hotels. **A** grade stands for a luxury hotel which doesn't have quite so many items on the *table d'hôte*, nor does it have night service; but the food is just as good and the atmosphere less restrained. **B*** grade stands for well-furnished and comfortable; some rooms have a bath, cooking is good and plain. **B** and **C** grades are clean, comfortable but limited, **B** offering more in the line of bathrooms and food. All Bord Fáilte graded hotels have heating and hot and cold water in the bedrooms. If you come across a hotel that is ungraded, it is because its grading is under review or because it has just opened, or does not comply with Bord Fáilte requirements. The prices of hotels vary enormously, no matter what grade they are, and the grading takes no account of atmosphere and charm. Many of the most delightful and hospitable country houses come under grades B or C, whilst some of the grade A hotels are very dull. All graded hotels are listed in the Bord Fáilte *Guest Accommodation* booklet and in the *Be Our Guest* booklet. Northern Irish hotels are listed in the *Where to Stay* guide.

Guest Houses

These are usually houses which have become too large and expensive to maintain as private houses. The minimum number of bedrooms is five. The grade **A** houses are just as good as their hotel equivalent, as are those graded lower down the scale, although the atmosphere is completely different. In fact, some of the best places to stay in Ireland are guest houses, particularly in Dublin.

If you decide to vary your accommodation from guest house, to town and country house or farmhouse, you will discover one of the principles of Irish life: that everything in Ireland works on a personal basis. If you are on holiday to avoid people, a guest house is the last place you should book into. It is impossible not to be drawn into a friendly conversation, whether about fishing or politics. You will get a large, thoroughly uncontinental breakfast, and delicious evening meals with a choice within a set meal. Dinner is always very punctual, at eight, after everyone has sat around by the fire over very large drinks. Lunch or a packed lunch can be arranged. All grades of guest house have hot and cold water, and heating in the bedrooms. Grade **A** guest houses have some rooms with private bathrooms, but their reputation is based on scrumptious food and comfortable surroundings. You can get full details of guest houses in the Bord Fáilte and Northern Ireland Tourist Board booklets entitled *Be Our Guest* and *Where to Stay in Northern Ireland*. As a general guide, a comfortable, even luxurious night's sleep will cost between IR£14 and IR£30, although the more basic guest houses do not cost more than a farmhouse B&B. A delicious meal ranges from between IR£11 and IR£20. Sometimes the owners provide high tea, sometimes the only meal they do is breakfast. Our selection of guesthouses is included in the list of places to stay at the end of each county section.

Often these family homes make your stay in Ireland, for you meet Irish people who are kind, generous and intelligent. This is also the most economical way to stay in Ireland if you don't want to stay in a tent or in a youth hostel. If you are not going to a place that is recommended, it is largely a matter of luck whether you hit an attractive or a mediocre set-up, but always watch out for the shamrock sign, the Bord Fáilte sign of approval. Wherever you go, you should get a comfortable bed (if you are tall, make sure it is long enough, as sometimes Irish beds can be on the small side), and an enormous breakfast: orange juice, cereal, two eggs, bacon, sausages, toast and marmalade, and a huge pot of tea or coffee. If you get rather tired of this fry-up, ask your hostess the night before for something different and she will be happy to oblige. Another thing—the coffee is invariably weak and tasteless; it's much safer to stick to tea! Nevertheless, breakfast is still a very satisfying meal, which means you don't feel hungry again until the evening.

Bed and breakfast per person ranges from IR£13 to IR£20 throughout the Republic and the North if you are sharing a bedroom (a single room is sometimes more expensive). You can get much cheaper weekly rates, with partial or full board. Very often you can eat your evening meal in the dining room of the B&B. Again, there will be masses to eat and piping hot—so much better than most of the restaurants and cafés. There is a great flexibility about breakfast and other meals: they happen when it suits you, but you should give notice before 12 noon if you want to eat dinner.

Some houses serve dinner at between IR£9 and IR£15, and some 'high tea', which is less costly (between IR£6 and IR£8). 'High tea' is a very sensible meal which has evolved for the working man who begins to feel hungry at about 6pm. You get a plate of something hot, perhaps chicken and chips, followed by fresh soda bread, jam and cakes and a pot of tea. Sometimes you get a salad. This leaves you with plenty of time to go out and explore in the evenings—whether to the pubs or the countryside! Some houses provide tea and biscuits as a night-cap for nibblers at around 10pm.

More and more establishments have en suite bathrooms with a loo, basin and bath or shower. You usually pay about IR£2 extra for this. If there is only a communal bathroom you will be charged a trivial amount for the hot bath—if you are even charged at all. Ask the woman of the house for a towel or, better still, carry your own, as those you are given are usually the size of a tea towel. Take your bath whenever you want; your hostess will ask you how many you had at the end of your stay. The bathroom is shared by everybody, family and guests, and it should be immaculately clean. Don't have your bath when it is obvious that everyone else is trying to use the bathroom.

For people hitching or using public transport, the town houses are the easiest to get to and find, but my favourites are farmhouses, followed closely by country houses. The farms concentrate on dairy, sheep, crop farming or beef cattle and often a mixture of everything. Tucked away in lovely countryside, they may be traditional or modern. The farmer's wife, helped by her children, makes life very comfortable and is always ready to have a chat, and advise you on the local beauty spots, and good places to hear traditional music or go for a *ceili*. Some of the town and country houses are on fairly main roads, but they are generally not too noisy as there is so little traffic about. The type of house you might stay in ranges from the Georgian to the Alpine-style bungalow, from a semi-detached to a 1950s dolls' house. There are a bewildering number of architectural styles in the new houses beginning to radiate out from small villages.

It is wise to book maybe a night or two ahead during July and August, though it is rarely necessary. This means that you do not have to be tied, and can dawdle in a place as much as you want.

Full details of Irish homes can be obtained from the Northern Ireland Tourist Board, and a booklet on farmhouses, town and country houses from any Bord Fáilte office or write to Irish Farmhouse Holidays, Glynch House, Newbliss, Co. Monaghan or the Secretary, Town and Country Homes Association, Killadean, Bundoran Road, Ballyshannon, Co. Donegal.

Renting a House or Cottage

This is very easy. Every regional office of Bord Fáilte has a list of houses and apartments to let; there is also a short list of self-catering houses at the back of the *Guest Accommodation* booklet. Places to rent range from converted stable blocks, modern bungalows to stone-built cottages.

For the north, ask the NITB for their self-catering bulletin (no. 11) or look in the back of the accommodation booklet and in newspapers. The Republic has a very popular Rent-an-Irish-Cottage scheme with centres in Counties Limerick, Galway, Mayo, Tipperary and Clare. On the outside the cottages are thatched, whitewashed and traditional; inside they are well-designed with an electric cooker, fridge and kettle—all the mod cons you could want. There are built-in cupboards, comfy beds, and linen. Simple, comfortable Irish-made furniture and fittings make it a happy blend of tradition and modern convenience. The cottages vary in size: some take eight, others five. Easter and May, June, July and August are the most expensive times with prices hovering around IR£250 to IR£400 a week, but in October, sometimes the nicest month in Ireland weather-wise, a cottage for eight is very reasonable at around IR£150 per week. The local people take a great interest in you because they are all shareholders in the scheme and so do their best to make you content! Write to Bord Fáilte for details of the scheme and other self-catering cottages.

Youth Hostels

The Irish YHA is called *An Oige* and has 44 hostels. These are distributed all over the Republic and there are a few in the Six Counties, often in wild and remote places, so that they are doubly attractive to the enterprising traveller. Members of the International Youth Hostel Federation can use any of these and the hostels in Northern Ireland. If you haven't got a card, you can join for IR£8.50; there is no age limit! All you have to do is buy something called an International Guest Card, by purchasing six welcome stamps costing IR£2 each. The stamps may be bought one at a time at six different hostels, if you like.

The youth hostels are often the most superb houses, and they range from cottages to castles, old coastguard stations to old military barracks. They are great centres for climbers, walkers and fishers, and not too spartan; many have a comfortable laxity when it comes to the rules. You must provide your own sheet and sleeping bag. A flap or pocket to cover the pillows can be bought at the *An Oige* office, and the hostel provides blankets or sheet bags. Bring your own knives, forks, spoons, tea towels, bath towel, soap and food. All the hostels have fully equipped self-catering kitchens, and most also provide breakfast, packed lunches and an evening meal on request.

Charges vary according to age, month and location; during July and August it is slightly more expensive, and it is vital to book. This applies also to weekends. All *An Oige* and YHANI (Youth Hostel Association of Northern Ireland) hostels may be booked from one hostel to another, or centrally by contacting the head office listed below. Most of the hostels are open all year round. It's quite a good idea to combine hostelling with staying at B&Bs (*see* under 'Farmhouses, Town and Country Houses', above.)

There are several rail/cycling holidays on offer to hostel members. The average approximate cost of staying overnight ranges from IR£4.50 to IR£5.90 from July to August and from IR£2 to IR£5.50 for other months. The Dublin International Youth Hostel is IR£7 for members and IR£7.50 for non-members. All enquiries, an essential handbook and an excellent map can be got from the *An Oige* Office, 61 Mountjoy Street, Dublin 1, ✆ (01) 830 4555, ✆ (01) 830 1610. For Northern Ireland, contact YHANI, 56 Bradbury Place, Belfast;, ✆ (0232) 324733. Independent Holiday Hostels of Ireland (IHH) is a completely separate organisation to YHA. It is a co-operative society of 112 hostels throughout Ireland, ranging from Georgian houses to restored mills. They are friendly, open to everyone (children are welcome in most hostels), and most have double and family rooms. All hostels will rent you sheets and all hostels provide duvets and blankets. The average price for a dormitory bed in high season is IR£6. Send off for a list of hostels to IHH Office, UCD Village, Belfield, Dublin 2, ✆ (01) 260 1634, ✆ (01) 269 7704.

Many other organizations such as the YWCA, ISSACS, and colleges of further education offer cheap and comfortable accommodation in central Dublin and in other parts of the country. Some of them have excellent eating facilities attached; for example, the hostel on the Aran Islands at Kilronan. Ask for a *Discover Young Ireland* brochure from the Bord Fáilte, Baggot Street Bridge, Dublin 2, ✆ (01) 676 5871.

Camping and Caravanning

The camping and caravan parks which meet the standards set by Bord Fáilte and the Northern Ireland Tourist Board are listed in a booklet available from the tourist offices. You can also order it direct from Ms A. Dillon, Irish Camping and Caravanning Holidays, 2 Offington Court, Sutton, Dublin 13. There is also a selection in the *Guest Accommodation Guide* republished every year by Bord Fáilte. The sites are graded according to amenities and many of them are in beautiful areas. Laundry rooms, excellent showers and loos, shops, restaurants, indoor games rooms and TV make camping easy and also more civilized, especially if you have children. It is possible to rent tents and camping equipment.

For a complete list of sites, write to the main Dublin tourist office, and the NITB in Belfast. Here are a few useful contacts: in Co. Cork you could try the Tent Shop, Rutland Street, off South Terrace, Cork City, ✆ (021) 316184. In Co. Dublin try O'Meara Holidays Ltd, Ossory Business Park, 26 Ossory Road, North Strand, Dublin 3, ✆ (01) 836 3233, and in Co. Sligo try Benbulben Caravans and Camping, Ballinode, Sligo, ✆ (071) 45618. It is also possible to rent caravans and motor homes. For full details check the *Caravan and Camping* booklet. Overnight charges in the camping parks vary between IR£5.50 and IR£7.00 per night, with a small charge per person at some parks and IR£1 for electrical linkup. If you are bringing your own caravan or camping equipment to Ireland, and have Calor gas appliances, the only ones on sale in Ireland which are compatible are those supplied by Gaz. Some caravan parks accept dogs if they are on a leash.

Farmers can be very tolerant of people turning up and asking if they can camp or park their caravan in a field. You must ask their permission first, and tell them how long you want to stay. Be polite, do not get in the way and you will find that they will give you drinking water, lots of chat, and even vegetables from their gardens.

Women Travellers

Irish men have an attitude towards women which is as infuriating as it is attractive. They are a grand old muddle of male chauvinism, with a dash of admiration and fear for their mothers, sisters and wives. Irish women have a sharpness and wit which makes them more than a match for 'your man' in an argument, but at the same time they work their hearts out.

If you are a lone female travelling through Ireland you will find an Irish man will always help you with your luggage, your flat tyre and stand you for a meal or a drink, without any question of you buying him a round. If one tries to chat you up in a bar, or at a dance, it is always a bit of 'crack', not to be taken seriously, and the game is abandoned at once if you get tired of it. They probably think that you ought to be travelling with somebody else, but it's only the women who will say so, saying, with a smile, that it must be a bit lonesome. If you walk into an obviously male preserve, such as a serious drinking pub, don't expect to feel welcome, because you won't be unless everybody is drunk and by that time you would need to scarper. A bit of advice, which does not apply just to women, was pithily put by an Irish politician: 'The great difference between England and Ireland is that in England you can say what you like, so long as you do the right thing. In Ireland you can do what you like, so long as you say the right thing.' If you are hitch-hiking on your own, or with another girl, you will get plenty of lifts, and offers to take you out dancing that night; your driver will never believe that you have to get on and be somewhere by a certain date, so the journey is passed in pleasant banter. You would be better off hitch-hiking with someone else if possible, although Ireland is pretty safe on the whole.

Topics

The people are thus inclined: religious, frank, amorous, sufferable of infinite paines, verie glorious, manie sorcerers, excellent horsemen, delighted with wars, great alms-givers, passing in hospitality.

(From *Holinshed's Chronicles*, 1577)

This description so aptly fits the Irish today that I can only add a few very superficial remarks on the subject. Conditions have changed radically. For a start, almost half of the population lives in the spreading cities. Still, compared to its near-neighbour, England, and to many other European countries, Ireland is a very rural place and even city-dwellers have close links with their country background. Wherever they live, Irish people have a healthy disdain for time and the hustle and bustle of business. Remember the old Irish saying as you travel around that, 'When God made time he made plenty of it.' You will become aware of a great sense of shared identity and neighbourly feeling, particularly towards those in trouble, or the very old.

The traits peculiar to the Irish which always reassert themselves, wherever they are in the world, are numerous. Amongst them is a delight in words and wordplay (reading anything by Flann O'Brien or James Joyce will give you a taste of it); a love of parties and crack (a good time), music, dancing and witty talk; a ready kindness which never fails; great hospitality and an interest in your affairs which is never mere inquisitiveness, but a charming device to put you at your ease. They are an untidy race—in their houses and in the countryside. This, mixed in with a certain sloppiness, leads to the phenomenon of rusty cars dumped in lonely glens, litter in any old place, and general mess. Not for the Irish the freshly painted doors and gateways of the Anglo-Saxon. There is a lot of ignorance and indifference in matters aesthetic. Old buildings go to rack and ruin, and vile ribbon development chokes the towns and the countryside around.

An Irish person never forgets an insult or a wrong, and this memory will go back for generations. It might have been a quarrel over land or the meanness of the local gentry. Oliver Cromwell is still remembered with hatred for his savage campaign in the 1650s. The Irish have a quarrelsome spirit which is quickly roused in the face of bland priggishness.

Each province and county of Ireland produces more individual traits: the northerners have a reputation for directness of speech and a fighting spirit. The Munster people are held in respect for their poetry. A Dubliner might be considered a bit of a know-all. The people of Connacht are famous for their hospitality and strength.

Finally, one last word in this briefest of outlines: the Irish still have a great sense of the spiritual. The Catholic Church is very strong, but so is the faith of Church of Ireland members, and of the Presbyterians, to judge by the numbers who attend their churches on Sundays. Religion is the great anchor; it pervades all aspects of living, which perhaps partially explains the paradox that in Ireland there is little thought for the future, and life is lived for the moment.

The Fairy People, or *Daoine Sidhe*, are a rich part of Irish folklore. According to peasant belief, they are fallen angels who are not good enough to be saved and not bad enough to languish in Hell. Perhaps they are the gods of the Earth, as it is written in the *Book of Armagh*; or the pagan gods of Ireland, the Tuatha dé Danaan, who may also have been a race of invaders whose origins are lost in the mists of time. Antiquarians have different theories but, whatever they surmise, these fairy people persist in the popular imagination; they and their characteristics have been kept alive in tradition and myth.

The Fairy People are quickly offended, and must always be referred to as the 'Gentry' or the 'Good People'. They are also easily pleased, and will keep misfortune from your door if you leave them a bowl of milk on the window-sill overnight. Their evil seems to be without malice, and their chief occupations are feasting, fighting, making love and playing or listening to beautiful music. The only hardworking person amongst them is the leprechaun, who is kept busy making the shoes they wear out with their dancing. It is said that many of the beautiful tunes of Ireland are theirs, remembered by mortal eavesdroppers. The story is that Carolan, the last of the great Irish bards, slept on a rath which, like the many prehistoric standing stones in Ireland, had become a fairy place in folk tradition, and forever after the fairy music ran in his head and made him the great musician he was. Some of the individual fairy types are not very pleasant, and here are brief descriptions of a few.

The banshee, from *bean sidhe*, is a woman fairy or attendant spirit who follows the old families, and wails before a death. The keen, the funeral cry of the peasantry, is said to be an imitation of her cry. An omen which sometimes accompanies the old woman is an immense black coach, carrying a coffin and drawn by headless riders.

The leprechaun, or fairy shoemaker, is solitary, old, and bad-tempered; the practical joker amongst the 'Good People'. He is very rich because of his trade, and buries his pots of gold at the end of rainbows. He also takes many treasure crocks, buried in times of war, for his own. Many believe he is the dé Danaan god Lugh, the god of arts and crafts, who degenerated in popular lore into the leprechaun.

The leanhaun shee, or fairy mistress, longs for the love of mortal men. If they refuse, she must be their slave; if they consent, they are hers, and can only escape by finding another to take their place. The fairy lives on their life, and they waste away, but death is no escape. She has become identified in political song and verse with the Gaelic Muse, for she gives inspiration to those whom she persecutes.

The Pook seems to be an animal spirit. Some authorities have linked it with a he-goat from *púca* or *poc*, the Gaelic for goat. Others maintain it is a forefather of Shakespeare's Puck in *A Midsummer Night's Dream*. It lives in solitary mountain places and old ruins, and is of a nightmarish aspect. It is a November spirit, and often assumes the form of a stallion. The horse comes out of the water and is easy to tame if you can only keep him from the sight of water. If you cannot, he will plunge in with his rider and tear him to pieces at the bottom.

Traditional Irish music is played everywhere in Ireland, in the cities and the country. Government sponsorship helped to revive it, especially through Radio an Gaeltachta (Irish-language radio) in the west. Now there is great enthusiasm for it amongst everyone: a nine-year-old will sing a lover's lament about seduction and desertion, without batting an eyelid, to a grandfather whose generation scarcely remembered the Gaelic songs at all. The 1845–49 famine silenced the music and dancing for a while, but today Ireland has one of the most vigorous music traditions in Europe. Irish ballads are sung the world over; each emigrant considers himself an exile still, and the commercial record industry churns out ballads. Most record covers tend to be decorated with the grinning features of a leprechaun and a few shamrocks for good measure.

Serious traditional music is not in this sweet folksy style. Listening to it can induce a state of exultant melancholy, or infectious merriment; whatever way, it goes straight to your heart. The lyrics deal with the ups and downs of love; failed rebellions, especially that of 1798; soldiering, dead heroes; religion and homesick love for the beauty of the country-side. Comparatively few deal with occupations or work!

The bard in pre-Christian society was held in honour and a great deal of awe, for his learning and the mischievous satire in his poetry and music. After the Cromwellian and Williamite wars, he lost his status altogether; music and poetry were kept alive by the country people who cheered themselves up during the dark winter evenings with stories and music.

The harp is, sadly, scarcely used nowadays, except when it is dragged out for the benefit of tourists at medieval banquets in Bunratty Castle, etcetera. The main traditional instruments used are the *uillean* pipes, which are more sophisticated than the Scottish bagpipes, the fiddle (violin) and the tin whistle. The beat and rhythm is provided by a handheld drum made from stretched goat hide. This instrument is called the *bodhran*, and the accordian, the flute, guitar and the piano are used by some groups as well. These are played singly or together.

The airs, laments, slip jigs, reels and songs all vary enormously from region to region, and you might easily hear a Cork man or a Leitrim fiddler discussing with heated emotion the interpretation of a certain piece. Pieces are constantly improvised on, and seldom written down; inevitably some of the traditional content gets changed from generation to generation. A form of singing that had almost died out by the 1940s is the *Sean-Nós*, fully adorned, sung in Gaelic and unaccompanied by instruments. Now the *Sean-Nós* section in music festivals is overflowing with entrants.

You will have no difficulty in hearing traditional ballads or folk music in the local bars or hotels; players usually advertise in the local newspaper or by sticking up a notice in the window. The group of players seem only too happy to let you join in, and as the atmosphere gets smokier the music really takes off. In 1951 Comhaltas Ceoltoírí Eireann was set up for the promotion of traditional music, song and dance. It now has two hundred branches all over the country, and their members have regular sessions (*seisiún*) which are open to all. Ask at the local tourist office or write to Comhaltas Ceoltóirí Eireann, 32 Belgrave Square, Monkstown, Co. Dublin, ✆ (01) 280 0295. There is bound to be a *fleadh* going on somewhere near you. The All-Ireland Fleadh is held at the end of August in a different town every year. There are 30 smaller festivals around the country each year. At these you can hear music of an incredible standard brimming over the streets from every hall, bar, hotel and private house. It takes a great deal of stamina and a lot of jars to see the whole thing through. Do not expect a formal concert-hall environment, as music and 'crack' thrive best in small intimate gatherings, and are often unplanned sessions in the local bar.

In Kerry, Father Pat Ahearn has got together a National Folk Theatre, which has performances in song, mime, and the dance of ordinary life set in rural Ireland years ago. They are based in two thatched cottages, in Finuge and at Carraig on the west tip of the Dingle Peninsula. Each cottage is known as *Teach Saimsa*, the house of musical entertainment. Contact: The National Folk Theatre of Ireland, Godfrey Place, Tralee, Co. Kerry, ✆ (066) 23055. Founded in 1974 to promote Irish Folk Culture through the medium of music and heavy emphasis on traditional Irish dancing and singing.

If you get a chance to watch the Orangemen marching with their flute bands (practising ground for the celebrated James Galway when he was a youngster), you will see how important music is to every Irishman. Boys beat the great Lambeg drums till their knuckles bleed, while the skilful throwing of the batons makes a great performance—well worth seeing, in spite of its sectarian associations.

Today Ireland is producing some good musicians of a completely different type from the folk groups. The local bands that play in the bars play jazz, blues, and a rhythmical and melodious combination of pop and traditional instruments. Look in the local newspaper of any big town or ask in a record shop; they will know what gigs are on and probably be able to sell you a ticket as well. Some of the top names on the rock and pop scene come from Ireland, for instance, Van Morrison, U2 and the Cranberries.

Sacred Trees

Certain trees have or had significance in Ireland: rowan, holly, oak and blackthorn. The distribution of the Irish word for *bile*, meaning tree, in place names indicates that the cult of the sacred tree was widespread. They were associated with ecclesiastical and inauguration rights, as at Doon Rock, in County Donegal, which was the place where the chieftains of Donegal, the O'Donnells, were throned.

In more modern days the list of sacred trees has dwindled to the whitethorn or hawthorn tree, which has come to be associated with the fairies. Bad luck invariably falls on anyone who cuts one down or interferes with it. You often see a lone tree in a field around which a farmer has painstakingly ploughed. Recently, the destruction of a bush in the course of the construction of the De Lorean car plant near Belfast is believed by some to have caused the collapse of that enterprise!

Boglands

Ireland is literally rich in boglands, formed over many hundreds of years. In the past, boglands were despised except as a source of fuel, but now we know how rich they are in flora and fauna. And a vast quantity of folklore has grown up around them, beautifully described in *Irish Folk Ways* by E. Estyn Evans. In many fairy stories the human is lured off the path into the bog by strange lights at night. Walking on bogs can be very mucky and sometimes dangerous, so keep to the few paths and try and go with a local to guide you. Many writers describe the great peace and well-being to be had from a day out on the bogs cutting turf. Even now, a Dubliner clings to his cutting rights on a piece of Wicklow hill, for there is something eminently satisfying about cutting the sods of rich blackness, and then, later, during the bitter cold winter nights, heaping it onto the open fire. Underneath the bog, well-preserved bodies, jewelled crosiers for bishops, golden cups, giant elks' antlers and brittle pots of butter have all been revealed as the turf is cut away.

In this extract from his poem, 'Kinship', Seamus Heaney focuses on the mysterious quality of the bogs, which when opened up reveal the past.

> *Quagmire, swampland, morass:*
> *the slime kingdoms,*
> *domains of the cold-blooded,*
> *of mud pads and dirtied eggs.*
> *But bog*
> *meaning soft,*
> *the fall of windless rain,*
> *pupil of amber.*
> *Ruminant ground,*
> *digestion of mollusc*
> *and seed-pod,*
> *deep pollen bin.*
> *Earth-pantry, bone-vault,*
> *sun-bank, embalmer*
> *of votive goods*
> *and sabred fugitives.*
> *Insatiable bride.*
> *Sword-swallower,*
> *casket, midden,*
> *floe of history.*
> *Ground that will strip*
> *its dark side,*
> *nesting ground,*
> *outback of my mind.*

From *North* (Faber and Faber)

About 14 per cent of Ireland's land surface is bog. The brooding immutability of the bog, the drizzling rain and winds which sweep it have surely contributed towards the Irish philosophy of fatality. There are two types of bogs—blanket and raised. The latter are mainly to be found in the midlands. In Ireland, wetness is a key factor in the formation of the peat which begins to grow on lakes and ponds as plants invade the water. Sphagnum moss is the vital plant because it holds water like a sponge and has a great capacity for trapping nutrients. Peat builds up because it releases acid which inhibits the breakdown of dead plants.

The Irish economy has been bolstered by the boglands. Bord na Mona, the Government-owned turf company, was set up in 1946 and has drained vast areas of peat, cutting it by machines and using the fuel to generate electricity. The sphagnum in the upper layers is baled as horticultural peat and sold for use in gardens all over Britain. But the draining of the bogs has consequences for rivers, and for those living near them in valleys, for the bogs act like huge natural sponges to soak up rainfall and release it very slowly. Thus, if the bog is stripped away there is danger of flooding. The stripping of the bog is also very costly ecologically, as gully erosion results. Some hand-cut bogs, when left, show signs of being colonised and healed by the bog-forming plants themselves. But this is unlikely to happen in machine-cut bogs. Sheep-grazing and burning also do damage.

A balance must be found between economic needs and conservation needs, because at the rate the machines can cut the turf there will be no more by the end of the century. All the insects, birds and animals that find a home in the bog will disappear if nothing is done. We will lose the flighting of the golden plover, the special mosses and flowers. Recently, the tourist and environmental interest of the boglands have been evaluated, and there is potential for wildlife conservation in 'cutaway' bogs - the bogs which are exhausted of peat. If you are interested there is a bogland centre at Lullymore, Rathangan on the Bog of Allan in Co. Kildare, ✆ (0762) 851102. A fine raised bog is the Clara Bog and Mongan Bog, Co. Offaly. For more information contact the Peatland Conservation Council, 3 Lower Mount Street, Dublin 2, ✆ (01) 872 2392; also the Peatlands Park, Lough Neagh, Dungannon, Co. Armagh, ✆ (0762) 851102.

Tracing Your Ancestors

If you have any Irish blood in you at all, you will have a passion for genealogy; the Irish seem to like looking backwards. When they had nothing left—no land, no Brehon laws, no religious freedom, they managed to hold on to their pride and their genealogy. Waving these before the eyes of French and Spanish rulers ensured that they got posts at court or commissions in the army. There is no such thing as class envy in Ireland: the next man is as good as you, and everybody is descended from some prince or hero from the Irish past. It is the descendants of the Cromwellian parvenues who had to bolster up their images with portraits and fine furniture. Now the planter families have the Irish obsession with their ancestors too!

The best way to go about finding where your family came from is to write to the Public Record Office in Dublin and the Public Record Office of Northern Ireland in Belfast. First you must have found out as much as possible from family papers, old relatives, and the records of the Church and State in your own country; your local historical or genealogical society might be able to help. Find out the full name of your emigrant ancestor, the background of his or her family, whether rich, poor, merchants or farmers, Catholic or Protestant. The family tradition of remembering the name of the parish or townland is a great help.

In America, immigrant records have been published by Baltimore Genealogical Publishing Company in seven volumes, and lists the arrival of people into New York between 1846 and 1851. In Canada, the Department of Irish Studies, St Mary's University, Halifax is very helpful. In Australia, the Civil Records are very good: try the National Library, Canberra, the Mitchell Library, Sydney, and the Society of Australian Genealogists, Richmond Villa, 120 Kent Street, Sydney.

The following addresses are important sources of information in Ireland:

The General Civil Registration of Births, Marriages and Deaths, The Registrar General, Joyce House, 8–11 Lombard Street East, Dublin 2, ✆ (01) 671 1000. Open Mon–Fri, 9.30–12.30 and 2.15–4.30. Marriages of non-Catholics were recorded from 1845. Registration of everybody began in 1864. Search fees are very reasonable.

The Genealogical Office, 2 Kildare Street, Dublin 2, ✆ (01) 661 8811. Consultations are by appointment only. This office handles enquiries into heraldry, genealogy and family history for the whole of Ireland, and will make searches for you for a small fee. It is also the contact address for a list of Research agencies in the Republic.

The Registry of Deeds, Henrietta St, Dublin 7, ✆ (01) 873 2233. Open Mon–Fri, 10–4.30. It has records of land matters from 1708 onwards. You may make your research in person for a small fee.

The National Library, Kildare St, Dublin 2, ✆ (01) 661 8811. Open Mon 10–9; Tues/Wed 2–9, Thurs/Fri, 10–5, Sat 10–1. It has many sources in its books, newspapers and manuscripts.

National Archives, Bishop Street, Dublin 8, ✆ (01) 478 3711. Open Mon–Fri, 10–5. Unfortunately, the Pubic Record Office in Dublin was burnt in 1922, and with it many of the Church of Ireland registers, but not all. It houses Griffith's Primary Valuation of Ireland, 1848–63, which records the names of those owning or occupying land and property, as well as other important genealogical sources.

The State Paper Office, Dublin Castle, Dublin 2, ✆ (01) 478 3711, ext. 2518. Rebellion reports and records relating to 1798, and convict records of those transported to Australia.

If your ancestors were Presbyterian, **the Presbyterian Historical Society,** Church House, Fisherwick Place, Belfast, may be able to help. **The Ulster Historical Foundation,** which is attached to the Northern Ireland Public Record Office, will undertake searches. The address to write to is the Secretary, UHF, 12 College Square East, Belfast, ✆ (01232) 332288. Local records are held at a county level dating from 1864.

Church records vary widely in age, and are an essential primary source. The parochial registers are in the keep of parish priests and Church of Ireland rectors all over Ireland. Wherever there is an enthusiastic historical society or heritage society and the co-operation of the parish priest, the process of indexing parish records within their own counties has begun. Seventeen Genealogical Centres have opened up all over Ireland which provide computerised information on Irish families. All parish and appropriate civil records are being collected and filed. For a list write to **Irish Genealogical Project,** 1 Clarinda Park North, Dun Laoghaire, Co. Dublin or the Kildare Street address above. For a listing, please enclose return postage.

Hibernian Researchers, 24 Bainagowan, Palmerston Park, Dublin 6, (01) 496 6522, employ full-time professional genealogists with plenty of experience; they will undertake searches for you. Another genealogical research agency is **Irish Genealogical Services,** 111 South Parade, Belfast, BT7 2GN, ✆ (01232) 646489.

The Scarteen Hunt and the Black and Tans

A unique combination of countryside and hounds makes hunting with the Scarteen Hunt and the Black and Tans in County Tipperary an experience that will always stay in your mind. The Ryan family has had eight masterships of this hunt, spread over three hundred years; every member of the family has been born and bred to the saddle. They have always kept the Black and Tan hounds, which are derived from the Kerry Beagle—not a beagle at all, but a 23-inch (53 cm) hound similar to a harrier. They were once hunted all over Ireland, but the 19th-century fashion for bringing in the English foxhounds led to the demise of the private packs of Kerry Beagles, and the Scarteen hounds are the only surviving example. The Ryans have bred them for as long as they can tell, and the pack is documented as far back as 1640. At that time the Abbot of St Hubert in France wrote to the Ryans asking for a draft of hounds. It has even been suggested by Muriel Bowen, in her book on Irish hunting, that the Chiens St-Hubert may have originally been started with the Irish hounds that accompanied the Irish monks to Europe in the 5th century. It is interesting that it was on a ship carrying a cargo of hounds that St Patrick escaped to France from Ireland and slavery in AD 406.

The hounds are a beautiful and rich combination of the colours of their name, with a longer face and longer, straighter hindlegs than a foxhound. Edith Somerville, co-author of *The Irish RM*, described them like this: 'Tall romantic creatures with long pendant unrounded ears and lovely eyes and pensive long-nosed faces with a cry of such poignant melancholy as, taken in conjunction with their sable robes, might suggest to their followers that they were being led to the chase by a company of bereaved widows'. Their voices do indeed sound splendid, like the notes of cellos, double basses, and violas. 'Mystical' is a word that has often been used to describe their rich timbre. Black and Tans are by instinct, temperament and breeding great scenting hounds. They are also independent-minded and, by English foxhound standards, rather unruly. It is essential that their master and whipper-in get the perfect balance of discipline and reward. They are happy, friendly beings and hate the whip, refusing to hunt at all if it is used to excess.

The Scarteen has the smallest county, but it is spread over fine heathery hills and boggy plains, with double and single banks and ditches, and there are few formal covets. The Master of the Hunt, Christopher Ryan, knows the country, its owners and inhabitants like his own and the hunt is very popular locally. The fame of the Scarteen has always attracted visitors, and so to keep the balance in favour of farmers and other locals, only up to 10 visitors are allowed each day, and then only if they are riding horses hired locally. The visitors' cap is IR£70 and preference is given to people who are also staying locally. The hunt season is from end of October to mid-February. Contact The Treasurer, Mr Dick Power, Hospital, ✆ (061) 390192 (evening only).

Historic Houses and Gardens

If you want to try to understand the Anglo-Irish, who have a very muddled status amongst most shades of opinion, the best thing to do is look round one of their houses.

The expression 'Anglo-Irish' has political, social and religious connotations. It is used to describe the waves of English settlers and their descendants who became so powerful in the land after the success of the campaigns of Elizabeth I of England. An optimistic view is held by some that Anglo-Irish is a tag that should only be applied to literature, and indeed it does seem ridiculous that after three hundred years of living in a place, these landowning families are not counted as truly Irish. On the one hand, it is a fact that the sons of the Ascendancy were educated in England, and served the British Empire as soldiers or civil servants, and that they beheld themselves as different from the native Irish; whilst on the other, many of these people felt a great and patriotic love for Ireland,

led revolts and uprisings against British rule and, starting with the Normans, became in the very apt, anonymous and undated Latin saying 'more Irish than the Irish'.

Ireland's big houses were built by families who would be most offended if you called them English, although as far as the Gaelic Irish are concerned that is what they are! 'The Big House' is another very Irish expression; it is applied to a landowner's house regardless of its size or grandeur. In fact, if you look through Burke's *Guide to Irish Country Houses* and the rather depressing, but fascinating, *Vanishing Houses of Ireland* (published by the Irish Architectural Archive and the Irish Georgian Society) you will get a very good idea of the variety and huge number of houses that belonged to the gentry.

The English monarchs always financed their Irish wars by paying their soldiers with grants of land in Ireland, and as the country was so unruly, the settlers lived in fortified or semi-fortified houses during the 17th century. There are only a very few examples of Tudor domestic architecture. Portumna Castle, County Galway, is a ruined mansion of this type, but the most famous is Ormonde Castle, Carrick on Suir, County Tipperary. It has the remains of 16th-century stucco-work including a plasterwork portrait of Elizabeth I; and look out for the early 17th-century plasterwork if you visit Bunratty Castle, County Clare. Another interesting house which it is possible to visit is Huntington Castle, County Carlow, a fortified Jacobean house built in 1620.

The most impressive and the first Irish building in the grand Renaissance style is the late-17th century Royal Hospital at Kilmainham in Dublin, which has been rescued from dereliction and restored. It is now the Irish Museum of Modern Art and is also used for art exhibitions; its staterooms are once more decorated with rich and costly furnishings. The victory of William of Orange over James II was complete when the Jacobites surrendered at the Treaty of Limerick in 1696. Within a few years the Penal Laws were introduced, which severely restricted the freedom of both Catholics and non-conformists. The majority of big houses were built in the hundred years following the 1690s when the Protestant landowners settled down to enjoy their gains. The civil and domestic architecture that survives from these times is both elegant and splendid, and is to be found in every county.

The chief centre of this 18th-century architecture was, of course, Dublin. Before the unfortunate Union of Ireland with England in 1801, it was a confident, learned and artistic capital. Today, in spite of the building developers, it has held on to its gracious heritage. When you are in Dublin, make a point of walking around the elegant residential squares of St Stephen's Green, Merrion Square and Fitzwilliam Square to the south of the city, and, on the north side, Parnell and Mountjoy Squares. The two great masterpieces of public building, the Custom House and the Four Courts, were built by James Gandon towards the close of the century and they still dominate the skyline. A few distinguished buildings were added to the city in the 19th century, including Gandon's last effort, the King's Inns, but, after the Union, building in Dublin tended to stagnate.

The 'Big House' usually consists of a square, grey stone block, sometimes with wings, set amongst gardens and parkland with stables at the back, and a walled garden. Sometimes it is called a castle, although the only attribute of a castle it may have is a deep fosse. A lingering insecurity must often have remained, for many are almost as tall as they are wide, with up to four storeys, rather like a Georgian version of the 16th-century tower house.

The buildings are completely different in atmosphere here from their counterparts in England. They have not undergone Victorian 'improvements' or gradually assumed an air of comfortable mellowness over the centuries. It was an act of bravado on the part of the Anglo-Irish to build them at all, for they had always to be on the alert against the disaffected natives, who readily formed aggressive agrarian groups such as the White Boys. They never had enough money to add on layer after layer in the newest architectural fashion; their houses remained as Palladian splendours or Gothick fantasies built during the Georgian age, when the fortified house could at last be exchanged for something a good deal more comfortable.

The big houses that remain are full of beautiful furniture, pictures, *objets d'art* and the paraphernalia of generations who appreciated beauty, good horses, hard drinking and eating, and were generous and slapdash by nature. It is against this background of grey stately houses looking onto sylvan scenes and cosseted by sweeping trees that one should read Maria Edgeworth, supplying some details yourself on the Penal Laws, the famine, the foreignness of the landlords and their loyalties. The literature on the 'Big House' is huge, and if you read Thackeray, Trollope, Charles Lever, Somerville and Ross, and more Maria Edgeworth on the subject, you will not only be entertained but well informed. The big house, the courthouse, the jail and the military barracks were all symbols of oppression and not surprisingly many of them got burnt out in the 1920s; but these houses echo with the voices of talented and liberal people: the wit of Sheridan, Wilde, the conversations of Mrs Delany, the gleeful humour of Somerville and Ross, whisper through the rooms as you wander around.

In England there is a whole network of organizations and legislation to protect the historic house. In the Republic of Ireland there is no equivalent of the National Trust, the Historic Building and Monuments Commission, no National Heritage fund. This means there are no grants for repairs to buildings, and no effective legislation to protect them from dereliction or neglect. Even now the big house is persistently regarded by the powers that be as tainted with the memories of colonialism and an oppressive age. They are labelled as 'not Irish', although the craftsmen who built and carved the wonderful details of cornicing, stucco-work and dovetailing, elegant staircases and splendid decoration were as Irish as could be. There are many desolate shells to glimpse on your travels, though it is still possible to go around quite a selection of well cared-for properties.

The National Heritage Council set up by Charles Haughey has helped to change official attitudes, but it is the Irish Georgian Society which so far has done most to secure the future of the 'big house'. Founded in 1958 to work for the preservation of Ireland's architectural heritage, the society has carried out numerous rescue and restorataion works on historic houses. Financed almost entirely by members and donations, one of its great achievements was the restoration work done on Castletown House in Co. Kildare, Ireland's largest and finest Palladian country house. It was bought by the Hon Desmond

Guinness in 1967, the founder and then president of the Irish Georgian Society, and they had their headquarters at Castletown until 1979. From 1979 the house was owned and maintained by the Castletown Foundation, a charitable trust who continued with the restoration work and kept the house open to the public. In January 1994 Castletown became the property of the State and is the responsibility of the Office of Public Works. The Georgian Society is now based at 74 Merrion Square, Dublin 2, ✆ (01) 676 7053. Another house of great importance which is open to the public through the enterprise and energy of a few individuals is Strokestown Park House, County Roscommon. The growth of tourism has been of great help in the survival of these great houses, and state-funded organizations have started to look after some of them. Malahide Castle on the outskirts of Dublin is one of particular importance, and it is today filled with a great collection of Irish portraits and furniture. The Talbot family, who lived there from the reign of Henry II until the mid-1970s, were unable to go on coping with the huge cost of its upkeep.

If these gracious buildings and their gardens and parkland interest you, book into the country-house hotels such as Ballymaloe House in County Cork, Hilton Park in County Monaghan, Newport House in County Mayo or Markree Castle in County Sligo which has been restored by a direct descendant of the family who built it. For more details of country-house lodgings, see **Practical A–Z**, 'Where to Stay', pp.55–62, and individual entries at the end of each county chapter.

There is a growing demand to stay in or rent an Irish castle and some of them are quite reasonable in price. Elegant Ireland is a company which will organize the most specialized of requests and holiday schedules. They have a range of very exclusive and attractive country houses where you can stay as the guest of friendly, interesting hosts, and where you can be sure of good food. They will also organize rented properties from a castle to a thatched cottage. For details contact Elegant Ireland, 15 Harcourt Street, Dublin 2, ✆ (01) 475 1665/475 1632, 🖷 475 1012. If you are in the US, you may call their agent Abercrombie & Kent at their toll-free number (800) 323 7308, or in their Oakbrook (Illinois) office, ✆ (708 954) 2944. Luxurious tours can be arranged, by which you can stay as a guest in some of these splendid buildings and be entertained to dinner by the owner. 'Hidden Ireland' is the collective name for a number of privately owned historic houses throughout Ireland offering accommodation and often dinner, ✆ (01) 668 1423.

John Colclough runs specialized tours of public and private houses and castles in Ireland. You can ontact him at Irish Country House Tours, 71 Waterloo Road, Dublin 4, ✆ (01) 686463. Aer Lingus offers holidays at three castles run as hotels. Details from Aer Lingus Holidays, 88 Staines Road, Hounslow, Middx, TW3 3JB, ✆ (0181) 569 4001. If you simply want to wander around ask for a list of houses, and castles open to the public from the Irish Tourist Board.

The National Trust has several properties in Northern Ireland whose restored glory seems to be in mocking contrast to their counterparts in the Republic. Castle Coole in County Fermanagh and Springhill in County Londonderry are favourites, the latter because it still has the atmosphere of a gracious house, whose owners were never wickedly rich, just thrifty in a typically Northern way. All these properties have entrance fees which vary from £2 to £4.

You could also combine classical music and architecture if you followed the AIB Music Festival, which takes place in June each year. Many of the houses chosen are not usually open to the public, which makes the occasion very special. For 10 days in June music-lovers can travel over a large part of Ireland to listen to top-class performers in Ireland's stately houses. Ask for details from the Irish Tourist Board or from Crawford Tipping, Festival Administrator, AIB Music Festival in Great Irish Houses, 1st Floor, Blackrock Post Office, Blackrock, Co. Dublin, ✆ (01) 278 1528, @ (01) 278 1529.

Later Architectural Forms

Palladian

The term used to describe a pseudo-classical architectural style taken from the 16th-century Italian architect, Palladio. Sir Edward Lovett Pearce introduced the Palladian style to Ireland, and it was continued by his pupil, Richard Cassels, also known as Castle. Carton and Castletown in County Kildare, and Russborough in County Wicklow are good examples of the Palladian style in which the central block of each house is flanked by pavilions. The most perfect Palladian house in the British Isles is Bellamont Forest in County Cavan, designed by Pearce, which has fortunately been restored recently, but is not open to the public.

Neoclassical

A style of building which is similar to that of Palladio, but was more directly inspired by the civilization of Ancient Rome. It became popular in the 1750s until the Gothic Revival.

Gothick

An amusing and romantic style which was popular in the late 18th century. It is spelt with a 'k' to distinguish it from the serious, and later, Gothic Revival. Gothick Castles were built by Francis Johnston and the English Pain brothers, who came over to Ireland with John Nash during the 1780s. Towers and battlements were added to more severe classical houses.

Gothic Revival

From the 1830s onwards many houses and churches were built in a style harking back to the Tudor and perpendicular forms; the popularity of these gradually gave way to the more severe style of the Early-English and Decorated Gothic. The English church architect Augustus Pugin (1812–52) equated Gothic with Christian and Classicism with pagan. He designed some churches and cathedrals in Ireland including St Mary's Cathedral in Killarney. J. J. McCarthy (1817–82), an Irish architect, was very strongly influenced by Pugin; you can see McCarthy's work at St Patrick's (Roman Catholic) Cathedral, Armagh.

Hibernio-Romanesque

A style which was popular in church architecture from the 1850s onwards. It fitted in with growing national feelings to lay claim to an 'Irish style' which existed before the Anglo-Norman invasion. A good example of it can be seen at the RC Church in Spiddal, County Galway.

Irish Rococo Plasterwork

The great period of rococo plasterwork in Ireland began with the Swiss Italian brothers Paul and Philip Francini, who came to Ireland in 1739 to decorate the ceiling at Carton, Maynooth, for the Earl of Kildare. They were great stuccodores, and modelled plaster figures, trophies, fruit and flowers in magnificent combinations. You can see their work at Castletown House, Celbridge, County Kildare and at Newman House, 85–6 St Stephens Green, Dublin.

The Irish craftsmen quickly learned the technique, and between 1740–60 many beautiful ceilings were created. These craftsmen tended to leave out figures, and concentrate instead on birds, flowers, and musical instruments. The ceilings are graceful, yet full of life, with a swirling gaiety which make Adam ceilings, which later became the fashion, seem rather stilted. A fine example of a Rococo ceiling and staircase is at 20 Lower Dominick Street, Dublin. The composition of birds, flowers and fruits is perfect. Robert West (*c.* 1730–90) was the architect, and he was also an accomplished plasterer—much of the modelling had to be done by hand on site. St Saviour's Orphanage run the building, and they very kindly allow visitors to see the plasterwork. Other splendid examples of this Rococo exuberance can be seen at Russborough, County Wicklow, and the Rotunda Chapel, Dublin.

Selected Architects

Richard Cassels, also known as Castle (*c.* 1690–1751). Cassels is responsible for some of the most beautiful country houses in Ireland. He was of Huguenot origin (his family came from Germany to England), and part of the circle surrounding Lord Burlington, the wealthy and scholarly aristocrat who did so much to bring neoclassicism to Britain. Cassels came to Ireland in the 1720s and designed Powerscourt House, in County Wicklow, which so sadly was burnt down in the 1970s. He also designed Carton House in County Kildare, the Rotunda Hospital in Dublin, many houses in St Stephen's Green, and Leinster House. He is credited with the designs for Parliament House (now the Bank of Ireland building), in College Green. Cassels was also involved in designing the Newry Canal, begun in 1730, which linked the coalfield of Coalisland in County Tyrone to Newry, a distance of 18 miles (28.8 km). It was the first major canal in the British Isles. He designed the Doric Temple and the Dining Halls in Trinity College Dublin.

James Gandon (1743–1823). Born in London of Huguenot origin, and apprenticed to William Chambers, the Scottish architect. He was invited to Ireland to build a new

Custom House in Dublin. He arrived in 1781 and it was completed the same year. He was later commissioned to make extensions to Parliament House in College Green. His classical Four Courts were finished in 1802. He also designed the King's Inns, although he resigned from the project in 1808 because of irritation with the Lord Chancellor, and it was completed by his partner, Baker. His buildings—highly original and harmonious combinations of elegant neoclassical and Palladian Baroque styles—set the seal on Dublin's character at the time of Grattan's Parliament.

Francis Johnston (1760–1829). An architect in Armagh, and responsible for many of the fine buildings there, such as the Observatory. He moved to Dublin in 1793 where he designed the Chapel Royal in Dublin Castle, and the GPO in O'Connell Street. He also supervised the rebuilding of the House of Commons. He made a huge contribution to founding the Royal Hibernian Academy of Painting, Sculpture and Architecture in 1823, and he was its president for many years. He designed some 'Gothick' castles such as Charleville Forest in County Cork.

Sir Charles Lanyon (1813–89). He was born in Belfast, and built the Custom House there in 1857. Lanyon was adept at creating country houses in the Italian style; imposing and florid buildings adapted from Italian palaces and villas of the High Renaissance Period.

Sir Richard Morrison (1767–1849). The Regency architect from West Cork who designed the neoclassical Fota House, in County Cork, where the estate buildings, including a huntsman's lodge, are scaled-down versions of the house. You can also see his fine courthouse in Galway City.

John Nash (1752–1835). English architect who designed grand country houses, amongst which are Killymoon Castle and Caledon in County Tyrone. His elegant neoclassical style can be seen in the planned terraces of Regent's Park, London, and in the Royal Pavilion, Brighton.

Sir Edward Lovett Pearce (1699–1733). He was born in County Meath, and served as a soldier. He visited Venice in his early twenties, where he made drawings of the buildings there and in other Italian cities. He was the leader of the Irish Palladians, and he designed the interior of the largest and most splendid of all Irish country houses, Castletown in County Kildare. Pearce became an MP and, in 1730, Surveyor-General. He worked on the Irish Houses of Parliament in College Green (the first purpose-built parliament house in the world, and now the Bank of Ireland), with his pupil Richard Cassels.

Robert West (c. 1730–90). Dublin architect and stuccodore. He was responsible for many of the fine houses in the Georgian squares of Dublin, including 20 Lower Dominick Street, which it is possible to visit.

Gardens and Arboreta

If you love the colours, shapes, textures and scents of peaceful and mature gardens, you can have a marvellous time touring the many gardens of Ireland. The climate is a fortunate one for plants and trees because it is temperate and rainy; there is a variety of rocks and soils, and the winter is so mild it allows for the cultivation of tender plants. The grass grows well and makes generous areas of green which interact with the formal hedges, herbaceous borders, impressive trees and romantic stretches of water which nearly always enhance the parkland of these gardens.

Gaelic Ireland does not have a long horticultural tradition. It began when the Anglo-Normans and later settlers introduced the idea of a pleasure garden, with its flowers and fruits. The unsettled state of Ireland, with its many hundreds of years of internal fighting and conquest, left little time for gardening until the 18th century. By then the country was calmer, and the new 'Ascendancy' began to build themselves comfortable houses, formal gardens and parklands. They planted their estates with fine oak and beech woods, and it is usually fairly obvious today where the lands around you formed part of a demesne because of the trees. Inevitably, these parks and gardens were regarded as symbols of conquest, and were often attacked by the landless peasants. An attitude still prevails in Ireland which does not value trees, except as firewood, and very few are left to grow on the lands of the small farmer. That said, one of the most attractive features of the Irish landscape is the way your eye is drawn to the top of ancient raths or ring forts which are crowned by graceful trees. These grow undisturbed because of their association with the fairies. Many landlords planted exotic species of trees around these forts and on small hillocks in the 19th century, and they do much to beautify the landscape.

The Huguenots who came to Ireland with William of Orange brought with them new fashions in evergreens, topiary, and flowers such as tulips, pinks and auriculas. Mazes were laid within clipped hedges, and there are still a few examples, as at Birr Castle in County Offaly and Kilruddery, near Bray, Co. Wicklow. Most of the Irish gardens which survive were started in the 18th and 19th centuries. The Dublin Florists' Club, founded in 1746, was a great stimulus to the propagation of flowers and trees. It sounds a very convivial society whose members (mainly aristocrats, army men and clergy), met in taverns and drank endless toasts to the King, the Royal Family and 'the glorious memory' (of William III). After these loyal toasts exhibits of carnations and auriculas were passed around to be admired. Specimens were named and premiums offered to plantsmen by the society. More recently, Ireland has become famous for its roses, cultivated by very famous breeders such as Dickens and McCredy's, and for its daffodils, bred by Guy Wilson near Broughshane, Co. Antrim and Lionel Richardson of Waterford.

The mid 18th century saw the fashion for naturalized parkland take over from formal gardening. In the 19th century William Robertson, who started life as an Irish garden boy in County Laois, led the revolution against bedding plants and artifice and became the advocate of wild gardens—where the plant was suited to the situation and the garden to the nature of the ground. Mount Usher in County Wicklow and Anne's Grove Gardens in County Cork are fine examples of his style. For those who love rock gardens designed as miniature mountain landscapes, the garden at Rowallane in County Down is a delight. Mount Stewart, also in County Down, is full of the bizarre, including fanciful topiary. There is a charming Japanese garden at Tully (part of the National Hunt Stud); and

Kilruddery and Powerscourt in County Wicklow are lovely examples of Italianate gardens with beautiful ironwork and classical statuary. The arboreta at Castlewellan, Fota, Birr and Powerscourt are very famous; and at Derreen in County Kerry the Australian tree fern has become naturalized. Howth Castle Gardens in County Dublin and Rowallane in County Down have superb rhododendron trees. Glenveagh Castle in County Donegal and Glin Castle Gardens in County Limerick are amongst my personal favourites. Both are a happy mixture of formal and wild gardens, with huge walled gardens filled with flowers, vegetables and herbs. Both have wonderful natural settings. Another great favourite is Birr Castle Gardens, right in the heart of Ireland. If you are in Dublin, do not neglect to go to the Botanical Gardens in Glasnevin which are really superb.

The list of treasures and rare species in Irish gardens open to the public is very impressive, and there are too many to mention here. Useful publications to travel with are *The Gardens of Ireland* brochure by Bord Fáilte, which can be picked up free at any tourist office, and the *Gardens of Ireland* by Michael George and Patrick Bowe (Hutchinson, 1986). The Royal Horticultural Society of Ireland holds flower shows, lectures, and garden visits. Details from Swanbrook House, Bloomfield Avenue, Morehampton Road, Dublin 4, ✆ (01) 668 4358. The Ulster Gardens Scheme organizes open days in many gardens. Details from the Northern Irish Tourist Board, 59 North Street, Belfast, ✆ (01232) 246609. A couple of useful publications to travel with are *The Hidden Gardens of Ireland* by Marianne Heron (Gill & Macmillan) and *Irish Gardens* by Terence Reeves-Smyth (Appletree Press). The entry fee to gardens open to the public varies between IR£2 and IR£4.

History

I found in Munster, unfettered of any
Kings and queens, and poets a many–
Poets well skilled in music and measure,
Prosperous doings, mirth and pleasure.
I found in Connaught the just, redundance
Of riches, milk in lavish abundance;
Hospitality, vigour, fame,
In Cruachan's land of heroic name
I found in Ulster, from hill to glen,
Hardy warriors, resolute men;
Beauty that bloomed when youth was gone,
And strength transmitted from sire to son.
I found in Leinster the smooth and sleek,
From Dublin to Slewmargy's peak;
Flourishing pastures, valour, health,
Long-living worthies, commerce, wealth.

from 'Prince Alfrid's Itinerary'
(version by James Clarence Mangan)

If you happen to fall into conversation with an Irishman in any bar the subjects of religion and politics are bound to come up. With any luck you will have a cool glass of Guinness in front of you, for discussions on Ireland are inevitably rather emotional. The Irish are good talkers and have very long memories, so when you are in Ireland it's a good idea to have some idea of their history.

Many of Ireland's troubles have stemmed from her geographical situation—too far from Britain to be assimilated, too near to be allowed to be separate. Queen Elizabeth I poured troops into Ireland because she appreciated the strategic importance of Ireland to her enemies. Throughout the centuries Ireland has been offered help in her fight for independence, but it was never disinterested help; whoever paid for arms and fighting men in Ireland wanted to further some military, political, religious or ideological cause of their own. France in the late-18th century supplied arms to Ireland to distract England from other policies; and in Northern Ireland some of the guns were supplied by foreign powers to the IRA. Things have not changed much.

General History

Pre-Celtic Ireland

The hills and river valleys are scattered with ancient monuments dating from the Stone, the Bronze and the Iron Age. Most of them suggest some religious significance, though the myths and legends of Ireland have swathed them in romance and heroic stories. These were recounted by the Celtic story-tellers or *shanachies* in the cottages and castles. Unfortunately only a few survive today as 'memory men'.

The earliest record of man in Ireland is dated between 8700 and 8600 years ago, as deduced from fragments found at a camp in **Mount Sandel** near Coleraine. The people of this time lived a nomadic life, hunting and trapping; they could not move around very easily as the countryside was covered by forest, interrupted only by lakes and river channels. They used *curragh* boats, similar to the ones used today by fishermen in the west of Ireland. They also built lake-dwellings or *crannogs*, many of which were used until a couple of centuries ago. No one is sure where these people came from but they had the island to themselves for 3000 years. Then came **Neolithic** man, who perhaps is the Fir Bolg in Celtic mythology: at this stage everything is very vague. These people were farmers and gradually spread over the whole of Ireland, clearing the forest as best they could with their stone tools. They evidently practised burial rites, for they built chambered tombs of a very sophisticated quality, decorated with spirals and lozenge shapes. For example, the Great Burial Chamber at Newgrange in the Boyne Valley is a superb piece of construction using a tremendous variety of building stones. The chamber is large enough to contain thousands of cremated bodies. These people must have been very well organized, with the energy and wealth to spare for such an ambitious project—similar in its way to the pyramids, and a thousand years older!

Around 2000 BC yet another race appeared, who were skilled miners and metal-workers. They were called the **Beaker People**; or the Tuatha dé Danaan, as they are known in Irish legend. They opened up copper mines and started to trade with Brittany, the Baltic and the Iberian Peninsula. They had different beliefs about burial: their dead were buried singly in graves lined with stone slabs and covered with a capstone. There are a thousand chambered graves, ring-shaped cairns, standing stones, rows and circles of stones left from these times, and the Boyne Valley culture; they hint at various rituals and, it has been suggested, at observations of the stars. You will glimpse them from the road: solitary forms in a ploughed field, often used as scratching posts for cattle. They are often called 'fairy stones', and the chambered graves have been nicknamed 'Dermot and Grania's bed'.

The Celts

The next invaders arrived about 500 BC. These people had iron weapons and defeated the Beakers, whose legendary magical powers were no defence against the new metal. Known as the **Celts** or **Gaels**, the new invaders had spread from south Germany, across France, and as far south as Spain. Today everybody in Ireland has pride in the 'Celtic' past: epic tales sing the praises of men and women who were capable of heroic and superhuman deeds, and the beautiful gold jewellery is carefully preserved as proof of their achievements. The Celts brought to Ireland a highly organized social structure, and the La Tène style of decoration (its predominant motif is a spiral or a whorl). Ireland was divided into different clans with three classes: the **free**, who were warriors and owned land and cattle; the **professionals**, such as the jurists, Druids, musicians, story-tellers and poets, who could move freely between the petty kingdoms; and, finally, the **slaves**. Every clan had a petty king, who in his turn was ruled over by the high king at Tara, County Meath.

The Gaels made use of many of the customs and mythology that had existed before their arrival, so their 'Celtic civilization' is unique. They were also very fortunate, for although they were probably displaced themselves by the expanding **Roman Empire**, once they got to Ireland they were isolated, and protected to some extent by England which acted as a buffer state. The Romans never extended their ambitions to conquering Ireland, so the Gaels were able to develop their traditions, unlike Celts elsewhere in Europe. They spent most of their time raiding their neighbours for cattle and women, who were used as live currency. They also had their religion. The stone images and pillars which have survived from those days have a strange and powerful aura. Most are head idols. The human head was all-important as a symbol of divinity and supernatural power—even when it was severed from the body it still retained its powers. The warriors used to take the heads of their slain enemies and display them in front of their houses. The Gaels also believed firmly in an afterlife of the soul: they would lend each other money to be repaid in the next world!

The Arrival of Christianity

Christianity was brought to Ireland in the 5th century AD by **St Patrick**, and quickly became accepted by the kings. One of them, **Cormac MacArt**, who ruled in Tara about a century and a half before St Patrick arrived, saw the light and told his court of Druids and nobles that the gods they worshipped were only craven wood! The Druids put a curse on him and soon afterwards he choked to death on a salmon bone; but before he died he ordered that he was not to be buried in the tomb of Brugh (Newgrange) but on the sunny east point by the River Rosnaree. When St Patrick lit a fire which signalled the end of Druid worship, legend has it that he was looking down from the Hill of Slane on to Rosnaree.

The Christians displayed great skill in reconciling their practices and beliefs with those of the pagans; a famous saying of St Columba was, 'Christ is my Druid'. The early Christians seem to have been very ascetic, preferring to build their monasteries in the most wild and inaccessible places. Today you can still see their hive-shaped dwellings on **Skellig Michael**, a windswept rocky island off the Kerry coast. Wherever they went, these early saints attracted followers and their monasteries expanded without much planning. The monasteries became universities renowned throughout Europe, which was submerged in the Dark Ages, and produced beautiful manuscripts like the famously beautiful *Book of Kells*. The abbots held great power as spiritual lords and landlords; many of the petty kings were relations and left all their precious goods in the monasteries, using them as a sort of bank. From the 6th century onwards, much of the missionary spirit of the Irish monks was directed outwards to the Continent. They founded Bobbio in Italy and other religious houses and the interchange of ideas between the Continent and Ireland was far greater than was once thought.

The Viking Invasion

The tranquillity of Ireland, 'land of saints and scholars', was brutally interrupted by the arrival of the **Vikings** or **Norsemen**. They were able to penetrate right into Ireland through their skilful use of the rivers and lakes. They struck for the first time in 795, but this was only the start of a 300-year struggle.

Much treasure from the palaces and monasteries was plundered, for the buildings had no defences; so the monks built round towers in which to store their precious things at the first sign of trouble. Never had the Gaels been threatened like this before. Eventually the Norsemen began to settle down and they founded the first city-ports—Dublin, Wexford and Waterford and started to trade with the Gaels.

Military alliances were made between them when it helped a particular king in the continuous struggle for the high kingship. After a short period of relative calm another wave of Norsemen invaded and the plundering began again; but **Brian Boru**, who had usurped the high kingship from the O'Connors, defeated the Vikings at Clontarf in 1014 and broke their power permanently. Unfortunately, for the Gaelic people, Brian Boru was murdered by some Vikings in his tent just after the victory at Clontarf. Now havoc and in-fighting became a familiar pattern, as the high kingship was fought for by the O'Briens, the O'Loughlins and the O'Connors. The Gaelic warriors wasted themselves and their people, for no one leader seemed strong enough to rule without opposition. The next invaders saw that their opportunity lay in the disunity of the Irish.

The Norman Invasion and Consolidation

In the mid 12th century the Pope gave his blessing to an expedition of **Anglo-Normans** sent by **Henry II** to Ireland. The Normans were actually invited over by the King of Leinster, **Dermot MacMurragh**, who had made a bitter enemy of **Tiernan O'Rourke** of Breffni by running off with his wife, Devorgilla. He also backed the wrong horse in the high kingship stakes, and the united efforts of the High King Rory O'Connor and O'Rourke brought about a huge reduction in MacMurragh's kingdom. So he approached Henry II, offering his oath of fealty in exchange for an invasion force of men with names like Fitzhenry, Carew, Fitzgerald, Barry—names you still see in Irish villages. The Normans were adventurers and good warriors: in 1066, William, Duke of Normandy had taken the crown of England by force with only 5000 men. Now, in 1169, several Norman nobles decided to try their luck in Ireland, and they found it easy to grab huge tracts of land for themselves. The Gaels had faced so few attacks from outside their country that they were unprepared to do battle. Their weapons were very inferior to those of the Normans; their main advantage was their knowledge of the bogs, mountains and forest, and their numbers. The Normans had a well-equipped cavalry, who rode protected by a screen of archers. Once they had launched a successful attack, they consolidated their position by building moats, castles, and walled towns. **Strongbow**, one of the most powerful of the Norman invaders, married MacMurragh's daughter and became his heir, but his successes and those of the other Norman barons worried Henry II. In 1171 Henry arrived in Ireland with about 4000 troops and two objectives: to secure the submission of the Irish leaders and to impose his authority on his own barons. He achieved both aims, but the Gaelic lords still went on fighting. In fact, the coming of the Normans began a military struggle which was to continue over four centuries.

The Bruce Invasion

In 1314 **Robert Bruce of Scotland** decisively defeated English forces at Bannockburn, and was in a position to try to fulfil his dream of a united Celtic kingdom, by putting his brother **Edward** on the throne in Ireland. At first his invasion was successful, but he left a trail of destruction behind him. The year 1316 was marked by famine and disease exacerbated by the war. His dream brought economic and social disaster to Ireland, and when Edward Bruce was defeated and killed at Dundalk few of his allies mourned his death. The Normans' control fluctuated within an area surrounding Dublin known as the Pale, and they became rather independent of their English overlord; in some cases, such as the de Burgos (Burkes), they became more Irish than the Irish. The Gaelic lords in the north and west continued to hold their territories. To do so they imported Scottish mercenary soldiers, called **gallowglasses**, who prolonged the life of the independent Gaelic kingdoms for more than two centuries after the defeat of Edward Bruce.

The Nine Years' War: Elizabethan Conquest and Settlement

Since the Norman invasion, Ireland had been ruined by continual fighting. By the late 16th century the country was in the doldrums and it is little wonder that **Queen Elizabeth** preached the need for a Crusade-style war to bring civilization to Ireland. Elizabeth had an interest in Ireland; many of the Irish nobles had been educated at her court, and she endowed and founded Trinity College, Dublin. However, the basic reason for her preoccupation with Ireland was security. She was determined to bring the Irish more firmly under English control, especially the Ulster lords who had so far maintained almost total independence. Elizabeth took over the Irish policy of her father which had never been fully implemented, her government decided that all the Gaelic lords must surrender their lands to the Crown, whereupon they would be regranted immediately. At this time Ulster, today the stronghold of Protestantism, was the most Gaelic and Catholic part of Ireland, and it was from here that the great **Hugh O'Neill** and **Red Hugh O'Donnell** launched a last-ditch struggle against Elizabeth. Initial successes bolstered the rebels' morale. Elizabeth, recognizing the gravity of the situation, sent over her talented favourite soldier, Essex.

Most of his troops died from disease and guerrilla attacks, and with no reinforcements he had little alternative than to make a truce with O'Neill. Disgrace and execution were his reward. In February 1600 Lord Mountjoy arrived in Ireland with 20,000 troops. Risings at Munster were crushed and with them the aspirations of Connacht and Leinster. The Gaelic chiefs seem to have been ruthless in their allegiances. They had hailed O'Neill as Prince of Ireland but now, anticipating defeat, they deserted him. O'Neill's hopes were raised by the long-promised arrival of Spanish troops at Kinsale in 1601, but they only numbered 4000. When they did do battle against Mountjoy, the Irish were left confused when the Spaniards failed to sally out as arranged.

The Flight of the Earls

O'Neill returned to Ulster on the 23 March 1603 and made his submission to Mountjoy, only to learn in Dublin later that Queen Elizabeth had died the very next day. He is said to have wept with rage. Amongst all the nobles, only he might have been able to unite the Irish and beat Elizabeth. O'Neill had his titles and lands returned to him, but the Dublin government, greedy for his property, began to bait him. It took his land at the slightest excuse and forbade him to practise Catholicism; so, abandoning hope and his followers, he sailed to Europe. This 'Flight of the Earls' took place on the 14 September 1607, from the wild and beautiful shores of the Swilly. It symbolizes the end of Gaelic leadership and a new period of complete domination by the English. The Irish lords took themselves off to the courts of France and Spain or into the foreign armies. If you glance through the lists of famous generals and politicians in Europe, a few Irish names will leap up at you from the pages: in Spain, Wall and O'Donnell; in Austria, the minister Taafe; in France, Admiral Macnamara and General Lally Tullindaly. The Flight of the Earls had become glorified in stories; but on the whole, the eponymous nobles were vicious and uncultured, contributing nothing to the mainstream of European thought. They had spent most of their energies warring among themselves and at the last moment deserted their country and left the Irish peasants with no leadership at all.

The Confederation, Cromwell and the Stuarts

By the 1640s, Ireland was ready for rebellion again—there were plenty of grievances. **James I**, a staunch Protestant, dispossessed many Gaelic and old English families in Ireland because they would not give up Catholicism, and he began the '**plantation**' of the most vehemently Catholic province, Ulster, with Protestants. Previous plantations had not worked because of inclement weather, but James knew that the Scots would be able to skip about the bogs as well as the Irish! When **Charles Stuart** came to the throne, many Catholic families hoped that they might be given some religious freedom and retain their estates, but nothing was legally confirmed. In 1633 **Black Tom**, the Earl of Strafford, arrived with the intention of making Ireland a source of profit rather than a loss to the king. In his zeal to do so he succeeeded in alienating every element in Irish society. His enemies amongst the Puritans in Ireland and England put pressure on the king to recall him and he was eventually executed. English politics became dominated by the dissension betweeen the Roundheads and the Cavaliers and the hopeless Irish took note. Their maxim was 'England's difficulty is Ireland's opportunity'. Charles tried to deal with the growing unrest in Ireland by giving everybody what they wanted, but he no longer had enough power to see that his laws were carried out. The Gaelic Irish decided to take a chance and rebel; many of them came back from the Continental armies hoping to win back their old lands. In October 1641 a small Gaelic force took over the whole of Ulster and there were widespread uprisings in Leinster. In Ulster, the Gaelic people had been burning for revenge and the new planted families suffered terribly. This cruel treatment has not been forgotten by Ulster Protestants.

The Dublin government was worse than useless at controlling the rebels, who continued to be successful. While the government waited for reinforcements from England, they managed to antagonize the old English, for they made the mistake of presuming that they would be disloyal to the Crown, and so viewed them with suspicion. The old English families decided to throw in their lot with the rebels since they were already considered traitors, but on one condition: a declaration of loyalty from the Gaelic leaders to the Catholic English crown which was now seriously threatened by the Puritans.

The Confederation of Kilkenny

By February 1642 most of Ireland was in rebel hands. The rebels established a provisional government at **Kilkenny**, and Charles began to negotiate with them hoping to gain their support against the Puritans. Things were too good to last. The destructive factors that had ruined many Irish uprisings before and since, came into play: personal jealousy and religion. The old English were loyal to the king and wanted a swift end to the war; the Gaelic Irish were only interested in retrieving their long-lost lands and were ready to fight to the bitter end. This disunity was exacerbated by the rivalry between the Gaelic commander, **Owen Roe O'Neill** and the commander of the old English army, **Thomas Preston**. In October 1645 the Papal Nuncio arrived and the unity of the Confederates was further split: he and O'Neill took an intransigent stand over the position of the Catholic Church, which Charles I could not agree to.

The rebels won a magnificent victory over the Puritan General Munro at Benburb, but O'Neill did not follow it up. The confederates, torn by disunity and rivalry, let opportunities slip past and they lost the initiative. Eventually they did decide to support the king and end their Kilkenny government, but by this time Charles I had been beheaded and his son had fled into exile. The Royalists were defeated at Rathmines in 1649 and the way was left clear for the Puritan leader, **Cromwell**, who landed in Dublin soon after. Cromwell came to Ireland determined to break the Royalists, break the Gaelic Irish, and to avenge the events of 1641 in Ulster. He shared the Puritan hatred for the Catholic Church: it is easy to forget how extreme both religious viewpoints were then. Cromwell thought that the priests had engineered the rising—of the Irish character and their grievances he knew little and cared less. He started his campaign with the **Siege of Drogheda**, and there are the most gruesome accounts of his methods. When his troops burst into the town they put Royalists, women, children and priests to the sword; in all 3552 dead were counted, whilst Cromwell only lost 64 men. Catholics curse Cromwell to this day. The same butchery distinguished the taking of Wexford. Not surprisingly, he managed to break the spirit of resistance by such methods and there were widespread defections from the Royalists' side. Owen Roe O'Neill might have been able to rally the Irish but he died suddenly. Cromwell's campaign only lasted seven months and he took all the towns except Galway and Waterford. These he left to his lieutenants.

By 1652 the whole country was subdued, and Cromwell encouraged all the fighting men to leave by granting them amnesty if they fled overseas. The alternative to exile was, for many families, something that turned out to be even worse: compulsory removal to Connacht and County Clare. Some had been neutral during all the years of fighting, but that was never taken into account. Cromwell was determined that anyone suspect should go to Hell or Connacht! So if you want to track down the really ancient Irish families, find out if they came from Connacht. The government had lots of land to play around with after that. First of all they paid off 'the adventurers', men who had lent them money back in 1642. Next, the Roundhead soldiers, who had not been paid their salaries for years, got Irish land instead. Thus the Cromwellian Settlement parcelled out even more land to speculators and rogues.

Stuart and Orange

After the **Restoration of the Monarchy** in 1660, the Catholics in Ireland hoped for toleration and rewards for their loyalty to the Stuart cause. They felt threatened by the fast-expanding Protestant community, mostly dissenters, who had been given religious freedom under Cromwell. Charles did not restore many Catholic estates because he had to keep in with the ex-Cromwellian supporters, but Catholics were given a limited amount of toleration. However, with the succession of Charles' brother **James**, who was a Catholic, things began to brighten up. In Ireland, the Catholic Earl of Tyrconnell became commander of the army in 1685 and, later, chief governor. By 1688 Roman Catholics were dominant in the army, the administration, the judiciary and the town corporations, and by the end of the year Protestant power in Ireland was seriously weakened.

James frightened all those Protestants in England who had benefited from Catholic estates. They began to panic when he introduced sweeping acts of toleration for all religions. His attempts to re-establish the Catholic Church alienated the country to such an extent that the Protestant aristocracy invited **William of Orange** over in November 1688 to relieve his father-in-law of his throne. James fled to France but soon left for Ireland, which was a natural base from which to launch his counter-attack. By the date of his arrival in March 1689, only Enniskillen and Londonderry were in Protestant hands.

The Siege of Londonderry and Battle of the Boyne

The subjugation of the city of Londonderry was James' first aim. In a famous incident celebrated in Orange songs, a group of apprentice boys shut the city gates to the Jacobite army, and so began the famous Siege of Londonderry. The townspeople proved unbreakable, even though food supplies were very low and they were reduced to eating rats and mice and chewing old bits of leather. Many did die of starvation during the 15 weeks of the siege, but just as they were about to give in, the foodship *Mountjoy* forced its way through a great boom built across the Foyle. This military and psychological victory was of enormous significance in the campaign. When William himself arrived at Carrickfergus in June 1690, James decided to confront him at the Boyne. William of Orange had an army of about 36,000 comprised of English, Scots, Dutch, Danes, Germans and Huguenots, against James' army of about 25,000, made up of Irish and French. William triumphed, as the result of his numerical and strategic superiority. James deserted the battlefield and Ireland with haste.

In the **Battle of the Boyne** James seems to have completely lost his nerve. The Jacobite forces had to retreat west of the Shannon to Limerick, and William promptly laid siege to it. So weak were its walls that it is said they could be breached with roasted apples. The defence of Limerick was as heroic as that of Londonderry. Patrick Sarsfield slipped out with a few followers and intercepted William's siege train and destroyed it. William then gave up and left for England leaving Ginkel in charge. The next year the French King Louis XIV sent over supplies and men to fuel the Jacobite cause, as he hoped to divert William in Ireland for a little longer. The Jacobite leader St Ruth, who landed with them, proved a disaster for the Irish; Sarsfield would have been a better choice. Ginkel took Athlone and Aughrim in June and July of 1691, after two battles in which stories of courage on the Jacobite side have provided inspiration to patriot poets and musicians. The last hope of the Catholic Irish cause was now Limerick.

The Treaty of Limerick

Sarsfield skilfully gathered together what Jacobite troops were left and got them back there. (St Ruth had been killed by a canonball, and rather typically had appointed no second-in-command.) Ginkel tried to storm the town from both sides, but still Limerick held out and he began to treaty with Sarsfield. Honourable terms were made for the Jacobites, and Sarsfield signed the famous **Treaty of Limerick** in October 1691. The next day a French fleet arrived and anchored off the Shannon estuary, but Sarsfield stood by the treaty. The treaty seemed to guarantee quite a lot. Catholics were to have the same rights as they had had under Charles II and any Catholic estates which had been registered in 1662 were to be handed back. Catholics were to be allowed free access to the bar, bench, army and parliament. Sarsfield was to be given a safe passage to the Continent with his troops. But the Treaty was not honoured, except for the last clause which got all the fighting men out of the country.

This was one of the dirtiest tricks the English played, and to be fair to William of Orange he wanted the treaty to be enforced, but being new and unsure of his support he complied with the treachery. Eleven thousand Irish Jacobites sailed away to join the French army, forming the Irish Brigade. Over the years many came to join them from Ireland, and were remembered in their native land as the **Wild Geese**.

The Orange/Stuart war still lives vividly in the imagination of the people today. The Siege of Londonderry has become a sign of Protestant determination: 'no surrender 1690' is scrawled, usually in bright red paint, on the walls and street corners of Loyalist areas in Northern Ireland. The Battle of the Boyne is remembered in a similar way. Here is an old, old anecdote. An old man is asked by a youth (or a foreigner), 'Who is King Billy?' His reply is , 'Away man, and read your Bible.'

The Penal Laws

The defeat of the Catholic cause was followed by more confiscation of land, and the **Penal Laws**. What had happened was that a bargain had been struck with the Protestant planters. They would be allowed to keep a complete monopoly of political power and most of the land. In return they would act as a British garrison to keep the peace and prevent the Catholics from gaining any power. To do this they passed a series of degrading laws. Briefly they were as follows. No Catholic could purchase freehold land. Any son of a Catholic, turning Protestant, could turn his parents off their estate. Families who stayed Catholic had their property equally parcelled out amongst all the children, so that any large estates soon became uneconomic holdings. All the Catholics were made to pay a tithe towards the upkeep of the Anglican Church. All priests were banished. No Catholic schools were allowed and spies were set amongst the peasants to report on 'hedge schools', a form of quite sophisticated schooling that had sprung up; priests on the run taught at these schools and celebrated Mass. A Catholic could not hold a commission in the army, enter a profession nor even own a horse worth more than £5. These anti-religious laws had the opposite effect to that intended: Catholicism took on a new lease of life in Ireland. In addition, **economic laws** were introduced that put heavy taxes on anything that Ireland produced—cloth, wool, glass and cattle—so that she could not compete with

England. The trading regulations were very disadvantageous to the non-co
Protestants and many of them left.

The worst thing about these Penal Laws was the moral effect. It became F
the law, and necessary to smuggle and steal; the country turned itself into
society using every means to outwit the authorities. To be a Catholic mean
to lie to protect your priest, and if you were a farmer there was no point in making a
profit—any Protestant was allowed to come and claim it. It was not always as bad as that;
the harshness of the laws did not reach to every part of Ireland. Sometimes a family, part
of which became Protestant, would come to an agreement. The Protestant end held on to
the Catholic property in trust and then handed it back when the laws were relaxed or
repealed. The Protestant landlords were nervous at first and grabbed as much as they
could while the going was good, until this became a habit. They felt under no obligation to
their Irish tenants, whom they tended to despise and could not understand. Many of them
never bothered to learn more than a few words of Gaelic. Not all of them were bad, but
they were resented anyway for being alien in religion, race and customs.

Then, gradually things began to relax; the Catholics had been well and truly squashed.
The Protestants began to build themselves grand and beautiful houses, the draughty, damp
tower houses could be left to decay. (Irish squires were famous for their hard drinking; the
expression 'plastered' comes from the story of a guest who was so well wined and dined at
a neighbour's housewarming party that he fell asleep against a newly plastered wall. He
woke up next morning to find that his scalp and hair had hardened into the wall!)

As the 18th century progressed, however, there were signs of aggression amongst the
peasantry; agrarian secret societies were formed with names like the **White Boys**, **Hearts
of Oak**, and the **Molly Maguires**. They were very brutal and meted out rough justice to
tenants and landlords alike. If any peasant paid rent to an unfair landlord, he was likely to
be intimidated or have his farm burnt down. In Ulster, peasant movements were dominated by sectarian land disputes. The Catholics were called the **Defenders** and the
Protestant groups the **Peep-O'Day Boys**. In the 1770s the Penal Laws were relaxed a
little and Catholics were allowed to bid for land, and they incensed the Protestants by
bidding higher. After a particularly bad fight between the two sides which the Protestants
won, the **Orange Order** was founded in 1795. A typical oath of one of the early clubs
was, 'To the glorious, pious and immortal memory of the great and good King William, not
forgetting Oliver Cromwell, who assisted in redeeming us from popery, slavery, arbitrary
power, brassmoney and wooden shoes'.

The **American War of Independence** broke out in 1775 and Ireland was left undefended. There were fears of an invasion by France or Spain and a general feeling that there
ought to be some sort of defence force. The **Volunteers** were organized with officers from
the Protestant landowning class; but as the fears of invasion receded they turned their
considerable muscle to the cause of political reform, and Britain began to fear that they
might follow the example of the American colonies. When America sought independence,
Irish Protestants and Catholics alike watched with approval, particularly since many of the
rebel Americans were of Ulster/Scots blood. The landowners had their own parliament in

, but all important matters were dealt with by London. A group of influential owners began to think that Ireland would be much better off with an independent ish parliament. In 1783, the British Government, influenced by the eloquence of the great speaker **Henry Grattan**, acknowledged the right of Ireland to be bound only by laws made by the King and the Irish parliament. Trade, industry and agriculture began to flourish, and the worst of the Penal Laws were repealed or relaxed.

Grattan's Parliament

Grattan's Parliament was really an oligarchy of landowners, but at least they understood the problems of the economy and tried to bring a more liberal spirit into dealings with Catholics and dissenters. Grattan wanted complete Catholic emancipation, but for that the Irish had to wait. Yet Trinity College was made accessible to those of all religious persuasions, although Catholics were forbidden by their bishops to go there. The great Catholic Seminary at Maynooth was founded, and endowed with money and land from the Protestant aristocrats, who were worried that the priests educated at Douai might bring back with them some of those frightening ideas of liberty and equality floating around France. Dissenters were given equal rights with the Established Church at this time.

Dublin was now a handsome Georgian city, a centre for the arts, science and society—duelling was the national pastime! All this pleasure was expensive so landowners began to sublet their estates to the landhungry tenants. All the dirty work was done by an agent who also pocketed most of the profits, but the system enabled landlords to live in idleness and keep large houses in Dublin. In the early 1790s, fear and anger swept through Europe in the form of the French Revolution and the governments of Europe, whether Catholic or Protestant, drew nearer together in mutual fear.

Many, who at first were delighted with the revolution in France, became disgusted with the brutality of its methods. The Irish government disbanded the Volunteers and got together a militia and part-time force of yeomanry. It was nervous of a French invasion and increasingly of a middle-class organization, the 'United Irishmen', who were sick of a government which only spoke for a tiny proportion of the population.

Wolfe Tone and United Irishmen

The aim of the United Irishmen was to throw open the Irish parliament to all Irishmen, irrespective of their rank or religion. Many United Irishmen were from Ulster non-conformist backgrounds. Initially the movement was to be non-violent, but when war broke out between England and France, all radical societies were forced to go underground. No liberal ideas could be tolerated during the war effort. **Wolfe Tone** was a Dublin lawyer and a prominent United Irishman; he crossed over to France to try and persuade the French Directory to help.

The Protestant Wind

Wolfe Tone succeeded brilliantly in arguing a case for French intervention and on the night of 16 December 1796, the last great French invasion force to set sail for the British Isles slipped past the British squadron blockading the port of Brest. Five days later 35 ships with 6000 men aboard arrived and anchored off Bantry Bay. Unfortunately, the frigate carrying the Commander-in-Chief, General Hoche, had become separated from the rest of the fleet during the journey and so it was decided not to land until he arrived. But their good fortune deserted them. After waiting through one clear, calm day the wind changed and blew from the east, and it is remembered in all the songs as a 'Protestant Wind'. The fleet endured the rain and storm for three days, then the ships cut cable and headed back for France. Only Wolfe Tone and his ship, *The Indomitable*, remained and, as Tone put it, 'England had not such an escape since the Armada'.

Meanwhile, in the Irish countryside, increasingly brutal attempts were made by the militia and the yeomanry to stamp out sedition. In Ulster, where the United Irishmen were strong, efforts were made to set the United Irishmen against the Orangemen, many of whom had joined the yeomanry. This continual pressure forced the society to plan rebellion. However, government spies had infiltrated its ranks, and two months before the proposed date many of the leaders were arrested. By this time many Irish peasants had joined the United Irishmen, inspired by the heady doctrine of Tom Paine's *Rights of Man*. The increased power of the Irish parliament had not meant more freedom for them; on the contrary the heretics and alien landlords now seemed to have more power to persecute them in the forms of tithes and taxes. Yet the Gaelic-speaking peasants had little in common with the middle-class agitators, and their anger was even more explosive.

The 1798 Rebellion

In May 1798 the rebellion broke out. The United Irish leaders had planned a rebellion believing that they could count on an army of over 250,000. However, the absence of leadership and careful, efficient planning resulted in local uprisings with no central support; even those which achieved some success were quickly crushed. In Wexford, the United Irishmen led by Father Murphy succeeded in capturing Enniscorthy and all the county except New Ross. It took a general, a month of warfare and a pitched battle lasting 12 hours to defeat the rebels. The battle of Vinegar Hill, with its grisly and indiscriminate reprisals against Protestants, ended in the rebels' defeat, and the usual brutal consequences. In Ulster there were two main risings, under **McCracken** and **Munro**. The risings both enjoyed brief success during which time the rebels treated any Loyalist prisoners well—a marked contrast to what had happened in other counties. But the sectarian battles between the Peep-O'Day Boys had already soured the trust of the Catholics, and many of them did not turn up to help the mixed bunch of United Irishmen. Poor Wolfe Tone and others who had started the society with such hopes for affectionate brotherhood saw their ideals drowned in a sea of blood. Nugent, the commander of the government forces in Ulster, decided to appeal to the rebels who had property to lose, especially those in the rich eastern counties, and he proclaimed a general amnesty if the Antrim rebels gave up their arms. The rebels of Down did not get off so humanely; when they had been routed and shot down they were left unburied in the streets for the pigs to eat. McCracken and Munro were executed.

The Races of Castlebar

Whilst the war between France and England became more embittered, Wolfe Tone succeeded in raising another invasion force. On 22 August 1798, **General Humbert** arrived in Killala Bay with 1000 men and more arms for the rebels, although most of them had dispersed. Humbert captured Ballina and routed 6000 loyalist troops in a charge called the 'Races of Castlebar'. But there were not enough rebels and Humbert had to accept honourable terms of surrender in September. Only a few weeks later, another unsuccessful French expedition arrived with Tone on board and entered Lough Swilly. It was overcome by some British frigates and Wolfe Tone was captured. He appeared before a court martial wearing a French uniform and carrying a cockade. The only favour he asked was the right to be shot, which was refused, whereupon he cut his own throat with a penknife and lingered in agony for seven days.

The rebellion of 1798 was one of the most tragic and violent events in Irish history, and it had the effect of making people try to bring about change in a non-violent way. In the space of three weeks, 30,000 people, peasants armed with pitchforks and pikes, women and children, were cut down and shot. The results of the rebellion were just as disastrous. The ideas of political and religious equality were discredited, because of the deaths and destruction of property. The British Government found that an independent parliament was an embarrassment to them, especially since the 'Protestant garrison' had not been able to put down the peasant rising without their help.

The Union

Pitt, the British prime minister, decided that union between Great Britain and Ireland was the only answer. First he had to bribe the Protestants to give up their power and many earldoms date from this time. Then the **Act of Union** was passed, with promises of Catholic emancipation for the majority. Pitt really did want to give them equality, for he saw that it was a necessary move if he wished to make Ireland relatively content. Unfortunately Pitt was pushed out of government, and **George III** lent his considerable influence to those opposed to Catholic emancipation. He claimed, with perfect truth, that the idea of it drove him mad. The Union did not solve any problems: the Catholics felt bitterly let down and the temporary Home Rule of Grattan's parliament was looked back to as an example. Irreconcilable nationalism was still alive and kicking. Union with England was disadvantageous to Ireland in the areas of industry and trade and many poorer Protestants were discontented—although from now on the Ulster non-conformists supported the Union, for many had been disillusioned by the vengeance shown towards Protestants by the Catholic peasantry. The terms of the 1801 Act were never thought of as final in Ireland, although the English failed to understand this.

The Liberator: Daniel O'Connell

Catholics still could not sit in parliament or hold important state offices or get to the senior judicial, military or civil service posts. Between the Union and 1828 many efforts to have something done about this came to nothing. Then the Catholics found a champion among themselves: a Catholic lawyer called **Daniel O'Connell**. Daniel O'Connell came from an old Catholic Irish family; he had been sent to school in France where his uncle was a general in the French army. His glimpses of the French revolutionary army had left him completely against violence whatever the political end. The rising of 1798 confirmed in him the belief that 'no political change is worth the shedding of a single drop of human blood'. O'Connell founded the **Catholic Association** which, amongst other things, represented the interests of the tenant farmers. Association membership was a penny a month and brought in a huge fighting fund. Most important of all, the Catholic priests supported him, and soon there were branches of the association everywhere.

A turning point for Irish history and the fortunes of Daniel O'Connell came with the Clare election in 1828, when the association showed its strength. O'Connell had an overwhelming victory against the government candidate when all the 40-shilling freeholders voted for him. The whole country was aflame: they wanted Daniel at Westminster. Wellington, the Prime Minister of the day, was forced to give in, and the **Emancipation Bill** was passed in April 1829. But this was not a gesture of conciliation, for at the same time he raised the voting qualification from 40 shillings to a massive £10. Protestant fears had been raised by the power of such a mass movement, for tenant farmers had dared to vote in opposition to their landlords, even though voting was public. To English Catholics Daniel was also a 'Liberator'.

For 12 years O'Connell supported the Whig government and built up a well-disciplined Irish party whose co-operation was essential to any government majority. He was then able to press for some very necessary reforms, and when the viceroy and his secretary were sympathetic much was achieved. But with the return of the Conservatives in 1840, O'Connell decided it was time to launch another popular agitation campaign, this time for the repeal of the Union. His mass-meetings became 'monster meetings', each attended by well over 100,000 people. The government refused to listen on this issue; British public opinion was firmly against it and in Ulster there was a distinct lack of enthusiasm. Daniel O'Connell arranged to have one of his biggest meetings yet, at Clontarf, where Brian Boru had defeated the Vikings. The Government banned it and O'Connell, unwilling to risk violence, called it off. He himself was arrested for conspiracy and sentenced by just the sort of packed jury he had been trying to abolish. Luckily for him, the House of Lords was less frightened and more just; they set aside his sentence. But by then O'Connell's influence had begun to fade, and some Irish began to look to violence to achieve their aims.

The Young Irelanders

Within the Repeal Association was a group of young men who called themselves the **Young Irelanders**. They had founded *The Nation* newspaper to help O'Connell, but they soon began to move in a different direction. They believed that culturally and historically Ireland was independent of England. They fed their enthusiasm on the painful memories of 1798 and composed heroic poetry which they set to old ballad tunes. They were useless at practical politics and did not have the support of the clergy. In 1848 they responded to the spontaneous and romantic uprisings in Europe with one of their own. It was a dismal failure and alienated many people who had been in favour of the Repeal of the Union. The movement was not to become respectable again until 1870.

The Great Hunger

The diet of an ordinary Irishman was six pounds of potatoes and a pint of milk a day, and he lived in miserable conditions. The Cromwellian and Williamite plantations, together with the effect of the Penal Laws, left the Catholics with only 5 per cent of the land. Except in the North, where a thriving linen industry had grown up, the people had to make their living from farming. Absentee landlords became more of a problem after the Union, their agents greedier and their rent demands even higher. It was the farmer at the bottom of the pyramid who paid heavily for what he got. From 1845–49 the **potato blight** struck, with tragic results.

The population of Ireland, as in the rest of Europe, began to rise quickly in the late 18th century, perhaps because the potato could feed large families on small plots of land. Anyway, the marriage age, which had previously been very high, dropped right down and more babies were born. The most deprived and populated area of Ireland was the west, where the potato was the only crop that would grow; it alone sustained the fragile equilibrium of large families on tiny holdings. The scene was set for agricultural and social catastrophe. As the potato rotted in the ground, people ate turnips, cabbage, wild vegetables and even grass, but these could not supply more than a few meals. Gradually, thousands of people began to die of starvation, typhus fever, relapsing fever and dysentery. You may ask yourselves what was done to help them? Very little by the government, quite a lot by individuals and private charities. Every day corn and cattle were leaving the country; nothing was done that might interfere with the principle of free trade and private enterprise. The government's attitude was rigid, though they did allow maize in, a crop in which nobody had any vested interest. Food distribution centres were set up and some relief work was paid for by the government. But this was not very sensible sort of work; mostly digging holes only to fill them in again. Something constructive like laying a network of railway lines might have interfered with private enterprise! Out of a population of eight and a half million, about one million died and another million emigrated.

Emigration

The Irish had been emigrating for years; first to escape persecution by fleeing to the Continent and then as seasonal labour for the English harvests. The Ulster Scots had set the first pattern of emigration to America. They had found that Ireland was not the promised land, after being lured over there by grants of land and low rents. Bad harvests, religious discrimination and high rents sent them off at the rate of 4000 a year. Not many Catholics followed, for there were still restrictions on Catholic emigration. After the Napoleonic wars and the agricultural slump, 20,000 of the brighter and wealthier Catholics went to America; by then America was more liberal in its attitude towards Catholics. Boat fares over were very cheap and the opportunities in the New World seemed less biased in favour of the rich upper classes. Many Irish went to Australia as convicts or free settlers. But the heaviest years of emigration were just after the famine, especially to the USA. The people travelled under appalling conditions, and boats were called 'coffin ships'. It took six to eight weeks to get to America in those overcrowded and disease-ridden conditions. By 1847 nearly a quarter of a million were emigrating annually.

Irish priests followed their flocks out to America and Australia and founded churches wherever they were needed, so a distinct Irish Catholic Church grew up. Such an influx of starving, diseased Irish Catholics was quite another thing to the steady flow of a few thousand Ulster Scots, and initially a lot of people were prejudiced against them. Most of the emigrants left Ireland loathing the British in Ireland. Their children grew up with the same hatred, and sometimes became more anti-British than the Irish left in Ireland. This bitterness was soon transformed into political activity, aided by the Young Irelanders who had fled to America. Many of the emigrants had come from the west where the Gaelic language and culture existed undisturbed. The rest of Ireland, especially the east, was quite anglicized and became more so with the development of education and transport.

America and Irish Politics

By 1858 the Irish Catholics in America had reorganized themselves as the **Fenian Brotherhood**. James Stevens founded a sister movement in Ireland called the **Irish Republican Brotherhood** (IRB). The Fenians called themselves after the legendary Fianna Warriors and were dedicated to the principal of Republicanism. In Ireland, aided by money from America, the Fenians started up the newspaper, *The Irish People*, which was aimed at the urban worker. When the American Civil War was over many Irish American soldiers came over to help the Fenians in Ireland, but their military operations were always dismal failures. In 1867 the government quickly crushed their uprising and felt confident enough to give the leaders long prison sentences. The clergy opposed any revolutionary secret societies and supported action only when it was through constitutional channels. But Fenianism remained a potent force. John Devoy in America and Michael Davitt of the Irish Land League, were imaginative enough to see that violence was not the only way to fight high rents. They made a loose alliance with Parnell, the leader of the Irish Party in the House of Commons.

John Devoy was head of the **Clan-na-Gael**, an organization which cloaked Fenianism. In America, through the Fenians, Parnell was able to collect money for the land agitators. John Devoy gave money and moral support to the revolutionaries in their fight for independence. The Clan created good propaganda for the Nationalists and, between the death of Parnell and the rise of **Sinn Fein** (the new Nationalist party), did everything it could to drive a wedge between the USA and England, and to keep the States neutral during the First World War. It even acted as an intermediary between Germany and the IRB who were negotiating for guns.

The Irish Americans played such an important part in Irish politics that it is worth jumping in time for a moment to recount subsequent events. In 1918 **Eamon de Valera**, born in America, was elected by Sinn Fein head of a provisional government. He came to America with high hopes during the War of Independence in Ireland. He wanted two things: political recognition from the government for the Dail Eireann—the Irish parliament set up in Dublin in 1919—and money. He failed in his first aim: he was rebuffed by President Wilson, himself of Ulster Scots blood, and very proud of it too. But the President belonged to the strain of Presbyterian emigrants who had flung themselves wholeheartedly into the making of America, and helped draw up the Constitution. They had forgotten the hardships they suffered in Ireland and did not continue to bear grudges. However, de Valera got plenty of money, 6m dollars in the form of a loan, but he fell out with Devoy. He founded a rival organization called the **American Association for the Recognition of the Irish Republic** (AARIA). When Ireland split over the solution of partition and there was a civil war, the Republicans, who rejected the partition, were supported by the AARIA, whilst the Free Staters had Devoy and Clan-na-Gael behind them. The leading spirit of the AARIA was **Joseph McGarrity**, who later broke with De Valera when he began to act against the IRA. His group and their successors have continued to give financial support to the IRA during the present troubles in Northern Ireland.

Now to return to the efforts of the British government to forestall the repeal of the Union and the efforts of various organizations to bring it about.

Tenants' Rights and the Land War

The Union Government was blamed by many in Ireland for the tragic extent of the famine, but the government was blind to the lessons it should have taught them. The famine had only intensified the land war and the 1829 Act simply enabled the impoverished landlords to sell their estates, which the peasants had no money to buy. So the speculators moved in, seized opportunities for further evictions and increased the rents. They cleared the land for cattle rearing and were more brutal towards the peasants than the old landlords. Tenant resistance smouldered, stimulated by the horrors of the famine.

Michael Davitt organized the resistance into the **National Land League**, with the support of Parnell, the leader of the Irish Party in the House of Commons. In the ensuing **Land War** (1879–82), a new word was added to the English language—'boycott'. The peasants decided not to help an evicting landlord with his crops and he had to import some loyal Orangemen from Ulster to gather in the harvest. The offending landlord was a Captain Boycott. The tenants wanted the same rights that tenants had in Ulster and fair rent, fixity of tenure and freedom to sell at the market value. They also wanted a more even distribution of the land. At that time 3 per cent of the population owned 95 per cent of the land.

But one of the greatest barriers to reconciliation was the mental block the English had about Ireland. Behind all the agitation at this time, and all the obstruction the Irish Party caused in parliament, was a desire for the repeal of the Union. But the politicians saw the problem as religion, over-population, famine, anything but nationalism. It did not enter English heads that the Irish might not want to be part of Britain. The Union, in their eyes, was surrounded by a sort of aura: with it, Irishmen were on an equal footing with the rest of Great Britain, they were part of the Empire. The Union was also a security against foreign attack and must stay. Only one man said anything sensible on the subject and he was not listened to. **J. S. Mill** said that England was the worst qualified to govern the Irish, because English traditions were not applicable in Ireland. England was firmly *laissez-faire* in her economic policies, but Ireland needed economic interference from the government. This the English politicians had resolutely refused to do during and after the famine. Gladstone and other Liberals were aware of the discontent. They tried to take the sting out of Irish Nationalism by dealing with the individual problems one by one, believing that then the nationalist grievance would disappear.

Killing Home Rule with Kindness

One of the first things to be dealt with was religion, for it could not be kept out of politics. The Protestant Ascendancy, by virtue of education, contacts, etcetera, still monopolized powerful positions, despite Catholic emancipation. This frustrated the middle classes and created an Irish Catholic national distinctiveness. There may have been no legal barriers any more, but there were unofficial ones.

The Anglican Church of Ireland still remained the Established Church until 1869, and until then the Irish peasant had to pay tithes to it. The Catholic hierarchy wanted a state-supported Catholic education, but the government tried to have interdenominational schools and universities. This never satisfied the Catholic Church and consequently, much later on, it supported the illegal nationalist organizations. Unfortunately the government were unwilling to establish the Catholic Church in Ireland as they would have had problems with the Protestants in Ulster, so although the Catholic Church had consolidated its position, it was not conciliated.

The distress of the peasant farmers had, by this time, become identified with nationalism, so the government set out to solve the economic problems, thinking that this would shatter the nationalists. But they acted too late. Only in 1881 were the demands of the tenants met. Large amounts of money were made available to tenants to buy up their holdings, and by 1916 64 per cent of the population owned land. (Many of these new owners had the same surnames as those dispossessed back in the 17th century.) But Britain was remembered not for these Land Acts, generous as they were, but for the Coercion and Crime Acts which Balfour brought in to try and control the unrest and anarchy which existed in some parts of the country. The **Land Purchase Acts** took away the individual oppressor and left only the government against whom to focus discontent. The peasants had been given more independence and the landlords were virtually destroyed, so the Union became even more precarious. The Nationalists could not be bought off.

Home Rule for Ireland?

Parnell forced the government to listen, often holding a balance of power in the House of Commons, and for a while he managed to rally the whole Nationalist movement behind his aggressive leadership. The bait of universal suffrage was enough for the Fenians to try and overthrow the Union from within the system. The **Secret Ballot Act** in 1872 made this even more attractive than abortive rebellions. But the Home Rule League did not succeed, even though Gladstone and the Liberals, who were at that time in Opposition, had promised to support it. First of all, Parnell was a weakness as well as a strength. His aggressive tactics alienated many Englishmen and his Protestant origins upset some of the Catholic hierarchy, who thought he should have concentrated a little more on pushing the Catholic university they wanted. Also, his affair with Kitty O'Shea and involvement in a divorce case shocked many Victorians and non-conformists in the Liberal Party. They demanded that he should be dropped from the leadership of the Irish Party, and when the Catholic hierarchy heard this, they also began to scold 'the named adulterer' and turned their congregations against him. Another reason for the failure of the Home Rule Bill was that the predominantly Protestant and industrial North of Ireland had no wish to join the South. The North thought that it would be overtaxed to subsidize the relatively backward agrarian South, and the Protestants were frightened of being swamped by the Catholics. Their fear gave them a siege mentality; Parnell's divorce case was like a gift from heaven and gave them a reprieve. English opinion was still against Home Rule and it was only because the Irish Party had made a deal with the Liberals that there was any hope of their succeeding. With the fall of Parnell, the Irish Party split and lost most of its importance.

Parnell's fall in 1891 and the failure of the 1893 Home Rule Bill initiated a resurgence of revolutionary nationalism. The younger generation were shocked by the way in which the Catholic Church within Ireland condemned Parnell over the O'Shea case. And, as the moral authority of the Church was cast aside, so was one of the barriers to violence. Parnell's failure to work things through Parliament seemed to indicate that only violence would work. Young people began to join the Irish Republican Brotherhood (IRB), founded by James Stevens, and even the Church began to show more sympathy because at least nationalism was preferable to the aesthetic socialism that was creeping into Dublin. Many of the priests had brothers and sisters in illegal organizations and it was inevitable that they would become emotionally involved.

Gaelic Cultural Renaissance

There was a new mood in Ireland at the end of the 19th century. The people were proud of being Irish and of their cultural achievements. Unfortunately only 14 per cent of the population spoke the Gaelic language (the famine and emigration that followed had seriously weakened its hold); English was taught in schools, knowledge of it led to better jobs and opportunities, and Irish music and poetry were neglected except by a few intellectuals. However, it was in the stories of Ireland's past greatness, her legends and customs, that many diverse groups found a common ground. In 1884 the **Gaelic Athletic Association** started to revive the national game—hurling. Everybody knows how important cricket is to the English village green. Now Irishmen were actively and publicly participating in something very Irish. In 1893 the **Gaelic League** was formed. Its president was **Douglas Hyde**, who campaigned successfully for the return of Gaelic lessons to schools and as a qualification for entry to the new universities. He never wanted the League to be a sectarian or political force, but it did provide a link between the conservative Catholic Church and the Fenians and Irish Nationalists. 'The Holy Island of St Patrick' developed an ideal: that of the Catholic, devout, temperate, clean-living Irishman. (England was seen as the source of corruption, whilst Patrick Pearse and de Valera made revolution seem respectable.) The Gaelic League and the Gaelic Athletic Association were used by the IRB as sounding boards or recruiting grounds for membership.

The Liberals returned to power in 1906 and things began to look brighter for Home Rule. In 1910 John Redmond led the Irish Party and held the balance of power between the Liberals and the Conservatives. In 1914 Asquith's **Home Rule Bill** was passed, although it was suspended for the duration of the First World War. But six years later Ireland was in the middle of a war of independence and the initiative had passed from the British into the hands of the revolutionary nationalists. Why did this happen? The British Government had left Home Rule too late; the time lag between when it was passed and when it actually might be implemented gave the Irish public time to criticize it and see its limitations. The nationalists began to despair of ever finding a parliamentary solution, for the British could now not force the North into Home Rule and were shutting their eyes to the gun-running which had been going on since the formation of the Ulster Volunteers. The Irish people were rather lukewarm about organizations like the IRB and its associated new Sinn Fein Party, founded by Arthur Griffith, but an event on Easter Monday in 1916 changed all that.

Easter Rebellion 1916

Plans for a national rising with German support were made. The support did not arrive and in a confused situation a rising commenced in Dublin. It happened very quickly. Suddenly the tricolour of a new Irish Republic was flying from the General Post Office in Dublin. Two thousand Irish nationalist volunteers, led by **Patrick Pearse** of the IRB, stood against the reinforcements sent from England and then surrendered about a week later. People were horrified at first by the waste of life, for many civilians got caught up in the gun battles; but then the British played into the hands of Patrick Pearse. All 14 leaders were executed after secret trials. The timing of the uprising was no coincidence. Pearse and the others wanted it to be a blood sacrifice and the resurgence of the nationalist spirit which followed after such a sacrifice was comparable to the resurrection of Christ.

The executions happened before there could be any backbiting as to why the whole thing had been a muddle. Suddenly they were dead, and pity for them grew into open sympathy for what they had been trying to obtain. The Catholic Church was trapped in the emotional wave which advocated revolution. The party which gained from this swing was the Sinn Fein; it was pledged to non-violent nationalism and was the public front of the IRB. John Redmond, the leader of the Irish Party at Westminster, had urged everybody to forget their differences with England and fight the common enemy which was Germany, but the Irish Nationalists, who were negotiating with the Germans, saw things in a very different light. Many Irishmen did go and fight for Britain, but the feeling was that Redmond was prepared to compromise over Home Rule and shelve it until it suited the British.

When in 1918 conscription was extended to Ireland even more people decided that **Sinn Fein** was the only party which could speak for them. It won all the Irish seats bar six. Redmond's party was finished. The only problem was that 44 of the Sinn Fein members were in English jails; those that were not met in Mansion House and set up their own Dail Eireann. American-born Eamon de Valera made an audacious escape from Lincoln prison and was elected the first President of the Irish Republic in 1919. The Irish Volunteers became the **Irish Republican Army** and war was declared on Britain.

The North

Meanwhile in the North they had found a leader to defend the Union in the Dublin-born **Edward Carson**. He was a leading barrister in London (he cross-examined Oscar Wilde in that notorious law suit), and was openly supported by the Conservatives in England. A solemn **Covenant of Resistance to Home Rule** was signed by hundreds of thousands of Northern Unionists. They would fight with any means possible not to come under an Irish parliament in Dublin. After the Easter rising of 1916, Carson was assured by Lloyd George that the six northeastern counties could be permanently excluded from the Home Rule Bill of 1914. When the **War of Independence** broke out in the South, the British offered them partition with their own parliament whilst remaining within Britain. Today they still feel their ties are with a liberal Britain, not the Catholic South. (Remember that in the Republic there is no divorce and limited contraception, mixed marriages are discouraged, and the Welfare State is very limited. Protestants find it disturbing that the Roman Catholic Church's influence is so strong in every facet of social and political life, although the old-fashioned strict Catholicism prevalent until the 1970s is definitely on the wane).

The War of Independence

The British Government had been caught out by the Declaration of Independence by the Dail. The British were engaged in trying to negotiate a peace treaty at Versailles and the Americans had made it very clear that they sympathized with the Irish. Ammunition raids, bombing, burning and shooting began in Ireland, mainly against the Irish Constabulary. The British government waited until the Versailles Conference had come to an end and then started to fight back. The **Black and Tans** were sent over to reinforce the police, and Lloyd George tried to play it down as a police situation. The Black and Tans got their name from the mixture of police and army uniform they wore. Their methods were as brutal as those of the IRA and it became a war of retaliation.

Michael Collins was in charge of military affairs for the IRA and he set up an intelligence system which kept him well informed about British plans; he waged a vicious, well-thought-out campaign against the Black and Tans. By July 1921 a truce was declared because the British public wanted to try to reach a compromise. In October an Irish delegation, which included Griffith and Collins, went to London to negotiate with Lloyd George. They signed a treaty which approved the setting up of an Irish Free State with Dominion status, similar to Canada. The British were mainly concerned with the security aspect and they made two stipulations; that all Irish legislators should take an oath of allegiance to the Crown and that the British Navy could use certain Irish ports.

Civil War

The Republicans (or anti-treaty side) in the Dail were furious. They regarded it as a sell-out. They did not like the oath, or the acceptance of a divided Ireland. Michael Collins saw it as a chance for 'freedom to achieve freedom' and when it came to the debate on it in the Dail, the majority voted in favour of the treaty. De Valera was against the treaty and, as head of the Dail, he resigned; **Arthur Griffith** succeeded him. In June, when the country accepted the treaty, civil war began. The split in the Dail had produced a corresponding split in the IRA; part of it broke away and began violent raids into the North. The remainder of the IRA was reorganized by Michael Collins into the Free State Army. When he was assassinated, a man just as talented took over, **Kevin O'Higgins**. This period is remembered as the **War of Brothers**, and it was bitter and destructive. Men who had fought together against the Black and Tans now shot each other down.

Finally, the Republicans were ready to sue for peace. De Valera, who had not actively taken part in the fighting but had supported the Republicans, now ordered a ceasefire. The bitterness and horror of the civil war has coloured attitudes to this very day. The differences between the two main parties, **Fine Gael** (pro-treaty) and **Fianna Fail** (anti-treaty), are historical rather than political, although perhaps in foreign policy Fianna Fail has taken a more anti-British line. Fine Gael held power for the first 10 years and successfully concentrated on building the 26-county state into something credible and strong. In 1926 de Valera broke with Sinn Fein because they saw the Dail and the government in power as usurpers, as bad as the British, and refused to take up their seats. De Valera founded his own party, the Fianna Fail. De Valera was a master pragmatist and succeeded in disappointing none of his supporters; the new state wanted a change and in 1932 he formed a government. He soon made it clear that Ireland was not going to keep the oath of allegiance or continue to pay the land annuities (the repayment of money lent to help tenants pay for their farms).

De Valera

In 1937 de Valera drew up a new **Constitution** for Ireland. It declared Ireland a Republic and seemed a direct challenge to the Northern Ireland Government. Article 5 went like this: 'It is the right of the Parliament Government established by the Constitution to exercise jurisdiction over the whole of Ireland, its Islands and territorial seas'. Article 44.1.2. recognized: 'The special position of the Holy Catholic, Apostolic Roman Church as the guardian of the Faith professed by the great majority of its citizens'.

Both parties had trouble with extremists in the 1930s; Fine Gael had to expel General O'Duffy of the Fascist Blue Shirt movement, and Fianna Fail were embarrassed by their erstwhile allies in the IRA. De Valera dealt with the situation by setting up a military tribunal and declaring the IRA an illegal organization. The IRA did not die but went underground and continued to enjoy a curious relationship with the government and the public. When it got too noisy it was stamped on; but the IRA continues to be regarded nervously and with respect, for its ideals and its members' intransigence seem to be in line with Ireland's dead patriots.

Northern Ireland

The North Today

It is very difficult to be impartial about the 'Troubles' in Northern Ireland—they have been tragic and frightening. With the ceasefire holding at the time of writing, there is hope for the future, albeit very cautious. The basic reason for the 'Troubles' is that the Catholic minority in the North did badly with all the reshuffling that went on in the 1920s, and once the State was set up they were treated as second-class citizens.

The series of events that lead up to the present situation is discussed in more detail below. Before you read on, you may find it useful to look at the glossary of Northern Irish political parties and terms at the end of this chapter.

Discontent Amongst Ulster Catholics, 1921–69

The Ulster Protestants make up two-thirds of the population of Northern Ireland, and the Catholics the rest. Under the leadership of Edward Carson and James Craig, the Ulster Protestants had managed to wrestle their bit of Ulster from the rest of Ireland, and preserve the Union with Britain. They utterly repudiated the idea of a Catholic Gaelic Republic of Ireland, and held themselves aloof from events in the Free State, later the Republic. The Unionists regarded the Catholics as the natural enemies of the state, and their treatment of them stored up plenty of trouble for the future. No attempt was made to woo the Catholic Nationalists, perhaps because the Protestant leaders directed all their energies into preserving the Union. Unionists have a beleaguered mentality because they are constantly in a great state of anxiety about being turfed out of the Union with Britain and into the Republic of Ireland. They were anxious in the 1920s, and they are so now. Remember also that, for hundreds of years, a distrust and rivalry had grown up between the two religious groups over land. The feeling was tribal, and compounded by bloodshed over land fights. The **Government of Ireland Act** in 1920 gave Westminster supreme authority over Northern Ireland. The **Ireland Act** of 1949 enshrined the constitutional guarantee which gave the Stormont Parliament the right to decide whether Northern Ireland would remain in the UK or not.

All Catholics were and still are regarded as supporters of the **IRA**, an organization which was indeed a real menace to this shaky state. It was seen as imperative that Catholics should never be allowed into positions of power and influence. Sir Basil Brooke (1888–1973) was typical of the type of blinkered cabinet minister who ran the government for years. He, along with James Craig (1871–1940), first Prime Minister of Northern Ireland, encouraged Protestants to employ only Protestants, for he, like others, believed that the Catholics were 'out to destroy Ulster with all their power and might'. He became Prime Minister in 1943 and played an active role in linking the Orange Order, of which he was a leading member, with the government of the time. In describing the situation one wants to use the word 'apartheid', although the set-up was not as extreme as that which existed in South Africa. Protestant businesses tended to employ Protestants and Catholics employed Catholics. There were few mixed housing areas or marriages. The Catholic priests fiercely defended their right to run Catholic schools—as they still do.

Government went on at a mainly local level through county and town councils. The Loyalists ensured that they always had a majority on the council through the use of gerrymandering. The local voting qualification also favoured Protestants, who were often wealthier, for the franchise was only granted to house-owners or tenants, and the number of votes allocated to each person could be as high as six, depending of the value of their property. Because the Protestant rulers controlled housing schemes and jobs, the working-class Protestants were given the lion's share of any housing or jobs that existed. Northern Ireland had a much lower standard of living than the rest of the UK, and any advantages were eagerly grasped by these workers, who displayed little feeling of worker solidarity with their fellow Catholics. They never could escape from their religious prejudices and preoccupations to unite against the capitalists, although the ruling class had feared their alliance during the 1922 riots over unemployment.

The Catholics themselves were ambiguous about the State; most of them in the 1920s were Republicans, and they never gave up hope that the Dublin Government might do something about it. Many believed that the Six Counties could not survive, and in the beginning Nationalist Republican representatives refused to sit at Stormont. On the other hand, others had watched with horror the bloodshed and bitterness which resulted from the Civil War in the Irish Free State. After being educated, the bright ones emigrated rather than fight the system. The IRA attempted over the next 50 years to mount a campaign in the North, but they never got anywhere. They managed a few murders, but a big campaign in 1956–62 which killed 19 people failed miserably. The local Catholics did not back them, and the **B Specials** (the Protestant-dominated special police force) did their job well. The trouble was, 'the Specials' irritated and harassed law-abiding Catholics, which left them with a feeling of injustice.

For the time being the Protestant Unionists were able to dominate Catholic Nationalists in elections in a proportion of about four-to-one. This gave them a feeling of security, which was also bolstered by the gratitude of the British government for their loyalty and help during the Second World War, when the North of Ireland had been a vital bulwark for the rest of the UK.

The Civil Rights Movement—British Troops Move in

Yet things had to change, for as young and educated Catholics and Protestants grew up they began to agitate about the obvious injustices, and the **Civil Rights Association** was formed in 1967. Unfortunately, the marches which drew attention to their aims also attracted men of violence on both sides, and as the marches turned into riots, the Protestant Loyalists, including the **Royal Ulster Constabulary** (RUC) and B Specials, seemed to be in league with the Protestant mobs against the Catholics. At this point the discredited IRA failed to seize their opportunity to woo the Catholics, who were confused and frightened. The Catholics welcomed the British troops, who were brought in to keep the peace after the Loyalists and police beat up Civil Rights marchers at Burntollet, and later the inhabitants of the Bogside in Londonderry, in January 1969.

At that time **Terence O'Neill** had taken over from Lord Brookborough as Prime Minister at Stormont. Although of the same Unionist Ascendancy stock, he realized that something must be done to placate the Nationalists. The few liberal gestures that he made towards the Catholics and the Republic opened up a Pandora's box of fury and opposition amongst the Protestant Unionists, who found a leader in the **Reverend Ian Paisley**. The reforms O'Neill planned over housing and local government came too late, and he was swept away by the Protestant backlash when he called a General Election in April 1969. The brutality with which the police had broken up the Civil Rights marches had stirred support for the IRA, and the Summer Marching Season was marked by even more violence.

The IRA Exploit Events

The IRA organized itself to exploit the situation. It split into two after an internal struggle, and the murders and bombings which dominated events after this time are mainly the work of the Provisional IRA, commonly called the IRA. The British army lost the confidence of the Catholic community it had come to protect through heavy-handed enforcement of security measures. Besides, the IRA posed as the natural guardians of the Catholics, so there were cheers amongst the Catholic Nationalists when the IRA killed the first British soldier in October 1970. The IRA aimed to break down law and order; any method was legitimate, and any member of the army or police was a legitimate target to their mind.

The Stormont government hastened to pass some much needed reforms between 1969 and 1972. The RUC was overhauled, and the B Specials abolished. A new part-time security force was set up within the British Army and called the **Ulster Defence Regiment** (UDR). In 1971 a new Housing Executive was set up to allocate houses fairly, irrespective of religious beliefs. The IRA managed to conduct a destructive bombing campaign in the cities; innocent civilians were killed or injured and buildings destroyed. British soldiers responded to rioting in the Bogside in January 1972 by killing 13 people. A cycle of violence begetting violence began to spiral, and society divided along even more sectarian lines than before. The legacy of hatred, psychological distress and bitterness that has built from this time is terrible to contemplate.

British Attempts to Solve the Problem

In 1972 the Stormont government and parliament were suspended by the British government, which had always retained full powers of sovereignty over it. Direct Rule from Westminster was imposed, and continues to be until a solution can be found. There is a **Secretary of State for Northern Ireland**, appointed by the British Prime Minister, and a body of English ministers and civil servants. Elected members from the different parties sit in Westminster and try to bring Northern Irish issues to the attention of the House.

Internment was brought in in August 1971, and large numbers of terrorist suspects were imprisoned without trial. This hardened Catholic opinion against British justice, and the practice was gradually phased out after a couple of years. Subsequently, the **Diplock system of Criminal Courts** was introduced, which means alleged terrorists are tried by judges who sit alone without juries. It was justified by the amount of intimidation that the jury could be subjected to. Various power-sharing initiatives between the largely Protestant Unionist parties and the Catholic and Republican SDLP did not get off the ground, so Direct Rule continues.The suspension of the Stormont Parliament removed the Constitutional guarantee of the 1949 Act but it was renewed in the 1973 Constitution Act which established the principle that any change would have to have majority consent.

The Sunningdale Agreement

In December 1973 the leaders of the Northern Irish parties, a new Executive, and Ministers from the United Kingdom and for the first time, the Republic of Ireland met together at Sunningdale, and agreed to set up a **Council of Ireland** which would work for consultation and co-operation between Northern Ireland and the Republic. The Agreement provided for a new type of Executive in Northern Ireland, in which power was shared as far as possible between representatives of the two communities in a joint government. It was the dawn of new hope for the province, but the Uni̶ the Republican terrorists did not want this new co-operation to work. Fac̶ strike called by the Ulster Workers' Council which paralysed the prov̶ ment did not use the army to break the strike, but allowed intimida̶ paramilitary organizations to win the day. The Unionist members ̶ resigned, and Direct Rule had to be resumed. Many people believe that i̶ Agreement had been implemented, much suffering could have been avoided, and the whole of Ireland might be a stabler place today.

The Victims of the 'Troubles'

Since then, the province has suffered sectarian killings, bombings, and the powerful propaganda of the hunger strike campaign by IRA prisoners in the early 1980s. The economy has been in the doldrums and the well-educated members of society, both Protestant and Catholic often leave; however there is now hope that things will improve, that the economy will pick up and foreign investors will look again at Northern Ireland. The Ulster people have suffered the gradual erosion of their society through violence, intimidation, and the subtler psychological effects that violence induces. On the positive side, the spirit and bravery of the Ulster people remains unbroken; manufacturing businesses continue to thrive and compete in international markets, and throughout the province you meet cheerful, humorous and down-to-earth people who are managing to cope. But the statistics in such a small population are grim. Between 1969 and 1994, around 3168 people have lost their lives, around 3300 people have been injured and maimed of which around 2200 have been civilians. The feelings of despair, fear and outrage in both communities led to extreme attitudes in the 1980s. The Reverend Ian Paisley and his colleagues have a huge following, whilst support for Sinn Fein increased considerably at the expense of the Constitutional Nationalists and the SDLP; more recently support for Sinn Fein has dropped.

The Anglo-Irish Agreement

In 1985, after initial efforts by **Garrett Fitzgerald**, the leader of the Fine Gael Party in the Republic, and **Margaret Thatcher**, the British Prime Minister, the New Ireland Forum met in Dublin. It was agreed that Northern Ireland would remain in the United Kingdom as long as the majority so desired, and that the Dublin Government should have an institutionalized consultative status in relation to Northern Irish Affairs.

The effect of the Agreement was largely positive, although gradual. Both governments made progress in the complicated area of extradition and cross-border security, especially after the general revulsion in the Republic against the IRA bomb attack in Enniskillen in 1987. Diplomatic tensions between Britain and the Republic eased. The British Government grasped the nettle of injustice over the conviction of the 'Guildford Four' and the 'Birmingham Six', prisoners convicted of bombings on mainland Britain. The reopening of these cases and the subsequent acquittal of these prisoners dissipated much bad feeling in the Republic of Ireland where there is great scepticism about British justice in relation to the Irish. One of the most important achievements of the Agreement was that

Government formally accepted 'the principle of consent' by the people of ern Ireland. Any change in the Constitution Act of 1973 had to have majority sent. The Unionists were not mollified by this, for it is enshrined in the constitution of _ie Republic that the Irish Republic claim the whole island, and this claim had not been given up. The Agreement made the world realise that the 'Brits out' solution would be no solution, because it would mean forcibly transferring a million-strong Protestant population into a united Ireland that did not really want them, and the probability of bloody civil war.

The strong emotional link between the English and the Northern Irish has changed since the beginning of the century. The Union was no longer regarded as sacrosanct; many English and Scots know little about the North, and resented the lives lost and money spent maintaining the Union. The Unionists understood this very clearly and felt even more threatened. The Nationalists had not rejected the IRA, who continued to work for the destruction of the six-county state through murder and bombing campaigns in Ulster. On mainland Britain and Europe, the IRA followed a campaign of bombing 'soft' British military targets, and assassinating British politicians, lawyers, and industrialists in order to turn British public opinion against the Union with Northern Ireland.

1990–1993

Inter-party talks began in Northern Ireland and before they broke down some progress was made in defining the three complicated relationships between the North and the UK, the North and the Republic, and the Republic and the UK. This meant there was a set of negotiating mechanisms for the peace process to be furthered. British policy continued to try and find the middle ground between opposing parties in the North, and it was hoped that the politics of the extremists would wither away.

The IRA carried out bombing attacks in the financial heart of London in 1992/93 and elsewhere. One such attack in a shopping centre in Warrington killed two children; there was worldwide revulsion, and a peace movement was launched in Dublin. The IRA could continue their campaign of violence indefinitely, but there were signs that key elements in the IRA wanted to try and change things through political action. In April 1993, **John Hume** of the SDLP started a dialogue with **Gerry Adams** of Sinn Fein. Both the British and the Irish Governments reacted furiously to this but popular nationalist support for the dialogue both North and South forced the governments to rethink their policy. Both Prime Ministers Major and Reynolds began a new policy of trying to draw the extremists into the political process and to aim at all party talks for a lasting constitutional settlement which would bring peace. The North had just suffered the horror in October 1993 of the IRA bomb in a Belfast chippie which killed 10 people; and then the terrible revenge by extremist loyalists who shot 14 people in a public house in Greysteel.

The Downing Street Declaration

On the 15th December 1993, both the Irish and British Prime Ministers presented a **joint Declaration** which successfully managed to address the competing claims of the Nationalists and the Unionists. The British Government declared in the document that

Britain 'had no selfish strategic or economic interest in Northern Ireland' and recognised the right of the people of Ireland North and South to self-determination. Both Governments affirmed that the status of Northern Ireland could only be changed with the consent of 'a great number of its people'. In the event of an overall political settlement the Irish Government declared it would drop its claim to the six counties contained in articles 2 and 3 of the Irish Constitution. The Irish Government would establish a forum for peace and reconciliation at some later date. Both governments offered a place at the negotiating table to the extremists on both sides if they renounced violence.

Ceasefire

After a disappointing reaction to the Declaration and prevarication for several months, the IRA eventually announced '**a complete cessation of military operations**' on 31st August 1994. In the following weeks the extremist unionist forces of the UFF, the UVF and the Red Hand of Ulster announced a **ceasefire**, conditional upon the IRA's continuing ceasefire. This outcome has brought great opportunities for eventual peace, and the fact that the day-to-day maiming and killing has ceased is a great relief to the people of Northern Ireland. Of course there are many irreconcilable aims on both sides of political opinion, and the politicians will have to make compromises. Amongst the many problems to solve is the great distrust on the Unionist side many fear a secret deal between Britain and the Republicans so the danger of a Unionist backlash is very real. Although the main Unionist party seems satisfied at the moment with British assurances, the Unionists have seen the British Government (Conservative) move from a unionist to a neutral position. They fear they may yet move, as Sinn Fein would like, to the role of 'persuading' the Unionists to join the Republic. All the people of Northern Ireland fear that the ceasefire may not be permanent—there have been ceasefires before, although this one has lasted the longest so far. Gerry Adams has said that a militant IRA could emerge in a few years' time if the causes of conflict are not resolved.

None of the terrorist groups has given up their arms (at the time of writing—February 1995). The IRA are demanding that the British Army and the RUC should disarm, and that all political prisoners be released. So there are major problems ahead over the question of IRA and UFF arms, and the future community policing in Northern Ireland. The IRA has been policing Catholic West Belfast for many years, to protect their own financial empire, and to control lawless youths. The RUC are not welcome in Nationalist areas, as the Nationalists see the RUC as a Unionist police force although the RUC has been trying hard to change its image. Historically there have always been very few Catholics in the RUC because of hostility to the force and fear of the IRA. One of the crucial issues to be worked out is who should police areas such as West Belfast. Another problem to be solved is the future of political prisoners, and how the rule of law can be reimposed on criminal activities and extortion rackets run by terrorist groups both republican and loyalist. However, the ceasefire is felt to be the irrevocable beginning of a new phase with the British Government slowly, and the Irish Government impatiently, moving towards the next step, a peace summit where the peace process can be decided.

The Irish Republic has a titular Head of State, a **President** who is elected for seven years by the vote of the people. The President is empowered on the recommendation of the Dail to appoint the Prime Minister (Taoiseach), sign laws and invoke the judgement of the Supreme Court on the legality of Bills. He is also supreme commander of the armed forces. The Irish parliament consists of the President and two Houses: the Dail and the Senate. The Dail is made up of 166 members (TDs) elected by adult suffrage through proportional representation. The Senate is made up of 60 members: 11 are nominated by the Taoiseach; 49 are elected by the Dail and county councils from panels representative of the universities, labour, industry, education and social services. The average length of an Irish Government is three years.

In the 1970s and 1980s each Irish government has had to face unemployment, growing emigration and a huge national debt—in 1989 it was IR£24,827 million. The Republic is a major supporter of the **EU** and the **Maastricht Agreement** and has done extremely well economically from EU funding. Six billion pounds was allocated in regional structural funds. For many years Ireland was at the lower end of the EU GDP average which meant it often qualified for extra regional assistance, but recently its GDP has risen to above 80 per cent of the average so it might no longer be eligible. However, the addition of the new Scandinavian countries is likely to raise the average GDP.

The principle of neutrality so long adhered to in foreign affairs is no longer certain. Ireland has recently attended as an observer the **Western European Union** (WEU) defence body. Economically Ireland has become very attractive to high technology and computer investment, partly because of its young well educated population. Economic growth rates have been good, and emigration has slowed down.

The traditional lines of Irish parties are also changing from the pro- and anti-treaty (of 1921) stances. Mary Robinson as the Head of State has brought a new flexibility and dynamism into politics here. Her enthusiasm and energy in helping all parts of Ireland, including the North, has won her great popularity and a world profile.

Irish Political Parties

The origins of the two major parties, the Fianna Fail and Fine Gael, hark back to the violent differences between those anti the Free State Treaty, and those pro it. **Fianna Fail** has managed to establish itself as the dominant ruling party, although this dominance is definitely under threat as the general public is disillusioned with the incompetence and corruption revealed by a number of celebrated cases. At the time of writing the Taoiseach and Fianna Fail leader, Albert Reynolds had been forced to step down after a series of polit-ical blunders. He was replaced as party leader by Bertie Ahern.

Fine Gael is a more Socialist-inspired party with strong European inclinations. The **Labour Party** has found it difficult to gain popular support in the country as people have, up to now anyway, been very conservative and voted as their family do—either Fine Gael or Fianna Fail. This is changing now as Labour have increased their powerbase in the last

10 years in Dublin and Cork and formed a coalition governments either with Fianna Fail or Fine Gael. Sinn Fein is the political arm of the Official IRA (which is a banned organization) but does not command much support in the Republic. The new government is a coalition of Fine Gael, led by the new Taoiseach, John Bruton, and the Labour Party.

A Glossary of Political Parties and Terms

The following labels and identities crop up in discussions on Northern Ireland again and again.

Unionist: refers to one who supports the Union with Great Britain, and has no wish to share an Irish nationality with the Republic of Ireland. There are two main Unionist parties in Northern Ireland. The Official Unionists were the original party and are, on the surface, more willing to discuss options to try and solve the crisis in the State. The Democratic Unionist Party (DUP), led by Ian Paisley, is more radical and Protestant. It is very anti any sort of co-operation with the Irish Republic, and anti the Pope.

Alliance: a label used for a party composed of moderate Unionists, both Protestant and Catholic, but it loses out to the more extreme parties.

Loyalist: a general term to describe anyone in favour of the Union with Great Britain.

Republican: a label which refers to anyone who supports a united Ireland. In Northern Ireland, the Socialist Democratic and Labour Party (SDLP), formed in 1970, is committed to achieving a United Ireland through peaceful and democratic means. It is linked, although only in its aims, to the Provisional Sinn Fein, the political wing of the IRA, which is less choosy about its methods.

Nationalist: is interchangeable with the label 'Republican'.

IRA: is the label used to describe the Irish Republican Army, which did not disband after the Civil War in Ireland ended (1920–21). The IRA is outlawed in the Republic of Ireland and the United Kingdom. The objective of its members is to fight by the gun and bomb until the whole of Ireland is free of the British, and the six counties reunited with the rest of Ireland. In 1969, with the start of civil disturbances, the IRA was reinvigorated. Firstly it reorganized itself and split into two. The Marxist Socialist-inspired members call themselves the Official IRA (OIRA) and the traditionalists call themselves the Provisional IRA (PIRA) after the 'Provisional' government of Ireland set up in the GPO after the Easter Rising of 1916. The ideals of the 'Provos' are straightforward: a United Republic of Ireland, whatever the cost in terms of violence. The Provisionals are generally referred to as the IRA, since the Officials have dropped out of the action.

UVF and **UDA:** both the Ulster Volunteer Force and the Ulster Defence Association are illegal Protestant terrorist organizations that recruit from the working class. They are usually involved in revenge killings after IRA attacks.

RUC: Royal Ulster Constabulary. Reorganized in the 1970s, this police force manages much of the security of Northern Ireland in co-operation with the British army. The Catholic Nationalists in Northern Ireland regard it with suspicion, believing it to be biased by its largely Protestant Unionist membership. Any Catholics who join it are singled out for death by the IRA.

The B Specials: were a special, part-time reserve force within the RUC with special powers to search out IRA members. Catholics maintain that they beat up alleged members. They operated from the 1920s until it was disbanded in the early 1970s.

The Orange Order: a sectarian and largely working-class organization that originated as a secret Protestant working-class agrarian society known as the Peep-O'Day Boys. William of Orange (William III of England) became their hero, and the society changed its name to the Orange Order in 1795. Its members have a traditional fear of the Catholic majority in Ireland and are Unionist in politics. Orange Lodges are still active in Northern Ireland.

The Summer Marching Season: is a reference to the Orange and Hibernian marches during July and August. Each side commemorates opposing events in the history of Ireland. In the past, drums and equipment were lent between the two sides, but the present conflict has distilled into bitterness and hatred, and this has ceased. The Orange marchers, in particular, frequently take provocative routes through Catholic areas.

Gerrymandering: refers to the policy of concentrating large numbers of Catholics with Republican views in unusually big electoral districts, whilst Protestant Unionists were in smaller districts. This meant that the Protestant Unionists were always certain to win a larger number of representatives, district by district. Londonderry was a prime example: 87 per cent of the large Catholic population were placed in one ward which returned eight seats, whilst 87 per cent of the much smaller Protestant population were placed in two wards and they returned 12 seats. Gerrymandering gradually became the norm from the late 1920s until the electoral reforms at the beginning of the 1970s.

Civil Rights Movement: began in the 1960s, and was inspired by the American Civil Rights campaigner, Martin Luther King. The Civil Rights Association, founded in 1967, called for jobs, houses and one man one vote. It was supported by both Catholics and Protestants, and the leadership of the Association has been described as 'middle-aged, middle-class and middle-of-the-road'. The Civil Rights Movement was hijacked by a more Republican and Socialist element and the mob violence that attended the Civil Rights marches, and eventually lost out to the IRA.

Direct Rule: the British Government had always retained full powers of sovereignty on all matters over the Northern Ireland government at Stormont. Thus, when the riots and bloodshed began to get out of control, and the Stormont government seemed unable to implement reforms or control the police, Direct Rule was imposed in 1972. The Stormont Government and Parliament is still suspended, and Northern Ireland MPs sit in the British House of Commons.

Religion

The reminders and symbols of a religious faith and deep love of God are everywhere to be seen in Ireland. The images which fill my mind are of a child in white, showing off her dress after her first Holy Communion, rags caught in brambles around a holy well; cars parked up a country lane, everybody piling out for Mass, umbrellas held high and skirts fluttering. The people of Ireland invoke and refer to the Virgin Mary and to Jesus often in their everyday talk. Roadside shrines to the Virgin are decorated with shells and fresh flowers, and many people still stop what they are doing to say the Angelus at noon and at sunset. Grey Neo-Gothic churches dominate the small country town, whilst in the smaller villages the chapel or church is a simpler building, planted around with dark yews and beeches above which the ceaseless cawing of the rooks can be heard.

In Ireland everybody knows what you are—whether Catholic, Presbyterian, Church of Ireland, Baptist or Methodist; anything else is classed as 'heathen', and they feel sorry for you if you are nothing! The history of Ireland has had much to do with this feeling of religious identity, and, unfortunately, in the North this mix of politics and religion has produced individuals whose extreme Catholic or Presbyterian attitudes are reminiscent of 17th-century Europe. The bigotry that characterizes such attitudes has been a major factor in the political situation in the North today. Efforts are made by some of the clergy to organize ecumenical meetings but mostly their congregations ignore them.

Pre-Christian Ireland

The Irish have been religious for five thousand years, and there are plenty of chambered cairns (mounds of stones over prehistoric graves) to prove it. The Celts who arrived in about 500 BC seemed to have been a very religious people, and they had a religious hierarchy organized by Druids. These people worshipped a large number of gods, and central to their beliefs and rituals was the cult of the human head. They believed that the head was the centre of man's powers and thoughts. Their stone masons carved two-headed gods and the style in which they worked has a continuity which can be traced right up to the 19th century. There are heads in the Lough Erne district which are difficult to date. They could be pagan, Early-Christian or comparatively modern.

The origins of the earlier Tuatha Dé Danaan are lost in legend: they may have been pre-Celtic gods or a race of invaders, themselves vanquished by the Celts. They are believed to have had magical powers and heroic qualities. Today they are remembered as the 'wee folk' who live in the raths and stone forts. Here they make fairy music which is so beautiful that it bewitches any human who hears it. The wee folk play all kinds of tricks on country people, from souring their milk to stealing their children, and so a multitude of charms have been devised to guard against these fairy pranks. I can remember being told about the fairies who used to dance in magic rings in the fields; the trouble was that if you tried to go up to them they would turn into yellow ragwort dancing in the wind.

Early-Christian Ireland

Christianity is believed to have come to Ireland from Rome in the 4th century, although St Patrick is credited with the major conversion of the Irish in the 5th century. The Irish seem to have taken to Christianity like ducks to water, although much of our knowledge of early Christianity comes through the medieval accounts of scholarly (but possibly biased) clerics. One explanation for the ease with which Christianity took over is that the Christians did not try to change things too fast, and incorporated some elements of the Druidic religion into their practices.

An example of the assimilation of the Druidic religion by the Christians is the continuing religious significance of the holy wells. Ash and rowan trees, both sacred to the Druids, are frequently found near the wells, and Christian pilgrims still leave offerings of rags on the trees as a sign to the Devil that he has no more power over them. Patterns (pilgrimages) and games used to be held at the wells, although they often shocked the priest, who would put the well out of bounds and declare that its healing powers had been destroyed. There are many other everyday signs of the way that the spiritual life of the Irish people harks back to pagan times. In cottages and farmhouses you might see a strange swastika sign made out of rushes. This is a St Brigid's cross, hung above the door or window to keep the evil spirits away. Fairy or sacred trees are still left standing in the field even though it is uneconomic to plough round them—bad luck invariably follows the person who cuts one down.

Monasteries in Early-Christian Ireland

By the end of the 6th century the Church was firmly monastic, with great monasteries such as Clonmacnoise in County Offaly, and Clonfert in County Galway. These centres were responsible for big strides in agricultural development and were important for trade; they also became places where learning and artistry of all sorts was admired and emulated. The Ireland of 'Saints and Scholars' reached its peak in the 7th century.

The monks sought an ascetic and holy way of life, although this was pursued in a fierce and warlike manner. The ultimate self-sacrifice was self-imposed exile, and so they founded monasteries in France, Italy and Germany. The abbots, by the 8th century, had become all-powerful in Irish politics. Missionaries continued to leave Ireland and contribute to the revival of Christianity in Europe, and there was a blossoming of the arts with wonderful metalwork and painted manuscripts. By the 9th century, the monasteries were commissioning intricately carved stone high crosses, such as you can see at Ahenny in County Tipperary.

Religious Discrimination

Religious discrimination is long-established in Ireland. Over the centuries Catholics and Protestants have suffered by not conforming to the established church, although Catholics have undoubtedly received the greatest share of discrimination and persecution. The

Huguenots arrived when Louis XIV revoked the Edict of Nantes in 1686. They were Calvinists and intermarried easily with the other Protestant groups. (The Huguenots were very skilled and established the important linen industry, as well as weaving and lace-making.) The Presbyterians were the biggest group of dissenters, most of whom were Scots who settled in Ulster during the 17th century. They had been persecuted in Scotland because of their religious beliefs and now they found that Ireland was no better: they were as poor as the native Irish, and many found life so hard that they emigrated to America. Quakers, Palatines (German Protestants), Moravians, Baptists and Methodists also settled in Ireland but their numbers have declined through emigration and inter-marriage.

Religion in Ireland Today

In the Republic of Ireland the Catholics make up 93% of the population, the Church of Ireland 2.8%, the Presbyterians 0.4%, the Jews 0.06%, the Methodists 0.2%, and the rest are small groups of other religious denominations or non-believers. In the Six Counties of Northern Ireland, the Catholics make up 34.9%, the Church of Ireland 24.2%, the Presbyterians 29%, the Methodists 5%, and others 6.9%. In the Republic the Catholic majority is obviously the controlling force in political and social life and the Protestant minority has bowed out gracefully. The Protestants used to represent almost 10% of the population but this figure has declined through mixed marriages.

In theory the modern state does not tolerate religious discrimination, and it is true that both Jews and Protestants have reached positions of importance and wealth in industry and banking. However, the Protestant classes had it so good during the hundreds of years of British Rule that it is not surprising that for a short time there was a legacy of antipathy towards anyone connected with the mainly Protestant Ascendency. Happily, the antipathy has nearly disappeared now, but instead there is an enormous amount of Catholic compla-cency, and the power of the Church is very powerful in the land. The bishops' exhortations on divorce, contraception, AIDS, etcetera are listened to with great earnest-ness by the politicians. The sanctity of the family is held to be of the greatest importance. Recently there was a national referendum on the introduction of divorce, which had the priests thundering in the pulpits; and in the end the bulk of the people voted against it! Another referendum on this may well be held in the near future. Contraception is now readily available but women still go to England for abortions. Of course, in Northern Ireland, the laws of the land are quite secular, being laid down by the British government, but divorce is still quite unusual there, too, and the principal UK legislation on abortion, the 1967 Abortion Act, has not been extended to the province.

The parish priest is always a person of great importance in Irish society and he is usually very approachable. You might easily meet him in the village bar having a drink and a chat. Nearly every family has a close relative who is a priest or a nun, and Irish priests and nuns leave their native land in great numbers to serve overseas, taking their particular brand of conservative Catholicism with them.

Schooling is mostly in the hands of the Church (incidentally, Ireland has a very high stan-dard of literacy and general education), and thankfully the days of the cane and the even crueller sarcasm of the priest-teachers described by so many Irish writers has disappeared.

The people in the top positions in Ireland today mostly went to Christian Brother Schools (look in the Irish *Who's Who*). So did many county councillors and petty officials who organize Ireland's huge bureaucracy. The old-boy network is very strong for getting favours done, grants approved, and planning permission granted.

Irish people practise their religion faithfully in rural areas. The churches are full on Sundays, and visits to Knock, Croagh Patrick, and Lough Derg are taken many times in a person's lifetime. Holy wells are still visited, and Stations of the Cross go on even in ruined churches and friaries. But in the cities more and more young people and other disillusioned individuals have moved away from the church and some religious orders are forced to advertise for their priests! The numbing censoriousness of Catholicism and Protestantism in Ireland has become part of the island's image, just as the green hills, and constant rain. But it is a theme which has been overplayed, and the reality is that people are really very tolerant of other religious communities within their society; this applies to Northern Ireland too. Great community involvement and care comes directly from the churches, and the social events are enjoyable and fun. The Irish are amongst the most generous when it comes to raising money for world disasters, and this charity work is usually channelled through the Church.

Death and weddings are always occasions for a bit of 'crack', and there is also a party whenever the priest blesses a new house. Irish couples spend more on their engagement rings and their weddings than their English counterparts; it's a really big occasion. The Irish wake has lost many of its pagan rituals—mourning with keening and games involving disguise, mock weddings, jokes and singing. Nowadays, the dead person is laid out in another room and people come in to pay their last respects, and then spend the rest of the evening drinking, eating and reminiscing.

Irish Saints

Every locality in Ireland has its particular saint. The stories that surround him or her belong to myth and legend, not usually to historical fact. One theory is that all these obscure, miraculous figures are in fact Celtic gods and goddesses who survived under the mantle of sainthood. Included below is a short account of lives of some of the most famous saints, about whom few facts are known.

Brendan (*c.* 486–575), Abbot and Navigator

This holy man is remembered for his scholastic foundations, and for the extraordinary journey he made in search of Hy-Brasil, believed to be an island of paradise, which he had seen as a mirage whilst looking out on the Atlantic from the Kerry Mountains. His journey is recounted in the *Navigato Brendan*, a treasure of every European library during the Middle Ages. The oldest copies are in Latin and date from the 11th century. The account describes a sea voyage which took Brendan and 12 other monks to the Orkneys, to Wales, to Iceland, and to a land where tropical fruits and flowers grew. The descriptions of his voyage have convinced some scholars that he sailed down the east coast of America to Florida. Tim Severin, a modern-day explorer, and 12 others recreated this epic voyage between May 1976 and June 1977. In their leather and wood boat, they proved that the Irish monks could have been the first Europeans to land in America. (It is possible to see the boat at the Lough Gur Centre in County Clare.) Christopher Columbus probably read the *Navigato*, and in Galway there is a strong tradition that he came to the west coast in 1492 to search out traditions about St Brendan.

The saint's main foundation was at Clonfert, which became a great scholastic centre. One of his monks built the first beehive-shaped cells on Skellig Michael, the rocky island off County Kerry. Other foundations were at Annaghdown in County Galway, and Inisglora in County Mayo. Brendan is buried in Clonfert Cathedral, and he is honoured in St Brendan's Cathedral in Loughrea, County Galway, where the beautiful mosaic floor in the sanctuary depicts his ship and voyage.

St Brigid (died *c.* 525), Abbess of Kildare

Brigid, also known as Briget, Bride and Brigit, is the most beloved saint in Ireland and is often called Mary of the Gael. Devotion to her spread to Scotland, England and the Continent. The traditions and stories that surround her describe her countless generous and warm-hearted acts to the poor, her ability to counsel the rulers of the day, and her great holiness. Her father was a pagan from Leinster and she was fostered by a Druid. (This custom of fosterage in Ireland existed right up to the 19th century.) She decided not to marry and founded a religious order with seven other girls. They were the first formal community of nuns and wore simple white dresses.

St Brigid has her feast day on 1 February, which is also the date of the pagan festival Imbolg, which marks the beginning of spring. She is the patron of poets, scholars, black-smiths and healers, and is also inevitably linked with the pagan goddess Brigid, the goddess of fire and song. There is a tradition that St Brigid's Abbey in Kildare contained a sanctuary with a perpetual fire, tended only by virgins, whose high priestess was regarded as an incarnation and successor of the goddess. The two women are further linked by the fact that Kildare in Irish means 'church of oak', and St Brigid's church was built from a tree held sacred to the Druids. There is a theory that Brigid and her companions accepted the Christian faith, and then transformed the pagan sanctuary into a Christian shrine.

Kildare was a great monastic centre after Brigid's death, and produced the now lost masterpiece, the *Kildare Gospels.* Tradition says that the designs were so beautiful that an angel helped to create them. The St Brigid's nuns kept alight the perpetual fire until the suppression of the religious houses during the Reformation.

Brigid was buried in Kildare Church, but in 835 her remains were moved to Downpatrick in County Down, because of the raids by the Norsemen. She is supposed to share the grave there with St Patrick and St Colmcille, but there is no proof of this. In 1283 it is recorded that three Irish knights set out to the Holy Land with her head; they died en route in Lamiar in Portugal, and in the church there the precious relic of her head is enshrined in a chapel to St Brigid. The word 'bride' derives from St Brigid. It is supposed to originate from the Knights of Chivalry, whose patroness she was. They customarily called the girls they married their brides, after her, and hence the word came into general usage.

St Columban (died 615), Missionary Abbot

Columban, also known as Columbanus, is famous as the great missionary saint. He was born in Leinster and educated at Bangor in County Down under St Comgall, who was famed for his scholarship and piety. Columban set off for Europe with 12 other religious men to preach the gospel and convert the pagans in Gaul (France) and Germany. He founded a monastery at Annegray, which is between Austria and Burgundy, in AD 575, and his rule of austerity attracted many. Lexeuil, the largest monastery, and then Fontaines, were all established within a few miles of Annegray. When Columban was exiled by the local king, he and his followers founded Bobbio in the Apennines, between Piacenza and Genoa. Bobbio became a great centre of culture and orthodoxy from which monasticism spread. Its great glory was its library, the books from which are scattered all over Europe and are regarded as treasures. There are still many parishes in the region dedicated to St Columban.

St Colmcille (c. 521–97), Missionary Abbot

Along with St Patrick and St Brigid, Colmcille, also known as Columba and Columcille, is probably the most famous of the Irish saints. He spread the gospel to Iona and hence to Scotland. St Colmcille was a prince of Tyrconnell (County Donegal), and a great, great grandson of Niall of the Nine Hostages, who had been High King of Ireland. On his mother's side he was descended from the Leinster Kings. He was educated by St Finian of Movilla, in County Down, and also by Finnian of Clonard, and Mobhi of Glasnevin. He studied music and poetry at the Bardic School of Leinster, and the poems he wrote which have survived are delightful. A few are preserved in the Bodleian Library, Oxford. He chose to be a monk, and never to receive episcopal rank. He wrote of his devotion: 'The fire of God's love stays in my heart as a jewel set in gold in a silver vessel.'

In AD 545 he built his first church in Derry, the place he loved most. Then he founded Durrow and later Kells, which became very important in the 9th century when the Columban monks of Iona fled from the Vikings and made it their headquarters. In all, Colmcille founded 37 monastic churches in Ireland, and he produced the *Cathach*, a manuscript of the Psalms. At the age of 42 he set out with 12 companions to be an exile for Christ. They sailed to the island of Iona, off the west coast of Scotland, which was part of the Kingdom of Dalriada ruled over by the Irish King Aidan. He converted Brude, King of the Picts, founded two churches in Inverness, and helped to keep the peace between the Picts and the Irish colony. The tradition that he left Ireland because of a dispute over the copy he made of a psalter of St Finian is very dubious. The legend goes that the dispute caused a great battle, although the high king of the time, King Diarmuid, had tried to settle the dispute and had ruled against Colmcille, saying: 'to every cow its calf, to every book its copy'. The saint is supposed to have punished himself for the deaths he had caused by going into exile.

Colmcille was famous for his austerity, fasting and vigils. His bed was of stone and so was his pillow. From the various accounts of his life, Colmcille emerges as a charismatic personality who was a scholar, poet, and ruler. He died at Iona, and his relics were taken to Dunkeld (Scotland) in AD 849.

St Enda of Aran (died c. 535), Abbot

Famous as the patriarch of monasticism. He is described as a warrior who left the secular world in middle life. He had succeeded to the kingdom of Oriel, but decided to study for the priesthood. He was then granted the Aran Islands by his brother-in-law, Aengus, King of Cashel. He is said to have lived a life of astonishing severity, and never had a fire in winter, for he believed the 'hearts so glowing with the love of God' could not feel the cold. It is said that he taught 127 other saints, who are buried close to him on the islands.

St Kevin of Glendalough (died c. 618), Abbot

Many stories surround St Kevin, but we know he was one of the many Irish abbots who chose to remain a priest. He lived a solitary contemplative life in the Glendalough Valley where many people followed him, attracted by his rule of prayer and solitude. He played the harp, and the Rule for his monks was in verse. He is supposed to have prayed for so long that a blackbird had time to lay an egg, and hatch it on his outstretched hand. His monastery flourished until the 11th century. In the 12th century St Lawrence O'Toole came to Glendalough and modelled his life on St Kevin, bringing fresh fame to his memory. The foundation was finally destroyed in the 16th century.

St Kieran (c. 512–549), Abbot

St Kieran, also known as Ciaran, is remembered for his great foundation of Clonmacnoise, where the ancient chariot road through Ireland crosses the Shannon River. Unlike many Irish abbots he was not of aristocratic blood, for his father was a chariot-maker from County Antrim, and his mother from Kerry. St Kieran attracted craftsmen to his order, and Clonmacnoise grew to be a great monastic school, where, unusually for Ireland, the position of abbot did not become hereditary. Kieran died within a short time of founding the school. Many kings are buried alongside him, for it was believed that he would bring their souls safely to heaven.

St Malachy (1094–1148), Archbishop of Armagh

Malachy is famous as the great reformer of the Irish Church. He persuaded the Pope, Eugenius III, to establish the Archbishops of Ireland separately from those of England. He also ensured that it was no longer possible for important ecclesiastical positions to be held by certain families as a hereditary right. For example, he was appointed Bishop of Armagh, although the See of Armagh was held in lay succession by one family. It was an achievement to separate the family from this post without splitting the Irish Church.

The saint was educated in Armagh and Lismore, County Waterford, and desired only to be an itinerant preacher. His great talents took him instead to be Bishop of Down and Connor, and in 1125 he became Abbot-Bishop of Armagh. He travelled to France, where he made a lasting friendship with Bernard of Clairvaux, the reforming Cistercian. The Pope appointed him papal legate in Ireland, and whilst abroad he made some famous prophesies; one was that there will be the peace of Christ over all Ireland when the palm and the shamrock meet. This is supposed to mean when St Patrick's Day (17 March) occurs on Palm Sunday.

St Patrick (c. 390–461), Bishop and Patron Saint of Ireland

St Patrick was born somewhere between the Severn and the Clyde on the west coast of Britain. As a youth he was captured by Irish slave traders, and taken to the Antrim coast to work as a farm labourer. Much controversy surrounds the details of Patrick's life. Popular tradition credits him with converting the whole of Ireland, but nearly all that can be truly known of him comes from his *Confessio* or autobiography, and other writings. Through these writings he is revealed as a simple, sincere and humble man who was full of care for his people; an unlearned man, once a fugitive, who had learnt to trust God completely. Tradition states that after six years of slavery, voices told him he would soon return to his own land, and he escaped. Later, other voices call to him from Ireland, entreating him 'to come and walk once more amongst us'.

It is believed that he spent some time in Gaul (France) and became a priest; perhaps he had some mission conferred on him by the Pope to go and continue the work of Palladius, another missionary bishop who worked amongst the Christian Irish. It is believed that some confusion has arisen over the achievements of Palladius and Patrick. Patrick, when he returned to Ireland, seems to have been most active in the north, whilst Palladius worked in the south. He made Armagh his primary see, and it has remained the centre of Christianity in Ireland. He organized the church on the lines of territorial sees, and encouraged the laity to become monks or nuns. He was very concerned with abolishing paganism, idolatry and sun-worship, and he preached to the highest and the lowest in the land. Tradition credits him with expelling the snakes from Ireland, and explaining the Trinity by pointing to a shamrock.

One of the most famous episodes handed down by popular belief is that of his confrontation with King Laoghaire at Tara, known as the seat of the high kings of Ireland, and the capital of Meath. It was supposedly on Easter Saturday in 432, which that year coincided with a great Druid festival at Tara. No new fire was allowed to be lit until the lighting of the sacred pagan fire by the Druids. St Patrick was camped on the Hill of Slane which looks onto Tara, and his campfire was burning brightly; the Druids warned King Laoghaire that if it was not put out, it would never be extinguished. When Patrick was brought before Laoghaire, his holiness melted the king's hostility and he was invited to stay. Although Laoghaire did not become a Christian, his brother Conal, a prince of the North, became his protector and ally.

Certain places in Ireland are traditionally closely associated with St Patrick, such as Croagh Patrick in County Mayo, where there is an annual pilgrimage to the top of the 2510-ft (765 m) mountain on the last Sunday of July; and Downpatrick and Saul in County Down. The cult of St Patrick spread from Ireland to many Irish monasteries in Europe, and in more modern times to North America and Australia, where large communities of Irish emigrants live. The annual procession on 17 March, on St Patrick's Day in New York has become a massive event, where everybody sports a shamrock and drinks green beer. However, quite a few Irish believe St Colmcille should be the patron saint of Ireland, not this mild and humble British missionary!

Oliver Plunkett (1625–81), Archbishop of Armagh and Martyr

This gentle and holy man lived in frightening and turbulent times, when to be a practising Catholic in Ireland was to court trouble. He was born into a noble and wealthy family whose lands extended throughout the Pale. He was sent to study in Rome, and was a brilliant theology and law scholar. He became a priest in 1654 and in 1669 was appointed Archbishop of Armagh. Oliver was one of only two bishops in Ireland at that time, and the whole of the laity was in disorder and neglect. Apart from the hostility of the Protestants, the Catholics themselves were divided by internal squabbles. Oliver confirmed thousands of people, and held a provincial synod. He did much to maintain discipline amongst the clergy, to improve education by founding the Jesuit College in Drogheda, and to promulgate the decrees of the Council of Trent.

Oliver managed to remain on good terms with many of the Protestant gentry and clergy, but was eventually outlawed by the British government. The panic caused by the false allegations made by Titus Oates in England about a popish plot was used by Plunkett's enemies, and he was arrested in 1678. He was absurdly charged with plotting to bring in 20 thousand French troops, and levying a charge on his clergy to support an army. No jury could be found to convict him in Ireland, so he was brought to England, where he was convicted of treason for setting up 'a false religion which was the most dishonourable and derogatory to God of all religions and that a greater crime could not be committed against God than for a man to endeavour to propagate that religion'. He was hanged, drawn and quartered at Tyburn in July 1681. His head is in the Oliver Plunkett Church in Drogheda, County Louth, and his body lies at Downside Abbey, Somerset.

The Province of Munster

Munster (*Cuige Mumhan*) is the largest province in Ireland and a mixture of everything you consider Irish: the purples of the mountains melt into chessboards of cornfields in which the stooks stand like golden pieces. Houses are whitewashed, glens are deep and the coastline is made ragged by the force of the Atlantic, with sandy bays and rocky cliffs.

It is a land of extremes: a large, placid, fertile plain, brooding mountain scenery, luxurious vegetation, and harsh barren land. The stately River Shannon flows along the border of Tipperary, and on out to the sea between County Clare and County Limerick. The extreme southwesterly coast is swept by westerly gales, and trees have been distorted into bent and twisted shapes. The moonscape of the Burren contrasts with the softness of Killarney; the dairy-land of Cashel of the Kings, where the lordly and the holy worshipped on that rock above the plains, contrasts with the thrashing sea around Dingle and the Iveragh Peninsula.

The Burren is the youngest landscape in Europe and its carboniferous limestone hills have been shaped by intense glaciation. Spring gentian, mountain avens, hoary primrose, milkwort and orchids are amongst the wonderful variety of plants that flourish here. A great collection of southern and northern plants grow together: the bog violet and arbutus in Kerry, and the alpine/arctic plants of the Burren. Wild goats still range the Burren and keep at bay the ever-invasive hazel scrub. The best time to visit for the flowers is May.

This is the land of the Mumonians; the 'ster' suffix is a Scandinavian addition to the more ancient name of Muma, as it is with Ulster and Leinster. The people are warm, relaxed and musical; they are also backward-looking and quarrelsome. Dubliners say that Munster is a little England. The Anglo-Normans certainly had a part in moulding the towns, so did some of the adventurer types of the Elizabethan times, but Cork city is the creation of lively Irish minds, whether Celts or later arrivals. Cork people think their city ought to be the capital rather than Dublin!

Munster has always been cut off geographically from the rest of Ireland—by the mountains of Slieve Bloom, the bogs of Offaly and the River Shannon. This has helped to develop a great mythological tradition, with mother-goddesses figuring prominently in legend and place-names. There is Aire of Knockaney in County Limerick, and Aibell of Crag Liath, who reappears in the 18th century to preside over the judgement in Brian Merriman's famous vision poem 'The Midnight Court' (*see* p.125). Anu is Mother of the Gods, whose breasts are represented in the Pap Mountains on the Kerry border. Most primitive of all is the ancient Hag of Beare, who spans many centuries and to whose activities many megalithic monuments are attributed. She is variously known as Digde,

Dige or Duinech, and we are told that she passed through seven periods of youth. She is also supposed to have written the marvellous 9th-century poem The Hag of Beare, which is a lament for lost beauty, and the struggle between bodily pleasure and salvation through the Christian way of repentence:

> Yet may this cup of whey
> O! Lord, serve as my ale-feast—
> Fathoming its bitterness
> I'll learn that you know best.

Also strong in the mythological tradition is Donn Firinne, the ancestor-God to whom all the Irish will journey after death. His house is believed to be somewhere in this province. Munster has been commonly accepted as being divided into two parts—between the ancient O'Brien Kingdom of Thomond and the MacCarthy Kingdom of Desmond. This was certainly a political reality by the 12th century until the 17th century.

A Way With Words

The Irish have a way with words but the Kerryman is something else: from the cradle he is taught that language was invented to conceal thought! At least this is what the rest of Ireland thinks. Not surprisingly, Kerry jokes, not Irish jokes, are common. Munster has a great tradition of poetry. Daniel Corkery did much in his book *Hidden Ireland* to highlight the Gaelic poets in Munster during the 18th century. Poetry in Ireland has always been a vehicle for not only evoking mood or passion, but also for social and historical discourse. In Gaelic society the poet had great power and his gift of Satire was feared more than any weapon. After the 17th century, the status of the poet faded as the native institutions which had supported Gaelic poetry disappeared under English rule, and the intelligentsia were killed or exiled. Fortunately, semi-professional poets still existed in the 18th and early 19th century in rural communities. They gathered together in 'Courts of Poetry', organized gatherings where they exchanged their verse. Many of them were from Munster and they all wrote in Gaelic. They were great story-tellers, and many lament the loss of the Irish aristocracy and the decline of their great houses, their hospitality and protection. The most famous amongst them are David O'Bruadair (c. 1625–98), Egan O'Rahilly (c. 1675–1729), Owen Roe O'Sullivan (1748–84), and Eileen O'Connell. She was the aunt of Daniel O'Connell (1775–1847), 'the Great Liberator', and wrote one of the greatest love poems in the Irish language, 'The Lament for Art O'Leary'.

Brian Merriman (1749–1805) wrote the long poem 'The Midnight Court', which deals—with wit and eloquence—a mighty blow for women in the never-ending struggle between the sexes. In the poverty-stricken farming communities, marriages were made late in life, and they were made around land and money. Often the husband waited until his parents were dead, so he had a bit saved, before he took a wife. In his poem, Merriman seems to be suggesting in a joky yet serious way that if Irish girls got to marry only old goatish men, who could not give them pleasure, it would be better to ignore the 'bond of the prelates', free the priests from their vow of celibacy, and practise free love! This extract is from the translation by Frank O'Connor, which was banned in 1946 by the Censorship Board as a filthy figment of O'Connor's imagination. De Valera, the president of the time, was trying to create a pure, Catholic Ireland!

...A starved old gelding, blind and lamed
And a twenty-year-old with her parts untamed.
It wasn't her fault if things went wrong,
She closed her eyes and held her tongue;
She was no ignorant girl from school
To whine for her mother and play the fool
But a competent bedmate smooth and warm
Who cushioned him like a sheaf of corn...

There is a summer school held in Brian Merriman's honour at different locations in Munster each year (*see* **Practical A–Z**, p.51) In this century, Frank O'Connor, Bryan MacMahon, William Trevor, Sean O'Faolain and Edna O'Brien are amongst those who keep up the Munster tradition of skill with words.

County Limerick

A limerick is a nonsense verse, and Limerick is also a lovely county in Ireland. The county existed long before the five-line stanza, but since Edward Lear popularized them in his nonsense book, limericks have become world-famous. The origin of these poems is intriguing and open to debate, but it is claimed that in the 18th century a group of poets known as the Poets of Maigue, who lived near Croom, wrote these witty verses in good-natured sparring and as drinking songs. James Clarence Mangan, himself a great poet, translated them into English in the 1840s and they became popularized in England. One of the poets, Sean O'Tuama, a tavern keeper, wrote:

I sell the best brandy and sherry
To make my good customer merry
But at times their finances
Run short as it chances
And then I feel very sad, very.

One of his customers, Andy MacCraith, replied:

O Tuomy! you boast yourself handy,
At selling good ale and bright brandy,
The fact is your liquor makes everyone sicker,
I tell you that,
I your friend Andy.

County Limerick itself is a quiet farming community dotted with the ruins of hundreds of castles and bounded on the north by the spacious Shannon, spreading like the sea, and on its other sides by a fringe of hills and mountains. Limerick has the peaks of the Galtees in the southeast, the wild Mullaghareirk Mountains of southwest Limerick and the rich Golden Vale of east Limerick. There are lovely forest walks in all these places and sailing to be had on the Shannon. The visitor will be fascinated by Lough Gur, and the Norman castles and monasteries which still survive amongst the green fields and old farmhouses lying snugly in the valleys. The best dairy cattle come from County Limerick and it is also famous for its horse-breeding, principally because of the fertility of the pasture land. (The glacial deposits spread long ago by the retreating glaciers left a rich topsoil.)

The population of County Limerick is around 160,000, of whom 60,000 live in towns. Besides work in the agricultural industry, there is some light industry, and the Shannon Free Airport Development Company provides a lot of jobs.

History

Not surprisingly in such fertile countryside, the monks founded important monasteries. That they were rich is proved by the bejewelled Ardagh Chalice found in a ring-fort in 1868, and now in the National Museum in Dublin. The Vikings, in search of new territory and loot, sought them out up the Shannon Estuary and destroyed many centres of learning. They founded a colony which was to become the city of Limerick. Next came the Anglo-Normans, also attracted by the rich lands. Amongst the principal families were the Fitzgeralds, the de Burgos, the de Lacys and the Fitzgibbons. But it was the Earls of Desmond, the head of the Fitzgeralds, who owned the most and ruled like independent princes, eventually quarrelling with their Tudor overlords in England. They and their supporters are known as the Geraldines. In the 16th century the Tudors tried to centralize their authority. So in 1571 the Geraldines, who by now were completely Gaelicized, started a revolt which ended in savage wars and ruin for their house.

Throughout the following centuries up to the present day, Limerick has played a significant role in the numerous uprisings against English rule. In 1650 there was the 12-month siege of Limerick against Cromwell which ended in capitulation. The Jacobite-Williamite war (1689–91) saw two more sieges in which the heroic General Patrick Sarsfield played his role (*see* 'Limerick City', below). William Smith O'Brien, a Limerick man, was one of the leaders of the abortive 1848 Rebellion, and three of the leaders of the 1916 Rising in Dublin were from the county. Edward Daly and Con Colbert were executed, but Eamon de Valera escaped that fate due to his American birth. Later he was one of the leaders of the War of Independence (1919–1921), and President of Ireland from 1959 to 1973.

Getting There and Around

By air: Shannon Airport.

By rail: There is a main railhead terminal in the City of Limerick, ✆ (061) 418666.

By bus: Limerick City railway and bus depots are on Parnell Street. Bus Eireann runs a reasonable service from Limerick City, ✆ (061) 418855 for details.

By car: cars available for hire from Shannon Airport. In Limerick City, contact Cara Rent-a-Car, Coonagh Cross, ✆ (061) 455811. Camper vans also available.

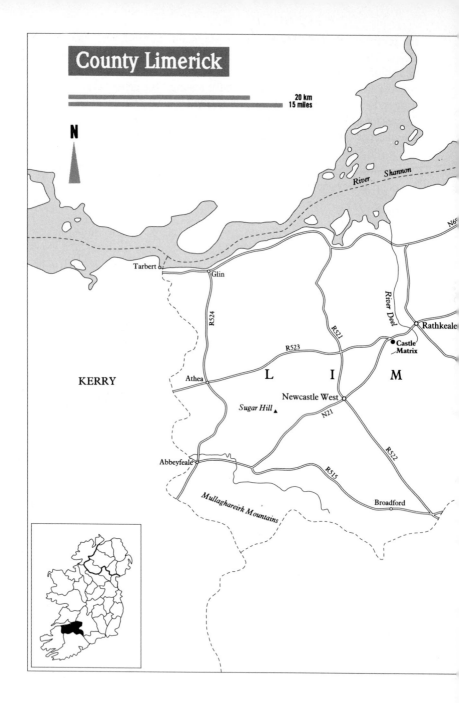

County Limerick

20 km
15 miles

N

River Shannon

River

Tarbert

Glin

N6

River Deel

Rathkeale

R524

R521

R523

Castle Matrix

KERRY

Athea

L   I   M

Newcastle West

Sugar Hill

N21

Abbeyfeale

R522

R515

Mullaghareirk Mountains

Broadford

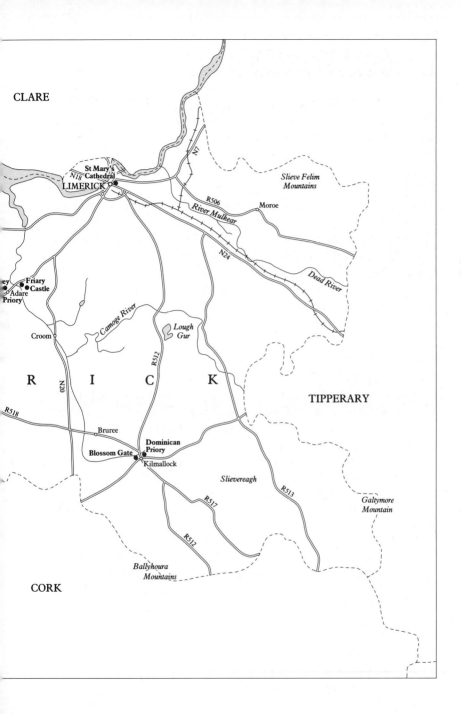

CLARE

St Mary's
N18 Cathedral
LIMERICK

Slieve Felim
Mountains

N7

R506
River Mulkear
Moroe

N24

Dead River

ey Friary
Castle
Adare
Priory

Camoge River

Croom

Lough
Gur

R512

R I C K

N20

TIPPERARY

R518

Bruree

Dominican
Priory
Blossom Gate
Kilmallock

Slievereagh

R513

Galtymore
Mountain

R517

R512

Ballyhoura
Mountains

CORK

By hovercraft: tours depart from Steam Boat Quay, Limerick, ✆ (061) 414147.

By bike: Raleigh Rent-a-Bike network operates throughout the county. Your local dealer in Limerick City is Emerald Cycles, 1 Patrick Street, ✆ (061) 416983.

Tourist Information

Arthur's Quay, Limerick City, ✆ (061) 317522, all year.

Shannon Airport, ✆ (061) 41664, all year.

Adare, ✆ (061) 396255, May to October.

Festivals

The dates of the festivals vary a little each year, and there may be one-off festivals in some towns, so do check details with the tourist offices.

17–25 March: The Band Music Festival, Limerick, ✆ (061) 410777. A mixture of concert bands, marching bands, parades and street entertainment.

May: Game and Country Fair, Adare, ✆ (061) 396770.

June: Paddy Music Expo, Limerick, ✆ (061) 400444. Showcase of traditional and contemporary Irish music.

July: The Ten Knights of Desmond Festival, Newcastle West ✆ (069) 62757/ (061) 317522.

End July/early August: Music Festival at Murroe, ✆ (061) 378219.

August: Limerick Agricultural Show, ✆ (061) 415519.

Limerick City

Limerick City has something rather drab about it which is hard to put your finger on. It is largely Georgian in character—a grid pattern of streets has been superimposed onto the older town which followed the curve of the River Shannon. The novelist Kate O'Brien came from the respectable middle class that moulded this city in the 19th century. She describes it as having , 'the grave, grey look of Commerce'. Yet Limerick is doing its best to forget the hard times of the 1940s, '50s and '60s and has recently been given a substantial facelift. It has a reputation for smart clothes shops, and the Art School here has produced some talented clothes designers. For a city of its size it also has a buzzy nightlife. There is a lot of unemployment and emigration still, but new industries have been set up, and there is an Arts Centre, the Bell Table, which produces excellent shows and exhibitions.

Like Londonderry it is a symbolic city, full of memories, and there is lots to see which reveals Limerick's more ancient past. It was founded in AD 922 by the Norsemen, and has always been an important fording place on the River Shannon. More concrete evidence of the past is the massive round tower of King John's Castle built in 1200, which is on the river guarding Thomond Bridge, and is one of the best examples of fortified Norman architecture in the country. In the wars of 1691 it was eventually surrendered to the Williamite Commander Ginkel after a fierce battering from his guns. The siege which preceded the surrender is stored away in the psyche of Irishmen. During the 1690s there were three struggles going on: the struggle of Britain and her Protestant allies to oppose the ascendancy in Europe of Catholic France, the struggle of Britain to subdue Ireland, and the struggle of the Protestant planter families and the Catholic Irish for the leadership of Ireland. The French supplied money and commanders to help Catholic James II wrestle his crown back from the Protestant William of Orange (*see* **History**, p.89). The majority of the Catholic Irish supported the Jacobite cause and many joined up. It is part of the Irish folk memory that the French commander, St Ruth, and King James were asses, and that the Irish Commander Patrick Sarsfield was intelligent, daring and brave. The Irish army had been beaten at the Boyne under St Ruth and had retreated to Limerick, where the walls were said to be paper thin. William began a siege whilst he waited for the arrival of big guns and artillery. Patrick Sarsfield led a daring raid on the siege train from Dublin and destroyed it. He rode through the night with 600 horses into the Clare Hills, forded the Shannon and continued on through the Slievefelim Mountains. Finally, he swooped down on William's huge consignment of guns and blew them skywards. His action saved Limerick from destruction for a time, whilst William abandoned the siege. When William III eventually did break through the Limerick walls, he sent in 10,000 men to wreak havoc, but the women and children of the city fought alongside their men, and they beat back the invaders. The second siege started the following year, and this time heavy losses were inflicted when the Williamite leader, Ginkel, gained control of Thomond Bridge. The promised help did not come, and there was nothing to do but negotiate an honourable treaty. This Sarsfield did, and he agreed to take himself and 10,000 Irish troops off to France, in what became known as 'The Flight of the Wild Geese'. But the terms of the treaty were not carried out and the Treaty Stone beside Thomond Bridge, where the treaty was supposed to have been signed, is now known as 'The Stone of the Violated Treaty'.

Old English Town and its Irish counterpart across the river are the most interesting parts of Limerick to wander in. The old Viking town of Limerick is on an island formed by the Shannon and what is called the Abbey River (a branch of the Shannon). It is known as English Town. The Vikings and later the Normans tried to keep the native Irish from living and trading in the city area so the Irish settled on the other side of the Abbey River—in Irish Town. A short circular walk takes you round the main places of interest. A great way of appreciating the beauty of the Shannon is to take a hovercraft trip up and down river (*see* 'Activities' below). From O'Connell street turn down Sarsfield street and cross the river by Sarsfield Bridge, then turn right up Clancy's Strand which gives you a good view of the city. Walk along until you come to Thomond Bridge which leads you into the Old Town, passing by King John's Castle. You may wander around the **Castle** (*open April–Oct, daily; Nov–Mar weekends only; adm; © (061) 411201*) which has recently had a couple of floors converted into an interpretative centre with displays of various instruments of early warfare and details of the castle's role in Irish history. A riverside walk leads you from the castle to the beautiful 18th-century Custom House, which has been restored and is housing the Hunt Collection in 1995 (*see* below). Close by is the tourist office in Arthur's Quay. Walk down Nicholas Street to St Mary's Cathedral, which is the only ancient church building left in the city and which was built in 1172 by Donal Mor O'Brien, King of Munster. Inside are some superb 15th-century oak misericords (choir stalls) carved into the shapes of fantastic beasts.

A few minutes' walk over Matthew Bridge brings you to the **Granary** in Michael Street. This is a fine example of a recently restored 18th-century Georgian warehouse, now the home of the City Library and archive. The Bell Table Arts Theatre is situated in 69 O'Connell Street, to the southwest, and various Irish travelling theatre companies stop off here; well worth a telephone call to find out what's on. There is also a small gallery which shows the work of many local artists and is part of the international EVA Art Exhibition held at various venues around the city.

After the 1760s when the city walls were dismantled, English and Irish Town merged and Georgian streets and squares were built. St John's Square is full of lovely old buildings of *c.* 1750, some of which are being restored after years of neglect. The **Limerick Museum** (✆ (061) 47826) is in Nos.1 and 2 on the west side, and houses an impressive collection of items from the Neolithic, the Bronze and Iron Ages, including the famous 'Nail' or pedestal, formerly in the Exchange (now gone, except for a fragment of the façade in Nicholas Street), where the merchants of Limerick used to pay their debts. Hence the expression 'paying on the nail'.

To the southwest, close to the entrance to the People's Park off Pery Square, is **Limerick Art Gallery**, which has a collection of modern Irish paintings and holds some very interesting exhibitions. Beautiful lace is made by the Good Shepherd Sisters in Clare Street, on the Dublin Road, ✆ (061) 415183. You can visit them during working hours, and buy something exquisite which might in time become a family heirloom! Three miles (5km) from the city centre, off the N7 to Dublin, the **Hunt Collection** (*open Tues–Sat, 10–5;* ✆ *(061) 333644*) is temporarily at the University of Limerick, but is due to relocate to the Granary in Michael Street in 1995. John Hunt was a noted art historian and Celtic archaeologist who died in the 1970s. His collection was gathered over 40 years and contains a mixture of Bronze Age weapons, 18th-century silver, jewels, paintings and medieval artefacts, including the 9th-century bronze Cashel Bell, the largest in Ireland, found near Cashel town in 1849, and Early Christian brooches.

There is greyhound racing at the town course several nights each week. Look in the local newspaper for details.

Adare and Surrounding Area

To the west of Limerick, only 16 miles (26km) away, Shannon Airport is a free port area in which customs duties and formalities are suspended. There are hundreds of bargains for those flying out.

About 10 miles (16 km) from Limerick, going southwest on the N20, **Adare** (*Ath Dara*: the ford of the oak tree), is set in richly timbered land through which the little River Maigue flows. There is only a wide main street, set on both sides with pretty thatched cottages, many of which are either antique shops, craft shops or restaurants. One of them is the local tourist office. The village is noted for its fine ecclesiastical ruins, but first notice the newly restored village washing pool—opposite the Trinitarian Abbey, just off the main street. You can imagine the stories and scandal exchanged as the village women washed their clothes. The finest ruin is the **Franciscan friary** founded in 1464 by Thomas, Earl of

Kildare. (The village belonged to the Kildare branch of the Fitzgeralds or Geraldines.) The friary was attacked and burned by parliamentary forces, but its ruins are very beautifully proportioned, and can be viewed at a distance from the long narrow bridge of 14 arches (c. 1400) on the outskirts of the village on the N20 going north. If you want to go right up to it, check with the golf club office at the entrance, as it is in the heart of the Adare Manor Golf Club.

The modern village has grown up around the rest of the ecclesiastical buildings. The **Augustinian priory**, now used as the Church of Ireland Church, was founded in 1315 by the Kildares. It was restored in 1807 by the first Earl of Dunraven. His family used to own the Gothic Revival-style manor house whose lush parklands surround the village. Adare Manor is now a luxury hotel. The church has some interesting carvings of animals and human heads, and gives a good idea of what an Irish medieval church must have looked like. **Desmond Castle**, on the banks of the Maigue, beside the bridge, was built in the 13th century on the site of an earlier ring-fort. It is a fine example of feudal architecture with its square keep, curtain walls, two great halls, kitchen, gallery and stables.

The area around Adare is known as the Palatine because of the number of Lutherans from Southern Germany who settled here in the 18th century. Their descendants, bearing such names as Ruttle, Shier, Teskey and Switzer, are still numerous in the area. **Rathkeale** (17miles/11km west of Adare) is the second-largest town in County Limerick, and is notable for its fine early-19th-century courthouse and doorways in the main street. It has a small museum devoted to the history of the palatines. **Castle Matrix** (*open 1 June– 1 Sept, Sat–Tues, 11–5; adm; © (069) 64284*) about a mile (2km) to the southwest, is a fine Geraldine Castle built about 1410. The poet-Earl of Desmond, whose style epitomized the courtly love genre, lived here in the 1440s. The castle has been restored and houses a unique collection of documents relating to the Wild Geese, Irish soldiers who served so nobly in the Continental armies of the 17th and 18th centuries. It has the reputation for being the first place in Ireland, where the potato was grown. The story goes that the poet Edmund Spenser met Walter Raleigh here in 1580, and they became great friends. They were both as yet young and unknown, seeking to make their fortune in Ireland, where they had both been granted land. When Raleigh returned from his successful voyage to America, he presented some potatoes to their host, Lord Southwell, who evidently cultivated them with some success. The Methodist movement in North America was initiated at Castle Matrix: Palatine refugees on the estate were converted by John Wesley, and in 1760 Philip Embury and Barbara Ruttle Heck sailed to New York and founded a church there. It is now the headquarters of the Irish International Arts Centre and Heraldry Society.

Croom, right in the middle of County Limerick, is celebrated as the meeting place of the 18th-century Gaelic poets of the Maigue. Fortunately, their poetry is available in translation, and is unforgettable for its wit and feeling. It is here that the light verse of the 'limerick' was first popularized. An old castle of the Geraldines is hidden behind a wall on the southern approach to the village. **Knockfierna Hill**, 6½ miles (10km) southwest of Croom, is a fine place for a walk. It is held sacred to the Dé Danaan, King of the Other World, or Death, Donn Forinne. From the summit, on a clear day, you can see a great expanse of Ireland with mountains and the Shannon Estuary.

Glin and Surrounding Area

Glin, a lovely village on the Shannon, is very near the car ferry at Tarbert which takes you across to County Clare. It is well worth a visit to **Glin Castle** *(open in May, 10–12 and 2–4, and at other times by arrangement with Madame Fitzgerald or Evelyne O'Sullivan, ℂ (068) 34112)* still the ancestral home of the Knights of Glin, part of the Fitzgerald tribe. (The present Knight of Glin is an art historian and stalwart campaigner on behalf of the historic buildings of this island which are so often left to decay.) The castle is Georgian Gothic and noted for its flying staircase, lovely plasterwork, and 18th-century furniture and paintings. The gardens are beautifully planned and tended, and are a fitting extension of this romantic house. *(Craft shop and restaurant at the Gate Lodge open Apr–Oct.)*

North of Glin is Foynes, a small port on a wide stretch of the Shannon Estuary. A very interesting hour can be spent at the Flying Boat Museum *(open Mar 31–Oct 31, 10–6; ℂ (069) 65416)*. Between 1939 and 1945 Foynes was famous as a base for seaplanes crossing the Atlantic. The radio and weather room with original transmitters, receivers and Morse code is fascinating. Many high-ranking British and American military officers passed through Foynes during the Second World War.

Following the border with Tipperary southwards you come to **Athea**, a centre for traditional music, and a pretty place. All around are lovely hill walks and drives. **Abbeyfeale**, on the N21 south of Athea, is surrounded by rolling hills and is another centre of traditional music, song and dance. It is also the gateway to Killarney and Tralee. To the east are the **Mullaghareirk Mountains** near the village of Broadford, which are mainly forested with the uniform evergreens so beloved of the Forestry Commission.

Lough Gur

Lough Gur, 11 miles (17km) south of Limerick City, is guarded by the remains of two castles built by the Earls of Desmond in an area rich in field antiquities. According to legend, the last of the Desmonds is doomed to hold court under the waters of Lough Gur and to emerge, fully armed, at daybreak on every morning of the seventh year in a routine that must be repeated until the silver shoes of his horse are worn away. As if to echo the story, the lake itself is horse-shoe shaped. Man has been here since 3000 BC and you can see stone circles, wedge-shaped graves and Neolithic house sites. The **Interpretative Centre** *(open 14 May–end Sept, daily, 10–6; adm; ℂ (061) 85186)* has an excellent audio-visual show explaining the history of the Lough Gur area from the Stone Age. The centre is very sympathetically built, inspired by Neolithic house styles.

Kilmallock to the Clare Glens

Kilmallock, about 11 miles (17km) south of Lough Gur on the R512, is in the rich land of the Golden Vale. It was built by the Geraldines (Fitzgeralds) and John's Castle still stands in the centre of town, while Blossom's Gateway is a remnant of the ancient walls. The town should have been as gracious as Adare, but nothing has been protected. There is a beautiful Dominican priory dating from the 13th century. A pillar in the aisle arcade shows the ball-flower ornament—very rare in Ireland, though common during the 14th century in England. **Bruree**, 4½ miles (7 km) to the west of Kilmallock on the R518, is the place where Eamon de Valera grew up. The school he went to is now the **De Valera Museum**. An old corn mill with a huge mill wheel makes a striking image as you enter the village from the west.

Murroe (also spelt Moroe) and the Clare Glens are on the northeastern borders of Limerick, about 10 miles (16km) from Limerick City on R506. Murroe lies under the foothills of the Slievefelim mountains, and is dominated by the 19th–century **Mansion of Glenstal**. Now a Benedictine monastery, it is famous as one of Ireland's public schools (run by the monks) and a centre for the promotion of ecumenicalism. The grounds are very beautiful in May and June when the rhododendrons are out. The monks will always make you welcome; they sell beautiful hand-turned wooden bowls etc. Glenstal used to be the family home of the Barringtons, who donated the **Glens of Clare** to the County Councils of Limerick and North Tipperary for the pleasure of the public. The Glens, a mile (2km) north of Murroe, are not so much glens as a scenic gorge with sparkling waterfalls. There is a nature trail which leads you through this beautiful wooded place. Murroe has traditional music recitals during the holiday season and is a pleasant area in which to stay. A further mile or so west, at **Clonkeen**, is a small rectangular church, about 12th-century, with a richly decorated Irish Romanesque doorway and north wall window.

Shopping

Chocolates: Leonidas Chocolates, O'Connell Mall, O'Connell Street, Limerick. Wonderful Belgian chocolates. Sonia's Chocolates, Denmark Street and 35 O'Connell Street, Limerick; delicious chocolates made in Limerick by the unemployed under the auspices of Sister Joan.

Crafts: Martin O'Driscoll, gold & silversmith, Potato market, Merchant's Quay, ✆ (061) 415914. Irish crochet from Margaret Hogan, Main Street, Foynes. General crafts, woollens and tweeds from Irish Handicrafts, Arthur's Quay Shopping Centre; ceramics and stained glass from Workspace on Michael Street, Limerick, ✆ (061) 416800. All these are open during normal working hours.

Foods: Wholefoods/cheese: an excellent variety of local cheeses, organic veg and breads from Eats of Eden, Spaight's Shopping Centre, Limerick, ✆ (061) 419400; Glen-O-Sheen Cheddar, Kilmallock, ✆ (063) 86140.

Ham: County Limerick is world-famous for its ham. A good source is Hogan's Bacon Shop, 74a Little Catherine Street, Limerick, ✆ (061) 412542.

Venison: Irish Venison Co-op at the Limerick Food Centre, Rahun, ✆ (061) 412542.

Lace: From the Convent of the Good Shepherd Sisters, Clare Street (the Dublin Road), Limerick, ✆ (061) 415183. Open Mon–Fri, 9.45am–4.45pm.

Pottery: Orchard Pottery, Castleconnell, ✆ (061) 377181. Stoneware decorated with colourful Celtic designs.

Woollens: Michelina Stacpoole, luxurious fashion knitwear, Adare, ✆ (061) 396409. Also available at La Femme, Cecil Street, Limerick.

Activities

Golf: Shannon, between the airport and the estuary, ✆ (061) 471020. Adare, in the Manor Demesne; ✆ (061) 396204 and in the grounds of the Manor itself ✆ (061) 396566.

Horse-racing: 4-day meeting in December at Limerick.

Hunting: This is great hunting country. Contact the County Limerick Hunt through the Hon. Secretary, Limerick County Hunt, Adelaisk House, Bruff, ✆ (061) 82114; the Stonehall Harrier Hunt Club, the Hon. Secretary, Askeaton, ✆ (061) 393286.

Pony-trekking: At Rathcannon, Kilmallock, ✆ (063) 392026 and Crecora Equestrian Centre, ✆ (061) 355139.

Sailing: On the River Shannon, ✆ (061) 76364/(067) 376622.

Where to Stay

luxury

Adare Manor Hotel, Adare, ✆ (061) 396566, is the original house of the Earls of Dunraven. A mixture of Victorian Gothic and Tudor Revival fantasy, it has beautiful grounds with horse-riding, clay pigeon shooting and an 18 hole golf course designed by Robert Trent Jones.

expensive

Dunraven Arms Hotel, Adare, ✆ (061) 396209, is an old-world hotel on the main street, with a colourful garden, pretty rooms and friendly staff. By contrast, **Jurys Hotel**, Ennis Road, Limerick, ✆ (061) 327777, is predictably modern and convenient.

moderate

The old-fashioned, comfortable **Railway Hotel**, Parnell Street, Limerick, ✆ (061) 413653, is family-run. **Castle Oaks House**, Castleconnell, ✆ (061) 377666, is a delightful Georgian house.

inexpensive

Mrs O'Shaughnessy offers comfortable accommodation in **Hollywood House**, Ballinvira, Croagh, Adare, ✆ (061) 396237, a very pretty Georgian house, 3 miles (4.8km) south of Adare. In another Georgian house, **Millbank House**, Murroe, ✆ (061) 386115, Mrs Keays makes guests welcome in a farm setting. There's trout- and salmon-fishing on the river which flows through the farm. From **Cooleen House**, Bruree, ✆ (063) 90584, Mrs McDonoogh's whitewashed

Georgian farmhouse, you can hear the rustling of the little river that flows beside the house. Very friendly service and fine old-fashioned bedrooms.

Convenient for Shannon Airport, Mrs Johnson offers warm hospitality and good food at **Ballyteigne House**, Rockhill, Bruree, ℂ (063) 90575. Mrs Sheedy-King provides excellent home-cooking at **Flemingstown House**, Kilmallock, ℂ (063) 98093. From **Jackson's Turrett**, Clancy Strand, Limerick, ℂ (061) 326186, there are lovely views of the Shannon in Mrs Caball's cosy, en-suite rooms. **Reens House**, Ardagh, ℂ (069) 64276 is the Curtins' 17th-century house on a dairy farm. **Limerick Hostel**, Barrington's House, George's Quay, Limerick, ℂ (061) 45222, has rooms for 2–4 people, singles for IR£6.50, but is a touch austere. **An Oige Hostel**, 1 Pery Square, Limerick, ℂ (061) 31462, is another cheap option.

self catering

Rent an Irish Cottage, Kilfinane, ℂ (061) 411109, offer traditional-type cottages. **Adare Holiday Cottages**, Avenue Row, Adare, ℂ (061) 396566, are modern and practical.

Eating Out
expensive

Restaurant de la Fontaine, 12 Upper Griffin Street, ℂ (061) 414461. Provincial France on the inside with robust but pricey country cooking and an extensive and exceptional French wine list. **The Mustard Seed**, Adare, ℂ (061) 396451. Delicious and imaginative food in a series of little dining rooms in pretty thatched cottage. Memorable smoked salmon with walnut oil.

moderate

Woodlands House, Knockanes, Adare, ℂ (061) 396118. Popular with locals; huge helpings of plain food. *Dinner and Sunday lunch only.* **The Silver Plate**, 74 O'Connell Street, Limerick, ℂ (061) 316311. Fish restaurant, cooking French-style. **Charcos**, Castleconnell, ℂ (061) 377533. Pub grub and restaurant with grill.

inexpensive/cheap

Bell Table Arts Centre Café, 69 O'Connell Street, ℂ (061) 319866. Tasty lunches and great choice of cakes. *Daytime only.* **O'Sheas**, 2 Little Catherine Street, Limerick, ℂ (061) Excellent snacks with good vegetarian options. Daytime only. **Vintage Pub**, Ellen Street, Limerick. Traditional pub with lunchtime snacks. **Foley's Pub**, Lower Shannon Street, Limerick. Lunchtime meals such as ham and cabbage, Irish stew. **The Jasmine Palace**, Mall on O'Connell Street, Limerick, ℂ (061) 412484. Cantonese. *Open lunch and dinner.* **Matt the Thresher**, Birdhill, ℂ (061) 379227. On the road into Limerick. Excellent barfood, home-made bread; barstools made out of tractor seats. *Open all day.* **Oscar's**, Savoy Cinema Complex, Henry Street, Limerick. Always has a few moderately priced vegetarian options. **Ivan's**, Caherdavin, Limerick, ℂ (061) 455766. A sandwich counter, take-away deli service and excellent breads. Good for picnic ingredients. *Open till 11pm.*

Entertainment and Nightlife

Lively arts: The Bell Table Arts Centre, 69 O'Connell Street, Limerick, ✆ (061) 319866. *Son et lumière* shows of Irish history at St Mary's Cathedral and King John's Castle, Limerick; adm, ✆ (061) 413157/310293.

Pubs and Clubs: Boxwell's, Patrick Street, Limerick; currently Limerick's 'hotspot' for the young and trendy. Brazen Head: O'Connell Street, Limerick. Popular pub and eatery which houses a club called 'Teds' for after-hours fun and frolics. The Works, Savoy Cinema Complex, Limerick, brand new 'hip' nightclub.

Traditional music: Nancy Blakes, Upper Denmark Street, Limerick, and at the Speakeasy on O'Connell Street, Limerick.

County Kerry

Kerry is packed with some of the most beautiful scenery in Ireland, and the friendliest people. It is a kingdom all of its own, whose people love to use words with flamboyance, skill and humour. An irregularly shaped county with long fingers of land reaching into the sea, it boasts the opulent lakes of Killarney at its centre—set amongst the wooded MacGillycuddy's Reeks, the grandest mountain range in the land. To the west are the peninsulas of Iveragh and Dingle, which are dear to every traveller who lands up amongst their splendour, and where mountains and sea are jumbled together in a glory of colour. The Beara Peninsula has an equal beauty but is relatively unexplored. Every year the small farmer re-creates a pattern of golden hayricks and cornfields, and wild flowers grow in the hedges and handkerchief fields where the black Kerry cow grazes, when she is not creating a traffic jam on the narrow country lanes.

Off the coast are some fascinating islands, which it is possible to visit with some perseverance. On the **Skelligs Rocks** the word of God has been praised and celebrated for six hundred years. **Valentia** is a soft, easy island by comparison; while the **Blaskets**, 3 miles (4.8km) out to sea, are beautiful but deserted.

The possibilities for enjoying yourself in County Kerry are numerous. If you are simply motoring around the narrow country lanes, you will see the most superb vistas of seascape, hill and valley. But do not try to do too much driving in one day, for the roads are very twisty and each bend holds more alluring beauty; the driver can end up doing too much, and it is possible to explore it all too quickly. The hotels and restaurants of County Kerry are generally of a very high standard, and the seafood and salmon are all that could be desired. Sailing, deep-sea fishing and water-skiing are all easy to arrange, as is golf, horse-riding, game fishing and walking in the heathery mountains. For those who most like to wander amongst gardens and into historic buildings, there are several properties open to the public. One of the most famous is, of course, **Derrynane House**, the house of Daniel O'Connell, 'the Great Liberator', who won Catholic emancipation. Whatever you

plan to do, expect some rainy weather and cloud, for Kerry is notoriously wet and warm. For those interested in the ancient past, Kerry is scattered with ogham stones, standing stones, forts and clochans (the stone huts of holy men). Interpretative centres have opened up to educate those interested in local history and to cater to the coach tours.

History

A brief historical outline must start, as always, back in the time of the Bronze Age, some 4500 years ago. Miners from Spain and Portugal were attracted by the precious metals to be found in the mountains, and it is still possible to find traces of their mines, and their assembly places which are marked with stone circles, rock carvings and wedge tombs. From the wealth of legend which remains of the later Bronze Age and Early Stone Age, (500 BC) it is possible to build up an accurate picture of society as it was then. It was hierarchical, aristocratic, and warlike. There were no towns and cattle-raising and raiding dominated everything. Farmers lived in ring-forts and on crannogs for defensive reasons. Writing was confined to an archaic form of Irish which you can see on the ogham stones scattered around Kerry. Kerry beaches were the landing places for many of the legendary invasions, voyages and battles of Ireland's past. The miners who sailed into the bays from Spain are recorded in legend, as were the other waves of settlers.

Christianity came in the 5th century and great changes began. The old tribal centres went into a decline, and powerful new kingdoms emerged, often with an abbot-prince at their heads. A strong monastic structure grew up and some monasteries became great centres of learning. The monks learnt the art of writing and recorded the legends and sagas. Many of these centres were in inhospitable locations—the 'dysart' of some place names. In Kerry there is the wonderfully preserved 7th-century foundation on Skellig Michael.

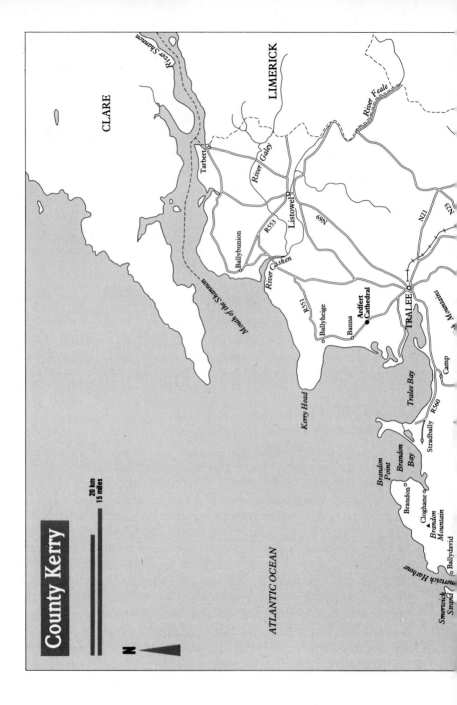

County Kerry

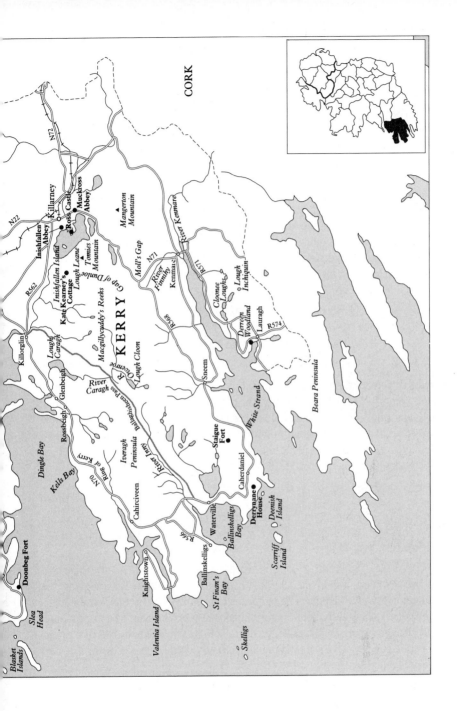

CORK

N72

N22

N71

Killarney
Ross Castle
Mucross
Abbey
Inishfallen
Abbey
Mangerton
Mountain

River Kenmare

Moll's Gap

Inishfallen Island
Kate Kearney's
Cottage

Tomies
Mountain
Lough Leane

River
Flesk

Kenmare

Lough
Inchiquin

Gap of Dunloe

KERRY

River
Finnihy

Cloonee
Loughs

R571

Derreen
Woodland
Lauragh

R574

Macgillycuddy's Reeks

Lough Cloon

R568

N71

Sneem

Killorglin

Lough
Caragh

Glenbeigh

River
Caragh

R. Owenroe

Beara Peninsula

Rossbeigh

Ballaghisheen Pass

White Strand

Dingle Bay

Kells Bay

Iveragh
Peninsula

Ring of Kerry

Staigue
Fort

Cahirciveen

River Inny

N70

Caherdaniel

Derrynane
House

Slea
Head

Knightstown

Waterville

R566

Ballinskelligs

Ballinskelligs
Bay

Deenish
Island

Scarriff
Island

Blasket
Islands

Doonbeg Fort

Valentia Island

St Finan's
Bay

Skelligs

141

In the upheavals and faction-fighting of the 11th and 12th centuries, three ruling families emerged in Kerry as definite clans: the MacCarthys south of Killarney; the O'Donoghues around Killarney; and the O'Sullivans around the Kenmare Rivers. These are names which crop up again and again in Kerry's history, right up to today. In the 13th century, with the arrival of the Anglo-Normans, the Fitzgeralds established strongholds throughout the region. They became the Palatine Earls of Desmond, and bought with them tenants and fighting men who introduced the common Kerry names of Browne, Landers, Ashe and Ferriter. The Earls of Desmond became so powerful that they were able to maintain an independence from the centralizing efforts of the English monarchs right up till the reign of Elizabeth I. They adopted many of the old Irish traditions; poetry and music flourished under their patronage. The last earl took part in a rebellion against Elizabeth, and lost his lands and his life, and the Gaelic way of life began to disappear. The country was reorganized in 1606 into the shape we know today, and the new landowners were largely English and Protestant. The political destruction of the 17th century is wonderfully recorded in the laments and satires of the poets of Munster. This short verse of David O'Bruadair (*c.* 1625–98) sums up what the poets felt:

> Sad for those without sweet Anglo-Saxon
> Now that Ormonde has come to Erin
> For the rest of my life in the land of Conn
> I'll do better with English than a poem.

Version by John Montague

Kerry produced perhaps the greatest Irish leader there has ever been in the shape of Daniel O'Connell, who in 1829 won Catholic emancipation, not only for the Irish, but for all Catholics under British rule. He came from an old Gaelic family who had managed to hold on to their lands and to get along with their Protestant neighbours. The famine of 1847 and the emigration that followed reduced the population of Kerry as it did everywhere in Ireland. Nowadays Kerry is a land of small farmers and relies on the tourist industry.

Getting There and Around

By air: From the small airport at Farranfore there are flights from London with Manx airlines or Aer Lingus via Dublin, ✆ (066) 64644.

By boat: If you are planning to go west to County Clare and Galway, you can avoid Limerick City by taking the car ferry at Tarbert, across the Shannon River to Killimer. The ferry sails from Killimer every hour on the hour, and from Tarbert every hour on the half-hour; it takes 30 mins. The nearest international ferryport is Ringaskiddy, near Cork City, which has ferries to the Continent. Ferry service around the Ring of Kerry from Dingle: Tues, Wed, Thurs, Sat and Sun, IR£10.

By rail: Kerry is linked to Dublin by a good rail line from Killarney and Tralee; call ✆ (064) 31067 for information.

By bus: Bus Eireann provides a good bus service to many parts of the county, ✆ (066) 21211/23566.

By car: car hire from Brien Sheehy, Boherbue Road, Tralee, ✆ (066) 21080. or McElligots, Rathass, Tralee, ✆ (066) 23011.

By bike: Raleigh Rent-a-Bike network operates in Kerry, ✆ (01) 261333. The local dealer in Killarney is O'Callaghan's, College Street, ✆ (066) 31175. In Tralee, Jim Catall Himself Ltd, Staughton's Row, Tralee, ✆ (066) 21654.

To the islands: to visit the Skelligs, hire a boat from Caherdaniel or Derrynane Pier, or from Valentia Island—a matter of trying your luck with the local fishermen. One contact is Des Lavelle, who operates a scuba-diving school, ✆ (066) 56124. He also organises cruises around the islands from the Skellig Heritage Centre ✆ (021) 273251 or (064) 31633. The Café Liteartha in Dingle, ✆ (066) 51388, often displays information in the window on boats and excursions out to the Skelligs and the Blaskets; there are now some 'official' boats that visit the islands—call the Skellig Heritage Centre, ✆ (066) 76306 for more information. Also, ask in Krugers Bar, Dunquin, ✆ (066) 56127, about hiring a boat to the Great Blasket. A small boat ferries day-trippers from Dunquin Harbour at 11am, returning late afternoon, ✆ (066) 56188 for more information. Bord Fáilte are loathe to recommend anyone because of the insurance requirements; the local boatman will not be covered and the trip is at your own risk.

Tourist Information

Killarney Town Hall, ✆ (064) 31633, all year.

Kenmare, beside Heritage Centre, ✆ (064) 41233, 9.30–7 in summer only.

Tralee, Godfrey Place, ✆ (066) 21288, all year.

Dingle, ✆ (066) 51188, April to end October.

Kenmare, ✆ (064) 41233, seasonal office.

Festivals

Easter: Easter Folk Festival. Call Mr O'Callaghan, ✆ (064) 33404.

May: Rally of the Lakes, car rally. Contact Mike Marshall, ✆ (064) 32026. Ballybunnion International Bachelor Festival, ✆ (066) 21288.

May–September: Siamsa Tire, The National Folk Theatre of Ireland, Godfrey Place, Tralee, ✆ (066) 23055, has a programme of evening entertainment based on Irish music, folklore and dance.

July: St Brendan's Festival, Dingle, ask for Rosie Ban, ✆ (066) 51466. Irish Music Festival, Dingle. Contact Fergus O'Flahertie, O'Flahertie's Bar, Dingle, ✆ (066) 51461.

August: Rose of Tralee Competition, ✆ (066) 21322. **10–12 August**, Puck Fair, Killorglin, ✆ (064) 31633/61193.

Kenmare and Surrounding Area

The route into Kerry via Cork is spectacular. However, instead of going straight to Killarney, you should explore around **Lauragh** and the **Cloonee Loughs**, for the waterfalls and lakes are lovely. An unmarked road off the R571 will take you up to a wonderful view over the Beara Peninsula and Inchiquin Lake. Across the lough is **Uragh Wood**, a survivor of the primeval oakwoods which once covered most of Ireland. These are sessile oaks, which are distinguished by their curious hunched branches. There is a beautifully planted garden at **Derreen Woodland** (*open April–end Sept, daily, 11–6; adm; ✆ (064) 83103*). near Lauragh, on the Kenmare-Castletownbeare road (R571). The moist climate has given the plants a tropical vigour. As you walk through the winding paths and tunnels of deep shade cast by the bamboo and rhododendrons, there are glorious glimpses of sea and wild mountain country. The land, and thousands of acres around it, used to belong to Sir William Petty, who was responsible for the mapping of two-thirds of Ireland after the Cromwellian Conquest.

This is marvellous walking country, and you can base yourself in **Kenmare**, a pretty 19th-century town. Savour the view of the Kerry Hills, the Macgillycuddy's Reeks, the Caha Range on the Cork border and the broad estuary of the River Kenmare. Kenmare itself is full of excellent craft shops, coffee houses, bars, restaurants and a heritage centre, so leave yourself at least a couple of hours to wander around it. Cleo in Shelbourne Street is especially tempting. The colours of woven rugs, jerseys and tweeds perfectly echo the beautiful surrounding countryside. There is a fine prehistoric stone circle along the banks of the River Finnihy. To get there, walk up a road to the right of the Market House. Follow this until you see a notice reading 'cul de sac', and walk up the little lane on the right to where it joins another lane to the left. On the left, behind a high ditch, is the stone circle. It is always accessible. On the square above the tourist office is the **Kenmare Lace and Design Centre** where you can look at a display of the point lace made locally and even see demonstrations. On the outskirts of town on the Killarney road (N71) is **St Mary's Holy Well**, which is still much visited as the waters are reputed to have strong healing powers. The road from Kenmare to Killarney (N71) is twisty but the landscape is spectacular. Once you have climbed to the top of the mountain and through Moll's Gap, you get wonderful views of Killarney's lakes and woods.

Killarney

Killarney is dedicated to making money out of tourists and no longer attractive in itself, yet the surrounding countryside remains beautiful and unspoiled. If you are willing to walk in the mountains and away from well-worn tracks, you will find that the luxuriant green of the woods, the soft air, the vivid blue of the lakes and the craggy mountains above will have the same charm for you as they have had for countless travellers since the 18th century. Remember to bring a raincoat, and expect at least one day when the mists will creep over everything.

Killarney does have one thing to offer sightseers: **St Mary's Cathedral**, built in silvery limestone in the 1840s to the design of Pugin. It is a very successful Early-English style building, austere and graceful. You will find it in Cathedral Place, a continuation of New Street. There are plenty of banks, shops, craft shops and restaurants to choose from, but avoid staying in the centre of the town as it gets so crowded. And expect to be approached by the jarveys, who gather with their ponies and traps on the street corner as you enter the town on the N71. They will guide you around the valley and take you for as long or as short a trip as you want. Be sure to negotiate the price for the ride before you start.

In July in Killarney Town are the **Killarney Races**, when the place is crowded with locals. They also come in their thousands for the **Killarney Rally** in May, part of the Benson and Hedges motor-racing circuit of Ireland. At about the same time, the Easter folk festival is held at various venues around the town.

Excursions from Killarney

A large part of the Killarney Valley is a National Park, at the centre of which is Muckross House and Abbey. The valley runs roughly north–south through a break in the great Macgillycuddy's Reeks range of mountains which run east–west. Lough Leane lies north of the range, and the Middle and Upper Lakes, mainly south of it.

It is possible to have great fun seeing the sights by pony and trap, also known as a jaunting car. Excursions from Killarney take up to a full day and during the trip you are regaled with stories by the jarveys. They have built up an international reputation for telling visitors exactly what they expect to hear—leprechauns, legends, you name it! A boat trip down the three lakes takes a whole day and is idyllic in good weather. There are half-day bus trips, and ponies may be hired to explore the Gap of Dunloe, on the outskirts of Killarney. This is only advisable for experienced riders. The Gap of Dunloe divides the Macgillycuddy's from the Purple Mountain and Tomies Mountain. The mouth of the Gap starts at Kate Kearney's Cottage (who was reputed to be a witch), a coffee shop off the Killorglin road 6 miles (10km) west of Killarney, and continues through to Moll's Gap on the Kenmare road (N71). Most people start from this end and hire a pony or sidecar. Cars are not welcome on this route until well after 7pm, as the horse traffic on the narrow unpaved road will not allow you to pass. The journey through the Gap is spectacular, with steep gorges and deep glacial lakes. A more detailed description is given below.

For those who prefer to be more independent and economical, hiking or biking will get you to the Gap of Dunloe, Muckross Abbey and Castle, Ross Castle and Innisfallen Isle. **Ross Castle** is 1.5 miles (2.4km) south west of the town centre on a peninsula. It is a fine ruin dating from the 15th century, consisting of a tower house surrounded by a bawn (fortified enclosure). On the left of it there is a 17th-century house built by the Brownes, who became Earls of Kenmare. It is not possible to go inside the castle but from here you can hire a boat to **Innisfallen Island** (*IR£3–IR£4 per hour*), which is like a country in miniature with hills and valleys, and dark woods. Holly and other evergreens grow very thickly here. Near the landing stages are the extensive ruins of **Innisfallen Abbey**, founded about AD 600, a refuge for Christians during the Dark Ages in Europe. The Annals of Innisfallen, a chronicle of world and Irish history written between AD 950 and 1380, are now in the Bodleian Library, Oxford. The monastery lasted until the middle of the 17th century when the Cromwellian forces held Ross Castle.

About 3 miles (5km) from Killarney is the **Muckross Estate** on the Kenmare road. Muckross House and Abbey are part of an 11,000-acre estate given to the nation by Mr Bowers Bourne of California and his son-in-law, Senator Arthur Vincent. They had owned the property for 31 years. The estate has been made into a National Park and covers most of the lake district, with walks and drives to all the beauty spots, although cars are not allowed to some parts of the estate. **Muckross House** (*open all year, daily, 9–7 in summer, 5.30 in winter; adm, gardens free; for a small extra fee you can visit a traditional working farm within the estate;* ✆ *(064) 31440*) was built in Tudor style by Henry Arthur Herbert in 1843, whose family were landlords in the area. The main rooms are furnished in splendid Victorian style. The rest of the house has been transformed into a museum of Kerry folklore with a craftshop in its basement. You can see a potter, a weaver and blacksmith at their trades. There is a very informative film of the geology and natural beauties of the park, which is put on every half-hour. The gardens around the house are delightful, and here you can see the native Killarney strawberry tree (arbutus)—an evergreen with creamy white flowers followed by fruits which resemble strawberries. Close by, overlooking the lower lake, is **Muckross Abbey**, a graceful Early-English ruin founded for the Observatine Franciscans in 1448. In fact, this area is a stage set for everything the tourist wishes to see, and the natural beauty of the setting is enhanced by superb gardens. There is a gigantic yew tree in the centre of the cloister.

The **Gap of Dunloe** can be approached further along the main Killarney–Kenmare Road (N71) and there is plenty to stop for en route. Notice the strawberry tree, or arbutus, growing among ferns and oaks, and the pink saxifrage on the wayside. All of the following are well-signposted. You can stop and take the woodland path to the **Torc Waterfall**, found by following a rough road on the left just before a sign cautioning motorists about deer. The walk is very short, leading you through splendid fir trees to the 60ft (18m) falls. It is also possible to drive there and park. Return to the main road. For another little detour to some falls, continue on past the Galway Bridge where you can follow the stream up into the hills to the **Derrycunnihy Cascades**. Maybe you will come upon a few sika (Japanese deer) or red native deer. The cascades are set in primeval oak woods, and this is a rich botanical site of ferns and mosses. Go back to the main road again (N71) and continue for 6 miles (9.7km) to **Ladies' View**, which gives you a marvellous view of the upper lake and a hideous tourist shop-cum-café. Now turn off right before Moll's Gap and right again along the dirt track. You are now in the **Gap of Dunloe**, a beautiful wild gorge bordered by the dark Macgillycuddy's Reeks, the Purple Mountain and Tomies Mountain. You can explore the Gap with some arduous walking. This is some of the best ridge-walking country in Ireland. If you do go walking, even for a short stroll, you should carry good waterproof gear, as the weather comes straight in from the Atlantic. The Macgillycuddy's Reeks include Carrantuohill, at 3414ft (1040m), the highest mountain in Ireland.

If you are interested in seeing a fine example of ogham stones, take the main road for Killorglin (R567), past the Dunluce Castle Hotel. Turn right down a hill to a T-junction, and right again, over the bridge and up the hill. A signpost points left to a collection of ogham stones in a wired enclosure high on the bank. This is the best place in Kerry to see the weird ogham writing, the only form that existed before the arrival of Christianity. The lateral strokes incised into the stone and crossing a vertical line give the name of a man long, long dead.

Another fine view of the Killarney lakes and mountains can be seen from **Aghadoe Hill**. It is not at all touristy. In pagan times, the hill was believed to be the birthplace of all beauty, and lovers still meet here. The legend goes that whoever falls in love on Aghadoe Hill will be blessed for a lifetime. To get there from the centre of Killarney, take the Tralee road until you see a sign for Aghadoe Heights Hotel. The view opens up around the hotel. One of the youth hostels is also in this direction (*see* p.158).

The Ring of Kerry

The road which makes up the **Ring of Kerry** is 112 miles (180km) long, and takes about three hours to drive without any detours. Starting back at Kenmare, one can take the N70 and follow the coiling road south around the coast—stopping to enjoy the views, and perhaps setting off down the tiny R roads to get a better look at **St Finan's Bay, Bolus Head** and **Doulus Head**. The ring ends at Killorglin. (You can, of course, travel the Ring anti-clockwise, starting from Killarney on the Killorglin road. The views are equally good.)

Detour to the Interior

Alternatively, as the Ring does not venture deeply into the interior of the Iveragh Peninsula, you could do just that by travelling to the lake area of Caragh, Glencar and Lough Cloon, which will take at least half a day. This wild, mountainous landscape was the hunting ground of the legendary Fionn MacCumhail (Finn MacCool) and it is absolutely delightful. Myriad little roads lead up to these parts. Perhaps the simplest is the lonely road through the **Ballaghisheen Pass**, which is unnumbered and runs between Killorglin and Waterville. It actually branches off the N70 just north of Waterville by Inny Bridge. The Caragh River is famous for its early salmon, and the Macgillycuddy's Reeks cast their great height against the skyline all the way. At the north end of Lough Cloon, up a small road to some farmhouses and then right along a track, is an ancient settlement with ruined clochans (beehive huts) and terraced fields. Up in the wild country, turn right at Bealalaw Bridge and continue on until you come to a right fork over the Owenroe River which takes you into the Ballaghbeama Gap and joins a larger road to Sneem. This takes you through a tortuous and breathtaking channel between two mountains, Knocklomena and Knockavulloge, named in Irish after the golden gorse which grows on their slopes. Traces of the Early-Bronze Age Beaker people have been found here in rock carvings. The Kerry Way, a signed route for walkers starts at Glenbeigh and follows a desolate and beautiful route through the Reeks.

Back to the Ring Again

Sneem is a quiet village (out of season) divided by the Sneem river. It has a good pub and was attractively laid out by an 18th-century landlord. On the central green is a recently erected monument to De Gaulle who once spent two weeks here; locals refer to it affectionately as 'Da Gallstone'.

About 10 miles (15km) west of Sneem, continuing on the N70, there is a signpost right to **Staigue Fort**—isolated at the head of a desolate valley, and about 2500 years old. The circular stone fort rises out of a field, and a large bank and ditch surround it. The fort has a tremendous atmosphere and ancient strength about it; the farmer who owns the field has been known to demand an entry fee. Beyond Castlecove village on the N70 is **White Strand**, which is superb for bathing.

West again on the N70, a mile (1.6 km) from Catherdaniel is **Derrynane House** (*open May–Sept, 9–6; Oct–April, daily, 11–5; adm; ✆ (066) 75113*), the home of Daniel O'Connell, 'the Great Liberator', who won Catholic emancipation in 1829. It contains many of his possessions and is beautifully kept as a museum. The mellow simplicity of the house is very appealing, and the video of his life well worth watching. He believed that 'no political change whatsoever is worth the shedding of a single drop of human blood.' His family typified the old Irish ways of hospitality. They got on easily with all their neighbours, whether the hard-drinking gentry or the fisherfolk. Daniel O'Connell himself was fostered out when a baby to some island people, a custom which has its roots in ancient Ireland. His aunt Eileen wrote a wonderful lamentation on the death of her husband, Art O'Leary, who was killed for refusing to sell his fine mare to a Protestant named Morris for the sum of £5. (Catholics under the penal laws of the time were not allowed to own a horse of greater value than this.) This extract is from the beginning, when she entreats his dead body to rise up:

> *My love and my delight*
> *Stand up now beside me,*
> *And let me lead you home*
> *Until I make a feast,*
> *And I will roast the meat*
> *And send for company*
> *And call the harpers in,*
> *And I will make your bed*
> *Of soft and snowy sheets*
> *And blankets dark and rough*
> *To warm the beloved limbs*
> *An Autumn blast has chilled.*

Translated by Frank O'Connor

The grounds have exceptionally fine coastal scenery, and form a park of 298 acres. **Derrynane Bay** has one of the most glorious strands in the country.

A few miles further round the coast, **Waterville** is the main resort of the Ring; palm trees and fuchsia imbue it with a Continental air. The people speak Gaelic, the Munster variety, and **Ballinskelligs Bay** is a favourite place for Gaelic-speaking students, who stay in the B&Bs here. The beach is very beautiful with splendid views. This area is a rich source of legend. The story goes that it was near Waterville that Cessair, the grand-daughter of Noah, landed with her father, two other men and 49 women. They were hoping to escape the Great Flood of the Bible story. The year, apparently, was 2958 BC! The women divided the three men amongst them but two of them died and the third, Fintan, was so reluctant to remain with the women that he fled and later turned himself into a salmon. This peninsula was also the landing point of another invasion: the coming of the Celts. The 12th-century manuscript The *Book of Invasions*, or the *Lebor Gabala*, describes it as follows. The Milesians had got to Spain, and there they built a watch-tower from which they saw Ireland, and it looked so green and beautiful that they set sail for it. Their poet, Amergin, sang a poem of mystical incantations as he first touched the Irish shore. The poem itself is rather beautiful, and this is part of what he sings:

> *I am the womb: of every holt,*
> *I am the blaze: on every hill*
> *I am the queen: of every hive,*
> *I am the shield: for every head*
> *I am the grave: of every hope.*

Version by Robert Graves

The *Book of Invasions* states that the Celts arrived on the 1 May 1700 BC. As you enter Waterville on the N70, on the skyline to your right is an alignment of four stones. This is supposed to be the burial place of Scene, wife of one of the eight leaders of the Milesians.

Cahirciveen to Killorglin

A theatrical tower guards the bridge and the inlet at **Cahirciveen**. It used to be the police barracks but is now a heritage and tourist information centre. The design is grandiose Victorian, and was used for many other police barracks all over the British Empire. This area is marked by turf-cutting and dominated by the holy mountain, **Knocknadobar**. From the summit at 2267ft (690m), you get a wonderful view of the Dingle Peninsula and the Blasket Islands. Closer to, Valentia Island and the little harbour village of **Knightstown** is a pretty place to stay. Valentia was chosen as the site for the first transatlantic cable in 1858; natives could get in direct contact with New York but not with Dublin! Above the village the famous blue-grey Valentia slates were quarried. The quarry is no longer in use, but has been converted into a religious grotto. The views across to the mainland are magnificent. The Skellig Heritage Centre is beside the road bridge that links the island to Portmagee (*see* below). The N70 continues around the peninsula, passing close to Knocknadobar Mountain and along Kells Bay, which is a good place to bathe. This wildly romantic landscape is peopled with heroes from Ireland's legendary past: Fionn MacCumhail and the warrior band, the Fianna, hunted these glens. Close by, in the locality of **Rossbeigh** and **Glenbeigh** the landscape is rich in memories of Oísîn the son of Fionn, who came back here after his long sojourn in the land of youth. He had left with Niamh, a golden-haired beauty he had met on the Rossbeigh strand. It is fascinating to visit the Bog Village Museum at Glenbeigh (*open Mar–Nov, daily; adm*) which depicts life in the rural 1800s.

If you turn off the Ring of Kerry road (N70) here and drive up to the Ballaghisheen Pass, you can remember that this is where Oísín went looking for his companions in the Fianna, and from this great height surveyed the glens and mountains. He did not understand that three hundred years had passed whilst he was enchanted, and that they were long dead. This area is also strongly associated with the story of Diarmuid and Grainne (*see* pp.576 and 578), who stayed in a cave at Glenbeigh. The Ring of Kerry ends with the attractive town of Killorglin, which grew up around an Anglo-Norman castle on the River Laune. The castle is now ruined, but you can explore a similar one nearby at Ballymalis. It has been partly restored, and you can climb to the top of the 16th-century tower, which is great fun. It is always open, entry free. **Killorglin** is famous for its cattle and horse fair held in August, when vestiges of an ancient rite are enacted: a wild goat from the mountains is captured and enthroned in a cage in the centre of town. He is a symbol of the unrestricted merrymaking to follow. The event is known as the **Puck Fair**, and it may date from the worship of the Celtic God, Lug. Certainly, the '*craic*' (fun and entertainment) is good; book in advance if you want to stay overnight in the town.

The Skelligs

A trip to the **Skelligs** will take a whole day and is a highpoint of any visit to this part of the country. These rocky islands lie at the mouth of Ballinskelligs Bay and rise dramatically from the sea. The Small Skellig is covered in thousands of gannets, whilst the Great Skellig, or Skellig Michael, has on it an almost perfect example of an early monastic settlement which was in use between the 6th and 12th centuries. The Gaelic word *sceilig* means splinter of stone, and you can only wonder at the skill of the men who cut and shaped that stone.

A sea cruise around the islands can be taken from the Heritage Centre on Valentia Island, Cahirciveen or Dingle. If you wish to go yourself and stop off at the islands, boats can be hired at Caherdaniel or Derrynane pier. (For details, *see* 'Getting Around'.) At the time of writing, landings have been limited to Sun, Mon, and Tues during the high season. Check with the tourist office. Take a waterproof jacket, flat shoes, a picnic, and, if you are keen on birdlife, a pair of binoculars. The trip out there can be very rough, and it illuminates something of the need for solitude that those holy men hungered for. You land to the noisy fury of the seabirds, and approach the monastery up a stairway 540ft (164m) long, hacked out of stone over a thousand years ago. On this barren rock half a mile long and three-quarters of a mile wide (800m by 1200m), there was little these holy men could do there except pray and meditate. The way of life must have been hard; sometimes the waves crashing around the rock reach enormous heights. You can see beehive huts, stone crosses, the holy well, oratories and cemeteries. These are laid out close together; the oratories and the medieval **St Michael's Church** are separated from the six cells or beehive huts by the holy well. The fresh water on this desolate island is provided from the rock fissures, which hold rainwater. The Vikings raided the monastery in AD 812 and 823, but in AD 956, Olaf Trygveson, the son of the King of Norway was baptized here. When he became king he introduced Christianity to Scandinavia. The monastery here grew independent of the authorities in Rome, as did the clerics in Ireland as a whole. The Celtic church refused to follow a 7th-century ruling about the time of Easter, and it was not until medieval times that the Skelligs fell into line. The **Skellig Heritage Centre** (*open May–Sept; ✆ (066) 76306*) interprets the life of the monks on Skellig Michael through film, graphics and models. It also gives information about the bird-life, water-life and the light-house service. Books, crafts and snacks for sale.

The Dingle Peninsula

Annascaul to Dingle Town

There are several ways into the peninsula. The most obvious is to continue on the N70 to Castlemaine and then to **Annascaul** on the R561, which passes the beautiful sandy beach at Inch. The spectacular way to get to Dingle, however, is via Camp on the R559, and the Glennagalt Valley—the Glen of the Madmen. Mad people were taken here to recover, helped perhaps by the magnificent scenery between the Beenoskee Massifs. (Incidentally, the Irish phrase for someone who has gone mad is, 'he's away with his head'.) This is the way the old railway used to go, dropping down to Annascaul where you can get a drink at the South Pole Inn, called so because the former proprietor, Tom Crean, was with Scott in the Antarctic.

Dingle is a big fishing town. It has developed in the most attractive way. The gaily painted houses and busy streets lead you to the harbour where the fishing boats move gently in the swell of the tide. The catches off this part of the coast are terrific, but the boats are small and high-tech methods have not yet arrived. This adds greatly to the charm of the scene. The Roman Catholic church in the centre of the town is a dim, calm place full of a feeling of welcome. In a different way the cafés and bars invite one to linger, and give the town a delightful holiday atmosphere. James Flahire's Bar by the harbour is full of clutter and old-fashioned furnishings, and in Dick Mack's in Green Lane you can buy not only a pint but also a selection of footwear. Ireland used to have many such places, but they are rapidly disappearing. There are several good craft shops to browse in. The local celebrity and major attraction, however, is undoubtedly Fungi, a playful dolphin who wandered into the bay some years ago. His fame is such that the writer Vikram Seth has planned an opera in his honour.

If you decide to base yourself in Dingle for a few days, there are many beautiful places to explore nearby. You can walk in the **Slieve Mish Mountains**, where there is not only wild beauty but a fund of archaeological remains. To the northeast of Annascaul, on the right summit of Caherconree Mountain, is a rare example of an inland promontory fort. It dates from about 500 BC and is associated with Cú Chulainn, the great Ulster hero. (Notorious for his attraction to woman, in this story he rescues a damsel in distress, and carries her off to the North of Ireland.) From the great **Strand of Inch** you have views of the Blasket Islands. In the pubs, after ten in the evenings, you can listen to traditional music or singing, which just happens when the locals get together. Dingle comes from the Irish *daingean*, meaning fortress, but nothing remains of one now. The local people speak

Irish amongst themselves, though you will find that they will switch to English when you are around, for courtesy's sake. West of Dingle is wonderful, austere country battered by the Atlantic wind and sea.

Ventry has a lonely white strand on which it is said the King of the other World, Donn, landed to subjugate Ireland. He had come to help the King of France avenge his honour as Fionn had run off with his wife and daughter. The great Fionn MacCumhaill and his Fenian knights won the day, of course (*see* **Old Gods and Heroes**, p. 578). On the road to Shea Head, just off the R559 at Fahan and about 3 miles (6km) past Ventry, there is a group of Early-Christian **clochans**—414 in all. Local farmers still build little clochans as storehouses for animals, and the continuity of style with the unmortared stone is such that you cannot tell the old from the new. Nineteen souterrains (underground passages and storage places) and 18 standing stones, two sculptured crosses and seven ring-forts are strewn all over the slopes of Mount Eagle; the most prominent is the powerfully built Doonbeg Fort, which can be seen from the road, surrounded by the sea on three sides. The fort is dated between 400 and 50 BC. It was well protected by several defensive, earthen walls and an inner stone wall. Inside, local people and livestock would have gathered when under threat by rival tribal groups. There is a souterrain leading from the inside of the fort to the entrance. The road from Fahan winds round the countryside to Shea Head, from where you can see the Blasket Islands.

The Blasket Islands

The Blaskets are made up of several tiny islands and the Great Blasket, all now uninhabited. Charles Haughey, the politician, owns one of them as a holiday retreat.

Some beautiful writing has sprung from the Great Blasket, produced just before the island way of life collapsed in the 1940s. The young emigrated because of the harsh living conditions, and the Great Blasket has been uninhabited since 1953. The accounts of island life left to us through the writing record the warmth and the fun, as well as the misery and heartbreak, of their hard way of life. Their acceptance of death and life has great dignity, as does their sense of comradeship with the others on the island. There are three autobiographies written in the 1920s and 1930s: *The Islandman* by Tomas O'Crohan, *Twenty Years a-Growing* by Maurice O'Sullivan, and the autobiography of Peig Sayers. All are worth reading for the humour, pathos and command of the Gaelic language, which comes through even in translation. The **Dunquin Heritage Centre** (*open daily in high season; adm*) focuses on the story of the Blaskets.

You can visit the Blaskets from Dingle or Dunquin Harbour. Kruger's Pub in Dunquin is the place to enquire about boats and departure times. You might be lucky and persuade a local to take you out there in a **curragh**, the boat used for centuries by the Island men to catch the shining mackerel found in these waters. When you arrive, you will see that the Great Blasket is full of memories. If you have read the literature, you will recognize the White Strand where the islanders played hurling on Christmas morning. But the stone walls around the intensively farmed fields have now tumbled, and the village is a ruin. Tomas O'Crohan wrote at the end of his account: 'somewhere there should be a memorial of it all...for the like of us will never be again.' It is a pleasant walk up to the ruined hill-fort and there are wonderful views.

Back on the mainland again, heading north up round the peninsula, at **Ballyferriter** there is an active, friendly co-operative which grows parsley to export to France. They are also very keen on preserving their heritage—the Gaelic language, antiquities, and beautiful scenery. You can look around their heritage centre (*call © (066) 56100 for times of opening*). At **Ballydavid** the ancient industry of curragh-making goes on. The beaches around here are magnificent, in particular **Smerwick Strand**. In any of these you might find Kerry diamonds—sparkly pieces of quartz, a nicer souvenir than anything you could buy.

East of Ballyferriter lies the perfectly preserved **Oratory of Gallarus**—a relic of early Christianity. It is built of corbelled stone and is so watertight that not a drop of rain has entered it for a thousand years. The only missing section of the original building are the crosses which stood at each end of the roof ridge. Always accessible, and entry is free. At the crossroads above Gallarus, turn sharp left for **Kilmalkedar Church**, built in Irish Romanesque style in the 12th century. There must have been an earlier pagan settlement here as there are some ancient carved stones around the site. Nearby is the Saint's Road up the Brandon Mountain. This ancient track leads up to **St Brendan the Navigator's Shrine**. St Brendan climbed up to its summit to meditate and saw in a vision Hy-Brasil, the Island of the Blessed, and afterwards he voyaged far and wide looking for this ideal land. People still climb up here on the last Saturday in June to pray. An easier climb can be made from the village of **Cloghane** and the views from it are magical. It's not surprising that St Brendan saw Utopia from here!

The main (unnumbered) road from Dingle to Stradbally and on to Tralee (R560) takes you over the **Connor Pass**, the summit of which is 1500ft (497m) with great views over Dingle Bay. There are dark loughs in the valley and giant boulders are strewn everywhere. At the foot of the pass, a branch road leads off to Cloghane and Brandon,-both good bases for exploring and climbing the sea cliffs around Brandon Point and Brandon Head.

Tralee is the chief town and administrative capital of County Kerry. It is famous outside Ireland for the lovely Victorian song 'The Rose of Tralee'. The town was the chief seat of the Desmond family, but nothing remains of their strong castle. The old Dominican friary that the Desmonds founded was completely destroyed by the Elizabethan courtier soldier Sir William Denny, who was granted the town when the Desmond estates were seized.

The town has suffered continually from wars and burnings, and today is largely mid-19th-century in character although there are some fine Georgian houses in the centre. The Courthouse has a fine Ionic façade, and in Derry Street is an impressive 1798 Memorial. The Dominican Church of Holy Cross is by Pugin and contains ancient carved stones. In Abbey Street there is a modern church with a lovely chapel dedicated to the Blessed Virgin Mary, which contains some fine work in stained glass by that great artist Michael Healy, who worked at the turn of the century. The Ashe Memorial Hall, an imposing 19th-century building off Denny Street, is a very fine **County Musuem** *(open all year, Mon–Sat 10–6, Sun 2–6; adm; ☎ (066) 27777)*. The displays trace the history of Kerry from 5,000 BC, and the exhibits include archaeological treasures found in Kerry. Another attraction is the reconstructed town of medieval Tralee, you travel through the streets in a 'time-car'. The Tralee steam train leaves from Ballyard station; the 3km jaunt takes you to Blennerville working windmill, complete with restaurant and craft shops. It is possible to buy a 'passport ticket' which covers all Tralee's attractions. **Crag Cave**, Castle Island is an underground cave system at least 4km long *(signposted off the N21 Limerick to Tralee road; open all year; adm ; ☎ (066) 41244)*.

North Kerry

North Kerry has none of the splendour of Dingle but a rather quiet charm, a taste of which you will get if you drive between Tralee and Tarbert on your way to County Clare.

Places to go in north Kerry include **Ardfert Cathedral** on the R551, a noble Early-English Romanesque building dating from the 13th century. Like many Irish ruins, it is rather neglected, but therein lies much of its charm. There are many modern graves built inside the ancient walls, and a stern warning (obviously ignored) from the Office of Public Works that this must stop. Open all the time, although restoration work seems to be ongoing. **Banna** and **Ballyheige** have lovely strands. **Listowel** has ambitions as a cultural centre and puts on a **Writers' Week** every year with a book fair, art and photography exhibitions, plus short-story-writing workshops *(dates change every year, so check with tourist office for details)*. The attractive town is situated on the River Feale, with a ruined 15th-century castle in the square. It belonged to the Fitzmaurice family, Anglo-Normans who later showed consistent disloyalty to the Crown. Many writers came from this area; of particular note is Bryan MacMahon, whose wonderful novel *Children of the Rainbow* will keep you entranced with its descriptions of the Kerry countryside. On the coast, some 10 miles (16km) southwest of Listowel on the R553 is the delightful resort of **Ballybunion**. Besides good sea bathing, you can have a hot seaweed bath, which makes you feel very relaxed and seems to take away any aches and pains *(see* 'Activities'). **Carrigafoyle Castle** north of Ballylongford is a 16th-century O'Connor Castle. Always accessible, you can walk to the battlements by a winding stone staircase from which you get a stunning view.

If you are taking the car ferry across to County Clare from **Tarbert**, you may visit **Tarbert House** *(open May–mid August, 10–12 and 2–4; ☎ (068) 36198)* with its fine Georgian furniture and lovely Irish Chippendale mirror.

Killarney crafts: The Bricui, High Street and College Street; Blarney Woollen Mills and Serendipity in College Street, and Avoca handweavers at Moll's Gap. McBeas is a good little department store.

Ring of Kerry crafts: The Homestead Craft Shop and Sneem Craft Workshops. Gleann Bhride Handweavers, Waterville. Clay Pottery and Gallery in Cahirciveen. Sheeog Irish Handcrafts in Killorglin. Nostalgia for linen sheets, De Barra for Celtic jewellery.

Kenmare crafts: Kenmare Homespuns, the Craft Shop, Cleo's for elegant tweed suits, linen and woven rugs. The Kenmare Lace and Design Centre, The Square, Street, sells locally made lace, ✆ (064) 41679. Quill's Woollen Market, Kenmare, Brenmar Jon on Henry Street, ✆ (064) 41138 for designer knitwear.

Dingle crafts: Commodum Craft Centre, Irish Crafts, Oliver McDonnell in Green Street, Dingle. Arts and Crafts in Strand Street, Dingle. Café Liteartha, Dykegate Street, Dingle, for Irish books and tapes. Pottery and tea shop in Ventry. Dunquin Pottery and Café in Dunquin. Handweaving and pottery by Louis Mulcahy in Ballyferriter at the Potadoireacht na Caoloigne Centre. Weaving by Lisbeth Mulcahy, Green Street, Dingle and silver jewellery by Brian de Staic, Green Street, Dingle.

Tralee crafts and clothes: Carraig Donn Knitwear, Bridge Street, Tralee. Penny's Pottery, The Square, Tralee, ✆ (066) 59962 Lots of chunky lavender-blue pottery.

Delicacies: wild smoked salmon from Ted Browne, Kilquane, Ballydavid, Dingle; ✆ (066) 55183. Delicious smoked bacon and black pudding from Norreen Curran, Green Street, Dingle; ✆ (066) 51398. Farmhouse cheese, yoghurt, pizzas and cheesecake from Lisette and Peter Kal, the White House, Tuosist, Kenmare, ✆ (064) 84500. (The Kals also hire out bikes and organize boat trips for fishing. Their house is signposted from the R571 going southwest from Kenmare.) The Pantry, 30 Henry Street, Kenmare, ✆ (064) 31326, for homemade bread, Capparoe goat's cheese, and other picnic ingredients. Seancara, Courthouse Lane, Tralee, for more excellent farmhouse cheeses, and homemade bread and lemon curd.

Activities

Deep-sea fishing: Mr N. O'Connor, Ventry, ✆ (066) 59947; Michael O'Sullivan, Waterville, ✆ (0661) 74255; George Burgum, Dingle, ✆ (066) 51337. Excellent deep-sea angling in the Kenmore River Estuary, Valentia Island and off Ballydavid Head.

Shore-angling: all round the Dingle Peninsula and Ring of Kerry. Ask in the Dingle tourist office for details.

Brown trout fishing: On Lough Leane and Lough Avaul and the Kenmare River.

Sea trout fishing: On the Inny River. Contact Club Med, ✆ (066) 74133; and the Butler Arms Hotel, Waterville, ✆ (066) 74144.

Salmon fishing: This is excellent on Lough Currane near Waterville. Contact the Waterville Fishery or Tourism development both on ✆ (066) 74366. Also, on River Laume and River Caragh. Contact Pat O'Grady on ✆ (066) 68228 or the Glencar Hotel, Glencar, ✆ (066) 60102.

Sailing and water-skiing: Parknasilla Great Southern Hotel, Parknasilla, ✆ (064) 45122. Dromquinna Manor, Kenmare, ✆ (064) 41657. The Aqua Dome, Ballyard, Tralee, ✆ (066) 28899. Waterworld complex.

Diving: in Ventry and Dingle Bays: You can go diving with an amazing and much loved friendly dolphin called Fungi who has been living in Dingle Bay for a few years. Boat trips to see him are organized by Mr Donegan, ✆ (066) 51720; or you can walk for 1km east of Dingle to the bay where he lives. Wet suits are available for hire from shops and boats, The Pier, Dingle or from Seventh Wave, ✆ (066) 51548, near the bridge, Dingle. Des Lavelle operates a scuba-diving school from Valentia, ✆ (066) 56124. Skelligs Aquatics, Caherdaniel, ✆ (0667) 5277.

Sea sports: Derrynane Sea Sports, Caherdaniel, ✆ (066) 75266, diving, sailing etc.

Surfing: Inch Strand, Srudeen Strand, near Dingle. (Bring your own surf board.)

Seaweed baths: Collins family, North Beach, Ballybunion, ✆ (068) 27469. Open June to beginning October. Cost IR£4.00.

Swimming: White Strand, near Castlecove, Derrynane beach, and Kells Bay near Rossbeigh. Beaches around Shea Head and Stradbally, Ballyheige and Banna Sands in North Kerry.

Lake tours: Killarney Waterbus; ✆ (064) 32638 or Lily of Killarney, ✆ (064) 31068.

Pony-trekking: in Tralee, ✆ (066) 21840. The management specializes in trekking through the Dingle Peninsula. For trekking in the Killarney National Park ✆ (064) 31686. Equestrian Centre, Ballintagart, Dingle, ✆ (066) 51454.

Horse-racing: in Killarney throughout May and July, contact Michael Doyle, ✆ (064) 31459 for details; in Tralee in August and in Listowel in September. Look in the local newspapers, or in the back of the free calendar of events available from any tourist office.

Horse-drawn caravans: D. Slattery, 1 Russel Street, Tralee, ✆ (066) 21722.

Golf: Waterville, ✆ (0661) 74133. Killarney, ✆ (064) 31034. Tralee, ✆ (066) 36379. Ballybunion, ✆ (068) 27146.

Walking: The Kerry Way, a signposted route between Killarney, the Black Valley, Lough Acoose and Glenbeigh; and the Dingle Way, between Tralee Camp, Annascaul and Dingle. Contact the tourist office in Killarney for detailed maps. For general advice and help, contact Irish Wilderness Experience, 50 Woodlawn Park, Killarney, ☎ (064) 32922; and Arbutus Lodge Apartments, Aghadoe; ☎ (064) 31497. The 1:50,000 Ordnance Survey map no.78 'The Reeks' is very good. For excellent information on walking, fishing, contact Tracks and Trails, ☎ (064) 54196 at 53 High Street, Killarney. Kerry Country Rambles, Killarney, ☎ (064) 54196.

Open farms: Muckross Traditional Farm, Killarney, ☎ (064) 31440; Churchtown Farm Park, Killarney, ☎ (064) 44440.

Where to Stay

luxury

Park Hotel, Kenmare, ☎ (064) 41200. A château-style hotel with every modern comfort in rooms furnished with fine antiques. Everything about it is professional and first-rate. **Sheen Falls Lodge**, Kenmare, ☎ (064) 41600. Beautiful location and sunny low-key décor. Food is lavishand imaginative. Helipad for visiting dignitaries.

expensive

Caragh Lodge, Caragh Lake, ☎ (066) 69115. Comfortable and well-furnished country house in a wonderful situation overlooking the lake, with a fine garden. **Parknasilla Great Southern Hotel**, Parknasilla, ☎ (064) 45122. Comfortable hotel in a 19th-century mansion on the banks of the Kenmare River. Ask for a room in the older part. **Butler Arms Hotel**, Waterville, ☎ (0667) 4144. A Grade A hotel and lovely place to stay if you like salmon or trout fishing.

moderate

Killeen House hotel, Aghadoe, Lakes of Killarney, ☎ (064) 31711. Friendly, cosy little hotel up in the hills of Aghadoe, 10 minutes from Killarney and away from the crowds. **Doyle's Townhouse**, John Street, Dingle, ☎ (066) 51174. One of the most enjoyable places to stay in the country. The rooms are full of comfort and individuality, and the downstairs sitting-room has shelves and tables groaning with interesting books over which you can linger by a warm fire. The bar and restaurant next door are famous for their conviviality and good food. **Smugglers' Inn**, Waterville, ☎ (0667) 4330. Family-run and on the beach. **Glendalough House**, Caragh Lake, ☎ (066) 69156. Josephine Roder is an excellent hostess and has furnished her house with great love and care. Great views over the lake. **Listowel Arms**, The Square, Listowel, ☎ (068) 21500. Old-fashioned country hotel. **Dromquina Manor**, Kenmare, ☎ (064) 41657. Very comfortable with lovely views over the water. Waterskiing nearby. **Lansdowne Arms**, Main Street, Kenmare, ☎ (064) 41368. Friendly family-run hotel. **Lios Dana Natural Living Centre**, Inch, Annascaul, ☎ (066) 58189. Holistic retreat holidays. Overlooking Dingle Bay. **Club Mediterranée**, Waterville, ☎ (066) 74133. Shedding its sun image, lots of activities for the fit.

Hawthorne House, Shelbourne Street, Kenmare, ✆ (064) 41035. Extremely comfortable modern house, all bedrooms en suite. The food is delicious and lavish. **Carriglea House**, Muckross Road, Killarney, ✆ (064) 31116. Very close to Muckross House and the National Park, so you can avoid the busy centre of town. Comfortable rooms, with own bathrooms. The **Sugan Youth Hostel** in Killarney Town is good although fairly small, as is the restaurant beneath it, ✆ (064) 33104. **Lavelle Family**, Valentia Island, ✆ (066) 76124. This peaceful place is a lovely base from which to explore. Fabulous views. Mrs McKenna, **Mount Rivers**, Carhan Road, Cahirciveen, ✆ (0667) 2509. Comfortable rooms with bath in Victorian house. The O'Shea family, **Benmore Farm**, Oughtive, Waterville, ✆ (0667) 4207. Old farmhouse on mountain road. They will arrange boat trips to the Skelligs. **Aisling House**, Castlegregory, ✆ (066) 39134. Wonderful guesthouse: clean, comfortable and cheap, with a delicious breakfast. **Alpine House**, Dingle, ✆ (066) 51250. All rooms with bath. Mrs Curran, **Greenmount House**, Dingle, ✆ (066) 51414. Recommended by readers. Freshly squeezed orange juice and lots of choice for breakfast. The **Old Stone Cottage**, Chiddaun, Dingle, ✆ (066) 59882. Comfortable little cottage. **Ferntock**, Killorgan, ✆ (066) 61848. Well-run modern B&B, well-situated for golf and the 'Puck' festival. Very cheap: The **'An Oige' Killarney International Hostel**, ✆ (064) 31240, is 2km outside Killarney at Aghadoe. A crumbly looking hulk of a building set in pretty grounds. A free bus meets trains from Dublin and Cork.

self-catering

Traditional 3-bedroom stone-built house in Ventry, ✆ (066) 59962. **Penny Sheehy** also has some recently built properties for rent. 2-bedroomed farmhouse in traditional style, **Patrick O'Leary**, ✆ (064) 45132. From £100 per week. **Ballintagart Hostel and Equestrian Centre**, Dingle, ✆ (066) 51454. Converted 18th-century hunting lodge. Open fires & CH. **Bog View Hostel**, Annascaul, Dingle Peninsula. Converted school with turf fires. Also does B&B and evening meals. Modernised farmhouse, sleeps 6, close to Ballyferriter. Contact **Ms Naughton**, 20 Vineyard Hill Road, London SW19 7SH, ✆ (0181) 946 4782. From IR£180 a week. 3-bedroomed/3-star timber chalet with lush garden, Sneem. Call **Thomas Stans**, ✆ (064) 45100/(021) 273251 £400–£500 per week.

Eating Out

luxury

The **Park Hotel**, Kenmare, ✆ (064) 41200. Delicious French cuisine in grand surroundings.

expensive

Doyle's Seafood Bar and Restaurant, Dingle, ✆ (066) 51174. In a room reminiscent of an old Irish kitchen with stone floor and mellow wooden furniture, you can eat deliciously prepared seafood chosen by the very friendly and welcoming proprietors, John and Stella Doyle. **Nick's Restaurant and Pub**, Lower Bridge Street, Killorglin, ✆ (066) 61219. Large portions of seafood and steaks. Packed with local people singing 'My Irish Molly' round the piano. Very friendly and great fun. The **Strawberry Tree**, 24 Plunkett Street, Killarney, ✆ (064) 32688. One of the best restaurants in KIllarney. **Sheen Falls Lodge**, Kenmare, ✆ (064) 41600. Michelin-starred. **Beginish Restaurant**, Green Street, Dingle, ✆ (066) 51588. Enthusiastic staff and delicious seafood with a conservatory at the back.

moderate

An Leath Phingin, 35 Main Street, Kenmare, ✆ (064) 41559. The Italian chef, Maria, makes her own fresh pasta and scrumptious sauces to go with it. **Foley's Seafood and Steak Restaurant**, 23 High Street, Killarney, ✆ (064) 31217. Delicious seafood and lamb, also good vegetarian dishes. **Gaby's Restaurant**, 17 High Street, Killarney, ✆ (064) 32519. Mediterranean-style café with delicious seafood. Very popular locally. It does not take bookings, so arrive early. *Lunch served Tues–Sat, and dinner at 6pm.*

The **Lime Tree**, Kenmare, ✆ (064) 41225. Newly re-opened as an American-style café. **The Half-door**, John Street, Dingle, ✆ (066) 51600. Excellent and imaginative food. Very good value. **The Forge**, Holy Ground, Dingle, ✆ (066) 51209. Steaks and seafood. The **Smugglers' Inn**, Cliff Road, Waterville, ✆ (066) 74422. Good seafood in a restored farmhouse set on the beach. You can stay here very reasonably too.

Stone House, Sneem, ✆ (064) 45188. A guesthouse which produces reasonable Irish food. *Dinner only.* **Teach Cullain**, Cahirciveen, ✆ (0667) 2400. Traditional Irish food, meat and fish. **Graney's Fish and Chip Shop**, Dingle. Excellent and cheap take-aways. **Loaves and Fishes**, Caherdaniel, ✆ (0667) 5273. Food hearty but stylish. **Packies**, Henry Street, Kenmare, ✆ (064) 41508. Informal fish restaurant. **D'arcys Old Bank House**, Main Street, Kenmare, ✆ (064) 41589.

inexpensive/cheap

Purple Heather, Henry Street, Kenmare, ✆ (064) 41016. Good for lunch-time snacks, homemade soups and seafood. Cosy fire in bar. **Sugan Bistro**, Michael Collins Place, Killarney, ✆ (064) 33104. Near the railway station, a cheap wholefood bistro. **Anne's Kitchen**, Annascaul. Healthy snack lunch. **An Café Liteartha**, Dykegate Street, Dingle, ✆ (066) 51388. Bookshop and café serving sandwiches and soup.

The Islandman, Main Street, Dingle, ✆ (066) 51803 Very elegant bar/café/bookshop serving tasty food all day. **Whelans**, on the Main Street, Dingle, ✆ (066) 51620. Good Irish stew. **Ashes Bar**, Camp, ✆ (066) 30133. Seafood platter at lunchtime. More elaborate *à la carte* menu in the evening. Traditional music in the summer. **Ruth's Wholefood Kitchen**, 76 Boherbue, Tralee, ✆ (066) 22665. On the road into Tralee, the restaurant has consistently good vegetarian food and fresh spring water from the owner's farm. **Pizza Time**, The Square, Tralee, ✆ (066) 26317. Good pizza. **Lord Baker's**, Main Street,

Dingle, ✆ (066) 51277. Good bar food. The **Blue Bull**, South Square, Sneem, ✆ (064) 45382. The **Blind Piper**, restaurant and bar, Caherdaniel, ✆ (066) 75126. Good lively atmosphere in this pretty hamlet. **An Tailann**, Brickwell Lane, off New Street, Killarney, ✆ (064) 33083. Vegetarian lunches and dinners in sweet little cottage. **Yer Man's Pub**, 24 Plunkett Street, ✆ (064) 32688. Authentic and cosy little pub, sandwiches at lunch and a good nightclub at the back. The **Horseshoe** pub, Main Street, Kenmare. Popular pub with cosy fire; tables outside; serves food. **O'Donnatham's**, Henry Street, Kenmare. Old-style new pub. Determined to establish a reputation for its traditional music.

County Cork

Imagine quiet flowing rivers in green wooded valleys, a coastline which combines savage rock scenery with the softest bays, hillslopes which are purple in the late summer with bell heather, an ivy-clad castle standing amongst hayricks in a field, and you have captured something of Cork County.

This is Ireland's largest county and includes some of the richest agricultural land in the northeast, the important ocean port of Cobh, as well as the most beautiful coastal and mountain scenery in the country. It is also the most suitable spot to indulge in the relaxing pastimes of eating and drinking: some of Ireland's best hotels and restaurants are located in attractive settings all over the county. If you are into sports and culture, there is wonderful sailing, deep-sea angling, salmon and trout fishing, beautiful stately homes, gardens and, of course, the Blarney Stone to kiss! The growth of tourism has not spoilt the coast: it has just encouraged better quality craft shops, pubs and hotels. Many of the most discerning visitors are the Corkonians themselves, who work hard in the city and play in the pretty coastal resorts of Kinsale and Crosshaven.

The city is something else: the country people may be slow, but the city people have produced a cosmopolitan centre humming with energy and confidence, full of grand buildings and shops, industry and culture, aided by a wit and business sense that would be hard to beat. Dubliners alternate between jealousy and heavy sarcasm in trying to describe the place—the best I heard was 'God's own place with the devil's own people'. Corkonians think nothing of nipping across to Paris for the weekend, and there is an air of cultural sophistication which seriously challenges Dublin as the cultural capital. The Triskel Arts Centre in the city centre is excellent, and puts on a great variety of events all year around.

Corkonians are a mixed bunch, consisting of the down-to-earth working class and the monied middle class, which includes a rather genteel Protestant element whose forebears manned the British Empire; as well as quite a few 'blow-ins'—English and Continentals who have come for a variety of reasons and settled down to enjoy the way of life. The Cork accent is very strong, slow and sing-songy, so you will probably have to concentrate hard to understand it.

History

The history of Cork is similar to that of the rest of Munster; its well-watered and fertile lands attracted human settlement as far back as 6000 BC, when people lived by hunting, fishing, and gathering roots and berries. Kitchen middens found around the shores of Cork Harbour date from this time. From the Megalithic period there are stone circles, standing stones, and wedge tombs to explore. Written history dates from the coming of Christianity. St Ciaran of Cape Clear is titled 'first born of the Saints of Ireland', and it is claimed that he arrived before St Patrick in the 5th century AD. Early church sites abound, and with the invasion of the Anglo-Normans in 1169 the Continental religious orders were set up in rich and beautiful abbeys. Some of their ruins remain. The Norsemen or Vikings mounted many raids on the Early-Christian settlements from the late 8th century onwards. They soon founded their own ports, settling down to trade with the native Irish, and so gradually became amalgamated into Gaelic society. The Anglo-Norman invasion brought advanced building techniques to Ireland: the Norman war-lords built themselves sophisticated castles, usually on a defensive site which had been used before. Their followers made themselves moated farmhouses. In the 15th century the ruling families built themselves tower houses; many ruins remain to add drama and interest to the countryside and coastline. Comfortable domestic architecture did not develop until the 17th and 18th centuries, for the county was very unsettled whilst Celt and Anglo-Norman fought, made alliances with and against each other, and largely ignored the laws issued from London.

The administrators sent to implement English rule were successful after the Elizabethan wars of the late 16th century, when the land was planted with families loyal to the crown. Huge tracts of land were granted to men like Richard Boyle, who became Earl of Cork; and Sir Edmund Spenser, who wrote the long poem *The Faerie Queene* at Kilcoman Castle whilst he was Lord Deputy of Ireland. Beautiful Georgian houses survive from the 18th century, when the new landowners began to feel secure in their properties and build, plant and garden. It is possible to stay in some of these fine houses, which are not huge, but perfect in proportion and decoration.

By contrast, the oppressive laws introduced to control the Catholic population in the 1690s, the Rising of 1798 and the ghastly famine of the 1840s, all combined to create a peasantry that was poverty stricken. The Irish War of Independence was fought with ferocity in County Cork; there were many burnings and cruelties on both sides, and the Civil War split family loyalties in two. Michael Collins (1890–1922), the dynamic revolutionary leader and one of the men responsible for negotiating the Anglo-Irish treaty of December 1921, was the son of a small farmer in Clonakilty. During the Civil War he was shot in the head by the anti-Treaty forces in an ambush between Macroom and Bandon.

Today, the memories of the Civil War are still alive, but the people are forward-looking and sophisticated. Industries such as whiskey, brewing, clothing, food processing, computers and pharmaceuticals have boomed around Cork Harbour, and the Cork City inhabitants enjoy the amenities of their beautiful county.

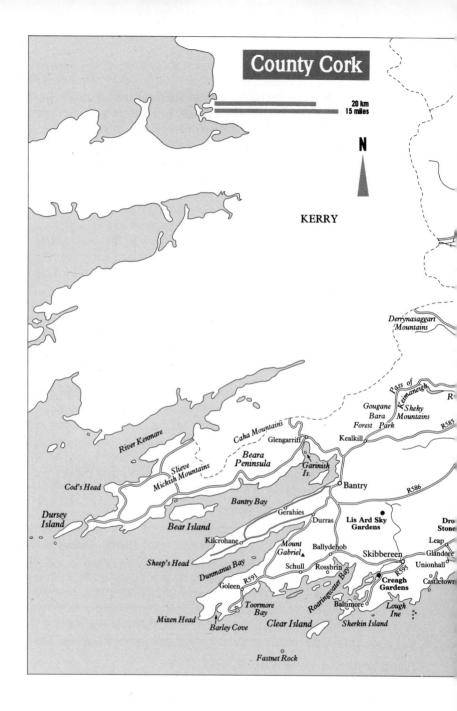

County Cork

20 km
15 miles

N

KERRY

Derrynasaggart
Mountains

Pass of Keimaneigh
R

Gougane   Shehy
Bara   Mountains
Forest   Park

R585

Caha Mountains

River Kenmare   Glengarriff   Kealkill

Beara
Peninsula   Garinish
Is.
Slieve
Mickish Mountains

Cod's Head   Bantry

R586

Bantry Bay

Dursey   Gerahies
Island   Durras   Lis Ard Sky   Dro
Bear Island   Gardens   Stone

Kilcrohane   Leap
Mount   Ballydehob
Gabriel   Ballydehob   Skibbereen   Glandore

Sheep's Head   Schull   Rossbrin   Unionhall

Dunmanus Bay   R591   Creagh
Goleen   Gardens   Castletown

Toormore   Baltimore   Lough
Bay   Ine
Mizen Head   Clear Island   Sherkin Island
Barley Cove

Fastnet Rock

162

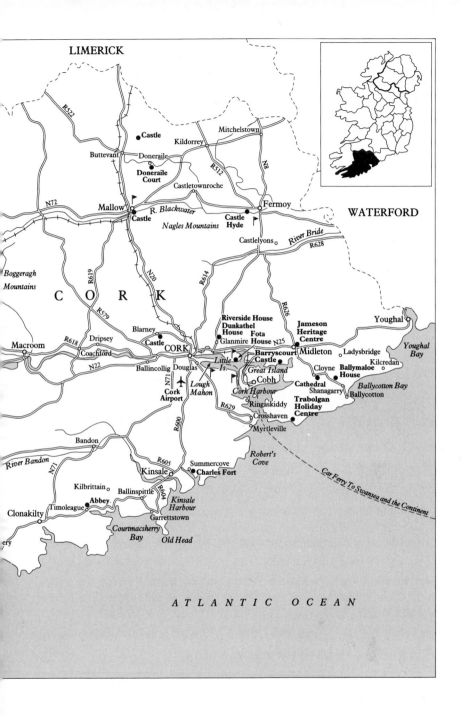

By air: Cork and Shannon International Airports.

By bus: Expressway buses from Dublin and other big towns, and a good local bus service in County Cork, ✆ (021) 506066/ 508188 Cork City Depot. Day tours and airport buses from Parnell Place, ✆ (021) 503399. Local buses from Patrick Street.

By rail: Cork is linked to Dublin and other areas by an excellent rail network. Trains from Kent Station, including a suburban service to Cobh. For all passenger enquiries, bus or train, ✆ (021) 504888.

By boat: to Ringaskiddy Ferryport near Cork City, between the Continent and Swansea, ✆ (021) 378036. Car and passenger ferry at Ringaskiddy Airport, 3¾ miles (6km) from the city centre, on the road to Kinsale. ✆ (021) 371185.

By car: car hire from Kevin O'Leary, Bandon, ✆ (023) 41264. Parking: disc system operates; tickets available from shops and post offices.

Taxis: Co-op, City Centre, Cork, ✆ (021) 272222; and ABC, ✆ (021) 961961.

By bike: bikes are available for hire from the Cycle Repair Shop, 6 Kyle Street, Cork, ✆ (021) 276255, Cycle Sane, 396 Blarney Street, ✆ (021) 301183, and from the Youth Hostel (central booking office), ✆ (01) 725399. Raleigh Rent-a-Bike network operates here. Your local dealers are Kramer's Bicycles, Glengariff Road, Newtown, Bantry, ✆ (027) 50278. Roycroft Bikes, Ilen Street, Skibbereen, ✆ (028) 21235/21810. Shortcastle Cycles, Shortcastle Street, Mallow, ✆ (022) 21843. J. O'Donovan, 4/5 South Main Street, Bandon ✆ (023) 41227.

getting to the islands

Sherkin Island: ferry from Baltimore sails seven times daily during the summer months and takes about 10 minutes, ✆ (028) 20125 for more details.

Cape Clear Island: during June, July and August, the island is serviced by two ferries: one from Schull and one from Baltimore. The Baltimore ferry runs at least twice daily, May to September, ✆ (028) 39119. The Schull ferry operates from June to September, ✆ (028) 28138.

Bear Island: off Castletownbere in Bantry Bay. Two ferries offer a frequent service in the summer months. Contact Colm Harrington, ✆ (027) 75000; or Patrick Murphy, ✆ (027) 75004.

Shearwater Cruises, Seaview Farm, Kilbrittain, ✆ (023) 49610, offers cruises to offshore islands leaving from Kinsale.

Tourist Information

Cork, Tourist House, Grand Parade, ✆ (021) 273251, all year.

Cork Airport, ✆ (021) 964347, June to September.

Skibbereen, Town Hall, ✆ (028) 21766, all year.

Youghal, Market House, Market Place, ✆ (024) 92390, June to September.

Bantry, ✆ (027) 50229, June to September.

Kinsale, ✆ (021) 772234, March to November.

Clonakilty, ✆ (023) 33226, July and August.

Glengarriff, ✆ (027) 63084, July and August.

Festivals

Cork City

End April/early May: Cork International Choral and Folk Dance Festival; contact ✆ (021) 308308, John Fitzpatrick.

June: Cork Dry Gin Round-Ireland Sailing Race, a biennial event held in even-numbered years, starting in Dublin. Contact the tourist office.

July: International Folk Dance Festival, Cobh. Contact Noel O'Driscoll, ✆ (021) 504233.

Mid-July: Cork Sailing Festival, held in even-numbered years. Based at Crosshaven, Royal Cork Yacht Club. Contact Donal Healy, ✆ (021) 831023.

August: Cobh Regatta, ✆ (021) 811237.

September/October: International film festival, ✆ (021) 271711, Anne O'Sullivan.

Late October: Cork Jazz Festival, ✆ (021) 270463.

Co. Cork

March: Ballydehob Races, ✆ (028) 37191.

May: Aquatic and Vintage Car Weekends in Kinsale, ✆ (021) 774026. Bantry Mussel Festival; ✆ (027) 50360.

June: Kinsale Arts Week, ✆ (021) 774026. Charlesville Cheese and Song Contest; ✆ (063) 81407.

July: Walter Raleigh Potato Festival, Youghal; ✆ (024) 92390. Festival of West Cork in Clonakilty, ✆ (028) 21766. Maid of the Isle Festival, Skibbereen, ✆ (028) 21200. Cahirmee Festival, Buttevant, ✆ (022) 23556. Kinsale Regatta, Castletownshead, ✆ (028) 36146.

August: Mallow Horse Races, ✆ (022)21338; Schull and Baltimore Regattas ✆ (028) 20125. Timoleague Harvest Festival, ✆ (023) 46120.

August: All Ireland Busking Festival, Youghal.

Sept/October: Gourmet Festival, Kinsale, ✆ (021) 774026 (Peter Barry).

Cork City

The name Cork comes from the Gaelic *Corcaigh*, which means 'a marshy place'. Ireland's second city, with a population of 135,000, is built on marshy land on the banks of the River Lee, and has crept up the hills. The river flows in two main channels, crossed by bridges, so that central Cork is actually on an island. It is a bit confusing if you are driving there for the first time, with its one-way roads and the crossing and recrossing of the river.

Until the Anglo-Norman invasion in 1179, Cork City was largely a Danish stronghold, though it first became known in the 7th century as an excellent school under St Finbarr. The Cork citizens were an independent lot and although after 1180 English laws were nominally in force, it was really the wealthy merchants who were in charge and decided things. In 1492 they took up the cause of Perkin Warbeck and went with him to Kent where he was proclaimed Pretender to the English crown—Richard IV, King of England and Lord of Ireland. They lost their charter for that piece of impudence, but Cork continued to be a rebel city. William III laid siege to it in 1690 because it stood by James II, and it had to surrender without honour. In the 17th and 18th centuries it grew rapidly with the expansion of the butter trade, and many of the splendid Georgian buildings you can still see were built during this time. In the 19th century it became a centre for the Fenian movement, which worked for an independent republic. During the War of Independence 1919–21, the city was badly burned by the Black and Tans and one of Cork's mayors died on hunger strike in an English prison. But Cork is also famous for a more moderate character, Father Theobald Matthew (1790–1856), who persuaded thousands of people to go off the drink, though the effect of his temperance drive was ruined by the potato famine and the general misery it brought.

Cork still has a reputation for clannish behaviour amongst its businessmen, and for independence in the arts and politics, but you would be hard put to it to find a friendlier city to wander around, and you can easily explore it on foot.

CORK

1 Bus Office	12 St Ann's Church, Shandon	22 English Market
2 Christchurch	13 St Finbarr's Cathedral	23 The Granary Theatre
3 Church of St Francis	14 The Lough	24 St Mary's Pro Cathedral
4 Crawford School of Art	15 Tourists Office	25 South Chapel
5 Fitzgerald Park	16 University College	26 To Cork Airport
6 G.A.A. Athletic Grounds	17 University Sports Ground, Mardyke	27 To Car Ferry at Ringaskiddy and Crosshaven
7 Mardyke Walk	18 Coal Quay	28 Cork Gaol
8 Marina	19 SS Peter & Paul Church, off Patrick St.	
9 Opera House	20 Court House	
10 Railway Station	21 Father Mathew Memorial Church	
11 Red Abbey		

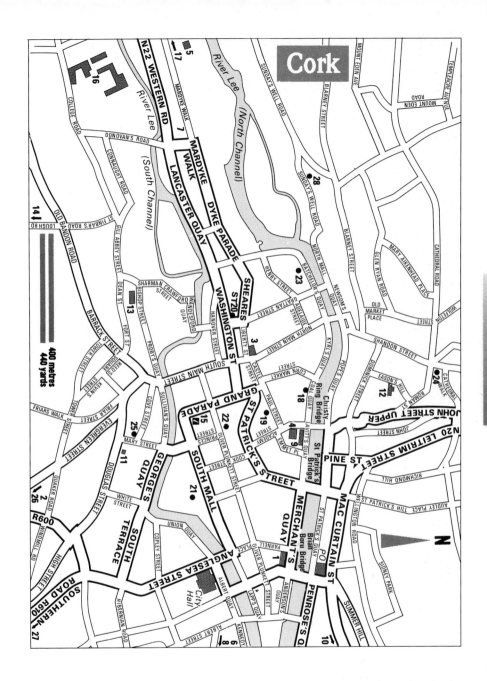

City Centre

Cork's business and shopping centre is crowded onto an island, with elegant bridges linking the north and south sides of the city. The first thing you will notice about the city is its skyline which, like Derry, is still 19th-century. Cork has spires and gracious wide streets. St Patrick's Street curves close to the river; one side of the street is lined with old buildings, the other by uninspiring modern office and shop fronts built after the burning in 1920. Here you will find a statue of Father Matthew. The covered **English Market**, off Patrick Street, is fun to wander round; notice the fountain with birds and bulrushes cast in iron. It mostly sells food, and is rather like Smithfield in London. **Cornmarket Street** has an open-air flea market, usually called Coal Quay, where you can bargain for trifles and observe the sharp-tongued store owners. Also off St Patrick Street is **SS Peter and Paul Church**, a Gothic-style building designed by the younger Pugin.

The South Mall to the south of the island, and the adjoining Grand Parade have some pretty buildings. In Washington Street, east of Grand Parade, is the magnificent Corinthian façade of the 19th-century **Court House**. Off South Mall is the **Father Matthew Memorial Church** facing Charlotte Quay with a fine-stained glass window dedicated to Daniel O'Connell, 'the Great Liberator'. Between South Mall and Grand Parade is the fine 18th-century **Christ Church**, used today to house the archives of the county. At the south end of the Grand Parade is a monument to Ireland's patriot dead, and the tourist office. **Crawford Art Gallery** in Emmett Place has a stunning collection of works by Irish artists such as Sean Keating, Orpen, and Walter Osbourne. There are also some very good 19th-century paintings. The Gallery Café is excellent after the exhausting pastime of art appreciation (*open daily; © (021) 273377 for more details*). Nearby, in Park Street, are excellent craft shops to browse in. Opposite North Mall, on Cork Island still, the **Old Maltings** buildings have been adapted for the use of the University of Cork. This complex includes a small theatre called **The Granary**. Swans, the symbol of Cork City, are fed near here, so there are often large flocks of them. Close to the maltings is the large Mercy Hospital, off Grenville Place, which incorporates the 1767 **Mansion House**, built as the official residence of the Mayor of Cork.

If you follow the river westwards along Dyke Parade and leafy Mardyke Walk, and then cut south across Western Road, you will come to the Oxbridge-style **University College**, which is grouped around a 19th-century Gothic square. The only modern building is the **Boole Library**, opened in 1985. It is named in honour of George Boole (1815–1864) who was the first professor of mathematics here, and who is credited with working out the principles of modern computer logic. The Roman Catholic **Honan Chapel** is a period piece of Celtic revivalism, copied from Cormac's Chapel on the Rock of Cashel. Close to the university is **Cork City Museum** (*open daily, Mon–Fri, 11–5, Sun 3–5, closed Sat; adm free, ☎ (021) 270679*), a pleasant Georgian house in the gardens of Fitzgerald Park. It is worth visiting for local information and history and silver, glass and lace displays.

North of the River

St Patrick Street leads to the St Patrick's Bridge. Once over it, you enter a hilly part of the city. Some of the streets here are literally stairs up the steep slopes, and open only to pedestrians. Off Shandon Street, the bell-tower of **St Anne's Church**, the lovely **Tower of Shandon** with its two faces in white limestone and red sandstone, looks down into the valley. The church, which is open daily, was built between 1722 and 1726 to replace the church destroyed during the Williamite siege. The peal of the eight bells which were made in Gloucestershire in 1750 are dear to every Corkonian heart. You may ring the bells of Shandon for a small fee, and conjure up Father Prout's lyrical poem about the wild spells that they wove for him a hundred years ago:

> *'Tis the bells of Shandon*
> *That sounds so grand on*
> *The pleasant waters of the River Lee.*

Skiddy's Almshouse, founded in 1584, stands in the churchyard. In about 1620, the Vintners Company of London settled a perpetual annuity of £24 for the benefit of 12 widows of Cork. Down by the river is North Mall, which has some fine 18th-century doorways. The 18th-century **Butter Market** used to be in this area, as was the slaughterhouse for vast numbers of cattle, which were then salted and used as provisions for the British Navy and many European ships before they made the long voyage to America. The **Old Butter Exchange** is now a centre for craft studios. The **Dominican Church of St Mary** by the River Lee was completed in 1839 and has a magnificent classical façade. It is in a very prominent position, which immediately dates it as post-Catholic Emancipation: Catholic churches built before that time were built away from the main centre of towns and cities. Further north is St Mary's Pro-Cathedral, begun in 1808, which has a fine tower. The Neo-Gothic **Cork City Gaol** on Sunday's Well Road (*open daily 9.30am–8pm ☎ (021) 542478*) has been restored as a museum which depicts the life of a 19th-century prisoner and the social history of the period.

South of the River

South of the river, between Bishop and Dean Streets, is **St Finbarr's Cathedral**, which was built in the 19th century by wealthy Church of Ireland merchants on the site of the ancient church founded by St Finbarr. If you don't have time for much sight-seeing this building and the **Art Gallery** are musts. The cathedral's great spires dominate the city, and it has a beautiful west front, with three recessed doors, elaborate carving and a beautiful rose window. The building itself is in the Gothic style of 13th-century France and was built between 1867 and 1879 by a convinced medievalist and English architect, William Burges. His eye for detail was meticulous as well as humorous, and the whole effect is vigorous—a defiant gesture to Catholic Ireland. Also on the South Side, off Douglas Street, is the grey limestone tower of **Red Abbey**, a remnant of a 14th-century Augustinian friary. Close by, on Mary Street, is **South Chapel**, built in 1766 on an inconspicuous site. At this time, the penal laws may have relaxed, but a show of Catholicism was discouraged and disliked by the ruling classes.

The Suburbs

The **Church of Christ the King** on Evergreen Road, to the south at Turner's Cross, was designed by an American architect, Barry Byrne, in the 1930s. The carved figure of Christ crucified with his arms spread above the twin entrance doors is very striking.

Riverside House at Glanmire, 3¾ miles (6km) from the city on the Cork–Dublin road (*open May–Aug, Thurs–Sat, 2–6; at other times by appointment; adm; © (021) 821205/ 821722*), was built in 1602, and has exquisite plasterwork by the Francini brothers. The brothers were Swiss-Italian stuccodores, who came to Ireland in 1734 and adorned the ceiling of the dining-room with allegorical figures representing Time rescuing Truth from the assaults of Discord and Envy. Dr Browne, the Archbishop of Cork, was responsible for remodelling the original house in the 1730s and it remained in his family until the early part of this century. It has been restored by its present owners, Mr and Mrs Dooley, with the help of the Georgian Society.

Dunkathel House, also in Glanmire (*open May to mid-October, Wed–Sun, 2–6; © (021) 821014; adm*) is a fine Georgian house, worth visiting not only to see the antiques, but also to buy some. Afternoon tea here is very pleasant too. The house was built by a wealthy Cork merchant in 1790, and has a wonderful bifurcated (forked) stair-case of Bath stone. There is a rare 1880s barrel organ which is still played for visitors. Gifts as well as antiques are for sale.

Twenty minutes' walk from the city centre via Barrack Street and Bandon Road is the **Lough**, a freshwater lake with feral geese. **Douglas Estuary**, via Tivoli (15 minutes from the centre by car), has hundreds of black-tailed godwit, shelduck and golden plover.

Cork City Environs

Approximately 5 miles (8km) southwest of Cork city on the N22 is **Ballincollig**, where you can visit the 19th-century **Royal Gunpowder Mills** on the River Lee (*open April– Sept; © (021) 874430*). This factory produced huge quantities for the British army. The restored visitor centre details the history of the mills; it also has an exhibition gallery, craft shop and café.

Blarney is 5 miles (8km) northwest of the city on the R617. This small village has a fame out of all proportion to its size because it is the home of the Blarney Stone. Legend tells that whoever kisses it will get the the 'gift of the gab'. This magic stone is high up in all that is left of **Blarney Castle**—its ruined keep (*open all year, Mon–Sat, 9–5 in spring; 9–6.30 in summer; and 9–sundown in winter; © (021) 85252; adm*). It is a magnet which attracts almost every visitor to Ireland, so expect to find the place crowded and full of knick-knacks. In the days of Queen Elizabeth I the castle was held by Dermot MacCarthy, who had the gift of plamas, the Irish word for soft, flattering or insincere speech. Elizabeth had asked him to surrender his castle, but he continued to play her along with fair words and no action. In the end the frustrated Queen is supposed to have said, 'It's all Blarney—he says he will do it but never means it at all.' The MacCarthy's forfeited their castle in the Williamite wars of 1690, and it was later acquired by the St John Jefferyes family. The stone is probably a 19th-century invention, and today you can even buy yourself a certificate which guarantees you have kissed it. Try showing that to your prospective employer! The castle is well worth seeing for its own sake, as it has one of the largest and finest tower houses in Ireland, built in 1446 by the MacCarthy clan. The landscaped gardens surrounding it are also superb. You can also visit **Blarney Castle House and Gardens** (*open Mon–Sat, June–mid-Sept, 12–6; adm;* ✆ *(021) 385252*), a Scottish baronial mansion with a charming garden.

Cobh (pronounced *Cove*) is 15 miles (24km) southeast of Cork city on the R624 off the N25. It is the great harbour of Cork and handles huge ships. There is an International Dance Festival here in July; it is a rather nice place to stay, near to the city but without its bustle. The town is nearly entirely 19th-century and is dominated by the Gothic **St Colman's Cathedral**, the work of Pugin and Ashlin (*open daily 10–6; adm;* ✆ *(021) 811562*). Between 1848 and 1950 two and a half million people emigrated to America from here with many a sad scene enacted by the quay. The history of the port with its strategic position in the North Atlantic, the sinking of the liner *Lusitania* by a German submarine in 1915, and the story of the emigrants is recorded at the **Cobh Heritage Centre** (*open daily 10–6;* ✆ *(021) 813591*) in the converted Victorian railway station. The Royal Yacht Club, near the railway station, was founded in 1720, and is the oldest in Ireland and Great Britain. It has a very good regatta in the summer. The views from the hill above Cobh facing south onto the land-locked harbour, islands and woods are superb. If you want a stroll, make for the old **churchyard of Clonmel**, a peaceful place where many of the dead from the Lusitania are buried.

Fota House and Estate (*open April–Sept, weekdays 10–5; Sun 11–5; rest of the year, Sundays and public holidays only;* ✆ *(021) 812678; adm*) over the Belvelly Bridge is on a magical little island in the River Lee Estuary. The arboretum surrounding the house is luxurious and mature, with a collection of semi-tropical and rare shrubs. The house, which is mainly Regency in style, was built as a hunting lodge, and has a splendid neoclassical hallway. Sadly, at the time of writing the house is closed to the public due to deterioration of its structure. The University of Cork has sold a large portion of the island to a British development company who have already made a golf course and plan to build an hotel and holiday houses here. The house, arboretum and seventy acres of parkland were withdrawn from the development after a public outcry. The fine collection of Irish landscape paintings have been transferred to Limerick University Museum. The future of Fota Island is uncertain, so see it whilst you have a chance. There is also a bee garden and a wildlife park.

Kinsale (*Cionn Saile*: tide head) is 18 miles (29km) southwest of Cork City on the R600. Its fame was established years ago as a quaint seaside town with delicious restaurants and carefully preserved 18th-century buildings; its popularity only seems to increase. It used to be an important naval port. In 1601 the Irish joined forces with Spain against the English, and the Spanish fleet anchored here before the disastrous battle of Kinsale, which led to the 'Flight of the Earls' and put an end to the rebellion against Elizabeth I and her reconquest of Ireland.

This is the perfect place for a relaxed holiday. **Multose Church** is the oldest building in town, parts of it dating from the 13th century. Inside are the old town stocks. The churchyard has several interesting 16th-century gravestones which in spring are covered in whitebells and bluebells, and in summer red valerian grows out of crevasses in every wall. There is an interesting museum in the old courthouse, with material associated with the life of the town and port through the centuries, ✆ (021) 77220.

To the south, on the R604, near **Ballinspittle**, is a ring-fort at about AD 600. There are some superb sandy beaches at the resort of **Garrettstown**, a little further south on the R604, and splendid cliff scenery at the **Old Head of Kinsale** at the end of the road. Round the Old Head of Kinsale, just 7 miles outside the attractive village of Summercove, the remains of a 15th-century **De Courcy castle** overlook the blue and white-flecked sea. **Charles Fort** in Summercove (*open mid-June–early Oct, daily, 10–5; mid-April–mid-June, Tues–Sat, 9–4.30, Sun, 11–5.30; rest of the year, Mon–Fri, 10–4; adm; ✆ (021) 772263*) was built in the 1600s (in the time of Charles II), as a military strong point. It is shaped like a star and you can wander round its rather damp nooks and crannies. The 18th/19th-century houses inside were used as barracks.

Crosshaven, 13 miles (21km) east of Cork city, on the Cork Harbour Estuary, is the playground of the busy Cork businessmen and their families. There are lovely beaches at **Myrtleville** and **Robert's Cove**, and a crescent-shaped bay filled with yachts and boats of every description. Approximately 11 miles from Cork City going east on the N25 is the attractive town of **Midleton**, which has benefited from the restoration of the 18th-century whiskey distillery. It is a fine building, self-contained within 11 acres, and you can take a tour around all the major parts—mills, maltings, corn stores, stillhouses and kilns. The waterwheel is still in perfect order, and you can see the largest pot still in the world with a capacity to hold more than 30,000 gallons. It stopped as a working distillery in 1975, and there is a mass of information charting the history of Irish whiskey. The **Jameson Heritage Centre** is off Distillery Road (*open March–Oct; ✆ (021) 682821 for more details*). Southwest of Midleton is the fine **Barryscourt Castle** (*open to the public daily*), a quadrangular keep with square towers surrounded by a lawn; it overlooks the inner reaches of Cork harbour. The fast main road (N25) to Midleton and Youghal means that many people do not explore the peninsula opposite Crosshaven. Turn off at Midleton and follow the R629 to **Cloyne**, if you wish to visit its vast and ancient cathedral. This dates from the 13th century, and the round tower beside it is one of the only two surviving round towers of the county. You are allowed to climb this one to the top and the view is superb. Amongst the monuments in the cathedral is an alabaster tomb to George Berkeley, the philosopher who was bishop here from 1734 to 1753.

The R629 from Cloyne leads down to **Ballycotton**, a little fishing village set in a peaceful unspoilt bay. There is a pretty view out to Ballycotton Islands, which protect the village from the worst of the sea winds, and a fine bird sanctuary on the extensive marsh by the estuary. Close by is the welcoming and attractive **Ballymaloe House**, which is now a hotel and famous for its restaurant, cooking school and craft shop. At Ladysbridge near Garryroe is a fine fortified house built of the local limestone, called **Ightermurragh Castle**. Over one of the fireplaces in Latin is an inscription which tells that it was built by Edmund Supple and his wife, 'Whome love binds in one', in 1641. Two miles (3.2km) to the southeast in **Kilcredan**'s 17th-century Church of Ireland church are some fascinating limestone headstones with a variety of imaginative motifs. Sadly, the church has suffered the fate of many of that faith and is without a roof, and the carved tomb of Sir Robert Tynte has been ravaged by the weather. Just to the south is **Shanagarry**, famous for its pottery, and the old home of William Penn, the founder of Pennsylvania. You can buy the simple earthenware and glazed pottery there or at the **Ballymaloe House** craft shop.

Youghal (pronounced 'Yawl', from *eochaill*: a yew wood) is one of the most attractive seaside towns in Ireland, approximately 30 miles (48km) east of Cork City on the N25. If you can, try to arrange your trip so that you approach it from the lovely **Blackwater Valley**, which has some of the best driving and walking country in Ireland—if you like wooded banks, green fields, old buildings and twisting, unfrequented roads. Youghal was founded by the Anglo-Normans in the 13th century and was destroyed in the Desmond Rebellion of 1579. The Fitzgeralds, earls of Desmond, were a powerful Anglo-Norman family who joined forces with the Gaelic lords from Ulster to try and repulse the armies of Elizabeth I. The town was handed over to Sir Walter Raleigh in the Elizabethan plantation period, when he became mayor of the town and lived in a gabled house called **Myrtle Grove** at the end of William Street (guided tours possible). Raleigh is said to have planted the first potato in the garden, an act which was to have far-reaching consequences for Ireland's population. The town holds a potato festival each year to celebrate the arrival of the new spuds. In the same street is the 15th-century Church of Ireland collegiate **Church of St Mary**. The inside of this large cruciform church is crowded with interesting monuments, including one to the Earl of Cork, Richard Boyle, looking very smug, surrounded by his mother, his two wives, and nine of his 16 sons. A memorial stands to the extraordinary lady, the Countess of Desmond, who died in 1604 at the age of 147 after falling out of a tree when gathering cherries. The church was founded by Thomas, the 8th Earl of Desmond, and restored in 1884, after being derelict for years. The most notable features are its Early-English west doorway, the massive pulpit, with its canopy of carved bog oak, and the large six-light east window (*c.* 1468) of stained glass with arms of the Desmonds, Sir Walter Raleigh, the Earl of Cork and the Duke of Devonshire.

The old part of town lies at the foot of a steep hill, whilst the new part has grown along the margin of the bay. The main street is spanned by a clock, weather vane and lantern known as the **Clock Gate** and erected in 1771. It houses the tourist office, art gallery and museum. Further down the street is the ruined **Tynte's Castle**, which was built in the 15th century. Portions of the old walls which once bounded the town still stand, but even in 1579 they were in a bad state, and were easily breached by the rebellious Earl of Desmond.

Fermoy to Mallow

Fermoy (*Mainistir Fhearmuighe*: the abbey of the plantations), 30 miles (48km) north of Cork City on the N8, used to be a garrison town for the British army and is built along both sides of the darkly flowing River Blackwater. People hereabouts are familiar with every fascinating detail of catching salmon. The town has an air of shabby gentility, for it has seen more prosperous days. Lord Fermoy, an ancestor of the Princess of Wales, is said to have gambled away his Fermoy estates in an evening. The Protestant church built in 1802 contains some grotesque masks.

Just outside Fermoy, overlooking the river to the west, is one of the most beautiful houses in Ireland, the late-Georgian mansion, **Castle Hyde**. This was the home of Douglas Hyde, the first President of the Irish Republic and the founder of the Gaelic League. Sadly, it is not open to the public. **Castlelyons**, a few miles outside the town (turn left off the N8 going towards Cork), is a quiet and pretty hamlet where intimations of past history compel you to stop. Here is the great house of the Barry's, a Norman family, in vast ruin, and the remains of a 14th-century Carmelite friary.

To the north, **Mitchelstown** is famous in Ireland for butter and cheese, an industry which employs a lot of people, although the cheese is rather boring—Cheddar and a sort of soft bland spread. It is also famous for its **caves**, a further 10 miles (16km) to the north on the Cahir road (N8) (*open daily throughout the year, 10–6; adm;* *(052) 67246*). The countryside around becomes richer as you travel west and enter the Golden Vein, a fertile plain which extends north of the Galtee Mountains. At Kildorrey, turn right off the N73 onto the R512 to go to Doneraile. Near here was the home of the novelist Elizabeth Bowen (1899–1973), whose works so beautifully describe the shades and subtleties of the Anglo-Irish. Her house, '**Bowens Court**', a beautiful 18th-century mansion, was demolished recently—a victim of the government's lack of interest in historic buildings.

Doneraile and Buttevant are in Edmund Spenser country, 40 miles (64km) north of Cork City, between the Blackwater and the Ballyhoura Mountains. Here he is said to have written *The Faerie Queene*, inspired by the sylvan beauty of the countryside, and so flattering Elizabeth I that she granted him lands. Tragically, Spenser's home, **Kilcolman Castle**, was burned and he and his wife had to flee, leaving their baby daughter to perish in the flames. **Kilcolman** is now a sombre ruin, in a field beside a reedy pool northeast of Doneraile. From 1895 to 1913 **Doneraile** was the parish of Canon Sheehan, who wrote wise and funny books about Irish rural life. His statue stands outside the Catholic Church. **Doneraile Court** is a wonderful Georgian house which has been saved from ruin by the Irish Georgian Society (*house will be open to the public once restoration work is finished; for details call (022) 24244*). For the time being, it is possible to view it from the beautiful oak-spread surrounding parkland. The park is being developed for tourists, and there are nature walks. Enter through the grand stone gates in the town. Doneraile Court is a house with an interesting story behind it: here Elizabeth Barry, wife of the first Viscount Doneraile, hid in a clock case to observe a masonic lodge meeting held in the house. Perhaps she laughed, but whatever happened she gave herself away, and all the masons could do was to elect her as a mason—the only woman mason in history. Nearby is the unique alkaline **Kilcolman Bog**. The home of many birds, you can arrange to visit it if you are involved in bird study. Contact the tourist office for details.

At **Buttevant** during July is the **Cahirmee Horse Fair**, which has been held for hundreds of years and is always good crack, with lots of other events happening at the same time.

Mallow, 10 miles (16km) south, used to be a famous spa where the gentry of Ireland came to take the waters and have a good time. In the 18th century the spa inspired the anonymous verse which begins:

> *Beauing, belling, dancing, drinking,*
> *Breaking windows, damning, singing,*
> *Ever raking, never thinking,*
> *Live the rakes of Mallow...*

The old spa house is now a private house and the once-famous water gushes to waste. The town has pretty 18th-century houses, a timbered decorated **Clock House** and **Mallow Castle**, which is a still-impressive, roofless ruin of a fortified 16th-century tower house. The **Mallow Races**, which happen intermittently throughout the spring, summer and autumn, is the only time the place really comes alive, though it is frequented by anglers and the **Folk Festival** in July is very cheerful. Just outside the town is **Longueville House** which produces delicious wine, and where you can eat and stay in great style.

At **Castletownroche** on the N72, 10 miles (16km) east of Mallow, notice the pretty Church of Ireland church on a rise above the river. To the north of it is **Anne's Grove** (*open Easter–end Sept, Mon–Sat, 10–5; Sun 1–6; adm;* © *(022) 26145*) with its tranquil woodlands and walled garden. The sloping grounds surrounding the beautiful 18th-century house are planted in the style made popular by William Robertson in the late 19th century. Nothing is contrived and the massed plants lead up winding paths to the river and gardens. Rhododendrons, magnolias, eucryphias, abutilons and primulas obviously love it here, so vigorously have they grown.

Now head west to **Killarney**, from Cork or Mallow, via Macroom. From Mallow, the country lanes which take you through the **Boggeragh Mountains** are a maze, and rather fun if you have time to get lost for a while. They have a wild mystery, heightened by the green glow from the overgrown hedges which form an arbour overhead. Twenty miles (32 km) further on, you arrive at **Macroom**, where J. P. Quilan's Pub is a welcome retreat for a drink or snack. The woodwork of the bar is superb and there is always a warm fire to welcome you. Macroom (*Maigh Chromtha*: sloping plain) is on the direct route to Killarney (N22), and is a favourite place for tourists and music enthusiasts. This is a gorgeous part of Ireland: scenes are lush with green pasture and bright-flowered with fuchsia and heather. The R618, west from Cork City, follows the lovely River Lee through **Dripsey** and **Coachford**. Dripsey woollen mills produce an excellent wool. If you are heading for Killarney try and plan your journey to include the **Pass of Keamaneigh** 5 miles (8km) west of Ballingeary on the R584 to Bantry. Here is one of the most beautiful forest parks in the country—**Gougane Barra**, 'the rock-cleft of Finbarr', a dramatic glacial valley with a shining lake in its hollow, into which run silvery streams. This is the source of the River Lee. In the lake is a small island, approached by a causeway, where St Finbarr set up his oratory in the 6th century. At the entrance to the causeway is **St Finbarr's Well** and an ancient cemetery. The island has a few 18th-century remains, some Stations of the Cross, and a tiny modern Irish Romanesque chapel which is often used for weddings. A popular pattern (pilgrimage) is made here every year on the Sunday nearest to the feast day of St Finbarr (25 September). After the Pass of Keamaneigh, strewn with massive boulders, you come into the colourful valley of the Owvane with a view of Bantry Bay. At **Kealkill**, 5 miles (8km) before Bantry, there is an ancient stone circle, reached by an exciting hilly road just off the R584.

Bandon to Baltimore

Before describing Bantry, here is a brief description of the very attractive south Cork coast, starting off from the market town of **Bandon**, 20 miles (32 km) southwest of Cork City on the N71. Bandon was founded by Richard Boyle, the Earl of Cork, in 1608. Over the gate of the then-walled town it is said that there were once the words, 'Turk, Jew or atheist may enter here, but not a papist.' A Catholic wit responded, 'He who wrote this wrote it well, the same is written on the gates of hell.' The River Bandon and its tributaries make for good

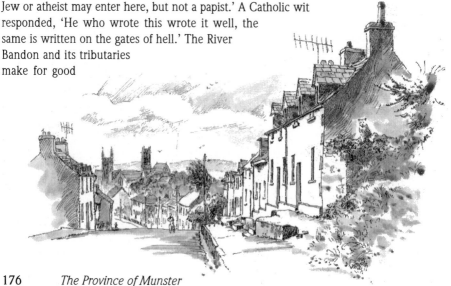

fishing and walking, and, if you want to explore, **Kilbrittain**, **Timoleague** and **Courtmacsherry Bay** are unspoilt. Motorists can get a good view of the wooded valleys, and rolling fields which do not have the hedges you find in Tipperary. **Timoleague** is dominated by the ruins of a **Franciscan abbey** founded in 1312. It has a fairly complete cloister and an outer yard, and is always accessible to the public. On the banks of the Argideen River are the varied and lush **Timoleague Castle Gardens** (*open daily from mid-May–mid-Sept, 11–5.30; adm; © (023) 46116 or (021) 831512*), with many rare and tender plants. To open shortly at **Clonakilty** is a model village which depicts village life in Ireland 40 years ago; it is typical of the theme approach to tourism that is becoming so common. Contact the Town Hall, Clonakilty for details. But it is still possible to experience the real thing and in this part of the country you find the typical Irish bar-cum-grocery shop, with old-fashioned lettering displaying the proud name of the owner. Courtmacsherry is a sea-angling centre. A little further west, **Rosscarbery** is a charming old-fashioned village. It had a famous school of learning founded by St Fachtna in the 6th century, and a medieval Benedictine monastery. The very attractive 17th-century Church of Ireland church is on the old cathedral site. Inland to the west, in the valley of the little River Roury stands the ruin of Coppinger's Court, a ruined Elizabethan or Jacobean mansion, burnt out in 1641, which gives shelter to cows in winter. It stands to the left, off an unclassified road between Leap and Rosscarbery. From Roury Bridge, a country road (R507) winds to **Dromberg Stone Circle**, from where you can see across pastures and cornfields to the sea. It is dated between the 2nd century BC and 2nd century AD. A cremated body was discovered in the centre of the circle when it was excavated. The beaches of **Owenahincha** and, to the east, the **Longstrand** have wonderful sand. **Union Hall** and **Glandore** are two pretty resort villages on a narrow inlet 5 miles (8km) west of Rosscarbery, whose harbours are filled with highly painted boats.

Round the next headland, **Castletownshend** is a neat Georgian village on a steep hill, in the middle of which grows a huge tree. The village used to be the home of Edith Somerville (1858–1949), co-author of the humorous *Reminiscences of an Irish RM*. She is buried in the pretty Church of Ireland graveyard here, with cousin and co-author Violet Martin (1862–1915), who wrote under the pen name 'Martin Ross'.

Skibbereen, linked to Castletownshend by the R596, is a market town famous for its own weekly newspaper the *Southern Star*, previously called the *Skibbereen Eagle*. It is good for a read and sheds a lot of light on local preoccupations. Between Skibbereen and Drimoleague off the R593, is an exciting and thoughtful enterprise still in the process of creation. The **Liss Ard Sky Gardens** (*open by appointment only © (028) 22368*) is a combination of artistic spaces and wildlife gardens extending for forty acres. Three and a half miles (5.6km) south of Skibbereen on the Baltimore Road are **Creagh Gardens** (*open all year, daily, 10–6; adm; © (028) 22121*), a romantic and informal garden planted amongst woods which lead to the river estuary. Best seen between April and June. All round Skibbereen and particularly to the west is some lovely country where knuckles and fingers of land reach into the sea, breaking off into islands like **Sherkin** and **Clear**. It is possible to get a boat from Baltimore (R595) to the islands. Negotiate with the local fishermen or take the regular ferry boat. St Ciaran was born on Cape Clear, and the remains of a cross and holy well mark the site of his church. There is an important bird observatory here, as the island is on a major bird migration route; and also a youth hostel. The familiar Fastnet Rock mentioned in shipping forecasts is just off Cape Clear. This region used to be an O'Driscoll stronghold (the local Gaelic sept or tribe) until it was sacked by Algerian pirates in 1631, and the Irish people captured and sold as slaves along the Barbary coast. Near to Baltimore is the beautiful **Lough Ine**, just the place for a walk or picnic.

Ballydehob to Mizen Head

Ballydehob is a colourful little village 10 miles (16km) away from Skibbereen on the N71, with a fine 12-arch railway bridge which lies at the head of Roaring Water Bay. About 2 miles (3.2km) south at **Rossbrin**, the ruin of an O'Mahony castle stands by the sea, the home of the 14th-century scholar Finin. A spectacular road runs from Schull, a few miles further west, up to **Mount Gabriel** (945ft/288m). If you decide to climb it, be careful of the prehistoric coppermines dug into the slopes. The view is out of this world. The R591 curls round the head of lovely **Toormore Bay**, past **Goleen** with its sandy beach (the Gulf Stream means that swimming is quite possible here), to Crookhaven with its boat-filled harbour. **Barleycove** is a sandy beach along which you can stretch your legs before you get to the splendid, sheer heights of **Mizen Head**. The soft, red sandstone cliffs banded with white fall down to the sea whilst flurries of birds glide on the air currents beneath you. The cliffs are high and nearly vertical, so be careful! A lighthouse on the islet below is linked to the mainland by a suspension bridge. Many ships have been wrecked here in the past. From the Mizen Head, the R591 goes to Durras at the head of Dunmanus Bay. The drive to Kilcrohane and Sheeps Head and then on to Gerahies is magnificent and very untouristy. The views spread across Bantry Bay and the Beara Peninsula.

Bantry has one of the finest views in the world. What you must not miss is **Bantry Bay House** (*open daily all year except Christmas Day, 9–6; open until 8 on most summer evenings; adm; tearoom and craftshop; also B&B accommodation—see 'Where to Stay', below; © (025) 50047*) which has a glorious view and is directly above the town so you do not see the ugly petrol stations below it. You can go round the house on your own (accompanied only by the faint strains of classical music), with a detailed guide written by the owner which you then hand back when you have finished. Rare French tapestries, family portraits and china still have a feeling of being used and loved. The house and garden have definitely seen better days, yet this is one of the most interesting houses in Ireland, and certainly one of the least officious that is open to the public. The house was built in 1740, and added to in 1765. The owner, Mr Egerton Shelswell-White, is at present embarking on restoration work. He is an enthusiastic patron of music, and there are many fine concerts held in the library. The dining room is a stunning shade of bottle blue against which the gold-framed portraits, the china and silver look magnificent. Two of the portraits are of King George II and Queen Charlotte. They were painted at the sovereign's order and given to the first Earl of Bantry, from whom Mr Shelswell-White is descended, as a token of thanks for his efforts in helping repel the French invasion force of 1798. In the side courtyard of the house is an exhibition devoted to the 1798 Bantry Bay Armada. There is a 1:6 scale model of a frigate in cross-section and extracts from Wolfe

Tone's Journal. Just outside the town on Glengarriff Road are the **Donemark Falls**, a pretty waterfall on an island. The owner of this land has made it into a rather eccentric garden, a mixture of natural and artificial charm with gnomes. The N71 takes you swiftly toward Glengarriff.

Glengarriff's humpy hills and wooded inlets look over limpid water and isles. (Mulroy Bay in Donegal is similar.) **Inacullin**, alias Garinish Island (*open May–Oct, daily 10–5; adm; © (027) 63040*), used to be covered only in rocks, heather and gorse until it was made into 37 acres of garden by a Scotsman, John Allen Bryce, in 1910. Now it is a dream island full of sub-tropical plants, with a formal Italian garden, rock gardens and a marble pool full of goldfish. It is an exceptional place, full of structure and outstanding plants, well worth the IR£4 plus return boat fares to the island. Bernard Shaw often stayed here. There are many boatmen willing to take you out to the island; in fact, they fight for your trade. You might walk in **Glengarriff Valley**, 'the bitter glen', and up to the hills hidden in the Caha Range, or drive up the Healy Pass Road, with its lovely mountain scenery gazing down on the indented sealine and the green woods. It is quite a testing zig-zag drive following the R574 road to Lauragh in County Kerry.

Shopping

Cork City and Environs

Antiques: Dunkathel, Glanmire, © (021) 821014. McCurtain Street, Cork (north side), has a variety of antiques and bric-a-brac. Also the flea market, Cornmarket Street.

Clothes: stylish linen and tweed for men and women from the House of Donegal, Paul Street.

Musical instruments: *uileann* pipes from A. Kennedy, St Johns, Clifton Road, Montenotte Park, Cork, © (021) 503762. Bodhrams (drums) from Crowleys Music Centre, 29 MacCurtain Street, © (021) 503426. Harps from L. Egar, Ardmuire, Herbert Park, Gardiner's Hill, Cork, © (021) 504832. Fiddles from Martin Faherty in the Shandon craft centre.

Crafts: a wide selection, of top-quality, from the Stephen Pearse Shop, Paul Street, and IDA Craft Centre, The Butter Exchange, Shandon.

Woollen goods: Blarney Woollen Mills. Blarney Castle Knitwear, Blarney.

Glass: Cork Crystal Glass Company, Blarney.

Hand-woven tweed: Rosemary Kelleher, 15 The Skiddys, Shandon, Cork, © (021) 501283.

Contemporary art: Cork Art Society, Lavitt's Quay, © (021) 277749.

Jewellery: Stephen O'Shaughnessy, 22 Patrick Street, Cork, © (021) 270011.

Chain stores: (including A-Wear and Marks & Spencer) St Patrick Street and Merchant's Quay Pedestrian Centre.

Books: The Mercier Press, French Church Street, produces a wealth of books of Irish interest, and novels by Irish authors.

Food and flowers: The English Market, between Patrick Street, Grand Parade and Oliver Plunkett Street. Natural Foods, 26 Paul Street, for delicious bread and buns.

If you need a quiet drink after shopping, make for the traditional, old-fashioned bar called the Vineyard in Market Place, off St Patrick Street.

Co. Cork

Crafts: Ballymaloe Craft Shop, Shanagarry, Midleton, ✆ (021) 652531. Bantry House Craftshop, Bantry.

Handmade baskets: Morbert Platz, Ballymurphy, Innishannon, ✆ (021) 885548.

Handmade kitchen knives: Ballylickey, Bantry, ✆ (027) 50032. Ballymaloe Kitchen shop, Shanagarry ✆ (021) 652032

Pottery: Macroom. Rossmore Country Pottery, Rossmore, Clonakilty, ✆ (023) 38875. Ian Wright, Corsits Pottery, Kilnaclasha, Skibbereen, ✆ (028) 21889. R. and J. Forrester, Bandon Studios, North Main Street, Bandon, ✆ (023) 41360. P. & F. Wolstenholme, Courtmacsherry Ceramics, Courtmacsherry, ✆ (023) 46239. Kinsale Pottery, Jagoes Mill, Kinsale, ✆ (021) 72771. Leda May Studios, Main Street, Ballydehob; ✆ (028) 37221. Stephen Pearce Pottery, Shanagarry, ✆ (021) 646807; West Cork Arts Centre, North Street, Skibbereen, ✆ (028) 22090.

Furniture: O'Donnell Design, Baltimore Road, Skibbereen.

Gift shop: Bantry House.

Leprechauns: Elizabeth Mans, Gort na Reagh, Kilcrohan, Bantry, ✆ (027) 67017.

Flutes: Colin Hamilton, Coolea, Macroom.

Smoked goods: Harbour Smoke House, Ballydevlin, Gooleen, Schull. Ummera Smoked Products, Ummera House, Timoleague, Bandon, ✆ (023) 46187. Telephone first to buy their delicious smoked-salmon sausage.

Cheese: Gubbeen Cheeses, Gubbeen House, Schull, ✆ (028) 28231. Wonderful soft cheese, visitors welcome at the farm. Milleens Cheese, Eyeries, Beara Peninsula, ✆ (027) 74079. Delicious soft cheese. Telephone first. Cleire Goat's Cheese, and goat's milk ice-cream, summer only, Cape Clear, Skibbereen, ✆ (028) 39126. Garlic and plain semi-soft cheese. Ardrahan Cheese, Ardrahan House, Kanturk, ✆ (029) 78099. Gouda-type cheese. Coolea Cheese, Coolea, ✆ (026) 45204, strong flavoured semi-soft cheese; Ardsallagh goat's cheese and milk, Ardsallagh, Youghal, ✆ (021) 92545. Also comes bottled with olive oil.

Delicacies: Mannings Emporium, Ballylickey, ✆ (027) 50456. Local cheeses and whiskey cake. Fields, 26 Main Street, Skibbereen, ✆ (028) 21400. Good locally made herb sausages, cheese, country butter. Essential Foods, Bantry, ✆ (027)

61171. Local organic vegetables; Hudson's Wholefoods, Main Street, Ballydehot, ℗ (028) 37211, seaweeds, local cheese and delicious ice cream; Twomey's Butchers, 16 Pearse Street, Clonakilty, ℗ (023) 33365. Famous Clonakilty Black Pudding.

Market: Carrigaline Country Market, The GAA Hall, Crosshaven Road, Carrigaline. Country market every Friday, 10–11. Good vegetables, home baking and gorgeous flowers.

Fish: Castletownbere Fishermen's Co-op, The Pier, Castletownbere, ℗ (027) 70045. Fresh fish every day except Sunday. Fresh fish also from The Pier, Ballycotton Bay, E. Cork. Usually about 2 every day. If you miss it there's a good fish shop on the main street, ℗ (021) 613122.

Activities

Salmon fishing: Carysville Fishery, Carysville House, Fermoy, ℗ (025) 31094/31712, book in advance. Derek Good, Inishannon, ℗ (021) 775133. Fishing tackle and local knowledge from J. O'Sullivan, 4 Patrick Street, Fermoy, ℗ (025) 31110; Vickery & Co, Main Street, Bantry; The Tackle Shop, 6 Lavitts Quay, Cork City; Trident Angling Centre, Kinsale, ℗ (021) 772301.

Deep-sea fishing: boat hire from Peter Manning, Ballycotton Angling Centre, ℗ (021) 646773. International Sailing Centre, East Beach, Cobh, ℗ (021) 841348. Charles Robertson, Roycestown, Carrigaline, Crosshaven, ℗ (021) 372896. Marc Gannon, Woodpoint, Courtmacsherry, Bandon, ℗ (023) 46427. Carberry Charters Ltd, Ballinatoma, Union Hall, ℗ (028) 33463. Ted Brown, Green Gorse, Baltimore, ℗ (028) 20438. Nick Dent, Cappaglass, Ballydehob; ℗ (028) 20164.

Sea-swimming: at Ballycotton, Longstrand, Owenahincha, Goleen Beach, Barley Cove, around Skibbereen and Schull.

Sailing schools: International Sailing Centre, 5 East Beach, Cobh, ℗ (021) 811237. Baltimore Sailing School, The Pier, Baltimore; ℗ (028) 20141.

Yacht charter: Rossbrin Yacht Charters, Rossbrin Cove, Schull, ℗ (028) 37165. Sail Ireland Charters, Trident Hotel, Kinsale, ℗ (021) 772927.

Hunting: Duhallow Hunt, ℗ (022) 21539. Muskerry Hunt, Mr Murphy, ℗ (021) 872966; South Union Hunt, ℗ (021) 293966.

Pony-trekking: The Rosscarbery Riding Centre, Rosscarbery, ℗ (023) 48232; The Henry Ford Homestead, Clonakilty, ℗ (023) 39117; Dunboy Riding Stables, Dunboy Castle, Castletownbere, ℗ (027) 70044.

Golf: Mallow Golf Club, Ballyellis, Mallow, ℗ (022) 21145. Fermoy Golf Club, Fermoy, ℗ (025) 31472. Muskerry Golf Club, Carrigrohane, ℗ (021) 385297. Cork Golf Club, Little Island, Cork City, ℗ (021) 353451. Douglas Golf Club, in the southern suburbs of Cork City, ℗ (021) 895297. Monkstown Golf Club,

Parkgarriffe, Monkstown, ✆ (021) 841225. Youghal Golf Club, Knockaverry; ✆ (024) 92787. Fota Island, ✆ (021) 883700.

Trabolgan Holiday Centre: indoor pool, children's safari jungle etc.

Ballymaloe Cookery School courses: Darina and Tim Allen, Kinoith House, Shanagarry, ✆ (021) 646785. Courses vary from three months to one day.

Where to Stay

Cork City and Environs

Jury's Hotel, Western Road, Cork City, ✆ (021) 276622 (*expensive*). Garden on the river, modern with sports facilities. **Lotamore House**, Tivoli, Cork City, ✆ (021) 822344 (*moderate*). Comfortable bedrooms with own bath. **Arbutus Lodge**, Montenotte, Cork City, ✆ (021) 501237 (*moderate*). Famous for its restaurant. Luxurious rooms. **The Metropole**, McCurtain Street, Cork City, ✆ (021) 508122 (*moderate*). Old-fashioned with delicious breakfasts. **The Gables**, Stoneview, Blarney, ✆ (021) 385330 (*inexpensive*). Old rectory, nicely furnished. **Isaac's**, 48 MacCurtain Street, Cork City, ✆ (021) 500011. Hostel with self-service restaurant in converted warehouse. **The Fitzgeralds**, Ashton Grove, Knockraha, ✆ (021) 821537 (*inexpensive*). Fine Georgian house, 7 miles (11km) north of Cork.

Co. Cork

Mrs Merrie Green, **Ballyvolane House**, near Fermoy, ✆ (025) 36349 (*expensive*). Lovely old Georgian house, beautiful grounds. Friendly family and lots of locally produced vegetables in the cooking. **Assolas Country House**, Kanturk, ✆ (029) 50795 (*expensive*). Set amongst mature trees which reach down to the river, this 17th-century house is a superb place to get away from it all. Tennis, fishing, croquet in the grounds. Delicious food. **Ballymaloe House**, Shanagarry, Midleton, ✆ (021) 652531 (*expensive*). Very pretty Georgian house, near the fishing village of Ballycotton. Elegant rooms, very friendly service, fabulous food, generous helpings. The whole Allen family are involved in the enterprise. You may be inspired to book into the cookery school here. Sea, river-fishing and riding can be arranged. **Longueville House**, Mallow, ✆ (022) 47156 (*expensive*). There is a maze at the back of the house, and the only vineyard in Ireland; and long sloping views to the river and the ruined Callaghan Castle in the front. The food is superlative, and the service attentive.

Larchwood House, Pearson's Bridge, near Ballylickey, ✆ (027) 66181 (*moderate*). Family atmosphere and delicious cooking. **Scilly House**, Kinsale, ✆ (021) 772413 (*moderate*). American owned. Attractive bedrooms with pretty views over garden and bay. The **Marine**, Glandore, ✆ (028) 33366 (*moderate*). Simple hotel with lovely view of cove. The **Commodore Hotel**, Cobh, ✆ (021) 811277 (*moderate*). Old-fashioned seaside hotel. **Bantry House**, Bantry, ✆ (027) 50047 (*moderate*). Stately house, built in 1750, with bright rooms furnished in the simplest, yet most cheerful way. Fantastic views. **Seaview Hotel**, Ballylickey, Bantry, ✆ (027) 50462 (*moderate*). Cosy, bright, Victorian house with spacious bedrooms. Two comfortable cottages for rent in the grounds. **The Old Presbytery**, Cork Street, Kinsale, ✆ (021) 772027 (*moderate*). Characterful B&B with brass beds and restaurant. **The Blue Haven**, Kinsale, ✆ (021) 772209 (*moderate*). The best hotel in Kinsale: small, cosy and comfortable with excellent food. Mrs Vickery, **Bow Hall**, Castletownshend, ✆ (028) 36114 (*moderate*). Lovely Queen Anne house. **Mrs Sharp Bolster**, Glenlohane, Kanturk, ✆ (029) 50014 (*moderate*). Comfortable Georgian house. Mrs Sherrard, **Glenview House**, Ballinaclasha, Midleton, ✆ (021) 631680 (*moderate*). Pretty 18th-century house, lovely grounds with tennis and croquet. Good food. **Aherne's Pub and Seafood Bar**, North Main Street, Youghal, ✆ (024) 92424 (*moderate*). Nice neat spacious bedrooms and wonderful seafood.

O'Donovan's Hotel, 44 Pearse Street, Clonakilty, ✆ (023) 33250 (*inexpensive*). Wonderful old-fashioned and characterful family-run hotel, with a fine public bar, in the town centre. **Seacourt**, Butlerstown, ✆ (023) 40151 (*inexpensive*). Historic and beautiful house built in 1760. View of Seven Heads Peninsula. *Open June till end of August.* **Glebe House**, Ballinadee, Bandon, near Kinsale. ✆ (021) 778294 (*inexpensive*). Splendid dinners and breakfasts in an attractive house. Mrs O'Mahony, **Grove House**, Ahakistra, Durras, ✆ (027) 67060 (*inexpensive*). Pretty old farmhouse on Sheep's Head Peninsula. For breakfast, honey from the garden and free-range eggs.

Mrs Hegarty, **Ahakista**, Bantry, ✆ (027) 67045 (*inexpensive*). Traditional farmhouse with lovely views. Mrs O'Shea, **Magannagan Farm**, Derryconnery, Glengarriff, ✆ (027) 63361 (*inexpensive*). Good high teas. Muckley Family, **Shangri La**, Glengarriff Road, Bantry, ✆ (027) 50244 (*inexpensive*). Friendly, cosy house. **Lettercollum House Hostel**, Timoleague, ✆ (023) 46251 (*inexpensive*). Excellent restaurant. **Gabriel Cottage**, Smorane, ✆ (028) 22521 (*inexpensive*). Vegan/vegetarian B&B. **Travara Lodge**, Courtmacsherry, ✆ (023) 46493 (*inexpensive*). Comfortable with views of the bay and good home cooking.

self-catering

Mrs Harte, Cahermore, Rosscarbery, ✆ (023) 48227 Renovated farmhouse, oil fired aga cooker, sleeps 6. From IR£150 per week. **Hollybrook House**, Skibbereen, ✆ (028) 21245. Several 19th-century properties on wooded estate. 8 luxury coastal cottages (sleep 6) with use of hotel facilities. **Terry Adams**, Courtmacsherry, ✆ (023) 46198. From £200 per week. Vary Knivett, **Shiplake Hostel**, Dunmanway, ✆ (023) 45750. Traditional farmhouse in the mountains, with self-catering kitchen where you can cook up the organic vegetables sold by the owners. They also sell wholemeal bread and delicious pizzas. **Blairs Cove House**, Durras, near Bantry, ✆ (027) 61041. Apartments, IR£90–400 per week. 18th-century apartments, Castletownshend, contact Mrs Salter-Townshend, **The Castle**, Castletownshead, ✆ (028) 36100. Mrs Salter-Townshend also does B&B.

Mrs Kowalski, **Ashgrove Lodge**, Cobh, ✆ (021) 812483. 18th-century house, sleeps 5. From IR£200 per week. **Cashman Family**, Garrison, Kanturk, ✆ (029) 50197 Thatched cottage, sleeps 6. From IR£130 per week.

Eating Out

Cork City and Environs

Arbutus Lodge, Montenotte, Cork, ✆ (021) 502893 (*expensive*). Well-established and excellent restaurant with a nationwide reputation. Moderately priced lunch; dinner is more lavish. **Cliffords**, 18 Dyke Parade, Cork City, ✆ (021) 275333 (*expensive*). Smart restaurant in converted Georgian building that used to house the city library. One of few Irish restaurants to have a michelin star. Imaginative menu and impeccable service. Also own a small cheaper bistro next door. **Glandore**, Jury's Hotel, Western Road, Cork, ✆ (021) 276622 (*moderate*). Good service and consistent quality. **Glassialley's**, 5 Emmet Place, Cork, ✆ (021) 272305 (*moderate*). Salads, roasts, seafood. **The Huguenot**, French Church Street, Cork, ✆ (021) 273357 (*moderate*). French cuisine. **Jacques Restaurant**, 9 Phoenix Street, Cork. ✆ (021) 277387 (*moderate*). Interesting cooking and good vegetarian dishes. The **Oyster Tavern**, Market Lane, ✆ (021) 272716 (*moderate*). Has the atmosphere of a gentleman's dining room with white-aproned waitresses. The seafood is excellent. **Isaac's Brasserie**, 48 MacCurtain Street, ✆ (021) 503805 (*moderate*). Fashionable 18th century converted warehouse. Zesty imaginative menu.

O'Reilly's, English Market (corner of Grand Parade), Cork, ✆ (021) 966397 (*inexpensive*). Tripe and drisheen (sheep's innards). **Baxters**, Lavitt's Quay, Cork. ✆ (021) 272139 (*inexpensive*). Cold meats and salads. *Lunch only Mon to Fri.* **Quay Co-op**, 24 Sullivan's Quay, Cork. ✆ (021) 317660 (*inexpensive*). Good wholefood vegetarian restaurant, open lunch and dinner. Also a wholefood shop and bookshop. **The Long Valley**, Winthrop Street, Cork, ✆ (021) 272144 (*inexpensive*). Pub selling delicious sandwiches. **Crawford's Art Gallery Café**, Emmett Place, Cork, ✆ (021) 274415 (*inexpensive*). Run by one of the Allen Family of Ballymaloe fame, you can eat light and original food here for lunch or early supper. Good fresh orange juice and gooey cakes for a snack. **The Triskel Arts Café**, Triskel Arts Centre, 15 Tobin Street, Cork, ✆ (021) 272022 (*inexpensive*). Filling lunchtime dishes. Very good soups. **Bewley's**, Cork Street (*inexpensive*). **The Gingerbread House**, Frenchchurch Street, ✆ (021) 276411 (*inexpensive*). Takeaway or eat in sandwiches, croissants and cakes.

Co. Cork

Ballymaloe House, Shanagarry, ✆ (021) 652532 (*expensive*). Famed throughout Ireland for its superb food, it never disappoints you. **Longueville House**, Mallow, ✆ (022) 47156 (*expensive*). Adventurous and generous cuisine. **Shiro Japanese Dinner House**, Ahakista, Durras, ✆ (027) 67030 (*expensive*). If you are staying anywhere near, arrange a meal here, for not only are you guaranteed a superb meal, but the whole atmosphere is magical. The husband-and-wife team have combined all the right elements of Japanese love of beauty and decoration in the rooms in which you eat, and in the preparation of the food. She is Japanese, he is German, and the view outside the window, pure Irish sea beauty. Dinner only; booking essential. **Blairs Cove House**, Durras, near Bantry, ℘ (027) 61127 (*expensive*). Situated in the stable building of a Georgian mansion, run by a French couple. Steaks and fish grilled in front of you. Dinner and Sunday lunch only. **The Blue Haven**, 3 Pearse Street, Kinsale, ℘ (021) 772209 (*expensive*). Very good restaurant in this cosy hotel. Seafood a speciality, steaks good too.

Max's Wine Bar, Main Street, Kinsale, ℘ (021) 772443 (*moderate*). Attractive old house. Varied menu. **Dunworley Cottage**, Butlerstown, Bandon, ℘ (023) 40314 (*moderate*). Very popular locally. Good for vegetarians. *Lunch and dinner.*The **Altar Restaurant**, Toormore, Schull, ℘ (028) 35254 (*moderate*). Good pâté and seafood. **Heron's Cove Restaurant and B&B**, Goleen, Skibbereen, ℘ (028) 35225 (*moderate*). Harbour-side setting, very good fish and shellfish dishes. Lunch and dinner. **Mountain View Hotel**, Glengarriff, ℘ (027) 63103 (*moderate*). Family-run hotel, cordon bleu cooking.

Bawnleigh House, Ballinhassig, ℘ (021) 771333 (*moderate*). Décor rather grim but creative, delicious food. (Closer to Half Way Village than Ballinhassig). **Mill House**, Rineen, Skibbereen, ℘ (028) 36299 (*moderate*). Seafood restaurant. **Aherne's Pub and Seafood Bar**, North Main Street, Youghal, ℘ (024) 92424/ 92533 (*moderate*). Good atmosphere and delicious seafood. **Lettercollum House**, Timoleague, ℘ (023) 46251 (*moderate*). Only 8 tables, booking essential, set menu, delicious. **Annie's**, Ballydehob, ℘ (028) 37292 (*moderate*). Good set meals and special portions for children. **Tra Amici**, Coomhola Road, near Ballylickey, ℘ (027) 50235 (*moderate*). Excellent Italian cooking. **Larchwood House**, Pearson's Bridge, nr Ballylickey, ℘ (027) 66181 (*moderate*). Friendly and informal atmosphere, good home-cooking.

Bushes Bar, Baltimore, ℘ (028) 20125 (*inexpensive*). Bar overlooking the harbour. **5A Café**, Banack Street, Bantry (*inexpensive*). Cheap, hippyish vegetarian café. **Achle's Bakery and Restaurant**, Main Street, Schull, ℘ (028) 28459 (*inexpensive*). **The Courtyard**, Main Street, Schull, ℘ (028) 28209 (*inexpensive*). Bar/restaurant/craftshop/delicatessen. **Mary-Anne's Bar**, Castletownshend, ℘ (028) 36146 (*inexpensive*). Excellent bar food and friendly atmosphere. **Dillon's Bar**, Timoleague, Bandon, ℘ (023) 46390 (*inexpensive*). Continental style bar/café. Good snacks.

O'Donovan's Pub, 44 Pearse Street, Clonakilty, ℘ (023) 33250 (*inexpensive*). Plain cooking and pub grub. **Johnny Barry's Bar**, Glengarriff (*inexpensive*). Inexpensive bar food. **The Snug**, The Quay, Bantry, ℘ (027) 50057 (*inexpensive*). Eccentric bar opposite the harbour with simple home-cooked dishes. **The Tin** pub, Ahakista (*inexpensive*). Wacky bar opposite Shiro Japanese dinner house.

Theatre, music and film: check the *Cork Examiner and Evening Echo*. In the evenings there is plenty to choose from but try to see a production by the Theatre of the South, at the Cork Opera House. They tend to produce only contemporary Irish writers' work which can be very good. The Theatre of the South is open for about eight weeks every summer. Opera House, Emmett Place, ✆ (021) 270022. Otherwise, go to the Everyman Theatre, McCurtain Street, ✆ (021) 501673, which does not restrict itself in any way—tragedy, farce and comedy, by any author as long as he or she is good. The Triskel Arts Centre, off South Main Street, ✆ (021) 272022/272023, hosts a wide range of events—music, exhibitions, drama, film seasons, poetry readings.

Clubs/pubs: Klub Kaos on Oliver Plunkett Street is currently the 'in' nightspot. Mollies on Tuckey Street is where to go for drinks beforehand; and a new club called Hysteria, near French Church Street augurs well. For music and a pint of Murphy's Stout, Charlie's, the Lobby, and the Phoenix, all on Union Quay often have music whilst An Bodhran, 42 George's Quay or An Spailpin Fanach on South Main Street specialise in traditional Irish.

County Waterford

Waterford is a fertile county with rugged mountain beauty and a pretty coastline dotted with fishing villages-cum-holiday resorts, and interesting ruins. The southeast coast also has the reputation of being sunny. The county is traversed by two mountain ranges, the Comeragh and the Monavullagh, set with tiny lakes, and planted conifer forests. The valley in which Waterford City lies is watered by the River Suir which flows into the River Nore, which in turn flows into the River Barrow—sister rivers, and the county is bordered by the Blackwater and the great Atlantic sea. In *The Book of Invasions*, or *Lebor Gabala*, a mythological account of the pre-history of Ireland, the first Celts described the site where Waterford City grew up as 'a sweet confluence of waters, a trinity of rivers'.

The county has absorbed the Celt, the Norse and the Norman, and all have contributed to the richness of its archaeological remains, castles and lovely church buildings. It was actually Norsemen who founded the city of Waterford about AD 850, and used it as a base from which to raid up the rivers to the rich valleys of Tipperary and beyond; the name Waterford is of Danish origin.

History

A brief sketch of the county's history must start with the great race of builders from the Boyne Valley who built Newgrange in County Meath. They spread down to Waterford and left impressive monuments of their civilization. The manner of their decorative carvings is unmistakable and it has been tagged the 'Boyne Valley style'. Their tombs and portal dolmens are particularily concentrated around the seaside resort of Tramore; and human remains that date from about 9000 BC have been discovered east of Cappoquin.

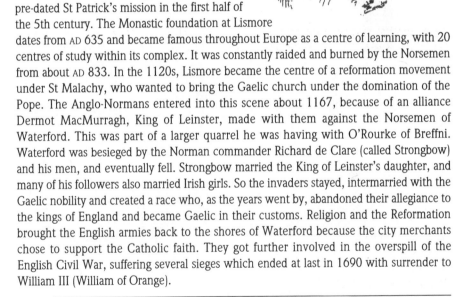

When the Celts invaded in about 500 BC, the main tribe in Waterford seems to have been the Deisi, who launched successful raids on Roman Britain. They held territory between the Blackwater and the Suir, and such was their impact that Waterford county is still referred to as 'the Decies'. The Norsemen kept to their patch round Vadrafjord or Waterford city, occupied with raiding and establishing trade-links. The early Christian monks made a great impact on the Decies. St Declan of Ardmore is supposed to have pre-dated St Patrick's mission in the first half of the 5th century. The Monastic foundation at Lismore dates from AD 635 and became famous throughout Europe as a centre of learning, with 20 centres of study within its complex. It was constantly raided and burned by the Norsemen from about AD 833. In the 1120s, Lismore became the centre of a reformation movement under St Malachy, who wanted to bring the Gaelic church under the domination of the Pope. The Anglo-Normans entered into this scene about 1167, because of an alliance Dermot MacMurragh, King of Leinster, made with them against the Norsemen of Waterford. This was part of a larger quarrel he was having with O'Rourke of Breffni. Waterford was besieged by the Norman commander Richard de Clare (called Strongbow) and his men, and eventually fell. Strongbow married the King of Leinster's daughter, and many of his followers also married Irish girls. So the invaders stayed, intermarried with the Gaelic nobility and created a race who, as the years went by, abandoned their allegiance to the kings of England and became Gaelic in their customs. Religion and the Reformation brought the English armies back to the shores of Waterford because the city merchants chose to support the Catholic faith. They got further involved in the overspill of the English Civil War, suffering several sieges which ended at last in 1690 with surrender to William III (William of Orange).

Getting There and Around

By air: Cork Airport is about 60 miles (96km) away. Waterford Airport has flights to Dublin, Manchester and London with Manx Air and Ryanair.

By boat: to ferry ports of Rosslare in County Wexford, and Dun Laoghaire and Dublin.

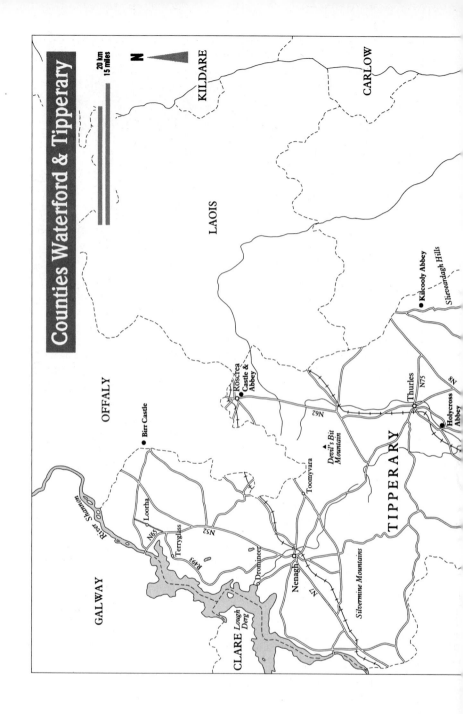

Counties Waterford & Tipperary

20 km
15 miles

N

KILDARE

CARLOW

LAOIS

OFFALY

Kilcooly Abbey

Slieveardagh Hills

Birr Castle

Roscrea
Castle &
Abbey

Thurles

N75

N8

N62

Devil's Bit
Mountain

Holycross
Abbey

River Shannon

Loorha

Terryglass

N65

N52

TIPPERARY

Toomyvara

GALWAY

R493

Dromineer

Silvermine Mountains

Nenagh

N7

CLARE Lough
Derg

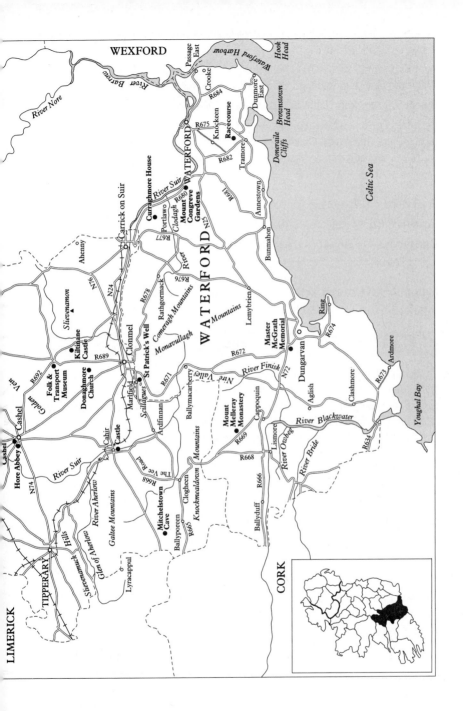

By rail: mainline train services connect Waterford City with Dublin, Limerick and Rosslare, ✆ (051) 73401

By bus: Express buses link Waterford City with Dublin. Local services from Waterford City to most small villages. Waterford Bus Station, ✆ (051) 73401.

By car: car hire from South-East rent-a-car in Waterford, ✆ (051) 21550.

By bike: The Raleigh Rent-a-Bike network operates throughout the county. Your local dealers are; Wright's Bike Shop, Henrietta Street, Waterford, ✆ (051) 74411; Murphy's toys and cycles, Main Street, Dungarvan, ✆ (058) 41376.

Tourist Information

Waterford, 41 The Quay, ✆ (051) 75788, all year.

Tramore, Railway Square, ✆ (051) 81572, June to beginning of September.

Dungarvan, ✆ (058) 41741, June to September.

Festivals

September/October: Waterford International Festival of Light Opera at the Theatre Royal; ✆ (051) 74402/32001.

Waterford City

Waterford is snugly situated on a curve of the River Suir before it opens out into the sea. It has a reputation for good wine bars and the old parts of it are attractive, though, as is too often the case, the modern surroundings are very ugly. A quick tour of the city should perhaps start with the **Waterford Crystal Glass Factory**, a mile or so (2km) west of the city on the Cork Road (N25). There are organised tours around the factory, see under activities. Most visitors will have heard of Waterford Crystal, which has a worldwide market. It is beautifully patterned cut glass with many different styles. The industry was started in 1783 and pieces dating from that time are now extremely valuable. You can see a wonderful example of Waterford glass in the cut-glass chandelier which hangs in the City Hall in the Mall. The Mall is right in the heart of Waterford, and from here you can see most of the buildings of interest in the city. An organized tour is available from June to Sept, 12–2, starting from the Granville Hotel. An alternative tour could include the Crystal factory, a quick look in at the City Hall, and then a browse in **Reginald's Tower** (*open all year, Mon–Sat; adm includes heritage centre;* ✆ *(051) 71227 for more details*) which guards the end of the Mall by the river. A massive circular fortress with a wall 10ft (3m) thick, it was built in 1003, and named after the Norse governor of the time. When the desperado Strongbow landed in 1170 and took the city, Reginald's Tower became a Norman stronghold and has since then served as a royal residence, a mint, a military barracks and a city prison. It is now the civic **museum** with a very interesting display of old artefacts and memorabilia from Waterford's past.

A quick walk down the Quay takes you past the ruined French Church, originally a Franciscan foundation built in 1240. It got the label 'The French Church' because it was used by Huguenot refugees who came to Ireland after the Revocation of the Edict of Nantes in 1696. It has a lovely east window and is always accessible. Turn third left after the French Church and you come to St Olaf's Church, which was founded by the Norsemen in about AD 870 and rebuilt by Normans. Walking back up towards the Mall is the Church of Ireland Cathedral, Christ Church, which was built in 1779 and is classical Georgian in style. Inside are several older monuments, one of them in remembrance of a man named Rice, who chose to depict himself in a state of decay with frogs, toads and other wriggling things emerging from his entrails. The cathedral was restored after fire in 1779 to plans created by a local architect, John Roberts. It was redecorated again in 1891. Another lovely building is the Chamber of Commerce in George Steet, built by the same architect as the cathedral. You can ask to see inside it. In **St Peter's Church**, Greyfriars Street, is a Heritage Centre (*open April–Sept, Mon–Fri, half-day Sat; ℗ (051) 73501*) where excavated artefacts from the Viking period are displayed. In September the Theatre Royal hosts the Waterford International Festival of Light Opera. Waterford City produced some great actors whose names are still revered in the acting world: Mrs Jordon in 1767, and Charles Kean in 1811. It is also where the Christian Brothers opened their first scholastic establishment in 1802. Edmund Ignatius Rice had his first foundation at Mount Sion in Barrack Street, since when the order has spread all over the world. **Mount Congreve Demesne and Wild Garden** at Kilmeadan, five miles (8km) west of Waterford city, stretches over 110 acres with one of the largest collection of rhododendrons in the world. (*Guided tours by appointment only; adm exp; ℗ (051) 84115.*)

The Coast from Portlaw to Annestown

Portlaw on the River Clodagh, northwest of Waterford on the R680, was founded as a model village by a Quaker family, the Malcolmsons, who had started up a cotton industry in the 19th century; unfortunately many of the quaint houses have been modernized and become dull in the process. Beside the town is **Curraghmore House and Gardens**, the family home of the Marquis of Waterford (*open from 1 April–30 Sept, every Thurs and public holiday, 2–5; adm; ℗ (051) 87101*). The family name is Beresford and they, the Beresfords, were noted for their dominance in the Church and Government; one of them was called 'Sand Martin' because of his skill in picking sinecures and plum jobs for his many friends. (A characteristic of the sand martin is to share his nest with a numerous extended family.) Curraghmore is worth visiting just to see the splendid, grey 18th-century house, in its parkland setting with gentle sloping hills rising behind. It is worth seeking out the 18th-century shell-house made by the Countess of Tyrone. The specimen trees have reached a magnificent size, they were mainly planted in the 19th century. The house is open by special arrangement.

Nearby on the Waterford Harbour is the village of Crooke. Roughly opposite and a little further down is Hook Head, interesting because the two—so it is claimed—are immortalized in the saying 'By Hook or by Crooke', a phrase first used by sailors. There is nothing much to see at Crooke, but Passage East further up the Barrow estuary is an atmospheric place which has been a ferry village for centuries, and an important port. It was here that Strongbow landed in 1170, and here that Henry II landed with 4000 men in 400 ships a year later, to make sure that Strongbow did not set up a rival kingdom and step into the shoes of his father-in-law Dermot MacMurrough, who had just died. He formally declared Waterford a Royal City, and tradition holds that it remained loyal to him and his heirs until the 16th century, and the change of the English monarchy from Roman Catholic to Protestant. Today, there is a car ferry across from here to County Wexford.

Dunmore East, 10 miles (16km) south of the city, is a little seaside place, rather like a Devon fishing village, with beautiful little headlands made of old red sandstone carved into cliffs and safe bathing beaches. Sea pinks grow along the cliff edges, which have some lovely peaceful places to walk. Just follow the coast path leading along to Brownstown Head, where there is the remains of a fort. You will meet the colourful fishermen in the bars, though they can be quite clannish. Dunmore was the centre of a thriving herring industry and the Irish terminal for a mail service from England in the early 19th century.

Tramore, 10 miles (16km) further south around the coast to the west, is the place to go if you want to meet Irish people on holiday rather than fellow foreigners. Its 3 miles (4.8km) of sand are swept by the Gulf Stream, which makes the sea fun for bathers and surfers. It has a well developed amenity complex beside the promenade, a miniature railway and boating lake, and a first-class racecourse. At **Celtworld** (*open March to May and October, daily 10–5.30; June–Sept, daily 10–8; adm*), the world of the 'celt' is described and 'interpreted' using the latest technology. A quick and pleasant walk to the west of the town leads by a coastal path to some steep cliffs known as the Doneraile Cliffs. The remarkable **Knockeen Dolmen** is near by, but quite difficult to find. Follows the signs off the Tramore to Carrick on Suir road (R682). Drive until you meet a three-forked road. Take the right fork and drive uphill until you come to a large white farmhouse. Opposite is a field gate and stile. The dolmen is in the shadow of the hedge on the far side of the field. It probably marks the grave of a local Deisi chieftain. This sort of tomb-building was going on when people moved from being hunter-gatherers to keeping domestic animals and growing their own food. Two large matching upright stones mark the entrance, with three smaller standing stones behind. The uprights support the heavy capstone, which is thought to have been raized up by a system of propping and levering.

Annestown, on the R675 nearby, also has a lovely beach. So does Bunmahon, further west, a small fishing village which is perched above some magnificent cliffs.

Dungarvan to Ardmore

Dungarvan is a pleasant seaside resort where the River Colligan broadens into Dungarvan Bay. There are the remains of an old Norman Castle and a pretty arched bridge. Most notorious is the very individual expression of decorative art in the Shell Cottage. It has become very well known, and bus tours of people stop to admire this very suburban-style house, whose every surface and garden is decorated with coloured shells in various patterns. You might think it kitsch but a lot of energy and dedication has gone into it. The work was done by a Shell oil company employee who on his many trips around the world collected every sort of shell. Religious knick-knacks, toys and other colourful objects have also been introduced into the shell patterns. His widow now continues his life's work. There is a small showroom in the house where shell souvenirs are sold to aid two leper colonies in Africa. Anyone in town will direct you there. In the graveyard of the Church of Ireland church by the river is a curious 'holed' gable with circular openings. Two and a half miles (4km) northwest of the town, on the fork of the R672 and N72, is the **Master Mcgrath Memorial** erected in 1873: a plain stone structure with an elegant spire. The tablet is engraved not with the name of some famous Victorian, but with the image of a greyhound. In case you didn't know, Master McGrath won the Waterloo Cup for coursing three times during the 19th century. The greyhound is still remembered in ballads, and by a brand of superior dog food. About 5 miles (8km) south on the R674 is the famous Irish-speaking village of Ring, where Irish scholars go to study.

Ardmore, further to the west along the coast on the R673, is an important ecclesiastical site. Just outside Ardmore Village are the remains of a 7th-century monastic settlement founded by St Declan, possibly as early as the 5th century. Some say St Declan was busy converting the pagans to Christianity whilst St Patrick was still a slave herding cattle. The ancient remains are spread out over a small area and interspersed with more modern gravestones and memorials. They include the most graceful round tower in Ireland, built in the 11th century of cut stone. Its entrance door is 10ft (3m) above the ground, so that the monks could store precious things up there: in times of trouble they entered it by means of a retractable ladder. There is also the remains of a 12th-century cathedral, a mixture of Hiberno-Romanesque and Early-English styles, with a wealth of figure sculpture spread over almost the whole of the west gable. The figures are badly weathered but it is just possible to make out the Judgement of Solomon, Adam and Eve with the Tree and the Serpent, and the Adoration of the Magi. In the nave and chancel are some ogham stones which suggest this was a burial place even before St Declan arrived. The lower portion of the building is believed to incorporate part of an earlier 7th-century church. Besides the cathedral and the tower, there is St Declan's Oratory in the eastern part of the graveyard. It is reputed to be where he is buried, and on 24 July many locals still make a pilgrimage to it. St Declan's Oratory is typical of the small, dark dwellings in which the early fathers used to live. Apparently this preference for separate cells grouped together comes from the Coptic Egyptian influence in the Irish Church, along with a rejection of the bodily senses and a deep suspicion of women. St Declan's Oratory was not in fact built until the 9th century, but Irish architecture seems to advance very slowly. This foundation was the recognized seat of a bishop as early as AD 1111. About half a mile to the east is St Declan's Holy Well. It was renovated in 1789, and many people still visit it. There is a stone chair, three stone crosses and stone basin for pilgrims to wash their limbs in. Most holy wells have pre-Christian associations of magical healing powers, which the early clerics modified to fit in with Christianity. Legend and fact become impossibly mixed up and this area is scattered with objects with folk stories behind them. Down on the strand is a crannog, visible only when the tide is out. There too lies St Declan's Stone at the end of the strand. It was supposed to have been used by the saint to carry his bell and vestments across the sea from Wales. It is reputed that if you crawl beneath it your aches and pains will be cured—although, of course, this manoeuvre is impossible for sinners. The old pilgrims' route between here and Cashel in Co. Tipperary is being opened up for walkers, this includes a 2½-mile (4km) route around Ardmore itself.

Cappoquin to Ballymacabry and the Nire Valley

The R671 runs from the southwest corner of the county, through Clashmore and Aglish to Cappoquin, following stretches of the Blackwater, which are lined by stately grey houses. **Cappoquin** is at the head of the tidal estuary of the River Blackwater. Graceful timbered hills surround it, whilst the northern slopes of the Knockmealdown Mountains rise to the north. This is an excellent place to fish for trout or roach. Four miles (6.4km) to the north off the R669 is the Trappist Cistercian Abbey of **Mount Melleray**. The monastery is modern, but in its precincts are five ogham stones. The order has built up an almost self-sufficient community which still keeps the old rule of monastic hospitality, so do not hesitate to accept if they offer you a meal. The monks have transformed the barren mountainous landscape into green farmland through great effort and determination. It is a place of prayer, contemplation and work, and everyone is welcome. At the foot of the hill on the road to the abbey is **Melleray Grotto** whose statue of the Virgin is said to move.

The N72 from Cappoquin to Lismore follows the River Blackwater, flowing smoothly between green fields and trees, overlooked by gracious houses. **Lismore** has one of the finest castles in Ireland which dates back in parts to the original built by King John in 1185. It belonged to Sir Walter Raleigh in 1589 and he sold it to the adventurer Richard Boyle, later the first Earl of Cork, who apparently said: 'I arrived out of England into Ireland, where God guided me hither, bringing with me a taffeta doublet and a pair of velvet breeches, a new shirt of laced fustin cutt upon taffeta, a bracelet of gold, a diamond ring, and twenty-seven pounds three shillings in monie in my purse.' His 14th child is remembered as the Father of Chemistry because in the late 17th century he established Boyle's Law, which proves that air has weight—a milestone in the dissociation of chemistry from alchemy. In 1814 the Lismore Crozier and the 15th-century manuscript *The Book of Lismore* were discovered in one of the castle walls. (The Lismore Crozier is on display in the National Museum in Dublin.) Eventually the castle passed through the female line to the Devonshire family, who still own it. The present castle was rebuilt in the mid-19th century by the 6th Duke of Devonshire. Lismore means 'great fort' in Irish, and this great pile of grey castellated stone hanging over the Blackwater River lives up to all one's expectations of what a castle should be. Unfortunately, it is not open to the general public but the **gardens**, and especially the Yew Walk, are very lovely (*entrance in the town of Lismore; open 8 May–8 Sept, 1.45–4.45, daily except Sat; adm; © (058) 54424*). It is said that Edmund Spenser wrote part of his *Faerie Queene* here. You are lucky if you can visit in late spring when the camellias and magnolias are in bloom.

Lismore is a place of ancient renown both for its learning and piety. Under St Colman in the 8th century it won the title of 'Luminary of the Western World', and men came from all over Europe to study here. The Norsemen, of course, were attracted to it as bees to honey, and looted the town and abbey frequently, but the monastery and abbey were finally destroyed by Raymond le Gros and his Norman mercenaries in 1173. The

Cathedral of St Carthach is one of the loveliest in Ireland and approached by a tree-lined walk. It dates from medieval times but was restored by the Earl of Cork in 1633. The graceful limestone spire was added in 1827. There is an interesting 1557 MacGrath tomb. The Heritage Centre in the Courthouse details the town's ancient history. On the R668, a few hundred yards north of the castle is a fine walk to Ballysagartmore Towers, a Gothic style gateway and tower which guards the entrance to a three arched bridge; a waterfall adds to the beauty of the scene.

To the west of Lismore, the nearby village of Ballyduff on the Lismore–Fermoy road (R666) is another centre to base yourself for salmon or roach fishing. To the northeast, the **Nire Valley** is fantastic for views, pony-trekking and walking. On either side are mountain slopes, clear tumbling streams and woods. (It lies between Comeragh and Knockmealdown ranges and can be approached from Clonmel to Ballymacarberry, or from the R671 off the N72 near Cappoquin.) **Ballymacarberry** is a welcome spot for pony-trekkers and walkers exploring the Nire Valley, and the heather-covered slopes of the Comeragh Mountains. The local bar is very friendly and hires out ponies, as does Melody's Riding Stables (*see* 'Activities', below). A superb car drive awaits you if you head for the village of Lemybrien on the junction of the Waterford/Carrick-on-Suir road to Dungarvan road (R676 and N25). Just north of it is a highly scenic drive through the Comeraghs which takes you up to the Mahon Waterfall. It is well signposted. Rathgormack on the R678, about 6 miles (10 km) from Clonmel, is a lovely little village on the northern side of the Comeragh mountains. It is a popular hiking centre, and boasts the remains of an early-medieval church and castle.

Shopping

Waterford crystal: Waterford Crystal Factory, Kilbarry, Waterford; ✆ (051) 73311.

Crafts: Aisling Crafts, Barronstrand Street, Waterford. Mrs Hackett, 68 Mill Street, Cappoquin, ✆ (058) 54107, for crochet. Woodcraft, Dunabrathin, Annestown; ✆ (051) 96110. John Glavey, hand-made fiddles, Passage East ✆ (051) 82406.

Activities

Golf: in Tramore; ✆ (051) 86170. Faithlegs Golf Club, Waterford City ✆ (051) 82241. West Waterford Golf and Country Club, Dungarvan ✆ (058) 43216; Waterford Castle ✆ (051) 71633.

Sea-angling: Cormac Walsh Gone Fishin', 42 Lower Main Street, ✆ (058) 43514 and Dungarvan Charter Angling, Kilosserva, Dungarvan, ✆ (058) 43286.

Fishing: for salmon and trout on the River Blackwater contact the Blackwater Lodge, Ballyduff, ✆ (058) 60235 and Clonanav Farm, Nire Valley, ✆ (052) 36141; salmon at Carysville Fishery, Fermoy, ✆ (025) 31094. Coarse fishing for roach and dace on the Blackwater just past the Cappoquin Bacon factory. Information and tackle from Mr J. O'Sullivan, 4 Patrick Street, Fermoy, ✆ (025) 31110.

Swimming: at Tramore, Dunmore East, Ardmore and Dungarvan. Splashworld, Tramore, ✆ (051) 81330. Indoor water-based adventure centre.

Surfing: championships in Tramore, ✆ (051) 86582.

Walking: through the Comeraghs on the Munster Way, a marked trail. Contact the tourist office for details. Orienteering, bird-watching, hill-walking and other activities organised through Shielbaggan Outdoor Pursuits Centre, Ramsgrange, New Ross, County Wexford, ✆ (051) 62108. For local walks in the Nire Valley contact Larry and Eileen Ryan, Clonanav Farm House, Ballymacarberry, ✆ (052) 36141. St Declan's long distance walk, Ardmore, ✆ (024) 94152.

Pony-trekking: Melody's Riding Stables, Ballymacarberry, ✆ (052) 36147.

Hunting: The Waterford Hunt, Woodstown, ✆ (051) 82549/82235. The West Waterford Hunt, C. Trigg, Tourtane House, Glencairn, ✆ (058) 54110. The Kilwatermoy Hunt, T. Murray, Dunmoon, Tallow, ✆ (058) 56122.

Horse-racing: at Waterford and Tramore in June and August.

Polo school: learn to play in days at the only international polo school in Europe. You stay in an attractive 18th-century mansion and pay about IR£200 a day according to how much instruction you want. Contact Major Hugh Dawnay, Whitfield Court Polo School, Waterford, ✆ (051) 84216.

Lively arts: Waterford Arts Centre, Garter Lane, 50 O'Connell Street, Waterford, ✆ (051) 55038/77153.

Where to Stay

expensive

Granville Hotel, Waterford, ✆ (051) 55111. Smart, old-world and central. **Waterford Castle**, The Island, Ballinakill, Waterford. ✆ (051) 78203. Two miles (3.2km) downstream from Waterford City, this Anglo-Norman castle is very luxurious, with excellent sporting facilities.

moderate

Blackwater Lodge, Upper Ballyduff, ✆ (058) 60235. A snug place for fishermen to swop stories in. **Ballyrafter House**, Lismore, ✆ (058) 54002. Comfortable Georgian house, ideal place to centre yourself for fishing or just exploring the lovely Blackwater Valley. **Prendiville's Restaurant and Guesthouse**, Cork Road, just outside Waterford, ✆ (051) 78851. Nice simple rooms in a restored stone gatelodge. **Richmond House**, Cappoquin, ✆ (058) 54278. Comfortable Georgian country house, en suite rooms.

Dooley's Hotel, Waterford, ✆ (051) 73531. Old, established, friendly. **Whitechurch House Hotel**, Cappagh, Dungarven, ✆ (058) 68182. Pretty Georgian house in lovely grounds. **O'Shea's Hotel**, Strand Street, Tramore, ✆ (051) 81246. Small family-run hotel, close to the beach.

Mrs Richardson, **Elton Lodge**, Rossduff, Dunmore East, ✆ (051) 82117. Set in a lovely wooded garden, this is a pretty Georgian farmhouse between Waterford City and Dunmore East. Mrs Nugent, **The Castle**, Millstreet, Cappagh, nr Dungarvan, ✆ (058) 68049. This has a lovely restored 15th-century wing. It is not a smart castle, but is very homely. Tennis, trout fishing, and riding are available on the farm. Mrs Ryan, **Clonanav Farmhouse**, Ballymacarberry, Nire Valley. ✆ (052) 36141. The family are experts on local walks and angling.

Dunmore Lodge, Dunmore East. Cosy rooms in an old cottage, ✆ (051) 83454. **Aglish House**, Aglish, ✆ (024) 96191. Nice stone farmhouse near River Blackwater. Mrs Moore, **Old School House**, Ballymacarberry, Nire Valley, ✆ (052) 36217 Hospitable and comfortable.

self-catering

Pretty thatched cottages outside Ardmore and overlooking the sea. ✆ (024) 94116. From IR£130 a week. Stone-built farmhouse near Cappagh, Dungarvan. **Shamrock Cottages UK**, ✆ (0823) 660126. Mews house in stable yard on wooded estate. Mrs Claire Chavasse, **Cappagh House**, Cappagh, ✆ (058) 68185 From IR£130 per week.

Eating Out

moderate

Candlelight Inn, Dunmore East, ✆ (051) 83215. Well-cooked food, featuring a lot of fish and shellfish. **The Ship Restaurant and Bar**, Dunmore East, ✆ (051) 83144. Casual, fun atmosphere. Good seafood. **Dwyers Restaurant**, 5 Mary Street, ✆ (051) 77478. In a converted barracks, cosy, comfortable ambience and good food.

inexpensive/cheap

Haricots Wholefood Restaurant, 11 O'Connell Street, Waterford. Very good homemade soups, and, a rarity in Irish restaurants, freshly squeezed juice! Delicious homemade ice cream and cakes. Open till 8 only. **Reginald Tavern**, The Mall, Waterford, ✆ (051) 55087. Good pub grub behind Reginald's Tower. **The Saddler's Tea Shop**, The Square, Cappoquin, ✆ (058) 54045. Good home-baking and light lunches. **Seanachie Restaurant**, Dungarvan, ✆ (058) 42242. Good bar food in traditional thatched bar with music at night. **Chapman's Restaurant**, 61 The Quay, Waterford, ✆ (051) 74938. Delicious pâté and ice cream. *Daytime only.* **McAlpin's Sun Inn**, Checkpoint, ✆ (051) 82182.Good pub grub. *Evenings only.*

Entertainment and Nightlife

Clubs: Flow Motion nightclub, above Egans, Barrowstrand Street, Waterford. Held every Friday, relatively young crowd, playing hiphop and indie sounds.

To get a clear idea of the beauty of Tipperary—and it is very beautiful, even though it lacks a stretch of coastline—walk to the top of Slievenamon, which in early summer is scented with the almond fragrance of gorse blossom. Slievenamon is a county landmark; a conical mountain north of Clonmel that rises to 2358ft (719m). Up there, you get the feeling of space and a wide, splendid view: to the south are the Comeraghs and silver ribbon of the Suir; to the west, the Galtees; and to the north, the Rock of Cashel rising out of the flat, rich farmland.

Slievenamon means, in Irish, 'mountain of the fairy women'. The story relates how Fionn and the Fianna warriors had dallied with these fairy women, so when Fionn decided to wed, to prevent any of them becoming jealous, he said he would marry the one who reached the summit of the mountain first. However, the wily man had set his heart on Grainne, the daughter of King Cormac, and so he whisked her up to the top the evening before the race. When the panting winner reached the top, 'there sat the delicate winsome Grainne and not a feather of her ruffled'. So much for legend. In music, the refrain 'It's a long way to Tipperary' entered the battlefields of the Somme as a favourite British marching song during the First World War.

So many people have heard of the county, without knowing of its glorious countryside and its wealth of 12th- and 13th-century church buildings and castles. For the angler there are rivers of brown trout; for the archaeologist, plenty of Stone Age and Iron Age sites. The horsey will be attracted by the hunting and the gourmet riding holidays you can join around Lough Derg. This is also a fine place for the breeding of horses, gun-dogs and greyhounds. But, for passing travellers, it is the story of Cashel of the Kings and the strength of Cahir Castle which hold the imagination. Another treasure is the border town of Birr, up in the north of the county, where the gardens and arboretum of the castle are amongst the finest in the Island and there is soon to be a splendid scientific centre.

History

The history of this county is very closely linked to that of the great Ormonde family. The founder of the family in Ireland was Theobald Fitzwalter, who came over in 1185 with Prince John, and was later appointed to high office as Chief Butler to the Lord of Ireland. Henceforth, the family surname was Butler, and its members generally maintained a policy of faithfulness to the interests of the British crown. This was in direct contrast to their kinsfolk, and arch enemies, the Geraldines. The Geraldines were close neighbours and split into two branches, Desmond and Kildare.

Tipperary was divided into two Ridings; with Clonmel as the capital of the South Riding, and Nenagh as the capital of the North Riding. This division dates from some early administrative peculiarity.

Tipperary has always been a rich prize for the winners of battles and uprisings, because of its fertile farms and pastures. In the 18th century is was a county of landlords and relatively prosperous peasants. The region was settled during this time by Palatines who were fleeing religious persecution. The potato famine hit hard in the 1840s; and later, during the uncertain times leading up to Independence, many landlords were burnt out.

Getting There and Around

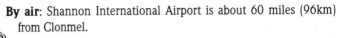

By air: Shannon International Airport is about 60 miles (96km) from Clonmel.

By rail: mainline routes pass through the county and stop at Thurles, Cahir, Clonmel, Carrick on Suir and Roscrea.

By bus: Bus Eireann serves many country towns and villages, ✆ Clonmel Bus Station, (052) 22622; or Roscrea Bus Station, (0505) 21198.

By car: many car-hire companies are based at Shannon Airport. Outside the airport, try Donal Ryan, Templederry Nenagh/Killinan, Thurles, ✆ (0504) 52243/21400; Shaun Crowe, Car Rentals, Limerick Road, Tipperary, ✆ (062) 51219.

By bike: The Raleigh Rent-a-Bike network operates throughout the county. Your local dealer in Nenagh is Raymond Moynan, 61 Pearse Street, Nenagh, ✆ (067) 31293.

Tourist Information

Cahir Castle, ✆ (052) 41453, July and August.

Cashel Town Hall, ✆ (062) 61333, April to September.

Clonmel, ✆ (052) 22960, June to early September.

Nenagh, ✆ (067) 31610, May to end of September.

Festivals

March: Thurles Music Festival: music, song and dance.

April: Cashel Point-to-point., ✆ (01) 800295 or the tourist office for details.

June: Clonmel Show with horse jumping.

End of July: Feile Rock Festival, Thurles, ✆ (0504) 22702, includes the best of Irish bands.

August: Literary gathering in honour of Charles Kickham 1848-82, novelist and revolutionary, at Mullinahone. ✆ (052) 53200 for details. There are lectures, field trips and poetry readings. Irish traditional music festival in Clonmel ✆ (01) 280 0295.

Late August: Festival in Tipperary Town. Details from the tourist office.

The Southeast and Around Clonmel

Clonmel, in the south of the county on the N24, means in Irish 'the honeyed meadows', and it has a lovely setting by the River Suir and the Comeragh Mountains. The town was important when the Norman family of Butler were all-powerful, and today it is the largest in the county, with prosperous food industries and bustling shops. It has a prosperous bright look about it, which is not surprising as most of Tipperary, particularly its central region around the Suir and the Golden Vein, consists of very fertile land.

The restored Franciscan Church in the town centre retains its old tower and a 15th-century Butler tomb with stone effigies of a knight and lady. The Art Gallery in the Library in Parnell Street has some good 20th-century paintings. Laurence Sterne, who wrote one of the first English novels, *Tristram Shandy*, was born here (in 1713); as was George Borrow, another English novelist (1803–81). The enterprising Italian pedlar Charles Bianconi, who gave Ireland its first public transport service when he ran his celebrated Bianconi Long Cars from Clonmel to Cahir in 1815, came to Clonmel as a poor vendor of holy pictures, and stayed. The Parish Church of St Mary has a fine east window. About 2 miles (3 km) east of town, off the N24 and near Marlfield, is St Patrick's Well. This is a noted local beauty spot, in a pretty glen and near the Scillogues twin lakes.

Further downriver, still following the N24, is the old town of **Carrick on Suir**, a thriving market town which in the past had a big woollen industry, founded by the Duke of Ormonde in 1640. His family, the Butlers, had long made Carrick their stronghold, and Black Tom the 10th Earl of Ormonde built himself the fortified Elizabethan mansion home you can see, known as '**The Castle**' *(open mid-June to Sept, daily, 9.30–6.30, adm; © (051) 40787*). He was loyal to Elizabeth I, and was evidently hoping for quieter times. There is nothing else quite like this Tudor mansion in Ireland, for when it was built the transition from the fortified castle to the undefended house had not yet begun, and when it did, the Tudor style gave way to other architectural fashions. The Office of Public Works has sympathetically restored it, returning to the long gallery the great carved fireplace that had adorned Kilkenny Castle for many years.

Ahenny (the ford of fire), about 3½ miles (6km) from Carrick on Suir on the R607 and the border with County Kilkenny, boasts two elaborately carved stone crosses from the 8th century in a sleepy old churchyard. The bases are carved with wonderful figure-scenes; and the crosses themselves with spiral, interlaced and fret designs. The art of the high cross has developed here from abstract decoration to the telling of a story in stone. There is a message on the base of the larger North Cross depicting Christ giving the Apostles their mission; and in the base of the South Cross, the scene of Daniel in the lion's den. Around the neighbourhood are some very extensive slate quarries. The vast spoil-heaps and water-filled holes are softened by many kinds of orchids, and yellow irises, known locally in Gaelic as *felistroms.*

Near Fethard, about 6 miles (10km) north of Clonmel on the R689, is Kiltinane Castle and Kiltinane Old Church where you can see some *sheila-na-gigs (see* p. 590) smothered in ivy. **Fethard** itself, 3 miles (4.82km) further north, has a lovely old church with fine 15th-century windows and a square tower. There is also a 14th-century Augustinian abbey, which has a fine collection of gravestones and beautiful arches beside the sanctuary. It is always open to view. On the Cashel road (R692) just outside the village is a **Folk and Transport Museum** *(open May–Sept, 10–6; adm; © (052) 31516 for more details)* with some interesting items from the agricultural past including a man-trap to catch poachers in. Three miles (4.8km) northeast of Fethard is the ruined **Knockelly Castle** with a fine town and 16th-century tower. And 5 miles (8km) south of the town is the ancient **Church of Donaghmore**, in a very ruined state. It still has a very beautiful carved Irish-Romanesque doorway.

Travelling northeast from Fethard towards the border with Kilkenny and the Slieveardagh Hills is **Killenaule**, on the R689. This is a fine example of an Irish village with an impressive Gothic-style Catholic church. There is a good view of Slievenamon from here. Ten miles (16 km) further north, again following the R689, you come to **Kilcooly Abbey**, on an unnumbered road which follows the wall of Kilcooly estate. The abbey is always accessible. Park your car outside the entrance gate as requested and walk a few hundred yards up the avenue. Take a path to the right past the Church of Ireland church, and through a field which has a marvellous stone dove-cot. Kilcooly Abbey is one of the most outstanding examples of Cistercian building in County Tipperary. (The other is the Abbey of Holycross, on the R660 between Cashel and Thurles.) It was founded in 1183 and nearly ruined in 1445, with subsequent reconstruction, but despite being a muddle it is a very handsome ruin with a superb six-light east window. The tomb flags are exquisitely carved by one Rory O'Tunney; and the south doorway is set in the midst of a highly ornamented screen with a carved crucifixion, and a scene of St Christopher bearing Jesus over a river symbolized by a shoal of fish. Amongst the other carvings is one on the doorway of the south transept, of a coy mermaid holding a looking-glass—a motif also found in Connacht. This region was settled by Palatines when some of them fled here in the 18th century from religious persecution in Germany. Their foreign-sounding names appear occasionally on shop and bar signs.

Cashel and Environs

South of Kilcooly, towards the middle of the county is the **Rock of Cashel** (*open daily, April–Sept, 9–7; Oct–March, Mon–Sun, 9.30–4.30; adm; © (062) 61437*): a steep outcrop of limestone rising out of the rich agricultural land of the Golden Vein, and crowned with the imposing ecclesiastical ruins of the ancient capital of the kings of Munster. The grouping of the bare, broken buildings against the sky is memorable and worth travelling many miles to see. There is an 11th-century round tower; a small chapel known as St Cormac's Chapel; a grand cathedral which was built in the 1230s; and a Vicars' Choral Hall, built around 1420. The Vicars' Choral Hall houses some exhibits including St Patrick's Cross. Outside on the rock is a replica of this cross, which was removed inside to protect it from erosion.

The Rock was the seat of ancient chieftains and later the early Munster kings, and upon this naturally well-defended high place there was very likely a stone fortress or caiseal. Legend records that in AD 450 St Patrick came to Cashel to baptize either Corc the Third or his brother and successor, Aengus. During the ceremony Patrick is supposed to have driven the sharp point of his pastoral staff into the king's foot by mistake, and the victim bore the wound without a sign, thinking that such pain was all part of becoming a Christian! From that time onwards, Cashel was also called St Patrick's Rock. Brian Boru, High King of Ireland, was crowned here in 977. In 1101 King Murtagh O'Brien granted the Rock to the Church, for its political importance had declined, and it became the See of the Archbishopric of Munster.

The Rock itself and the buildings are in the care of the Office of Public Works, and the guided tour of 40 minutes or so is very interesting and well-done. If you want to walk around on your own, you will find **Cormac's Chapel** on your right as you face the main bulk of the cathedral buildings, in the angle formed by the choir and south transept of the cathedral. It was built in the 1130s by the Bishop-King Cormac MacCarthy, and is a fascinating building architecturally, often described as Hiberno-Romanesque. The most Irish thing about Cormac's Chapel is its steep stone roof. As for the rest—the twin towers, the storeys of blank wall arcading, the high gable over the north dooorway and most of the stone-cut decoration—it could be German. Inside, is a spendid but broken stone sarcophagus of 11th-century work. The ingenious pattern of ribbon and wild beast decoration with which it is decorated was probably reintroduced into Ireland by the Vikings. Inside the sarcophagus a gilt copper crozier head was found. The head, which is now preserved in the National Museum in Dublin, is late-13th-century French, and richly ornamented with animal and fish forms in enamel, turquoise and sapphire. The French and German influences at Cashel are not surprising: there are documented links between Cashel and the Irish monasteries of Cologne and Ratisbon, and before the chapel was built monks were always travelling to and from the Continent. The fascinating carved-stone heads are a feature of Romanesque architecture, also originating in France. One is reminded of the Celtic head cult, and perhaps both Irish and French carvings derive from ancient Celtic monuments, such as can be seen in Roqueperteuse and Entremont in southern France.

As you enter the complex of buildings through the restored **Vicar's Choral Hall** you will see the Cross of St Patrick, probably of the same date as the sarcophagus. Christ is carved on one side and an ecclesiastic, perhaps St Patrick, is carved on the other. The massive base on which it is set is reputed to be the coronation stone of the Munster Kings. The immense ruins of the cathedral built beside Cormac's chapel date from the second half of the 13th century, and were the scene of two deliberate burnings during the Anglo-Irish wars of the Tudors and Cromwell. In 1686 the cathedral was restored and used by the Church of Ireland, but then it was left to decay until Cashel became a National Monument and everything was tidied up. What remains now is a fine example of austere Irish Gothic architecture with a rather short nave, the end of which is taken up with what is known as **The Castle**, a massive tower built to house the bishops in the 15th century. Everything about the cathedral is superbly grand and delicate in marked contrast to Cormac's Chapel. The round tower is about 11th-century. You can see the top of it perfectly if you climb to the top of The Castle, plus a wonderful view of the Golden Vein, the hills to the east and west, and Slievenamon in the south. There is a gap in the hills to the north, which is said to correspond exactly to the size of the Rock. Legend tells that the Devil bit off a great block and spat it onto the plain below, hence the name of the mountain: Devil's Bit. Just below, on the plain, is **Hore Abbey**, built by the Cistercians from Mellifont. It is always accessible if you want to visit it. The Rock looks superb at night, particularly during the summer when it is floodlit.

Cashel Town is a thriving place with a very good hotel, the Cashel Palace. It used to be the residence of the Church of Ireland archbishops and was built in gracious Queen Anne style in 1730. The architect was Edward Lovett Pearce (1699–1733), who also built the Irish Houses of Parliament in Dublin. It is worth having at least a coffee there so you can get a glimpse of the panelling and carving. The Diocesan Library, in the precincts of the St John the Baptist Cathedral, has one of the finest collections of 16th- and 17th-century books in Ireland. There are several on exhibition, but you have to contact the Dean if you want to get inside the cathedral. The Roman Catholic Church, also called after St John the Baptist, is in direct contrast to the simplicity of the cathedral—exotic and full of statues. The shop fronts in Cashel's main street are very colourful and the plastic age has not made too much impact. There's a lively folk music and dance centre at Brú Ború. (*open most of the year;* © *(062) 61122*). The town has a very good craft shop specializing in handwoven Shanagarry tweed and leather-work. In Padraig O'Mathuna's Gallery you can buy enamel and silver *objets d'art.*

Between Thurles and Cashel on the banks of the lazy Suir, deep in the countryside, reached by a road (R660) hemmed in by hawthorn hedges, is **Holycross Abbey**. Unfortunately, it is right next door to a rather tatty lounge bar. The abbey was built so that a portion of the True Cross presented by Pope Paschal II in 1110 to Murtagh O'Brien, King of Munster, might be properly enshrined. In 1182 the abbey was transferred to the Cistercians, who magnificently embellished it so that it became a popular place of pilgrimage. The building was rebuilt and changed over many centuries, and most of the finest work belongs to the 15th century. Inside is a sedile (seats reserved for the clergy) of perfect workmanship and design, so delicate that it resembles the work of a woodcarver rather than a mason working in limestone. The abbey is in full use today, having been restored by skilled workmen, who had to give their best to equal the standard of past centuries. It is open for prayer all day, and there is a craft shop in the courtyard.

Three miles (5km) north of Holycross on the R660 is **Thurles**, a busy market town situated on a plain by the River Suir. It was important as a strategic base during the Anglo-Norman conflict. And it is famous for its sugar beet factory, and for the founding of the Gaelic Athletic Association in 1884 by Archbishop Croke; there is a statue of him in Liberty Square. He is buried in the fine cathedral in the town centre; this was modelled on the one in Pisa, and has a pretty bell-tower. The Cathedral is the centre of the archdiocese of Cashel (R.C.), one of the four into which Ireland is divided. The town has a race-course, and the remnants of two keeps known as Bridge Castle (guarding the south side of the bridge) and Black Castle (in the town centre).

Cahir (the stone fortress), 8 miles (12.8km) south of Cashel at the meeting of the N8 and N24, is the nicest sort of Irish town, on the River Suir, with old-fashioned shops, colourfully painted houses and a wide main square, with plenty of space to walk and park. It has a magnificent, fully restored 15th-century castle on an island in the river; the largest of its period in Ireland. **Cahir Castle** (*open mid-June–mid-Sept daily, 9–7.30; April–Oct, 10–6; rest of the year 10–4.30; adm; for other times of opening,* © *(052) 41011*) was granted to James Butler, the third Earl of Ormonde, in 1375, and through many vicissitudes it remained in that family until Victorian times. The Ormonde Butlers were a

Norman family who became all-powerful in the county. They also became rather too inde-pendent of their monarch in England, and the massive fortifications of the castle came under fire from the cannon of the Earl of Essex in 1599. It was the only important success of his Irish Campaign. A visit to the castle is memorable as the guides are so enthusiastic and bring the defensive tactics of the besieged to life. One's head is set spinning with the ingenuity of the portcullis and the holes for burning oil. The Great Hall and other rooms within the castle are furnished and there is plenty of information about the lifestyle of the day. There is also an excellent audio-visual show outlining the archaeological and ecclesi-astical sites of importance in the area. The town of Cahir is very attractive and has several old buildings including the town house of the last Butler, the Earl of Glengall, in the square. This is now a typical Irish country hotel, the Cahir House Hotel. On the outskirts of Cahir is the newly restored **Swiss cottage** (© *(052) 41144 for opening times*), a delightful folly designed by John Nash for Lord and Lady Cahir in the early 19th century. It is the epitome of the rural idyll, with a higgledy-piggledy thatched roof, and grotto chairs . The Church of Ireland church here was also by Nash.

Ardfinnan, 5 miles (8km) south of Cahir, has a ruined castle built by the Earl of Morton, afterwards King John of England. It is always accessible. The River Suir is so wide here it needs a 14-arched bridge to span it.

The Vee Road (R668) from Cahir passes beautifully wrought iron gates and then plunges you deep in the countryside, eventually taking you through the Knockmealdown Gap which crosses the county border into Waterford. Ten miles (16km) south of Cahir, you pass through Clogheen, before the road curves up the slopes thick with pine forest, then it suddenly turns back on itself in a wide vee or hairpin and you get the most fabulous view over the patchwork of fields—from 1114ft (340m) above sea-level. Forest gives way to bracken and heather and a lonely mountain tarn; the steep cliff rising up behind it is covered in a bright green mass of oak and rhododendron. It is sometimes quite misty, and as you go down towards Lismore in County Waterford, you look through the rain and sparks of sunlight at shifting vales. Just before Lismore the trees, oak and beech, grow with tropical thickness, festooned with moss and ferns, then suddenly the spires of Lismore Cathedral stand against the skyline. Off the Vee Road, just west of Clogheen on the R665, Ballyporeen has become famous for its connection with the family of Ronald Reagan. His great-grandfather was baptized in the church here, and there is a pub named after him. Four miles (6km) away is the **Mitchelstown Cave** (*open throughout the year, 10–6; adm*). It is well signposted from Ballyporeen and 2 miles (3km) off the N8 Mitchelstown/ Cahir road. The system is very exciting to visit as the dripstone formations, stalactites, stalagmites and columns are fantastical. The caves have been given a variety of names such as the Altar Cave, where the formations are remarkably ecclesiastical, and the two caves known as The Lords and The Commons, after the Houses of Parliament. They were often used by rapparees or rebels on the run. The prominant rebel, the Sugane Earl of Desmond, took refuge in them in 1601 and was betrayed to the English by his kinsman Edmond, the last White Knight, who was paid £1000 for his treachery. A rare species of spider, *Porrhomma myops*, is found in the network of caves. You must explore with the guide, who is a fascinating source of stories and information about the caves.

The **Glen of Aherlow** between the Galtee mountains and the Slievenamuck Hills is not really a glen, but a lush and colourful valley. The R663 runs parallel with the River Aherlow, and signposts point to the numerous tarns and lakes set in the beautifully shaped Galtees.

Tipperary and the Galtees

Tipperary, lying in the Golden Vein, is a great farming centre. The town has a fine bronze figure of Charles Kickham (1828–82), a patriot and novelist. Read his novels *Knocknagow* and *The Homes of Tipperary* if you can. The Manchester Martyrs and John O'Leary (1830–1907), a Fenian leader and journalist, have memorials worth looking at. Also try to take a look at the Catholic church, a Gothic limestone building.

The Galtees are a magnificent huddle of peaks, formed from a conglomerate mixture of old red sandstone and silurian rocks, and stretching from Tipperary into Limerick, where they merge with the Ballyhoura Hills which border Cork. The ridge-walking is fantastic, especially around Lyracappul. The mountain splendour between the Silvermine Mountains (still mined for silver and zinc) and Toomyvara on your way to Nenagh is worth exploring. Around here you will hear stories of Ned of the Hill, the local Robin Hood, who plundered the English planter families and made up the lovely song 'The Dark Woman of the Glen'.

The North Riding of Tipperary

Nenagh is the administrative capital of the north riding of Tipperary. It has an impressive 100ft (33m) circular keep called the **Nenagh Round**, which was built as part of a strong pentagonal castle in 1200 by the first of the Ormonde line, and is one of the best examples of its kind in the country. The Bishop of Killaloe did it an injustice in 1858 by adding a castellated crown, but it is still beautiful. Across the road in the 19th-century gaol and governor's house is the **Nenagh Heritage Centre**, ✆ (067) 32633. Permanent displays and temporary exhibitions are held on view here; one, 'The Hurler', gives you an insight into that very national sport. The centre also provides a genealogical service. **Terryglass** and **Lorrha** are pretty villages beside Lough Derg. The former has a good craft shop. Lorrha is well worth a detour, for its architecture is still that of an unspoilt Irish village with a smithy, old school, and single-storey buildings. There are some remnants of 9th-century high crosses, a Norman motte, and a finely decorated doorway in the Norman church of the

Canons Regular. At the other end of the village is an attractive Roman Catholic church. Nearby is a splendid tower house encompassed by a cared-for lawn, and the remains of a 13th-century **Dominican priory** which has some lovely carved tombs of about 350 years old. Five miles (8km) from Nenagh is the holiday centre of **Dromineer** on the edge of Lough Derg. It has a fine ruined castle by the harbour, and the place has been sympathetically developed as a sailing, fishing, cruising and water-skiing resort. The wooded islands which cluster in the 25mile- (40km-) long lough are fun to explore, and there are regular cruises if you do not want to navigate a boat yourself (*see* 'Activities' below).

Roscrea and Surroundings

Two wonderful artefacts from the Early-Christian era have been found in these parts: the early-9th-century silver Roscrea Brooch, with its gold and amber decoration; and the mid-8th-century *Book of Dimma*, which contains the four *Gospels* and is enclosed in a shrine of bronze with silver plates ornamented with Celtic interlacing. Both treasures are now in Dublin. You can see the *Book of Dimma* in Trinity College, and the brooch in the National Museum. At the entrance to the little town of Roscrea, St Cronan's Church and Round Tower is all that remains of a monastery founded by St Cronan in the early 600s. The west façade of this 12th-century Romanesque church has survived and the rest was demolished to make way for an 1812 Church of Ireland church in the churchyard. There is a 12th-century high cross there too. The Roman Catholic **Church of St Cronan** in Abbey Street is built on the site of a 15th-century Franciscan friary, of which the square tower and part of the church remain. The altar piece is very attractive. You must go to the **Roscrea Castle Complex** in Castle Street, which contains **Damer House** (*open June–Sept, 9.30–6.30; © (0505) 21850 for other hours of opening and special exhibitions; adm*). This early-18th-century town house is in the curtilage of a 13th-century Norman castle built by the Ormondes. It was rescued by the Georgian Society and has a wonderful carved pine staircase which took years of loving care to restore. The panelling and proportions of the rooms are very attractive. The town Heritage Society now runs the centre with an annexe for cultural and historical exhibitions; it also has a craft and book shop and tourist information.

Birr on the north tip of County Tipperary is one of the prettiest towns in Ireland, with wide Georgian streets and mature trees. It is a border town, actually just in County Offaly (*see* pp.479–80). **Birr Castle** (*open all year round; adm; © (0509) 20056 for hours of opening and exhibitions*), built by the Parsons family, Earls of Rosse, is magnificent. As you enter through the imposing gates, it is like a magic world where the trees are greener and the flowers vivid, and the fruit-trees are always laden. The castle itself is only open for rare events such as the Festival of Music in Great Irish Houses (*see* p.18). However, there is an exhibition hall which always has something of interest, usually to do with the Parsons family, after whom the town was once named, and who seem to have been talented, intellectual and artistic. In 1845 one of their descendants built what was then the world's largest telescope, which you can see. A scientific centre is planned for the near future. The landscaped park, with its lake and waterfalls, the formal garden, box hedges and huge magnolia tree will entrance you.

Shopping

Crafts: J. Shanaghan, Chapel Street, Carrick on Suir for woven baskets. The Basket Case, Summerhill, Nenagh; Hanley Tweeds, Clare Street, Nenagh; Cashel: The Gift Shop, Padraig O'Mathuna (jewellery and silver), Rossa Pottery. Sarah Ryan Ceramics, Palmer's Hill; Shanagarry Weavers, Cahir Road, Cashel, ✆ (062) 61028. Tom's Pottery and Craft Shop, the Old Church, Terryglass, ✆ (067) 22125.

Glass: Tipperary Crystal, Clonmel Road, Carrick on Suir, ✆ (051) 41188

Cheese: Cashel Blue Cheese, Beechmount, Fethard, ✆ (052) 31151. Telephone first if you wish to buy from the farm. Baylough Cheese, Mount Anglesby, Clogheen, ✆ (052) 65275, for handmade herb cheeses. Cooleeney Cheese, Cooleeney House, Moyne, Thurles, ✆ (0504) 45112, for delicious Camembert-style cheese. Check for availability.

Wholefood: The Honey Pot, 14 Abbey Street, Clonmel, ✆ (052) 21457. Shop and restaurant with organic vegetable market on Thursdays and Fridays.

Activities

Fishing: Brown trout fishing also on the River Suir and its many tributaries: The Southern Regional Fisheries Board, Anglesea Street, Clonmel, ✆ (052) 32971 or the Tourist Board.

Hunting: Tipperary is famous for its hunting over banks, ditches, walls and hills, and in woodland. Contact: The Golden Vale Hunt, Mark Molloy, Crossogue House, Ballycahill, Thurles, ✆ (0504) 54123. The North Tipperary Hunt, Val Cope, Timona, Ballycommon, Nenagh, ✆ (067) 24376. The Ormonde Hunt, Mr Cahalan, South Park, Ballingarry, Roscrea, ✆ 067 21105. The Scarteen Hunt (also known as the Black and Tans), Dickie Power, near Fethard, ✆ (061) 390192. The Tipperary Hunt, Mrs Betsy O'Connor, ✆ (052) 31130.

Horse-riding: Scrammon trekking, Lorthal, Nenagh, ✆ (0509) 47132. The Dagg family organises rides around Lough Derg. They can also organise hunting and pony-trekking for short periods.

Horse-racing: in Tipperary, Thurles and Clonmel throughout the year.

Sailing: Learn to sail at Knightswater Sports Centre, Dromineer, Nenagh, ✆ (067) 24295.

Cruising: on Lough Derg. Knightswater Sports Centre, Dromineer, ✆ (067) 24295. They also organize water-skiing, dinghy sailing, wind-surfing etc. Try also the Derg Line, Killaloe, County Clare, ✆ (061) 376364; or Emerald Star Line, 47 Dawson Street, Dublin 2, ✆ (01) 679 8166.

Golf: at the very pretty Clonmel Course 3 miles (5km) outside Clonmel at Lyreanearle, ✆ (052) 21138. Ballykisteen Golf and Country Club, Monard, ✆ (062) 51256. Tipperary Golf Club, Rathanny, ✆ (062) 51119.

Walking: The Cahir Way is a signposted route from Cahir to Ballydavid through the Galtee Mountains. There are also trails between Carrick on Suir, Clonmel and

Clogheen near 'The Vee' in the Knockmealdown Mountains. For details contact the local tourist office or Cospoir, 11th floor, Hawkins House, Dublin 2, ✆ (01) 873 4700 ext. 2524.

Where to Stay

County Tipperary has really got its act together for well-run bed and breakfasting in lovely country houses. The following establishments are in beautiful places, have comfortable rooms, and produce delicious food for breakfast and dinner.

luxury

Cashel Palace Hotel, Cashel, ✆ (062) 61411. Luxurious living in a historic and beautiful house just off the main street of the town.

expensive

Michael and Bessie Wilkinson, **Gurthalougha House**, Ballinderry, ✆ (067) 22080. Country house set in 150acres (60ha) of private forest, overlooking the Shannon on its way through to Lough Derg. If you are an early riser you will see plenty of wildlife along the river and wooded walks, and gain a good appetite for the delicious breakfasts. **Dundrum House**, Dundrum, near Cashel, ✆ (062) 71116. Country hotel furnished with Victorian period furniture. Elevators make access easy for the handicapped. Good food, and excellent sporting facilities.

moderate

Lismacue House, Bansha, ✆ (062) 54106. A beautiful lime tree avenue leads you to this warm and gracious 17th-century house. **Kylenoe**, Ballinderry, Nenagh ✆ (067) 22015. Stone farmhouse with modern extension. Excellent breakfasts and dinners. **Knocklofty House**, Clonmel, ✆ (052) 38222. Overlooks the river Suir, is central and very comfortable. Mr and Mrs Quigley, **Ballycormac House**, Aglish, nr Roscrea, ✆ (067) 21129. Spacious 300-year-old white-washed cottage with open fires in the pretty sitting rooms. Riding, hunting and shooting can be arranged locally and there are stables on the premises. Write to them for their brochure. **Riverrun House**, Terryglass, Nenagh, ✆ (067) 22125. Well run B&B in the village. **Ros-Guill House**, Kilkenny Road, Cashel, ✆ (062) 61507. Great views of the Rock of Cashel and tasty breakfasts.

inexpensive

Mrs Sherwood, **Killaghy Castle**, Mullinahone, ✆ (052) 53112. An 18th-century farm manor house with its own Norman castle attached. Lovely quiet location, horse-riding close by. The village of Mullinahone is noted for its memorabilia and the grave of 19th-century novelist and revolutionary Charles J. Kickham. **Carrigeen Castle**, Cork Road, Cahir, ✆ (052) 41370. Lovely but small rooms. Mrs Shesgreen-Flannery, **Otway Lodge**, Dromineer Harbour, Dromineer, ✆ (067) 24133. Comfortable, convenient location for those wanting to explore Lough Derg. **Parkstown House**, Horse and Jockey, near Cashel, ✆ (0504)

44315. Georgian country house, 7 miles (11.2km) north of Cashel; friendly, elegant and tranquil. Mrs Murphy, **Indaville**, Cashel, ✆ (062) 61933; friendly and comfortable. Farmhouse hostel, ✆ (052) 41906. On an organic farm with kitchen facilities, 4 miles SW of Calin off Mitchelstown Road.

self-catering

Gillies Macbain, **Cranagh Castle**, Hostel, Templemore, ✆ (0504) 53104. Run by an enthusiatic member of the Irish Organic Growers Association, this lovely Georgian house is called a castle because of the medieval tower house attached to it. Plenty of traditional farm animals. Self-catering with cheaper accommodation in the dormitory. 17th-century coach house, sleeps 6, very comfortable. Contact **Mrs Nicholson**, Lismacue, Bansha, ✆ (062) 54106 From IR£295 per week. **Kilcoran Farm Hostel**, Kilcoran, Cahir, ✆ (052) 41906. Organic smallholding with comfortable kitchen. **The Old Rectory**, Lorrha, Nenagh, ✆ (0509) 47010. Converted coach house. Rent-an-Irish cottage, ✆ (061) 411109. Old-style houses in Terryglass.

Eating Out
expensive

Chez Hans, Cashel, ✆ (062) 61177. In an old church, excellent food cooked by Hans, who is German. Dinner only. **Cashel Palace Hotel**, Cashel. ✆ (062) 61411. You can choose between the formal Four Seasons Restaurant and the attractive cellar, where traditional Irish food is a speciality and more moderately priced. **Dundrum House**, Dundrum, ✆ (062) 71116. Excellently prepared plain Irish cooking. **The Foxes' Den**, Modreeny, Cloughjordan, ✆ (0505) 42210. Converted cellar resturant in 18th century country house.

moderate

The **Glen Hotel**, Glen of Aherlow, ✆ (062) 56146. In the most spectacular position overlooking the wooded valley, you can get a reasonable meal here. **Mulcahy's Restaurant**, Gladstone Street, Clonmel. Pub lunch. **Gurthalougha House**, Ballinderry, ✆ (067) 22080. Candle-lit dinner in a country house. Delicious food. *Dinner only.* **The Spearman**, Main Street, Cahir, ✆ (062) 61143. Good for a light lunch.

inexpensive/cheap

Abbey Restaurant, Abbey Street, Clonmel, ✆ (052) 21457. Wholefood and vegetarian restaurant in an old warehouse. Good range of soups and stir-fry. Daytime only. **Paddy's Pub**, Terryglass, for a pub lunch and dinner. Traditional music at night and in the **Derg Inn** next door. **The Whiskey Still**, Dromineer, ✆ (067) 24129, traditional old pub, good grub and music. **Crock of Gold**—opposite Cahir castle. Small restaurant above craft shop handy for snacks and afternoon tea. **Honeypot**, 14 Abbey Street, Clonmel, ✆ (052) 21457. Tasty wholefood restaurant, crunchy salads and bakes. **Goosers** pub, Ballina, ✆ (061) 376792. Some of the best pub grub in the area. More expensive restaurant at the back. **Matt the Thresher's**, Birdhill, ✆ (061) 379227. All-day pub food. Organic bread, seafood and Limerick ham.

County Clare

Until the 4th century Clare was part of Connacht, after which it became known as the Kingdom of Thomond. It is a wild and beautiful county, still marked with signs of a tempestuous past: there are 2300 stone forts or 'cahers' dating back to pre-Celtic times. It is unspoilt by tourism, even though it has huge Shannon Airport in the south. The locals earn money from farming, tourism and fishing, and the airport gives a lot of employment to the surrounding area. Nearly three-quarters of the county boundary is formed by water and the Shannon Scheme is the largest hydro-electric scheme in the country. It is separated by the Shannon Estuary from County Kerry, its neighbour in the south, though there is a car ferry from Tarbert to Killimer.

Most people go inland, almost to the centre of Ireland, to find the Limerick bridge, and then only shoot through Clare on their way to the delights of Connemara. But Clare has its plunging cliffs and strange karst landscapes to attract the more adventurous. The west Clare coast ends in the dramatic Cliffs of Moher. To the north, overlooking Galway Bay, the Barony of the Burren looks like some misplaced section of the moon—white, crevassed and barren, but springy turf grows in the earth-filled fissures, and cattle manage to graze quite happily around the cracks that could catch them in a leg-breaking fall. The Burren region extends over some 25 miles (40km) from east to west and 15 miles (24km) from north to south-between Galway Bay on the north, the Atlantic coast on the west, and a line drawn roughly through Doolin, Kilfenora, Gort and Kinvara. In late May the place becomes starred with gentians, cranesbill, geraniums and orchids. Arctic alpine mountain avens sprawl lavishly over the rocks and Irish saxifrage tufts cover sea-sprayed boulders. Sheltered in the damp clefts of limestone are shade loving plants such as the Maidenhair fern. The plentiful rainfall disappears into the limestone and into a pot-holers dream of passages and caverns. Impermanent lakes known as turloughs appear when the ground water floods through the fissures after a lot of rain. No one has yet been able to explain fully how such a profusion of northern and southern plants came to grow together, some of which are unknown in continental Europe. The temperate winter and warm limestone beneath the turf suit the plants, and their colonies have grown up unhindered because the arid land has never been cultivated, only grazed by cattle. The Burren is very rich in antiquities left by Stone Age farmers who cleared the hills of forest. By medieval times, the hills were treeless, and the wide expanses of fissured rock exposed. The Burren certainly stimulates many questions, but there has been much controversy over the siting of an office of Public Works Interpretative Centre right in the middle of this unique area. A local action group has for the moment stopped work on the site, but the battle continues. Many people are keen for the extra work and money such a centre would bring in, but it seems sad that a nearby village could not be chosen for the centre or the existing one at Kilfenora expanded. The pollution, erosion and visual destruction to this magical landscape will destroy much of the beauty and atmosphere people come to enjoy. There are many places to bathe and fish around the coast, whilst the scenery and walking around the lakes and hills of Slieve Bernagh, which rise on the west side of the long stretch of Lough Derg, are some of the best you will ever find. In the last few years a few of the wonderful carved stone heads to be found in the ancient holy sites have been stolen, apparently hacked off and driven away. The Office of Public Works may have to substitute replicas for the originals if this continues.

History

The 12th-century *Book of Invasions*, or *Lebor Gabala*, connects Clare with the Fir Bolgs, but we know little about these shadowy people. Many centuries later, it was a Clare man, Brian Boru of the clan O'Brien, who conducted a vigorous and successful campaign against the Vikings and defeated them at Clontarf in 1014. He became High King of Ireland in 1002, and built the Palace of Kincora as his royal residence in 1012. Sadly, he was killed in his tent after the battle of Clontarf, and the fragile national unity he had managed to create disappeared very fast. There is nothing left of Kincora today.

In the tales of ancient Ireland the countryside was fraught with the battles of the land-owning Celtic clans: O'Briens, O'Deas, MacNamaras and MacMahons who, when they were not waging fierce war on foreigners, filled in the time by fighting amongst themselves. In 1172 the incumbent chief of the O'Briens, Donal Mor, enlisted the help of a new group of invaders, a party of Norman mercenaries, in his war against the O'Conors of Connacht. Despite this initial foothold in the country, the Norman-English forces did not make much of a mark in County Clare until the accession of Henry VIII in 1534 and his acknowledgement as King of Ireland. The O'Briens were made Earls of Thomond, and remained more or less loyal to the English crown until the Cromwellian conquest (*see* **History**, p.88). After that time, Clare and neighbouring Connacht became a seat of rebellion against English rule. Clare is part of the wild west of Ireland: when Cromwell heard that a large part of Clare had no trees to hang a man, nor enough water to drown him, nor enough earth to bury him, he thought it would be just the place to banish the rebellious Irish whom he had thrown off the land in other parts of the country.

Getting There and Around

By air: Shannon International Airport, ✆ (061) 471444.

By boat: Kerry-Clare ferry from Killimer. Single car ticket costs IR£7, return is IR£9. The ferry departs from Killimer on the hour between 7am and 7pm, Mon–Sat (9pm April–Sept).

By rail: Limerick is the nearest main terminal, ✆ (061) 418666. Ennis train station, ✆ (065) 40444.

By bus: Good local services, ✆ (065) 24177.

By car: cars are available for hire at Shannon Airport; Dan King, Shannon Road, Newmarket-on-Fergus, ✆ (061) 368126; Tom Mannion, O'Connell Street, Ennis, ✆ (065) 24211.

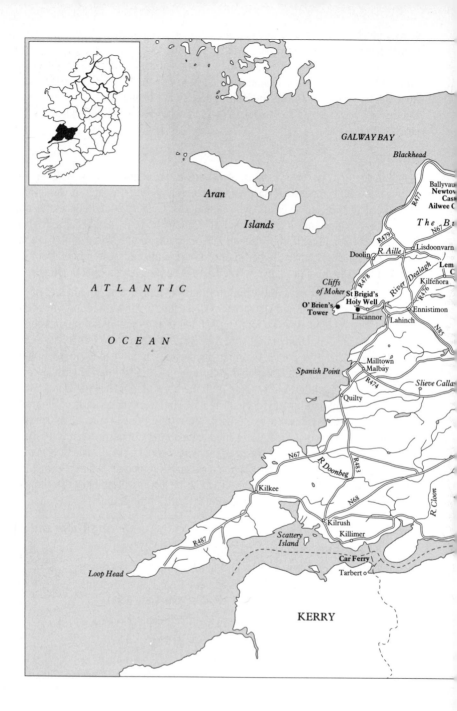

GALWAY BAY

Blackhead

Aran

Islands

Ballyvau
Newtov
Cas
Ailwee C

R477

The B

N67

Doolin

R479

R. Aille

Lisdoonvarn

Lem
C

ATLANTIC

Cliffs
of Moher

R478

River Dealagh

Kilfenora

R476

St Brigid's
Holy Well

O' Brien's
Tower

Liscannor

Ennistimon

Lahinch

N85

OCEAN

Milltown
Malbay

Spanish Point

R474

Slieve Calla

Quilty

N67

R. Doonbeg

R483

Kilkee

N68

R. Cloom

Kilrush

Killimer

Scattery
Island

R487

Car Ferry

Loop Head

Tarbert o

KERRY

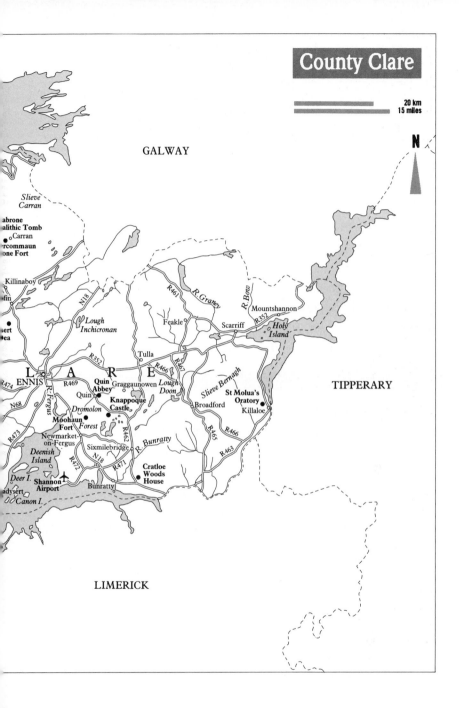

County Clare

20 km
15 miles

N

GALWAY

Slieve
Carran

abrone
alithic Tomb
○Carran
rcommaun
one Fort

Killinaboy

ofin

Lough
Inchicronan

sert
ea

Killaloe

Tulla

R352

N18

R461

R Graney

R. Bow

Mountshannon

Feakle○

Scarriff

R352

Holy
Island

L   A   R   E
ENNIS

R469

R466

R462

Quin
Abbey

Graggaunowen

Lough
Doon

Slieve Bernagh

St Molua's
Oratory

TIPPERARY

Quin

Knappoque
Castle

Broadford

Killaloe

R474

R Fergus

N68

Dromolon

Forest

R466

Moohaun
Fort

R473

Newmarket-
on-Fergus

Sixmilebridge

Bunratty

R465

R463

Deenish
Island

R472

N18

R471

Deer I.

Shannon
Airport

Bunratty

Cratloe
Woods
House

adysert

Canon I.

LIMERICK

213

By bike: The Raleigh Rent-a-Bike network operates all over Clare, ✆ Dublin (01) 6261333. Your local dealer in Ennis is Michael Tierney, 17 Abbey Street, ✆ (065) 29433.

Tourist Information

Ennis, Limerick Road, ✆ (065) 28366, all year.

Lisdoonvarna, ✆ (065) 74062, June to beginning of October.

Lahinch, ✆ (065) 81474, 15 May to September.

Cliffs of Moher, ✆ (065) 81171, May to December.

Shannon Airport, ✆ (061) 471664, all year.

Festivals

May: The Wildlife Symposium, Ballinalacken Castle, Fanore, ✆ (065) 76105.

Late May: The Fleach Nua, a festival of traditional music, dancing and singing, in Ennis in the last weekend of the month, ✆ (065) 24143/(01) 280 0295.

Early June: Ennistymon Festival of traditional singing.

Early August: Carnival of Music, Lisdoonvarna, ✆ (065) 74042.

August: Feakle Festival of Music, ✆ (061) 924131.

September: Match-Making Festival of Ireland, Lisdoonvarna, ✆ (061) 362422.

Central Clare

Around Killaloe and Bunratty

Killaloe is right on the great Shannon and connected to Ballina in Tipperary by a bridge of 13 arches. Not far from the bridge, on the west bank of the river, is the gem of Killaloe, **St Flannan's Cathedral**, the fine 12th-century building built by Donal O'Brien on the site of an earlier church founded in the 6th century by St Lua. There is a magnificent Hiberno-Romanesque door which is better than anything else of its kind in Ireland, and is said to be the entrance to the tomb of Murtagh O'Brien, King of Munster, who died in the same century the cathedral was built. The bold and varied carvings of animals and foliage on the shafts and capitals, and the pattern of the chevrons on the arches are not merely decoration: they are modelled to make the entire conception an organic whole. Nearby is **Thorgrim's Stone**, the shaft of a cross bearing a runic and ognam inscription of about the year AD 1000. The view from the top of the square cathedral tower is superb. You can see all the mountains that crowd round the gorge of Killaloe, and the beautiful Lough Derg. In the grounds of the cathedral is **St Flannan's Oratory** with a lovely high stone roof, with its Gothic doorway a splendid contrast to the cruciform cathedral.

The oratory, which dates from the 12th century, has a Romanesque west door but the inside is dark and gloomy. It dates from the 12th century. The Roman Catholic church standing high above the town is believed to be on the site of Kincora, the great palace of Brian Boru where riotous banquets were the order of the day. Inside the church are some fine stained-glass windows by Harry Clarke, who worked upon many church windows in the early decades of this century. His style is fantastical and fairylike in the manner of the English illustrator Aubrey Beardsley (1872–98), and the colours are exceptionally vivid. In the grounds is **St Molua's Oratory**, a very ancient ruin reconstructed here after being removed from an island in the Shannon, before it was flooded by the Shannon hydro-electric scheme in 1929. Killaloe is a centre for fishing and boating. There are facilities for water-skiing and sailing, and a large marina (*see* 'Activities', below).

A mile (1.6km) or so out of Killaloe on the R463 is **Crag Liath**, known locally as the Grianan, overlooking the road northwards to Scarriff. It was written in 1014 in the annals of Loch Ce that this fort was the dwelling place of Aoibhill (also known as Aibell), the celebrated banshee of the Dalcassian Kings of Munster, the O'Briens. (In Irish, *Dal gCais* means sept or tribe of Cas. A banshee (*bean-sidhe*) or fairy woman is a ghost peculiar to people of old Irish stock; her duty is to warn the family she attends of the approaching death of one of its members.) Thus it was that Aoibhill appeared to Brian Boru on the eve of Clontarf and told him that he would be killed the next day, though not in the fury of the battle. This is exactly what happened, for he was murdered in his tent when the battle was over and the victory his. The short climb to the fort is lovely. All around is beauty: woods, water and mountain. (*The fort is always accessible; adm free.*)

If you cross the Shannon at Limerick, you will find yourself heading for **Bunratty Castle** on the Newmarket road (N18). Bunratty is a splendid tower house standing beside a small stone bridge over River Ratty; a perfect, restored example of a Norman-Irish castle keep. The present castle dates from 1460, though it is at least the fourth to have been built on the same spot. It was built by the McNamaras, who were a sept of the O'Brien's, and it remained an O'Brien stronghold until 1712. It was then occupied by the parliamentarian Admiral Penn, the father of William Penn who founded Pennsylvania. After years of neglect it was bought by Lord Gort in 1954, who restored it with the help of Bord Failte and the Office of Public Works. They have managed to recreate a 15th-century atmosphere and there is a wonderful collection of 14th- to 17th-century furniture. In the evenings it provides a memorable setting for medieval-style banquets. In the grounds surrounding the castle, a **folk park** (*open daily throughout the year, 9.30–5.00 (7pm June–Aug); adm; ✆ (061) 361511*) has gradually grown up with examples of houses from every part of the Shannon region; many of them were re-erected after being saved from demolition during the Shannon Airport extension. You can see butter-making, basket-weaving and all the traditional skills which made people self-sufficient in days gone by. There is also a very good collection of agricultural machinery. There is a good craft centre at the Ballycasey Workshops about 3 miles (5km) west on the N18.

It is also worth making an expedition to **Cratloe Woods House** (*open June–mid-Sept, Mon–Sat 2–6; adm; ✆ (061) 87306*), on the main Limerick/Shannon to Ennis Road (N18), about 5 miles (8 km) from Limerick. Cratloe Woods is an ancient O'Brien house, and the only surviving example of an Irish long house that is still lived in as a home. It is packed with interesting history, and there is a good tea and craft shop. The woods themselves have some of the only primeval oak forest left in Ireland, and if you climb the hill you will get a fine view.

Around Lough Derg

Broadford, Tulla and Feakle are all pleasant villages where you can stay in farms or town and country houses and explore the Clare lakelands. Lough Graney is especially beautiful, with its wooded shores. Most of the loughs are well stocked with bream and pike. Near Feakle the witty and outrageous poet Brian Merriman earned his livelihood as a schoolmaster (see p.125). Here, also, is the cottage of Biddy Early, the wise woman about whom at the turn of the century Lady Augusta Gregory collected stories for her book *Visions and Beliefs of the West of Ireland.*

From the pretty village of Mountshannon on Lough Derg it is possible to get a boat to Iniscealtra, also known as Holy Island, about ½mile (1km) from the shore. (It is easy to hire a boat at the harbour, which is a main stopping place on the lake for hire-cruisers and sailing boats.) The Christian settlement on the island is attibuted to St Carmin, who lived here in about AD 640. Today there are five ancient churches, a round tower, a saint's graveyard, a hermit's cell and a holy well. St Carmin's Church, beside the incomplete round tower, has a wonderful Hiberno-Romanesque chancel arch, impressive in its simplicity. The festival at the holy well was famous for the Bacchanalian revelry that accompanied it. It was stopped by the priests, sometime in the last century, because the local squireens would steal the girls at it. The memorial stones are still in place in the saint's graveyard for the period covering the 8th to the 12th centuries. Unfortunately the whole effect is rather spoiled by modern tombstones and garish plastic wreaths.

Around Ennis

Newmarket-on-Fergus takes its name from a 19th-century O'Brien, Lord Inchiquin, who was very enthusiastic about horses. In the grounds of his Neo-Gothic mansion, now a luxury hotel, is **Mooghaun Fort** (also spelt Maughaun), one of the largest Iron Age hill-forts in Europe, enclosing 27 acres (11ha) with three concentric walls. Maybe it was people from this fort who buried the enormous hoard of gold ornaments which was discovered nearby in 1854 by workmen digging the way for a railway line. Unfortunately much of it was melted down, probably by dealers, but a few pieces of 'the great Clare gold find' have found their way to the National Museum in Dublin. You can reach the fort through Dromoland Forest. Access is by foot via a forestry car park signposted to the left off the N18 road between Newmarket-on-Fergus and Dromoland.

At **Craggaunowen** off the Quin-Sixmilebridge Road (R469) there is a reconstructed *crannog* or lake dwelling, and a four-storey tower house (*open May–Oct, daily, 10–6, adm;* © *(061) 367178*). This is a fascinating centre which gives a good idea of how our ancestors lived. The valley surrounding it is beautiful, and if you are there at teatime, the scones at the reception cottage are delicious. On display is the Brendan, a replica of the original boat used by St Brendan on his voyages. Tim Severin, a modern-day adventurer, sailed it to North America via Iceland and Greenland, with the purpose of demonstrating that St Brendan could have been the first to discover America, in the 6th century. Nearby, at Quin (about 8 miles (13km) northwest of Bunratty), is **Knappoque Castle**, run on the

same lines as Bunratty Castle with medieval banquets in the evening (*open daily, April to end Sept, 9.30–5, adm. The medieval banquets are held twice-nightly at 5.45 and 8.45, May–end Sept; ✆ (061) 368103*).

At the next crossroads, to the east of the town, a right-turn leads to **Quin Abbey** (*always accessible; adm free*) which is very well preserved, and therefore subject to countless coach tours. It was founded for the Franciscans in 1402 and incorporated with a great castle built by one of the de Clares. The monastic buildings are grouped around an attractive cloister and there is a graceful tower. Buried here is the famous duellist with the wonderful name of Fireballs MacNamara.

Ennis (*Inis*: river-meadow), the county capital, is sited on a great bend of the River Fergus. The streets are narrow and winding, and in the centre is a hideous monument to the great Daniel O'Connell, who successfully contested the Clare seat in 1828 even though the repressive laws of the time disqualified Catholics. Right in the middle of the town is **Ennis Friary**, a substantial ruin (*open May–Sept, 9.30–6.30; rest of the year key with caretaker, Mary Kearns, ✆ (065) 22464*). The friary was founded for the Franciscans by Donchadh O'Brien, King of Thomond, just before his death in 1242. It is rich in sculptures and decorated tombs although the building itself has been rather mucked about, with additions and renovation. On one of the tombs is the sculptured device of a cock crowing. The story goes that, standing on the rim of a pot, he cries in Irish, 'the son of the Virgin is safe', a reference to the Bible story of the cock that rose from the pot in which it was cooking to proclaim that, 'Himself above on the Cross will rise again', to the astonishment of the two Roman soldiers who had questioned the prophecy.

There is a small **museum** (*open Mon–Fri*) in Harmony Row which specializes in objects associated with famous Clare people. Fans of Percy French (1854–1920), the painter and entertainer, can look at the old steam engine immortalized in his song, 'Are you right there, Michael, are you right?' This song about the West Clare Railway, and the engine's habit of stopping at places other than stations, led to a libel action with the directors.

Around Corrofin

On the way to Corrofin (off the N85 to Ennistimon, and 2 miles (2.5 km) off the R476), is the famous religious settlement of **Dysert O'Dea**. It was started in the 7th century by St Tola, but he probably lived in a cell of wattle and daub. The present ruin is a much-altered 12th-century Hiberno-Romanesque church with a badly reconstructed west doorway that now stands in the south wall. The door is sumptuously carved, and the arch has a row of stone heads with Mongolian features and proud but rather sad expressions. The idea for the heads came from northern France. (Monks and scholars moving between Ireland and the Continent had much more influence on building and style than was once thought.) Beside the church is the stump of a round tower, and about a hundred yards (91m) east is a high cross from the 12th century. Christ is shown in a pleated robe, and below him is a bishop with a crozier. A decisive battle fought here in 1318 drove the Anglo-Normans out of the surrounding area for several centuries, when the O'Brien chief of the time defeated Richard de Clare of Bunratty and expelled him.

Corrofin village lies between two pretty lakes, the Inchiquin and Atedaun. There is good game and coarse fishing here, and plenty of caves, for this is marginal shale and limestone countryside in which the River Fergus plays some tricks. The **Clare Heritage Centre** (*open all year, daily (exc Sundays in winter) 10–6; adm; © (065) 37955*) in the old Church of Ireland hall offers a 'tracing your ancestor' service, and displays give a very interesting guide to rural Ireland 150 years ago.

About 2 miles (3.2km) further up on the R476 is **Killinaboy**, a small village close to the northern tip of Lough Inchiquin which is also spelt Kilnaboy on some maps. The remains of a round tower rest in the graveyard of a ruined church which dates from the 11th century. Over the south door is a *Sheila-na-Gig*, a grotesque and erotic figure of a woman. These *Sheila-na-Gigs* are often carved and fixed to ecclesiastical buildings, probably as a sort of crude warning to the monks and laity of the power of feminine sexuality. There are many gallery graves around here. A mile (1.6km) northwest of Killinaboy at **Roughan**, just over a stile and in a field, is the Tau Cross, shaped like a T with a carved head in each of the arms. Several like this have been found in a Celtic sanctuary at Roquepertuse in France, and it is likely that this is pre-Christian.

On the main road leading to Kilfenora (R476) is the ruined **Lemaneagh Castle** which belonged to the O'Briens. It is a really lovely old ruin with a tower dating from 1480 and an early-17th century fortified house. Sir Conor O'Brien, who built the four-storey house, had a very strong-minded wife called Red Mary, many of whose exploits have passed into folklore. After Sir Conor died, she married an influential Cromwellian to ensure the inheritance of her son, Donat, and to prevent the expropriation of her lands. The story goes that when one day he made an uncalled-for remark about her first husband, she promptly pushed him out of the window.

The Burren

Kilfenora is a place of ancient importance on the fringe of the Burren. It is worth staying a while, not only to look at the **Burren Display Centre** (*open daily, Mar–Oct 10–5, June 10–6, July and Aug 9–7; adm; ℗ (065) 88030*) which explains the flora, fauna, butterflies and rock formations of the area, but also because it has four 12th-century carved crosses, all of the same excellent standard, which suggests they might have been produced by the same workshop or even by a single carver. The small 12th-century Church of St Fachnan is called 'the Cathedral', and its bishopric is still held by the Pope!

The district is generally called 'the Burren' after the ancient Barony of that name. It extends some 25 miles (40km) from east to west and 15 miles (24km) from north to south, between Galway Bay and the Atlantic Ocean, with the villages of Doolin, Kilfenora, Gort and Kinvarra forming its southeastern border. One of the amazing things about the Burren is that its 50 square miles (130sqkm) are dotted with signs of ancient habitation— stone forts and megalithic tombs, which blend perfectly with a landscape strewn with strangely shaped rocks.

On the R480 to Ballyvaughan, 6 miles (9.7km) past Lemaneagh Castle, is the great dolmen of Poulabrone (the pool of sorrows) with a massive capstone; and nearer Killinaboy in the upland part of the Burren is the great stone fort of Cahercommaun. To get to it, turn left in Carran village and left again at the next junction. Look out for a shrub-lined avenue to the left which leads to a car park. From here you go a short way by foot. The fort is situated on a cliff edge across some ankle-breaking country, but notice the flower life between the stones. A Harvard excavation team reached the conclusion that the fort was occupied during the 8th and 9th centuries by a community that raised cattle, hunted red deer and cultivated some land for growing grain. Also on the road to Ballyvaughan, a mile (1.6km) out of Kilfenora, is one of the finest stone forts in Ireland, known as Ballykinvarga. This has a very effective trap for those trying to launch an attack: chevaux de frise, which are sharp spars of stone set close together in the ground. The great fort of Dun Aengus on the Aran Islands has a similar arrangement.

At Ballyvaughan on the north of the Burren you can rent yourself an Irish cottage and explore Black Head, which looks over the shimmering Galway Bay and gives clear views of the Aran Islands and the Cliffs of Moher. The islands are made of the same grey lime-stone as the Burren and have the same bright flowers in the springtime. Ballyvaughan village is set in a green wooded vale, an oasis after the bleached plateaux of limestone, mighty terraces and escarpments to the south. The village has good craft shops, and the harbour is the starting point for boat trips to the islands (*see* 'Aran Islands', pp.256–261). There are a couple of tower houses built in the 16th century to explore: Gleninagh, sign-posted between Ballyvaughan and Lisdoonvarna, was occupied by the O'Loughlins until 1840; Newtown Castle is unusual in that it is round with a square base. It is not sign-posted; you will find it down a lane, 2 miles (3.2km) south of Ballyvaughan.

The **Aillwee Caves** (*open daily, Mar–early Nov 10–6.30, July and Aug 10–7.30; adm;* ✆ *(065) 77036*) are 2 miles (3.2 km) southeast of Ballyvaughan on the N67. All over the Burren there are hundreds of caves formed by the underground rivers—great sport for the speleologist. Aillwee Caves date back to 2 million BC. When the river dried up, or changed its course, they became the den of wild bears and other animals. Today the entrance has been tamed to make it easier for the less intrepid, and the caverns are festooned with stalagmites and stalactites.

By taking the corkscrew road to **Lisdoonvarna** (*Lios Duin Bhearna*: the enclosure of the gapped fort), you get a series of lovely views of Galway Bay. Since the decline of Mallow, Lisdoonvarna is the most important spa in Ireland. The waters are said to owe much to their natural radioactivity; there are sulphur, magnesia and iron springs, a pump room and baths for those who come to take the waters. Hotels, guest houses and bed and breakfasts have sprung up everywhere, for the place is very crowded in the summer, and there is much courting, inspired no doubt by the invigorating properties of the water. There are also plenty of dances and concerts during the spa season. Excitement is at its height in September with the **Match-making Festival**. Spinster ladies come all the way from America for the fun. There is a sandy cove at **Doolin**, 3 miles (4.8km) away, good for fishing but dangerous for bathing. This little fishing village is famous for its traditional music, and you can get a boat from here to Innisheer, the smallest of the Aran Islands, a crossing that takes about 40 minutes (*for more information ✆ (065) 74455/74189*).

In the area are curious mineral nodules formed by limestone and shale which look just like tortoise shells. There are three of these built into the wall beside the Imperial Hotel in Lisdoonvarna. From here, the coast road (R478) leads to the **Cliffs of Moher**, which drop down vertically to the foaming sea. Seabirds somehow manage to rest on the steep slopes; guillemots, razorbills, puffins, kittiwakes, various gulls, choughs and sometimes pere-grines. The cliffs stretch for nearly 5 miles (8km) and are made of the darkest sandstone and millstone grit. On a clear day there is a magnificent view of the Twelve Bens and the mountains of Connemara. **O'Brien's Tower** was built in 1835 by a notorious landlord as an observation post; behind it is an Information Centre (*open Mar–Oct*).

On the R478 southeast of the cliffs is **Liscannor**, a little fishing village where the fish-ermen still use curraghs. John P. Holland (1841–1914), who invented the submarine, was born here. However, it is more famous locally for the **Holy Well of St Brigid**, about 2 miles (3 km) northwest of Liscannor on the R478, near the cliffs of Moher. The well is an important place of pilgrimage. An aura of faith and devotion lingers in the damp air and amongst the trivial offerings of holy pictures, bleeding hearts and plastic statues of the Pope. You approach by a narrow stone passage, probably still feeling slightly amazed by the life-sized painted plaster model of St Brigid next to the entrance of the well, which is sufficiently naturalistic to be macabre when first glimpsed.

Lahinch, 1 mile (1.6km) south of Liscannor, is a small seaside resort with a pretty arc of golden sand and waves big enough for surfing. The golf course at Lahinch is champi-onship-standard, but as a guest you are most welcome. There is an amusing story of one enthusiast who putted a winner and got the trophy. He remarked with the skill and colour only the Irish can summon, 'I declare to God I was that tense I could hear the bees belchin'. **Ennistymon**, with its colourful shop fronts, is 2½ miles (4km) inland on the N85, in a wooded valley beside the cascading River Cullenagh.

Southwards, following the N67 down the coast from Lahinch, you come to Spanish Point (just off the R482), where a great number of ships from the Spanish Armada were wrecked. Those sailors who struggled ashore were slaughtered by the locals on the orders of the Governor of Connacht. **Milltown Malbay**, opposite Spanish Point on the N67, has a summer school, held as a tribute to Clare's greatest piper, Willie Clancy (1921–73), who was not only a musician, but also a folklorist and master carpenter. He was especially noted for his beautiful rendering of slow Irish airs on the *uileann* pipe. The summer school, held at the beginning of July for 10 days, comprises lectures, recitals, concerts, workshops and traditional music. It is a splendid time to visit for all the fun (*see* 'Festivals').

From Milltown Malbay, you can have a swim at the silver strand of **Freach**, just to the north of the town, or climb **Slieve Callan**, the highest point in west Clare, and on the way rest at the little lake at **Boolynagreana**, which means 'the summer milking place of the sun'. To get there, follow the R474 southwards for 6 miles (9.6km) to the Hand Crossroads, and then walk over rough land for about a mile (1.6km). All round these foothills the ancient agricultural practice of transhumance was pursued. This is known in Ireland as 'booleying' and involves moving livestock to mountain pasture during the summer months. Booleying has fallen into disuse with modern feeding methods.

Back on the coast road (N67) you will find **Quilty**, a strange name for an Irish village which comes from the Irish *coillte*, for woods, but there are no trees on this flat part of the coast. The great lines of stone walls are bestrewn with seaweed being dried for kelp-making. The seaweed is either burnt, and the ash used for the production of iodine, or exported for the production of alginates which produce the rich, creamy head on Guinness. The church here is reminiscent of the Early-Christian churches, but in fact it was built in 1907, with money given by some French sailors who were rescued by the villagers when their ship was wrecked one stormy night.

Southwest Clare

Kilkee to Killimer

Kilkee (*Cill Chaoidhe*: Church of St Caoidhe), about 12 miles (19.2 km) south on the N67, is a grand place for a holiday by the sea. It is built along a sandy crescent-shaped beach, and the Duggerna Rocks, acting as a reef, make it safe for bathing at any stage of the tide. The coast lying southwestwards for about 15 miles (24km) from here to Loop Head is an almost endless succession of caverns, chasms, sea-stacks and weird and wonderfully shaped rocks. The cliff scenery is on a par with the Cliffs of Moher. There is a colourful legend about Ulster's hero Cú Chulainn, who was generally well loved by women, but this time was being pursued relentlessly by a termagant of a woman called Mal. Eventually he came to the edge of the cliffs on Loop Head and leapt on to a great rock about 30ft (9m) out to sea. Mal was not to be outdone and made the same leap with equal agility and success. Cú Chulainn straight away performed the difficult feat of leaping back to the mainland and this time Mal faltered, fell short, and disappeared into the raging ocean below. Out of this legend came the name Loop Head, Leap Head in Irish. As for poor Mal, she must have been a witch, for her blood turned the sea red and she was swept northwards to a point near the Cliffs of Moher called Hag's Head.

Kilrush (*Cill Rois*: the Church of the Promontory) is a busy place overlooking the Shannon Estuary with a newly built marina at **Cappagh**. Two miles (3.2km) out into the estuary, **Scattery Island** (Cathach's Island), found by St Senan in the 6th century, has some interesting monastic remains. An island in the broad Shannon was easy meat for the Vikings, who raided it several times. The round tower is very well preserved and has its door at ground level, so the unsuspecting monks must have been surprised by the aggressive Norsemen. The five ruined churches date from medieval times. Boat trips from Cappagh to Scattery Island are available in the summer (*call Atlantic Adventures ☎ (065) 52133 or Stephen Brennan on ☎ (065) 52031*).

The **Fergus Estuary**, where the mouth of the River Shannon gapes its widest, is a paradise of forgotten isles, untouched and deserted, with names like Deer Isle, Canon Isle and Deenish. You can base yourself near **Killadysert**, on the R473 going north to Ennis, and have great fun exploring them. The McMahon family still farm on Canon Isle, and if you make enquiries they may take you out there in their boat.

Shopping

Crafts: from Knappoque Castle, Cratloe Woods House and the Shannon Airport Duty Free Shop, which you can visit only as you are leaving the country. Woven clothing, candles and prints from Bunratty Folk Park. Crafts, books and Tim Robinson's map of the Burren from the Aillwee Caves Complex, near Ballyvaughan. The Manus Walsh Craft Shop, Ballyvaughan sells paintings, silver, jewellery and enamels. The Design Yard in Lahinch sells designer woollens by Lyn Mar. Close to Shannon Airport on the junction of the N18/N19, The Ballycasey Craft Workshops, Ballycasey, ☎ (061) 364115, have a great selection of tweeds, Arans, pottery, woodwork etc.

Delicacies: The Farmshop, Aillwee Cave Co. Ltd, Ballyvaughan, ☎ (065) 77036, sells food for picnics or to take home-all made by the Johnston family. They also bottle the natural spring water from the caves, and Ben makes his own cheese, Burren Gold. Open Sesame wholefood shop, 29 Parnell Street, Ennis, ☎ (091) 31315, sells organic veg and local cheeses. Sausages are made by Gerry Howard, La Verna, Lisdoonvarna town centre. Unglert's Bakery in Ennistymon produces German rye breads and strudels.

Cheese: Annaliese Bartelink Gouda-style cheeses flavoured with herbs in person or by post from Poulcoin, Kilnaboy.

Shellfish: Oyster Shell Company, New Quay, The Burren (behind Linnaue's Bar); ☎ (065) 78105.

Mead: The Bunratty Winery, Bunratty (behind Durty Nelly's Bar); ☎ (061) 362222.

Local cartographer Tim Robinson has produced an excellent large-scale map of the Burren. Available locally, IR£3.25

Activities

 **Cruising**: at Killaloe through Derg Line Cruisers, who also organize water-skiing and day cruises, ✆ (061) 376364. Mount Shannon Harbour across the lough is a great place from which to make boat trips up the lovely River Graney (also known as the Scariff).

Yacht charter: Yachting International, Trident Hotel, Kinsale, ✆ (021) 772301. Shannon Sailing Centre, Dromineer, Co. Tipperary, ✆ (067) 24295. This company charters yachts that can be picked up in Kilrush, and also organizes wind-surfing, canoeing, water-skiing, day cruises and sailing on Lough Derg.

Fishing: for brown trout on the lakes. M. Tierney, 17 Abbey Street, Ennis, ✆ (065) 29433 or Michael Mammon, Lough Derg Angling Centre, Killaloe, ✆ (061) 376329; Tom Burke, Burke's Shop, Main Street, Corrofin, ✆ (065) 37677.

Deep-sea fishing: Atlantic Adventures, Cappa, Kilrush, ✆ (065) 52133; Dermot Collins, Clare Coast Charter, Ballyvaughan, ✆ (065) 21131/77014; William O'Callaghan, Rosslevan, Ennis, ✆ (065) 21374. Kieran O'Driscoll Marine Charter, Fanore, ✆ (065) 76112/088 575163.

Sailing: sailing in traditional Galway Hookers, Ballyvaughan, ✆ (091) 37539.

Swimming: in Lough Graney, and in the sea at Lahinch and around the coast by Spanish Point, Fanore and Doonbeg.

Caving: John MacNamara, Admiral's Restaurant, Fanore, ✆ (065) 76105. Kilshanny Outdoor Centre, Lisdoonvarna, ✆ (065) 730230.

Spa: Sulphur baths at Lisdoonvarna, ✆ (065) 74023. IR£6 for a bath in this little-changed Victorian spa well.

Golf: At Lahinch, ✆ (065) 81003. At Shannon (between the runways of the airport and the estuary), ✆ (061) 61020; Dromoland Castle, ✆ (061) 368444.

Pony-trekking: Residential Riding Holidays at Clonmore Lodge, Quilty, ✆ (065) 87020. Cliffs of Moher Equestrian Centre, Liscannor, ✆ (065) 81283. Trekking through the Burren with the Yellow Rose Riding Centre, Ballinagaddy, Ennistymon, ✆ (065) 71385.

Hunting: Clare Hunt meets from early November to mid-March, ✆ (061) 364146/368329.

Conducted walks: in the Burren area to look at flora, ✆ (065) 20885 or (065) 74603/74580; Burren Education Centre, ✆ (065) 78066.

Traditional music: Clare is particularly famous for its music sessions. Ennistymon boasts some good venues, as does Doolin. Try McGann's, O'Connors or Vaughans in Kilfenora. For a quiet drink in Ballyvaughan, try O'Lochlain's which is more traditional than the touristy Mark's. For a spot of knee-bending, Lois na h Abhna on the Gort road, outside Ennis organises 'Ceilidhs' (traditional Irish dancing). Set dancing and music, ✆ (065) 20996 for details.

Where to Stay

luxury

Dromoland Castle, Newmarket-on-Fergus, ✆ (061) 368144. Owned by the consortium that also operates Ashford Castle, the hotel has beautiful grounds, golf course and delicious food; the atmosphere is a bit impersonal. Lord Inchiquin, **Thomond House**, Newmarket-on-Fergus, ✆ (061) 368304. Conor O'Brien, the 18th Baron Inchiquin, is the O'Brien of Thomond. The exquisite Georgian-style house overlooks Dromoland Castle and its lake, the original home of the O'Briens which is now a luxury hotel. There is salmon fishing, deer stalking, riding and golf, all of which need to be arranged in advance.

expensive

Gregan's Castle, near Ballyvaughan, ✆ (065) 77005. Not actually a castle, but an old manor house with delicious food and comfortable rooms. Set at the top of Corkscrew Hills, in green gardens which are in fantastic contrast to the Burren moonscape, with wonderful views over Galway Bay. The **Falls Hotel**, Ennistymon, ✆ (065) 71004. This had a very good reputation 50 years ago, and it still has a spectacular view of the river. Full of atmosphere and faded charm.

moderate

Ballinalacken Castle Hotel, Lisdoonvarna, ✆ (065) 74025. Beautifully situated overlooking the beach. Recently upgraded from guesthouse to hotel. **Ballykilty Manor**, Quinn, ✆ (065) 25627. Set in wooded grounds with fishing on the River Rine. **Keane's Hotel**, Lisdoonvarna, ✆ (065) 74011. Small family-run hotel. Carnelly House, Castlecastle, ✆ (065) 28442. Early Georgian house with wonderful Francini ceiling. Elegant en suite rooms. Only 9 miles from Shannon Airport. **Sheedy's Spa View Hotel**, Lisdoonvarna, ✆ (065) 74026. Friendly, family-run hotel with a popular restaurant.

inexpensive

Fergus View, Kilnaboy, Corrofin, ✆ (065) 27606. Farmhouse with good home-cooking. Mary Kelleher makes all her own yoghurt and museli. **Caherbolane Farm**, Corrofin, (065) 27638. Simple but good cooking. **Ballymarkham House**, Quin (065) 25726. Fine country house. Kelleher family, **Inchiquin View**, Kilnaboy, ✆ (065) 37731. Comfortable modern farmhouse. **Smyths Village**, Feakle, ✆ (0619) 24002. Cosy fishing hotel. Mrs O'Connor, **Clohaunincy House**, Seafield, Quilty, ✆ (065) 87081. Good home-cooking.

Halpin's Hotel, 2 Erin Street, Kilkee, ✆ (065) 56032. Good service and comfort in cosy hotel. Dilly Griffey and family, **Lahardan House**, Crusheen, Ennis, ✆ (065) 27128. Old family house, comfortable rooms with en suite baths, and delicious home-cooking. **Parochial House**, Cooraclare, ✆ (065) 59059. Relaxed, family home in former priest's residence. Good for children and handy for Killimer car ferry. The **Doolin Hostel**, Doolin, ✆ (065) 74006. Modern with a shop and kitchen facilities.

self-catering

Old-style farmhouse. Contact **Mrs O'Callahan**, Blean, Killydysart, ✆ (065) 26594. Mount Shannon Village: traditional-style cottages, close to the harbour and sailing club. Contact **Bridie Cook**, Gortatleva Bushypark, Galway, ✆ (091) 25295. IR£130–430 a week, depending on the season.

Rent-an-Irish-cottage, Ballyvaughan. Pretty, traditional cottages, ✆ (061) 411109. Bellharbour traditional-style cottages, on the coast between Ballyvaughan and Kinvara. Contact Jacinta Stacey, **Trident Holiday Homes**, Unit 2, Sandymount Village Centre, Dublin 4. ✆ (01) 683534. IR£140–410 per week.

Traditional Irish Cottages, Feakle, in the east Clare lakelands. Contact the Secretary, Mrs B. Purcell, **Irish Cottages**, Feakle, ✆ (061) 924053.

Traditional farm cottage near Mullagh, with sea-view. Contact **Mrs Torpey**, Mullagh, Ennis, ✆ (065) 87031. From IR£150 a week.

5-bedroomed old Georgian house, Corrofin. **Mr Cronin Magle**, Corrofin, ✆ (061) 411773. IR£475–575.

Eating Out

expensive

MacCloskey's Restaurant, Bunratty House Mews, Bunratty, ✆ (061) 364082. In the cellars of an attractive house built in 1846 by a hopeful son waiting to inherit the castle from his father. The décor and atmosphere reflect that feeling of a vanished leisurely way of life. Exquisite food. *Evenings only.*

moderate

Au Tintean Restaurant, Main Street, Doonbeg, ✆ (065) 55036. Seafood restaurant with Swiss chef. *Evenings only.* **Gregan's Castle**, near Ballyvaughan, ✆ (065) 77005. Delicious food all day in the Corkscrew Bar, where the cosy fire and low-beamed ceiling is especially welcome after a long hike. **Claire's Restaurant**, Ballyvaughan, ✆ (065) 77029. Small and unpretentious with a vegetarian dish as standard, great atmosphere. Very popular locally.

Medieval banquets at Bunratty and Knappoque Castles through Castle Tours, ✆ (061) 61788 (*see* pp.215 and 216–7). The Orchard Restaurant in **Sheedy's Spa View Hotel**, Lisdoonvarna, ✆ (065) 74026. Surprisingly sophisticated food in this family run hotel. **Mr Eamons**, Lahinch, ✆ (065) 81050. **Barrtia Seafood Restaurant**, Lahinch, ✆ (065) 81280. Simple but good seafood restaurant just outside Lahinch with views of the bay. **Manuel's Seafood Restaurant**,

Corbally, Kilkee, ✆ (065) 56211. Fabulous views over the bay and, on the other side, the River Shannon and the Kerry Mountains. *Dinner only.*

inexpensive

Lantern House, Ogonnello, Killaloe, ✆ (061) 23034. Home cooking, overlooking Lough Derg. **Aillwee Cave Restaurant**, Ballyvaughan, ✆ (065) 77036/77067. Eating in a cave is rather a novel experience. Delicious soups, pies, cakes. Lunch only. **Roadside Tavern**, Lisdoonvarna, ✆ (065) 74084. Wood-panelled pub-cum-smoking house. Delicious smoked trout, salmon and chowder.

The Cloister, Abbey Street, Ennis, ✆ (065) 29521. Old World bar. Good soups, local cheeses and nutty brown bread during daytime; at night becomes more formal (and expensive) as a restaurant. **Mac's Pub**, Mount Shannon. Good atmosphere and bar snacks.

Durty Nelly's, Bunratty, ✆ (065) 364861. Pub and eating house popular with locals as well as visitors. **An Fear Gorta**, Pier Road, Ballyvaughan, ✆ (065) 77023. Tea room and restaurant, good cakes and seafood.

Linnane's Bar, New Quay, ✆ (065) 78120. Pub that specialises in lobster and oysters. **Monk's Bar**, Ballyvaughan. Delicious mussels and brown bread. Traditional music at night.

The Province of Connacht

The province of Connacht (*Cuige Chonnacht*), also spelt Connaught, is made up of Counties Galway, Mayo, Roscommon, Sligo and Leitrim. Oliver Cromwell thought of Connacht as a Siberia to which he could banish the troublesome Catholic landowners, and here on the crowded, stony farms the famine struck the hardest in the 1840s. Today, it seems a wild paradise of mountains, heather and lakes into which the Atlantic makes spectacular entrances with black cliffs, golden beaches and island-studded bays. This is the wild west, which was for centuries remote from Dublin and fashionable values; where in some parts the local people still speak Gaelic, and where they have clung to their own traditions in spite of the past invaders and the more insidious advance of modern life.

On a bright day in this region, you might think that Cromwell did those 'transplanted Irish' a good turn: your aesthetic feelings are satisfied, and you know that a good meal is waiting at the next hotel! The dismal grey rocks, the scraggy sheep, the turf ricks and misty mountains are transformed into a tumble of brownish purple, with streaks of silver and cornflower blue where the lakes reflect the sky in the deep valleys. This is why the monks in Early-Christian times turned their backs on the court of Tara and the rich Celtic princes, and built their tiny churches on the windswept islands off the coast.

Farming and fishing in this part of the world is a risky business, and the history of Connacht closely reflects the barren countryside. The Norman invaders seem to have been less successful here, or less persistent, than in other provinces; or else they became Irish themselves, like the family de Burgo who changed their name to Burke. It is rather ironic that the Connacht people, who so strongly ignored outside influences for hundreds of years, should be more Anglicized now because of TV and the tourist trade than they ever were under the British. But the areas known as the *Gaeltachta*, where Gaelic is still the first language, are protected by the government, and incentives by way of grants have encouraged people not to move off to America or England for jobs.

It would be a mistake to think that all Connacht is wild mountain scenery. A large part of it belongs to the limestone plain which covers the centre of Ireland, making it rather saucer-shaped, with its mountains on the rim. The whole of Roscommon, part of Leitrim, South Sligo and much of Galway is made up of neat fields, trees and heather, dotted with lakes and lined by the lovely River Shannon. The Shannon rises in the Iron Mountains of Cavan and flows southwest into Leitrim, where it curves to form a moat round the eastern boundary of Connacht. This part of the province is wonderful, but it has not the instant splendours of Connemara or Joyce's Country. The Shannon widens to engulf huge lakes, rather like a snake swallowing down its prey whole, while it continues to coil down the countryside.

The climate of the west is mild, though a misty rain often falls, leaving you soaked through. The mountains seems to nudge the clouds above them into rain, but there is always a glimmer of sunshine about and in summer it can get superbly warm. Scarlet fuchsia grows along the coast roads in place of the overbearing hawthorn hedges. In parts where you would be hard put to it to find a blade of grass, a giant hogweed plant will grow in early summer, and purple rhododendron grows profusely. All of Connacht, but especially Connemara, is rather like a piece of tweed cloth with a thread of grey running through it—a speckled look given by the thousands of little stone walls.

History and Legend

Connacht has a lion's share of heroes, legends and battles. Back in the mists of pre-history, tradition holds that the Fir Bolgs, who had lived thinking themselves alone on the island, bumped into the tall, fair Tuatha Dé Danaan and there was a battle on the plain on Moytura. The Fir Bolgs were defeated and had to retreat to the islands and mountains of the west. Here they built themselves the marvellous ring-forts of *Dun Aonghus* and *Dubh-Chathair* on the Aran Islands. Here, they clung on whilst the centre of power shifted from the Dé Danaans to the invading Celts. The legendary Dé Danaans are supposed to have brought with them the *Lial Fail*, or Stone of Destiny, which was used in Ireland as the coronation seat. At some period it was taken to Scone in Scotland and has now landed up in Westminster Abbey!

Connacht has produced two infamous queens. One told Queen Elizabeth I not to patronise her, and was a sea pirate who ruled from Clare Island. Her name was Grace O'Malley. The other was Maeve, a legendary Queen remembered in the epic tale, 'The Cattle Raid of Cooley'. What happened was this...

Maeve and her husband were measuring up their worldly possessions and found that they were equal in all things except one. He owned the most magnificent white bull which outclassed anything she could produce. However, there was a brown bull in the Kingdom of Ulster that was equal to his and she was determined to have it. At certain times of the year, the Red Branch Knights, who were the guardians of Ulster, became as feeble as kittens because of the spell put on them. So choosing this time of the year, her raiding party thought the whole expedition would be easy; but at a crucial fording point, the young and untried hero, Cú Chulainn, who was free of the spell, challenged each Connacht man to fight, and he slew them all. Maeve, undaunted, decided to get the bull for herself and succeeded; only when she got the bull home it went into a mad frenzy and fought with the white bull until the earth shook. At last, the bull of Cooley caught the white bull by the horns and shook it to pieces, causing a loin to fall by the Shannon, giving the town Athlone its name.

Maeve is said to be buried at the top of Knocknarea Mountain in County Sligo. Nearby, on the slopes of the hauntingly beautiful Ben Bulben, the legendary hero Diarmuid met an untimely death in a boar hunt arranged by his enemy Fionn MacCool (see **Old Gods and Heroes**, p.576).

County Galway

County Galway (*Gaillimh*) is the second-largest county in Ireland, and 50 per cent of its population still speak Gaelic as their first language. It stretches from the wild and beautiful region known as Connemara in the west to the banks of the Shannon and Lough Derg in the east, and includes the island-studded Lough Corrib. It is truly a county of contrast. There is bog and rich farming land that a Meath man would not sniff at; whilst amongst the mountains and along the coast the tiny clochan of whitewashed stone cottages tells of a different way of life, where the Atlantic winds blow strongly and the cheerful red hens scratch away amongst a soil made fertile with layers of seaweed.

For those of you in search of peace and solitude, miles of lonely valleys and hills and huge golden beaches await you. Anglers will be in paradise fishing on Lough Corrib and the other countless lakes, and the salmon rivers of Owenglin and Dawros. Some very good restaurants have been set up, and serve delicious fresh seafood in imaginative ways. As for drinking, the bars are the friendliest you could hope to find. Ancient Stone Age fortifications and early monastic churches add more fascination to the county. A trip to the Aran Islands is not only an adventure in itself, but gives you a chance to see Conor Fort on Inishmaan, built of massive great stones. Romantic ruins of 15th-century castles add their charm and stories to the landscape, and some have been restored for the public to look around. Galway City is a very attractive and civilized place, with plenty of cultural life: music, theatre, good bookshops and cosy bars in which to discuss all you have seen and heard.

History

The names that crop up again and again in the history of County Galway are O'Flaherty, de Burgo, and Lynch. They each represent a different and conflicting group who battled it out for centuries. The O'Flahertys were a warlike Gaelic tribe from Connemara, also known as *Iar-Chonnacht*. The de Burgos were Norman adventurers who were granted the land around Galway City in 1226, at which time it was a small fort. Richard de Burgo fortified it stongly to keep out the O'Flahertys, but over the years the de Burgos became Irish in their ways and lost their allegiance to the Crown. During the reign of Edward I in the 13th century, 14 Anglo-Norman and Welsh families had settled in the town, and were passionate Royalists. They controlled all the civic powers and kept themselves to them-selves, excluding any Irish from the town, including the de Burgos or Burkes as they were now called. (Quite when this name change happened is not recorded.) In 1518 the Corporation resolved that no inhabitant should receive into his house, 'at Christmas, Easter no feast else, any of the Burkes (Burgos) MacWilliams, Kellys, nor any sept else without licence of the Mayor and Council, on pain to forfeit £5, that O nor Mac shall strut nor swagger through the streets of Galway'. The chief of these 14 families or 'tribes' as they were known, were the Lynches, and through the enterprise and resourcefulness of such families Galway City became rich trading in wine and other commodities with Spain.

The tribes of Galway were able to hang on to civic power in their city until 1654, when Cromwellian forces took the city after a siege of months and shattered it. The Williamite wars in the 1690s brought about another siege, and spelt the end of Galway's independence and importance.

Galway City was the administrative centre for the west of Ireland during British rule in the 18th and 19th centuries. The famine years of 1845–49 bought desolation and horror to the countryside and massive emigration followed for several generations. However, the Congested Districts Board set up in 1890 to promote the development of traditional crafts and fishing industries started to improve matters. At the turn of the century, Nationalists used the west of Ireland as a powerful symbol of 'Real Ireland', because the people remained un-Anglicized and still spoke Gaelic; despite the widescale emigration and the national school system, which between 1831 and 1904 taught no Irish. After the establishment of the Irish State, the Congested Districts Board evolved into the *Roinn na Gaeltachta* (the Department of State responsible for Irish-speaking districts), and special grants were made available to encourage people to stay in the county. The IDA (Industrial Development Authority) has also had great success in attracting sophisticated industrial companies. Galway City has its own university, the second-largest regional technical college in the country, and a flourishing arts community. The attempts to preserve the Irish language are bolstered by *Radio na Gaeltachta* and Irish summer colleges, where students from all over Ireland speak Gaelic, learn *ceili* dancing, and stay in the houses of Irish-speaking families. The struggle to preserve the Gaelic speaking districts is always present: tourism and television undermine it, and the young continue to emigrate to other parts of Ireland and abroad. Many people have a sister or brother working in America or England because the work prospects are so much better there.

Getting There and Around

By air: Galway City has an airport with daily flights to London (Luton). Shannon International Airport is approximately 1½ hours' drive from Galway City. Dublin Airport is approximately 3½ hours' drive from Galway City.

By sea: to Larne, Dublin and Rosslare Ferry Ports.

By rail: mainline trains serve Ballinasloe and Galway City ✆ (091) 64222.

By bus: Bus Eireann, the national company, serves all the major towns with Expressway buses, and there is a good local network. Galway Bus Depot, ✆ (091) 62000/635555.

By car: car hire available in Galway City from Avis, ✆ (091) 68886.

By bike: The Raleigh Rent-a-Bike network operates throughout County Galway. Local dealers are John Mannion, Railway View, Clifden, ✆ (095) 21160; Europa Bicycles, Earls Island, Galway City (also arrange tours), ✆ (091) 63355; and Renvyle Stores, Tullycross, ✆ (095) 43450. Bicycles can also be hired from P. Clarke, Dunlo Street, Ballinasloe, ✆ (0905) 42417; O'Connor's Garage, Cong, ✆ (092) 46008.

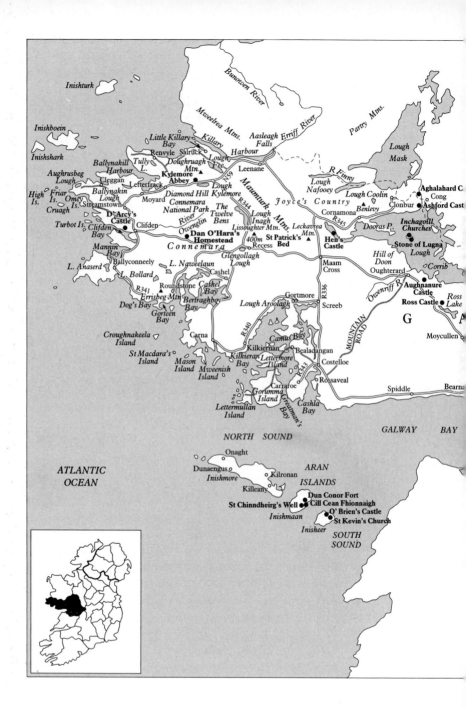

Inishturk

Inishboein

Inishshark

High Friar Is.
Is. Omey Is.
Cruagh Is. Streamstown

Turbot Is. Clifden
Bay

Mannin
Bay

L. Anaserd

Dog's Bay

Croughnakeela
Island

St Macdara's
Island

Bunowen River

Mweelrea Mtns.

Aasleagh
Falls

Erriff River

Little Killary
Bay

Killary

Harbour

Leenane

Parry Mtns.

Lough
Mask

Aughrusbeg
Lough

Ballynakill
Harbour

Renvyle Salruck
Tully
Doughruagh
Mtn.
Kylemore
Abbey

Lough
Fee

R Finny

Lough

Cleggan

Letterfrack

Lough

Ballynakin
Lough

Diamond Hill Kylemore

Connemara
National Park

Moyard

D'Arcy's
Castle

Clifden

The
Twelve
Bens

Owenglin
River

Dan O'Hara's
Homestead

Connemara

Ballyconneely

L. Naweelaun

Cashel

Roundstone Cashel
Bay

Errisbeg Mtn

R341

Bertraghboy
Bay

Gorteen
Bay

Lough
Inagh

Maumturk Mtns.

Joyce's Country

Lough
Nafooey

Lough Coolin

Benlevy

Cornamona

Lough

Lissoughter Mtn. Leckavrea
Mtn.

400m
Recess

St Patrick's
Bed

Glengollagh
Lough

Gortmore

Lough Aroolagh

Carna

Camus Bay

Kilkiernan

Aghalahard C.
Cong

Clonbur Ashford Cast

Inchagoill
Churches

Dooras P.

Hen's
Castle

Maam
Cross

Stone of Lugna
Lough

Hill of
Doon

Oughterard

Corrib

Aughnanure
Castle
Ross Castle

Ross
Lake

Screeb

G

Moycullen

St Chinndheirg's Well

Mason
Island

Kilkieran Lettermore
Bay
Island

Mweenish
Island

Lettermullan
Island

Gorumma
Island

Kilronan

Bealadangan

Costelloe

Rossaveal

Carratoe

Cashla
Bay

Spiddle

Bearna

NORTH SOUND

Onaght

Dunaengus
Inishmore

Killeany

Inishmaan

Inisheer

ARAN

ISLANDS

Dun Conor Fort

Cill Cean Fhionnaigh
O' Brien's Castle
St Kevin's Church

SOUTH
SOUND

GALWAY BAY

ATLANTIC
OCEAN

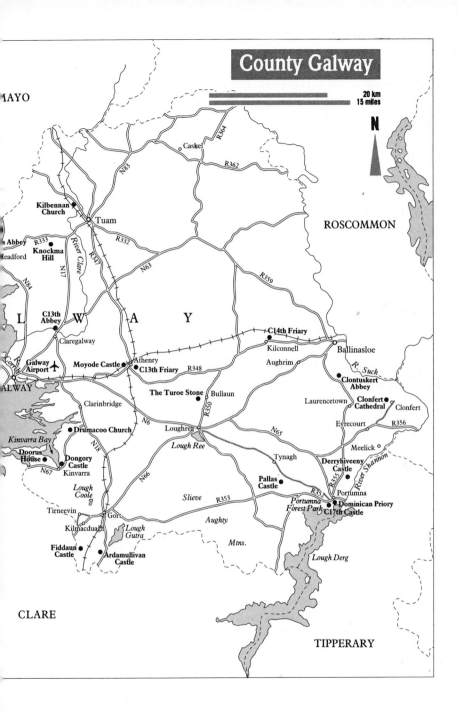

County Galway

20 km
15 miles

N

MAYO

ROSCOMMON

Cashel

R364

R362

N83

Kilbennan Church

Tuam

R332

s Abbey   R333

Knockma Hill

Meadford

River Clare

R341

N63

N17

N84

R359

C13th Abbey   W   A   Y

L

Claregalway

C14th Friary

Kilconnell

Ballinasloe

Galway Airport

Moyode Castle

Athenry

C13th Friary

Aughrim

R. Suck

R348

ALWAY

Clontuskert Abbey

The Turoe Stone   Bullaun

Clarinbridge

N6

R350

Laurencetown   Clonfert Cathedral   Clonfert

Drumacoo Church

Loughrea

Eyrecourt   R356

Kinvarra Bay

Lough Ree

Meelick

Doorus House

Dongory Castle

N18

Tynagh

Derryhiveeny Castle

River Shannon

N67

Kinvarra

Lough Coole

N66

Slieve   R353

Pallas Castle

R355

Portumna

Tirneevin

Gort

Aughty

Portumna Forest Park

Dominican Priory
C17th Castle

Kilmacduagh

Lough Gutra

Mtns.

Fiddaun Castle

Ardamullivan Castle

Lough Derg

CLARE

TIPPERARY

233

Thoor Ballylee, ✆ (091) 31436, May to September.

Ballinasloe, ✆ (0905) 42131, July to August.

Tuam, ✆ (093) 24463, July to August.

Galway, Aras Fáilte, Victoria Place, ✆ (091) 63081.

Clifden, ✆ (095) 21163. May to September.

May: Ballinasloe Coarse Fishing Festival, ✆ (0905) 42512/42582.

Mid-July: Galway Arts Festival, ✆ (091) 63800 for details.

Early July: Galway Film Fleadh, ✆ (091) 66744.

Late July/early August: Galway Races, Ballybrit Course. Contact the tourist office for details.

Mid-August: Connemara Pony Show, Clifden, ✆ (095) 21863.

September: Clarinbridge Oyster Festival is early in the month, ✆ (091) 96342. Lots of drinking, oyster-opening competitions, traditional music, dances and fun.
Late September: Galway Oyster Festival, ✆ (091) 22066.

East Galway

Gort (*Gort inse Guaire*: Field on Guaire's Island), the main town on the road from Galway to Ennis, Shannon, Limerick and the south, stands in a natural gap between the Slieve Auchty mountains and the Burren—the traditional roadway between Munster and Connacht. Guaire is the name of the 7th-century king who built a castle here; he was supposed to have been so generous that his right hand, his giving hand, was said to be longer than his left. One day as he sat down to a sumptuous meal, the plates of food suddenly flew out of the windows; he naturally followed his meal on horseback, intrigued by such magic. After a few miles he came upon St Colman, who had just that minute finished a seven-year fast by gobbling up the feast. Instead of being angry the king was impressed, and even more so when he found Colman was a relation, and he granted him the lands of Kilmacduagh where the saint founded a monastery.

Kilmacduagh, about 4 miles (7.4km) southwest of Gort on the R460, has one of the most interesting collections of church buildings in Ireland. There is a 12th-century monastic church, called a cathedral. It is roofless now but has good carvings; one on the jamb of the door is an incised comic face with earrings. The round tower near the small lake was built in the 11th or 12th century. It is one of the most perfect in Ireland; its angle has something in common with the Tower of Pisa. The monks used to build the door of such towers about 25ft (7.6m) from the ground, so that when marauders attacked they could whip up the ladders when they were safely installed with their treasures. In **Tirneevin**, just north of Kilmacduagh, is a small church with a very fine stained-glass window of Christ the sower, by George Campbell. Four miles (6.4km) south of Gort lies Lough Cutra, and amongst some beautiful woods on the southwest edge of the lough is a castellated mansion, built in 1810 to designs by John Nash for Lord Gort (*not open to the public*).

Around Gort there are many little streams which suddenly disappear into the limestone; the River Beagh emerges to flow through a ravine called the Ladle and then into the Punchbowl. This is a huge funnel-shaped hollow, surrounded by trees, with water swirling dangerously at the bottom. It is only a few yards from the road, so it is not difficult to see even if you are in a hurry. The Gort area is full of literary associations: in 1917, W. B. Yeats bought a ruined tower house for £35 and called it **Thoor Ballylee** (*open daily, May–30 Sept, 10–6; adm; © (091) 31436 for more details*). Now Bord Fáilte have carefully restored it, and many rare first editions of Yeats' work are on exhibit there. He lived here until 1929, whereupon it once more fell into ruin. You will find it just off the N66 north of Gort. It is a romantic building with a wonderful view from the top. An audio guide to the tower and grounds is available in different languages. Lady Gregory's old home, **Coole Park**, is about 2 miles (3.2km) northeast of Gort. She was a writer and co-founder of the Abbey Theatre in Dublin. Many remarkable people from the Irish literary scene stayed here, including Yeats, who found it a refuge when he was ill and little-known. Nothing is left of the house which was demolished for the value of its stone (such things always happen in Ireland), but the lovely spreading copper chestnut which was Lady Gregory's visitors' book still grows in the walled garden. You can make out the initials of A. E. (George Russell, the mystical painter), Jack Yeats, Sean O'Casey and a bold G. B. S.—George Bernard Shaw. It is protected from nonentities by a high iron railing. The demesne has been taken over by the Forestry Commission and is a wildlife park open to all. Signs point the way to Coole Lake where Yeats saw nine and fifty swans and wrote a poem about them.

Five miles (8km) south of Gort are the ruins of the 16th-century **Ardamullivan Castle**, an O'Shaughnessy stronghold. They were the ruling sept in these parts before they were dispossessed by Cromwell. Another of their strongholds is **Fiddaun Castle**, 5 miles (8km) south-southwest of Gort. It has a fine bawn (fortified enclosure), and is also in ruins.

Around Kinvara

Kinvara is a charming fishing village at the head of a bay where there is a restored 16th-century castle called **Dunguaire**, also known as Dungory (*open mid April–30 Sept, daily, 9.30–5.30; adm; medieval banquets twice-nightly, May–Sept; © (091) 37108 for more details*). It is sited on a little jutting promontory beside the bay; a tower house stands within the strong walls of its close-fitting bawn. On summer evenings you can savour the delights of a medieval banquet, whilst you listen to readings from Irish literature. The Great Hall is rather bijou but the Irish dancing and singing are fun, and through the windows of the castle to the north you look over the waters of Galway Bay to the hills of Connemara. To the south you can make out the grey and hazy hills of the Burren in County Clare. The road from Kinvara goes past the head of the peninsula, on which is **Doorus House**, where Yeats and Maupassant used to stay. It is now a youth hostel. Northwards from Kinvara the N67 runs inland with little side-roads turning west to the island waters of Galway Bay. One of these roads leads to the ancient monastic site of Drumacoo, which is dedicated to a nun, Sister Sorrey. Here there is a very beautiful south doorway decorated in Early Gothic style *c.* AD 1200. There is also a very weedy holy well outside the churchyard wall.

At **Clarinbridge**, on the main Galway-Limerick road (N18), the bars come alive in September with oyster enthusiasts gathered there for the **Oyster Festival**. Whatever the time of year, you should take the tiny side-road for Moran's on the Weir in Kilcoghan, signposted in Clarinbridge, for delicious Guinness and seafood of all sorts. This pub-restaurant is a main venue for the Festival (*see* p.234). Recently the small native oyster has been attacked by a disease which is devastating stock—an economic and culinary disaster.

Around Portumna

Fifteen miles (24km) east of Gort on the R353 is **Portumna** (*Port Omna*: the Landing Place of the Tree Trunk). This market town stands at the head of the huge and intricate Lough Derg, the furthest downriver of the Shannon lakes, and a major cruising centre with plenty of shops and bars. To the west of Portumna is good walking country on the forested slopes of Slieve Aughty. The R353 from Gort dissects the mountain, and there are numerous unnumbered roads from which you can climb to a vantage point and see the extensive views of Lough Derg and the surrounding countryside. The climb up the Slieve Aughty mountains is not too strenuous an exercise, for the highest point is 1207ft (368m). On the edge of the town is the forested demesne of the Earls of **Clanrickarde**, now a lovely **forest park** with nature trails and picnic spots bordering Lough Derg. There is a small car parking fee. The 17th-century castle is being restored by the Office of Public Works (*always accessible*). A stone set in the crumbling walls of the double staircase is an affectionate epitaph to a dog that died in April 1797: 'Alas poor Fury, she was a dog taken all in all, I shall not look upon her like again'. Near the castle is a Dominican friary founded in 1410, with beautiful windows.

There are two castles in this area you should go out of your way to see: Derryhivenny and Pallas. **Derryhivenny Castle** is 3 miles (4.8km) northwest of Portumna. Built in 1653 by Donal O'Madden, it is well preserved and one of the last tower houses built in Ireland. **Pallas Castle** is about 6 miles (9.7km) from Portumna on the Loughrea road (N65). Built in the 16th century by the Burkes, the lower storeys are defensive, as in most castles, and any openings are few and purely utilitarian—terrible places to have actually lived in! Amongst the lush and peaceful Shannon valley about 15 miles (24km) northeast of Portumna and 10 miles (6km) northeast of Eyrecourt on the R355 is a monastery founded by St Brendan the Navigator in AD 563. There is a superb example of Irish Romanesque art in the doorway of the minuscule church known as **Clonfert Cathedral** (*open daily*). Six receding planes are decorated with heads, foliage and abstract designs; within the pediment, sculptured heads peer down at you. The 15th-century chancel arch is decorated with angels, rosettes, and a mermaid admiring herself in a mirror. **Clonfert Catholic Church** houses a 13th-century wooden Madonna and child, found in a tree hole. It was probably hidden during Cromwell's time. **Meelick**, close by on the River Shannon, has mooring facilities for boats.

Around Loughrea

Loughrea (the Town of the Grey Lake), is a bright, colour-washed town, situated on a lovely lough. The pubs are venues for fine traditional music which is very popular here. It started life as a stronghold of Richard de Burgo, whose family turned into Burkes and later Clanrickardes; you will often come across the name. The town is very affluent because at Tynagh there are lead and zinc mines.

What you must not miss if you stop in Loughrea is **St Brendan's Catholic Cathedral**. It is not very inspiring from the outside, but inside the decoration epitomizes the development of the ecclesiastical arts and crafts in Ireland from 1903 to 1957. The stained-glass windows are by Sarah Purser and other members of her Tower of Glass. This was a stained-glass workshop founded in 1903 in Dublin which attracted other talented artists such as Evie Hone. The statue of the Virgin and Child is by John Hughes, and embroidered sodality banners are by Jack Yeats. **Loughrea Museum** in Dunkellin Street (irregular opening times) traces the hundred-year history of the Gaelic Athletic Association, an organization which became linked with Nationalist ideals. Contact the tourist office in Galway for details. The Carmelite monastery is a fine early-14th-century ruin, and next door to it is an active Carmelite abbey. A most impressive curiosity is the **Turoe Stone**, which is found 4 miles (6.4km) north of town, signposted from the hamlet of Bullaun. It is a rounded pillar about 3ft (1m) high. A swirling mass of opposed spirals is carved upon the upper part. It must have had some ritual purpose, dates from the 1st century AD, and is the finest of its type in Ireland. It was moved to its present position from a ring-fort called Rath of the Big Man. The stone has been linked with the Celtic La Tene style of decoration that is found in Brittany, and also with the Omphalos Stone in Delphi which was seen as the navel or centre of the world by the ancient Greeks.

The family who live in the house close by have sought to benefit from the tourists, and opened a pet farm and coffee shop (*open April–Oct, daily; adm;* ✆ *(0905) 42140*) which has changed the ambience somewhat. There's a duck pond, small animals, a playground with swings and a collection of old farm machinery, and a wishing well.

Around Ballinasloe

Ballinasloe (*Beal Atha na Sluaighe*: town of the ford of the Hostings), 20 miles (16km) east on the N6, is famous for its **Horse Fair** in early October, when the quiet streets suddenly bustle with carnival events which last for eight days, and show-jumping competitions (*see* 'Festivals'). Horses are still put for sale on the fair green, but not in the number that the ballads reminisce about. (Horse fairs used to be common all over Ireland up until the 1950s when the tractor and car took over.) A tower is all that remains of the castle, which used to command the bridge over the River Suck—an excellent river for coarse fishing. Ballinasloe Angling Week, one of the biggest coarse angling competitions in Ireland, takes place here annually (*see* 'Festivals'). **St Michaels Church** contains some of the best stained-glass by Harry Clarke (1889–1931) and Albert Power (1883–1945), both highly regarded artists.

Kilconnell village, about 6 miles (9.7km) away on the R348 to Galway, has a **Franciscan friary**, founded in 1353 by William O'Kelly. In the 17th century it was unsuccessfully besieged by Cromwell. In the north wall of the nave are two 15th to 16th-century tomb chests, one with flamboyant tracery. The west tomb is divided into niches with the carved figures of Saints John, Louis, Mary, James and Denis. Under the tower the corbel shows a little carving of an owl in high relief. Tradition alleged that the incompetent French general, St Ruth, who led the Irish against King William in 1691, was buried here after the Battle of Aughrim. West of Ballinasloe on the N6 is the site of the battle, and the **Aughrim Interpretative Centre** (*open May–Sept, daily, 10am–6pm; adm;*Ⓒ *(0905) 73939*). The main causes and results of the battle are explored in displays, documents and an audio-visual show.

The well-preserved ruins of the **Abbey of Clontuskert** lie on the way to Laurencetown (R355). The abbey, which stands on the site of a monastery founded in the 9th century, was rebuilt by industrious Augustinian monks in the 14th century, with money from the sale of 10-year indulgences. The monks ignored the Reformation, and carried on until Cromwell finally wrecked the place. The abbey has an unusual and pretty west door of 1471, depicting saints, a mermaid, and various creatures.

Around Athenry

Athenry (*Baile Atha an Ri*: Town of the King's Ford), is pronounced Athenrye, and was founded by Meiler de Bermingham, a Norman warlord, in the last half of the 13th century. The strong walls that were later built round it still remain in fragments. In the central square stands the remains of a 15th-century cross showing the Crucifixion on one side and the Virgin and Child on the other. **St Mary's Parish Church** was built in 1289, if not before. It became collegiate in 1484, and was suppressed in 1576 and burnt by Clanrickarde's sons (even though the mother of one of them was buried there). The graceful spire in the grounds dates from 1828. Now ruined, but full of interest is the **Dominican priory** founded by de Bermingham in 1241. It has been a university and a barracks, and has now been tidied up by the Office of Public Works. The tracery work of the east window dated 1324 is very fine. The church was the burial place of the Earls of Ulster and many of the chief Irish families of the west, but their graves were destroyed by Cromwell's soldiers. In a recess a small carving of a monk grins forever, and there is an interesting grave slab dated 1682 to Thomas Tannain, on which are carved the bellows, anvil, auger, pinchers and horseshoes of his blacksmith's trade. In North Gate Street is a heritage cottage: a recreated traditional cottage furnished as it would have been early this century. Access through the tourist information point.

Moyode Castle, 2 miles (3.2km) southwest of Athenry, is a ruined mansion with an ancient castle in its grounds. Here in 1770 the nucleus of what was to become the Galway Blazers Foxhounds was formed. The big house, which is now a ruin, was taken over in the Nationalist cause by Liam Mellows and his Galway followers for several days during the Easter Rising in 1916. Mellows was a socialist leader who was executed during the Irish Civil War in 1922. **Claregalway** on the River Clare is now a suburb of Galway. It has the remains of a 13th-century **Franciscan abbey**.

Around Tuam

Tuam (Grave Mound), pronounced *Choom*, is a very uninspiring place: the streets smell of beer and chips. But that was on a rainy dark day. Tuam has a long history and during the 12th century was the seat of the O'Connor kings of Connacht. The presence of a fine 12th-century cross in the town square, and an imposing **Church of Ireland cathedral** are reminders of its past glory. Although the latter is a Gothic-revival structure, it still has a splendid, wide and lavishly carved chancel arch of rosy sandstone which dates from the 12th century. The imposing church door is surrounded by carved decoration: on one of the splays you can see the Devil pulling Adam's ears. The **Mill Museum** in Shop Street also provides tourist information in the summer.

Four miles (6.4km) north of Tuam is **Tollenfal Castle**, ancestral home of the Lallys—one of whom was the famous French general Baron de Lally, who has his name inscribed on the Arc de Triomphe in Paris. It is not open to the public. **Lisacormack Fort**, 1 mile (1.6km) east on the Dunmore road (N83), is the largest of the numerous earthworks scattered round this area. The fort is on private land. On the Ballinrobe road (R332), 2½ miles (4 km) from Tuam is **Kilbennan Church**, in Gothic style with 16th-century detail. Beside it is a 10th-century round tower. **Barnaderg Castle**, 4 miles (6.4 km) to the southeast of Tuam on the R332 to Barnaderg, is believed to be one of the last castles built in Ireland. On the keystone over the door is a *Sheila-na-Gig*.

Headford (*Ath Cinn*: the ford head), 10 miles (17km) west of Tuam, is set in countryside divided by stone fields. It is tidy and neat and a favourite angling centre, where it is possible to stock up with fishing tackle and groceries. The surrounding countryside contains the ruins of many Norman castles. **Knockma Hill**, about 7½ miles (12km) east of Headford on the R333, is traditionally held to be the home of King Finbarr and his Connacht fairies, and the burial place of Queen Maeve. It is the only hill for miles. **Ross Errilly Abbey**, just outside Headford, is an important and well-preserved 14th-century ruin; the cloister remains intact, although not ornate, and the domestic buildings are complete, exhibiting perfectly the arrangements of a Franciscan friary in the Middle Ages. There is a round hole in the floor of the kitchen: it is not a well but a fish tank, so the monks would always have fresh fish on Fridays. You will often notice that the Abbot knew how to choose the best architects, the finest land and best-stocked rivers for himself.

South Connemara

Connemara is not an area firmly drawn by boundary lines; it is the name given to the western portion of County Galway which lies between Lough Corrib and the Atlantic, bounded in the north by Killary Harbour.

Around Oughterard

Here, at **Moycullen**, the real splendours of the west begin, although it is worth stopping only when you get to **Oughterard**. A pretty river, the Owenriff, runs through the charming town, which is right on the upper shores of Lough Corrib and a good place to base yourself if you are keen on salmon and trout angling. If you are either coming from **Costelloe** on the coast road, or going there from Oughterard, take the mountain road which joins the two towns cross-country, and gives you a vast panorama of watery landscape as you go up through a small hill pass. The region is very wild, and the locals turn to stare at you as they load the turf into creels on the back of asses. There are shreds of shining water where you might find brown trout, and turf cuttings, which gleam with black wetness when they have been newly cut. **Aughnanure Castle**, 3 miles (4.8km) southeast of Oughterard (*open mid-June–mid-Sept, 9.30–6.30 daily; adm. Guided tours on request. The key is with a caretaker the rest of the year*; ✆ *(091) 82214*), is an O'Flaherty building and said to be one of the strongest fortresses at the time Cromwell was blockading Galway. The six-storey tower stands on an island of rock. In the days of its prosperity a portion of the floor of the hall was made to collapse: one of the flagstones was hinged downwards and an unwelcome guest might well find himself tipped into the fast flowing stream below. Nothing of the hall stands today: it too collapsed into the stream, as did the cavern over which it was built. But the castle has been restored, and you can climb right to the top. **Ross Castle** (not open to the public), 5 miles (8km) southeast of Oughterard beside the shores of Ross Lake, was the home of the Martins, who bankrupted themselves trying to help out in the famine times of the 1840s. One of them, 'Humanity Dick', was instrumental in setting up the Society for Prevention of Cruelty to Animals; and Violet Ross (1862–1915) was the Martin Ross of Somerville and Ross fame. Her cousin Edith Somerville lived in Cork, but they succeeded in collaborating to produce some exquisitely humorous novels and stories. *The Reminiscences of an Irish RM* and *Cousin*

Charlotte are the best. Follow the road from the village down to Lough Corrib for a lovely drive along its wooded shores. It leads you to the Hill of Doon and a good view of the largest island on the lake, Inchagoill.

Inchagoill

Inchagoill (*Inis an Ghaill*: the island of the devout stranger) is the prettiest and most interesting of the hundreds of islands on Lough Corrib. There is a 5th-century church, *Teampall Pharaic*, and one of 10th-century origin further to the south which was reconstructed in 1860. Then there is the Stone of Lugna, called after the navigator of St Patrick. This 2ft (72cm) high obelisk bears engraved Roman characters. It is supposed to be the earliest Christian inscription in Europe after the catacombs.

Clonbur is a centre for fishermen, situated on the limestone isthmus between Lough Mask and Lough Corrib. If you want to climb the Connemara, Maamturk or Partry Mountains, Clonbur is well-placed. One mile (1.6km) to the west rises the lovely mountain area known as Joyce Country, where it is said the Fir Bolgs assembled before they made their last stand against the Dé Danaan at the Battle of Moytura, long ago in the mists of legend. In the foothills leading up to the highest peak, Benlevy (1370ft/418m), is Lough Coolin, which in Edwardian days was the setting for lavish picnic parties which used to sally out from Ashford Castle about 5 miles (8km) away. Ashford Castle, just over the border in Cong, County Mayo, is now an extremely luxurious hotel. You can get there by car although the road is very narrow. It is a peaceful, dreamy sort of place.

Cornamona is on the northern corner of Lough Corrib on the Dooras Peninsula. It is in one of the most popular Irish-speaking districts in North Connemara, on the edge of Joyce Country. Joyce Country is named after a race of Welshmen who settled in Connacht after Richard de Burgo conquered it in the 13th century. The native O'Flahertys and the Joyces eventually got on rather well and used to go and mob up the 'plainsmen'. As they often crossed swords on the isthmus it became known as the Gap of Danger. Not one of the roads around here is dull and the fishing on the little loughs, as well as Loughs Mask and Corrib, is good. On the R345 to Maam is a spectacular ruin, **Hen's Castle**, on an island in the Corrib. It is said to have fallen into ruin after an O'Flaherty ate the hen which had been given to his family generations before by a witch. Cold historical fact states that the castle was built by the O'Connors.

At **Maumeen** (*Maimean*) in the Corcogemore Mountains (part of the Maamturk range) is **St Patrick's Bed and Holy Well**, reached by a footpath off the R336. Pilgrims have travelled here for centuries, as the well is reputed to have strong healing powers. The annual pilgrimage, on the last Sunday of July, has undergone a revival recently, with many people attending. **Lough Nafooey** is one of the most beautiful in Connemara and in Irish means 'the lake of the spectre'. It is off a mountain road that leads up the Finny River, and can also be approached by another road halfway between Maam and Leenane off the R336. Lots of little streams run into the lake so there is never a ghostly stillness, for the music of gurgling water plays continually in early summer accompanied by the smell of gorse and pine trees.

Barna to Carna

This section includes most of the Irish-speaking parts and stretches along the north coast of Galway Bay, and from there along the Atlantic to Carna. Its northern boundary runs from Gowlaun (*Gabhla*) through Maam Cross to Barna (*Bearna*). This part of the world is hilly and remote, for there are very few roads into it. From Galway to Spiddal (R336) it is disappointingly built-up, although you do get glimpses of the Aran Islands, looking far or near according to the clarity of the weather.

Rossaveal (*Ros An Mhil*) at the mouth of Galway Bay has a cabin-cruiser called *Aran Flyer* which runs regularly to Aran doing a brisk trade in turf, as Aran has no fuel resources of its own (*see* section on getting to the Aran Islands, p.256). By now you may have noticed the black beetle-like boats which the fishermen in Connacht use. The type of curragh you see in Ireland varies considerably from the Donegal coast to the Kerry coast in the south. Here, they are very light and it needs a skilful man to handle the long, heavy oars that have no blade. It is astonishing how much they can carry: a load could include cement and livestock—pigs and sheep with their legs tied and muffled.

From Rossaveal you follow the road north for just a mile to **Costelloe**, which has a wonderful coral strand and a good salmon-fishing river. There is quite a meeting of the roads here and you can go either to Maam Cross or follow a little road to Carraroe (*An Cheathru Rua*). At Bealadangan (*Beal An Daingin*), which is on the way to the islands of Lettermore, Gorumna and Lettermullen, you can rent a traditional-style cottage. This is rather deserted country, probably because the islands look dark and forbidding; but they attracted holy men long ago, for there are remains of ancient churches and holy wells where now only the sheep munch.

Back on the main road again you come to Screeb (*Scrib*). By turning left here you come to Lough Aroolagh and Gortmore (*An Gort More*). Here on a ledge of hillside above a small lake in the townland of **Turlough** you can go round the whitewashed cottage **Rosmuc**, where the patriot Patrick Pearse used to write plays and poems (*open daily, June–Sept, 9–6.30. In the winter the key is available at the house on the main road*). Patrick Pearse built this cottage as proof of his interest in Irish language and culture. He believed that if the Irish language died, Ireland would die as a nation. During the Rising of Easter Week 1916, he was Commander-in-Chief of the forces of the Irish Republic. After a week of fighting he and his fellow fighters surrendered, and he was courtmartialled and executed. Back on the R340, 4 miles (6.4km) further on is the village of **Kilkieran**. Here is scenery typical of the west: scattered houses with no nucleus nor clear distinction from the next village. You can see the brooding island of Lettermore and, if the wind is in the right direction, smell the rich seaweed which is dried in a factory here. Kilkieran and **Carna** are lobster-fishing centres, and there is a research station for shellfish, but you will find it difficult to buy a lobster for yourself—most of the seafood caught goes abroad or to the hotels. A side-road from Carna over a bridge takes you to **Mweenish Island** with its beautiful sandy beaches.

You can get a boat from Carna to **St MacDara's Island** where you get a marvellous view of the mountains of Connemara, and the hill of Errisbeg across Bertraghboy Bay. MacDara was a 5th-century saint who was greatly honoured by the people of Iar Chonnachta, so much so that in the age of sailing boats, the fishermen used to dip their sails three times before passing the island. Most of the villages have halls where *ceili* (the traditional Irish dances) are held and you can hear Irish singers, musicians and storytellers in the bars and hotels. The people who live here are very proud of their music and customs.

West Connemara

This is the district west of Maam Cross to the Atlantic, extending northwards to Killary Harbour and the Partry Mountains. It is a superb part of the world, much more exciting and untouched than the road that leads you round South Connemara.

Getting Around

By sea: to Inishbofin Island by mail boat, a 45-minute journey each way. The boats leave Cleggan pier at 11.30 am, 2 and 6 and return from Inishbofin at 9am, 2.45 and 5. Tickets IR£10 return, purchased at the pier bar. Sailings depend on the weather, so always check by telephoning ✆ (095) 44261.

Maam Cross to Roundstone

Maam Cross is a place that you see signposted constantly. In fact it is the most unprepossessing place, but it is the centre of magnificent scenery, and everybody travelling round Galway ends up here. If you climb Leckavrea Mountain (1307ft/402m) there are great views of the Twelve Bens, Maamturks and Lough Corrib.

From Maam Cross you could take the N59 past Recess, and take the R340/342/341 for Roundstone. **Recess** is a pretty village, where suddenly you come upon woods and Glendollagh Lough after driving through some spartan scenery. Lissoughter Mountain at 1314ft (400m) is worth climbing and you can see over to Lough Inagh and the mountains either side. This is where the green Connemara marble is quarried. It was formed millions of years ago by the action of strong compressive forces and heat on limestone. The oldest rocks in the county are exposed in this central area: the Twelve Bens (or Pins) and the Maamturk Mountains.

Cashel village is on a minor road (R342) right on Cashel Bay, an inlet of Bertraghboy Bay. It became famous overnight when General de Gaulle spent his holidays there. All these inlets and the mountain roads leading into the interior are bathed in the most superb colours. Even when the weather is gloomy, a shaft of light will pattern the deep purples and blues with greens and yellows. The luxury Cashel House Hotel is worth stopping at for a walk around the wonderful sub-tropical gardens or tea on the lawn.

Roundstone is a pleasant 19th-century village. The name is an awful English corruption of the Irish *Cloch na Ron*, which means 'rock of the seals'. There is a pretty harbour which looks across the water to the low-lying islands in Bertraghboy Bay; and a good, friendly bar, O'Dowd's, where the fisherman contrast starkly with the Dubliners in their smart Aran sweaters. Incidentally, there is a woman who occasionally sells lovely hand-knitted jerseys from her house which is next door to the village post office. Just outside Roundstone on the R341 Ballyconneely road is a government-sponsored craft centre, **Roundstone Park**, where you can buy exceptionally attractive ceramics and traditional musical instruments. Errisbeg Mountain (987ft/300m) towers above the village. It is a short climb but the views are superb; and look out for the flowers and plants, for this is a place beloved of botanists as well as artists. Two miles (3.2km) on towards Ballyconneely are two of the best beaches in Connacht. You will have seen their silver lines beside the blue sea if you climbed Errisbeg. They are called **Gorteen** and **Dog's Bay**. The latter is another terrible mistranslation into English: from *Port na Feadoige*, 'bay of the plover'.

Ballyconneely is on the isthmus about 9 miles (14.4km) from Roundstone. The road along this coastline is called the 'brandy and soda' road because of the exhilaration of the air. Beside the wide Mannin Bay is Coral Strand, so-called because of the white sand-like debris of a seaweed which looks like coral. Four miles (6.4km) south of Clifden is the site where Alcock and Brown came to ground after the first ever transatlantic flight.

Clifden (*An Clochan*: stepping stones) is generally called the capital of Connemara. It has a population of only just over a thousand, but it is simply the biggest place around in a countryside of scattered hamlets and farms. The town sits in a sheltered bay, and if you walk half a mile (1.6km) to the Atlantic shore and gaze out, you are looking straight towards America. It is a well-planned early 19th-century town founded in 1812 by John D'Arcy, and the two spires of the Protestant church and the Catholic cathedral give it a distinctive outline.

There are plenty of places to eat, and Millar's craft/tweed shop in the main street stocks the lovely floor rugs, shawls and tweed that the Gaeltacht home industries have revived. Clifden is the centre for the **Connemara Pony Show** in August. The ponies are diminutive, shaggy little animals that look after themselves. But much more goes on here besides selling and showing: there are bands, craft and cookery exhibitions, and the wide streets overflow with people speaking Gaelic and an English which keeps the idiom and expression of the Gaelic language.

Travelling around this part of Connemara, you pass through lakes, rivers, forests and mountains where there is little hint of pollution or industry. Even the machinery used on the farms is fairly traditional. At Dan O'Hara's Homestead Farm, Lettershea, 6km from Clifden, just off the N59 (*open April–Sept, daily 10am–6pm; adm*) you can see an eight-acre farm being run as a 19th-century farm would have been run. The farm is organic, and there is a reconstructed Crannog, ducks, pony and trap rides, a craft shop and tearoom.

There is a lovely road signposted 'Sky Road' which takes you further north round the indented coast. Amidst sprays of fuchsia it climbs high above Clifden until it is above **D'Arcy's Castle**, the baronial-style ruin of the D'Arcy who founded the town. From here you can see the waves crashing onto the rock islets of Inishturk and Inishbofin, whilst beyond to the north is Clare Island. The road continues into the quiet, seaweed-fringed Streamstown Bay, where white Connemara marble is quarried. **Cleggan**, 10 miles (16km) north of Clifden, is the main centre for the fishing industry in northwest Connemara; and it is the port for Inishbofin and the other islands.

Inishbofin Island

Inishbofin has a very varied history. In the 7th century St Colman founded a monastery here, and in the 13th century the O'Malleys won it off the O'Flahertys to add it to their seaboard empire. Grace O'Malley is said to have fortified it, although the locals say she could not dig through the rock to finish the deep ditch she was making. In 1652 Inishbofin was surrendered to the Cromwellians and was used as a sort of concentration camp for monks and priests. The barrack above the harbour has room for six cannons but now there are only red-beaked choughs to sound the alarm. Inishbofin has two hotels, so it is easy to get something to eat while you are there. The beaches are beautiful.

Letterfrack to Leenane

Letterfrack, a pretty village, was founded by the Quakers. There are wonderful bays for swimming and, along the coastal approach from Moyard onwards, there are excellent craftshops. Nearby is the sparkling Diamond Hill (1460ft/445m). **Connemara National Park** (*open all year*) extends over 3800 acres (1540ha), and is of outstanding ecological value, as well as being very beautiful. There is a Visitors' Centre with exhibits, and an audio-visual room which describes the geology, the flora and fauna of the area (*open April–Nov, 10–6.30*). Short- and long-distance walks have been laid out. The Kylemore Valley lies between the Twelve Bens and the forested Doughruagh Mountains in the north. The Twelve Bens and Maamturks, with their beautiful varying shapes, are not much above 2000ft (610m) at their highest. If you are going climbing, even though it may be sunny and dry at sea level it will be very wet underfoot. On the floor of the valley, trees and rhododendrons grow beside the three lakes and the Dawros River, which are well stocked with salmon and sea trout. There is a splendid mock castle (*not open to the public*) in the woods at **Lake Kylemore**, which is now a girls' school and a convent for the Benedictine Nuns of Ypres. The nuns run a restaurant and an excellent craft shop, and cultivate beautiful grounds around which you can wander (*open all year*). The wealthy Liverpudlian merchant who built the castle also built a fine mock Gothic chapel with pillars of Connemara marble inside. Nearby is a pre-Christian chamber tomb.

There is a lovely route (R344) just beyond the lake, dominated by the conical peaks of the Maamturks and the Bens, which cuts through the Inagh Valley to Recess. But if you follow the N59, you descend to the beautiful shores of **Killary Harbour**, a narrow fiord which reaches inland to Leenane. If you have time, go to **Salruck** on little Killary Bay. Here shades of pagan customs existed even as late as 1960, when tobacco pipes smoked at the wake of the deceased would be laid on the grave. The road from here to Renvyle follows a wild coastline, and if you look towards Killary Harbour the Mweelrea Mountain rises bare and massive. A fascinating tour may be made of **Heather Island**, once the home of Oliver St John Gogarty, surgeon and writer (*by appointment only, contact Heather Island House, Tully Lake, Renvyle; © (095) 41028; adm*).

The road to the mouth of Killary Harbour is set between the dark blue fjord and green hill slopes that are rilled so as to give the effect of crushed velvet. This is one of the safest natural anchorages in the world, keeping an almost constant depth of 13 fathoms, and sheltered from the wind by the mountains around. Douglas pine, beech, hawthorn and purple rhododendron add to the luxury of colour. The Erriff River comes tumbling over the Aasleagh Falls at the bridge just north of Leenane. **Leenane**, situated at the head of Killary Harbour, has plenty of accommodation if you want to base yourself here for walking or fishing. There is an excellent woollen craft centre just above the village on the N59. It also has information on local history, places of interest to visit and an audio-visual display. ✆ (095) 42323. Leenane recently featured as the location for the film *The Field*, and you will find constant references to it all over the village.

Galway City

Galway is a bustling city which has been the centre of trade for the whole of Connacht since the 13th century, despite a decline in the 18th and 19th centuries. The wine trade with Spain, and the enterprise of its citizens, has given it an independence and character which marks it out from the other provincial towns of Ireland.

History

There had always been some sort of settlement here, because of the ford on the Corrib River, but it never achieved any importance until the arrival of the Anglo-Normans. The de Burgos built a castle in 1226. By the end of the 13th century many Welsh and English families had been encouraged to settle here, and they built themselves strong stone walls to keep out the now dispossessed and disgruntled de Burgos and the wild O'Flahertys. There were 14 main families and they became known as the tribes of Galway. Fiercely independent, they made an Anglo-Norman oasis in the middle of hostile Connacht. In 1549 they placed this inscription over the west gate: 'From the fury of the O'Flaherties, good Lord deliver us'. (It is no longer there.) They also put out edicts controlling the presence of the native Irish in the town. So an Irish settlement grew up on the west side of the

Corrib following completely different traditions. They spoke only Gaelic and earned a livelihood through fishing. The settlement is now renowned for the Claddagh Ring, which you will notice on the fingers of many Irish exiles: a circle joined by two hands clasping a heart that was used as a marriage ring. Now, the romantic but poverty-stricken Claddagh settlement which appealed to Victorian travellers is gone, and the thatched and white-washed one-storey cottages have been replaced by a modern housing scheme.

The chief tribe of Galway was the Lynch family and there is a colourful story about the Lynch who was mayor in 1493. The tribes grew very prosperous through trading in wine with Spain and Bordeaux; and this Lynch had the son of a Spanish merchant staying in his house who aroused the jealousy of Walter, his son. Walter stabbed the young guest to death, and because he was so popular nobody could be found to hang him. So his father, having pronounced the sentence, did the deed himself and, filled with sadness, became a recluse. Near the Church of St Nicholas, in a built-up Gothic doorway on Market Street, there is a tablet commemorating the event.

Galway City Centre

Galway was an important administrative centre during the days of the British, from the 17th century until Independence, and now has a strong cultural identity with its own university where courses are followed in Irish and English, a large technical college and vigorous and high-quality theatre, traditional music and song.

The city itself is small enough to walk around in half a day. The planned 18th-century part centres around Eyre Square, which you come into immediately when approaching the city from the east. It is fairly easy to park in. The Galway tourist office, Aras Fáilte, in Victoria Park, is just a block away, close to the railway and bus station. The Gardens in Eyre Square are dedicated to John F. Kennedy, who received the freedom of the city only a few months before his assassination. In the gardens is a fine steel sculpture by Eamon O'Doherty based on the sails of the Galway 'hookers' or fishing boats; and a statue to Padraic O'Conaire (1883–1928), who wrote short stories only in Gaelic, and pioneered the revival of Gaelic literature. He was born on the High Street. The narrow streets of medieval Galway wind down to the river, and there are many fine bars and restaurants in which to while away the time. Fragments of buildings and mutilated stone merchant houses still exist amongst the fast-food signs and modern shop fronts. You have to go and seek out the strange and memorable animal carvings which have survived, and the fine doorways and windows. The best example is Lynch's Castle in Shop Street which now houses a branch of the Allied Irish Bank Ltd.

The **Church of St Nicholas** in Market Street is rather attractive, and worth a visit for the fine carvings inside. You may hear the eight bells peal, which make a lovely sound over the city. In Bowling Green, close by, is **Nora Barnacle House Museum** (*open May– Sept, Mon–Sat, 10–5; adm; © (091) 64743*), once the home of James Joyce's wife. The little museum contains memorabilia of the couple and their links with Co. Galway. A proud tradition exists that Christopher Columbus stopped at the church for Mass on his way to discover America. A Saturday market of organic vegetables, German sourdough breads and local cheeses is held in its shadow, and its atmosphere revives shades of medieval Galway. The modern **Catholic cathedral**, beside the salmon weir on the river, is an imposing hotchpotch of styles, and dominates the skyline. It was completed in 1965. The weir is in fact one of the nicest places to go and idle away the hours. Shoals of salmon making their way up to the spawning grounds of Lough Corrib lie in the clear river—the only entrance from the sea to 1200 miles (1930km) of lakes.

Elizabeth Tudor confirmed the city's charter in 1579, and appointed the mayor as admiral with jurisdiction over Galway Bay and the Aran Islands. The town was fully walled with 14 towers, but now there is only a fragment left near the quay, called the **Spanish Arch**. The office of Mayor, which had been in decline and abolished in 1840, was restored and given statutory recognition in 1937. The mayor's silver sword and great mace dating from the early 17th century are on display in the Bank of Ireland, 19 Eyre Square. The mace, a fine piece of Galway silver, was returned to the city by the Hearst Foundation of the USA in 1961. By the Spanish Arch there is a **museum** (*open daily in the summer;* ✆ *(091) 67641*). It has displays on the history of Galway and folklife. The **Kenny Art Gallery** in the high street holds exhibitions of ceramics, sculptures and paintings by contemporary artists. The **Grain Store** on Lower Abbeygate Street shows work in wood and metal. The **University of Galway Gallery** also holds occasional exhibitions; ✆ (091) 24411 to find out what's on and when. The **Druid Lane Theatre Company** based in Chapel Street produces very exciting and well-acted performances and they have built up something of an international reputation for their mostly contemporary repertoire. Interesting theatre is also produced by **An Taibhdhearc**, which concentrates on Irish-language works, as well as traditional music and bilingual folk presentations. The local newspapers, the *Galway Advertiser*, *Connaught Tribune* and free paper the *Galway Sentinel*, as well as the tourist office, will have the details of what's on. Good traditional music is played in the bars and the atmosphere can verge on the raucous.

Galway City is always a lively place, partly due to the youthfulness of its inhabitants, but the week of the races, late July, the **Arts Festival** (also July) and the **Oyster Festival** in September bring an extra sparkle and sense of enjoyment to the place. The Oyster Festival is a great time to be around: even more musicians busk on the streets; the bars are full of 'crack', singing and music; and serve delicious, plump oysters with glasses of cool, creamy Guinness. The festival centres around the oyster-opening championship which attracts participants from all over the world. The affair snowballs into dances, dinners, shows and speeches from local worthies, and maybe a celebrity or two. The famous **Galway Races** take place 2 miles (3.2km) from the city at Ballybrit Racecourse. The most exciting races are held at the end of July and feature the Galway Plate and the Galway Hurdle—a mixture of high society and sweet-talking bookies.

If you want to study the local history, join a summer course for foreign students at the University College. Reference material and books may be consulted in the Reference Library of the Court House on Woodside Quay. A good bookshop is Kenny's on the main shopping street, which has a substantial stock of Irish literature.

Salthill is a seaside resort which merges with the city. Many local people holiday there or come on day trips. Hotels, fun-parks and bingo halls line the seafront; it's a bit run-down, like many old seaside resorts all over the British Isles. But at night the place lights up as the strip opens up its clubs and discos, catering primarily to the youthful population of Galway City.

Shopping

East Galway

Crafts: from shops at Thoor Ballylee and at Dunguaire Castle, Kinvara. Craft shop at the Mill Museum, Shop Street, Tuam, ✆ (093) 24436.

Cut glass: Clarinbridge Crystal, ✆ (091) 96178.

West Connemara

Crafts: Connemara Handicrafts; China, pottery and a coffee shop, ✆ (095) 41058, Letterfrack. Goatskin bodhrans, tin whistles and harps in the IDA Park, Roundstone, ✆ (095) 35808.

Woollen goods: The Weaver's Workshop, Main Street, Clifden. Miller's Tweed Shop, Main Street, Clifden, ✆ (095) 21038. Rosmuc Knitwear, Gort Mor, Rosmuc, ✆ (091) 74172, for hand-loomed sweaters, and Leenane Cultural Centre for general woollen goods.

Pottery: Connemara Pottery, Ballyconnelly Road, Clifden. Roundstone Ceramics, IDA Park, Roundstone, ✆ (095) 35874. The handcrafted pottery here is imaginatively and colourfully decorated with fishes, snakes and other weird and wonderful designs.

Glass: Connemara Celtic Crystal on the outskirts of Moycullen, ✆ (091) 85157.

Delicacies: Smoked salmon from Salt Lake Manor, Clifden, ✆ (095) 21278. Ring for an appointment. If you have just caught your own salmon, the French owners will smoke it beautifully for you. Goat's cheese from Creeshla Farm, Cushatrower. ✆ (095) 35814. Home-made fudge and Thai curries from Fried Green Tomatoes delicatessen, Clifden.

Bodhrans and other traditional instruments from Roundstone Musical Instruments, ✆ (095) 35875.

Galway City

Crafts: The Grainstore, Lower Abbeygate Street, ✆ (091) 66620, for carved wood bowls. Curiosity Corner, Cross Street, wicker baskets and other odds and ends.

Woollen goods: Lots of knitwear shops on lower part of High Street; Taffee's, further up is a bit raggedy, but cheap. House of James, Castle Street is good.

Antiques, books: Cross Street, Galway City. Kenny's Bookshop, High Street. *Sheila-na-gig*, Middle Street. Cobwebs, Quay Lane, ✆ (091) 64388.

Tackle shops: Freeney's, High Street, ✆ (091) 62609; and Duffy's, Mainguard Street, ✆ (091) 62367.

Markets: Galway City Saturday Morning Market by St Nicholas' Cathedral sells cheese, herbs, vegetables, sausages and homemade jams.

Delicacies: Evergreen Wholefoods, High Street. They also sell lovely breads. McCambridges Grocery, 38 Shop Street. For cheese and preserves. Goya's Cake Shop, 19 Quay Street, ✆ (091) 67010, for some of the best patisseries this side of Paris. Small coffee shop attached.

South Connemara

Baskets: Loch na Fooey Basketry, Finney, Clonbur. Tom's baskets, Inis Oirr, Co. Galway.

Activities

East Galway

Fishing: for brown trout on River Clare and Lough Rea contact Freeny's, High Street, Galway City, ✆ (091) 62609; Duffy's, Mainguard Street, Galway City, ✆ (091) 62367; or The Rod and Reel, River Street, Ballinasloe; Mr Salmon, Main Street, Ballinasloe, ✆ (0905) 42120 for tackle and information.

Coarse fishing: on the River Suck for bream, rudd, perch and pike. Contact the Secretary, Angling Committee, Ballinasloe, ✆ (0905) 42512; the Western Fisheries Board, Earl's Island, ✆ (091) 63118 or Mr Ellis, ✆ (0905) 42582.

Hunting: with the Galway Blazers, ✆ (091) 46387; the East Galway Hunt and the North Galway Hunt, ✆ (093) 24326.

Pony-trekking: Aille Equestrian Centre, Aille Cross, Loughrea, ✆ (091) 41216. They also organize week-long trails in Connemara here. Clonboo Riding School, Corandulla, ✆ (091) 91362.

South Connemara

Fishing: For brown trout, sea trout, and salmon fishing on Lough Corrib, contact the tourist office in Galway City for details and regulations. Advice and help on boat hire and fishing from Thomas Tuck, Main Street, Oughterard, ✆ (091) 82335 and from Faherty's Angling Centre, Lakeland's, Oughterard, ✆ (091) 82146/ 82121; or from the Tourist Information Point in Monahan's Craft shop. For coarse fishing in Moycullen, call ✆ (091) 85555.

Swimming: at Costelloe in Cashla Bay.

Riding: Cashel House Hotel Riding Centre, Cashel, Connemara, ✆ (9095) 31001.

Pony-trekking: Connemara Trail Riding Holidays. Contact Mr Leahy, Aille Cross Equestrian Centre, Loughrea, ✆ (091) 41216.

Curragh races: contact the tourist office in Galway for details.

Golf: At Oughterard Golf Club, ✆ (091) 82131.

West Connemara/Galway City

Fishing: for information on salmon, sea, and brown trout contact: Kylemore Abbey Fisheries, Kylemore House, Kylemore, ✆ (095) 41145/41143; Delphi Fishery, Leenane, ✆ (095) 42213; Erriff Fishery, Leenane, ✆ (095) 42232; Galway Weir Fishery, Nun's Island, Galway, ✆ (091) 62388; Gowla Fishery, c/o Zetland Hotel, Cashel, ✆ (095) 31111; Inagh Fishery, Recess, ✆ (095) 34670/34608; Culfin Fishery, c/o R. Willoughby, Salruck, Renvyle, ✆ (095) 43498/43414. For fishing Ballynahinch Castle River/Owenmore River, call ✆ (095) 31006. For fishing Lough Corrib, Faherty's Angling Centre, Oughterard, ✆ (091) 82146 or c/o Currarevagh House, Oughterard, ✆ (091) 82312 (mostly limited to guests). Brochure and information on sea trout fisheries from the Hon. Sec., Western Game Fishing Association, Delphi Lodge, Leenane; ✆ (096) 42211.

Sea-angling: Deep-sea fishing boats can be hired in Roundstone, Clifden, Letterfrack and Renvyle. Contact: Pat Conneely, Roundstone, ✆ (095) 35854; John Ryan, Sky Road, Clifden, ✆ (095) 21069; J. Mangan, Letterfrack, ✆ (095) 43473.

Swimming: Water fun, Leisureland, Salthill, ✆ (091) 21455.

Sea bathing: all along the coast in the various inlets. Fine, sandy beaches at Ballyconneely and Tullycross.

Sailing: courses in Galway Bay. Contact Galway Bay Sailing Centre, 8 Father Griffin Road, Galway; ✆ (091) 63522. Clifden Boat Club, Clifden, ✆ (095) 21711.

Cruising: The Corrib Princess cruises for 90 minutes on Lough Corrib. Leaves from Woodquay, ✆ (091) 68903.

Golf: At Blackrock, Salthill; ✆ (091) 22169 and Ballyconnelly, ✆ (095) 23502.

Riding and pony-trekking: Errislannan Manor, Connemara Pony Stud and Riding Centre, Clifden, ✆ (095) 21134.

Adventure sports: Little Killary Adventure Centre provides weekly or weekend courses in canoeing, sailing, rock-climbing, etc. Contact the centre in Salruck, Renvyle, ✆ (095) 43411.

Walking tours: Connemara Contours, Island House, Market Street, Clifden, ✆ (095) 21379/34682. Walking amongst mountain and coastal scenery.

Where to Stay

East Galway

Ardilaun House Hotel, Taylors Hill, Galway, ✆ (091) 24133 (*expensive*). Large mansion house converted into attractive hotel with wooded grounds. Good food. **Skeffington Arms Hotel**, 28 Eyre Square, Galway, ✆ (091) 63173 (*expensive*). Small and central. **Brennan's Yard Hotel**, Lower Merchants Road, ✆ (091) 68166 (*expensive*). Comfortable, friendly service and pleasant bedrooms with lots of stripped pine and locally-made pottery. **Oranmore Lodge**, Tuam Road, Oranmore, ✆ (091) 94400 (*moderate*). Typical hotel décor with plush carpets. Comfortable with good food. **O'Deas Hotel**, Bride Street, Loughrea, ✆ (091) 41611 (*moderate*). Comfortable and unpretentious. **Hayden's**, Dunlo Street, Ballinasloe, ✆ (0905) 42347 (*moderate*). Lovely hotel, with landscaped gardens. Fifty rooms. **Cregg Castle**, Corrandulla, ✆ (091) 91434 (*moderate*). 17th-century castle, friendly, ideal for children. Traditional music in the evenings.

The McDonagh family, **Balrickard Farm House**, Headford, ✆ (093) 35421 (*inexpensive/cheap*). Unpretentious farmhouse which has a special deal for game anglers. Mrs M. Cunningham, **Hazel House Farmhouse**, Manusrevagh, Headford, ✆ (091) 91204 (*inexpensive/cheap*). A modern bungalow with a traditional Irish welcome, tea and scones when you arrive. Matt, the man of the house, plays the accordion, banjo and fiddle, and he is happy to play to his guests. Seamus and Patricia Kavanagh, **Hazelwood House**, Oranmore, ✆ (091) 94275 (*inexpensive/cheap*). Georgian-style bungalow, close to the sea in its own woodland. They can arrange hunting with the Galway Blazers. Delicious home-baking and local seafood for dinner. **Ballindiff Bay Lodge**, Linmnagh, Corrandulla, ✆ (091) 91195 (*inexpensive/cheap*). On the edge of the Lough Corrib. Good angling facilities.

South Connemara

Harry and June Hodgson, **Currarevagh House**, Oughterard, Connemara, ✆ (091) 82312/82313 (*expensive*). This country house is in the most beautiful setting on the edge of Lough Corrib. A charming and friendly atmosphere reigns amongst the cosy Victorian rooms. The passages are crammed with books, stuffed fish and fishing tackle. The food is comforting in an old-fashioned way, right down to the dinky coffee percolators. The Hodgsons are extremely helpful and have some of the best wild brown trout fishing in Europe, which they will organise for guests.

Mrs Casburn, **Moycullen House**, Moycullen, ✆ (091) 85566 (*moderate*). An Edwardian sporting lodge designed in 'arts and crafts' style in a lovely woodland garden of azaleas and rhododendron overlooking Lough Corrib. Fishing and boating organized by the Casburns.

Mrs B. Curran, **Ard Aoibhinn**, Cnocan Glas, Spiddal, ✆ (091) 83179 (*inexpensive*). Irish-speaking family. Close to the sea. Comfortable rooms with en suite bathrooms.

self-catering

200-year-old reed-thatched traditional cottage by the sea. Three bedrooms from IR£185 a week. Contact **John O'Toole**, Annaghvane, Bealadangan, ✆ (091) 72120.

West Connemara

Rosleague Manor, Letterfrack, ✆ (095) 41101 (*expensive*). Pretty first-class hotel overlooking Ballinakill Bay. Delicious food, and friendly atmosphere. **Cashel House Hotel**, Cashel, Co. Galway, ✆ (095) 31001 (*expensive*). A very luxurious but at the same time cosy house full of fine furniture and *objets d'art* picked up at country house sales. Superb garden overlooking beautiful sea inlet. Riding can be arranged.

Zetland House, Cashel Bay, ✆ (095) 3111 (*expensive*). Converted hunting lodge run by John Prendergast who trained at the Ritz in Paris. Superb food. **Ballynahinch Castle**, Ballinafad, Recess, ✆ (095) 31006 (*expensive*). Magnificent setting at the base of one of the Twelve Bens, and overlooking Owenmore River. Relaxed and informal atmosphere. It used to be the residence of an Indian Maharajah! **Cnocnaraw House**, Moyard, ✆ (095) 41068 (*expensive*). Small and cosy country house, with tastefully decorated rooms and lots of pretty, striped Connemara woollen rugs. Delicious and well-prepared food.

Days Hotel, Inishbofin Island, ✆ (095) 45803 (*moderate*). Well-established family-run, clean, friendly hotel right on the pier. The son runs the musical evenings. Children are welcome and there are facilities for divers. The **Ardagh Hotel**, Ballyconneely Road, ✆ (095) 21384 (*moderate*). Dutch-run small hotel, wonderful food.

Mrs Brand Voormolen, **Kille House**, Kingstown, Clifden, ✆ (095) 21849 (*moderate*). Pretty Georgian-style house with comfortable rooms and good food. **The Quay House**, Beach Road, Clifden, ✆ (095) 21369 (*moderate*). Restaurant with rooms. **Doonmore Hotel**, Inishbofin, ✆ (095) 45804 (*moderate*). Simple and clean and good local seafood.

Rose Cottage, Rockfield, Moyard, near Clifden, ✆ (095) 41082 (*inexpensive*). Simple, clean and attractive old-style cottage, in stunning countryside. Mrs K. Hardman, **Mallmore House**, Ballyconneely Road, Clifden, ✆ (095) 21460 (*inexpensive*). Comfortable, friendly country house, close to Clifden. Mrs King, **Killary House**, Leenane, ✆ (095) 42254 (*inexpensive*). Friendly farmhouse in superb situation.

self-catering

At Renvyle, nine thatched cottages of various sizes. Contact **Connemara West plc**, Renvyle, ✆ (095) 43464. IR£115–360 per week. Self-catering cottages on

Delphi Lodge estate, Leenane, ✆ (095) 42211. **The Masters's House**, Cleggan, ✆ (095) 44746. Hostel.

Galway City

Great Southern Hotel, Eyre Square, ✆ (091) 64041 (*expensive*). Rambling, Victorian and central, with comfortable rooms and a rooftop swimming pool.
Arch View Hostel, Dominick Street, ✆ (091) 66661 (*inexpensive*). Bed only. **Woodquay Hostel**, ✆ (091) 62618. New and well-equipped. Mr and Mrs Keogh, **Norman Villa**, 86 Lower Salthill, ✆ (091) 21131 (*inexpensive*). The best of the myriad B&Bs in Salthill. Sophisticated food.

Eating Out

East Galway

Dunguaire Castle Medieval Banquet, Kinvara, ✆ (061) 61788 (*expensive*). Poetry is read whilst you wine and dine on typical Irish fare. **Haydens**, Dunlo Street, Ballinasloe, ✆ (0905) 42347 (*moderate*). Good pub snacks and excellent dining room. The **Oranmore Lodge**, Tuam Road, Oranmore, ✆ (091) 94400 (*moderate*). Rich Irish cooking. **Meadow Court Restaurant/Bar**, Loughrea, ✆ (091) 41633/41051 (*moderate*). International menu and seafood. **Aughrim School House Restaurant**, Aughrim, ✆ (0905) 73936 (*moderate*). Simple and good food. Cre-Na-Cille, High Street, Tuam, ✆ (093) 28232 Game, meat and seafood. **The Moorings Restaurant**, Main Street, Oranmore, ✆ (091) 90462 (*moderate*). Good value.

Paddy Burke's, Clarinbridge, ✆ (091) 96107 (*inexpensive/cheap*). Oysters in particular to be taken with a glass of creamy stout. Obviously, if you order a lavish amount of seafood the price will creep up. **Moran's** on the Weir, Kilcolgan, near Clarinbridge, ✆ (091) 96113 (*inexpensive/cheap*). Seafood bar in old cottage overlooking their own oyster beds in Galway Bay.

Kinvara Coffee and Wholefood Shop, Kinvara harbour. **Imperial Hotel**, Tuam, ✆ (093) 24188 (*inexpensive/cheap*). Good-value and filling lunches. **Sullivans Royal Hotel**, The Square, Gort, ✆ (091) 31257 (*inexpensive/cheap*). Home-cooked food.

South Connemara

Drimcong Restaurant, Moycullen, ✆ (091) 85115 (*expensive*). The owners create the most delicious and original combinations of tastes, yet never overdo the novelty. You can be sure that you will get the best of what the season offers. The restaurant itself is in a lovely 17th-century house, and there are always turf fires in the rooms. Vegetarian and children's meals.

Boluisce Seafood Bar, Spiddal Village, ✆ (091) 83286 (*inexpensive/cheap*). Delicious seafood snacks. Try the fish chowder with home-made brown bread.

West Connemara

Cashel House Hotel, Cashel, ✆ (095) 31001 (*expensive*). Super food in fancy country-house surroundings. *Dinner only, booking essential.* Not suitable for children. **Drimcong House Restaurant**, Moycullen, ✆ (091) 85115 (*expensive*). So good! Very imaginative menu is widely regarded as one of the best in the country. **Erriseask House Hotel**, Ballyconnelly, Clifden, ✆ (095) 23553 (*expensive*). Unexpectedly imaginative cooking. **Quay House**, Beach Road, Clifden, ✆ (095) 21369 (*expensive*). Friendly, relaxed atmosphere in Old Harbour Master's house. Very high standard of cooking. **Zetland House**, Cashel Bay ✆ (095) 31111 (*expensive*). Wonderful seafood. **Ardagh Hotel**, Clifden, ✆ (095) 21384 (*expensive*). Delicious continental food. Also very good value open sandwiches as a cheap lunch option.

Beola Restaurant, Roundstone, ✆ (095) 35871 (*moderate*). Seafood as a speciality. **O'Grady's Seafood Restaurant**, Market Street, Clifden, ✆ (095) 21450 (*moderate*). Traditional seafood restaurant with a good menu and friendly service. **Destry Rides Again**, The Square, Clifden, ✆ (095) 21722 (*moderate*). Lively bistro-style restaurant named after the Marlene Dietrich film, laid-back and delicious modern cooking. Same owners are just opening a new dinnertime restaurant called the **Quay House** on the quays, which will apparently be just as good as Destry's, ✆ (095) 21369 (*moderate*). **Portfinn Lodge**, Leenane, ✆ (095) 42265 (*moderate*). Great seafood **High Moors Restaurant**, Clifden, ✆ (095) 21342. Very good food, be sure to book.

Days Hotel, Inishbofin, ✆ (095) 45803 (*inexpensive/cheap*). Good seafood and soups. **Peacockers Restaurant**, Maam Cross, Recess, ✆ (091) 82215 (*inexpensive/cheap*). Good lunches.

Galway City

Claddagh Room, Great Southern Hotel, Eyre Square, ✆ (091) 64041 (*expensive*). Good seafood. **Royal Villa**, 13 Shop Street, ✆ (091) 63450 (*moderate*). Good quality Chinese. **Tigh Neachtain**, Cross Street, Galway. A great pub with above average bar food. Lunch weekdays only. Dinner in their pricier restaurant upstairs. **Seventh Heaven**, Courthouse Lane, ✆ (091) 63838 (*moderate*). Spare ribs and the like. **Skeffington Arms Hotel**, 28 Eyre Square, ✆ (091) 63173 (*moderate*). Sophisticated food. **Nimmo's**, Spanish Arch, ✆ (091) 63565 (*moderate*). Seafood. Atmospheric café downstairs and restaurant upstairs. Lovely location. **The Malte House**, High Street, ✆ (091) 67866 (*inexpensive/cheap*). Excellent soups and bar snacks. **Fat Freddies**, The Halls, Quay Street, Galway (*inexpensive/cheap*). Fresh pizza, and strong Nicaraguan coffee. **Taafe's Bar**, Shop Street (*inexpensive/cheap*). A pub with good food. **McDonagh's Fish Café**, Key Street (*inexpensive/cheap*). Excellent eat in or take away fish and chips. **Pierre Victoires**, 8 Quay Street (*inexpensive/cheap*). Excellent value French food. **Mezza Luna**, Quay Street (*inexpensive/cheap*). Cheap and cheerful. Salads and pasta. **Goya's**, 19 Quay Street, ✆ (091) 67010. (*inexpensive/cheap*). Delicious cakes and coffee.

Entertainment and Nightlife

Traditional music: Ballad-singing and traditional music in the local bars. During the summer months try the Pucan Bar, Foster street; the Crane Bar, off Sea Road; Taaffes, Shop Street; and Taylor's, Dominick Street, all in Galway City. Teach Ceoil (Irish music house) at Tullycross, ✆ (095) 43446.

Jazz: The Quays Bar, Quay Street; the Blue Note, and the King's Head, on High Street, all in Galway City.

Theatre: Druid Lane Theatre, Chapel Lane, Galway City, ✆ (091) 68617. Taibhdhearc na Gaillimhe, Middle Street, Galway City, ✆ (091) 62024.

Medieval banquets: at Dunguaire Castle, Kinvarra, ✆ (091) 37108.

Art galleries: University College, Galway City, ✆ (091) 24411. Kennys, High Street, Galway City, ✆ (091) 62739.

The Aran Islands

The people and the islands of Aran have been described sensitively by the playwright John Millington Synge in his notebooks and in his play *Riders to the Sea*. If you read them, you will long to visit these windswept islands in Galway Bay. Liam O'Flaherty, another great Irish writer, was born here in 1818, the year before Synge first came to the islands. He describes the hard life of the island people in his short stories, *The Landing* and *Going into Exile*. Recently Tim Robinson, a stranger who came and lived on the islands, has produced a wonderful book called *Stones of Aran*, well worth searching out in Kenny's bookshop in Galway City.

The Aran Islands today are much the same as they were in John Synge's time, although in the summer the irritations and ugliness which tourism always brings does diminish some of their peace and unique culture, particularly on Inishmore.

Getting To and Around the Islands

By air: **Aer Arann** operates daily flights from Connemara (19 miles from Galway) to all the islands. It takes about 10 minutes actual flying time. Contact Aer Arann at Dominick Street, Galway, ✆ (091) 93034. They will also arrange scenic flights for groups.

By sea: two companies operate ferries out to all three of the islands, although the main point of call is Kilronan on Inishmore. **Island Ferries** have two boats: the *Island of Discovery* and *Aran Seabird*, both of which operate between Rossaveal and Inishmore Island on a daily basis from June to August. The crossing takes 40 minutes to an hour. *Island of Discovery* makes the journey daily during the winter. **Aran Ferries** have two boats: the *Galway Bay*, which operates between Galway City and Inishmore, and the *Aran Flyer*, which operates between Rossaveal and Inishmore on a daily basis from June to August. Timetables are determined by the tides and you can get them from CIE, ✆ (091) 62141, or the Galway Tourist Office, ✆ (091) 63081. The cost is IR£12.

These companies also go to Inishmaan and Inisheer. Contact: Aran Ferries, ✆ (091) 68903; Island Ferries, ✆ (091) 61767.

By minibus: for tours of Inishmore, contact Michael Hernon, ✆ (099) 61131; Michael Mullin, ✆ (099) 61132; or R. Gill, ✆ (099) 61169.

By bike: bicycle hire at several places in Kilronan. Try Aran Bicycle Hire, ✆ (099) 61132.

By jaunting car: details from Galway and Kilronan tourist offices.

Tourist Information for the Aran Islands

Galway, Victoria Place, ✆ (091) 63081, open all year.

Inishmore, Kilronan, ✆ (099) 61263, mid-June to mid-September.

Festivals

Last weekend in June/early July: Festival of Saints Peter and Paul Inishmore. Music and curragh races.

The Islands

There are three Aran Islands: Inishmore (Great Island), Inisheer (East Island) and Inishmaan (Middle Island). They can be reached by air from Galway City, or by a regular ferry boat from Galway Harbour, and by motorboat from Rossaveal. Most tourists come for the rugged beauty, the sweeping views, and to visit the prehistoric and early monastic ruins. The landscape is similar to that in the Burren, County Clare. It is made up of porous limestone, which you will notice is eroding into great steps, as you approach by boat. Gentian, maidenhair fern, wild roses and saxifrage blossom on the 11,000 acres (4450ha) which make up the three islands, but only 6 per cent of the land is rated as productive. The soil has been built up over the years with layer upon layer of seaweed, animal manure and sand from the beaches, so that these limestone rocks can support a few cattle and asses, and rows of potatoes.

The people of the islands speak Irish amongst themselves, but out of politeness they will switch to English if there is a stranger around. Many of them have been to America or England for work. There used to be a distinctive Aran dress but this has died out, except for the waistcoat of unbleached wool called a *bainin* or *bawneen*. Sometimes you still see the thick tweed trousers, and the gay woven belt which is worn to keep them up and is now sold to tourists as the Aran *kris* or *crios*. The women used to knit the *bawneens* and heavy Aran sweaters with the family pattern, so that it would be easier to identify the bodies of drowned fishermen. The women's dress of thick woollen shawl and red flannel skirt has disappeared, as in the rest of the west.

The Aran Islands currently have a population of approximately 1450 with 900 on Inishmore, 300 on Inishmaan and 250 on Inisheer. The young people tend to disappear to the mainland or further for jobs, and seldom come back. When John Millington Synge came to the islands between 1899 and 1902, he felt very aware that they were the European hinterland of culture, and he was strongly drawn to the islanders' faith in God. This is what he wrote of a young girl on Inishmaan: 'At one moment, she is a simple peasant, at another she seems to be looking out at the world with a sense of prehistoric disillusion, and to sum up in the expression of her grey-blue eyes, the whole external despondency of the clouds and the sea.'

There are seven stone forts on the islands, four on Inishmore; two on Inishmaan, and one on Inisheer, all believed to go back as far as the Early-Celtic period 2500 years ago. Mythology states that they were built by the Fir Bolg after they were defeated by the Tuatha Dé Danaan at the Battle of Moytura (*see* **Old Gods and Heroes**, p.578). One theory reinforces that story: that those who built the forts were making a last stand against their enemies. Some of the forts have no wells or water supplies, which is rather a puzzle because they would have been unable to withstand a siege.

The people who lived on the islands became Christians in the 5th century, converted by St Enda. Monastic schools were set up which became famous over the centuries, and people came from far and wide to study there. In the Middle Ages, the O'Flahertys of Galway and the O'Briens of Clare fought endlessly over the ownership of the islands. The English ended the dispute by building and garrisoning a fort known as **Arkin Castle** in the late 16th century. It is along the shore of the bay as you arrive at Inishmore. It was occupied at various times by Royalists, Cromwellians, Jacobite and Williamites.

The Aran Islands are wild and rugged, with so many attractions you might wish to stay there for months. The views around the forts and churches are magnificent, and you can wander around the rough roads, amongst the limestone rocks, watching for the little flowers and plants that somehow manage to grow. There are beaches on Inishmore and Inisheer, and the water is comparatively warm. It is best to ask locally about the various beaches, and about sea-angling, which can be done from a curragh or the cliffs. Every evening in the summer there are ballad sessions in the public houses.

Inishmore

Inishmore is the largest of the islands, being about 8 miles (12.9km) long. When you get off the steamer you can either hire a bicycle, or a sidecar and jarvey, to see the sights. The capital, **Kilronan**, has become rather touristy, but the people remain cheerful and courteous, in spite of the insensitive approach of tourists taking endless photos.

Kilronan is linked by road to a chain of villages, and if you want to get to a friendly drinking-house after the gruelling voyage, Daly's pub in **Killeany** (*Cill Einne*) is the place. Amongst the fields separated by loose stone walls (the effect is rather maze-like), you will come upon ancient ecclesiastical sites and the forts. The people of Aran, who could be descended from the Fir Bolgs, never bother with gates—they are too expensive to import. Instead, if they are herding livestock through different fields, they undo stone walls and then calmly build them up again when the animals have got through.

Here is a brief description of some of the forts and monastic remains. **Dun Aonghus** or Dun Aengus is on the south coast, on the summit of a hill which rises straight up from the sea. It covers some 11 acres (4.5ha) and consists of several concentric ramparts, 18ft high and 13ft deep (5.5m by 4m), which form a semi-circle with the two edges ending on the brink of the cliffs that fall nearly 350ft (107m) to the Atlantic. The approach is designed to cripple you if you do not advance with caution, for outside the middle wall, sharp spars of stone set closely in the ground form a *chevaux de frise*. At the time of writing Dun Aonghus is inaccessible because the farmer who owns the land is frightened of insurance claims from visitors who may injure themselves. It is to be hoped that the law can be changed to protect the owner. Enquire at the tourist office for the latest position. **Dun Eoghanacha**, another stone ring-fort, is to the south of the village of Onaght on the north-east coast, and is circular in shape. The fields to the west and south are full of ancient remains. One and a half miles (2.5km) west of Killeany on the southern side of the island, is **Dubh Chathair**, some of which must have disappeared over the steep cliffs, for it was even larger than Dun Aonghus. At Kilchorna, Monasterkieran and Teampall an Cheathrair are more evocative ruins. **Monasterkieran**, just northwest of Kilronan, has the ruins of a transitional period church, early cross slabs, an ancient sundial and a holy well. Kilchorna, about a mile southwest of Kilronan, has two clochans. **Teampall an Cheathrair** ('the church of the four comely saints'), is near the village of Cowrugh. It is a small 15th-century building outside of which four great flagstones mark the supposed graves of the saints. **Teampall Bheanain**, just south of Killeany, is 6th-century, only 10ft by 7ft (3m by 2m), and a unique example of an Early-Christian Church.

With the coming of Christianity and St Enda in AD 483, the island became Aran of the Saints. At Killeany, 2 miles (3.2km) southeast of Kilronan, there are the graves of 120 saints. All Enda's followers seem to have reached the glorious state of sainthood after living their lives in the narrow confines of clochans. The site also contains the remains of a small, early church and the shaft of a finely carved high cross. A few yards to the north-west of the doorway is a flagstone which is said to cover the grave of St Enda.

Inishmaan

Inishmaan is not usually visited by tourists, who tend to go to Inishmore on a day-trip only. If you do go to Inishmaan or Inisheer, see if you can go by curragh. Although an air strip links all the islands to the Galway mainland, it is an exciting and quite alarming experience to drop into the bouncing frail-looking craft and leave the security of the mail boat. Curraghs are made of laths and canvas and then tarred over. If you see one on land, being carried upsidedown, it looks just like a giant beetle. The fishermen of the west handle them with innate skill and they are often heavily loaded.

You can see the huge **Fort of Dun Conor** or *Dun Chonchuir* from the sound as you approach the shore of Inishmaan. Dun Conor is the most impressive of all the Aran forts. It is in the middle of the coastline and faces out to Inisheer. Its three outer walls have disappeared, with the exception of the remnants of the inner curtain, but the massive fortress wall, built of stones which only a race of giants could lift easily, is almost intact. Nearby is a freshwater spring which never dries up, called **St Chinndheirg's Well**; it is supposed to have curative properties. In the same area is one of the most interesting churches on the island, known as **Cill Cean Fhionnaigh** (`church of the fairheaded one'). It is one of the most perfect primitive Irish churches in existence, and there is another holy well here.

Inisheer

As you come through Foul Sound towards **Inisheer**, you see **O'Brien's Castle** on the rocky hill south of the landing place—a 15th-century tower set in a stone ring-fort. Inisheer is the smallest island, only about 2 miles (3.2km) across, but it greets you with a broad, sandy beach. It also boasts a tiny **10th-century church** dedicated to St Gobhnait, the only woman allowed on the three islands when the saintly men ruled these shores. Situated to the southeast of the landing place is the **Church of St Kevin** (*Teampall Chaomham*). This ancient building is threatened with shifting sand, but the locals clear it every year, on the saint's feast day, 14 June. It has a Gothic chancel, and an earlier nave. Islanders are still buried in the ground around the church.

Synge wrote this of the men of Inisheer: 'These strange men with receding foreheads, high cheek bones, and ungovernable eyes seem to represent some old type found on these few acres at the extreme border of Europe, where it is only in the wild jests and laughter that they can express their loneliness and desolation'.

Shopping

Crafts: Carrigdown Crafts, Main Street, Kilronan. Snarmara Craftshop (Islanders' Co-operative), Main Street, Kilronan. Inis Meain Knits, Inishmaan, ✆ (099) 73009. Open 8.30–5.00. Probably the nicest traditional jumpers in the country; they do an enormous export trade to Italy. Heritage House, Inisheer is also a good source of crafts.

Activities

Sports: no organised sport; fishing by private negotiation only.

Museums: *Ionad Arainn*, museum of folklife in Kilronan, with material about the Gaelic League. Open April–Oct 10–7. *Museum Na nOilean*, Inishmaan, folklife museum, with some books of J. M. Synge, and others about the Island. Open mid-June–Aug, 9.30–5, ✆ (099) 73009 or (099) 61355.

Where to Stay

Inishmore

Johnston Hernon's **Kilmurvey House**, Inishmore, ✆ (099) 61218 (*moderate*). Friendly owners at this guesthouse in an old stone house. Good basic meals served. The **Gill Family**, Cliff House, The Scrigeen, Kilronan, ✆ (099) 61286 (*inexpensive*). Top marks for comfort and excellent food. **Mainistir House Hostel**, Inishmore, ✆ (099) 61169 (*inexpensive*). Great value accommodation. Multi-lingual, friendly atmosphere, good music and an excellent vegetarian restaurant.

Inishmaan

Mrs A. Faherty, Creigmore, Inishmaan, ℰ (099) 73012 (*inexpensive*). Typical Aran farmhouse where you get a fine welcome. No evening meals.

Inisheer

Mrs Poil, *Radharc An Chlair*, Castle Village, ℰ (099) 75019 (*inexpensive*). A cosy, friendly establishment with heart-warming cooking.

Eating Out

Inishmore

An tsean Cheibh (The Old Pier), Kilronan, ℰ (099) 61228 (*moderate*). Good home baking and fresh fish. There is also a good fish-and-chip place in the same building. **Dun Aengus Restaurant**, Kilronan, ℰ (099) 61104 (*moderate*). Seafood in a traditional stone house. **Cliff House**, Kilronan, ℰ (099) 61286 (*moderate*). Wonderful cooking

Man of Aran Cottages, Kilmurvey Bay, ℰ (099) 61286 (*inexpensive*). A daytime café which serves soup, sandwiches and a lobster lunch. The owners are thinking of opening a one-room B&B here. **Mainister House Hostel**, Kilronan, ℰ (099) 61169 (*inexpensive*). Wonderful vegetarian buffets, but be sure to book, and turn up for 8pm as it disappears fast. **Peig's Café**, Kilronan (*inexpensive*). Sandwiches and cakes during the daytime. **Joe Watty's Pub**, Kilronan, ℰ (099) 61155 (*inexpensive*). Good chowders.

Inishmaan

De Bácam's pub (*inexpensive*) serves smoked salmon, Irish stew and fish chowder.

County Mayo

Mayo is a large county which towards the east is made up of limestone plains. These are interrupted by the sandstone hills of the Curlews and, further north, by the Ox Mountains or Slieve Gamph. From Ballinrobe in the southeastern corner to Ballintobber and Claremorris, heading for the central plains around Lough Mask, you might turn a corner and see the most unexpected things: perhaps a hedgehog or an otter, a beautiful shining lake, or a vast grey dolmen. If you stray to the southwest of the county, to the stunningly beautiful coastline, and explore right up to the Mullet Peninsula and Portacloy, you will find yourself amongst some of the most spectacular and lonely scenery in the west: quartzite, schist, and gneiss rocks form dramatic mountains and cliffs, and the Atlantic is a wonderful backdrop for the fuchsia-covered inlets, the sandy beaches, the soft green drumlins and the stretches of wild boggy country.

Mayo is one of the loveliest of counties, especially the loughs of Furnace and Feeagh, and the hillside country looking to the Holy Mountain, Croagh Patrick, and the wild Nephin

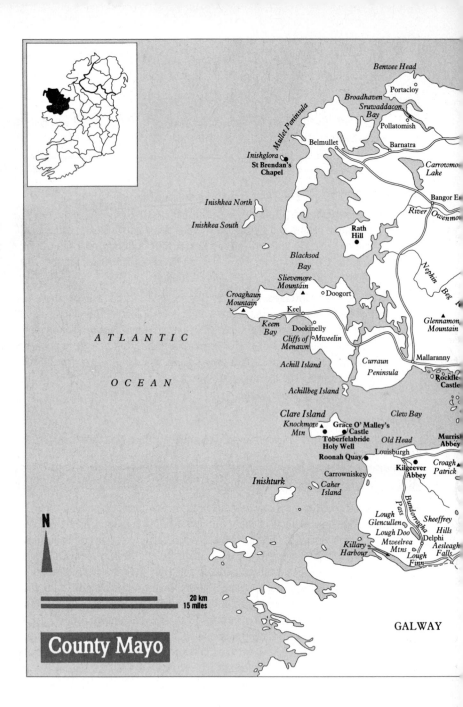

Benwee Head

Portacloy

Broadhaven
Sruwaddacon
Bay

Pollatomish

Mullet Peninsula

Belmullet

Barnatra

Inishglora
**St Brendan's
Chapel**

Carrowmo
Lake

Bangor E

River Owenmo

Nephin Beg

Inishkea North

Inishkea South

**Rath
Hill**

*Blacksod
Bay*

*Slievemore
Mountain*

Doogort

*Croaghaun
Mountain*

Keel

▲ *Glennamon
Mountain*

*Keem
Bay*

Dookinelly

Cliffs of Mweelin
Menawn

Achill Island

*Curraun
Peninsula*

Mallaranny

**Rockfle
Castle**

Achillbeg Island

A T L A N T I C

O C E A N

Clare Island

Clew Bay

*Knockmore
Mtn* ▲

Grace O' Malley's
Castle

**Toberfelabride
Holy Well**

Old Head

**Murris
Abbey**

Roonah Quay

Louisburgh

Croagh ▲
Patrick

Carrowniskey

**Kilgeever
Abbey**

Inishturk

*Caher
Island*

*Lough
Glencullen*

*Bundorragha
Pass*

*Sheeffrey
Hills*

Lough Doo

Delphi

*Killary
Harbour*

*Mweelrea
Mtns*

*Aesleagh
Falls*

*Lough
Finn*

N

20 km
15 miles

GALWAY

County Mayo

262

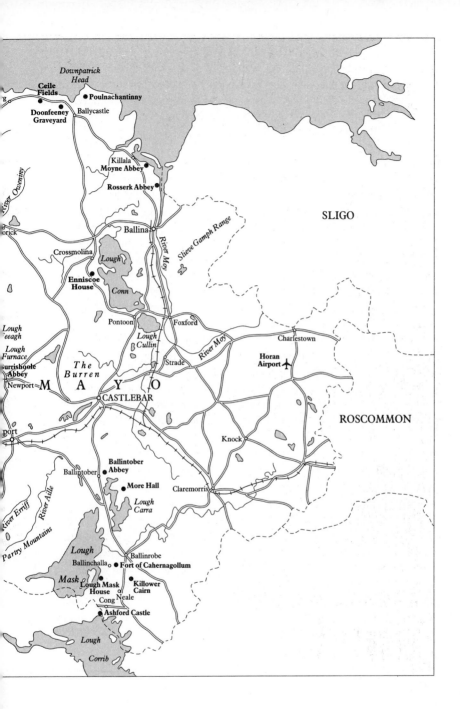

Downpatrick
Head
Ceile
Fields
g
• Poulnachantinny
Doonfeeney   Ballycastle
Graveyard

River Owenmy

Killala
Moyne Abbey •

Rosserk Abbey •

orick
Ballina

Crossmolina
Lough

River Moy

Slieve Gamph Range

SLIGO

Enniscoe
House   Conn

Lough
eeagh

Pontoon   Foxford

Lough   Lough
Furnace   Cullin

River Moy

Charlestown

urrishoole   The   Strade
Abbey   Burren
Newport M   A   Y   O
CASTLEBAR

Horan
Airport ✈

ROSCOMMON

port

Knock

Ballintober
Ballintober   Abbey

River Erriff
River Aille

• More Hall   Claremorris
Lough
Carra

Partry Mountains

Lough
Ballinchalla o • Fort of Cahernagollum
Mask Lough Mask   • Killower
House   Cairn
Cong Neale
• Ashford Castle

Lough

Corrib

263

range. The salmon and trout fishing here is marvellous, and there is an outdoor educational centre on Achill Island where you can spend the weekend or longer canoeing, rock-climbing, wind-surfing, snorkling, hill-walking or orienteering. Similar courses are available in the beautiful Delphi Valley near Louisburgh and Leenane. Between the lonely mountain bogs are some charming villages, excellent eating places and comfortable houses in which to stay. Westport is a very attractive 18th-century town where you can indulge in some culture and tour its stately mansion, Westport House.

History

Historically, County Mayo has its share of fascinating archaeological remains—mainly court cairns in the northwest of the county. The legendary battle of Moytura, between the Tuatha Dé Danaan and the Fomorians, was fought on the Mayo plains in the 303rd year of the world! The written history of Mayo starts, as it does for the whole of Ireland, with the coming of Christianity and St Patrick, who fasted for 40 days on the mountain which is now called Croagh Patrick in his honour. Important monastic remains are scattered about the county. Their names, such as Cong and Ballintubber, reverberate with past associations of learning and devotion to God. Ballintubber Abbey has celebrated Mass daily since it was founded in 1216, and was a stopping place for pilgrimages on their way to climb the holy mountain of Croagh Patrick. The Celtic people arrived in about 300 BC, and gradually evolved into septs with identifiable surnames such as O'Connor and O'Malley. The Anglo-Norman invasion in the 12th century bought a new influx of peoples with names such as Joyce, Burke (de Burgo originally), Walsh and Prendergast. They became in time more Irish than the Irish, often marrying the Celtic Irish and allying themselves with various factions. The English monarchs eventually determined to subjugate Ireland, as most of the Anglo-Normans had lost their loyalty to the Crown, and from 1600 English rule was firmly established. The county was shired about 1570 and called Mayo after a small hamlet within its eastern borders. In Irish, Mayo means 'plain of yew trees'.

After the Cromwellian victories of the 1640s many Irish from all over the country were dispossessed of their fertile lands and sent 'to hell or Connacht'. Many hundreds of small landowners arrived, and had to make a living out of moorland and bogs of Mayo. In the following century the Rebellion of 1798 brought great hope, and ultimately great loss of life to Mayo. The whole nation rose up against English rule, and the French Directory in Paris, who were eager to export their revolution, sent 1100 Frenchmen to join the United Irishmen. The French General Humbert landed in Killala, and inflicted a humiliating defeat on the English General Lake at Castlebar. The Irish peasants were armed only with pitchforks and other rudimentary weapons, but in the euphoria of victory, a 'Republic of Connacht' was set up with John Moore (ancestor of George Moore, the novelist), as its president. But massive English reinforcements soon put an end to the new Republic, and the uprising all over Ireland was put down. Many people were hanged.

During the Napoleonic Wars, all horses were commandeered for the British Army, and that was when the donkey which is so associated with this part of the country, was introduced. The potato blight between 1845 and 1847 bought huge suffering and loss of life.

The peasants barely survived in a good year, but several years of partial crop failure, and then the complete loss of their staple crop, meant that families died in their thousands. In the years that followed, many emigrated. Great bitterness and loss of hope followed until the land-leaguers started to organise tenant resistance to evictions and land clearance in the 1860s. (Speculators had moved in to buy land off impoverished landowners and they had few scruples about evicting peasants.) Michael Davitt, a Mayo man from Straide, and Charles Stewart Parnell, were the leaders of the land agitation, and eventually the government bought huge tracts of land and redistributed it to the people who worked it. An incident during this time of agitation gave a new word—'boycott'—to the English language. What happened was this. In 1880, the local people refused to co-operate with Lord Erne's land agent at Lough Mask House. The harvest was ripe for cutting, but nobody would lift a hand to help him. The agent's name was Captain Boycott, and the affair drew a lot of attention to the issue of land rights. About the same time, the Virgin Mary is said to have appeared at Knock, and this small village in the southeast of the county has since become a place of international pilgrimage.

Today much of the population of County Mayo earns money from tourism, in some form or another, and from keeping hill-sheep and fishing. Foreign companies have been encouraged by the state to set up here, and at Killala, in north Mayo, there is a huge Japanese Asahi chemical textile plant. The land is sparsely populated, and the locals are very friendly and helpful. The Mayo Gaeltacht (Irish-speaking area) covers parts of northwest Mayo including Curraun, parts of Achill and the Mullet Peninsula, plus a small area around Tourmakeady—the centre of the Gaeltarra Eireann knitwear industry, which uses soft colours and traditional patterns.

Getting There and Around

By air: Dublin International Airport and Horan International Airport, Charlestown.

By rail: to the main towns of County Mayo.

By bus: C.I.E. runs Expressway buses to the main towns, and there is a local network. Westport Depot, ✆ (098) 25253/25218; Ballina depot, ✆ (096) 71800.

By bike: Raleigh Rent-a-Bike operates here. Your local contact is J. Breheny, Castlebar Street, Westport; ✆ (098) 25020. Gerry's Cycle hire, Ballina, ✆ (096) 70455.

connections with the islands

To Clare: The mail boat operates between Clare and Roonagh Quay every day, and from 1 June to 31 August twice daily. Mr Chris O'Grady operates a service out to the island, and can organize sea-fishing and boating. Contact Bay View Hotel, Clare Island, ✆ (098) 26307.

To Inishturk and Caher: also from Roonah point. Getting on to a boat is a matter for negotiation with local fishermen, or Chris O'Grady.

East Mayo

    Knock, ✆ (094) 88193, May to September.

    Knock Airport, ✆ (094) 67247, June to August.

Southwest Mayo

    Achill, ✆ (098) 45384, July and August.

    Westport, The Mall, ✆ (098) 25711, all year.

    Louisburgh, ✆ (098) 66400, July and August.

North Mayo

    Ballina, ✆ (096) 70848, May to September.

    Castlebar, ✆ (094) 21207, May to September.

Festivals

June: Westport International Sea Angling Festival and Horse Show. Contact the tourist office in Westport.

Late June: International Four-day Walking Festival, Castlebar, ✆ (094) 24102.

July: Ballina Salmon Festival, ✆ (096) 70905.

Early August: Western Rose Festival, Charlestown. Beauty contest, floats, traditional music, ✆ (092) 54309.

August: International Fishing Festival, Killala Bay, ✆ (096) 22442.

October: Westport Arts Festival. Contact the tourist office.

East Mayo

Cong to Ballinrobe

Mayo has many holy sites and one of them, **Cong**, is beside the island-studded Lough Corrib, just over the border from County Galway. Cong means isthmus, and the Corrib and Mask Lakes are connected by a river which flows underground for part of its course, forming caves in the limestone. At some stage, a canal was built so that you could take a boat between the lakes, but the water never stayed in the porous limestone. Cong is a very friendly place, and has one of the nicest ancient abbeys and a most attractive modern Catholic church. They are beside each other down by the tree-lined river, off the main street, and the graceful stone of the old abbey merges with the flat grey asbestos sheets of the new parish church. **Cong Abbey** was founded in the 7th century by St Feichin. It became the favourite place of the O'Connors, Kings of Connacht, who for a time were also high kings of Ireland. Turlough O'Connor rebuilt the abbey for the Augustinians in 1120, after it was destroyed by the Norsemen, and the last high king of Ireland, Rory O'Connor, spent his final years here after the traumas of the Norman invasion. There are four fine doorways left. The cloisters were restored in the late 19th century by Benjamin Lee Guinness, who made his money from the famous black stout. Nearby, on a platform overhanging the river is the monks' fishhouse, a tiny stone building without a roof. It must have been a lovely place in which to contemplate while waiting for a salmon to take the bait. These monks became very rich because they possessed a fragment of the True Cross. Turlough O'Connor commissioned the most exquisite case in which to enshrine it, and people came from far and wide to pray beside it (you can see it in the National Museum in Dublin).

The demesne of **Ashford Castle**, which was also built by Benjamin Lee Guinness, borders the river here. Ashford is a mid-19th-century fantasy castle, with castellated towers which overlooks Lough Corrib. It is now a renowned luxury hotel, but anyone may walk in the beautifully planted grounds for a small fee. Because of the carboniferous limestone, the river flows underground here, and the tunnel through which it flows can be reached by various openings with intriguing names, such as Horse's Discovery, which is close to the village of Cong. A mile away in beautiful woods are other caves. Captain Webb's Hole was named after an individual who pushed his unfortunate mistresses down it. Apparently mistress number thirteen had the sense and strength to push him into the hole instead! The Pigeon Hole is the most impressive. You climb down the steep steps to the underground stream which is said to contain two white trout, an enchanted maiden and her lover.

About half a mile (0.8km) from Cong you might notice *crusheens* or little heaps of stone upon which a crude cross has been stuck. They mark the makeshift graves of famine victims; funeral processions still stop to pray by them. From here, you could take the road north to **Ballinrobe**, the fishing and touring centre of South Mayo. Loughs Corrib, Mask, Conn, Carra and Cullin are in easy reach. There are race meetings in the summer and a four-day wet fly-fishing competition is held here annually, usually in August.

On the way between Cong and Ballinrobe on the R345/R334 is a bizarre local site, the **Neal** (pronounced 'nail'), which is approached through the gates of an old estate, and set in an area rich in ring-forts. The Neal demesne contains 'the gods of Neal', which is a medieval tomb-carving with a 19th-century inscription claiming that 'the gods go back to the year of the world 2994'. To get a glimpse of the private ruin of **Lough Mask House**, 4 miles (6.4km) southwest of Ballinrobe, turn right off the R334 just as you leave town, and go through the little hamlet of Ballinchalla. This was the home of the Charles Boycott who was ostracized by his tenants during the land agitation of the 1880s. The ruined castle nearby was built by the De Burgos in 1480. Also in the same direction, about 2 miles (3.2 km) from town is the great stone fort of **Cahernagollum**, and a mile (1.6 km) further on is **Killower Cairn**, dating from the Bronze Age.

Castlebar and Knock

On the N84 travelling north to Castlebar, you pass by the fretted shores of Lough Carra. On the eastern shore is the ruin of **Moore Hall**, burned in 1923; it was the home of George Moore (1852–1933), the novelist. His three-volume autobiography is still widely read. He was something of 'a terror' in Irish literary circles, and fell out with W. B. Yeats and Lady Gregory, moving to England for the last 20 years of his life. He is buried on an island in the lake. His family are rather interesting because the Moores were Irish exiles who made a lot of money in the wine trade in Spain, and returned to County Mayo in the 18th century. Another member of the Moore family was proclaimed president of the Republic of Connacht after the success of the French invasion force at the Races of Castlebar, when they routed the English in 1798. The demesne is now a forest park with a picnic site, walks and lakeside scenic views. To reach it, take the unnumbered road to Carrownacon and turn left a mile before the village.

Situated 1 mile (1.6km) off the N84 to the east is **Ballintubber Abbey**, known as 'the Abbey that Refused to Die'. Mass has been said there, continuously, for seven and a half centuries. The fame of Ballintubber goes even further back—to St Patrick, who baptized his converts in a holy well there and founded a church. It was in the early 13th century that the king of Connacht, Cathal of the Wine Red Hand, built the abbey for the Augustinian order.

The abbey was nominally suppressed in 1542 and was attacked and burnt down by Cromwellian soldiers in 1653, but the stone-vaulted chancel survived, and services continued. When the guesthouse to the abbey was excavated many burnt stones were found near the stream over which it was built. These reveal how the monks heated their water: red-hot stones thrown into water brought it to the boil within minutes. There is a pilgrim path from here to Croagh Patrick. The foot-weary pilgrims must have been in need of a good wash when they returned, for the holy mountain is 20 miles (32km) away to the west. The restored abbey is very plain, with bright, modern glass in the windows. The Chapter House has a fine four-order west doorway with a pointed arch. It is freely accessible to the public.

Another noted place of pilgrimage is **Knock**, situated in the Plain of Mayo, 7 miles (11.3km) from the freshwater fishing centre of Claremorris. Here, in 1879, the Blessed Virgin Mary, St Joseph and St John appeared to 14 people. Although it rained heavily on the witnesses, the area around the apparition remained dry. Mary was wearing a white cloak and a golden crown on her head. Over 750,000 visitors and pilgrims visit the shrine annually. Unfortunately, the quiet little village of Knock has been turned into a very ugly, commercialized centre with chapels, monuments and a huge basilica. Holy water comes from chromium taps and there are endless car parks. Knock recently had a very dynamic priest who persuaded big business companies and the government that this part of the country needed an international airport. The Horan Airport near Charlestown was opened in 1986, and now has regular scheduled services from Stansted by Ryanair. It was regarded as a big joke when Monseigneur Horan first thought of it, and no one really believed the airport would ever appear. Couples come from all over the world to be married at the shrine, and the cemetery is expanding fast, for many people who are not local decide to be buried there. *For further information, write to the Presbytery, Knock, ☎ (094) 88100; or the Secretary, Knock Shrine Society, Bridgemount, Belcarra, Castlebar.*

Delphi Valley to Louisburg

At the head of the Killary inlet are the handsome **Aasleagh Falls**. Here you can take a beautiful and lonely route up to Louisburgh through the pass of Bundorragha (R335), with the Mweelrea Mountain on your left and Ben Gorm on your right. You soon come to **Delphi**, which is rather an apt name, for the mountains and the wilderness have a sort of wisdom which you can sense in the peace around you, in the birdsong and the lapping water. Lord Sligo was so impressed by its resemblance to Delphi in Greece that he renamed it from Fionnloch. Three lochs lie beside the road: Fin Lough, which means bright lake; Doo Lough, dark lake; and Glencullin Lough, the lake of the holly tree glen. An adventure sports centre is based here, and Delphi Lodge, hotel and fishing centre.

Louisburg, pronounced 'Lewisburg', is a pretty village near to Clew Bay. It has numerous pubs offering traditional music on various nights. The Derrylahan also has entertainments at weekends. There are fine sandy **beaches** at Old Head and further to the southwest at Carrowniskey. The purple-blue mountain ranges give the village a marvellous backdrop. If you take a minor road from here and travel west for a couple of miles over some low hills, you will get to Roonah Quay. From the quay you can take a boat or curragh to Clare Island, Caher Island and Inishturk. Planning a trip to any of these islands depends on the weather, but if you have to wait a day or so in Louisburg there are some nice places to stay and quite a lot to see. **Kilgeever Abbey** is 2 miles (3.2km) east of Louisburg, and has an ancient well and church; pilgrims to Croagh Patrick still include it in their itinerary. Then there is **Murrisk Abbey**, 7 miles (11.3 km) further to the east, on the R335 to Westport, which was founded by Tadhg O'Malley in 1457. It has a beautiful east window. Just above it is the pub where the thirsty pilgrims refresh themselves before and after the tough climb up Croagh Patrick.

Croagh Patrick is a sacred and beautiful mountain where St Patrick is believed to have spent 40 days and nights in fasting and prayer. For this magnificent feat of endurance he is supposed to have extracted a promise from God that the Irish would never lose the Christian faith he had brought them. The mountain is made up of quartzite which breaks up into sharp-edged stones, so it is not very comfortable walking—some pilgrims do it in bare feet. At the top is a small modern chapel, 2510ft (765m) above sea level. The materials for building the chapel, including 716 bags of cement, were carried up to the top of the mountain by devout pilgrims. If you are not interested in the religious aspects of the mountain, climb it just to see the magnificent views. Clew Bay lies below, its inner waters cluttered by green teardrop islands, formed by a glacier millions of years ago. Croagh Patrick has been in the news lately, as it is threatened by multinationals moving in to mine gold and bauxite. There is a lot of local protest.

This part of the coast and the islands off it are associated with a warrior woman who outshone all her male contemporaries in qualities of leadership. Granuaile, otherwise known as Grace O'Malley, was an amazing woman; she was a pirate captain, and her symbol was the seahorse. People still talk of her, even though she died in 1603. Her territory includes Clare, Caher, Inishturk and Inishbofin. Her family had been Lords of the Isles for two hundred years, and in the 40 years which it took the Tudors to extend their power to Ireland, Granuaile was the mainstay of the rebellion in the west. One of the stories which seems to explain her best is as follows. At the age of 45 she gave birth at sea to her first child, Toby. An hour later, her ship was boarded by Turkish pirates. The battle on the deck was almost lost, when she appeared wrapped in a blanket and shot the enemy captain with a blunderbuss. After that her men rallied, captured the Turkish ship and hanged the crew. Her story is documented in the **Granuaile Centre** in Louisburg, an excellent interpretative exhibition on permanent display (*open May–Oct;* ✆ *(098) 66195; adm*).

Clare Island

Clare Island has more land given over to farming than the other islands, though its higher slopes are covered in heather. It has superb cliffs up to 300ft (91m) high, but even these are overshadowed by the Knockmore Mountain which drops from 1550ft (472m) in a few hundred yards to join the cliffs. As you come into the small stone pier you will see **Grace O'Malley's Castle**, converted into a coastguard station during the 19th century but now a ruin. This large square stone tower still dominates the bay. Legend has it that the young sea pirate was in the habit of mooring her ships by tying them together, then passing the main rope through a hole in her castle walls, and retiring to bed with the rope wound round her arm, in order to be ready at the first alarm. Her last years were fraught with difficulties and she was forced, aged 63, to sail up the Thames to parley with Elizabeth I. Elizabeth offered her a title, but Grace replied that she was a queen in her own right! Finally they made a deal: Grace would retain some of her old lands, including Clare, and in return she would keep down piracy.

There is a holy well at **Toberfelabride**, but the gem of Clare is its abbey which is about 1½ miles (2.4km) west of the harbour. **Clare Abbey** is a 15th-century church with a tower, and is believed to be a cell of the Cistercian monastery of Abbeyknockmoy in County Galway. Grace O'Malley is buried here. On a plain round arch leading from the roofless nave to the chancel, there is a coat of arms topped by a horse rampant with the words '*Terra Mariq[ue] potens O'Maille*' (O'Malley powerful on land and sea). The most notable thing about the friary is the trace of fresco painting on the plastered ceiling of the vaulted roof; it is seldom that fresco painting has survived in Irish medieval churches. The friary is always accessible.

You can walk to the lighthouse at the north end where there are spectacular views from the cliffs. The lighthouse has been converted and restored and you can see round parts of it.

You could easily spend a couple of days on Clare although there's not a huge amount to occupy you (population 140). There is a diving centre on the island, and a hotel, but it is possible to come just for the day, and have a picnic.

Inishturk Island

Inishturk has a wonderful beach on its south side, and its little farms are full of wild flowers. About 90 people live here and make a living from fishing.

Caher Island

This island evokes the mood of early monastic settlements better than any other. The church here is small and roofless, and around it are 12 stone crosses, the most recent of which is not less than a thousand years old. One on the hilltop shows a human face, another a pair of dolphins. In the graveyard is **St Patrick's Bed** with impressions said to be the mark of his hands, feet and hips. This used to be part of the Croagh Patrick circuit, but few people come nowadays to lie in his bed and hope for a miraculous cure. It is a lovely grey-green place of walls, donkeys, sheep and green pastures. Nobody lives here now.

Louisburg to the Curraun Peninsula

From Louisburg, the R335 winds its way to Westport with lovely views of Clew Bay. **Westport** is a highly planned town, unusual in the west. James Wyatt, the well-known Georgian architect, planned it for the Marquess of Sligo. There is a pretty walk called the Mall which runs beside the River Carrowbeg and is overhung with trees.

In June the place is overflowing with people. There is the **Westport International Sea Angling Festival** at the beginning of June, followed by the Westport Horse Show. In July there is a **Street Festival** with sports, art displays, beauty competitions, music and dancing. There are ballad sessions in the pubs and hotels in the summer. In October the town hosts the **Westport Arts Festival**. Here too, you can walk around one of the few stately homes of the west of Ireland—**Westport House** (*open 1 June–31 Aug daily, 2–6; 15–31 May and 1–11 Sept, daily, 2–5; adm; ✆ (098) 25430*). The house, which is to the west of the town, is full of old Irish silver, family portraits and lovely furniture, and there is a miniature zoo in the grounds. It was built by Colonel John Browne and his wife, ancestors of the present Marquis of Sligo. He was a Jacobite, and she was the great, great grand-daughter of Grace O'Malley. There is a gift and tea shop, and the basements have been set up for family entertainments, fruit machines etc. The sea-angling grounds in Clew Bay are amongst the best in Europe, and deep-sea fishing boats can be hired locally (*see* 'Activities'). **Newport**, on the N59, has a superb country house hotel overlooking the river. **Newport House** used to be the home of the O'Donnells, once the Earls of Tir Connell, who were often in the forefront of opposition to English rule. The modern Irish Romanesque style church of St Patrick has some fine Harry Clarke stained glass windows depicting the Last Judgement.

The coastline around here is full of little islands and inlets. However, about ½ mile (0.8km) outside Newport on the N59, take a little road signposted to Furnace; this takes you to the wild mountain country of the **Nephin Beg** range. When it's sunny the lakes go a deep, sparkling blue; and the air is very bracing, rather like Switzerland. Lough Furnace (there used to be an old iron furnace here), is now a salmon research station, as is the next lake along, Lough Feeagh. If you decide to explore the wild territory of the interior between Glen Nephin and Bangor Erris, follow the old mountain road on past the lakes and past Glennamong Mountain (2063ft/629m) until it joins the R312. Then turn northwards until it joins the N59 at Bellacorick. The old grey house, wrapped in trees, which overlooks Lough Feeagh, is now a youth hostel. The route is very beautiful. Everywhere fuchsia, and rhododendron mingle with the stone walls and natural rock. The **Salmon Research Agency** has a very interesting visitor centre on Lough Furnace (*open June to end August © (098) 41107*). Wild salmon have a fascinating life cycle, and the centre provides details of this and how a fishery is run, together with the latest salmon research.

On the N59 to Mulrany there is a turn-off to **Burrishoole Abbey**, a 15th-century ruin, and a very charming and peaceful place where the sea laps all about. It is always accessible. The next stop-off is further along the coast at **Rockfleet Castle** (also known as Carrickahooley Castle). It stands on firm but seaweedy rock, a complete tower house looking over Newport Bay. Much of the charm of the place is in the story which goes with it. This four-sided 15th-century castle was built by the Burkes and passed to Grace O'Malley by means of a trick. She married Richard Burke on the understanding that either of them could end the marriage after a year by a simple declaration. She used the year to garrison the castle with her own men and kept it when she declared the marriage ended.

Numerous tantalizing beaches fringe the road. When you get to **Mulrany** on the neck of the Curraun Peninsula, you will find it has a beautiful long strand looking out to Croagh Patrick across Clew Bay. The climate is mild and rhododendrons bloom with even greater luxury than is usual in the west. There are myriads of yellow flags growing in the fields, which is another common and lovely sight in Connacht, though not so to the local farmers. You will also notice lots of guest houses and B&B places along this road, for this area is very popular in the summer.

The **Curraun Peninsula** is a wild nob of land through which you can pass on the way to Achill Island. There are three mountain peaks over 1700ft (518m) high, and lovely views over the sea to Clare Island and Achill. The single-track road round the Curraun gives you a fine introduction to Achill Island, which has all the most attractive characteristics of Connacht. Amongst them are the sleepy whitewashed cottages you can see across the water and the smell of burning turf floating with the breeze. Placid-looking donkeys are everywhere.

Achill Island

Achill is connected to the mainland by a bridge, and because it is one of the easiest islands to reach, it is the most touristy. The dramatic cliff scenery and long golden beaches make it very popular. The island has a splendid atmosphere, you wind up and down through the valleys, past lakes, where a few swans idle, and see before you the surging ocean where the Achill fishermen hunt for basking sharks.

Achill is 53 square miles (137¼ sq km) and the largest of the Irish islands, so the best introduction to it is to take the **Atlantic Drive**. This is signposted clearly as you leave the little hamlet of Achill Sound beside the causeway. You pass a small, ruined 12th-century church and then a slender tower house, Kildownet, which is supposed to have belonged at some time to Grace O'Malley. There is always a boat or two drawn up by the little quay beside it, which adds to its charm. The road follows the line of the shore round the south tip and passes Achillbeg Island, which contains the remains of an old hermitage. The road now goes north winding high up the sides of the cliffs—a route not recommended for horse or motor-drawn caravans.

Keel is a big village with restaurants and craft shops. It has the attraction of a large, sandy beach. The west-facing **Cliffs of Menawn** to the south of Keel have been wrought by the sea and wind into fantastic shapes, which are best viewed from a boat. Particularly note-worthy are the **Cathedral Rocks**, which are covered in fantastic fretwork. If you walk 3 miles (4.8km) to the end of Menawn Strand, you come to a holy well; and if it is low tide you can see clearly the Gothic arches and pillars of the rocks, above which rises Mweelin Mountain. It is an easy climb, if approached from Dookinelly. Keem Bay is a lovely sandy cove obvious from the cliff road. It is a favourite haunt of the basking shark but have no fear if you want to bathe: its food is plankton, not human flesh.

Doogort is a little fishing hamlet in the shadow of Slievemore Mountain (2204ft, 672m). Nearby are some sea caves. The village of Doogort has a contentious history. In the early 19th century, a Protestant missionary outpost was established in order to convert the local Catholics through both religous and physical example. The Mission acquired title to the rights of three-fifths of Achill in a short time, and resentment amongst the Achill people ran high. This was intensified when, apparently, soup and bread was given out to islanders during the famine only if they became Protestants. The Mission closed down in the late 19th century, but it did help start the first hotel on the island. On the lower slopes of Slievemore is a deserted village, a place of tumbled stone and lichen. This was an old 'booley village', occupied only during the summer months when the herds were brought to the upland pastures. Along the coast here are the **Seal Caves**. You can hire a boat to get to them, and enjoy the superb bathing beaches. The people of Achill are friendly and helpful, though one woman confessed that she much preferred the winter, when they had the island to themselves.

For mountain-climbers, Croaghaun drops 2000 sheer feet (610m) into the sea and its crescent arms provide impressive scrambling. The western sky with its tumbled cloud formation is one of the beauties of the west, and the rocks, mountain and crouching cottages on Achill must be seen in relation to it.

Northwest Mayo

From Mularany, the N59 runs over a vast bog; the edges are enlivened by splashes of purple rhododendrons and a few fir trees. Turf, which for hundreds of years has been cut from the bog, is used much less nowadays in heating and cooking; bottled gas has made life much easier for the housewife. But many farmers and country people have rights to turf turbaries, which they cut every year. The tool used to cut the neat sods from the bog is called a slane; while the man cuts, the women and children gather the sods and arrange them in little piles to dry. The pattern of the piles varies from area to area but they often resemble little clochans, such as the early Christians built.

Bangor Erris is a small place on the long, lonely road to Belmullet. This region is still known as Erris, one of the ancient Norman baronies of Ireland. **Belmullet** is one of the loneliest towns in Connacht. It stands on a slender piece of land just wide enough to prevent the Mullet from becoming an island. All the commerce of the peninsula is channelled through Belmullet, so on market day it is surprisingly full. If you want to base yourself here before exploring the wild and lonely peninsula, there is plenty of accommodation. Belmullet is famous for sea-angling, and there is an **international fishing festival** here in August. The Mullet is almost divided into little islands by the deep bays which cut into it on either side. The beaches and fishing are excellent and there are superb views of Achill, the Nephin Beg range, and the mystical islands of Inishglora and Inishkea. The grey and red-necked phalarope nests in the crevices and rocks along the coast, and the peninsula is scattered with prehistoric remains. Out in Blacksod Bay lies the wreck of *La Rata*, a large Spanish galleon which went down in the wild seas of September 1588—part of the Armada which threatened England. The islands of Inishglora and Inishkea are uninhabited, and hardly ever visited by tourists. Getting out to them is a matter of negotiation with local fishermen, and they can only be reached in calm weather. A walk around each one takes at least one hour. Always bring your own picnic and drinks.

Inishglora

On **Inishglora** (the 'Island of the Voice'), the Children of Lir regained their true form after being turned into swans by their jealous stepmother. The spell was to be broken when St Patrick's bell was heard ringing out over Ireland, but, unhappily for the Children of Lir, their immortality only lasted whilst they were swans. They came ashore, blind, senile and decrepit, to die almost at once. Inishglora has been a sacred island for thousands of years. It is only one mile from the Mullet Peninsula, and its ecclesiastical remains are associated with St Brendan, the Navigator. Some of the buildings definitely date from the 6th century. The most complete is the 12th-century **St Brendan's Chapel**, which is built of dry-stone masonry. Close by are the ruins of a church for men, and a church for women, and the holy well here is supposed to turn red if the water is touched by a woman's hand. It is said locally that lots of bones are uncovered where the soil is washed away by rain and sea-spray, for it was believed that the more serious a dead man's crimes, the more important it was to have him buried on an holy island. This not only improved his chances of salvation, but ensured that he could not come back to haunt you, since the spirits of the dead cannot pass over water.

To the southwest are the Islands of Inishkea.

Inishkea South and North

Inishkea means 'isle of the lonely heron'. Legend tells of Mulhenna who was unfaithful to her husband and banished here for a thousand years, condemned to take the form of a heron. **South Island** has a little deserted hilltop village, though fishermen camp here when they are fishing round the shores. The islanders moved to the mainland after ten men were drowned in 1927, during a freak gale. Moondaisies, grass, sheep and sandy beaches will be your reward, if you persuade a boatman to bring you out here. Both islands have the remains of ancient churches, incised stone crosses and some prehistoric signs of occupation.

Ballycastle to Ballina

On the mainland again, make your way up to the fishing hamlet of Pollatomish on Sruwaddacon Bay. Take the unnumbered road west of Barnatra on the R314. Close to the cliff edge is **Dooncarton Stone Circle** and megalithic tomb. Further north is the little harbour village of **Portacloy**, which is surrounded by high cliffs. You approach it by an unclassified road northwest of Glenamoy, a hamlet on the R314. The scenery is marvellous, and it is fun to explore the caves gouged out by the furious sea. This is possible only by boat. Ask locally, and you may find somebody to take you out. This is invigorating country for the walker. Some people like to tramp along the cliffs between Benwee Head and Belderg, and admire the view from the Cliffs of Ceide. Ceide Hill and the surrounding area is probably one of the world's most extensive stone age monuments. A **Visitor Centre** run by the Office of Public Works (*open mid-Mar–Oct, daily, 10–5, 6.30 in summer; adm;* © *(01) 661 3111 ext 2386 or (096) 43325*) has opened at Ceide Fields just off the R314 to explain the archaeology and geology of the area. For hidden in the bogs is evidence of a well-organised farming community dating from more than 5,000 years ago. Extensive patterns of stone walled fields, and corrals have been revealed under the bog. The centre has a small restaurant. A detailed map is also available from here detailing a series of wonderful walks that may be made following the Sculpture Trail. Sculptures commissioned to celebrate the social and cultural history of Mayo have been scattered on various sites along the spectacular coastline from Blacksod Bay to Ballina.

On the R314, in the northeastern corner of the county, **Ballycastle** is typical of the villages in the west. The streets are wide, the air smells faintly of turf, and everybody seems to be asleep. There is much to explore and very few tourists in the summer. The cliffs of Downpatrick Head are full of wheeling birds, terns, gulls, skuas, razorbills and guillemots, plus less active ones such as puffins; all seem to have nests somewhere on the edges of the cliffs. There are picnic tables set out overlooking the Atlantic, but it does not look as if anyone has ever eaten off them and now the birds and seapinks have taken over, visited by the occasional hare. There is ugly wire fencing on the head to prevent you from falling into the crevasses and holes around the cliff edge. One of the most spectacular holes is a puffin hole called Poulnachantinny. The story is that St Patrick was having a fight with the Devil, and dealt him such a blow with his crozier that the Devil was hammered clean through the rock and down into the sea-cave below. In their fight they also knocked a bit of the headland off into the sea: the stack of **Doonbristy** is proof! An old promontory fort was built on Doonbristy, before it became separated from the headland. It is a ruin now, of course. There is a pattern (pilgrimage) to the holy well and ruined church of St Patrick on Garland Sunday in May.

About 2 miles (3.2 km) northwest of Ballycastle, on the R314, is **Doonfeeney Graveyard**, where there is a ruined church and a standing stone, about 18ft (5.5m) high, with a cross carved on it. A large ring-fort stands close by, where, according to old beliefs, fairies hold their revels. The graveyard is scattered with ancient stone slabs and it is rather a quiet, secret place.

In spring, on the way east to Killala Bay, still following the R314, the banks of the roadside are covered in daisies and primroses. Killala was the scene of French landings in 1798, when Humbert brought 1100 French soldiers, plus uniforms and weapons for the rebels. Killala Bay is rather like a lagoon, having calm sheltered waters. Before you get to the town, a road to the left leads you past **Rathfran Abbey**, a ruined but fine Dominican friary dating from 1274. **Killala** town is very pretty and rather higgledy-piggledy, with a round tower rising from the middle of it. The tower is of a later date, and the doorway is almost 13ft (4m) from the ground. It is now thought that such towers are the work of skilled builders who moved around the country from site to site. This tower is of a lovely blue limestone with a greenish cap. Also at Killala, there is a small, plain 17th-century Church of Ireland cathedral and an attractive quay. Two miles (3.2 km) west is a 15th-century ruin called **Moyne Abbey** on the estuary of the lovely salmon river, the Moy, reputedly one of the best in Europe. Just a mile or two upstream is another abbey, **Rosserk**, which is rather more complete and is regarded as one of the finest Franciscan friaries in the country. It has some good carvings on the double piscina, one of which is of a round tower. The buildings include a square tower, nave, chancel, south transept, cloister and conventional buildings. There is a lovely arched doorway and east window. Very often friaries are referred to as abbeys by the local people. Moyne is, in fact, a friary too. It and Rosserk were burned in 1590 by Sir Richard Bingham, the English govenor of Connacht. Both are always accessible to the public.

Ballina to Castlebar

Ballina, pronounced *bally-nah*, is a port town on the estuary of the River Moy and is a good place to stay if you are in Ireland for the fishing. It is a very good shopping centre as well, especially after the remoteness and lack of choice in Erris. West of Ballina, off the R315, and 3km south of Crossmolina is the **North Mayo Family History Research and Heritage Centre** (*open all year;* ✆ *(096) 31809*). It is in the outbuildings of Enniscoe House which is also an extremely attractive and comfortable place to stay. There are lots of interesting farm implements on display in the Centre.

Foxford, 10 miles (16km) due south of Ballina, is a convenient place to stay if you are fishing on the Loughs Conn and Cullin. It has a visitor centre at its thriving wool and tweed mill in St Joseph's Place. This area is very attractive, the summit of Nephin Mountain is of whitish quartzite so it looks perpetually snowcapped, and when the sun is shining it is a lovely background to the deep-blue waters of Lough Conn. **Pontoon** is on the isthmus between the two loughs, and there are two hotels there.

It is worth stopping at **Straide**, if you are going to Castlebar. Straide is the birthplace of Michael Davitt (1846–1906), who started the Land League. His family were evicted from their small farm when he was five, and they emigrated to Lancashire, where he worked as a child in the cotton mills and lost his right arm in the machines. The Land League, founded in 1879, was a national agrarian movement in which the land workers refused to co-operate with landowners who tried to enforce evictions. Eventually the government passed the Land Act of 1881 which gave the tenants fair rent, fixity of tenure and free sale. The League went on to press for landownership, which came about in 1885. The **Michael Davitt National Memorial Museum** (*open in the summer, Tues–Sat, 10–6; adm; ✆ (096) 31022 for more details*) in Straide has a large collection of historical documents and photographs relating to the league. Opposite the museum is a ruined Franciscan abbey founded in the mid-13th century. It was transferred to the Dominicans in 1252. It has a wonderful series of sculptures. The *Pieta* is especially good. The Virgin sits with the limp body of Christ in her lap, guarded by two angels. There is an elaborate 15th-century tomb chest in the same style with figures of saints.

Castlebar is the administrative centre of Mayo and is busy enough to have a small airport. The town started as a settlement of the de Barrys. It became more important in 1611 when James I granted it a charter, and is remembered for the ignominious scattering of the British garrison in 1798 when the French General Humbert advanced with a motley crowd of French and Irish troops. The event is known today as the 'Races of Castlebar'. The remains of John Moore, the first and only president of the Connacht Republic, are buried in the Mall and there is a memorial to 1798 beside his grave.

Shopping

Crafts: from many shops in Westport, concentrated on the High Street, the Mall, Shop Street and Bridge Street. Earthenware from Terrybaun Pottery, Bofeenaun, Ballina, ✆ (094) 56472. Westport pottery, The Quays, Westport, ✆ (098) 26239.

Delicacies: J. Clarke & Sons, O'Rahilly Street, Ballina, for smoked wild salmon. Next door in Brendan Doherty's old-fashioned grocery, you can buy farm butter. For fish fresh off the sea, the Fisherman's co-op, Achill Sound, ✆ (098) 45123

Wool and fabric: handloomed arans from Carraig Donn Industries, Westport, County Mayo; ✆ (098) 25566. Gaeltarra Knitwear, Tourmakeady, ✆ (092) 44015. Foxford Woollen Mills, Foxford; ✆ (094) 56756. Brackloon Weavers, Westport, ✆ (098) 26236, for shuttle woven natural fibres.

Bellows: D. Benson, The Quay, Westport, ✆ (098) 26589.

Marble: G Lisibach, Station Road, Castlebar, ✆ (094) 22187.

Hats: Hats of Ireland, Newport Road, Castlebar, ✆ (094) 21144.

Activities

East Mayo

Fishing: for brown trout on Loughs Mask, Carra and Corrib. Tackle information from Pat Quinn Tackle, Main Street, Castlebar. In Ballinrobe, contact D. O'Connor, ✆ (092) 41083.

Walking: The Western Way, the 45-mile (73km) signposted trail over the mountains to Westport, starts at Oughterard. Details from Cospoir, 11th floor, Hawkins House, Dublin 2, ℗ (01) 673 4700.

Pony-trekking: contact Claremorris School of Equitation, Lisduff, Claremorris, ℗ (094) 71684.

Golf: Ashford Castle Hotel, Cong, has a golf course in its grounds. ℗ (092) 46003. Ballinrobe Golf Course, Claremorris, ℗ (092) 41148.

Southwest Mayo

Sea-fishing: boats can be hired from Mr F. Clarke, The Mews, Rosbeg, Westport, ℗ (098) 25481. Mr R. Roynan, Rosmoney, Westport, ℗ (098) 26514.

Fishing: for salmon and trout near Newport, contact Newport House Hotel, ℗ (098) 41222; and the Delphi Fishery, Leenane, ℗ (095) 42213.

Sailing: Glenans Sailing School, based on Cullenmore Island, Westport. Contact the Dublin office, ℗ (01) 6611481. All water sports facilities are available.

Pony-trekking: Drummindoo Stud and Equitation Centre, Castlebar Road, Westport, ℗ (098) 25616.

Golf: at Keel, Achill Island. Visitors welcome without reservations, ℗ (098) 45172. There is also a course at Westport which has memorable views and holes, ℗ (098) 25113.

Adventure sports: canoeing, rock-climbing, surfing, hill-walking and snorkelling. At Newport contact Mrs Pauline McDermott, Skerdagh Centre, ℗ (098) 41500. For Delphi Adventure Sports Centre, Delphi, Leenane, contact Mr Noone, ℗ (095) 42208. For facilities on Achill Island, contact Achill Outdoor Education Centre, Bunnacurry, Cashel, ℗ (098) 47253; and Achill Adventure and Leisure Island Holidays, Doogort, ℗ (0902) 94801.

Traditional music: a number of pubs in Westport and Louisburg have traditional music on various evenings.

North Mayo

Deep-sea fishing: contact Mr Michael Lavelle, Blacksod Bay, Ballina, ℗ (097) 85669; and John Walkin, Tackle shop, Tone Street, Ballina, ℗ (096) 22442.

Fishing: for salmon and salmon trout on the River Moy. Contact the Moy Falcon Fishery, c/o Mount Falcon Hotel, Ballina, ℗ (096) 21172. Fishing for brown trout on Loughs Conn and Cullin. Tackle shops and advice on local fishing: O' Connors, Main Street, Ballycastle; V. Doherty, Bridge Street, Ballina; William Coyle, American Street, Belmullet; J. O'Connor, 15 Spencer Street, Castlebar.

Traditional music: informal sessions at McDowell's Hotel, Slievemore Road, Doogort, Achill Island.

Clare Island Safaris: Contact Peter Gill, ℗ (098) 25048

East Mayo

Ashford Castle, Cong ✆ (092) 46003 (*luxury*). Opulent Victorian furnishings. Very comfortable, with stunning grounds, but rather impersonal because of its large rooms. Irish entertainment in the Dungeon Bar. **Partry House**, Ballinrobe, ✆ (092) 43004 (*moderate*), set on the shores of Lough Carra, warm and welcoming country house. Wonderful cooked breakfasts. **Ballyhowley House**, the Merrick family, Knock, ✆ (094) 88339 (*inexpensive*), lovely old house near Knock, set on the river. Mrs Bourke, **Woodlands**, Caherduff, The Neale, near Cong, ✆ (092) 46067 (*inexpensive*), comfortable modern house in the middle of the countryside.

self-catering

1817 cut-stone coach houses in the Cong area. Two bedrooms. Contact Mrs Hall, The Old Rectory, Cong, ✆ (092) 46396. From IR£210 per week.

Southwest Mayo

Newport House, Newport County Mayo, ✆ (098) 41222/41154 (*expensive*), superb country-house hotel in a beautiful creeper-covered Georgian house overlooking the river. Beautiful Irish 18th-century furniture adds to the elegance and beauty of the house. Notice the rococo Chippendale mirror hanging over the fireplace in the dining room. Old-fashioned formal service and delicious food, including their own home-smoked salmon. Information on local sights and fishing. **Delphi Lodge**, Delphi, ✆ (095) 42211 (moderate). Very comfortably converted sporting lodge in wonderful wild position. Own salmon and trout fishery. **Bay View Hotel**, Clare Island, ✆ (098) 26307 (*moderate*), the only place on the island to stay: friendly and comfortable. **McDowell's Hotel**, Doogort, ✆ (098) 43148 (*moderate*), family-run and full of atmosphere.

Mrs Sammon, **Cuaneen House**, Carrowmore, Louisburg, ✆ (098) 66460 (*inexpensive*), modern farmhouse in a beautiful location overlooking Clew Bay. Good home-cooking and very friendly family. John and Mary O'Brien, **Rath-a-Rosa**, Rosbeg, Westport, ✆ (098) 25348 (*inexpensive*), modern bungalow, only a hundred yards from the sea. Comfortable; friendly hosts with plenty of local knowledge. Mrs Margo Cannon, **Teach Mweewillin**, Currane, Achill Island, ✆ (098) 45134. Modern hillside bungalow overlooking Achill. Mrs Patten, **Island House**, Dookinelly, Keel PO. ✆ (098) 43180 (*inexpensive*). Very adequate lodgings. Mrs Stoney, **Rosturk Woods**, Mulrany, Westport, ✆ (098) 36264 (*inexpensive*), lovely family house on Clew Bay. Children welcome, elegant and comfortable.

self catering

Renovated apartments within the Old Coach House, and farm cottages on the Westport Estate. Sleeps six to 10. From IR£207 a week. Contact **Westport House Estate**, Westport, ✆ (098) 25141.

North Mayo

Enniscoe House, Mrs Susan Kellett, Castlehill near Crossmolina, Ballina, ✆ (096) 31112 (*expensive*), beautiful Georgian house set in parklands that edge Lough Conn. Grand and spacious rooms filled with elegant family furniture and portraits. Four-poster and half-tester beds in the pretty bedrooms. Huge log fires, and superlative cooking using seasonal ingredients to their best advantage. Susan Kellett is also very knowledgeable about the North County Mayo Heritage and Genealogical Society. A centre with family records has been set up in the stables of the house, along with a small museum which concentrates on rural life. Woodcock shooting available in the winter for small groups. Good brown trout fishing on Lough Conn; boats and gillies can be easily arranged. **Mount Falcon Castle**, Ballina, ✆ (096) 21172 (*expensive*), comfortable and sprawling Victorian country house crammed with all sorts of curios. A great sense of fun and atmosphere, which can be wholly attributed to the wonderful 85-year-old owner Constance Aldridge, who dines with her guests every night. Rich but glorious food and salmon fishing on the River Moy. During the winter rough shooting can be arranged. The Moffat family, **Kilmurray House**, Castlehill, Crossmolina, ✆ (096) 31227 (*inexpensive*), friendly, cosy, old farmhouse. Mrs Moffat organizes and cooks the meals very well, and her husband is a keen fisherman who will give you lots of advice. Mrs A. Reilly, **Highdrift**, Haven View, Ballina Road, Belmullet, ✆ (097) 81260 (*inexpensive*), modern bungalow. Mrs N. Carey, **Rathoma House**, Killala, ✆ (096) 32035, pleasant farmhouse in the depths of the country. Lots of farm activities, and horse riding can be arranged.

self-catering

Small cottages available in the grounds of Enniscoe House for short lets (*see above*). A group of 10 traditional-style cottages at Ballycastle. Sleeps six to eight. Contact Ireland West Tourism, Aras Fáilte, Galway, ✆ (091) 63081.

Eating Out

East Mayo

Ashford Castle, Cong, ✆ (092) 46003 (*expensive*), Irish-style food in sumptuous setting. **Echoes**, Main Street, Cong, ✆ (092) 46059 (*moderate*), cheerful home-cooking. **Davitt Restaurant**, Rush Street, Castlebar, ✆ (094) 22233 (*inexpensive*), good-value lunch. **Mulligans Pub**, James Street, Claremorris, ✆ (094) 71792 (*inexpensive*). Traditional Irish pub with good steaks.

Southwest Mayo

Newport House, Newport, ✆ (098) 41222 (*expensive*). It is a treat just to see inside this house, with its elegant furniture. The food is good too, especially the home-cured fish. **The Boley House**, Keel, Achill Island, ✆ (098) 43147 (*moderate*). Good, well-prepared and thought-out menus in a stone cottage.

Salmon, seafood, steaks. Dinner only. **McDowells Hotel**, Slievemore Road, Dugort, Achill Island, ✆ (098) 47205/43148 (*moderate*). Home-cooking. **Quay Cottage**, The Harbour, Westport, ✆ (098) 26412 (*moderate*). Folksy shellfood restaurant. Very cosy, with good bread and a vegetarian menu as well. **The Cork**, The Octagon, Westport, ✆ (098) 26929 (*moderate*). Tasty dishes for vegans, vegetarians and carnivores. **The Moorings**, The Quay, Westport ✆ (098) 25874 (*moderate*). Small with cordon bleu cooking. **Calvey's Restaurant**, Keel, Achill Island, ✆ (098) 43158 (*inexpensive*). Good basic food. **The Chalet**, Keel, Achill Island, ✆ (098) 43157 (*inexpensive*). Good fish and chips. The **Continental Café**, High Street, Westport, ✆ (098) 26679 (*inexpensive*). Homemade soup, excellent cheese, and German sourdough bread. Lunch only. **Circe's**, Bridge Street, Westport. Café and craft shop. Great sandwiches and chocolate cake.

North Mayo

Mount Falcon Castle, Ballina, ✆ (096) 21172 (*expensive*). Wonderful food taken at a long table with the charming and eccentric owner Connie Aldridge. Vegetarian food can be arranged. Dinner must be booked. **Breaffy House Hotel**, Castlebar, ✆ (094) 22033 (*moderate*). Good hotel-restaurant. **Gaughan's Pub**, O'Rahilly Street, Ballina (*inexpensive*). Excellent brown bread, smoked salmon from the shop next door and all the accoutrements one might need for pipe-smoking.

County Roscommon

Roscommon is a wonderfully green and fertile county, with shining sheets of water encircling it and scattered through it. It is the only county in Connacht without at least a touch of seashore, but the many lakes and rivers give it a different charm to that of its windswept neighbours facing the Atlantic. The placid River Shannon forms its eastern boundary, engulfed as it is by the beautiful Lough Ree for several miles. The River Suck, beloved of coarse fishermen, forms the boundary with County Mayo in the west; and Lough Key, Lough Gara and Lough Boderg encircle the county in the north. In the east and west there is bogland, but in the centre rich pastureland divides into fine cattle and sheep farms. (The population in the 1981 census was 54,543, all of whom live in predominately rural surroundings.)

The flood meadows on either side of the River Suck provide the perfect environment for birdwatching. Great flocks of wigeon come here to graze, as do whooper swans, golden plovers, black-tailed godwits and white-fronted geese. Snipe, curlew and lapwing are common. The familiar and beautiful cry of

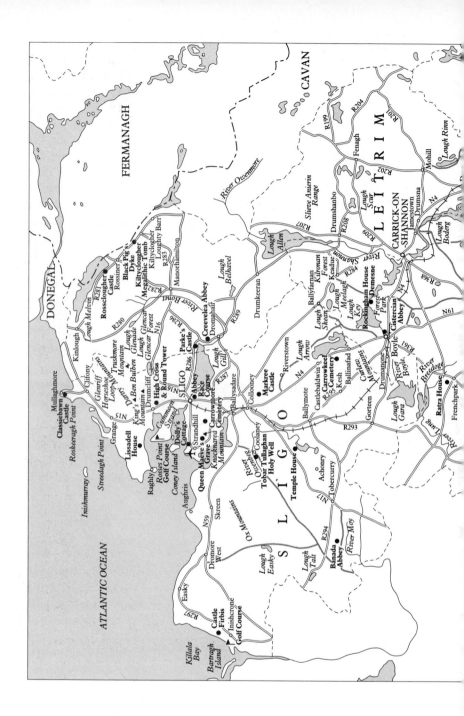

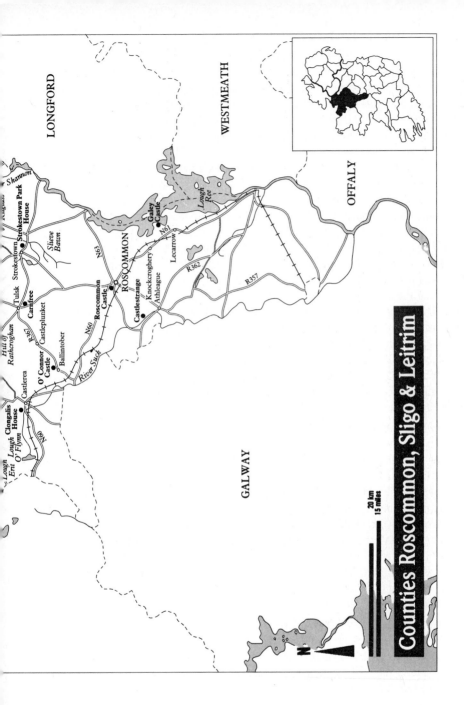

LONGFORD

WESTMEATH

OFFALY

Shannon

Strokestown Park
House

Strokestown

Slieve
Baun

N63

Galey
Castle

Lough
Ree

N6

Lecarrow

R362

R357

Tulsk

Carnfree

ROSCOMMON

Knockcroghery

Athleague

Castleplunket

Roscommon
Castle

Castlestrange

N60

Castlerea

Ballintober

River Suck

O'Connor
Castle

Hill of
Rathcroghan

Castlerea

R361

Lough
Erne

Lough
O'Flynn

Clongalis
House

N60

GALWAY

20 km
15 miles

N

Counties Roscommon, Sligo & Leitrim

the curlew, as it turns and wheels above the green fields where it has been grazing, is a sound peculiarly reminiscent of the Irish countryside.

There are many prehistoric monuments to see—burial mounds, megalithic tombs and ring-forts, and the most powerful Norman and Gaelic leaders of the medieval period built strong castles and abbeys here which have survived, although in a ruined state. The Cistercian abbey in Boyle is perhaps the most impressive, but the countryside is scattered with charming Church of Ireland churches dating from the 17th and 18th centuries which nowadays have hardly a congregation at all. The Protestant English and Scottish invaders who built these churches also planned and constructed impressive estates. The wealth of design and craftsmanship which went into making these large houses and their parks is only just beginning to be appreciated today; for years they were branded as the symbols of oppression by a race that has a long memory for wrongs and past injustices. One such great house belonged to the Kings of Rockingham, near Boyle. The house itself was destroyed by fire in 1957, but the gardens and surrounding parkland form what is now the Lough Key Forest Park. Unfortunately, the character and splendour of the place has been lost, and the park has been planted with conifer trees. You could spend a melancholy few days touring the ruined 'big houses' of County Roscommon, as you can everywhere in Ireland. The list of sad remains in this county is long: Kilronan Castle near Ballyfarnon, Mantua near Castlerea, Mount Plunkett near Athlone, Mount Talbot, Athleague, the Bishop's Palace in Elphin, and Ballanagare House in Ballanagare. Ballanagare House was built by the O'Connors, who were in pre-Norman times high kings of Ireland. Their main seat at Clonalis, near Castlerea—not a very attractive late 19th-century house—is open to the public, and houses an interesting collection of early-Irish papers and books (✆ (0907) 20014).

The other great Gaelic family of Roscommon were the MacDermotts; the head of the family was known as the MacDermott Prince of Coolavin. They survived as property-owners right up to the early-20th century. There is a lovely story about this family which illustrates the pride and interest in genealogy which is an Irish characteristic. This extract was related by Nina MacDermott, a nun who was the last MacDermott of Ramore in neighbouring County Galway. 'It is interesting,' she said, 'to learn how the status of the MacDermotts was regarded by the natives of the country. My father, when a boy of ten, was visiting his maternal grandparents at Cregg Castle. At the dinner table was an itinerant friar; they were always welcome to a meal wherever they happened to be at dinner time. He asked his host, James Blake—the Blakes were of Norman stock—who the boy was, and on being told he was a MacDermott the friar said, 'Ah, yes, the MacDermotts were princes in the land when the Blakes were hewers of wood and drawers of water.'

A very interesting house, which has survived intact, is Strokestown Park House. To visit it will uplift your spirits because its future is full of hope, with plenty of community involvement to sustain it. It was bought in 1979 by the local garage-owner in partnership with the present curator, and they have had the foresight to restore it. It also houses a small recently opened famine museum.

By air: Dublin and Shannon International Airports are 91 and 96 miles (145 and 153km) from Roscommon Town, respectively. Knock International Airport is only a few miles from Boyle, over the border in County Mayo. Ryanair flies there from several centres in the UK, and also to Galway City, which is 51 miles (82km) from Roscommon Town.

By rail: The rail link between Dublin and Sligo passes through Boyle. The Dublin-Westport-Ballina line passes through Roscommon Town and Castlerea.

By bus: Express bus services from Dublin to Roscommon Town, Strokestown, Elphin, Ballaghaderreen, Ballanagare and Boyle. Good local bus network. For details, ✆ (0902) 72651.

By car: car hire at Galway and Sligo Airports.

By bike: bicycles can be rented from Brendan Sheerin, Main Street, Boyle. ✆ (079) 62010.

Boyle, ✆ (079) 62145, May to September.

Roscommon, ✆ (0903) 26342, July and August.

Galway, ✆ (091) 63081, all year.

Late July/early August: Boyle Arts Festival, ✆ (079) 62163.

Early August: O'Carolan Harp and traditional Irish Music Festival, Keadue, Boyle, ✆ (078) 47204.

Keadue to Boyle

Keadue is near the Sligo and Leitrim borders. It is in one of the most attractive parts of the county, with the **Slieve Anierin Range**, also known as the Arigna Mountains, rising to the east. The R284 mountain road from Sligo to Ballyfarnon, further north, gives one a magnificent view over Lough Meelagh and Lough Skean. The R284 between Keadue and Ballyfarnon passes close to the edge of **Lough Meelagh**, on whose shore is an ancient church site and a holy well called Kilronan; both are associated with St Lasair and St Ronan. St Lasair was the daughter of St Ronan, who founded the original church in the 6th century. It has been twice burned down, and was last rebuilt in the 17th century. You are far away from the bustle of life in this enchanted and weed-high graveyard, and in the ruined church is a modern monument to Turlough O'Carolan, who died in 1733, and was the last in a line of harpists and poets who used to have such status in the Gaelic kingdoms. He is supposed to have composed the melody of 'The Star Spangled Banner'. He was born blind, and somehow came to the home of Mrs MacDermott Roe of Alderford, Ballyfarnan, who befriended and educated him. She provided him with a horse so that he could wander the country playing his harp at the big-house estates. He is buried in the graveyard, and to commemorate his memory the **O'Carolan Festival** is held annually in August. Traditional, folk and harp music is the basis of the festivities. Nearby, surrounded by the ash trees so sacred to the Druids in ancient times, is a lovely clear well which flows into the lough. Rosaries and rags ornament the ground, and a large rectangular stone slab, is supposed to heal those suffering from backache. The cure entails crawling under the slab, which is balanced on two other stones. A pattern (pilgrimage) is made to the well on the first Sunday of September every year.

Boyle is an attractive town, situated between Lough Key and Lough Gara. The Curlew Hills rise to the northwest and the River Boyle flows through it. The main street was once the avenue to the castle of the King family who later moved to Rockingham House (*see below*). It is now sadly dilapidated, and was used at one time as a military barracks. By the river bank is a **Cistercian abbey** (*open mid-June–mid-Sept, daily, 10–6; the key is with the caretaker in the neighbouring guesthouse for the rest of the year; adm; © (079) 62604*) in ruins, founded in 1161 and closely associated with its brother house, the great Mellifont Abbey in County Louth. It was not completed until 1218 and reflects the change of fashion from the round arches of the Romanesque period to the pointed lancet of the Early-English Gothic style. There is a mix of the different styles of arches and lavishly decorated capitals. The monastery was suppressed in 1569 and occupied by Cromwellian soldiers later on; you can see their names carved on the door of the porter's room. The Office of Public Works has cut down the ivy and done a lot to preserve the abbey. Looking onto the River Boyle is **Frybrook House** (*open April–Sept, Tues–Sun, 2pm–6pm; adm*) which has beautiful 18th-century plasterwork. It is right next to the Main Street. Another interesting 18th-century house, **King House** (entrance from the Main Street), has recently been restored and opened as an Interpretative Centre (*open May–Sept, Tues–Sun, Oct–April, weekends; adm; © (079) 63242*). It was once the seat of the Kings, who later moved to Rockingham House near Lough Key. The exhibition explores the history of Celtic chiefs such as the MacDermotts, and the 17th-century English families who ammassed huge estates.

East of the town is the great demesne of **Rockingham House**, which was burnt to a shell in 1957. Its grounds have been planted with conifers and form part of the **Lough Key Forest Park**, 4¾ miles (3km) east of Boyle on the N4 (*car park adm; © (079) 62214*). There are forest walks, a bog garden, picnic sites, a caravan and camping park, boating, fishing and cruising.

About 2 miles (3.2km) away at **Drumanone** is one of the largest dolmens in Ireland, known locally as **Druid's Altar**, which may have been a monument to someone living in the Bronze Age. You will find it beside the R294, just beyond the railway line; it is found by following a grassy lane to a railway crossing. Close by, on the waters of Lough Gara, three hundred *crannogs* (artificial islands) have been found. These *crannogs* were used by Iron Age farmers as defensive sites for themselves and their cattle. Some were in use up until the 17th century. Thirty-one dug-out wooden boats were excavated at the same time.

Around Frenchpark

Southeast of Lough Gara is **Frenchpark**, the birthplace of Douglas Hyde (1860–1949), founder of the Gaelic League and the first president of Ireland. His great cultural and social achievement was to collect stories and folklore from the peasantry. Some of the stories are at least a thousand years old, and had been transmitted by word of mouth generation after generation. They were in grave danger of being lost altogether as the use of Gaelic was declining. He was born in the rectory and retired to **Ratra House** in his old age. You pass the house as you enter Frenchpark from the direction of Ballaghaderreen on the N5 (it is not open to the public). The Church of Ireland church and graveyard in which he is buried is typical of many: a grey, simple Planter's Gothic with a garden of gravestones, flowers and grasses. It is now an Interpretative Centre (*open May–Sept, closed Mondays;* ✆ *(0907) 70016*). In the grounds of Frenchpark House is a five-chambered souterrain. Like all souterrains it is difficult to date, but was used between the Bronze Age and the 5th century AD. Frenchpark House was a beautiful house built to the designs of Richard Castle (or Cassels), Ireland's greatest Palladian architect. Its interior was dismantled in the 1950s, and the ruin demolished in the 1970s.

Six miles (9.7 km) southeast of Frenchpark is the **Hill of Rathcroghan**, a beautiful place just off the N5 going southeast to Tulsk. Rathcroghan is a flat-topped, almost circular mound of about 68yards (62m) in diameter. In the 1st century AD Queen Maeve or *Medb* (*see* **Old Gods and Heroes**, p.579) had a palace here. A little to the south of the mound is an enclosure known as the **Graveyard of the Kings**. This contains the remains of stone sepulchral chambers, and is well known as one of the three royal burial places of prehistoric Ireland—along with Kells in County Meath, and Brugh (Newgrange) in County Louth. In the graveyard is an old redstone pillar known as the **Pillar Stone of Daithi**. Daithi was a pagan king of Ireland who, according to the *Book of Leinster*, conquered Scotland, invaded the Continent and died in the Alps from a stroke of lightning about AD 428. All around in a radius of 3 miles (4.8km) forts are scattered.

Three miles to the southeast of Rathcroghan, just outside Tulsk, is **Carnfree**, the inauguration mound of the O'Connors, kings of Connacht. It is not much to look at-a grassy mound of earth and stones about 8ft (2.4m) high and 40ft (12m) in circumference; but the views are wonderful. It is reputed to be the burial ground of Conn of the Hundred Battles and the three Tuatha Dé Danaan Queens: Eire, Fothla and Banba. Here at Croghan, Queen Maeve launched her expedition to capture the Brown Bull of Ulster. It is difficult to imagine these legendary figures and this place as the seat of power, for the plain is crisscrossed by stone walls and modern farms.

Castlerea to Roosky

Off the N60, just east of **Castlerea**, a market town on the River Suck, stands **Clonalis House** (*open May–June, Sat and Sun, 2–6; 19 June–10 Sept, Sat 11–5.30, Sun 2–5.30; adm*), the ancestral home of the clan O'Connor. The family can trace itself back to Feredach the Just, a petty king in AD 75. The O'Connors produced 24 kings for Connacht, and 11 high kings for Ireland. At Clonalis, an inauguration stone not unlike the Stone of

Scone at Westminster Abbey symbolizes the O'Connors' royalty and prestige. The existing, rather ugly Victorian house was built in 1880, and the old 18th-century house is derelict after storm damage in 1961. The land itself has belonged to the O'Connor family for at least 1500 years, in spite of war and the penal laws. Besides furniture and family portraits, the house contains a unique collection of Early-Irish documents. Amongst them is a copy of the last Brehon (Gaelic) Law judgement handed down in about 1580. Also on show is the harp of Turlough O'Carolan, who composed beautiful and haunting airs, and three planxtys (lively pieces of dance music) to his O'Connor patrons.

Four miles (6.4km) southeast on Clonalis on the R367 is **Ballintober of Bridget** (named after St Bridget's Well), where there is a **ruined O'Connor castle** (*accessible at all times*) that withheld many sieges, including one by the Cromwellians. The 13th-century castle was the O'Connor's principal seat after the Anglo-Norman invasion in the 12th century until the beginning of the 18th century, when they moved to Clonalis. It is now an extensive ruin, quadrangular in shape, with towers at each corner, and two other towers defending the main entrance on the east. **Glinsk Castle**, south of Ballintober and just over the border into County Galway, is well worth a visit. (It is approached on an unnumbered road between the R364 just south of Ballymore and the R362. Turn left at the Kilcroan crossroads.) Glinsk is the shell of one of the best fortified houses in Connacht, with four storeys of mullioned and transomed windows, and stacks of chimneys, now used by the starlings and crows. Sir Ulric Burke, who died in 1708, is supposed to have built it, but its machicolated appearance suggests an earlier design. Always accessible.

Returning northeast via the R367 to Tulsk, and on the N5, is **Strokestown**. It sits at the foot of Slieve Bawn, which at 864ft (263m) is quite something in this low-lying country-side. The town is very handsome, with a wide main street laid out by Maurice Mahon (created Baron Hartland in 1800), who was impressed by the Ringstrasse in Vienna. At the eastern outskirts of the town in **Strokestown Park House** (*open 1 May–30 Sept and Bank Hols, Tues–Sun, 11–5; adm; ✆ (078) 33013*), the ancient ancestral home of the Mahon family from 1660 to 1979. Most of the house was designed by Richard Castle (Cassels) in the 1730s, but it contains both 17th- and 19th-century interiors. There is a still-room where the mistress of the house dried herbs and concocted remedies for minor illnesses. The kitchen gallery is a very unusual thing to find in Ireland. From the gallery, the mistress of the house could observe and communicate with her cooks and underser-vants without having to trail down to the kitchen herself. Apparently, weekly menus were dropped from the balcony every Monday. The nursery is full of lovely old toys, and there is an archive of documents relating to the famine years in the mid-19th century. The stables have magnificent groin-vaulted ceilings with Tuscan pillars. The house and lands were bought by the present owners intact, with all the paraphernalia of centuries. The ballroom-cum-library still has its original furniture. In the parkland surrounding the house, pheasants and sheep graze, unconcerned by the occasional car and village boys who have made it their own adventure land. A new garden has ben made within the walls of the old: pleasure gardens with a richly coloured herbacious border, yew arbours, walks and a maze. One of the most fascinating places to visit in Ireland. In the centre of Strokestown, in the former Church of Ireland church is **St John's County Heritage Centre** (*open 1*

May–30 Sept on weekdays except Mon, 10–6; weekends, 2–6; adm free; ℂ (078) 33380 for more details). The church was built in 1819, reputedly to the design of Sir John Nash, and has a fine octagonal nave. The centre has a permanent display on pagan Celtic society, the monuments of Rathcroghan, and the epic tale of the *Taín Bó Cuilgne*—the Brown Bull of Cooley. For those who want to trace their County Roscommon ancestry, the centre offers a research service. The **Slieve Bawn Co-operative Handicraft Centre**, also in the middle of the town, produces wicker baskets, tweeds, woollens and other crafts. To the east is **Roosky** on the River Shannon, where you can hire boats and go fishing on Lough Kilglass.

Around Roscommon

Roscommon is the county town and the main shopping centre of the county. It is also a popular angling resort. The dominating features of the town are the castle, the Dominican friary and the **old jail** in the Main Street. The last hangman of the jail was not a man, but a woman known as Lady Betty. She is supposed to have agreed to do this grisly job to save her own head from the noose. The Georgian **court-house**, opposite, is worth a visit. Its lovely rounded windows have

been rescued by the Bank of Ireland. In the 8th century St Coman founded a monastery here from which the town gets its name, but there is nothing left of it today. South of the town centre, off Abbey Street, is the ruined **Dominican friary** founded by Felim O'Connor, king of Connacht in 1253. His tomb is sculptured with figures representing gallowglasses—the fierce warriors from the west of Scotland who were hired by the Irish kings to fight the Norman and English invaders.

Roscommon Castle, north of the town off Castle Street, was built in 1269 by Roger d'Ufford, Lord Justice for Ireland. Four years later it was razed to the ground by the Irish, built anew, and taken again by the O'Connors in 1340, who held it for more than two hundred years. It is a typical Anglo-Norman fortress, quadrangular, with a tower at each angle, and one on each side of the gateway. It began to fall into decay in the last years of the 17th century. It is always accessible. The **Roman Catholic church of the Sacred Heart** off Abbey Street is built of local cut limestone and was completed in 1925. Over the main door are lovely glass mosaics constructed by the famous Italian firm of Salviati & Co. It also has a replica of the famous processional Cross of Cong, made in Fuerty in 1123 of oak decorated with animal designs in bronze gilt. Five miles (8 km) to the west of Roscommon on the R366 is the village of **Fuerty**, with the remains of a Franciscan church in which at least a hundred priests were massacred in Cromwellian times by a Colonel Ormsby. The colonel, who is buried here, was known as *Riobard na nGligearnach* (Robert of the jingling harness), whose cruelties are still remembered in local stories. Between Fuerty and Athleague, on an unnumbered road by the River Suck is the **Castlestrange** demesne. The house is a ruin, but under some trees is an Iron Age boulder known as the Castlestrange Stone. This is egg-shaped and covered in whorls and spirals, which seem to have been potent ornamental symbols and were often used in the pre-Christian Celtic La Téne style. The land is privately owned, but it is unlikely that anyone will object to you visiting it.

The N61 from Roscommon to Athlone stays close to the Lough Ree, but not close enough to get a proper look at it. If you cut down a small country lane to **Galey Castle**, just beyond Knockcroghery village, you will see the island of Inishcloraun in Lough Ree, where the legendary Queen Maeve retired to ponder on her eventful life and to find some peace (*see* **Old Gods and Heroes**, p.579). She used to bathe in a clear, fresh pool here, but an enemy pursued and killed her with a stone.

From **Lecarrow** another minor road leads you down to the **Castle of Rindown** (*always accessible*), a great fortress in the 13th century, with a rectangular keep within curtain walls. In the shelter of its stone walls a medieval village grew up along Norman lines. A defensive ditch was built across the peninsula on which it was built, and it became one of the bases for the conquest of Connacht. Now it is an ivy-covered ruin and place of peace, for hardly a soul wanders down the mile-long peninsula.

Shopping

Crafts: The Old Barrel Store, The Quays, Carrick-on-Shannon; ✆ (078) 20911. The Bastion Gallery, 6 Bastion Street, Athlone, ✆ (0902) 94948. Naomh Padraig Handcrafts, Cloonshee, Strokestown, ✆ (078) 37077.

Mainly rush baskets. Timepieces, Main Street, Roscommon, ✆ (0903) 25408. Clocks, jewellery and crafts.

Activities

Fishing: coarse fishing on the River Suck and its tributaries at Glinsk, Castlecook, Ballygar and Ballyforan. Also on Errit Lake, Hollygrove Lake, and in the Ballyhaunis area, Eaton's Lake, and Lakehill Lake. Fishing for brown trout on the upper stretches of the River Suck, River Derryhipps, and on Lake O'Flynn, a 600-acre (242ha) limestone lake. Contact W. T. Wynne, Main Street, Boyle. Two other contacts happy to help with fishing information are Mr Fitzpatrick, ✆ (079) 62444 and Brian Flaherty, Carrick Road, ✆ (079) 62053, who can also supply tackle, bait and a ghillie.

Golf: Boyle Golf Club, ✆ (079) 62594. Roscommon Golf Club, ✆ (0903) 26382.

Horse-riding: Munsboro Equestrian Centre, Munsboro Lodge, Sligo Road, ✆ (0903) 26449.

Boat trips: on Lough Key, during the summer only. Rowing boat hire from Mr Walsh, ✆ (079) 67037.

Horse-racing: on Roscommon Town course in April, May, June, Aug, Sept and Oct.

Where to Stay

moderate

The **Abbey Hotel**, Roscommon, ✆ (0903) 26240. Attractive Georgian building with only 20 bedrooms, and bathrooms en suite. Pyers and Marguerite O'Connor Nash, **Clonalis House**, Castlerea, ✆ (0907) 20014. An opportunity to stay with the descendants of Ireland's last High Kings. Victorian Italinate house on lovely wooded estate. Shooting and fishing can be arranged.

inexpensive

Mrs A. Harrington, **Glencarne House**, Ardcarne, Carrick-on-Shannon, ✆ (079) 67013. Very close to Lough Key Forest Park, a fine Georgian farmhouse with comfortable rooms and lovely old furniture. Well-cooked meals. The Burke Family, **Riversdale House**, Knockvicar, near Boyle, ✆ (079) 67012. Another period farmhouse in the middle of the country, with its own lake and river fishing.

self-catering

Large modern house on outskirts of Boyle. Five bedrooms. From IR£200 a week. Contact Mrs Candon, **Abbeyvilla**, Carrick Road, Boyle, ✆ (079) 62249. Mrs Candon will help with all kinds of local accommodation queries. Converted Mews house on Clonalis Estate. Four bedrooms. Contact Mrs O'Connor-Nash, **Clonalis House**, Castlerea, County Roscommon, ✆ (0907) 20014. From IR£140, top-season.

Eating Out

expensive

Abbey Hotel, Abbeytown, Galway Rd, Roscommon, ✆ (0903) 26240. 18th-century house with excellent French-style cooking. Cromleach Lodge, Lough Arrow, Castlebaldwin, ✆ (071) 65155. Set in the hills above Lough Arrow and in County Sligo, although close to Boyle. Traditional, hearty Irish cooking. *Dinner only.*

moderate

The **Royal Hotel**, Bridge Street, Boyle, ✆ (079) 62016. Coffee shop serves salads and casual lunch, and the restaurant serves more exotic fare. The **Royal Hotel**, Castle Street, Roscommon, ✆ (0903) 26317.

inexpensive

The **Crews Inn**, Roosky, ✆ (078) 38017. Extensive bar menu and a proper restaurant with plain cooking. **Maloney's**, Boyle. Good for a quick pub lunch. The **West Deli**, Castle Street, Roscommon, ✆ (0903) 25382. Soups, salads, hot main dishes. *Open until 7.* **James Clarke**, Patrick Street, Boyle. Traditional pub selling delicious Irish coffee.

County Sligo

Writing in the 19th century about her tour of Ireland, Mrs S. C. Hall dismisses Sligo in a few words with these lines: 'in scenery and character it so nearly resembles the adjoining county of Mayo that we pass over Sligo'. Nothing could be further from the truth. Sligo is somehow civilized, unlike the other counties in Connacht: there is order among the lakes and the glens, the great table mountains and open beaches.

From an artistic standpoint, Sligo is W. B. Yeats (1865–1934), just as Wessex is Hardy, for there is hardly a knoll or stream which did not stir his imagination. His brother Jack (1871–1957) uses paint instead of words to capture the faces of old men at the Sligo races, or the special quality of light which bathes the figures on the beaches. This light is very like that which plays around the coast of Brittany. Jack is always quoted as saying, 'Sligo was my school and the sky above it', and it was William Butler Yeats' wish that he should be buried under 'bare Ben Bulben's head'. All the places which inspired W. B. Yeats are still largely untouched; they are brought to your notice occasionally by discreet Bord Fáilte notices which quote the name and the line from the poem in which they are mentioned. The two brothers became intimately bound up in Sligo through their maternal grandparents, the Pollexfens, who were millers and small shipowners. They used to spend their school holidays with them, travelling from London where their father, John, tried to earn a living as a portrait painter.

The two Yeats brothers occupy such an important part in the artistic and literary history of Ireland in the early 20th century that one can hardly do justice to them in a guide book. Suffice to say that, if you obtain a copy of William Butler's collected poems, and make sure you visit the county museum to see the paintings by Jack, you will know why.

Besides being so beautiful, Sligo is famous for its traditional music, especially fiddle music, for fishing and for its prehistoric remains. It is easy to reach from Dublin by rail or road (133 miles/212km), and it has its own flourishing airport. The people are mainly sheep- and cattle-farmers. The climate is similar to the rest of Ireland; and it has that wonderful light which bathes all of the west coast of Ireland.

Sligo is fabulously rich in archaeological remains. In the vicinity of Carrowmore there is a huge cemetery with tombs dating from the Mesolithic and Neolithic Stone Ages. Close by is the romantic Knocknarea Mountain, crowned by Maeve's Cairn, one of the highlights of a Sligo tour. The cairn is traditionally believed to have been built for the legendary Queen Maeve or *Medb* around the time of Christ. Yet archaeologists believe that within the cairn there may be a passage tomb similar to that at Newgrange, County Meath, which was built by Stone Age farmers about 3000 BC. Ring-forts and *crannogs* (lake dwellings) are spread over the county and date from the Bronze Age. (At this time, the local king or chief-tain would have lived in the fort and ruled over a small area. There were no towns, and cattle were highly prized. So it is understandable that the epic story of the *Taín Bó Cuilnge*, in which Queen Maeve plays such a central part, should describe a war over a bull; *see* p.229) When the Christian monks established themselves in the 6th century, they built their churches within such forts, although the petty kings later granted them separate lands on which to build their monasteries. In the 12th century, the monastic system gave way to the bishoprics and dioceses of the Roman hierarchical system. A diocese was linked to the size of the petty Celtic kingdom whose king was usually closely related to the bishop of the area. Thus dioceses of today hark back to Celtic Ireland before it was shired by the English. Incidentally, the reforms of the 12th century coincided with the arrival of the architectural style of the Romanesque, as can be seen still at the ruined Abbey of Ballisodare.

History

The chief Gaelic families of Sligo were the O'Haras, O'Connors and O'Dowds, and, as the Anglo-Normans did not reach Sligo until the mid-13th century, these families continued with their own private quarrels and territorial struggles. When the Normans did arrive, in the persons of the Fitzgeralds and the Burkes and their followers, they failed to maintain their grants of land. Therefore, up until the early 17th century, the Celtic culture and native Behon laws continued to function alongside the English administrative structure.

From 1585 onwards there was a gradual change in land ownership, and in the Celtic order of society. Elizabethans and, later, Cromwellian soldiers were granted lands, which in numerous cases were unoccupied church lands, or lands which had never been perma-nently settled before. The population of Ireland was very small at that time, and many of the farmers moved their cattle from one pasture to another. Of course, some tribal lands were confiscated and granted to new settlers, but on the whole, English families settled into Sligo fairly peacefully. The names Phibbs, Crofton, Perceval, Ormsby, Parke, Irwin, Gore, Jones and Cooper date from these times. You can stay with the O'Haras at Coopershill House, or with the Percevals at Temple House; each family represents a strand in Sligo's history. Today their descendants farm the land, and keep up their wonderful houses by opening them up as guest houses.

Sligo Town was badly sacked and burned in the 1641 Rebellion, and later was held for the Jacobites in the wars of the 1690s. The whole county suffered terribly during the famine of the 1840s. Thousands died or emigrated to the New World, and this struck the death knell for the peasant Gaelic culture which had survived the vicissitudes of the centuries since the English invaded. The Gaelic tongue ceased to be the everyday language of the peasants, and many of the folk stories and traditions would have been lost forever, if it had not been for enthusiasts and antiquarians such as Lady Gregory (1852–1932) and W. B. Yeats. They and others collected much folk material and later, in 1904, she, Yeats and J. M. Synge (1871–1909) set up the Abbey Theatre, which produced many Irish sagas and is still the premier theatre in Dublin. In Sligo you can enrol in the Yeats Summer School, which has as its theme his poetry, plays and prose, and his historical background; plus Irish myths, legends and the history of the Abbey Theatre (*see* 'Summer Schools' in **Practical A–Z**). In the 18th and 19th centuries Sligo Town was a large port. Its industries were distilling, brewing, linen manufacture, milling, rope and leather-making. The famine hit the economy very hard, and it took years to recover. Today, the county is prosperous, with most people working in the agricultural industry.

Getting Around

By air: Sligo Airport (Strandhill) offers a daily service to/from Dublin during the week.

By rail: daily service from Dublin on weekdays and Sundays.

By bus: Expressway buses operate daily between Sligo and Dublin, and all major provincial towns. Local bus services link the villages of Inniscrone, Tobercurry (or Tubbercurry). For details contact Sligo Bus Station, © (071) 60066.

By bike: The Raleigh Rent-a-Bike network operates in the county. Your local dealer is Conway brothers, High Street, © (071) 61370.

Tourist Information

Sligo, Temple Street, © (071) 61201, all year.

Tobercurry (or Tubbercurry) has a tourist information point in Killoran's Restaurant.

Inniscrone has a tourist information point at Maughan's in the centre of the village.

Festivals

Late August: Fleadh Cheoil na Eireann, Traditional Music Festival, Sligo Town. Contact Comhaltas Ceoltoiri Eireann, © (01) 280 0295 or (071) 41148.

Spring: Western Drama Festival, Tobercurry. Contact Sligo Tourist Office or St Brigid's Hall, Tobercurry.

Sligo is the largest town in the northwest of Ireland. It has a great deal of colourful charm, and a feeling of centuries-old importance and prosperity. People come from their farms in the countryside to shop, socialize, go to the cinema or theatre, and to attend the large hospital. The town centres around two bridges over the River Garavogue. There are attractive 18th-century buildings, and some more rather ugly 20th-century office blocks, hotels and supermarkets. The streets are always busy and quite congested with traffic, so it would be wise, if you have a car, to park it in the car park off Wine Street. Fennigan's Pub in Wine Street has been modernized and spoilt, but if you want a good jar before or after your explorations of the town try **Hargadon's** in O'Connell Street. This is an old-fashioned pub with cosy snugs, old Guinness advertisements and mirrors which are decorated with painted gold slogans of whiskey and Guinness.

In the **Anglican cathedral** in St John Street, designed by Richard Cassels, is a brass memorial to Susan Mary Yeats, the mother of William and Jack. The cathedral itself dates from the 14th century, and has been restored several times. It is a cruciform shape, in the perpendicular style, with a huge tower. The **Catholic cathedral**, made out of local limestone, is next door. This Romanesque building has a beautiful high altar, and a fine peal of bells. It was completed in 1874. **Sligo Abbey**, a graceful ruined Dominican priory off Abbey Street, was founded in 1252, but was rebuilt in the 15th century after being burnt. It then suffered the usual fate of Irish monasteries, and was destroyed by the Cromwellians. The abbey ruins have been tidied up, and some conservation work has been carried out by the Office of Public Works. Inside are monuments to the local Gaelic nobility, and some very fine cloisters. The tower and the cloister, the east window and the high altar were added in the 15th century. The key to the abbey is available at any time from the caretaker; directions to his house are on the entrance gate. **Sligo Town Hall** and **Courthouse** were erected in the late 19th century, and you can visit them in the course of an interesting walking route devised by and available from the tourist office in Temple Street. On every weekday morning during the summer there is a conducted walking tour, also from the tourist office. As you wander, one of the things you may notice is the shabby backyards of the houses sloping down to the River Garavogue, although the owners of the shops and pubs in the streets have made an effort to retain and look after their handsome Edwardian fronts.

You can easily spend a delightful couple of hours in the **Municipal Art Gallery** housed in the County Library building in Stephen Street. The custodians are charming and interested in their subject, and the collection of pictures by Jack Butler Yeats, Paul Henry, Nora McGuinness, Sean Keating and others is inspiring. The **Sligo County Museum** (*open all year; © (071) 42212*) in the building attached to the library has exhibits of prehistoric interest, and items on folk life and the Anglo-Irish war of 1919–1921. It also has a special section on the Yeats family—W. B., his brother Jack, and sisters Lily and Holly. At one time they set up a publishing press and started different cottage industries. W. B. Yeats won the Nobel Prize in 1923 and this is proudly displayed. The **Sligo Art Gallery**

(© *(071) 45847*) at Hyde Bridge, holds impressive travelling art shows by national and international artists. It also contains papers and books of special interest to Yeats' scholars.

The town is lucky in having a large municipal park bordering the River Garavogue. **Doorly Park** has some lovely walks with wonderful views of Lough Gill and the mountains. Inside the park is **Sligo Race-Course**, where races take place in April, June and August. In the evenings during the summer, Sligo Drama Circle put on plays in the Town Hall every Tuesday and Thursday, usually by Irish playwrights. The **Hawk's Well Theatre and Conference Centre**, beside the tourism centre in Temple Street, puts on entertainments of all kinds throughout the year. Attractive hand-thrown pottery is sold in the **Sligo Craft Pottery Workshop** in Market Yard.

One of the highlights of a tour of Sligo is a boat ride, to watch the pretty wooded lake scenery of Lough Gill pass by. You depart from Riverside in Sligo town, in a fully covered all-weather boat. The trip takes 2½ hours, and what is most appealing is that at various places en route the poetry of W. B. Yeats is recited. It cannot fail to impress in such a lovely setting. Many of his poems refer to places on Lough Gill, one of the most famous being 'The Lake Isle of Innisfree'. The boat stops for 30 minutes at the Lake Isle Craft Shop, and you can buy tea or coffee and snacks here. It is of course possible to drive right around Lough Gill, taking the R286 to Dromahair in County Leitrim and then the R287 until it joins the N4 going back into Sligo Town. Do not neglect to go round **Parkes Castle** (*open June–mid-Sept, daily, 9.30–6.30; adm*), a fine example of a fortified manor house of the Plantation period. It has been restored beautifully and overlooks Lough Gill on the R286, just a couple of miles before Dromahair. There are also boat rides on the lake from Parkes Castle, as well as Dooley Park (*see* listings).

Strandhill to Carrowmore

If you take the R292 going west of Sligo Town, after 3 miles (4.8km) you come to **Strandhill**, a popular sea resort. It has too much concrete and consequently is not very attractive, but the strand is superb. The hard sand stretches for miles and the waves are good for bodysurfing. Huge sand dunes dominate the shore to the southwest of the seafront car park; and you might find beach pebbles with interesting fossil remains. Just as you enter Strandhill on the R292 is **Dolly's Cottage** (*open during July and Aug, daily, 3–5, all day on Wednesdays; adm*), a typical example of an early-19th century rural dwelling. It consists of a few rooms simply furnished, a mudfloor and a thatched roof.

From every direction in this area you can see **Knocknarea Mountain**, topped by its cairn. To climb this, continue along the R292 for a few miles and take the little road marked Glen, which ascends the lower slopes of Knocknarea Mountain. (You will know if you have gone too far because just beyond the turn off for the Glen road is a restaurant called Glen Lodge.) From the Glen road, you get a lovely view of the hummocky green fields down to the shore. You will come to a farm, where it is possible to leave your car, as long as you are tactful and polite. The walk to the summit (1978ft/603m) is along a track of curiously moulded limestone, with orchids and primroses growing either side. The cairn itself is 33ft (10m) high by 197ft (6m) wide, a huge mound of weather-beaten stone. It is reported to be the burial place of Maeve (*Medb*), the Queen of Connacht, who challenged the forces of Ulster to a legendary battle over a bull (*see* **Old Gods and Heroes**, p.579). The story is contained in the *Táin Bó Cuilgne*, the longest and most important of the Ulster cycle of heroic tales. The origins of the Tain are ancient, and pre-Christian, although it was actually written down by monks in the 12th century. Queen Maeve herself is thought to have lived around the time of Christ, but the cairn may well be Bronze Age. As yet, no one has excavated it, probably because it would be very expensive to undo its massive structure, and it would be sad if they did.

If you continue on through the crossroads at Knocknarea Church, and instead of rejoining the R292 take the turn southeast, you will be on the right road for **Carrowmore**, about 3 miles (4.8km) further on. This amazing megalithic Stone Age cemetery spreads over many small fields; the excavated burial chambers contain cremated remains dating from 3000 BC. There are circles, passage graves and dolmens; each one has a little notice warning that it is a national monument, but unfortunately since the 19th century over a hundred passage graves and dolmens have been destroyed, and only 40 remain.

Heading back towards Sligo town you see **Cummeen Strand**, which stretches up to Rosses Point. This expanse of sand and water is mentioned in Yeats' poem 'Red Hanrahan's Song', and here the River Garavogue flows into the sea. You can walk or drive out to **Coney Island** from the Strandhill side when the tide is out. Coney is supposed to have given its name to the New York pleasure island. A few people live on it, and the beaches surrounding it are tranquil. You will be able to watch wild duck and waders, and during the winter months Brent geese feed on the mud flats. The island has a convivial pub.

Rosses Point to Glencar

Rosses Point, a seaside village and resort, is 5 miles (8km) north of Sligo, reached by following the R291 along the curving arm of Sligo Bay. The village is long and straggling, with plenty of pubs and places to eat. It has a first-class golf course, which is used for the West of Ireland Amateur Open Golf Championship every year during the Easter weekend. At **Dead Man's Point**, the yacht club and an open-air swimming pool are a hive of activity and colour. The point owes its name to a foreign seaman who was buried rapidly at sea because the boat had to be away before the tide changed. He slid into the water, accompanied by a loaf of bread in case he was not yet quite dead! During the summer, pleasure boat trips around Sligo Bay go daily from Rosses Point pier.

A trip to **Glencar** is a very pleasant excursion if you are staying in Sligo Town. Leave Sligo on the N16 for Manorhamilton, and after about 10 miles (16km), a left-turn will signpost you to Glencar Waterfall. The road takes you along the edge of Glencar Lough, and steep-sided mountains rear up against the sky. The Differeen River feeds the lough whilst the Drumcliff River runs out the opposite end. This spot is well thought of by salmon and sea trout anglers. A small car park marks the path to Glencar waterfall, which drops 49ft (15m) and is very impressive after heavy rains. In Yeats' poem 'The Stolen Child', he talks of the Glencar pools 'that scarce could bathe a star'. Unfortunately the pools now have a concrete path, but are still very beautiful with a noisy stream and a mass of rhododendrons.

Drumcliff to Lissadell House

If you follow the N15 northwards towards Donegal you will find yourself, after 5 miles (8km), in **Drumcliff**, an ancient Christian monastic site which still has the remains of the old monastic enclosure, and a fine 10th-century high cross carved with biblical scenes. The road divides the site in two with the cross on your right and the stump of a round tower on the left. The graveyard of the Church of Ireland church, also to your right, contains the burial place of W. B. Yeats (*see* below).

St Columba founded a monastery at Drumcliff in the 6th century before sailing away to Iona. Colourful stories have grown up around the lives of all Irish saints, which have no historical foundation. The following is one such story.

Among saints, St Columba seems to have been the *enfant terrible*, for whilst a guest of St Finian he borrowed a psalter and secretly copied it out. Finian found out and said that the copy should be his, but Columba refused to hand it over. The high king was asked to settle the dispute and he ruled in favour of Finian, saying that just as every calf belongs to its cow, so every copy belongs to the book from which it is made. St Columba did not accept the king's judgement and gathered an army. He fought the king and won, but with the loss of three thousand lives. Columba's friend, St Molaise of Inishmurray, advised him to leave Ireland for ever, as a penance, and convert as many people as he had caused to die. (For more about St Columba, or Colmcille, *see* p.119.)

W. B. Yeats' great-grandfather was the rector of the simple Protestant church built at Drumcliff in Georgian times, and the poet is buried in the graveyard here, under his beloved Ben Bulben. He has a very plain headstone with his own epitaph 'Cast a cold eye on life, on Death/Horseman, pass by'. In Yeats' Tavern across the road they serve very good Guinness.

Just past Drumcliff to the west, an unnumbered road via Carney leads you to **Lissadell House** (*open June-mid Sept, daily except Sun, 2–4.15; adm; © (071) 63150 for more details*), its grounds swallowed up in Forestry Commission conifers. The house is the home of the Gore-Booths, a family who came to Sligo during the early 17th century. Like many of the Irish gentry, the Gore-Booths were great travellers and worked all over the British Empire. They brought home all sorts of weird and wonderful things, and Lissadell is a rich repository of furniture, pictures and books. Sir Robert Gore-Booth built the house during the troubled years which culminated in the famine of the 1840s. He mortgaged the estate to help the poor during the famine. His son, Sir Henry, sailed to the rescue of the Arctic explorer Leigh Smith. The following generation included Eva and Constance, both of whom were great friends of W. B. Yeats, who stayed in the house frequently during the second decade of the 20th century. Constance married a Polish artist and became Countess Markievicz. She also became deeply involved with the struggle for Irish independence. Having won a seat for the Sinn Fein party, she, like the rest of them, refused to take up her seat in Westminster, and sat instead for the Revolutionary Parliament called the Dail Eireann as the minister for Labour.

These are W. B. Yeats' reflections on past and present memories of the Gore-Booth sisters:

> *The light of evening, Lissadell,*
> *Great windows open to the south,*
> *Two girls in silk kimonos, both*
> *Beautiful, one a gazelle.*
> *But a raving autumn shears*
> *Blossom from the summer's wreath;*
> *The older is condemned to death,*
> *Pardoned, drags out lonely years*
> *Conspiring among the ignorant.*
> *I know not what the younger dreams-*
> *Some vague Utopia—and she seems,*
> *When withered old and skeleton-gaunt,*
> *An image of such politics.*
> *Many a time I think to seek*
> *One or the other out and speak*
> *Of that old Georgian mansion, mix*
> *Pictures of the mind, recall*
> *That table and the talk of youth,*
> *Two girls in silk kimonos, both*
> *Beautiful, one a gazelle.*

The building is in plain Georgian style, with a cavernous porch. It is in a lovely situation looking onto the sea, Knocknarea and Ben Bulben, but it is also very large and a little run down; it takes courage to try and keep it going. In the centre is a two-storey hallway lined with Doric columns leading to a double staircase of Kilkenny marble. Downstairs in the vast kitchen; you can have tea and coffee, made under conditions reminiscent of the 1920s. There is no drinking-water or electricity in this part of the house, and buckets of water have to be lugged down the stairs.

The forestry lands around Lissadell House have picnic sites and in the winter months you may be lucky and see skeins of barnacle geese wheeling in the sky, as there is a huge colony of them here. The two south-facing beaches which border the forest are reported to be the warmest in the county.

Raghly to Gleniff Horseshoe Scenic Drive

The road past Lissadell continues left towards the tiny fishing harbour of **Raghly**, which is surrounded by stunning views of Drumcliff Bay and the mountains all around. On the way there you will pass **Ardtermon Castle**, a 17th-century ruin, built as a semi-fortified manor house by an ancestor of the Gore-Booths. It is privately owned, and has been restored. Continuing along the coast on this tiny unnumbered road, you will see, on your left, **Knocklane Hill**. This was the site of a Celtic promontory fort, and a martello tower built as a lookout post in the uncertain times of the Napoleonic era. It is a short and exhilarating climb to the top of the hill, and on a fine day you will be rewarded with views it would be difficult to surpass. The beaches along this stretch of coastline are very isolated, and there is much bird-life. Sand used to cover much of the headland until bent grass was sown in the 19th century by Lord Palmerston, the British prime minister. **Ellen's Pub** at Maugherow, which is signposted along this road, is a tourist attraction with its thatched roof and traditional music sessions. The beach at **Streedagh**, signposted to the left, has magnificent sand dunes, and the limestone rocks contain fossil coral formed about four million years ago.

All around the coast are wrecks of the warships of the Spanish Armada. 'The Rock of the Spaniards', just north of Streedagh, was the place where in 1588 three Armada ships foundered. Contemporary accounts tell us that 1100 bodies were laid out on the beach at a time, and that most who reached the shore were stripped and killed. The storms and fierce gales that batter this part of the coast keep the vegetation low and stunted, but the glancing light is beautiful.

It is not surprising that the people of **Inishmurray**, 4 miles (6.4km) off the coast, abandoned their lands and houses in the 1950s, for life here was very hard. Inishmurray used to be famous for its brand of poteen. Now it is famous for the Early-Christian relics which have survived: beehive huts, small rectangular stone oratories, open-air altars, pillars and tombstones are dotted all over the island. The **monastery**, in the middle of the island, was probably built on a Druidic site, for one of the oratories is known as the Temple of Fire, and round about are quite a few stones thought to be used in Druidic rituals and known as cursing stones. After the Vikings struck in AD 807, the monks left and the islanders took over the old monastic buildings; one oratory became the men's chapel, and another the women's. Trips out to the island can be organized easily throughout the summer months (*see* 'Activities', p.306).

In **Grange**, a village just to the left of the N15, you can watch craftsmen hand-cut crystal at **Sligo Crystal Factory**, located a little to the right as you join the main road again.

North of Cliffony, a rock peninsula projects into Donegal Bay. Its sandy beach has encouraged the growth of the small resort of **Mullaghmore**. On the headland here you will see a Victorian Gothic castle—**Classiebawn**, once the home of Earl Mountbatten of Burma. This place became the tragic focus of world attention when in 1979 Lord Mountbatten, and members of his family and crew, were killed when his boat was blown up by the IRA in the bay below. The house is not open to the public.

Return to the N15, and at the hamlet of **Creevykeel** by the crossroads, stop for a look at the court tomb which is regarded as one of the finest in Ireland. It consists of a circular ritual court bounded by upright stones. Opposite the entrance are two burial chambers under a lintel which date from between 3500 and 3000 BC. Cross over the N15 and continue for 5¾ miles (9km) along the unnumbered road leading to Ballaghnatrillick Bridge. Cross the bridge and take the right-hand turn onto the **Gleniff Horseshoe Loop** road. The road runs into the heart of the Dartry Mountains with their tumbling streams and desolate, grey limestone cliffs. A left-turn off here takes you to Truskmore Mountain, which rises to 2115ft (645m). From the car park for the RTE transmitter station, a short walk takes you to the top, and a wonderful view of the surrounding countryside. Close to the summit are the entrances to Ireland's highest caves. These form part of an ancient underground system truncated by the glacier that formed the Gleniff valley. One of these caves is supposed to be where Diarmuid and Grainne slept when they were fleeing from the wrath of King Fionn MacCumhail. Diarmuid and Grainne are the Irish equivalent of Tristan and Iseult: every cave, dolmen and cromlech seems to be named after them (*see* **Old Gods and Heroes**, pp.576 and 578). From here, you can follow the loop road to Cliffoney and back on to the N15, or turn left along the old route and rejoin the N15 at the Mullaghnaneane crossroads.

West Sligo

Inniscrone to Tobercurry

The western parts of County Sligo make up a variety of handsome seascapes, mountainous bogland and pretty lakes. The coastal stretch has been developed for holiday-makers, whilst the mountains behind are wild and relatively unexplored. The R297 branches off the N59 between Sligo and Ballina in County Mayo and meanders through the villages along the coast. **Inniscrone** (also known as Enniscrone) is a holiday resort on Killala Bay with a long, sandy strand ideal for bathing. It has a marina, with berths for yachts, and deep-sea fishing boats for hire. There is an excellent bath-house offering salt-water seaweed baths, and steam baths in your own little wooden box; it's a luxurious and very relaxing experience and there is a nice tea-room attached. The 18-hole golf course is beautifully situated overlooking Bartragh Island. The pier and breakwater provide excellent fishing and bird-watching, and there is lovely walking country up the Moy estuary to Ballina. At the north end of town in ruins is **Nolan's Castle**, an early-17th century semi-fortified manor house.

This area is dotted with the ruins of castles, some of which have rather romantic associations. **O'Dowd's Castle**, 3 miles (4.8 km) to the south of Inniscrone, is one such ruin. The story is that one of the O'Dowds captured a beautiful mermaid and stole her magic cloak, and so was able to change her into a mortal woman. She bore him seven children, but always longed to return to the sea. When she at last regained her cloak, she changed back into a mermaid, took her children to a site called Cruckacorma, in Scurmore close to the castle, and transformed them into pillar stones. She then returned to the sea. The pillar stones are actually on a tumulus, and are known locally as the Children of the Mermaid. Two miles (3.2km) north of Inniscrone is **Castle Firbis**, the ruined stronghold of a family well known for their poetry and annals. The MacFirbis Clan were the hereditary poets and historiographers to the O'Dowds between the 14th and 17th centuries. They had a school of learning here and many important manuscripts were compiled. The most important to survive are *The Yellow Book of Leacan* (*c.* 1391), now in Trinity College, Dublin; *The Great Book of Leacan*, compiled between 1416 and 1480, now in the Royal Irish Academy, Dublin; and *The Book of Genealogies of Ireland*, compiled between 1585 and 1671, and now in the University College, Dublin. One of the last MacFirbis scribes was employed by Sir James Ware (1594–1666) to prepare transcripts and translations from the Gaelic for him. Sir James Ware, an antiquary and historian, was responsible for preserving

and collecting valuable historical material on Gaelic Ireland. As a member of parliament, and the auditor-general for Ireland, he was in a good position to help native Celts like the MacFirbis clan.

Easky is a fishing village 8 miles (12.9km) from Inniscrone on the coast road. The village is guarded by two martello towers, built to raise the alarm if Napoleon tried to invade. It is famous for its surfing waves in winter, and it has become something of a surfer's hangout, although there are other water sports facilities. Two miles (3.2 km) east on the R297, by the roadside is the split rock also known as **Fionn MacCumhail's Fingerstone**. This is said to have been split by MacCumhail's sword (Irish heroes always have superhuman strength), and is very impressive. It may, in fact, have been created in the Ice Age. Legend tells that the rock will close on anybody who dares to pass through the split three times!

From Dromore West, the R297 road joins the N59. Take the mountain road, signposted on the left, along a scenic route to Easky Lough. If you continue on into the Ox Mountains, just after the hamlet of Moss Hill you can turn right for Gleneask and **Lough Talt**. The views in this wild and isolated country are fabulous, and it is possible to walk between Lough Easky to Mullaney's Cross. Ask in the local tourist office for the *Irish Walks Guide 3, Northwest*, by Simms and Foley, which details this route. The R294 traverses the region and leads to the market town of Tobercurry (*see* below). Just before you reach Tobercurry at **Banada** is the ruin of **Corpus Christi Priory**, beautifully situated on the River Moy. The priory was the first Irish house of the Augustinian Friars of the Regular Observance, founded by the O'Haras in 1423.

Skreen to Coolaney

Another lovely route can be taken into the Ox Mountains from **Skreen**, which is a tiny little place just off the N59 between Ballysodare and Dromore West. It is worthwhile to stop off at the **Church of Ireland graveyard** to see the carved box tombs which date from between 1774 and 1866. The Black family tomb is a masterpiece of carving, on the northside it shows a ploughman in a top hat, tail coat, buckled shoes guiding a plough. The west end has a cherub's head and a skull and crossbones carved in high relief. The minor road leads you past tumbling streams and grand mountain scenery, past Lough Achtree and on to the scenic route signposted 'Ladies Brae'. New afforestation has changed the face of the mountains: the subtle browns, greens and purples have given way to the standardized green of the sitka spruce and lodgepole pine. But the skies and the shapes of the mountains are still magnificent, and the forests will one day yield a good cash-crop. As you journey closer to Coolaney, the road runs close to the Owenboy River, which makes a very pleasant picnic spot. And as you enter **Coolaney**, you might notice the Pack Horse Bridge which has many arches, but is in a very bad state of repair with several trees growing up in it.

Just outside Coolaney, about 1½ miles (2.4km) east on an unnumbered road leading to Collooney, is the **Holy Well of Tobar Tullaghan**, also known as Hawk's Well. This tranquil place used to be a place of pilgrimage for many; during the medieval period it was regarded as one of the Wonders of Ireland, apparently gushing forth fresh water at one time and salt water at another. It is still thought that the water in the well ebbs and flows with the tide. Close to Collooney and just off the N4 is **Markree Castle**, which was until very recently an example of a huge and derelict Gothic-style pile. Now Charles and Mary Cooper, who ran an excellent restaurant in the neighbourhood, have opened the castle as a hotel, and it has been beautifully restored. This is an especially satisfactory state of affairs because Charles Cooper is a descendant of the Coopers who acquired the estate in the 17th century. The castle was built in 1802, when the 18th-century house was transformed by the designs of Francis Johnston (1760–1829). Johnston was the architect of many famous buildings in Dublin, including the GPO. The owners will probably tell you that Markree was used as the setting for the ramshackle Majestic Hotel in the TV series *Troubles*, but that is all it has in common with the place!

Aughris to Ballysodare

The coastal stretch between Ballysodare and Skreen is very pretty, and it is fun to visit the little fishing harbour of **Aughris**, to walk around Aughris Head, and have a jar in the Beach Bar, which is famous for its Saturday-night traditional music sessions. The bar has been very badly modernized, with space invaders and the like, but you can admire the views from a cosy bench outside. The cliff ledges of Aughris Head hold the nesting places of many different bird species, and Dunmoran Strand to the east is a lovely sandy beach. **Ballisodare** is a bit of a thoroughfare for traffic leaving Sligo Town for Ballina, but it has the remains of a pre-Romanesque church and a 7th-century monastery founded by

St Feichin of Fore in County Westmeath. The church overlooks the wooded edge of Ballisodare Bay. Close by is the ruin of a 15th-century church which is almost buried in rubble from the quarry. By the bridge on the Dublin Road is **The Thatch**, a well-known traditional music pub.

South Sligo

Around Tobercurry

Tobercurry (also known as Tubbercurry), is a busy market town which holds the **Western Drama Festival**. The local drama group organizes one-act plays in autumn and three-act plays in spring. The festival is very well thought of for the quality of the productions, and the range of different styles and interpretations. The town is also a good centre for anglers, being close to Loughs Gara, Key, Arrow, Easky and Talt. Brown trout, pike and perch are the usual catches. Another excellent fishing centre to the north is **Ballymote**, which also has a ruined square Norman **castle** (*always accessible*) which was used as a major defensive post up until the 1690s. You get to it through the car park of the St John of God's Nursing Home near the railway station. Whilst you are in the area, you could take the opportunity to stay in the intriguing 18th-century **Temple House** situated off the N17 about 5 miles (8km) to the north. This is a great stone pile of a house, kept alive by the enthusiasm, enterprise and energy of its owners, who are also organic farmers. Close by is **Achonry**, an Early-Christian monastic site in a very ruined state which boasts a Church of Ireland cathedral, the **Church of St Nathy**. It dates from 1823, and to its east side are the ruins of a 15th-century church with a lofty square tower.

Gorteen to Lough Gara

To the south of Tobercurry is the village of **Gorteen**, which is recognized by traditional music-lovers as the centre of the distinctive Sligo flute-and-fiddle style. Sometimes you can hear the evocative airs and dancing tunes at the **Traditional Restaurant** and the **May Queen** in the centre of the town. Impromptu dancing may start up, which is the greatest fun. On the R294 2 miles (3.2km) southeast of Gorteen at the Mullaghroe crossroads overlooking Lough Gara, is a 16th-century square stone castle consisting of a walled enclosure with six square towers, and the remains of a curtain wall. It was the stronghold of the O'Garas, a ruling Gaelic family of that time. Fergal O'Gara was a patron of the monks who compiled the *Annals of the Four Masters* between 1623 and 1626. The annals are an important source of much of Ireland's history, and the monks who compiled them had to move from safe house to safe house between County Donegal and County Leitrim because of the troubled times. Lough Gara itself is set with many tiny islands, some of them man-made crannogs which were inhabited by Iron-Age farmers. In the winter it is possible to see many species of duck, white-fronted geese and whooper swans.

Keshcorran to Carrowkeel

To the northeast, over wooded and boggy lands, is the summit of **Keshcorran**, from which there are fantastic views of the surrounding countryside. (You can get there by travelling cross-crountry on the minor road from Mullaghroe to Kesh. Just before you get to Kesh you cross the R295 running between Ballymore and Boyle.) Keshcorran has many caves on its west face, all associated with legendary characters such as Cormac MacArt, the wise and generous high king who ruled over the heroes of the Fianna (*see* **Old Gods and Heroes**, pp.576 and 577). On Garland Sunday (the last Sunday in July), locals still gather by the caves for prayers and chat, in a tradition that stretches back thousands of years to celebrations in honour of the Celtic God Lug. Close by on a hill-top of the Bricklieve Range are the Bronze-Age **passage graves of Carrowkeel**. You reach these via an untarred mountain road, just off the N4 between Castlebaldwin and Ballinafad, which takes you round the base of the hill-top on an approach from the northwest for a couple of miles (3.2km). The burial chambers were obviously elaborately planned, set in round cairns and commanding panoramic views of the now relatively treeless landscape. The cruciform passage graves have narrow passages and are roofed with large lintel stones, whilst the larger chambers are roofed with corbelled stone.

County Sligo has many interesting archaeological remains that possibly link up with the mythological stories of Ireland's past. The great and legendary battle between the Fomorians and the Tuatha Dé Danaan, which is related in the *Book of Invasions*, or *Lebor Gabala*, is reputed to have taken place near here, and it is said the slain were buried here. Fourteen cairns are located on the spurs of promontories but there is also a 'village' of 14 clochans or beehive huts. It is possible to enter a few of the tombs, one of which is lit up by the setting sun on the longest day of the year. This is in contrast to the great passage tomb at Newgrange in County Meath, which is lit by the sun at sunrise on the shortest day of the year. If you wish to stay in this area, there is a beautiful Georgian country house called **Coopershill**, near Riverstown. It is a fine 18th-century mansion of attractive grey stone, furnished with well-loved and beautiful period furniture.

Shopping

Wool: Mullaney Bros, O'Connell Street, Sligo Town, for tweeds and cashmeres. Dooney's, O'Connell Street, Sligo, ✆ (071) 42274, for stylish hand-knits for men.

Pottery: in Market Yard, Sligo Town.

Books: of Irish interest from Keohane's, Castle Street, Sligo Town.

Crafts: Lake Isle Craft Shop, Innisfree. The Cat & the Moon, 25 Market Street, Sligo, ✆ (071) 43686, for pretty handicrafts and jewellery.

Crystal: Innisfree Crystal, Collooney, ✆ (071) 67340.

Delicacies: Tír na nóg, Gratton Street, Sligo Town, ✆ (071) 62752, for fresh vegetables, Irish cheeses, seaweed, herbs, shampoos and soaps. N. Woodeson, Coolenamore, Strandhill, ✆ (071) 68127, sells oysters wrapped in seaweed from the house. Telephone first. Gary's, 34 Market Street, Sligo Town, ✆ (071) 43564, for wild salmon, other fish and fruit. Gourmet Parlour. Bridge Street, Sligo, ✆ (071) 44617. Ballymaloe-trained. Delectable chocolate cakes and breads. Also do catering. Cosgrove's, 32 Market Street, Sligo. Old-fashioned deli crammed with goodies. Farmhouse cheese and breads from the Weiland's at Ballycastle, Cliffoney. For lovely German cheesecakes, call in advance, ✆ (071) 66399.

Uileann pipes: made by Charles Roberts, Creagadoo, Glencar, ✆ (071) 43967.

Activities

Fishing: coarse and game fishing on the Owenmore River and the lakes in its system, which produce marvellous pike, bream and rudd. Advice from the Ballymote and District Angling Club, Ballymote. Tackle and advice from Rogers', Main Street, Ballymote; and Barton Smith, 4 Hyde Bridge, Sligo Town. The sister river of the Owenmore, the Owenbeg, is known for its sea trout, as is Glencar Lough. Contact the Sligo Anglers Club, Sligo, ✆ (071) 42356.

Sea angling: from the shore at Inniscrone Strand, Inniscrone Pier, Easky Quay, Kilrusheighter Strand, Mullaghmore Peir, Mermaids Cove and Milk Haven. Angling boat hire from Jim Byrne, Alpine Hotel, Inniscrone, ✆ (096) 36144/36252; and Colm Ridge, Rosses Point, ✆ (071) 77244.

Pony-trekking: Horse Holiday Farm Ltd, Grange; ✆ (071) 66152. Besides pony hire on a daily basis, there are also 7- to 14-day trail rides through the mountains and along the magnificent coastline. You stay in B&Bs en route or, with a more expensive package, in country-house hotels.

Horse-racing: Sligo Race-course April, June to August.

Hunting: with the Sligo Harriers. Contact Mrs Siberry, Glen Cottage, Knocknahur, Sligo, ✆ (071) 68369.

Walking: Several walks are detailed in *The Irish Walk Guide 3*, Northwest by Simms and Foley, for sale in local bookshops and at the Sligo tourist office.

Golf: County Sligo Golf Club, Championship Links Course, Rosses Point, ✆ (071) 77134. Inniscrone Golf Club, Inniscrone, ✆ (096) 36297. A high-quality course amidst magnificent scenery.

Seaweed bath: Kilcullen's Bathhouse, Inniscrone, ✆ (096) 36238. Open Easter to October, during weekends in winter. An unmissable experience.

Surfing: at Easky, Enniscrone and Strandhill.

Boat trips: on Lough Gill from Parkes Castle, Dromahair or Doorly Park, ✆ (071) 64266. For cruiser hire on the lough, contact the Blue Lagoon Bar, Sligo, ✆ (071) 42530/45407. For weekend cruiser hire, contact Frank Armstrong, 14 Riverside, Sligo, ✆ (071) 41462.

Excursions: to Inishmurray Island. Contact Rodney Lomax, Mullaghmore; ✆ (071) 66124 or Mr McAllion, Rosses Point, ✆ (071) 42391. The boat goes out between April and October.

Where to Stay

expensive

Markree Castle, Collooney, ✆ (071) 67800. County Sligo goes in for rather grand country houses. This castle with its impressive castellated façade has three interconnecting reception rooms which are wonderfully grand, with tall mirrors and Louis Philippe-style plasterwork dating from 1845. The castle has been sympathetically restored by the owners, Charles and Mary Cooper, who built up a reputation for skill in creating imaginative food and a pleasant ambience at their Knockmuldowney Restaurant, now part of the hotel. All the rooms are very comfortable with private bathrooms, and the views over the surrounding countryside are superb. The lovely formal gardens lead down to the River Unsin. **Coopershill House**, Riverstown, ✆ (071) 65108. This Georgian mansion set in its own wooded parkland contains the most delightful aspects of a gentleman's residence. Large spacious rooms are filled with beautiful furniture and books, and warmed by crackling log fires. The bedrooms contain a fourposter-bed, a table to write at, and fragrant soaps in a cosy connecting bathroom. Everything is kept in tiptop shape. **Cromleach Lodge**, Castlebaldwin, ✆ (071) 65155. Delicious dinners and breakfasts and charming views over Lough Arrow.

moderate

Temple House, Ballymote, ✆ (071) 83329. A huge and rambling mansion which was made even grander in the 1860s by a nabob ancestor of the present occupants. It has a lovely, slightly faded Victorian feel, with original half-tester beds in huge bedrooms, ancient curtains and oriental *objets d'art*. The Perceval family are committed to organic farming; and their breakfasts are particularly delicious; don't miss the porridge! Boats are available to fish for pike and perch on Temple House Lake. Shooting for woodcock, snipe and duck on the estate can be arranged. Please be aware that Sandy Perceval is chemically sensitive, so scented cosmetics and perfumes should not be worn. **Glebe House**, Collooney, ✆ (071) 67787. Simple, comfortable rooms and delectable home-cooking French-style, using herbs and vegetables from the garden.

inexpensive

Mrs Carter, **Primrose Grange House**, Knocknarea, ✆ (071) 62005. This farmhouse was built as a charter school in the 18th century, and has a splendid situation overlooking the glen and the sea. The owners have won an award for their delicious breakfasts. Stuart Family, **Hillside**, Kilsellagh, Enniskillen Road, Sligo, ✆ (071) 42808. Friendly and comfortable old farmhouse, home cooking and log fires. Mrs Hill-Wilkinson, **Ross House**, Riverstown, ✆ (071) 65140. Comfortable and friendly farmhouse accommodation. Good for children as there is lots of activity on the farm. Gemma Healy, **Urlar House**, Drumcliffe, ✆ (071) 63110 Old fashioned farmhouse with 5 bedrooms, two en suite. **Tolen Lodge**, Culleenamore, Strandhill, ✆ (071) 68387. Faces the sea with Knocknarea in the background. Great food.

White Hill Hostel, Markievicz Road, Sligo, ✆ (071) 45160. Cottages to rent by Sligo Bay. Contact Charles Henry Ardtarmon, Ballinfull, ✆ (071) 63156. From IR£150 per week.

Eating Out

expensive

Knockmuldowney Restaurant, Markree Castle, Collooney, ✆ (071) 67800. Delicious food, an excellent wine list, and relaxed and friendly service in an impressive and atmospheric early-19th-century castle. **Reveries Restaurant**, Rosses Cromleach Lodge, Castlebaldwin, ✆ (071) 65155 Michelin rated.

moderate

Glebe House, Collooney, ✆ (071) 67787. Delicious and homely French cooking, with lots of herbs and vegetables from the garden. It is necessary to book in advance. **Truffles**, 11 The Mall, Sligo, ✆ (071) 44226. Tasty and imaginative pizzas, such as pizza with seven Irish cheeses. Very popular locally, although only open evenings. **Bistro Bianconi**, 44 O'Connell Street, Sligo, ✆ (071) 41744. Pasta and pizza to take away or eat in. Pleasant modern interior.

inexpensive/cheap

Hargadon's, O'Connell Street, Sligo, ✆ (071) 42974. Atmospheric old pub with cosy snugs and lunchtime pub fare. **Kate's Kitchen**, Market Street, Sligo. Deli selling salads and sandwiches to take away.

Entertainment and Nightlife

Theatre: The Hawkswell Theatre, Sligo, ✆ (071) 61518/61526, show some revivals and contemporary Irish theatre.
Music: Traditional music in the Trades Club, Castle Street. Tuesdays and Thursdays, 9.15, during the summer.

County Leitrim

Leitrim is a very individual county, with a secret, forgotten feel to it; a good place for a quiet holiday. The region is long and narrow with a foothold in the sea, stretching back to mountains, hills and streams. It is divided in two by Lough Allen, one of the many lakes of the Shannon river. It shares the beauty of Lough Gill and Lough Melvin with County Sligo, and has countless lakes of its own. The conversation in hotels and bed and breakfast places will invariably be about fishing. The lakes, by all accounts, are teeming with bream, pike, perch, salmon and trout. The renovation of the 19th-century Ballinamore and Ballyconnell canal provides the link between the Shannon and the Erne. Cruisers will be able to travel for 470m (750km) along tranquil inland waterways. Ballinamore, Leitrim and Keshcarrigan have fully serviced moorings.

If you are a walker and anxious to be alone, the mountains around Manorhamilton are full of wistful beauty; you will pass the remains of many deserted cottages on the slopes where only sheep and cattle graze. The people of Leitrim are mainly small-farmers, and the land has attracted quite a few outsiders or 'blow-ins', who are keen to own a smallholding and try organic methods to produce crops. Trees seem to thrive here, and the district immediately north of Lough Allen is planted with conifers. The county south of Slieve Anierin is covered by a belt of drumlins. These teardrop-shaped hills were left behind by retreating glaciers, and are composed of gravel debris. Most of the Leitrim boundary with County Roscommon to the west is formed by the River Shannon, as it winds through boggy fields and scrublands.

History

Before the county was 'shired' in around 1585 by Elizabethan administrators, it was known as West Breffni. The principal family or sept of this area was O'Rourke, whose members lived around the tiny settlement of Leitrim. In the centuries leading up to the Anglo-Norman conquest the O'Rourkes were continually involved in dynastic struggles for the high kingship of Ireland. In the 12th century, Tighernan O'Rourke was allied to Rory O'Connor, the high king. Dermot MacMurragh, the King of Leinster wished to be high king. A struggle began. MacMurragh raided Breffni in 1152, and stole Devorgilla, O'Rourke's wife. This led to the banishment of MacMurragh in 1166, and the coming of the Normans in 1169 to help him win his kingdom back. For Ireland, it was the beginning of a long and traumatic relationship with England. However, Breffni was hardly affected by the Normans, who kept to the south, and the Gaelic system under the lordship of the O'Rourkes lasted until Elizabeth I mounted her conquest of Ireland. Brian O'Rourke, the chieftain of the time, was one of the few Irish recorded who tried to rescue some of the Spanish sailors wrecked off the Sligo-Leitrim coast after storms drove the 1588 Armada onto the rocks. In reprisal he was taken prisoner and hung at Tyburn in 1590. His son, known as Brian of the Battleaxes, fought endlessly against the English, and joined in the Nine Years' War against the Elizabethan Conquest with the Ulster Lords O'Neill and Red Hugh O'Donnell. Their defeat at the Battle of Kinsale in 1601 spelled the end of their power; and the O'Rourke estate and castles were handed over to English and Scottish planters. The names Hamilton, St George, Harrison, Gore and Clements date from that time.

The Gaelic system took a long time to break down. Turlough O'Carolan, the famous blind harper, composer and poet (1670–1783) lived in Mohill for a while, succoured by the Gaelic system of patronage, and welcomed into the houses of peasants and gentry with his music. The Irish people everywhere still spoke Gaelic and remained fervent Catholics, which set them far apart from the new colonialists. The 1798 Rebellion bought bloodshed to Leitrim as the peasants joined in the French General Humbert's march to Ballinamuck, County Longford, from County Mayo. Many of them were slaughtered. The potato famine and emigration took its toll in the 1840s. By 1851, the population had dropped from 155,000 to 43,000. Today the population is about 28,000. One of the heroes of the Irish struggle for independence came from Leitrim. Sean MacDiarmada (1884–1916), who was born in Kiltyclogher, was one of the seven signatories of the proclamation of the republic in Easter Week 1916. He was court-martialled, and executed in May 1916.

Getting There and Around

By air: Carrick-on-Shannon is three hours from Dublin Airport.

By rail: Carrick-on-Shannon has a rail link with Dublin. There are three daily services during the week, and two on Sunday.

By bus: Expressway buses link Carrick-on-Shannon with Dublin and there is a good local network. Details from Sligo Bus Depot, ✆ (071) 60066.

By car: Car hire from Westward Garage, Strokestown, County Roscommon, ✆ (078) 33029.

By bike: The Raleigh Rent-a-Bike network operates in the county. Your local dealer is Gerharty's, Main Street, Carrick-on-Shannon, ✆ (078) 21316.

Tourist Information

Carrick-on-Shannon, Bridge Street, ✆ (078) 20170, May to September.

Sligo, ✆ (071) 61201, all year.

Festivals

Mid-June: An Tostal, Drumshanbo. Dancing and traditional music; one of the best, ✆ 078 41013.

August (usually): Wild Rose Festival, Manorhamilton. Beauty competitions, traditional music, floats and general entertainment.

North Leitrim

Around Manorhamilton

Manorhamilton is situated at the meeting of four valleys in a setting of steep limestone hills and narrow ravines. It was founded by Sir Frederick Hamilton whose fine 17th-century mansion is now a ruin cloaked in ivy overlooking the town. It is a good place to stop and explore the various roads that spiral out from it. You can take a boggy little road signposted right, a few miles down the main road to Belcoo (N16). It leads to some cashels or stone forts, known as **Tallyskcherny**, built about 500 BC; in the misty morning light they looked mysterious and remote; with only a pheasant's cry of alarm breaking the silence. The land around here belonged to the O'Rourke chieftains who took part with O'Neill and O'Donnell in the last great rebellion of the Irish nobility against Elizabeth I in the last decades of the 16th century. North of Manorhamilton, the Bonet Valley narrows towards the source of this pretty river into an equally pretty lake, the **Glenade**. This is a superb example of a glacial valley. The R280 runs beside its waters which are thickly edged with trees. The hills are high in the east, and to the west a line of crags rise from the grassy slopes. The road slopes down to **Kinlough**, a neat little village on Lough Melvin only 3 miles (4.8km) from the sea. If you want to taste the delights of **Bundoran**, a highly developed seaside resort in Donegal, it is only a few miles further on. The many-islanded

Lough Melvin extends for 8 miles (12.9km), and a scenic road follows its southern side from Kinlough to Rossinver. A sign by the road points to **Rossclogher Abbey and Castle**. The small ruined abbey was founded by St Mella, whilst the deserted castle was a stronghold of MacClancy, a sub-chieftain of the O'Rourkes. In 1588 nine survivors of the Spanish Armada took refuge here. You have to leave your car or bicycle and walk over long grass to reach both buildings, but it is worth it, for the view of the lough is superb. Notice the line of rushes, probably an underwater causeway, going out to the castle, which is on a little island or crannog. The abbey is easy to wander around, but you have to cross shallow water to reach the castle, and it is easiest viewed from the shore.

At **Rossinver**, at the head of the southern end of the lake, are to be found the remains of a church, and a monastery of St Mogue which dates from the 6th century. The church itself is 13th century and there is a holy well nearby. Modern gravestones look out of place in the graveyard. The road south to Kiltyclogher passes over the ancient earthwork called the Worm Ditch or the **Black Pig's Dyke**, which extends intermittently from Bundoran in the west to Newry in County Down. It was probably built by the Scotti, people who lived in the north between 300 and 200 BC, to prevent encroachment from the south. Legend as usual tells a much more colourful story: the ditch was formed by the slithering of a huge serpent over the land; or if it was not a serpent, then it was a monstrous pig that snuffled and rooted around, throwing up the earth as it went.

In the centre of **Kiltyclogher** village stands Albert Power's statue of Sean MacDiarmada who was executed for his part in the 1916 uprising. The cottage where he was brought up is a short distance away in the townland of Corranmore (*open to the public*). Follow the R283 to a rock at **Laughty Barr** where people used to go to hear Mass during the times of the Penal Laws. Signposted from the road is Kiltyclogher megalithic tomb, a court cairn built between 2000 and 1500 BC, and known locally as **Prince Connell's Grave**. From Manorhamilton to Sligo there is a lovely valley in which lies **Glencar Lough and Waterfall**; the spray when it is in full spate would soak you in seconds on a windy day. Yeats wrote a poignant poem about this place, called 'The Stolen Child'. There are always ballad sessions in the local lounge bars, but the big event in Manorhamilton is the **Wild Rose Festival** in August, which has music, dancing and other fringe events.

Around Dromahair

Dromahair is a very pretty village, about 8 miles (12.9 km) from Manorhamilton, through which the River Bonet flows until it gets to Lough Gill. The road N16/R286 from Manorhamilton has the most beautiful views of Lough Gill, and in the wooded country around (approached from the R286/R287), are the ruins of **Creevelea Abbey,** founded in 1508 by Margaret, wife of Owen O'Rourke. The abbey has a pretty pillar with a carving representing St Francis talking to the birds in a tree. The branches and roots of the tree grow in Celtic patterns. In the middle of the town are the sparse remains of **Breffni Castle**, stones from which were used to build another mansion, known as the Old Hall, beside it in 1630. The old castle was the chief stronghold of the O'Rourkes and it was from here that in 1152 Devorgilla, wife of Tighernan or Tiernan O'Rourke, eloped with Dermot MacMurragh at the age of 44. But she regretted her action, for Dermot turned out to be even crueller than Tiernan, and one day she slipped back to be reconciled with him. Her elopement was the turning point in the history of Ireland, for it eventually led to the flight of Dermot MacMurragh from Ireland, and his alliance with Henry II which resulted in the Anglo-Norman invasion of Ireland.

On the scenic R286 round Lough Gill, on the way to Sligo, there are plenty of lay-bys where you can park and look out over the water to the many islands. Following this route, you pass the 17th-century **Parke's Castle** (*open 2 June–mid-Sept, 9.30–6.30 daily; adm*), a fine example of a planter's insecurity. The manor house was well fortified against the Irish, and is surrounded by high bawn walls with picturesque turrets and steep sloping roofs. It has been restored and contains a permanent exhibition which provides information on many of the monuments in the area. An excellent audio-visual show is available, as are guided tours. From Dromahair, take the R289 which joins the R280 for Drumkeeran and Drumshanbo. This road twists through hills, past Lough Belhavel and Lough Allen. From now on the emphasis is on fishing, and along the roads you will notice signposts naming the various lakes and the sort of fish you are likely to catch. Lough Allen is noted for its large pike. Fish over 30lb (13.6kg) are not uncommon. There is good bream fishing from the banks of the 20 lakes within the 5 mile (8km) radius of Drumshanbo. **Drumshanbo** is a tidy and well-kept town. In mid-June it hosts an annual festival which celebrates Irish music and singing. Many people come to pray here at the enclosed community of Poor Clare Sisters. The Slieve Anierin range, or Iron Mountains, dominate the landscape. Iron was mined here two hundred years ago, but the industry ceased when the timber in the neighbourhood, which was the source of fuel for the smelting furnace, was used up.

South Leitrim

Carrick-on-Shannon was always an important crossing place but during the plantation of Leitrim in the reign of James I it was fortified and garrisoned to protect the new settlers. It is the county town and the centre of river cruising on the Shannon. It is a pretty place with very good fishing-tackle shops, a marina, hotels, pleasure crafts and countless river cruisers. Within 6 miles (9.6km) there are 41 lakes, and fishing is free and unrestricted. Many coarse fishermen make it their base for fishing up and down the Shannon. Worth a look is the **Costelloe Memorial Chapel**, which is the second smallest chapel in the world. Erected by Edward Costelloe in 1877 in remembrance of his wife. Both are now buried there, in crumbling coffins, which are visible through glass in sunken pits at either side of the entrance. If you feel a little spooked, you can always drop into Armstrongs next door, which sells drink amongst all the shoes and jumpers. It looks like nothing has changed here since Edward Costelloe passed away. Following the N4, just over the border into County Roscommon, you will come to the **Lough Key Forest Park** (*open all year, and has a restaurant and mooring facilities for boats; car park adm*). The park is very beautifully laid out, with bog gardens and nature trails, and there are boat trips on the lake. Still following the N4 towards Dublin, you keep close to the Shannon and pass through **Jamestown**, founded in the reign of James I. The next village of interest is **Drumsna**, which is on a hill overlooking the Shannon. The river scenery is lovely. When the Shannon was used for transporting produce, Drumsna was quite an important trading centre. Anthony Trollope lived here for some time and wrote his novel *The MacDermotts of Ballycloran*.

Dromod and **Roosky** are pretty little villages on the edge of the Shannon. Roosky has fine berthing facilities for river cruisers. If you retrace your steps to Dromod and take the R202 to **Mohill**, you come into drumlin country-a place of little hills whose hollows are filled with lakes. Mohill is a favourite angling centre. Between Mohill and Dromod, 6 miles (9.6km) off the N4 Sligo–Dublin road, on the shores of Lough Rinn, is a lovely estate which was once owned by the earls of Leitrim. The Victorian walled terraced gardens of **Lough Rynn House** are very attractive, and tours are available over the whole estate, which has many beautiful walls, redwoods and rhododendrons, as well as 600 fishable acres (243ha) of Lough Rinn (*open end May–mid-Sept; adm; ✆ (078) 31427 for more details*). The estate was rescued by an American, Mike O'Flaherty, who saw it advertised in a real estate office in the USA, flew over, and bought it. **Fenagh**, up in the hills, has the ruins of two medieval Gothic churches. They are all that remain of the monastery St Columba founded and which, under the rule of St Caillin, his close friend, became internationally famous as a school of divinity. This is a lovely lake-starred area where you can fish to your heart's delight. Close to the little village of **Drumcong** on the R210, on an island in Lough Scur, is a ruined Elizabethan castle which in the past was often attacked by the O'Rourkes of Breffni. Above the lough is **Sheebeg**, a small hill with a prehistoric mound on its summit. It is one of the many resting places attributed to the legendary Fionn MacCumhail. On the road (R202) back to Carrick-on-Shannon is the sister hill of Sheemore, which also has a pre-historic cairn, and a huge cross to mark Holy Year 1950. Both are easy to climb.

Shopping

Delicacies: Co-op Shop, Main Street, Manorhamilton. Eden Plants and Herbs, Rossinver, ✆ (072) 54122, sells an astonishing range of fresh herbs and vegetables.

Activities

Coarse fishing: local contacts include Sean Fearson, ✆ (078) 20313, or Jim Dolan, ✆ (078) 20014.

Fishing: tackle and information from Conroy's, Roosky, Carrick-on-Shannon; and The Creel, Main Street, Carrick-on-Shannon, ✆ (078) 20166.

Cruiser hire: Athlone Cruisers, Jolly Mariner, Athlone, ✆ (0902) 72892. Emerald Star Line, 37 Dawson Street, Dublin 2, ✆ (01) 6718870. Carrick Craft, P.O. Box 14, Reading, RG3 6TA, England, ✆ (0734) 422975 or (078) 20236. Tara Cruisers, Rosebank Marina, ✆ (078) 20736. Riversdale Barge Holidays ✆ (078) 44122. Shannon-Erne Waterway Holidays, ✆ (079) 67028.

Pony-trekking: Horse Holiday Farm Ltd, Grange, County Sligo, ✆ (071) 66152.

Walking: Cairns Hill Forest Park, near Dromahair.

Golf: at Bundoran Golf Club, ✆ (072) 41302.

Where to Stay

expensive

Cromleach Lodge Country House, Castlebaldwin, ✆ (071) 65155. Just over the border in neighbouring Sligo. Beautiful views over Lough Arrow, excellent traditional cooking.

moderate

The **Bush Hotel**, Carrick-on-Shannon, ✆ (078) 20014. Solid Irish cooking. Small, friendly and central.

inexpensive

Agnes Harrington, **Glencarne House**, Ardcarne, Carrick-on-Shannon, ✆ (097) 67013. Although just over the border in County Roscommon, this solid stone farmhouse is only 3 miles (4.8km) from Carrick-on-Shannon. Your hostess is an excellent cook, and has a good eye for attractive objects and furniture. The Thomas Family, **Riversdale**, Ballinamore, ✆ (078) 44122. Edwardian farmhouse with light and spacious rooms, good home-cooked food, and delightful hosts. They also run Riversdale Barge Holidays, so you can take a trip up the newly opened Shannon–Erne Waterway. The farmhouse base has an indoor swimming pool and squash court. Maloney Family, **Glebe House**, Ballinamore Road, Mohill, ✆ (078) 31086. 19th-century rectory. Fishing and riding can be arranged and there's a pony for the children. Minimum stay 2 nights. Mrs McGowan, **Drummond House**, Glencar, ✆ (072) 55197. Dogs welcome. Mrs Dee, **Ard-na-Greine House**, Carrick-on-Shannon, ✆ (078) 20311. Modern house with fresh clean rooms. Home-cooking. **Stanfords Village Inn**, Main Street, Dromahair, ✆ (071) 64140. Traditional Irish bar with bottles stacked high to the ceiling, hard stools and a cosy fire. Well away from the 'crack' in the bar are comfortable, clean bedrooms.

Eating Out

moderate

Maguire's Cottage, Drumshanbo, ✆ (078) 41033. Friendly restaurant with open fire and traditional furnishings. Big helpings, steaks, prawn cocktail, salads. *Evenings only.* **Glenview**, Ballinamore, ✆ (078) 44157. Restaurant as part of a B&B. Lovely setting beside the Woodford river. *Call in advance.*

inexpensive

Stanfords Village Inn, Main Street, Dromahair, ✆ (071) 64140. Cosy Irish pub with a simple restaurant overlooking a garden. Set dinner. **Cryan's Pub**, Riverside, The Bridge, Carrick-on-Shannon. Basic pub lunches. The coffee shop next door sells quiche and pizza. **Lough Rynn Estate Restaurant**, Mohill, ✆ (043) 23320. Chips and snacks. *End April to mid-September.*

The Province of Ulster

The Ulster border has meant much through the ages: *Cú Chulainn*, the Hound of Ulster, was perhaps its most famous guard when he defended it against the host of Ireland during the epic battles of the Brown Bull of Cooley. It is interesting to contemplate how myth and history support each other over this enmity between North and South. Irish archaeologists have just concluded that a great earthen wall was built two thousand years ago to separate Ulster (*Ulaidhstr*: Land of the Ulstermen) from much of the South of Ireland. It consisted of two pairs of double ramparts—the largest of which was 90ft (27m) wide, 18ft (5.5m) high and 1½ miles (2.8km) long, and formed part of a defensive border along the line of the upper reaches of the Shannon River. It is thought that the wall was built by tribal rulers in central Ireland as a defence against the warlike tribes of Ulster: to prevent two of the major fords across the Shannon, at Drumsna and Carrick in County Leitrim, being used by Northern invaders. The Drumsna wall cuts off a loop of the Shannon and is broken only by an entrance complex which formed a huge gateway into tribal territory—probably the Kingdom of Connacht. Another earthwork, built in the third or second century BC and known as the Black Pig's Dyke, stretches intermittently from Donegal Bay to the Dorsey and Newry Marshes in the east. This time the defence was built by the Ulstermen against the Southerners. It is likely that the two earthworks reflect different stages in the armed conflict between these two major prehistoric tribal groupings. It may even be that the legendary Connacht Queen Maeve or *Medb* built the Carrick and Drumsna defences during the great battles over the Brown Bull of Cooley.

The Northern Ireland you will see today has suffered most in the towns from the last 25 years of the 'Troubles'. This has paradoxically brought about planned and attractive public housing and public buildings for the most part. The countryside is as beautiful, and perhaps more accessible than anywhere else in Ireland because of the development of forest parks and guardianship of bodies such as the British National Trust. The North is also different because it was industrialized during the 19th century and so endured the more ugly stages of capitalist development, while Southern Ireland is trying to pull itself out of its agriculturally based economy and build factories now.

Having said all that, the visitor should not ignore Northern Ireland, thinking it is a foreign country within Ireland, because it certainly is not. One great plus point for the North is its teeming lakes and rivers. Coarse fishermen find nothing like it anywhere else in the British Isles. The vast majority of Northen Irish people are friendly, hard-working, witty and very kind. The North and the South, as the two states of Ireland are colloquially referred to, co-operate in many areas, especially the arts and tourism. A major example of this co-operation has been the reopening of the 19th-century Ballinamore and Ballyconnell canal that links the Shannon and Fermanagh lake systems. It fell into disuse over a hundred years ago, and its restoration has been funded by both governments, the EU and the International Fund for Ireland.

The six counties which make up the North are Antrim, Armagh, Down, Fermanagh, Londonderry and Tyrone. They are included in the ancient province of Ulster together with Cavan, Monaghan and Donegal.

History

Some experts on the Irish race maintain that in ancient times the North was full of Picts and the South full of Milesians—another Celtic tribe from Spain whose invasion is recorded in the ancient manuscript the *Lebor Gabala*, or *Book of Invasions*. They probably arrived a couple of centuries BC. What is more sure is that later, in the 17th century, Ulster was the most systematically planted province, because of its continued fierce resistance to the English. Thus the hardy Scots were introduced into the province to provide a loyal garrison.

The sign of Ulster is the Red Hand. This symbol is the result of the race for the overlordship of Ulster between the Gaelic MacDonnells and the Norman de Burghs, in the 12th century. The first to reach land would take the prize and as the two contestants struggled through the shallows off the Antrim coast, MacDonnell, fearing that de Burgh, who was leading the race would win, cut off his own hand and threw it far onto the strand where it lay covered in blood. Thus the symbol of this fair land is oddly prophetic of the many bloody struggles for its conquest.

The two great clans of the west are descended from the sons of the great high king of Ireland, Niall of the Nine Hostages (AD 379–405). Their names were Conal and Eoghan and they gave their name to districts in this part of the province: Tyrconnell and Tyrone. When Brian Boru, the great high king of the 11th century, instituted surnames in Ireland, the followers and descendants of Conal and Eoghan took the names O'Donnell and O'Neill respectively, and it was they who rebelled against English rule.

County Fermanagh

This is the lakeland of Ireland, bounded with limestone mountains in the southwest and scattered with drumlins which speckle the lakes with islands. A third of the county is under water: the great lake system of the Erne with its mass of lakelets in the upper lough, and the great boomerang of lower Lough Erne. Then there are the two Lough MacNeans in their mountain fastness, which together with the county's share of Lough Melvin have until recently discouraged incoming populations, so it is a place of long-lasting traditions and folklore. Even today, few strangers settle in this area, although the lakes attract summer visitors.

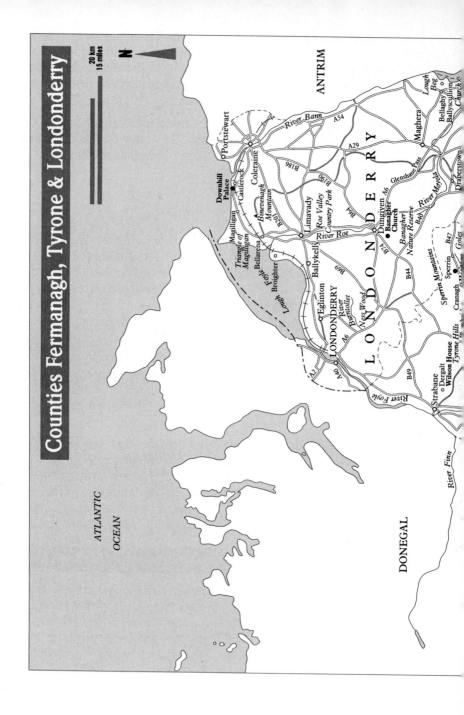

Counties Fermanagh, Tyrone & Londonderry

20 km
15 miles

N

ATLANTIC
OCEAN

DONEGAL

ANTRIM

Lough
Beg

Bellaghy
Ballyscullion
Church

Maghera

Draperstown

River Bann

A54

A29

B186

B190

B64

Glenshane Pass

River Moyola

Portstewart

Coleraine

Downhill
Palace

Castlerock

Binevenagh
Mountain

B201

Dungiven

Banagher
Church

A6

Banagher
Nature Reserve

B47

Magilligan

Triangle of
Magilligan

Bellarena

Limavady

Roe Valley
Country Park

River Roe

Ballykelly

B69

Sperrin

Cranagh

Sperrin Mountains

Goles

Foyle

Lough Broughter

Ballykelly

Ness Wood

LONDONDERRY

Eglinton

River
Burntollet

B44

B49

A6

A2

Strabane

Dergalt

Wilson House

Tyrone Hills

A40

River Foyle

River Finn

L O N D O N D E R R Y

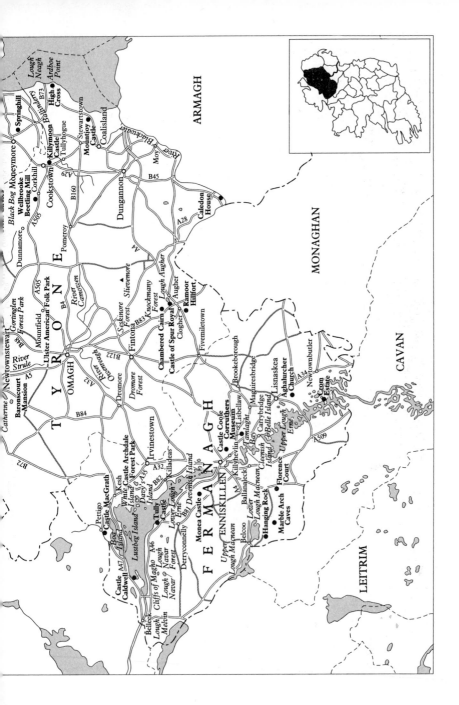

The countryside in which these beautiful lakes are scattered is mostly composed of little rushy farms where sheep and cattle graze. The higher ground is covered in hazel scrub, whilst in the limestone upland to the western edge of the country the soil is so poor that natural species have survived undisturbed by the tractor or fertilizers of the farmer. There are some lovely ash woods at Hanging Rock and Marble Arch. Here too are the famous Marble Arch Caves on Cuilcagh Mountain, which you can explore with a guide. The county also has two exquisite Georgian mansions under the care of the National Trust— Castle Coole and Florence Court. The coarse fishing is legendary, and every year in May fishermen have great fun at the Ulster Fishing Festival which spreads events all over the myriad lakes. You can explore the lakes by chartering a cabin cruiser and there are plenty of opportunities for water-skiing. The waterways of the upper and lower Erne are now connected to the great waterway of the Shannon by the newly restored Ballyconnell and Ballymore canal, which passes through some really unspoilt scenery.

History

The history of this county is similar to that of the rest of Ulster. The Maguires were the chief Gaelic family here before the plantation. In the 17th century, Scottish undertakers arrived to provide a population loyal to the English crown. Many grand and lovely houses were built by the big landowners in the 18th century (two of these are mentioned above).

Fermanagh has a vast and largely unrecorded ancient history, which you will get glimpses of through the beautiful carvings and stone statues still to be seen in graveyards and the Enniskillen Museum.

Those of you of a reflective turn of mind will be fascinated by the pagan idols; their impassive stone heads are to be found on the islands and secret peninsulas of Lough Erne. Usually they are mixed up with the gravestones of the newer religion, Christianity. The two seem to mingle quite happily. There are many remains of Christian hermitages, and on Devenish Island on Lough Erne is a superb collection of ecclesiastical ruins dating from the 6th century. The headlands of the loughs are wooded and often enough their interest is enhanced by the ruins of Plantation castles from the 17th century. This county and the town of Enniskillen has unfortunately suffered greatly since the 'Troubles' started in 1969: many lone Protestant farmers have been murdered by the IRA, and British soldiers ambushed on the narrow country roads which follow the curves of the lakesides. The most notable tragedy has been the IRA bomb blast which killed and maimed so many people gathered at the cenotaph at Enniskillen on Remembrance Sunday in 1987. Remarkably, the townspeople have worked selflessly to try to restore their community, rather than turn in on bitterness.

Fermanagh has never been a rich county. Its population have always lived by farming, fishing and, nowadays, tourism. The local people welcome tourists.

Getting There and Around

By air: From Belfast International Airport.

By rail: There is no train service.

By bus: Six Ulsterbus express buses run daily from Belfast to Enniskillen; two from Dublin. Good local bus links from Enniskillen to country areas. Enniskillen Bus Station, ℗ (0365) 322633.

By car: Car hire from Lochside Garage, Tempo Road, Enniskillen, ℗ (0365) 324366.

By bike: Bicycle hire from Mr Walker, Cycle Ops, Mantlin Road, Kesh, ℗ (0365) 31850; Lakeland Canoe Centre, Castle Island, ℗ (0365) 32456; Cycling Safari Holidays, ℗ (0365) 323597. Bike hire plus organised trips for one day or longer.

Tourist Information

Enniskillen, Lakeland Visitor Centre, Shore Road, ℗ (0365) 323110/325050.

Festivals

There are lots of tiny festivals and sporting events in villages thoughout the summer. Ask at the tourist office. The following are amongst the most interesting:

May: Coarse fishing festival.

Late June: Fiddlestone Festival, Belleek. Fiddlers come from all over Ireland to play in honour of a notable 18th-century fiddler from this little village.

August: Fishing Festival on Lough Melvin, based at Garrison. West Ulster Hound Show and Drag Hunt, Lisbellaw.

Enniskillen and Environs

Enniskillen is built on a bridge of land between Upper and Lower Lough Erne, and at first sight the medieval conglomeration of town and castle makes you think this is a very ancient town, although modern shops, supermarkets and offices unfortunately soon spoil the illusion. Before the plantation, the Maguires held sway over this lakeland area and used it as the centre for their watery dominions. Enniskillen's name comes from Cathleen, one of the women warriors of the Fomorian invaders. Her husband, Balor, was head of a pirate gang quartered on the rock island of Tory, off the Donegal coast. He later resurfaced as the Celtic god of darkness, whose one eye could strike you dead (*see* **Old Gods and Heroes**, p.575). Enniskillen is famous for its home regiments (the air of the Inniskillings became the tune of 'The Star Spangled Banner'), so you might say that there is a certain fighting tradition down here. Visit the **County Museum** (*open all year, Tues–Fri, 10–5; Sat–Mon, 10–1; adm;* ℗ *(0365) 325000*), which is housed in Maguire's Keep, a 15th-century building. Attached to it is the **Water Gate**, a fairytale building with towers and fluttering standards. The museum is one of the best and friendliest of local museums. It displays some of the strange head sculptures found in the locality, and explains the history of Fermanagh from the Middle Stone Age to the end of the Early-Christian period. There is also an audio-visual display on the Maguires of Fermanagh. British regiment enthusiasts will be interested in the soldiering relics of the Royal Inniskilling Fusiliers which can be seen in the same building.

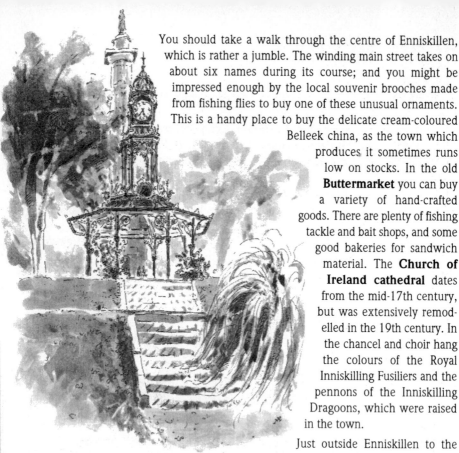

You should take a walk through the centre of Enniskillen, which is rather a jumble. The winding main street takes on about six names during its course; and you might be impressed enough by the local souvenir brooches made from fishing flies to buy one of these unusual ornaments. This is a handy place to buy the delicate cream-coloured Belleek china, as the town which produces it sometimes runs low on stocks. In the old **Buttermarket** you can buy a variety of hand-crafted goods. There are plenty of fishing tackle and bait shops, and some good bakeries for sandwich material. The **Church of Ireland cathedral** dates from the mid-17th century, but was extensively remodelled in the 19th century. In the chancel and choir hang the colours of the Royal Inniskilling Fusiliers and the pennons of the Inniskilling Dragoons, which were raised in the town.

Just outside Enniskillen to the northwest is the **Portora Royal School**, founded in 1608. As a public school it had amongst its more famous pupils Oscar Wilde. About 1¼ miles (2.4km) southeast of the town on the main Belfast to Enniskillen road (A4) is **Castle Coole** (*open 2–6 during April and May only on weekends and bank holidays; June–end Aug, 2–6 Fridays through Wednesdays; open daily at Easter; adm; ✆ (0365) 322690*), an assured and beautiful neoclassical house which has recently been carefully restored by the National Trust. This entailed replacing the Portland stone blocks of the façade. It was built between 1790 and 1797 with an agreeably simple symmetry, and the main block with colonnaded wings was designed by James Wyatt. Inside, 18th-century furniture is still in the rooms for which it was made. The English plasterer Joseph Ross, who had worked for Adam at Syon and Harewood, made the long journey to supervise the creation of the ceilings. The building accounts of the house survive, and since the cost of the construction exceeded the estimates, restraint may have been exercised in the decoration, keeping it elegant but simple. In the parkland surrounding the house there is a lake which has a very long-established colony of greylag geese. The saying is that if they leave Castle Coole, so will the Lowry-Corrys, Earls of Belmore, whose seat it is.

The Islands in Lower Lough Erne

Lower Lough Erne stretches in a broad arc with a pattern of 97 islands, with Belleek at one end and Enniskillen at the other. There is nothing nicer than exploring islands, and Lough Erne's scattered islets hold many treasures. You should not miss **Devenish**. Here St Molaise founded a monastic community in the 6th century, which was probably a more than usually perilous venture in that remote water kingdom, where paganism persisted long after Christian practices had taken hold in more accessible parts. However, there is a legend which credits these parts with a visitation by a character from the Old Testament, for the prophet Jeremiah is said to have his grave in the waters of Lough Erne. His daughter was married to the son of a high king of Ireland, and she brought as her dowry the Stone of Destiny, the coronation stone of Scone, the same stone that Fergus, who also cropped up in County Antrim (*see* p.355) took to Scotland. This story is almost as good as the variation of the Old Testament flood story recounted by the 9th-century cleric annalists, in which Beith, Noah's grandson, landed in Ireland with a whole ark of beautiful women—which is said to account for the comeliness of all Irish women today! Devenish island has a complete round tower, with an elaborately decorated cornice. Another ruin on the island incorporating some outstanding decoration is the 12th-century Augustinian **Abbey of St Mary**. Here St Molaise rested from his labours, listening spellbound to bird song which, it was said, was the Holy Spirit communicating. The reverie lasted a hundred years, and when he looked around after that interval this abbey had been built. You will find it a few miles outside Enniskillen off the main road to Omagh (A32). For transport to the island *see* 'Activities', p.328.

Another island with more tangible supernatural associations is **White Island**, in Castle Archdale Bay, north of Enniskillen, famous for its eerie statues. All eight of them are lined up in a row against the wall of a 12th-century church. Like many of the sculptures found in Fermanagh and nearby districts, there is a pagan quality about these objects. To what time in the distant past are they linked? What was their significance? They convey the potency of a sacred and magic object, of man's striving to harness the forces of the unknown. There are conflicting theories about just what the figures represent. Possibly they are of Christian origin employing archaic pre-Christian styles, dating between the 7th and 10th centuries. It is sometimes possible to hire a boat from Castle Archdale to Inismacsaint, a tiny island which has an ancient cross, possibly dating from a 6th-century monastery of which nothing remains, although there is a romantic ruin of a medieval church.

Boa Island, joined to the mainland by a bridge at each end, is the largest of the islands. Its name comes from *Badhbha*, war goddess of the Ulster Celts, and traditionally it remained the centre of the Druidic cult long after Christianity had arrived in Ireland. In the old cemetery, Caldragh, at the west end of the island, there is a strange 'Janus' figure with a face on each side. Such figures (several have been found in the Fermanagh area and in Cavan) are thought to have had ritual significance; a hollow in the figure's head may have held sacrificial blood. To find it, follow the A47 past the village of Kesh for about 5 miles (8km). Look for an insignificant signpost to Caldragh on the main road, then climb over a gate and through a field to this half-forgotten graveyard, full of bluebells in the spring.

The Northern Shore of Lough Erne

Killadeas is a fishing village looking on to Lough Erne. In the graveyard of the chapel there are some ancient, sculptured stones. One called the Bishop's Stone depicts a man with a crozier and bell. It is certainly pre-Norman. There is also a carved stone figure in the churchyard which dates from the 9th century. The country round the lough is full of the dips and hollows of the glacial-drift drumlins. Because of flooding problems in former years, you will notice few waterside town settlements although there are plenty of rushes, a source of thatching material. Just beyond the lough is **Castle Archdale Country Park** (*open from early morning till dusk; adm free; ✆ (03656) 21588*) on the B82. It is an old demesne now opened up for walking in the beautiful forest along nature trails; and for camping, boating and fishing. There is a marina here, café and shop. Also an exhibition centre (*open from Tuesday to Sunday from June to Sept*). The old castle is a pretty ruin. The ferry to White Island goes from here. From the jetty you overlook **White Island** and **Davy's Island**; it is a good place for setting off by boat to some of the nature reserve islands. Perhaps the loveliest aspect of this part of the shore is the flowers that decorate the water's edge.

Kesh is a busy little fishing village on the A35 where you can hire cruise boats. It is possible to learn the old skills of spinning and weaving at Ardess, near Kesh (*see* 'Summer Schools' in **Practical A–Z**). As you might expect, there is a boat-building industry here; traditional broad-beamed eel boats are still built, for this is a centre for eels (though subsidiary to Lough Neagh). From Kesh you can make your way to the pretty little island of **Lustybeg**, which has holiday chalets for hire. Another 'Janus' figure was discovered here, and is now in the Enniskillen Museum. Following the curve of the shoreline west you reach **Pettigo**, which is just in County Donegal, with newer houses straggling on and over the border into Fermanagh. Pettigo is an angling village which has grown up by the River Termon about a mile from where it flows into Lough Erne. It was on the pilgrims' route to Lough Derg, which lies in Donegal about 4 miles (6.4km) away, so it is busy in summer. The ruins of the 17th-century **Castle Magrath**, with its keep and circular towers at the corners, are on the outskirts of the village, next to the rectory. The B136 joins up with the A47 here and leads you to **Castle Caldwell**, which is situated on a wooded peninsula jutting out into the lough—a romantic situation for a romantic and enterprising family. One of the Caldwells had a barge on which music used to be played for his pleasure. Unfortunately, a fiddler overbalanced on one of these occasions and was drowned! You can see his fiddle-shaped monument with its warning:

> On firm land only exercise your skill
> There you may play and safely drink your fill.

In the 19th century the Caldwells promoted the original porcelain industry at nearby Belleek, using clay found on their estate. This clay has a high feldspar content, which gives this delicate china its texture and robustness. Now their castle lies in ruins. Visitors can wander in their gardens above the shore, admiring the view that in 1776 made Arthur Young the agriculturalist exclaim that there was 'shelter, prospect, wood and water here in perfection'. You can use the special wildfowl hides to watch the plentiful ducks, geese and other birds; these grounds also have the largest breeding colony of black scooters in the British Isles.

Further up the River Erne, at **Belleek** you reach another border village. For anglers there's a joky saying that you can hook a salmon in the Republic and land it in Northern Ireland. But it's more famous for its distinctive lustreware, which is produced as attractive ornaments rather than anything utilitarian. The 19th century **pottery factory** is very attractive; it has a small museum and guided tours of the pottery. Also in Belleek is an exhibition detailing the history of Lough Erne through exhibits and video. Contact the Erne Gateway Centre, ✆ (03656) 58866.

The Southern Shore of Lough Erne

On your way along the southern shore, on the A46, the road hugs the waterline, for limestone cliffs loom overhead, rising to the height of 2984ft (909m) at Magho. You may be tempted to venture above the lough and see how the countryside looks from the mountainous and wooded roads around Lough Navar. To visit the forest, go inland via Derrygonnelly on the B81, which is off the A46. From the **Lough Navar Forest** viewpoint you can see the splendid sight of the lough spread out in front of you, with the hills of Donegal in the distance, and the ranges of Tyrone, Sligo and Leitrim in a grand panorama. The forest entrance, opposite Correl Glen, is about 5 miles (8km) west of Derrygonnelly. It takes you on a 7-mile (11km) scenic road which is full of nature trails and little lakes, and has a camp site. The Ulster Way footpath runs through the forest up to a height of 1000ft, and runs down to Belcoo, between Upper and Lower Lough MacNean. This mountainous area is full of caves.

The plateau on the southern shore is covered with forest lands, and behind them are the Cuilcagh Mountains rising to the south. If you stick to the loughside you will pass the plantation-era **Tully Castle** and, further inland towards the south, a better-preserved castle at **Monea** (*open April–Sept, 10–7; Tues–Sat, 2–6; adm*). Both show the Scottish style brought to this country by Scottish settlers. Monea was built in 1618 by Malcolm Hamilton, a rector of Devenish Island. The castle front shows two circular towers which are square on the top storey, and the crow-stepped gables add to its Scottish air.

Up into the Western Mountains

For spectacular sights, nature has more on her side than architecture, so head towards the mountains in the west. You can take winding, confusing roads cross-country from Monea, but for a simpler route take Enniskillen as a starting point and follow the A4.

At **Belcoo** you reach a village lost in the mountains, situated on a narrow strip of land separating the two Lough MacNeans. In this place patterns (pilgrimages) to the St Patrick's Well are held on Bilberry Sunday, the last Sunday in July—the date of the Celtic *Lughnasa* or festival of fertility, a tradition which surely indicates the chain of pagan and Christian practices which have lingered on here longer than anywhere else and which gave the playwright Brian Friel the name for his highly successful play *Dancing at Lughnasa*.

If you go back by **Lower Lough MacNean** you will see the **Hanging Rock** from the minor road which goes to Blacklion across the border. Limestone has endowed this place with characteristic caverns. They stretch in a sort of underground labyrinth through the Cuilcagh Mountains, and some remain to be explored. Do not go pot-holing by yourself; apart from anything else, streams run into the caverns. You can see this for yourself from the scenic Marlbank loop road (unnumbered but signposted off the A4 Enniskillen–Sligo road), which takes you round from Florence Court to Lower Lough MacNean where the Sruh Croppa stream disappears into a crevice called the Cat's Hole. (*Marble Arch Show Caves are open seven days a week in July and Aug, from 11am; more limited times in April, May and Sept; last tour 5pm; adm. A 1¼-hour tour includes an underground boat trip. Take a jumper and flat shoes. It is wise to ring before setting out.* © (036) 348855.)

The wooded demesne of **Florence Court** is situated under the steep mountain of Benaughlin. This means 'Peak of the Horse', in Gaelic, and the white limestone showing through the scree at the foot of the eastern cliff did indeed once portray the outline of a horse, though it is getting more and more difficult to distinguish. Florence Court (*open April–May and Sept, Sat–Sun, 1–6; 1–5 during April; June–Aug daily except Tues; grounds open all year from 10am to one hour before dusk; adm;* © (0365) 348249), home of the Coles, earls of Enniskillen, is about 8 miles (13km) southwest of the town they helped to fortify in the plantation times, on the A4 and A32 Swanlibar road. Built in the mid-18th century for Lord Mountflorence, sadly the house has suffered fire damage, but there is still some fine Rococo plasterwork. It is beautifully situated in woodland with views across to the Cuilcagh Mountains. In the gardens is the original Florence Court yew, from whose seedlings grew *Taxus baccata fastigiata*, now found all over the world.

Upper Lough Erne

Upper Lough Erne and the maze of waters from the Erne river system provide quite a challenge for the explorer, so arm yourself with a good map. This area bridges the less water-strewn area of East Fermanagh whose pretty towns you may pass through. Some bear names of founder planter families. **Brookeborough** is on the A4, near the home of the Brooke family, who were prominent in Northern Irish affairs. Basil, the first Viscount Brookeborough (1888–1973) was Prime Minister of Northern Ireland and is remembered, perhaps unfairly, for his laager mentality towards Roman Catholics. The town of **Maguiresbridge** is called after the reigning chieftains, who were deposed by the planters.

This area is rich in folk tradition; you might meet someone with the secret of a cure, both for animal and human ailments. If you are interested in the distinctive sculptures you may have seen at the Enniskillen Museum or elsewhere, go and search out **Tamlaght Bay** near Lisbellaw on the A4, where at **Derrybrusk Old Church** you can see some more strange carved heads on a wall. At nearby **Aghalurcher Churchyard**, near Lisnaskea off the A34, you can see gravestones carved with what seems to be a rather macabre funerary motif, typically found in Fermanagh: the skull and crossbones. **The Crom Estate** (*open Easter–end Sept daily, 2–6; car park fee*) on the shores of Upper Lough Erne is a huge acreage of woodland, parkland and wetland. It is under the protection of the National Trust and is an important nature conservation area. You approach it on a minor road off the A34 in Newtownbutler. **Lisnaskea,** also on the A34, is rather an interesting market town with a restored market cross whose ancient shaft has fine carving. In the middle of the town is a ruined 17th-century castle built by Sir James Balfour, which was burnt down in the 19th century. On the main street is a folk-life display at the library (*open Mon, Tues and Fri, 9.15–5; Wed, 9.15–7.30; Sat, 9.15–12.30; adm free*). A cruise boat leaves the jetty here for 1½-hour tours of Upper Lough Erne (*see* end of chapter).

The upper reaches of Lough Erne are scattered with 58 little 'islands'. Meandering streams cut through the marshy wetlands creating these prettily named islands which are really tiny districts or townlands, not islands at all, for most of them are easy to walk and drive around. Some of them are inhabited, though on an increasingly part-time basis. You need to hire a boat to explore them properly. One sad story illustrates the difficulties attendant on island living even in these easier days: a postman living on Inishturk Island was frozen to death when his boat was trapped in ice during the hard winter of 1961. **Cleenish Island** can be reached from Bellanaleck on the A509 by a bridge. There are some remarkable carved headstones in the graveyard. Even more interesting is the collection of carved slabs on **Inishkeen,** accessible by causeway from Killyhevlin, which is just off the Dublin Road (A4) on the outskirts of Enniskillen. **Belle Isle** is a townland (it is hardly discernible as an island any more, being linked to the mainland by roads), which claims to be the spot where the *Annals of Ulster* were compiled in the 15th century by Cathal MacManus, Dean of Lough Erne. **Galloon Island** is large, with another ancient graveyard where you may, if you persevere, discern the curious carvings on the 9th- or 10th-century cross shafts which depict a man hanging upside down. Some think this might be Judas Iscariot, or else St Peter. There is a marina at **Bellanaleck** and **Carrybridge,** near Lisbellaw, where it is possible to hire cruisers and rowing boats with which to explore this secret wetland area, where cattle enjoy grazing the distinctive grasses and there is plenty of coarse fishing. If you wish to walk about here, be sure to wear long wellington boots. A mile west of Lisbellow, on Carrybridge Road, Tamlaght is a small private **museum** (*© (0365) 87278; adm*) with exhibits collected by the Corrothers family. Birds eggs, fossils, newspapers and letters sent from the Front, conjure up a lost world.

Shopping

Crafts: Belleek china, fishing-fly brooches and Irish lace in giftshops in Enniskillen main street. Also at the Belleek Visitor Centre in Belleek itself, where you can have tea. Ardess Craft Centre, Kesh, sells a range of local pottery, woven rugs and other crafts. Enniskillen Craft and Design Centre, The Buttermarket, Down Street, © (0365) 324499.

Pottery: Ann McNulty Pottery, Enniskillen Enterprise Centre, Down Street, Enniskillen, © (0365) 24721.

Antiques: Crock of Gold, Church Street, Enniskillen, © (0365) 323761; Forge Antiques, Circular Road, Lisbellaw, © (0365) 87774; R. Robinson, Drumduff, Florencecourt, © (03653) 48466.

Flowers: Tempo Flowers, 35 Townhall Street, ✆ (0365) 324969; Erne Flowers, 26 East Bridge Street, ✆ (0365) 325444.

Activities

Cruising: over 300 square miles (800 sq km) of island-studded lakes and rivers, with over 70 free jetty moorings and only one lock. Many companies rent out cruisers by the day or week. Prices range from £300 a week for a four-berth cruiser in the low season and £900 for an eight-berth in the high season. They welcome complete novices and give free lessons or how to handle boats. You can get a complete list from the tourist office in the Lakeland Visitor Centre, Shore Road, Enniskillen, ✆ (01365) 323110. Here are the telephone numbers of a few: Carrybridge Boat Company, Lisbellaw, ✆ (01365) 325511, has a fine reputation for service; Lakeland Marina Ltd, Kesh, ✆ (013656) 31414; Manor House Marine, Killadeas, ✆ (013656) 28100. With the restoration of the old canal between Ballinamore and Ballyconnell (in Co. Leitrim), it is now possible to cruise from the Erne to the Shannon Waterway system. Erincurrach Cruising, at Blaney, Enniskillen operates a one way boat rental between the Erne and the Shannon, ✆ (01365) 641737. Shannon Erne Waterway Holidays, ✆ (079) 67028.

Cruiser Tours: The Kestrel cruise boat leaves from the Round O Quay in Enniskillen for cruises round the islands every day from July to September, and includes a stop at Devenish Island. Price £3, ✆ (01365) 322882. There is a ferry service May–June 2.30pm daily, July–Aug 10.30, 2.15, 4.15; Sept at 2.30 on Tues, Sat and Sun. Cost £3, ✆ (013657) 322122 for more details. It is possible to hire launches and rowing boats. Ask at the Lakeland Visitor Centre, Shore Road, Enniskillen. Another cruiser tours Upper Lough Erne from 24 March to the end of September, with sailings in the morning and afternoon. Price £3, ✆ (013657) 322122 for more details. Boats over 10hp must be registered with the Portora Locks Warden, ✆ (01365) 322836. The Share Centre, Lisnaskea organises tours of Upper Lough Erne on a powered Viking Longship, Easter to Sept, ✆ (013657) 22122. Ferry to White Island from Castle Archdale (off the B82) every day except Monday, June–Sept 10am–7pm, Sunday 2–7pm, fare £2. Ferry to Devenish Island from Troy point, 3 miles north of Enniskillen. Junction of A32/B82. April–Sept, Tues to Sat 10am–7pm, Sunday 2–7pm, fare £2.

Water-skiing: through the cruiser-hire companies listed above or The Water Sport Centre, Drumrush Lodge, Kesh, ✆ (013656) 31578/31025 or Killeadeas Pavillon, (013656) 28202.

Fishing: The Fermanagh lakelands are renowned for their coarse fishing. Brown trout and salmon fishing are also excellent in the rivers and loughs. Lough Melvin is notable for three unusual species of trout: the gillaroo, the sonaghan and the ferox. The Lakeland Visitor Centre in Enniskillen stocks permits, licences and a booklet on local fishing waters, ✆ (01365) 323110. Alternatively contact the Hon. Brian Mulholland, Belle Isle, Lisbellow, ✆ (01365) 87231.

Golf: Enniskillen Golf Club in Castle Coole Estate, ✆ (01365) 325250.

Flying: pleasure flights and flying lessons from The Flying Club, St Angelo Airfield, Enniskillen. £70 per hour, £35 for half an hour.

Swimming and badminton: Fermanagh Lakeland Forum, Enniskillen, ✆ (01365) 324121.

Pot-holing: Marble Arch Caves, Florencecourt, ✆ (01365) 348855.

Belleek Visitor Centre—20 minute guided tour of the pottery, ✆ (013656) 58501.

Where to Stay

expensive

Killyhevlin Hotel, Dublin Road, Enniskillen, ✆ (01365) 323481. Comfortable modern hotel overlooking its own little lake. The bar is a great chatting place for fishermen. **Tempo Manor**, Tempo, ✆ (036 554) 247. Victorian Manor house overlooking gardens and lakes.

moderate

Mr A. Stuart, **Jamestown House**, Magheracross, near Ballinamallard, ✆ (01365) 81209. A gem of a Georgian house. Superb cooking and lots to do all around— water-skiing, fishing, riding. Lord and Lady Anthony Hamilton, **Killyreagh**, Tamlaght, Enniskillen, ✆ (01365) 87221. Comfortable 19th-century country house. Fishing, riding and tennis arranged.

inexpensive

Mrs Armstrong, **Tullyhona House**, Marble Arch Road, Florence Court, ✆ (01365) 48452. The pretty countryside could not fail to charm you, and your welcome is warm. Nice old house, set in its own grounds. Mrs Fawcett, Riverside **Farm Guest House**, Gortadrehid, Culkey, Enniskillen, ✆ (01365) 322775. Secluded, warm and friendly house with private fishing. **Castle Archdale Country Park Hostel**, ✆ (013656) 28118. Beds for £6 with family rooms available. Mrs Pendry, **Ardess House**, Kesh, ✆ (013656) 31267. All bedrooms en suite. Wholefood cooking. Courses run at the craft centre in the grounds. **Riverside Farm**, Gortadrehid, Culkey, Enniskillen, ✆ (01365) 322725. The River Sillies at the bottom of the farm holds the record for coarse fishing. Comfortable and friendly.

self-catering

The following are for rent by the week:

Lusty Beg Island Chalets, Boa Island, ✆ (013656) 32032. From £350 high season. **Ely Island Chalets**, Ely Lodge, Enniskillen, ✆ (01365) 341777. From £350 high season. Log cabin-style chalets on a large private estate. **Rose Cottage**, a National Trust cottage on Florence court Demesne, ✆ (01365) 348249. £150 low season. **Crom Cottages**, Crom Estate (National Trust) near Lisnaskea, ✆ (01396) 881204. 7 converted cottages available.

Eating Out

moderate

The Cedars, Castle Archdale, Drumall, Lisnarick, ✆ (013656) 21493. Excellent steaks and a homely atmosphere. **Franco's Pizzeria**, Queen Elizabeth Road, Enniskillen, ✆ (01356) 324424. Fun atmosphere. Food includes pasta, pizza and fish. **The Sheelin**, Bellanleck, ✆ (01365) 82232. Excellent for lunch or dinner. A traditional cottage with climbing roses round the door. Delicious brown wheaten bread.

inexpensive

Florence Court House, ✆ (01365) 348249. Lunch only: quiche, stews, wheaten bread. **Wild Duck Inn**, Lisbellaw. Pub grub. **Melvin House and Bar**, 1 Townhall Street, Enniskillen, ✆ (01365) 322040. Good pub lunches. The **May Fly Inn**, Kesh, ✆ (013656) 31281. Pub grub. **Reihill's Restaurant**, Innishcorkish Island, ✆ (013657) 21360. Lunches, soups and snacks. **Belleek Pottery Restaurant**. **Hollander**, 5 Main Street, Irvinestown, ✆ (013656) 21231. Delicious and original menu. **Le Bistro**, Ernside Centre.

Entertainment and Nightlife

Theatre: Ardhowen Theatre, Enniskillen, ✆ (01365) 325400.

Disco-dancing: Tipplers Brook, Enniskillen, ✆ (01365) 322048.

County Tyrone

This is the heart of Ulster, the land called after *Eoghan* (Owen), one of the sons of High King Niall of the Nine Hostages, who lived in the 4th century AD and was the progenitor of the O'Neill dynasty. The least populated of the six counties, Tyrone is celebrated in many a poignant song by emigrant sons (some of whom found fame and fortune in America).

The Sperrin mountains cover a large part of the north, the highest at 2240ft (683m) being Sawel, which is on the border with County Londonderry. In these lonely hills locals have panned for gold for hundreds of years, and recently excitement has been generated by the discovery of large deposits of this precious metal. Lough Neagh forms Tyrone's eastern border for a few miles in the east, but the county's main attraction is its chattering burns, flora and fauna, and peaceful glens. It is a land of hillside, moorland and good fishing.

Only in the southeastern area is it well-wooded, and there is a much quoted tag about 'Tyrone among the bushes, where the Finn and Mourne run'. The land in this region is more fertile and well-planted with trees; the farmers here keep cattle as well as sheep. Many of the farmhouses are still of whitewashed stone with gaily painted doorways. The linen industry is important at Moygashel, and there are many small businesses in the main towns, such as milling.

The plantation families have their traditions and big houses in the southeast too. Some of the loveliest, such as Caledon, are still occupied by their original families, whilst the most unusual, Killymoon Castle, was saved from ruin by a farmer who bought it for £100 in the 1920s. Neither of these houses is open to the public, but it is possible to stay in the grounds of another large Georgian mansion at Baronscourt, the home of the Duke of Abercorn. Here there is a golf course and coarse fishing, and water sports on Lough Catherine. There is fishing on the Rivers Mourne, Owenkillew, Camowen and Glenelly for brown trout and salmon. There is much to attract the walker and naturalist too, in the forests and moorland of the Sperrin Mountains.

Tyrone is an undiscovered county without the romance of Donegal or the reputation of the Antrim Coast, but it inspires pride and praise from its native dwellers. Tyrone people are well known for their music and their talent with language, both the spoken and written word; notice how many writers and poets come from this part of the world, the most notable being William Carleton, John Montague and Brian Friel.

History

This region is rich in folklore and ancient ways. Its history lives on in the language: some of the local expressions recall the Gaelic, although it is no longer spoken, and a few turns of phrase will take you back to the days of Elizabeth I. For example, a 'boon' is a company of people in the house, to 'join' is to begin, to 'convoy' is to accompany, and 'diet' is the word for food.

County Tyrone's past is similar to that all over Ulster, and it can be well illustrated by concentrating on the ownership of the lands and estate of Caledon, a small village close to the border with County Monaghan. This was O'Neill territory, and the natives fought vigorously against the English forces from the mid-17th century on, but by the 18th century the region was planted with Scottish undertakers. The story of Captain William Hamilton is typical of that of many of the new landlords. Captain William Hamilton, a Cromwellian soldier and one of the Hamiltons from Haddington in East Lothian, was granted the Caledon estate of Sir Phelim O'Neill after the Battle of Benburb in 1646. By 1775 the Hamilton line, which had intermarried with the Osserys—Earls of Ossery and Cork, had become very extravagant. As a result of the family's debts, the property was sold to a Derry merchant's son, James Alexander, who had acquired a vast fortune in the service of the East India Company. The most distinguished member of this family (which still owns the estate) was Viscount Alexander of Tunis.

The tenants and small farmers in this area are for the most part descended from Scottish Presbyterians, but in the hilly Sperrins there are still a good many Catholics—descendants of the ousted O'Neills and their septs.

Today, the fortunes of County Tyrone have been caught up in the 'Troubles', particularly because it is so close to the border.

Getting There and Around

By air: Belfast International Airport and Dublin Airport are about 70 and 86 miles (112 and 137km) from Omagh, respectively.

By rail: There is no railway line running through County Tyrone. The nearest station is Portadown, ✆ (01762) 351422.

By bus: Ulsterbus maintains a good service to all parts of the county. Omagh Bus Station, ✆ (01662) 242711. Strabane Bus Station, ✆ (01504) 382393.

By car: cars for hire from Johnston King Motors, 82 Derry Road, Omagh, ✆ (01662) 242788.

By bike: Conway Cycles, 157 Loughmacrory Road, ✆ (016627) 61258.

Tourist Information

48 Molesworth Street, **Cookstown**, ✆ (016487) 66727. Open April–Sept.

Cranagh, Sperrin Heritage Centre, 274 Glenelly Road, ✆ (0126626) 48142, June–Sept.

Strabane, Abercorn Square, ✆ (01504) 883735, mid-June–Sept.

Omagh, 1 Market Street, ✆ (01662) 247831. All year.

Festivals

Late May/early June: Omagh *Feis* with Irish dancing and music.

Last week of July: Bilberry Sunday *Feis* with traditional music and dancing at Altadaven, 2 miles (3.2km) south of Favour Royal.

July: Omagh Agricultural Show.

July: Sheepdog trials in Plumbridge.

August–Sept: Sheepdog trials in Gortin.

Strabane and Environs

Strabane (*An Srath Ban*: the white holm), is a border town and almost the twin of Lifford, across the Foyle in Donegal. The Finn joins the Foyle here as well. Strabane and its environs enjoy a notoriety in EU figures, for this area is an unemployment blackspot. However, going through it you are not struck by this sombre thought because it is a bustling town with friendly people. It is also the birthplace of John Dunlap, printer of the American Declaration of Independence. You should try to visit Grays (*open 24 Mar–end Sept, daily except Thurs and Sun, 12–6; adm*), the 18th-century printing shop in Main Street where he worked, which is owned by the National Trust. There is a collection of 19th-century hand-printing machines in working order. The stationers itself, which is not National Trust, is open all year (*✆ (01504) 884094*). Another Strabane-born notable is that curious wit Brian O'Nolan, alias Flann O'Brien. He wrote *The Poor Mouth* and other stories, and his column in *The Irish Times* between 1937 and 1966 became a byword for a debunking type of humour. There is not much else of particular interest in the town, except the fishing tackle shops near the bridge and a factory that produces a phenomenal amount of ladies' tights.

East of Strabane you pass into the **Tyrone Hills** which consist mainly of the Sperrin mountain range, extending into County Londonderry. This is perfect walking country, full of glens and mountain passes to beyond Plumbridge. At Gortin, a tiny hill village with a broad street, the B45 heads south to Omagh through Gortin Gap, a pretty mountain pass.

The Tyrone Hills

Plumbridge is a small crossroads village at the western end of the beautiful Glenelly Valley. A few miles on, following the B47, is the **Sperrin Heritage Centre**, situated between the villages of Cranagh and Sperrin. Here there is a comprehensive and interesting display of Sperrin wildlife, showing all the animals and birds you might be lucky enough to see whilst walking in the glens around here. One very special bird you might see is the hen harrier. Look out for the cloudberry, an alpine species which grows low to the ground on a single patch west of Dart Mountain. The Heritage Centre (*open June–Sept; adm; ✆ (016626) 48142*) also has a craft shop and tea room, and plenty of historical and cultural information. One of the great saints of Ireland, St Brigid, is strongly associated with this area; there are not many houses which do not have a St Brigid cross hanging above the door to ward off evil. These crosses look rather like swastikas, and are made of rushes. Most of the people living up in these moorlands are sheep-farmers, and regularly during the Spring and the Autumn there are great **sheep fairs** and **sheep dog trials** in Gortin. The Glenelly and Owenkillew Rivers are very good for trout fishing. You need a Foyle Fisheries Commission rod licence, which is available from tackle shops in nearby towns. If you follow the B47 from the Centre onwards to Draperstown (a scenic route), you pass Goles Forest, planted with conifers. Alternatively, the B48 from Gortin to Omagh passes through the wild and beautiful **Gortin Glen Forest Park**, where there are nature trails amongst the conifer trees. The Ulster Way also passes through it. (This signposted route for walkers covers most of Northern Ireland.) The country lanes around about are bright with gorse and primroses in Spring, and the lambs make a very pretty sight. Another Visitor Centre, **The Ulster History Park** (*✆ (016626) 48188; adm*) traces human settlement and society from 8000 BC to the 17th century. You find this on the B48, at Cullion, 7 miles north of Omagh.

A couple of miles southeast of Strabane on the pretty, unnumbered Plumbridge road, at **Dergalt**, is the Wilson homestead, maintained by the National Trust. This comparatively humble dwelling is where President Woodrow Wilson's grandfather (among many other children) was reared before he set off for the States to become a newspaper editor. The house is thatched and 19th-century, and provides a preview of what is available on a grander scale at the **American Folk Park**. The farm next door is lived in by Wilson family members. **Newtownstewart**, on the A5 10 miles (16km) south of Strabane, is a 17th-century plantation town with a tourist office in the old school yard. It is attractively laid out on a large main street. Nearby on the B84 lies Baronscourt Estate, which has an excellent garden centre. There are cottages for rent, coarse and game fishing, pony-trekking, golf and water-skiing on Lough Catherine.

Ulster American Folk Park

Open Easter–early Sept, Mon–Sat, 11–6.30, Sun 11.30–7; from late-September to Easter Monday, Fri 10.30–5; adm; ℂ (01662) 243292.

The Folk Park is between Newtownstewart and Omagh, sandwiched between the A5 and the Plumbridge road. It was developed by funds made available by the Mellon family of Pittsburg, in order to illustrate the conditions of life the emigrants left in Ireland and those they encountered in their new land, by reconstructing the buildings they inhabited. The Irish village has a meeting house, the central focus of the Ulster Presbyterian's worship; a forge, a school house and county shop. The New World buildings include log cabins, a clapboard farmhouse and various barns complete with implements. To complete your instruction you can go into the exhibition centre. While you are here, look out for the Ulster tartan, for near here a piece of tartan material was discovered in a bog, with the result that the so-called 'Ulster tartan' is full of tanned browns! The ancestral home of the Mellons, and the boyhood home of Archbishop John Hughes of New York, are very spartan and simple, and established showpieces. There is a fair bit of outdoor walking, so take along some good strong shoes and a raincoat.

Omagh

Omagh, capital of Tyrone, is separated from the other large town of the county, **Cookstown**, by the Black Bog which accounts for the turfcraft souvenirs you may find as a welcome alternative to the more usual Irish linen hankies or crochet also displayed for your attention. Turfcraft is made from compressed and heated peat. Some people tell you that there is something French about this town, with its twin-spired church and a reputation for liveliness. Brian Friel, the playwright, is a native. Any of his plays are worth making a special effort to see, he gives a profound and lyrical insight into Irish culture. *Translations* is particularly good—it deals with the loss of the Irish language. Omagh is a good spot for those seeking good fishing, which can be found on the Camowen and Owenreagh Rivers. Those wanting to hear the musical talent should try and time their visit to coincide with the West Tyrone *Feis* in May, also known as the Omagh *Feis*, which has plenty of Irish music and dancing.

From Omagh to Cookstown

Omagh is near other forest areas: **Seskinore Forest**, near Fintona, and **Dromore Forest**, further west. Should you wish to strike across the moor country you can go by Mountfield on the A505 from Omagh, which will take you by the Black Bog, a nature reserve; any other little roads you encounter may take you past some of the many antiquities which testify to Bronze or earlier Stone Age inhabitants of this area.

At **Pomeroy**, on the B4 15 miles (24km) east of Omagh, high in the mountains, equidistant from Cookstown and Dungannon, there are the remains of seven stone circles. More famous are the **Beaghmore Stone Circles**, outside Cookstown and near Dunnamore; these intricate alignments (on a northeast axis) represent the remarkable architecture of the late Stone Age or early Bronze Age. Their formation has been likened to a clock pointing for the last six thousand years towards the midsummer sunrise. They certainly look very impressive in the wild landscape which surrounds them. To get there, take a minor road off the A505 through Dunnamore, and travel on a few miles going north. Near to Cookstown at Corkhill is **Wellbrook Beetling Mill** (National Trust) (*open Easter and July–Aug, daily except Tuesday, 2–6; April–June and Sept, weekends and bank holidays, 2–6; adm; ✆ (016487) 51735*), a hammer mill powered by water for beetling. (This alarming-sounding process is the final stage of linen manufacture.) The mill is situated about 4 miles (7km) west of Cookstown, half a mile off the A505 Cookstown–Omagh road, in a lovely glen with wooded walks along the Ballinderry River and the mill race.

Cookstown is situated in the middle of Northern Ireland, near the fertile heartland which traces its course beside the Bann in Londonderry and continues down by Lough Neagh. There are two Nash buldings in its environs. On the outskirts southeast of the town is **Killymoon Castle**, a battlemented towered construction which contrasts with the simple Church of Ireland parish church known as St Laurane's at the southeast end of the main street. The conspicuous Puginesque Catholic church, sited on a hill in the middle of town, provides a good landmark. Dairy farming and linen are very important industries here.

Arriving at Cookstown you will be impressed by the long wide main street; if you are of a cynical turn of mind you may think it a good street for leading a charge against insurgents. Cookstown has a good Nationalist tradition, exemplified by the energetic Miss Bernadette Devlin, now McAliskey, who was active in the Civil Rights Movement and Nationalist Party in the 1970s. There is also a strong Scottish Protestant tradition with the ancestors of those who settled here in the 17th century.

Places to visit nearby include the loughside **Ardboe High Cross**, about 10 miles (16km) east on the shore of Lough Neagh. The cross is a 10th-century monument with 22 remarkable sculptured scriptural panels covered with scenes from the Old and New Testaments. These scenes are easily recognizable, unlike those on many of the other high crosses you may see, which are usually so weathered that you need to concentrate to read the theme. South of Cookstown in **Tullaghogue Rath** (pronounced '*Tullyhog*'), the O'Neills, the great chieftains of Tyrone were inaugurated. In 1595 Hugh O'Neill gave in to the British, and seven years later the Lord Deputy Mountjoy had the throne smashed to prevent any future ceremonies. At the foot of Tullaghogue hill, in what is now Loughry Agricultural

College, is the mansion where Jonathan Swift stayed while writing *Gulliver's Travels*; the portraits of his two loves, Stella and Vanessa, still hang in the house. It is sometimes possible to visit it; ask at the door. **Drum Manor Forest Park** close by, to the east of Cookstown on the A505, has a butterfly garden and a forest trail for the disabled (*open all year daily 10am–dusk; adm; parking fee; © (018687) 58256*).

Dungannon, a city on a hill, looks like your average planter town, with a planned main street and a Royal School founded in the time of James I of England. It was, in fact, the centre for the great O'Neills until the 'Flight of the Earls' deprived the Gaels of their native leaders (*see* **History**, p.00). It is now a quietly prosperous town with a long-established textile industry specializing in Moygashel fabrics, and a more recent Tyrone crystal-glass factory. At the beginning of the 17th century, in order to promote good Protestant education, James I of England and Ireland (James VI of Scotland) provided Royal Schools as well as charters for land. You may notice **The Royal School, Dungannon** which is on Northland Row in the centre of the town. The present building dates from 1786 and outside it is a statue of one of its most famous 'old boys', Major General John Nicholson, whose exploits in India inspired such legendary respect that there was even a sect called 'Nikkul Seyn'. Another Indian connection is the **police station** in the town centre, which looks like a castle with projecting apertures for missile-throwing. Apparently it was built according to plans for a fort in the Khyber Pass because some clerk in Dublin got into a muddle. This is the usual explanation for many of these exotic-looking stations which are scattered about Ireland.

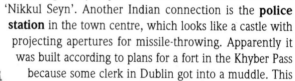

Tyrone has its River Blackwater, though it is not in the same league as the other Blackwater which flows through Cork and Waterford. It creates a watery border with County Armagh, and flows through **Moy** with its Italian-styled square created by one of the Charlemont family; and through **Caledon** on the A28, with its unspoiled Georgian look. James, first Earl of Charlemont, was famous for the lead he gave with Henry Grattan to the Volunteer Movement and his opposition to the Union in 1800. Perhaps more intriguing to the traveller is the

Clogher Valley, which is border country with the Republic and so enjoys that anomalous status of being either frontier outpost or lost territory. A narrow gauge railway used to run through the valley connecting the two sides. This place evidently has a long history of habitation, for many ancient earthworks have survived. The countryside is very pleasant and fertile, and extends for 25 miles (40km). There are some interesting villages and the River Fury runs through the valley.

Just north of **Augher**, off the B83, is the **Knockmany Forest**, a government-run forestry plantation on Knockmany Hill. At the top, look for the **Knockmany Chambered Cairn** said to be the burial place of Queen Aine, Queen of Oriel, a 6th-century kingdom whose centre was Clogher. The cairn is a passage grave dating from Neolithic times. This type of monument consists of a stone-built passage leading to a terminal chamber, often cruciform in shape, and covered by a mound or cairn of stones. The remarkable thing about this grave is its incised decoration, in patterns of concentric circles, zig-zags and other designs, which are similar in style to the great earthworks in the Boyne Valley, County Meath. This country, besides being a fisherman's haunt, is well forested. The 19th-century landlords who once owned vast tracts of land have disappeared, but their old estates, such as Favour Royal and Fardross, gave their names to public parkland and forests where it is possible to camp and have picnics.

If you are interested in the way things used to be on these large estates, it is worth seeking out the work of Miss Shaw, a governess whose photographs from the turn of the century are incorporated in an anthology called *Faces of the Past* by B. M. Walker. Another docu-mentor of earlier ways was the prolific William Carleton (1794–1869), the Irish Dickens, who was born at Springtown just outside Augher, and who made no bones about the hard-ships of peasant life, paying tribute to some of the great spirits who existed unsung in rural isolation. His most famous work is *Traits and Stories of the Irish Peasantry*. If you are interested in Carleton's work, ask to see the archival material in the Library in Fivemiletown.

Augher and Clogher are within striking distance. **Augher** lies between the Blackwater River and Augher Lake. You can see the 19th-century **Castle of Spur Royal** just to the west of the village as you pass by on the A4. It is possible to stay there.

Clogher village is on a site of prehistoric importance, as well as being of great ecclesias-tical significance. It was the original seat in the 5th century of the diocese of Clogher, one of the oldest bishoprics in Ireland. In the porch of **St MacCartan's Cathedral** there is a curious stone called 'the *Clogh-oir*' or Gold Stone. There are two 9th-century high crosses in the graveyard, and you can climb the tower and get a stunning view of the Clogher Valley. Ask at the rectory for access.

Behind this centre of ancient Christianity is the even older hill-fort of **Ramore**. Achaeologists have investigated it for evidence about the Iron Age, and perhaps the myste-rious '*Clogh-oir*' comes from an idol of those times. Nobody knows. It was certainly the site of the palace of the kings of Oriel; the tradition of the dynasty survives but not the dates, other than that they were pre-5th century. The hill-fort itself is now just a grassy mound, and always accessible.

Glass: Tyrone Crystal, Oaks Road, Dungannon, ✆ (018687) 25335. The glassworks give you a guided tour, and you can buy imperfect glassware very cheaply.

Designer clothes: Paul Costelloe clothes stocked at Carl Martyn's, Thomas Street, Dungannon, ✆ (018687) 22856.

Delicacies: Cookstown bacon and sausages.

Market: for household goods and vegetables at Aughnacloy on the 1st and 3rd Wednesday in the month.

Antiques: Viewback Antique Auctions, 8 Castle Place, Omagh, ✆ (01662) 246271. Killy Corran Hall, Garlaw Road, Clogher (signposted off the A4 South of Clogher), ✆ (016625) 48267. Kingsbridge Antiques, 31 Dungannon Road, Cookstown, ✆ (016487) 63426.

Fishing: for brown trout, sea trout and salmon on the River Blackwater, near Omagh, and on the Mourne River System which includes the Strule, Owenkillew and Glenelly. Licences from Foyle Fisheries Commission, Derry, or local fishing tackle shops. For the Ballinderry River, you need a Fisheries Conservancy Board game rod licence and permission (from tackle shop or tourist offices). Permits are available from tackle shops in Caledon, Cookstown, Omagh, Moy and Aughnacloy. Try the Strule, Drumreagh, Camowen and Owenkillen rivers for brown and sea trout. Maps of fishing area and permits from Tyrone Angling Supplies, Bridge Street, Omagh. The Department of Agriculture, ✆ (01232) 523434 offers pike and perch fishing in Creeve Lough and White Lough, and brown trout fishing in Brantry Lough.

Walking: in the valleys of the Glenelly, Owenreagh, Owenkillew and Camowen Rivers; in the 12 Sperrin forests, in particular Drum Manor, near Cookstown, and Gortin Glen Forest Park with its nature trails and wild deer. Other forest parks with nature trails: Favour Royal, Gollagh Woods, and Fardross Forest where you can see red squirrels. Riverside walks by Wellbrook Beetling Mill, near Cookstown. The Ulster Way signposted walking trail goes through the Sperrins. For details and a map write to the Sports Council, House of Sport, Upper Malone Road, Belfast, ✆ (01232) 381222.

Rough shooting: over the Sperrin Mountains. Applications to the Game Farm, Seskinore Game Farm, ✆ (01662) 841243. Also contact Ian Whiteside at Sperrin Sports, 112 Seskinore Rd, ✆ (01662) 840149.

Pony-trekking: at Edergole Riding Centre, Cookstown, ✆ (016487) 62924.

Water sports: fishing, water-skiing and windsurfing on Lough Catherine (and also golf), organized by Baronscourt Leisure Pursuits, Fairways, Golfcourse Road, Newtownstewart, ✆ (016626) 61013.

Golf: at Killymoon Golf Club, Cookstown, an 18-hole parkland course, ✆ (016487) 63762. Newtownstewart Golf Club, ✆ (016626) 61466. Omagh Golf Club, an 18-hole parkland course, ✆ (01662) 243160.

Open farm: Altmore Open Farm, 175 acre sheep farm in the Sperrins. Rare breeds and poultry. Open daily. 3 miles south of Pomeroy.

Guided tour: Benburb Valley Heritage Centre. Guided tours of 19th-century linen mill on the banks of the Ulster Canal. Ten miles south of Dungannon. Open Tues–Sat, 10–5, Sun 2–5, ✆ (01861) 549752.

Where to Stay
expensive

Captain R. M. Lowry, Blessingbourne, near Fivemiletown, ✆ (013655) 21221. You can imagine you are staying in the time of leisurely house parties when you stay in this attractive Victorian mansion set in wooded grounds. You are made to feel part of the family. The rooms are very comfortable, and the cooking first-rate.

moderate

Mrs N. Brown, **Grange Lodge**, Grange Road, Moy, near Dungannon, ✆ (018687) 84212. Comfortable Georgian house by the Blackwater River. Confident, delicious traditional food. **Inn On The Park**, Moy Road, Dungannon, ✆ (018687) 25151. 15 ensuite bedrooms, tennis court and attractive gardens. The **Valley Hotel**, 60 Main Street, Fivemiletown, ✆ (013655) 21505. Comfortable, cheery, grade B accommodation. The **Royal Arms**, 51 High Street, Omagh, ✆ (01662) 243262. Traditional hotel in the town centre.

inexpensive

Mr & Mrs McNeice, **Charlemont House**, 4 The Square, Moy, Dungannon, ✆ (018687) 84755. Georgian townhouse with period furnishings and lots of atmosphere with a view of the Blackwater River at the back. Nice garden.

self-catering

Baronscourt Cottages, Golf Course Road, Newtownstewart, ✆ (016626) 61013. Nine cottages by a private lake. **Capt. R. M . Lowry**, Blessingbourne, ✆ (013655) 21221. Two apartments.

Eating Out
expensive

Mellon Country Inn, 134 Beltany Road, Newtownstewart, ✆ (016626) 61224. Good steak. **Grange Lodge**, 7 Grange Road, Moy, ✆ (018687) 84212. Has a good reputation and good traditional homely food. Try their salmon in filo parcels. *Friday and Saturday evenings only.*

inexpensive

Try the local pubs for toasted sandwiches and soup. **Tommy's Bar** in Moy is very authentic. **Rosamund's Coffee Shop**, Station House, Augher, ✆ (016625) 48601. Homemade stew during the day. The **Caledon Arms**, 44 Main Street, Caledon, ✆ (01861) 568161. **Cookstown Courtyard**, 56 William Street, Cookstown, ✆ (016487) 65070. Set lunch, homemade pies and puddings.

County Londonderry

This is a rich and varied region. The traditions of war and tumult vie with the gifts of learning and song in the people who inhabit this friendly land. The countryside ranges from stormy sea coast and wild mountain ranges to sheltered valleys, well-wooded from years of far-sighted planting. The coastline from Magilligan to Downhill is scattered with golden strands. Historic Derry is a spire-dreaming city which arouses fierce passions in the hearts of its inhabitants.

The city and the whole county have suffered because of the 'Troubles', which started in the 1960s. The fighting in the streets, the bombing and the upset to normal life have taken their toll on the lives of the inhabitants. Yet some good things have happened: new housing schemes have been implemented, sports centres built and, where shops and stores were destroyed, new buildings have gone up. The people of the province are determined to survive, and not give in to the men of violence. None the less, people still live in tribal areas, either Catholic or Protestant; those who have tried to live in a mixed estate have been intimidated into moving out. This is true of Belfast also. Sinister forces are still at work, murdering off duty policemen, or citizens who have had the misfortune to be singled out by one or other of the paramilitary organizations.

The economy of County Londonderry is subsidized heavily by the British Government, and there is a lot of unemployment in places like the Bogside. Dupont and other international companies have set up factories and there are traditional linen and shirt factories.

History

The O'Neills were the overlords here before the county was planted with settlers who came over with the London City Companies. These London City Companies became owners of huge tracts of land, through grants from James I in the early 1600s. It was at this point that the county and its main town became Londonderry. Previously, it had been known as Derry-Colmcille after the oak grove in which it once stood, and after St Colmcille who had established a religious settlement here in AD 546. A subtle point is made to those 'in the know' whether reference is made to Londonderry or Derry. The former perhaps indicates Loyalist politics; but the county and its city are generally known as Derry, so this is how they are named in this text. Derry was granted to the Irish Society of London 'for the promotion of religion, order and industry'. The city had been ruined in the fighting between the English forces and those of O'Neill and O'Doherty, the chief Irish septs (clans) of the region. It was rebuilt with strong walls which protected it during three major sieges in the 17th century, earning it the title 'Maiden City'.

Derry is a terminal for railway and bus services, and is a useful halfway house for those moving east or west.

By air: to Belfast Airport. The City of Derry Airport has flights to Manchester, Glasgow and Jersey.

By sea: to Larne and Belfast ferryports.

By rail: mainline services from Belfast to Derry link the coastal towns along the way, ✆ (01504) 42228.

By bus: Ulsterbus connects Derry with Belfast, and there is a good local bus network, ✆ (01504) 262261.

Tourist Information

Derry, Bishop Street, ✆ (01504) 267284, all year.

Derry, Bord Fáilte Information Centre, Foyle Street, ✆ (01504) 369501.

Limavady, ✆ (015047) 62226, all year.

Festivals

Festival information: ✆ (01504) 267284/365151.

February/March: Derry *Feis*. Easter week: *Feis Dhoire Cholmaile*.

March: Celtic Film Festival.

May: Southern Comfort Jazz Festival, ✆ (01504) 260516.

June: Derry Summer Festival, ✆ (01504) 267284 for details.

July/August: The Apprentice Boys Marches in Derry, Castle Dawson and many other towns in County Londonderry. Contact the Apprentice Boys Memorial Hall, ✆ (01504) 263571; or look in the local newspapers—*The Derry Journal* or *The Sentinel*.

October: Banks of the Foyle Festival.

Early November: Northwest Arts Festival, mainly located in Derry.

Eglinton to Magilligan

The A2 takes you along the Foyle Plain and by-passes Eglinton (the site of the airport where the Loganair flights arrive from Glasgow, Dublin and Manchester), and travels through **Ballykelly**. This town was settled by people brought in by the Fishmonger's Company of London in 1618. It is close to a British army base, and in 1970 hit the headlines when off duty soldiers were blown up in a pub here. The next town along the coast, still following the A2, is **Limavady**. The people of this little village are Loyalist to the hilt, judging by the graffiti on their walls, much of which harks back to the siege of Londonderry in 1689, and the Battle of the Boyne in 1690. Before the Fishermongers Company arrived, Limavady was an important centre of the territory of the O'Cahans, a sept under the lordship of the O'Neills. There is no trace of their castle now. The town is very beautifully situated in the Roe Valley with fine mountain scenery to the north and southeast. It is associated with the famous 'Londonderry Air', which was noted down by Miss Jane Ross in 1851 from a passing fiddler called Denis O'Hempsey (*see* below). Thomas Connolly, speaker of the Irish House of Commons before the Act of Union in 1800, and builder of the beautiful Castletown House near Dublin, was the son of a Limavady blacksmith.

Precious gold representations of a masted boat, collars and a necklace fashioned in the Celtic La Tène style were found at Broighter near the coastal marshes surrounding the estuary of the River Roe. They can be seen in the National Museum, Dublin. Further up the coast, underneath the forest-covered Binevenagh Mountain, is the triangle of **Magilligan**. Although there is a huge army post here, and a scenic Martello tower, the strand is better known for its shells, the herbs that grow among the dunes, the birds and for the plagues of rabbits commemorated in a special Magilligan grace. This part of the world has connections with the Irish music tradition. At the end of the 18th century, interest in the Gaelic cultural achievement began amongst a group of scholarly men; foremost amongst them was Edward Bunting who did so much to preserve Irish airs and ancient music. He helped to organize a great assembly of Irish Harpers in Belfast in 1792. One of the oldest harpers, a blind man called Denis Hempsey, or O'Hempsey, lived near Magilligan. He provided Bunting with many old tunes and airs and had played before Prince Charles Edward Stuart at Holyrood Palace in 1745. It is rather symbolic that so many of the last Irish harpers were blind, as if they suffered physically the fate which had befallen their culture. Men like O'Hempsey or Carolan continued to play the old Irish airs and to wander through Ireland, yet they had no status in the English framework of society. The Gaelic lords who had given them a home and patronage had fled, and the Gaelic society in which they had played no longer existed. It is only fair to say, however, that the anglized Earl of Bristol and Bishop of Derry presented O'Hempsey with a house near Magilligan. The Magilligan Field Centre (*open all year*) at **Bellarena**, southwest of Magilligan on the A2, has a little museum, full of information on the flora, fauna and geology of the area.

Downhill to Coleraine

From Limavady you can cut inland through the Roe Valley to Dungiven on the B68 and pass through the Country Park which has many fine picnic spots. However, if you want to take advantage of the superb coastline you should go on from Magilligan following the A2 to Downhill, and on up to the pretty resort of **Castlerock** which has a superb sandy beach stretching for miles. A really worthwhile expedition can be made to the **Palace of Downhill** (*open April–June and Sept, Sat and Sun, 2–6; July–Aug and Easter, daily 2–6, and the glen and grounds are always open; adm free*), a ruined castle just off the A2 at Downhill village, built by the famous Earl-Bishop, Frederick Augustus Hervey (1730–1803), one of the most interesting and enlightened Church of Ireland bishops. The palace and the surrounding coastline is in the care of the National Trust. At the entrance the caretaker has planted a marvellous garden of primulas and cottage flowers, and the palace itself is sited on a windswept hill with wonderful views of the Inishowen hills and the Antrim headlands. The Earl-Bishop who built it was extravagant and well-travelled; the Bristol hotels you find all over the Continent take their name from him. He built up a great art collection with the episcopal revenues from his Derry bishopric (which in the 18th century was the second-richest in Ireland), and a second princely residence at Ballyscullion near Bellaghy, which is totally ruined. Downhill was built in the late 18th century. The landscaped estate which still remains includes the Mussenden Temple perched on a cliff overlooking the sea, the ruins of the castle, family memorials, gardens, a fish pond, woodland and cliff walks.

The bishop was a great advocate of toleration, contributing generously to Catholic and Presbyterian churches and their clergy. One of his amusements was party-giving. If you go down to the Mussenden Temple, the story of the great race he organized between the Anglican and the Presbyterian ministers before a dinner party is recounted. There was some suspicion that he was more of a Classicist than a Christian: his temple, on a cliff edge, is modelled on the Roman temple of Vesta, and it certainly suggests a certain independent interpretation of religion! The ruins of the palace lie within the boundaries of a farm, but the temple and the little valley beside it provide splendid picnic spots.

Eastwards along the coast is **Portstewart,** a seasoned little resort town which is overlooked by the castle-style convent (*not open to the public*). Inland from Portstewart is **Coleraine** (*Cuil Raithin*: fern recess), which is supposed to have been founded by St Patrick. Most of what you see was developed by the Irish Society of London. Whiskey from Coleraine is now made by Bushmills Distillery, although called Coleraine, is still held in high repute and indeed is supplied to the House of Commons, although Bushmills is probably the more famous of the two.Tours of Old Bushmills Distillery ✆ (012657) 31521.

The Coleraine campus of the University of Ulster is a centre for talks and tours during the summer, and there is a good **theatre** here called the Riverside. The campus has a rare collection of Irish bred daffodils and narcissi. In full bloom mid to late April. Free access always. The River Bann runs through the town and was the scene of early habitation. At **Mount Sandel**, on Coleraine's outskirts, Mesolithic flints have been found which indicate the presence of the earliest settlements in Ireland. There is much archaeological evidence to suggest that they date from 9000 BC. Later the mound of Mount Sandel became a royal seat of local Celtic kings, and finally, a Norman Fort. There is nothing to see now. If you are in the British Museum in London you will see some of those Bannside antiquities, the most spectacular of which is a huge hoard of Roman coins, evidently seized by Irish pirates, and now returned to England.

The Bann Valley

Bellaghy to Moneymore

You can follow the River Bann through its valley by taking the A54. The valley is farmed by the industrious descendants of Scots and English, who were tenants of the London Companies and arrived in the region in the early 17th century. The countryside is very pretty in a cultivated way. Before the Bann reaches Lough Neagh it broadens out into Lough Beg, and in the marshy area around the lake is Church Island, so called because of its ruined church and holy well. A spire has been constructed among the ruins—one result of Earl-Bishop Hervey's building ventures. He wanted to be able to see the spire from his palace at Ballyscullion. The local people still leave offerings at the holy well on the island. The birdlife around the lake is superb; and many water fowl, snipe and swans can be seen. Seamus Heaney, the poet, comes from this area.

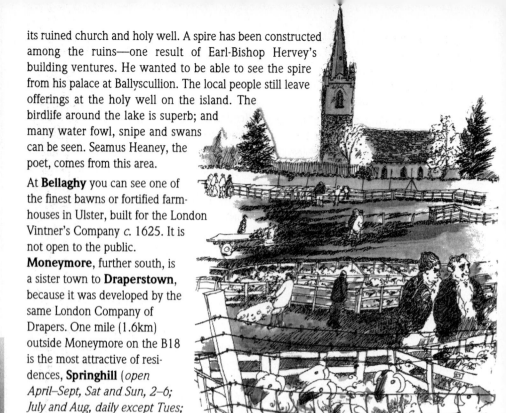

At **Bellaghy** you can see one of the finest bawns or fortified farmhouses in Ulster, built for the London Vintner's Company *c.* 1625. It is not open to the public.

Moneymore, further south, is a sister town to **Draperstown**, because it was developed by the same London Company of Drapers. One mile (1.6km) outside Moneymore on the B18 is the most attractive of residences, **Springhill** (*open April–Sept, Sat and Sun, 2–6; July and Aug, daily except Tues; adm; ☎ (016487) 48210*), built in the late 17th century as a fortified manor house by the Lennox-Conynghams, a settler family, with its outbuildings in Dutch style. It is a proper country gentleman's house with soft shadowed interiors, a lovely library and portraits, including one with a following gaze. The artist's trick was to paint the eyes so that they seem to be watching you wherever you stand. You can almost imagine you are a guest of the house when you go there. There is a small costume museum, and implements are on show in the outbuildings. The grounds are beautiful. The yew thicket is said to be a vestige of the ancient forest of Glenconkeyne, and there is a herb garden—essential for any household in the 17th and 18th centuries. Refreshments are available in the old servants' hall and there is a National Trust shop.

Maghera to Londonderry

Maghera, the mountain heartland of the county, is a small and busy town at the foot of the Glenshane Pass. It is said to be the meeting place of the mountain and plains people, rather like Dungiven on the other side of the mountain (*always accessible, adm free*). At the southeast end of the town there is an ancient church with a square headed doorway, dating perhaps from the 18th century. The massive lintels are decorated with a carved, interlaced pattern, and a sculpture of the crucifixion.

Up on the moor in the Sperrin Mountains, sheep-farming is practised and the government is planting conifer forests. At the top of **Glenshane Pass** on the A6 between Maghera and Dungiven, nature trails and picnic spots are laid out. You will pass thickets of native woods and plunging streams. Close by, to the west, is Sawel, at 2240ft (683m) the highest mountain in the Sperrin range.

Further south on the B40 from Draperstown you will find **Banagher Glen**, which has a **nature reserve**. North of the forest, off the B74 from Feeny, is **Banagher Church**, founded by a St Muriedach O'Heney. The church itself is probably 12th-century, with a square-headed doorway and massive lintels. In the graveyard is a stone-roofed tomb or oratory with the figure of O'Heney in relief—he who bequeathed to his descendants the power to be lucky with the sand from his tomb. Perhaps the poet Seamus Heaney makes occasional pilgrimages here! The church is always accessible to the public. On the eastern side of Dungiven (on the A6) is a fine ruin of an **Augustinian priory**, only the chancel with a Norman arch remains. The elaborate altar tomb erected in the late 14th century is very striking. It is carved with a figure in Irish dress grasping a sword, and commemorates an O'Cahan, whose family were the lords of this territory before the plantation.

This area is a delight for those of an exploratory nature, for the countryside is wild and full of romantic ruins, streams and forests. It also is noted for its prehistoric megaliths, which you can learn about at the Sperrin Heritage Centre, 274 Glenelly Road, Crancagh, near Gortin in County Tyrone (*open all year*). The **Ulster Way**, a signposted walking trail, passes through the Sperrin Mountains on its way from the Antrim Coast to Lough Erne in County Fermanagh.

On the A6 from Dungiven to Derry is **Ness Wood**, another attractive forest park, and the pretty River Burntollet runs through this area. At Burntollet Bridge on the A6 one of the opening conflicts of the recent troubles took place, on the occasion of a Civil Rights march in 1969.

Derry City

Londonderry (*Doire*: oak grove) is a symbolic city situated on the River Foyle. Before the 1960s it was probably best known for its association with the pretty 'Londonderry Air', but has until the recent ceasefire been one of Northern Ireland's trouble-spots. The strife is not unprecedented, for it has survived three sieges.

History

Derry was first besieged during the rebellion of 1641, then during the Cromwellian wars of 1649; and finally there was the historic siege of 1689. This last siege still plays a very important part in the mind of the Ulster Unionist, for it sums up the courage and righteousness of the Protestant settlers who resisted with the cry, 'No surrender!' The city was being assailed by James II, who had lost his throne in England and was trying to repair his fortunes in Ireland with the help of Louis XIV of France. Thirteen apprentice boys rushed to the gates of the city and shut them in the faces of his approaching army. This secured Londonderry for William III, who had been invited to take over from James II by the

English parliament. The siege that followed resulted in many deaths, for the city had no stores of food. Citizens ate rats, dogs, and the starch for laundering linen. A boom was placed across the River Foyle to prevent food supplies reaching the city, but this was eventually broken after 105 days, and the city was relieved by the forces of the Lord Deputy Mountjoy, commanded by Captain Browning, at Ship Quay on 28 July. Every year, the anniversary of the shutting of the gates is celebrated on 18 December, and the Raising of the Siege on 12 August. There are marches around the city, with bands and drummers.

The land on which the settlement of Derry grew up was granted to St Colmcille (St Columba), by Aimire, Prince of the O'Neills, in AD 546. St Columba built a monastery on the oak-crowned hill. He eventually left the monastery, and founded many other religious settlements, the most important of which was Iona, the isle off the west coast of Scotland. From here Christianity spread over Scotland. St Columba wrote, homesick for this place:

> Derry, mine own small oak grove,
> Little cell, my home, my love.

St Columba never outgrew his love for the city. He would have sympathized with the emigrant families who left Derry for America during the 18th and 19th centuries, among them the forebears of such famous figures as Davy Crockett and President James K. Polk.

In the 17th century Derry acquired its prefix 'London' because of the position occupied by the London Livery Companies in the building and development of the city. The city and the county were granted by James I to these companies, who rebuilt the walls and planned the streets, which still remain. Derry is the most complete walled city in Ireland: with early 17th century walls about a mile (1.6km) in circumference, pierced by seven gates, six bastions and many cannon.

City Centre

The city is now a modern industrial centre, noted for its manufacturing of clothing, but its skyline is still unmarred by too many 20th-century concrete intrusions, and a walk around the walls gives you a good view of the **docks** and the wide River Foyle. Big ships don't harbour here very frequently, although in the days of the British Empire they carried exotic cargo such as silk from Bombay. The **walls** and **gates** can be walked around in this order: Ship Quay Gate, opposite the Guildhall; then west to Magazine Gate, and on to Bishops Gate, where a triumphal arch was raised in 1789. It is constantly being disfigured with graffiti, for which Derry is famous, of course; then go further around to the Double Bastion. One of the cannons preserved here was used during the 1689 siege and is known as 'Roaring Meg'. Further to the north is the Royal Bastion, where the citizens of Londonderry raised the red flag of defiance, and a monument some 90ft (27m) high to the memory of Walker, who encouraged and led the defence of the city. This historic monument was destroyed by a bomb. There are a few more bastions before the circuit is finished. In summer, guided tours of the city walls leave from the tourist information centre in Bishop Street.

The old city is bounded by its walls. To the northwest of them is the Republican and historical **Bogside**, with its much-repainted 'Free Derry' monument and colourful murals.

Southeast across the Craigavon Bridge is the **Waterside**. The **Tower Museum** (*open daily in summer; rest of year, Tues–Sat, 10am–5pm (closed for lunch);* ✆ *(01504) 262746; adm*) in O'Doherty Tower, in Union Hall Place, preserves the treasures of the Corporation of London, including a two-handed sword said to belong to Sir Caher O'Doherty, who raided Derry in 1608. The tower is very attractive and has been rebuilt in the last ten years in soft grey stone. The tunnels date from the 17th century. An exhibition details the history of Derry and uses models and video to bring it to life. Artefacts from the Spanish Armada ships wrecked off the coast in 1588 are also on display. It is possible to tour the Guildhall, which has very good stained-glass

windows depicting the history of Derry. From Derry Quay, behind the Guildhall, thousands of Irish emigrants sailed to America. Next to the Guildhall, you will notice some attractive Georgian houses, some with medieval foundations. At the top of the hill on the Diamond, the central square of the old town, excavations were undertaken to try to uncover an early settlement, possibly the Columban foundation. However, they revealed domestic material from the early 17th century settler population. You should try to visit the Church of Ireland cathedral called **St Columb's** (*chapter house open to visitors daily, 9am–5pm*), which lies between Fountain Street and Bishop Street, and is an example of Planters' Gothic . The building was founded by the Corporation of London in 1633, and restored in 1886. The roof rests on stone corbels carved into heads representing past bishops of Derry. The bishop's throne incorporates the chair which was used at the consecration of the cathedral in 1633. The cathedral bells ring out through the city on every important religious, civic or national occasion; the peal is made up of 12 bells, eight of them dating from the 17th century. The cathedral was damaged a few years ago by a bomb which shattered some of the windows, but it has been repaired. It has a number of exhibits illustrating the spirit of the 17th-century siege.

The **Craft Village**, which is a reconstructed portrayal of Derry between the 16th and 19th centuries is worth a look, not least for a coffee break in the Boston Tea Party—or a browse amongst the craft shops.

The Courthouse (1813) in Bishops Street is a good example of Greek Revival architecture. Close by, just outside the city walls, is the interesting 18th-century **Church of St Columba**, also called Long Tower Church. It is built on the site of a 12th-century monastery called Templemore. Saint Columba is further commemorated in a boys' school of that name further down the street. **St Eugene's Roman Catholic Cathedral** off Infirmary Road and Great James Street has a fine east window and high altar. It was built in Gothic style in 1873. **The Orchard Gallery** in Orchard Street (✆ (01504) 269675), and the **Gordon Gallery** in London Street are within easy reach of each other, and will give you a taste of modern Irish art. **The Derry Heritage Centre** in Butcher Street (✆ *(01504) 269792*) preserves genealogical data from 1663.

Shopping

Chain stores: Boots, Next, Marks and Spencer and various others in the Richmond Centre, Ferryquay Street, Derry.

Art: The Gordon Gallery, 7 London Street, Derry, ✆ (01504) 374044. Exhibitions and sale of works by modern Irish artists. Also available are silver, ceramics and glassware.

Health food: Life Tree, Spencer Road, Derry, ✆ (01504) 42865.

Antiques: Forge Antiques, 24 Long Commons, Castlerock, ✆ (01265) 51339. Bygones, 73 Carlisle Road, Derry. The Smithy, 782 Coleraine Road, Portstewart. Alexander Antiques, 108 Dunluce Road, Portrush.

Crafts: The Donegal Shop, 8 Shipquay Street, Derry, ✆ (01504) 266928. Tower Museum Shop, Craft Village, Derry, ✆ (01504) 374404.

Activities

Coarse fishing: Lough Beg, River Bann.

Deep-sea fishing: between Lough Foyle and Portrush. Boat hire from: Robert Cardwell, 119 Bushmills Road, Coleraine, ✆ (01265) 822359; Joe Mullan, Portrush, ✆ (01265) 822209.

Game fishing: for brown trout and salmon on the Agivey, Clady, Roe Bann and Faughan Rivers. Game rod licence from Foyle Fisheries Commission, 8 Victoria Road, Derry, ✆ (01504) 42100. Information and gillie service from River Faughan Angler's Association, 26 Carlisle Road, Derry, ✆ (01504) 267781, in the afternoons only. Also, from Bann Systems Ltd, ✆ (01265) 44433.

Swimming and leisure centres: in Templemore, Lisnagelvin, St Columba's Park and Brooke Park—all in Derry.

Golf: Benone Golf Course, Downhill, ✆ (05047) 50555, is a seaside course. Castlerock Golf Club, 65 Circular Road, Castlerock, ✆ (01265) 848314. Royal Portrush Golf Course, Portrush, ✆ (01265) 822311. City of Derry Golf Club, 49 Victoria Road, Derry, ✆ (01504) 46369.

Pony-trekking: Ballylagan Equestrian Centre, Aghadowey, ✆ (01265) 868463; Hilltop Farm, Castlerock, ✆ (01265) 848629; Maddybenny Farm, Portrush,

℗ (01265) 823394/823603. The Island Equestrian Centre, Coleraine, ℗ (01265) 42599. Timbertop Riding Centre, 160a Curragh Road, Aghadowey, ℗(01265) 85788. Calmore Stables, 68 Main Street, Tobermore, ℗ (01648) 43988.

Talks and tours: University of Ulster in July and August. Contact the University, ℗ (01504) 265621.

Railway Museum: you can take a trip on a 1934 diesel railcar on the 1¾ mile track beside the Foyle. Open May to Sept, Tues–Sat, 10am–5pm; adm; ℗ (01504) 265234. On Foyle Road, Derry, close to Craigavon Bridge.

Where to Stay

expensive

Everglades Hotel, Prehen Road, Derry, ℗ (01504) 46722. Overlooking the River Foyle. Bland and comfortable. **Beechhill Country House Hotel**, 32 Ardmore Rd, Derry, ℗ (01504) 49279. One mile outside Derry. Well known for excellent cuisine. Mrs Welch, **Drenagh**, Limavady, ℗ (015047) 22649. Comfortable, fun country house. Excellent food.

moderate

Blackheath House, 112 Killeague Road, Blackhill, Coleraine, ℗ (01265) 868433. Fine 18th-century building with a good restaurant in its cellars, and spacious bedrooms with en suite bathrooms.

inexpensive

Mrs Hegarty, **Greenhill House**, Aghadowey, Coleraine, ℗ (01265) 868241. Your hostess loves to chat and bring you every comfort. Her home is a pretty Georgian farmhouse and her cooking is superb. Bedrooms with en suite bathrooms. Mrs Swinerton, **Moyola Lodge**, Castledawson, ℗ (0648) 68224. Another Georgian house, with free salmon fishing for its guests. Delicious raspberries and cream in summer. Mrs Craig, **Ballycarton Farm**, 239 Seacoast Road, Bellarena, ℗ (05047) 50216. Modern farmhouse in very scenic area close to Magilligan Nature Reserve. **Magee University College**, Northland Road, Derry, ℗ (01504) 265621. Impersonal, cheap and central. Mrs Henry, **Carneety House**, 120 Mussenden Road, Castlerock, ℗ (01265) 848640. Old farmhouse on the A2, just outside Castlerock. Mrs Kane, **Ballyhenny House**, 172 Seacoast Road, Limavady, ℗ (05047) 22657 Farmhouse with good home cooking and comfortable rooms. **Brown Trout Inn**, 209 Agivey Road, Aghadowey, ℗ (01265) 868209. Pretty grounds, near the river, with good food. Mrs Josephine King, **Camus House**, 27 Curragh Road, Coleraine, ℗ (01265) 2982. Listed 17th-century house overlooking the River Bann. Can offer lots of advice on fishing and have won an award for their breakfasts. Mrs Elizabeth Buchanan, **Elagh Hall**, Buncrana Road, Derry, ℗ (01504) 263116. 18th-century farmhouse, 2 miles (3.2km) from the city centre, overlooking the hills of Donegal.

Lough Beg Coach Houses, Ballyscullion Park, Bellaghy, ✆ (01648) 386235. 6 well-appointed cottages on large estate, sleeps 6. Full Irish breakfast and dinner can be ordered. Close to game and coarse fishing.

Eating Out
expensive

Macduffs, 112 Killeaque Road, Blackhill, Coleraine, ✆ (01265) 868433. The **Cellar Restaurant** of Blackheath House (*see* above). Intimate surroundings, with award-winning food based on freshly grown vegetables and local game and seafood.

moderate

Beech Hill Country House, 32 Ardmore Road, Derry, ✆ (01504) 49279. Delicious imaginative food such as home-made tagliatelle with chicken and sumptuous pies for dessert. **Ballycarton Farm**, 239 Seacoast Road, Bellarena, ✆ (015047) 50216. Good home cooking. Evenings only. **India House**, 51 Carlisle Road, Derry, ✆ (01504) 260532. Spicy well-cooked and reasonably priced menu. **Brown Trout Inn**, Mullaghmore, Aghadowey, ✆ (01265) 868209. Well-established, with good pub food. **Salmon Leap**, 53 Castleroe Road, Coleraine, ✆ (01265) 52992. Good buffet lunch. **Browns**, 1 Victoria Road, Derry, ✆ (01504) 45180. Simple, well-cooked food.

inexpensive/cheap

Austins Coffee Shop, The Diamond, Derry. Good for a cheap snack lunch and very central. **Morelli's**, The Promenade, Portstewart. Ice-cream and pasta. **Johnny B's**, 59 Victoria Road, Derry, ✆ (01504) 41078. Wine bar/restaurant serving satays, good salads and burgers. **Fiorentini's**, 67–69 Strand Road, Derry, ✆ (01504) 260653. Italian-style café selling cappuccino, ice-cream and sandwiches. The **Boston Tea Party**, Craft Village, Derry. Good snacks during the day. **Copper Kettle**, 4 Main Street, Castlerock, ✆ (01265) 848229. Stews, lasagne. Open in the daytime only. **Dungloe Bar**, 41 Waterloo Street, Derry, ✆ (01504) 267706. Pub grub and traditional music. **Metro Bar**, 3 Bank Place, Derry, ✆ (01504) 267401. Soup and stew.

Entertainment and Nightlife

Classical music/theatre: The Guildhall Master Music, ✆ (01504) 365151; Foyle Arts Centre, Lawrence Hill, ✆ (01504) 26657; Rialto Entertainment Centre for drama and exhibitions, ✆ (01504) 262567. The Playhouse, Artillery Street, ✆ (01504) 373538.

County Antrim

The coast has a well-deserved reputation for being one of the loveliest and most spectacular in Europe. The Antrim coast road (A2) passes through exquisite little fishing villages and areas of protected beauty. The famous Giant's Causeway—one of the wonders of the natural world—the wild beauty of Fair and Torr Heads, and the ruined Dunluce Castle, all contrive to make a trip here more than worthwhile. A little way inland are the Nine Glens of Antrim, which have been celebrated in poetry and song the world over because of their scenic beauty. This is from a poem called 'The Glens' by John Hewitt, who died recently.

> *Groined by deep glens and walled along the west*
> *by the bare hilltops and the tufted moors*
> *this rim of arable that ends in foam*
> *has but to drop a leaf or snap a branch*
> *and my hand twitches with the leaping verse*
> *as hazel twig will wrench the straining wrists*
> *for untapped jet that thrusts beneath the sod.*

Especially beautiful is Glenariff, with its waterfalls. The 'Mare's Tail' being the most spectacular. The glen is an excellent example of a post glaciation U-Valley. It is virtually geometric. The valley of the River Bann extends along the Londonderry border to Lough Neagh, the largest inland sheet of water in Britain: 150 sq miles (388 sq km) in all.

The weather on the east coast is variable, as it is in all parts of Ireland, although it is more inclined to be sunny and dry with a brisk breeze off the sea. The traveller who can brave the cold Atlantic water will enjoy the breakers which roll into Whitepark Bay, and the fine sandy beaches around Portrush. The bicyclist will find the roads quite strenuous, with hills and hairpin bends, but will be well rewarded with the views; whilst the walker can follow the Ulster Way, a marked trail which explores the Antrim Coast and Glens. A splendid adventure is to take the boat out to Rathlin Island and spend the day watching the huge sea bird population on the cliffs there, and just revelling in its clean and unspoilt beauty.

County Antrim shares Belfast, the capital city of Northern Ireland, with County Down, and it is dealt with separately (*see* p.371). Despite the 'Troubles', Belfast is a vigorous and industrious city with plenty of interest, especially for the historically and politically minded. It is still an important linen and ship-building centre and port, with a wonderful position on the River Lagan and Belfast Lough.

History

Antrim lies very close to Scotland with only a narrow strip of water in between, so it is not surprising that there are great links between the two. Even the accent of the peoples are similar. Before the Celts invaded, the Scotti people moved easily between Scotland and Ireland, crossing the Moyle or North Sea Channel here. (Today, the ferry links to mainland Britain are by far the shortest here, and the same shifting of populations goes on.) The word Scots is derived from the 4th-century Irish verb 'to raid', and the Romans called Ireland 'Scotia' because it was from here all the raiders came. It was not until the 12th century that its meaning was transferred to the country now called Scotland.

The precise dates of these developments can only be guesswork, but up until the 6th century the ancient Kingdom of Dalriada extended from the Antrim Coast, including the islands of Rathlin and Iona, to the west of Scotland. By the late 14th century the clan MacDonnell held the balance of power and their territory straddled both sides of the

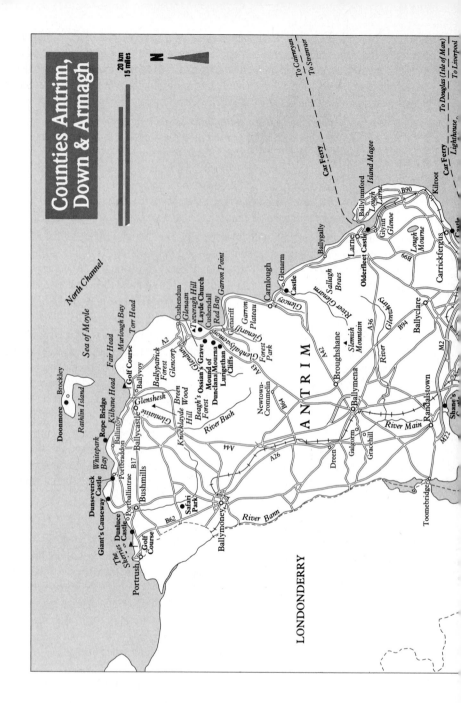

Counties Antrim, Down & Armagh

N

20 km
15 miles

North Channel

Sea of Moyle

To Carnlyon
To Stranraer
To Douglas (Isle of Man)
To Liverpool
Lighthouse
Car Ferry
Car Ferry

Ballylumford
Lough Larne
Island Magee
Kilroot
B90
Castle

Car Ferry

Glynn
Glenoe
Larne
Olderfleet Castle
Lough
Mourne
Carrickfergus
B99

Doonmore
Brockley
Rathlin Island
Whitepark Bay
Rope Bridge
Kilbane Head
Fair Head
Murlough Bay
Tor Head
Golf Course
Ballyvoy

Dunseverick Castle
Giant's Causeway Castle
The
Skerries
Dunluce
Castle
Portballintrae
Portbraddon
Ballintoy
B17
Ballycastle
Glenshesk
Glentaisie
Knocklayde Hill
Glensheshe
Brern Wood
Ballypatrick Forest
Glencorp
Cushendun
Glenaan
Layde Church
Cushendall
Red Bay
Garron Point
Glenariff
Tieveragh Hill
A2

Portrush
Golf Course
Bushmills
Safari Park
Ballymoney
River Bann
B62

Beagh's Ossian's Grave
Mound of
Dunclana/Mourna
Lurigethan
Cliffs
Glenariff/Glenann
Garron Plateau
Forest Park
Glenarm
Carnlough
Castle
Glencoy

A44
A26
River Bush
Newtown-Crommelin
B64
Sallagh Braes
River Glenarm
Broughshane
Slemish Mountain
A2
A36
Glenwhirry River
Ballyclare
B94
M2

Dreen
Galgorm
Grachill
Ballymena
River Main
M12
Randalstown
Shane's

A N T R I M

Toomebridge

LONDONDERRY

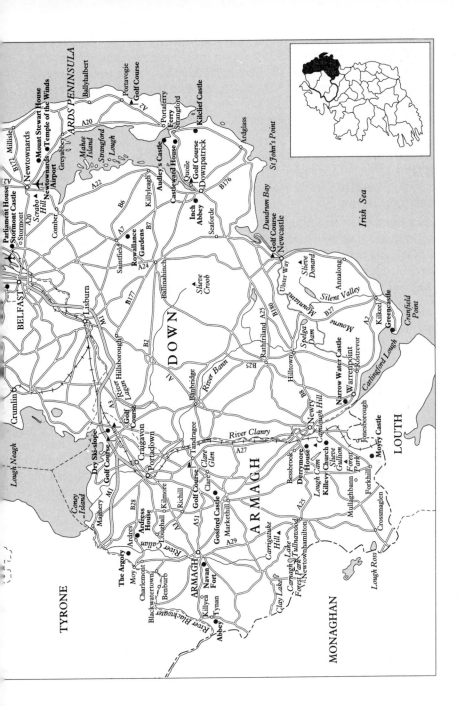

Atlantic up until the Elizabethan era. The time of the Dalriadic kings and the Scotti people is shrouded in half-myth and legend, but it has given rise to some interesting theories on who are the true natives of this land. The Scottish Presbyterians, whose forebears were settled here in the Jacobite plantations, have claimed that they were coming back to their original home, and that the Catholic Celts who were driven into the mountains were in fact the interlopers who had come up from the south.

Whatever the theories of the past may be, today the Jacobite plantations continue to have an effect, in that there are pockets of staunch Presbyterians loyal to the union with Britain who would man a Unionist army given half a chance. These Unionists live mainly in the rich plains, whilst there is a Catholic Nationalist fringe along the coast and in the glens, and never the two will mix.

Stepping back into the mists and fantasy of legend, there are stories of Fionn MacCumhail (Finn MacCool) and of Oísín, his son; stories of the sons of *Uísneach* who died for Deirdre's beauty; and of the Children of Lir, condemned to spend their lives as swans on the waters of the Moyle. The place-names of prehistoric remains, glens, mountains and caves abound with allusions to these myths (*see* **Old Gods and Heroes**, pp.574–80).

Getting There and Around

By air: Belfast International Airport is about 25 miles (40km) from Larne.

By sea: Stranraer or Cairnryan in Scotland are ferry rides of only about 2¼ hours from Larne. Seacat, Stranraer–Belfast, ✆ (01) 661 1731.

By rail: There are frequent train services from Belfast to Larne, which connect with ferries, and with buses travelling to the villages in the glens.

By bus: Ulsterbus coach tours around the Antrim Coast road depart from Ballycastle, Larne and Belfast. Ulsterbus and the Old Bushmills Distillery operate an open-topped bus between the 27 June and 28 August from Coleraine along the Giant's Causeway, via Portstewart, Portrush, Portballintrae, Bushmills, and return, ✆ Coleraine (01265) 3334 for information.

By car: Avis, Rent-a-car, Ferry Terminal, Larne Harbour, ✆ (01574) 260799. Hertz Rent a Car, Ferry Terminal, Larne Harbour, ✆ (01574) 278111.

By bike: The Raleigh Rent-a-Bike network operates in Ballymena, at R.F. Linton and Sons, 31 Springwell Street, ✆ (01266) 652516. Causeway Coast Cycles, Bath Street, Portrush, (01265) 824334.

getting to Rathlin Island

By boat: daily crossings from Easter to September. From September to Easter, a limited service is arranged by the Tourist Office, 7 Mary Street, Ballycastle, ✆ (012657) 62024. The mail boat leaves Ballycastle at about 10.30am every Monday, Wednesday and Friday. A return ticket costs £5. Be prepared to stay overnight, since the mailboat does not always return to Ballycastle on the same day.

Ballymena (Council Offices Ardiveen, 80 Galgorm Rd), ✆ (01266) 44111, all year.
Giant's Causeway, Visitor Centre, ✆ (012657) 31855, all year.
Portrush (Town Hall), ✆ (01265) 823333, April to September.
Antrim, Pogue's Entry, Church St., ✆ (01849) 428331.
Ballycastle, ✆ (012657) 620024, all year.
Belfast, St Anne's Court, 59 North Street, ✆ (0232) 246609.
Carrickfergus, ✆ (09603) 63604.
Cushendall, ✆ (02667) 71180.
Larne, Larne Harbour, ✆ (01574) 260088.

Festivals

June/July: *Feis na n gleann*—Gaelic music, crafts and sports in the Glens of Antrim.

Mid July: Ulster Steam Traction Engine Rally, Shane's Castle, Antrim, with vintage car rallies and side-shows as well. The Lughnasa Medieval Fair and Craft Market, Carrickfergus Castle. Lughnasa was a quarterly feast of the old Irish Calendar.

Last weekend of August: Ould Lammas Fair, Ballycastle.

The Antrim Coast from Belfast to Larne

If you start off from Belfast for the Antrim Coast, take the A2 loughside road passing the industrial districts and comfortable suburbs of Whiteabbey and Greenisland to the oldest town in Northern Ireland, **Carrickfergus**.

The town takes its name from one of the Dalriadic kings, Fergus, who foundered off this point on one of his journeys between Antrim and Scotland. The kings of Scotland were descended from his line and, therefore, the kings and queens of England. He is said to have brought his coronation stone from Ireland to Scone. Certainly the rock of red sandstone embedded with pebbles, now in Westminster Abbey, is like rock found along the Antrim coast. The town is lovely, very well kept and pedestrianised in parts with some good craft shops.

Carrickfergus Castle (*open April–Sept, Mon–Sat, 10–6, Sun, 2–6; Oct–Mar, Mon–Sat, 10–4, Sun, 2–4; adm*) is the most prominent sight in the town: a massive, rectangular, unbuttressed four-storey tower built by John de Courcy in the years after 1180. (John de Courcy and his kinsmen were very successful Normans who conquered much of Counties Down and Antrim.) The castle, which is extremely well-preserved, has a very interesting history. In 1210, King John of England slept here during his tour of Ireland. Powerful Norman lords such as the de Courcys and de Lacy's renewed their oath of allegiance to him at this time, but in reality they were very much a law unto themselves. The building was captured by the French for a brief period in 1760, and in all it has been militarily occupied for 750 years. Since 1928, however, it has been a museum, with an impressive array of weapons and armour on display, plus the history of such Irish regiments as the Inniskilling Dragoons. The video and costumed guides give a lively and exciting insight into the 800 years of the castle's history. Beside this splendid fortification lies the grand marina, where there are pleasure boats and rowing boats for hire. It is the largest of its kind in the six counties. Carrickfergus has an old **parish church** founded by St Nicholas in 1185, and rebuilt in 1614. The famous Ulster poet Louis MacNeice (1907–63), who was associated with the group which included C. Day Lewis, Auden and Spender, wrote charmingly of the skewed alignment of the aisle:

> *The church in the form of a cross but denoting*
> *The list of Christ on the cross in the angle of the nave.*

His father was the rector here for a while. There's also a monument to Sir Arthur Chichester here, one of the loveliest pieces of 17th century craftsmanship in Ulster. A new development is the Knight Ride in Antrim Street, a heritage exhibition and ride through history in the best Disney traditions. You can buy a joint ticket for this and the castle (*open April–Sept, Mon–Sat, 10am–6pm; Sun, 12–6pm; © (01960) 366455*).

On your way north out of Carrickfergus you pass **Kilroot**. Here in the Church of Ireland church, now a ruin, Dean Swift (1667–1745) began his clerical life. This fascinating man is remembered for his savage and ironic book *Gulliver's Travels*. At Whitehead, less than a mile up the coast, there are excursions on vintage trains every Sunday in June, July and August. Locomotive enthusiasts can indulge in train rides on early vehicles. You can go up the coast as far as Portrush on the Portrush Flyer from York Street. The train is formed from preserved coaches and is hauled by a powerful mainline locomotive. The road to Larne takes you along by the lough, which is almost landlocked by Island Magee, a small peninsula with popular beaches such as Brown's Bay and Mill Bay. There is a ferry from Larne to Ballylumford on Island Magee and it is fun to walk along the Gobbins, basalt cliffs on the east side of the peninsula.

Before you get to Larne you will pass one of the glens that break through the Antrim plateau—**Glenoe**, with four waterfalls. It is now under National Trust care. The little village of **Glynn** is actually on the shore of Larne Lough, and was the setting for a film called *The Luck of the Irish.*

Although there are some hideous buildings and unecological views produced by the industrial sites round **Larne**, it is an important port and the gateway to the Antrim coast proper, so you cannot very well avoid it. There are railway services at regular intervals to and from York Street Station in Belfast. These connect with the sailing times of the boats between Larne, and Stranraer and Cairnryan. It's the shortest sea crossing from Ireland to Scotland, taking only 70 minutes once you are in open sea. **The Railway Bar** on the Main Street is good for a jar, if you have time to spare before a crossing.

On **Curran Point**, a promontory south of the harbour, you can see **Olderfleet Castle**, a corruption of the Viking name *Ulfrechsfiord.* The castle is 13th-century and ruined, with free access. If you have time to spare whilst waiting for a ferry, a brisk 15-minute walk will take you past the Cairnyan ferry dock to Chaine Memorial Road where a replica of a medieval round tower, 95ft (29m) tall, looks out to sea. Around here, so many Middle Stone Age artefacts have been found that the term 'Larnian' is often used to describe the Mesolithic culture of Ireland. You may not be surprised perhaps to learn that the discovery of so many early sites in the Black North (i.e. in 'Protestant' areas like Larne or Mount Sandel, near Coleraine), has given rise to an interesting theory of history: that there were anthropological differences between the two warring factions of the northeast—the aboriginal Protestants (heirs of the Dalriadic kingdom who came back from Scotland to claim their land), and the Celtic Catholic invaders. A rather incredible figure from Larne's more recent past was the romantic novelist Amanda McKittrick Ros, who was wife of the stationmaster here. *Delina Delaney* and *Poems of Puncture* were among her better known works; the young Aldous Huxley and his mates, while at Oxford, formed a reading circle to admire their awfulness. She died in 1939, convinced that she would still be remembered in a thousand years. It seems she did not realize that people responded to her writings with derision, or at best kindly laughter. Still, her work has just been republished again! Here is an example of her ghastly prose. In *Delina Delaney* we are told that the blood of Madame de Maine 'boiled to overflowing as she thickly smutted her handkerchief with its carmine stain'. Next she feels her every nerve in her body 'dance to the quivering tune of her bloody pores'.

From Ballygally to Ballycastle

Beyond Larne, still on the A2 coast road, some 60 miles (96km) of wonderful maritime scenery stretches ahead of you. This area is like a pictorial textbook, with examples of nearly every rock formation and epoch. For the average visitor, this means views of lovely mountains, looming white cliffs, glens, trout streams and beaches. For the geologist, it is fascinating: there are Archean schists over 300 million years old which formed the first crust over the once-molten earth, lava fields, glacial deposits, raised beaches and flint beds. The red sandstone which colours the beaches was formed from the sands of a desert which existed 110 to 150 million years ago in the Triassic epoch. This was succeeded by a sea which formed Lias clays, which in turn were changed into chalk by a later invasion of the sea. This happened between 120 to 170 million years ago, and we have the white headlands of **Fair Head** to remind us. After the Ice Age, the Glens of Antrim were formed by the movement of the inexorable glaciers which gorged out the valleys. It is best to imagine the glens as being part of a giant hand with 10 fingers, and the spaces in between forming a series of short steep valleys running out towards the sea from the eastern edge of the Antrim plateau. The glens drain in a northeasterly direction and look straight across the sea of Moyle to Scotland. They were isolated from the rest of County Antrim by the difficult terrain of the Antrim plateau with its bogs and high ground near Glenarm. Today on the Garron plateau it is still possible to lose oneself, and to see wild ponies and goats grazing. These are remote areas, uninhabited by man.

The A2 coast road links each of the nine glens. From south to north, they are Glenarm, Glencloy, Glenariff, Glenballyeamon, Glenaan, Glencorp, Glendun, Glenshesk and Glentaisie. The glens are rich in legend and history and are really spectacular. Most of the favourite characters of Irish legends make an appearance somewhere. The Children of Lir, who were changed into white swans by their wicked stepmother, were sentenced to spend three hundred years swimming on the bleak sea of Moyle—an ancient name for this stretch of the North Channel, which lies along the northeastern shores of the glens. Thomas Moore (1779–1852) tells their sad story in the 'Song of Fionnuala':

> *Silent, oh Moyle be the roar of thy waters,*
> *Break not ye breezes your chain of repose,*
> *While mournfully weeping Lir's lonely daughter*
> *Tells to the nightstar her sad tale of woes!*

Deidre and the sons of Uisneach landed near Ballycastle after they had been in exile, and were lured from there to their death at Emain Macha, near Armagh. Fionn MacCumhail (Finn MacCool) mistakenly killed his faithful hound Bran in Glenshesk, and his sonOísín (Ossian) is buried in the glens. His grave is marked by a stone circle in **Glenaan**. Other relics of the past are the megalithic monuments built by agricultural people about five thousand years back, and the raths dotted all over the area. These were lonely farmsteads 1500 years ago.

The glens have had a turbulent history. Originally Richard de Burgh, Earl of Ulster, conquered them, and they were sold to the Bissetts in the early 13th century. Five genera-tions later the last of the Bissetts, Margery, the daughter of Eoin Bissett and Sabia O'Neill, became the sole heir to the glens. At this time John More MacDonnell of Kintyre, Lord of the Isles, was looking for a wife and he came to woo her. They were married in 1399, and from then on the glens have been in possession of the MacDonnells who became known as the MacDonnells of Antrim. They still live at Glenarm Castle, and have the more modern title of Earls of Antrim which they got in the 17th century. The MacDonnells did not keep the glens easily; they spent a lot of time and energy fighting other claimants to their territory, particularly the McQuillans, the O'Neills and Sir Arthur Chichester. In

1559 Sorley Boy MacDonnell tricked the McQuillans by spreading rushes over the bog holes which lay between the hostile camps above Glendun; and when the McQuillans and their allies the O'Neills led a cavalry charge, their horses sank into the swamps and their riders became easy prey to the arrows and axes of the MacDonnells. Even today there is a saying, 'A rush bush never deceived anyone but a McQuillan'.

The remoteness of the glens and their inaccessibility—until 1834 when the Antrim coast road was built by the engineer Ball—has caused the people of these parts to have a great sense of regional unity and an affinity with their neighbours on the Scottish coast. They also retained the Irish language until the last quarter of the 19th century. When the Gaelic League set out to revive the Irish language at the beginning of this century, they held a great *feis* (festival) in 1904 at which people competed in Irish dancing, singing and instrumental music, story-telling, crafts and hunting. A *feis* has been held every year since in one of the nine glens in late June.

From Larne you follow the A2 beneath cliffs and through the Black Cave Tunnel to **Ballygally**. Here there is a very Scottish-style castle, now a hotel. It is well worth a look inside to see the interior of a Scottish Bawn House. You can also have a drink in the bar in the dungeon. A couple of miles inland you can get a panorama of the Scottish coast, with the 'beehive' outline of Ailsa Craig from the Sallagh Braes. **Glenarm**, 'glen of the army', is one of the oldest of the glen villages, dating from the 13th century. The castle here belongs to the MacDonnells, who are descended from Queen Elizabeth's great enemy, Sorley Boy. It is not open to the public, but if you go into Glenarm Forest you can look back at this turreted castle, which reminds many of the Tower of London. Those who are looking for folk music may well find it in the village itself.

This part of the coast is full of chalk and limestone. Glenarm exports it from the little harbour, and there used to be quarries at **Carnlough**, which is the town at the foot of Glencloy (glen of the hedges) although it is not particularly interesting. This area has long been inhabited and farmed, with dry-stone walls enclosing the land. Although Carnlough attracts local holiday-makers because of its sandy beach, solitude can be found on **Garron Moor**, and in the other little glens. On your way round the Garron Point to Red Bay you will notice a change in the geology from limestone to the Triassic sandstone exposed on the shore. All along the A2 coast road you will find breathtaking sea views. The road was built from 1834 to ease the hardships of the glens' people—as a work of famine relief—but it also gave them a route out, resulting in a much diminished population.

Glenariff (Ploughman's glen), is the largest and most popular of the glens with its waterfalls: *Ess na Larach* (Tears of the Mountain) and *Ess n Crub* (Fall of the Hoof). With names like these you can understand how easy it was for poets to praise these valleys. Moira O'Neill, one of the 'landscape rhymers', wrote the *Songs of the Glens of Antrim*, which encapsulate the simple lifestyle and pleasures of the 19th-century glensfolk.

Waterfoot is at the foot of the Glenariff River, by the lovely Red Bay, so called because of the reddish sand washed by the streams from the sandstone. There are caves in the cliffs above which were once inhabited. The village is often the venue for the Glens of Antrim *Feis*. In the glen you will see steep climbing mountains and a green narrowing valley floor which gives some aptness to Thackeray's description, 'Switzerland in miniature'. This is perfect ground for nature rambles, with lovely wild flowers and the moorland of **Glenariff Forest Park**. This magnificent national nature reserve has a camp site and visitor centre in the glen. There is a beautiful walk beside the waterfalls and cascades of the glen. You can spend an hour or a whole day's hike here, and it is best to bring walking boots.

Along the east flank of the valley you can see the remains of a narrow-gauge railway which a century ago transported iron. On the west side, at the Alpinesque cliffs of Lurigethan, you can look for the mound of **Dunclana Mourna**, home of Fionn MacCumhail and his son, the poet Oísín. According to legend, the warrior Finn was the leader of a mighty band called the *Fianna*; he was renowned for his wisdom gained through eating the Salmon of Knowledge; for his shining beauty (Fionn means fair); and for his bravery. His deeds were recounted in the legends and epics of Scotland, as well as Ireland. Finn is the giant of the Giant's Causeway at the northern point of the county. He took up a sod of land to throw at another giant, leaving a hole which became Lough Neagh in the southeastern corner of the county, and forming the Isle of Man.

Continuing on the coast road we get to **Cushendall**, called the capital of the glens. It lies at the foot of the **Glenballyeamon** (Edwardstown Glen), a somewhat lonesome glen, and the two glens **Glenaan** (Glen of the Colt's Foot or Rush Lights) and **Glencorp** (Glen of the Slaughter). Cushendall is delightfully situated on the River Dall, and there is an excellent golf course and camping facilities and a nice bar called **Pat's Bar**. An interesting building is **Turnley's Tower** at 1 Millstreet, right at the crossroads of the town. This served as a curfew tower and gaol. Built in 1820 as a 'Place of confinement for idlers and rioters', its garrison of one man lived in the tower until very recently. On **Tieveragh Hill** you can get marvellous views over the coast, and muse on the fact that you might be standing on the capital of the fairies—they are supposed to live inside it. (It is actually a rounded volcanic plug.) **Oísín's Grave** is at the end of a path on the lower slopes of Tieve Bulliagh about 2½ miles (3km) west of Cushendall, in Glenaan. It is in fact a megalithic tomb and stone circle, but as is usual in Ireland, a lovely story is associated with it. This Celtic Orpheus was entranced by a vision of the golden-haired Niamh, and followed her to her father's kingdom of Tír na Óg. He returned to find his companions dead and St Patrick preaching. He died unconverted, for the clerks' (priests') music was not sweet to him after that of his father, Fionn. Further up the road is **Beagh's Forest**, which stands in splendid open country from where you can look back at the mountains Trostan and Slemish, where St Patrick spent many lonely hours in his youth watching sheep. A mile out of the village, on the way to Cushendun and by the sea, are the ruins of **Layde Church** which contains many monuments of the MacDonnells and was in use up to 1790.

Cushendun village and its beach are in the care of the National Trust. Clough Williams-Ellis, who designed the pretty cottages here, also designed the seaside village of Port Meirion in Wales. There are marvellous walks around the village and surrounding area, and a camp site. The River Dun is famous for salmon and sea trout, but you have to ask the local Cushendun fishing club for permission to fish. Within the hidden glen of **Glendun** (Brown Glen) and its wood, Draigagh, there is a mass rock carved with a crucifixion scene, supposedly brought over from Iona. The poet John Masefield, whose wife came from here, was perhaps thinking of this glen, when he wrote 'In the Curlew Calling Time of Irish Dusk', for it is full of wildlife and flowers. Continue along the A2 northwards to **Ballypatrick Forest**, where there is a scenic drive, a camp site, picnic area and walks. Opposite the entrance to Ballypatrick Forest is **Watertop Open Farm**, where you can see the animals at close quarters and hire a pony for trekking.

You have not finished with the glens yet, but you have some wonderful views from the headlands coming up. Go by **Torr Head**. It means traversing a twisty road from Cushendun through Culraney Townland, which remained an enclave of Scots Gaelic speakers until about 60 years ago. Here you can look to the Mull of Kintyre, only about 15 miles (24km) away. You can understand why this part of Ireland felt nearer to Scotland than any other kingdom. Between here and Fair Head is **Murlough Bay** where the kings of Dalriada had their summer residence. There are no remains, but the tree-fringed beach is charming. It is in the care of the National Trust, and the best way to reach it is from Drumadoon. At **Fair Head**, reached from Ballyvoy, you can look down from the highest cliffs in the northeast, but still more impressive is the heather-covered top with its three lakes.

Ballycastle is a particularly attractive resort towns. Although it's fairly lively with lawn tennis courts in the old harbour, golf and other amusements nearby, this is the landscape for the two saddest stories of Ireland. According to legend, round the waters of this part of Antrim coast the Children of Lir were said to have spent some of their years of imprisonment in the swan form their wicked stepmother condemned them to. At the east end of the Ballycastle sands is a rock called *Carrig-Usnach*, where the ill-fated Deirdre landed with her lover and his two brothers, the sons of Uisneach, at the treacherous invitation of King Conor who, desiring her beauty, had lured them back from Scotland.

Ballycastle is divided into the market end and the harbour end. The diamond-shaped market place is the site of the Ould Lammas Fair held at the end of August. Visitors from the Scottish islands such as Islay travel over for this ancient, famous fair. It was given a charter in 1606 and is, therefore, the oldest of Ireland's big traditional fairs, although keep away if you don't like swarming crowds. There are large cattle and sheep sales, about five hundred stalls selling hardware, food and crafts; and fun at night, with dancing in the street. There is a rhyme that goes:

> *Did you treat your Mary-Ann*
> *To dulse and yellowman*
> *At the Ould Lammas Fair in Ballycastle?*

Ballycastle Museum (*open July–Aug, 2–6, other times by appointment; ☎ (012657) 62024*) in Castle Street is worth a visit. Ballycastle was a stronghold of the MacDonnells. At the ruined **Bonamargy Friary**, east of the town, the great coffins of some of these redoubtable chiefs lie in the vault. It is possible to walk around it. The other family associated with the town was the Boyd family who developed the coal mines; the entrances to these may be seen if you go across the golf course to the foot of Fair Head. **The Corrymeela Community House** is also along here. (*Corrymeela* means 'Hill of Harmony'.) This place is an interdenominational conference centre, and groups of Catholic and Protestant children come and spend a holiday together here. The town is also famous for its tennis tournament on the well-drained grass courts which overlook the sea. It is possible to play on them for a small fee. There is a fine beach; friendly pubs, and plenty of old-fashioned shops where you can buy things like film, shrimping nets, buckets and spades. There is a forest drive around the beehive-shaped **Knocklayd Hill** and good fishing in the River Margy.

County Antrim is very well endowed with home bakeries, and the potato bread, known as 'Fadge,' is quite a speciality around Ballycastle. Also sold here is the dulse and yellowman of the fair rhyme: dulse being dried seaweed, salt and chewy; and yellowman being one of the most delicious confections you can imagine—a bit like the inside of Crunchie bars. In fact this part of the world is not great for restaurants; your best bet is to stick to picnics, although Ballycastle is a splendid touring centre. The other glens which make the quorum of Nine Antrim Glens can be visited from here. **Glenshesk** (the Sedgy Glen), is well wooded, lying east of Knocklayd Hill. **Breen Wood**, at the head of the Glen, is a nature reserve with very old oaks which probably witnessed the fights between the O'Neills and MacDonnells for mastery of the area. On the other side of the Hill of Knocklayd lies the last glen, **Glentaisie**, called after Taisia, a princess of Rathlin. She seems to have been something of a warrior, winning a great battle on this broad glen which now carries the main road (A44) from Ballycastle to Armoy. Another short expedition that can be made from the town is to **Kinbane Head**, a couple of miles to the northwest and stronghold of Colla MacDonnell, Sorley Boy's brother. Now it stands as a picturesque ruin on its narrow white promontory, reached from the B15 going to the Giant's Causeway. A better known tourist attraction is the swinging **Carrick-a-rede** rope bridge, north of Ballycastle, and about a mile (1.6km) on from Kinbane Head. It used to be a real dare to cross on this apparently slight causeway to the rock on which there is a salmon fishery house. The bridge is now a narrow, bouncy bridge of planks with wire handrails, and it still gives a thrill to cross it. The views are tremendous. (The bridge is dismantled between September and April.) One of the prettiest towns on the coast is **Ballintoy**: if you catch it on a good day it looks like a Mediterranean fishing village with its white church and buildings. The harbour is reached by a precipitous little road. You can walk west from here to **Whitepark Bay**, a great curve of beach with sand dunes which is a National Trust property. On the edge of the cliffs is **Dunseverick Castle**, of which only one massive wall remains. In under the cliffs is the little hamlet of **Portbraddan** with a tiny church dedicated to St Gobhan (patron saint of builders). You will get a good close up view of traditional salmon netting at this hamlet of four houses. The nets are set out to catch the salmon swimming along the coast to find the river where they were spawned. You should take your time here; beachcombers can find fossils, flower enthusiasts can examine the dunes, and there is even evidence of a Stone Age settlement at the east end.

Rathlin Island

Fair Head gives you a good view of **Rathlin Island**, called Raghery by the local people. The story goes that Fionn MacCumhail's mother was on her way to get some whiskey for him in Scotland, and she took a stepping stone to throw in her way across the Moyle. This was Rathlin. This L-shaped island lies about 8 miles (12.8km) from Ballycastle, and 14 miles (22km) from the Mull of Kintyre, rising with white cliffs from the sea. It is populated by families who retained their Scots Gaelic longer than any other community; and it has a fascinating history, mostly of battles and competition for its strategic position. Pirates and smugglers throughout the centuries have used it as a refuge and a hiding place for contraband. It was a good hideout for Robert the Bruce: he had to take refuge in one of the caves underneath the east lighthouse, and here he saw the persevering spider that inspired the saying, 'If at first you don't succeed, try and try again.' This was in 1306 when, with renewed resolve, he returned to fight on and gained the Scottish throne at Bannockburn. In Early-Christian times, the island's remote position provided a tranquil home for monks, until the Vikings came to plunder in the 9th century. There are traces of a monastic settlement and a stone sweat house at Knockans, between Brockley and the harbour; and a prehistoric mound-fort known as Doonmore, near the Stone Age settlement at Brockley. East of the harbour is a Celtic standing stone. In more modern times Rathlin was used in an experiment to establish a wireless link with Ballycastle by Marconi, the discoverer of the wireless. In 1898 his assistant successfully managed it. The island is inhabited by about a hundred people who farm and fish. A recent record-breaking transatlantic balloon flight by Richard Branson ended off their shore, with some 'salvage money' being earned. There is a guesthouse and restaurant. If you decide to pitch a tent, do ask at the appropriate farmhouse first.

As you approach Rathlin in the boat, you will see the beautiful white cliffs of the island and the endless wheeling of the sea birds which rest all over it. The most dramatic place to watch them is from the West Lighthouse where the volcanic rock stacks are covered with puffins, fulmars, kittiwakes, razorbills, shearwaters and guillemots. Buzzards, waders, wild geese, ravens and peregrine falcons can be seen at different times of the year. There are no cars for hire on Rathlin which is a blessing, and the roads are silent except for the odd tractor and car belonging to one of the families who live there. The island is small enough to walk around in a day if you are a strong walker or even better you can hire a bicycle. The verges of the roads are starred with wild orchids and there are hardly any bushes, let alone trees, to block the magnificent views of mountainy bog and little lakes. You might hear a corncrake calling, which is rare enough nowadays. You should be able to arrange to go lobster fishing with one of the locals; the best place to ask is in the pub on the quay. There is good sport to be had catching eels around the wreck of the cruiser *Drake*, which was torpedoed in the First World War. There is good shore fishing, and deep-sea angling boats may be hired at Ballycastle, Ballintoy, and Portballintrae. Scuba-diving trips are organized by a local (*see* 'Activities', below). Getting to Rathlin is easy, although you may have to spend the night if the weather turns bad or the mail boat does not return to the mainland on the same day (*see* 'Getting Around').

The Giant's Causeway and Environs

The **Giant's Causeway** is a UNESCO world heritage site (the only one in Ireland), and this accolade only confirms what tourists have known for centuries: that the mix of black basalt columns, white chalk, sea, moorland and sandy beaches makes for a spectacular coastline. About 60 million years ago there was great volcanic activity, and basalt lavas poured out to cover the existing chalk limestone landscape. It actually baked the chalk into a hard rock—very unlike the soft chalk of southern England. These lava flows and eruptions were separated by several million years, allowing tropical vegetation and soils to form. The cooling of the basalt lavas was very variable. When exposed to the air or water, they cooled rapidly and formed skins like that on the top of custard. If they cooled slowly at depth, they shrank to form remarkably even polygonal columns like the Giant's Causeway. Here the Ice Ages have eroded the cliffs and graceful arches have been formed by the action of the sea and weather.

There is a 5-mile (8km) circular walk past the strange formations. The National Trust, which owns and manages the causeway, has made great efforts to make the site accessible to the thousands who visit each year, and to retain the beauty and natural habitat of the area. No souvenir shops and ice-cream vans mar the scenery as they do in other parts of this beautiful coastline. The Trust now owns 104 acres (42ha) of the North Antrim cliff path between the causeway itself and the ruins of Dunseverick Castle beside Whitepark Bay. You will find the Giant's Causeway on the B146, a looproad off the A2 between Ballycastle and Bushmills. Car parking is provided, but access to the causeway is by foot only. The **Visitors' Centre** (*open July–Aug, daily, 10–7; earlier closing time during the rest of the year; car park adm; © (012657) 31852 for more details*) at the entrance includes a tea room and shop, as well as comprehensive interpretative displays, and information on the geology and history of the area . Next to the Centre is the **Causeway School Museum** (*open July and August, 11am–4.30pm*) which takes you back to a small country school circa 1920.

You can walk a couple of miles north along another coastal path to **Portballintrae**, a picturesque fishing village, past a huge strand with strong Atlantic rollers (be careful of the undertow), called Runkerry. Here, a Spanish galleon, the *Girona*, was sunk off the Giant's

Causeway. It contained the most valuable cargo yet found. You can see the recovered treasures in the Ulster Museum, Belfast.

Bushmills, which lies on the A2 inland from Portballintrae, is famous for its whiskey distillery which claims to be the oldest in the world. Whiskey (coming from the word *usquebaugh, uisce beatha* or sweet water), is one word that the English have taken from the Irish. Before whiskey became a genteel drink, 'the best Coleraine' was admitted to be a connoisseur's drink. Peter the Great in 1697 on his study tour of Europe was amongst many to appreciate the Northern Irish liquor. Bushmills distillery can be visited (*a tour of the distillery takes about one hour; © (012657) 31521; adm*).

If you like adventure stories of the old-fashioned historical variety, read one of George Birmingham's novels—say, *Northern Iron.* He lived between 1806 and 1872; his books are amusing and give a great insight into 'Victorian Ireland'. He used to live round here, and incorporates scenes from Irish life on this part of the coast and elsewhere in the North in his work. Many of Charles Lever's (1806–72) novels are set round here too. His books are more thrilling, on the lines of a Dennis Wheatley, and they helped to create the tradition of the rollicking devil-may-care young Irishman.

From the quiet little town of Bushmills you can move via the A2 onto North Ireland's biggest seaside resort, **Portrush.** Before you reach this mecca of amusements and fish and chips, visit **Dunluce Castle** (sometimes translated as Mermaid's Fort) (*open April–Sept, Mon–Sat, 10–7, Sun, 2–7; Oct–Mar, Mon–Sat, 10–4, Sun, 2–4; adm*), whose bold ruins keep watch over the magnificent coastline. The castle is well worth a visit . You can see it from the A2, 3 miles (4.8km) before you reach Portrush. Its long, romantic history isset out in a leaflet available at the entrance. Its kitchen actually fell into the seas while it was inhabited. Anyone approaching it along the shore (you can scramble from the White Rocks, a range of chalk cliffs accessible from the main road), may see the rare meadow cranesbill flower called the Flower of Dunluce. Portrush is on a promontory jutting out into the Atlantic. It has a small harbour which is popular with yachtsmen sailing in the west, and from here you can take boat cruises to see the Causeway Coast and the Skerries, a group of rocky islands where the great auk (now extinct), used to nest. Although it is crowded in the summer, it is a friendly place. You will find the Victorian/Edwardian main buildings have their own contribution to make to the unique flavour of a Northern coastal resort. **Waterworld**, with its jacuzzi, aquarium, craft shops and water flumes is great fun for children. Just west, in Londonderry, is **Portstewart**, another resort which like Portrush has excellent golf courses and camping facilities. The huge sandy beach is pounded by great surf waves.

Mid-Antrim

As you set off through mid-Antrim via **Ballymena** you will be passing through the richest farmland in the North. The farmers here are among the most modern and hardworking in Ireland. If you are here during the summer you will see the Loyalist flag, with a white background and red hand on a red cross, fluttering from many a household. This area has also benefited from the linen industry, which was greatly boosted in the late 17th century by the Huguenot weavers, who sought refuge here from the religious intolerance of Louis XIV of France. Louis Crommelin is credited with having started the linen industry, and northeast of Ballymena on the B64 is the little village of **Newtown-Crommelin** which is called after him. It is now a lonely sheep-rearing settlement, though in the past bauxite was mined on the moors around it. Ballymena itself is a very prosperous town; the rumour is that all the farmers roundabout have bank accounts in the tax haven of the Isle of Man! In fact a riddle asks—'Why are pound notes green?'—Ballymena men pick them before they are ripe! There is a good market for livestock, clothes and food every Saturday.

Another spot worth stopping at is the little Moravian settlement of **Gracehill** just outside Ballymena, where you can see some of the communal buildings dating from the 18th century around the green. These Moravians came from Eastern Europe. Their Protestant sect, also known as the United Brethren, was founded in Saxony, before they came to Ireland in 1746. Their style of living was communal although they lived as brothers and sisters in separate houses. The village is linked to **Galgorm** by a bridge over the River Main. You can get a glimpse of the 17th-century Galgorm Castle, which is surrounded by a lawn and stately trees. The little village itself is delightful, with thatched cottages along one main street which runs by the river to the castle.

Off the A26 to Coleraine, just on the outskirts of Ballymoney, a busy town in the Bann Valley, is **Leslie Hill Historic Park and Farm** (*open April–May and Sept, Sun and public holidays, 2–6; June, Sat and Sun, 2–6; July and August, Mon–Sat, 11–6, Sun, 2–6; adm; ✆ (012656) 66803*). The owners have restored the 18th-century farm buildings, which include the Bellbarn (a threshing barn), a dovecote, a typical cattle byre and the payhouse. You can also see the old stables which now house newborn piglets. The famous traveller and agriculturist Arthur Young visited Leslie Hill in 1776, and much admired the lovely grounds, pretty lake and island. The estate has been lived in by the Leslie family for nearly 350 years, and the big house is a classic Georgian stone-cut building dating from 1760 (*only open to groups and advanced booking is advised*).

The Causeway Safari Wonderland (*open every day from June to August; ✆ Dervock (012657) 41474*) off the Ballymoney to Portrush road (B62) at **Ballybogey** is very popular. There are children's amusements, picnic places, and a café. Motorists can drive around the reserve and see the lions moving about freely. When you make your way down to Antrim Town and Lough Neagh you will see the distinctive shape of **Slemish Mountain**, east of Ballymena, where St Patrick spent his youth after capture by Irish pirates. To get to it, take the B94 from Broughshane; turn left after a mile (1.6km), right after 3 miles (4.8km) (signposted), right after half a mile (0.8km) and follow the road between dry-stone walls to Slemish car park. From the top, which is a steep climb of about 700ft (213m), you get a wonderful view. This lonely, extinct volcano has been a place of pilgrimage on St Patrick's Day, 17 March, for centuries. At **Broughshane**, a mile beyond the village on the A42, is **Carncairn Daffodils Centre** (*adm free*) where you can buy bulbs which have frequently won prizes in the Chelsea Flower Show and are directly descended from the stock developed by Guy L. Wilson, the celebrated daffodil-breeder. At **Dreen**, near Cullybrackey, is the ancestral home of US President Chester Arthur

(1881–5). It is a thatched cottage which has been restored and furnished (*open to the public from April to September in the afternoons; adm*).

Two miles south of Templepatrick on the A6 is **Patterson's Spade Mill** (*open Easter– April, 2–6; April, May and Sept, Sat and Sun, 2–6; June to August, daily except Tues, 2–6 ✆(01849) 433619; adm*). It is the only water-driven spade mill left in Ireland, and a traditional forge where nine different and regional types of spades are produced. The place has been restored by the National Trust and there is a fascinating guided tour. It is a great place for children and the busy glowing workshop is full of exciting bangs and clangs showing the way things used to be done. Best of all you can go away with your own sturdy spade.

Antrim Town stands a little way back from Lough Neagh. The town has an old nucleus with a 9th-century round tower in almost perfect condition on Steeple Road (north of the centre), but it is being encircled by new housing and shopping centres. The ruined **Antrim Castle**, built in 1662, former seat of Viscount Massereene and Ferrard, is on the unmarked road to Lough Neagh, and an Anglo-Norman motte lies next to it to the north. The 17th-century gardens in the old demesne of **Massereene** have been restored and include geometrical borders, and a wooded walk. All are within a short walking distance from the city centre (*free access*).

Another way to the see the lough is on the **Shane's Castle Railway**. This is on Randalstown road, and is Ireland's only working narrow-gauge railway. The Shane's Castle **Railway and Nature Reserve** combine for a great day out (*open from Easter to the end of Sept; closed Monday and Friday; ✆ (018494) 63380 for details and bookings*). There is wildlife, rare plants, picnic areas and light refreshments at Shane's Castle Station. The trains run along the shore, and you can watch water birds from hides. The castle, which is a ruin, was for many centuries associated with the O'Neills of Clandeboye; the sculptured head in the south wall of the tower, about 30ft (90m) from the ground, is known as the Black Head of the O'Neills. The tradition is that, if anything should happen to the head, the O'Neill family will come to an end.

Lough Neagh, the largest stretch of inland water in the British Isles, is surrounded by flat marshy land, so you do not get a good view of it from the road. It is famous for the eels, which spawn in the Sargasso Sea, swim across the Atlantic, and struggle up the Bann in springtime, all 20 million of them (though now, as many as possible are captured at Coleraine and brought to Lough Neagh in tankers). The eels take about 12 years to mature, and the main fishery is at **Toomebridge**, a very large co-operative managed by local fishermen and farmers.

Lisburn in the Lagan Valley in the southern tip of County Antrim has a **Planters Gothic Cathedral**. Louis Crommelin lived here and there is an excellent **museum and Irish Linen Centre** which includes a re-creation of a linen-weaving workshop; the workshop produces specialist linen which you can buy (*open all year; ✆ (01846) 663377*).

Bread: good bakeries all over the county; especially good soda and potato breads.

Whiskey: The Old Bushmills Distillery, Bushmills, ✆ (012657) 31521. Tours and free sampling.

Delicacies: dulse (seaweed) and yellowman (confectionery) in Ballycastle grocery shops. Also wonderful sausages and black pudding at Wysner Meats, 18 Ann Street, Ballycastle, ✆ (012657) 62372.

Crafts: Giant's Causeway and Cushendun National Trust Shops, open April to September. Dunluce Centre, Portrush.

Markets: For vegetables and clothes at Ballymena on Saturdays, the Market Car Park beside the leisure centre on the Larne Road link.

Fresh eels: Lough Neagh Fishermans' Co-operative Society, Toomebridge, ✆ (01648) 50618.

Daffodil bulbs: from Carncairn Daffodils Centre, Broughshane.

Angling: The Bann, Main, Braid, Clough and Glenwhirry rivers have an abundance of brown trout, and salmon. Lough Neagh has its own variety of trout called dollaghan. The Inver, Glynn, Bush, Carey, Margy, Dun and Roe are all excellent for sea trout, salmon and brown trout. Telephone the local Tourist Offices for details.

Sea and shore-fishing: is very good all along the Antrim Coast. Boats can be hired. For a full list of operators and their addresses, refer to the Northern Irish Tourist Board *Information Bulletin 9*. Also, Ulster Cruising School, Carrickfergus Marina, Carrickfergus, ✆ (019603) 68818, for details of hiring self-hire open-decked angling boats off the Carrickfergus Coastline. Contact Christopher McCaughan, ✆ (012657) 62074. Approximately £50 for five hours. Best contacts for local sea fishing knowledge are: Joe Mullan, Tackle shop, 74 Main Street, Portrush, ✆ (01265) 822209; Frank O'Neill, Londonderry Arms Hotel, Carnlough, ✆ (01574) 885255/885458.

Cruising: on Lough Neagh and the River Bann. Contact Ulster Cruising School, Carrickfergus, ✆ (019603) 68818. Also contact Antrim Borough Council, The Steeple Antrim, ✆ (01849) 463113.

Orienteering: Contact Ardclonis Activity Centre, High Street, Cushendall, ✆ (012667) 71340.

Scuba-diving: off Rathlin Island. Contact Tommy Cecil, The Harbour, Rathlin, ✆ (012657) 63915.

Water sports: information on all water sports including fishing from The Recreation Department, Carrickfergus Borough Council, ✆ (019603) 51604.

Turbo thrill Ride at Dunluce Centre, Portrush; myths and legends multi media show, native quizz touch computers, ✆ (01265) 824444.

Pony-trekking: through the Ballypatrick forest at Watertop Farm, 188 Cushendall Road, Ballyvoy, Ballycastle, ✆ (012657) 62576. Also at Mourneview Stables, 33 Paisley's Road, Carrickfergus, ✆ (019603)64734.

Golf: the best of many courses are: Ballycastle, a lovely seaside 18-hole course, ✆ (012657) 62536; Cairndhu Golf Course, outside Larne, 18-hole parkland course, ✆ (01574) 83324; Royal Portrush Golf Course, three links courses by the sea, ✆ (01265) 822311.

Train trips: the railway preservation society of Ireland runs the Portrush Flyer between Belfast and Portrush on several Saturdays each summer. The journey takes two hours and costs about £12 one way, ✆ (019603) 53567 for details and dates, as these change every year. Shane's Castle Railway, Randalstown, is Ireland's only working narrow-gauge railway, ✆ (018494) 63380. This is under review and may not be open. For further details, ✆ (018494) 28216.

Tennis: The Ballycastle Tennis Club has grass courts, ✆ (012657) 63022.

Walking: The Ulster Way runs through the Antrim Coast. A copy of the relevant leaflet can be had from the Northern Irish Tourist Board in Belfast, ✆ (01232) 246609; or the Sports Council, Upper Malone Road, ✆ (01232) 381222.

Open farms: Leslie Hill, Ballymoney, ✆ (012656) 66803; Watertop Farm, Ballycastle, ✆ (012657) 62576.

Animal sanctuary: Talnotry Cottage, 2 Crumlin Road, Crumlin, ✆ (018494) 22900. Homemade scones in an ornamental garden, whose owners have a collection of endangered species of pheasant and quail. Open April to September daily. At other times by arrangement.

Where to Stay

luxury

Sir William and Lady Moore, **Moore Lodge**, Kilrea, Ballymoney, ✆ (012665) 41043. Very up-market, with excellent fishing on the River Bann. There are five bedrooms in all, three with private bathrooms.

expensive

Dunadry Hotel and Country Club, 2 Island Reagh Drive, Dunadry, ✆ (018494) 32474. Comfortable, modern hotel near the airport. **Galgorm Manor**, Ballymena, ✆ (01266) 881001. A spectacular 17th century castle with lovely lawns recently transformed into a plush hotel.

moderate

Bushmills Inn, Main Street, Bushmills, ✆ (012657) 32339. Comfortable, good service, excellent food. The owner used to work at the Europa in Belfast, the most bombed hotel in the world. This place, by contrast, is blissfully peaceful. **Auberge**

de Seneirl, 28 Ballyclough Road, Bushmills, ✆ (012657) 41536. Delicious French cooking here, plus the opportunity to sample excellent Black Bush whiskey—a liqueur whiskey which is pleasantly sweet. There are five bedrooms with their own bathroom, and a very high standard of comfort throughout.

Maddybenny Farm, 18 Maddybenny Park, Portrush, ✆ (01265) 43403. Comfortable, easy going atmosphere, with the best breakfast in Northern Ireland. There is also a riding school on the property. The **Londonderry Arms Hotel**, 20 Harbour Road, Carnlough, ✆ (01574) 885255. This was originally built as a coaching inn by the Marchioness of Londonderry, whose mother was the Countess of Antrim. It later came into possession of her grandson, Sir Winston Churchill, who sold it in 1926. It has a delightful old-world atmosphere. There are 15 bedrooms with private bathrooms.

inexpensive

Mrs Peel, **Ben Neagh House**, 11 Crumlin Road, Crumlin, ✆ (08494) 52271. An excellent B&B near Belfast International Airport, in a pretty Georgian farmhouse. Mrs Mills, **Derrin House**, 2 Princes Gardens, Larne, ✆ (01574) 73269.

Mr and Mrs McCurdy, **Rathlin Guesthouse**, The Quay, Rathlin Island, ✆ (012657) 63917. This is a very friendly guest house from where you can explore the beautiful island. Mrs White, **Maddybenny Farm House**, 18 Maddybenny Park, Portrush, ✆ (01265) 823394. Breakfasts are delicious and filling, with a great variety. 3 en suite rooms.

self-catering

Ballinlea Mill, 34 Kilmahamoque Road, Ballycastle. Restored mill house, sleeps 8. From £200 low season per week, ✆ (012657) 62287.

Briarfield, 65 Dickeystown Road, Glenarm, ✆ (01574) 841296. Cottage sleeps 4; from £110 per week low season.

Eating Out

expensive

The **Ramore Restaurant**, The Harbour, Portrush, ✆ (01265) 824313. You can promise yourself a super meal here: the chef has won many awards. It ranks alongside **The Auberge** in Bushmills (below), and is a delightful find in a coastline for the most part full of takeaways. Good value food during the day in the winebar downstairs. The **Auberge de Seneirl**, Ballyclough Road, Bushmills, ✆ (012657) 41536. Great atmosphere and delicious French cuisine. The **Londonderry Arms**, Carnlough, ✆ (01574) 885255. Very good fish, and wonderful views of the sea and glens. **Dunadry Inn**, 2 Islandreagh Drive, Temple Patrick, ✆ (08494) 32474. The wine bar here is open during the day. It is conveniently close to the airport, and unexpectedly good. **Galgorm Manor**, Ballymena, ✆ (01266) 881001. Opulent dining in new four-star hotel.

Bushmills Inn, Main Street, Bushmills, ✆ (012657) 32339. Delicious cold salmon and salads in a bistro-style restaurant. **Manley**, State Cinema Arcade, 70a Ballymoney Road, Ballymena, ✆ (01266) 48967. Cantonese and Peking cooking. **Water Margin**, 8 Cullybackey Road, Ballymena, ✆ (01266) 652320. Cantonese cooking. **Dobbins Inn**, 6 High Street, Carrickfergus, ✆ (019603) 51905. Rich *à la carte* food and bar meals. **Hillcrest Country House Restaurant**, 306 Whitepark Road, Giant's Causeway, ✆ (012657) 31577 *À la carte* and high tea. Also a B&B.

Harbour Bar, Portrush. Great Atmosphere. **National Trust Tearooms**, Cushendun, ✆ (01266) 74506. Light meals during the day, 12–6. Summer only. **Giant's Causeway**, ✆ (012657) 31582. Open Mar to Oct during the daytime only. **Brown Jug**, 23 Main Street, Ballymoney. Salads, quiche. Daytime only. **Rathlin Guesthouse**, The Quay, Rathlin Island, ✆ (012657) 63917. Snacks, sandwiches, high tea. **McCuaig's Bar**, The Quay, Rathlin, ✆ (012657) 63974. Pub grub. **YMCA**, Lancastrian Street, Carrickfergus, ✆ (019603) 63223. Soup and stew.

Belfast

Belfast is probably known to most people through the exposure brought by the recent 'Troubles', which started in the late 1960s. Press and television news reports have recorded the bombings, the military involvement and the sectarian murders, giving the impression of a war-torn city, constantly in a state of unrest and dangerous to visit. This is simply not the case. The visitor will be surprised at how 'normal' the streets are—full of people shopping at Marks & Spencer and the various chain stores which now proliferate in all British cities. Theatres, cinemas, restaurants and pubs all operate. The Belfast people are friendly and sympathetic to the tourist, answering any queries with the good-humour and interest which is a characteristic of the Irish.

Belfast (in Gaelic *Beal Feirst*: the mouth of the sandy ford) is the county town of Antrim, and the administrative centre of the six counties that make up Northern Ireland. It has one of the most beautiful natural settings of any city: ringed by hills which are visible from most parts of the town, and hugging the shores of the lough. It has been a city officially only since 1888. In the 19th century it grew from an insignificant town by a river ford into a prosperous commercial centre and port, with great linen mills and the famous shipyards of Harland & Wolf. The Titanic, built here and so tragically sunk by an iceberg, was considered an outstanding engineering feat.

Architecturally, Belfast is made up of some grand Victorian public buildings and the red-brick streets which characterize many British towns. The prosperous 'big houses' which make up the smart Malone Road area, and line the lough on either side, were built by the wealthy middle class who had benefited from the linen industry. The workers in the factories and shipyards divided themselves between the Catholic Falls Road area and the Protestant Shankill area. Today, both Catholic and Protestant communites are used to poverty and unemployment. Unemployment became worse as the linen and ship-building industries declined, nurturing the conditions in which the terrorist armies could thrive.

Getting There and Around

By air: Belfast International Airport, ✆ (018494) 22888, is 19 miles (30km) from the city. The airport coach leaves every hour from the Great Victoria Street Bus Station (just behind the Opera House entrance on Glengall Street). Belfast City Airport, ✆ (01232) 457745, is 4 miles (7km) from the city centre. It is served by local UK airlines only—no international flights. Take a train to Sydenham Halt from Central Station or bus or taxi from City Hall, Donegall Square.

By boat: Larne to Stranraer Ferry, ✆ (01232) 327525. Larne to Cairnryan Ferry, ✆ (01574) 274321. Belfast to Isle of Man steam packet, ✆ (01232) 351009. Belfast car ferries to Liverpool, ✆ (051) 9441010. The Larne ferry service always links in with a train to Belfast. The station is just beside the ferry terminal building. Hoverspeed Sea Cat, Belfast–Stranraer, 4 crossings per day; journey takes 1½ hours, ✆ (01304) 240241 (Dover).

By rail: from Belfast Central Station, East Bridge Street, trains go to all destinations except Larne Harbour. Larne Harbour is served by York Road Station. All rail transport enquiries, ✆ (01232) 230310 or 230671.

By bus: Ulsterbus operates within the city and throughout the province. Their coaches also go to the Irish Republic, and mainland UK, ✆ (01232) 320011. The main Belfast bus stations are: Great Victoria Street (entrance in Glengall Street), ✆ (01232) 320011/320574 for destinations in Counties Armagh, Tyrone, Londonderry, Fermanagh and West Down; Oxford Street, ✆ (01232) 320011/232356 for destinations in Counties Antrim, Down, Londonderry and the Cookstown area. City bus enquiries, ✆ (01232) 246485.

By car: rentals available from Belfast Harbour and Belfast International Airports. In the city, try Avis, ✆ (01232) 240404; or Godfrey Davis Europcar, ✆ (01232) 757401.The centre of Belfast is taboo for parking. It is very clear where not to park: there are large security notices on the pavements and double yellow lines. Excellent car parks and pay-and-display areas ring the centre of the city.

By bike: Bike It, 4 Belmont Road, Belfast, ✆ (01232) 471141.

Tourist Information

Northern Ireland Tourist Information Centre, 59 North Street, ✆ (01232) 246609.

Bord Fáilte, 53 Castle Street, ✆ (01232) 327888.

useful addresses

Emergency Services, ✆ 999.

Victoria Hospital, Grosvenor Road, ✆ (01232) 240503.

AA, 108/110, Great Victoria Street, ✆ (01345) 500600.

RAC, 79 Chichester Street, ✆ (01232): 240261.

Car Rescue Service (24 hours), ✆ (01232) 323333.

Youth Hostel Association, 56 Bradbury Place, ✆ (01232) 324733.

Festivals

November: Belfast Festival at Queens. Festival Box Office, College Gardens, 8 Malone Rd, ✆ (01232) 665577/667687. The arts scene really hots up for three weeks. Classical, jazz, pop and folk music events are on in church halls and every available space. So too are films, plays and art exhibitions. The most successful fringe shows from Edinburgh come to the city, and the festival proper attracts internationally known stars. Events take place mainly around the university area.

Central Belfast

The indiscriminate bombing of the 1970s seems to be over, and the streets are safe. The city centre is pedestrianized for security reasons and there are iron gates barring the exits and entrances. These are being phased out now (Feb 1995). Your possessions are searched before entering, and you are likely to see military vehicles cruising amongst the traffic, but you will see nothing else out of the ordinary, unless you are extraordinarily unlucky. The centre of Belfast is not very attractive, being rather grey, and the shopping arcades are tacky. Since the 1970s it has been bisected by motorways.

Because Belfast is a 19th-century town it lacks the graciousness of Dublin; its city fathers were plutocrats, rather than aristocrats. Two of the most attractive buildings are on Great Victoria Street: the **Grand Opera House** and the **Crown Liquor Saloon**. If you want a good evening out you can eat and drink at the bar of the latter, a gas-lit High-Victorian pub decorated with richly coloured tiles. It has been preserved by the National Trust, but it has not been gentrified and its old clientele still drink there. Afterwards, go on to the Opera

House for a play or concert. Touring companies from all over Britain perform here. The Opera House was also designed in High-Victorian style (by Robert Matcham, the famous theatre architect) with rich, intricate decorative detail, including carved elephants. It was restored in the 1970s by the architect Robert McKinstry, and painted on the ceiling is a fine fresco by a modern-day Irish artist, Cherith McKinstry. Even if you don't have an evening to spare, both buildings are worth a quick visit—it won't cost you anything!

Although many of the splendours of Belfast date from its period of mercantile importance, there was a great quickening of spirit here in the 18th century. United Irishman Henry Joy McCracken, whose family first published *The Belfast Newsletter* in 1737 (the longest-running morning paper in the United Kingdom), was a son of the city. Other 18th-century personalities include William Drennan, who coined the phrase 'the Emerald Isle' and founded the **Royal Academical Institution**, a distin-guished building between College Square East and Durham Street designed by Sir John Soane, the eminent London architect, classical scholar and collector. It was built between 1808 and 1810 in a style that is classical in proportion. The institution is now a school, but it is possible to look around it. The prospect is a little spoiled by the great College of Technology, built on the corner of the lawn. The **City Hall** in Donegall Square was built between 1896 and 1906—a grand composition with a central dome and corner towers borrowed from Wren's St Paul's Cathederal, which make it a good landmark (*guided tours available but must be booked in advance; adm free; © (01232) 320202 ext. 227*).

BELFAST

1 Central Library	12 Linenhall Library	23 Ulster Hall
2 Central Rail Station	13 Lyric Theatre	24 Arts Council Gallery
3 Civic Arts Theatre	14 NITB	25 Lyric Players Theatre
4 Bord Fáilte	15 Ormeau Park	26 Queen's University Film Theatre, off Botanic Ave.
5 Botanic Gardens	16 Queen's University	27 Cannon Cinema
6 Botanic Rail Station	17 St Anne's Cathedral	28 Royal Courts of Justice
7 Bus Station, Gt Victoria St.	18 Transport Museum	29 To Airport
8 Bus Station, Oxford St.	19 Ulster Museum	
9 City Hall	20 Windsor Park football ground	
10 Grand Opera House	21 Crown Liquor Saloon	
11 Law Courts	22 Royal Academical Institute	

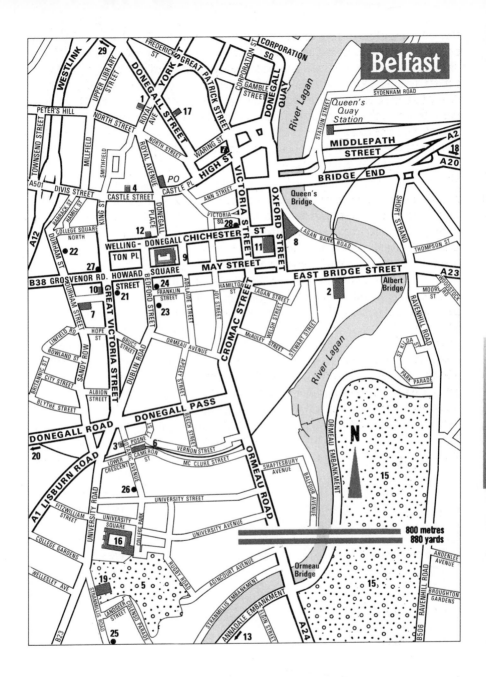

Belfast

River Lagan

CORPORATION SQ

CORPORATION ST

GAMBLE STREET

SYDENHAM ROAD

Queen's Quay Station

MIDDLEPATH STREET

A2

18

A20

BRIDGE END

Queen's Bridge

LAGAN BANK ROAD

SHORT STRAND

THOMPSON ST

FREDERICK ST

GREAT PATRICK STREET

YORK STREET

DONEGALL STREET

WESTLINK

29

UPPER LIBRARY STREET

PETER'S HILL

NORTH STREET

TOWNSEND STREET

MILLFIELD

SMITHFIELD

DIVIS STREET

A501

A12

BARRACK ST

HAMILL ST

KING ST

DURHAM ST

COLLEGE SQUARE NORTH

22

27

CASTLE STREET

CASTLE PL

PO

DONEGALL PLACE

WELLING-TON PL

DONEGALL SQUARE

12

9

HOWARD STREET

GROSVENOR RD.

B38

10

7

21

24

BEDFORD STREET

FRANKLIN STREET

23

GREAT VICTORIA STREET

HOPE ST

LINFIELD RD

ROWLAND ST

BRITANNIC ST

CITY STREET

SANDY ROW

BRUCE STREET

ALBION STREET

BLYTHE STREET

DUBLIN ROAD

ORMEAU AVENUE

DONEGALL PASS

DONEGALL ROAD

20

LISBURN ROAD

A1

LOWER CRESCENT

BOTANIC AVENUE

CAMERON ST

POSNE

3

6

26

VERNON STREET

MC CLURE STREET

UNIVERSITY STREET

FITZWILLIAM STREET

UNIVERSITY ROAD

UNIVERSITY SQUARE

16

COLLEGE PARK

COLLEGE GARDENS

UNIVERSITY AVENUE

WELLESLEY AVE

19

5

RUGBY ROAD

AGINCOURT AVENUE

STRANMILLIS EMBANKMENT

STRANMILLIS ROAD

LANDSEER ST

COLENSO PARADE

B23

25

13

ANNADALE EMBANKMENT

EGLIN STREET

ELGIN STREET

A24

NORTH STREET

ROYAL AVE

ROYAL AVENUE

1

17

WARING ST

HIGH ST

ANN STREET

VICTORIA SQ.

28

CHICHESTER ST

VICTORIA STREET

OXFORD STREET

MAY STREET

11

8

EAST BRIDGE STREET

A23

Albert Bridge

2

MOORS ST

MOORSTOCK

RAVENHILL ROAD

ST KILDA

PARK PARADE

River Lagan

ORMEAU EMBANKMENT

N

15

800 metres
880 yards

Ormeau Bridge

15

ARDENLEE AVENUE

BROUGHTON GARDENS

RAVENHILL ROAD

B506

ORMEAU ROAD

SHAFTESBURY AVENUE

BALFOUR AVENUE

BEECH STREET

APSLEY STREET

ORMEAU AVENUE

CROMAC STREET

HAMILTON ST

LAGAN STREET

JOY STREET

WELSH STREET

STEWART STREET

McAULEY STREET

ADELAIDE STREET

MAY STREET

SQUARE

The **Customs House** and **Courts of Justice**, and the **Ulster Hall** with its impressive organ, are all rather grey self-important buildings in heavy Victorian style. Unfortunately the 18th-century Donegall Square has been replaced with a medley of different styles since the 19th century. The **Linen Hall Library** here is a rich storehouse of books of Irish interest; and one of the last survivors in the British Isles of the subscription library movement, which was so important to civilized Europe in the late 18th/early 19th century. It has a comfortable room where you can sample periodicals, magazines and the day's flurry of newspapers. The librarians are polite and helpful, and the prints which line the walls echo the feeling of an earlier age.

Just along the way is the Robinson and Cleaver Building, overlooking Donegall Place. This flamboyantly Victorian department store is no more but houses a mixture of boutiques. In Corporation Square is **Sinclair Seamen's Church** designed by Charles Lanyon and built in 1853. The pulpit incorporates the bows, bowsprit and figurehead of a ship, the organ displays starboard and port lights and the font is a binnacle!

About 10 minutes' walk away from Donegall Square, down Great Victoria Street, is the university area. You pass the imposing Tudor-style red-brick Queen's University building to go into the **Botanical Gardens** (*gardens open from sunrise to sunset; Palm House Mon to Fri, 10–5, weekends 2–5*), which are small but beautifully laid out with formal flower beds. The recently restored Victorian Palm House is a splendid combination of graceful design and clever construction. Richard Turner, a Dubliner whose iron-works produced it, was also responsible for its design. It is made of sections which comprise the earliest surviving cast-iron and curvilinear glass architecture in the world. Inside the Palm House are tender and exotic plants.

Set inside the Botanical Gardens is the **Ulster Museum** (*open Mon–Fri, 10–5, Sat 1–5, Sun 2–5; adm free except for special exhibitions*). It has a variety of well-displayed and informative collections ranging from giant elk antlers to patchwork, jewellery and Irish antiquities. Of special interest is the outstanding modern art collection with a good representation of Irish artists including Sir James Lavery, whose wife was the Irish colleen on the old Irish pound notes. The Ulster Museum also has a unique collection of treasure from the wreck of the Spanish Armada vessel, the *Girona*. In 1588 Philip II of Spain ordered the greatest invasion fleet ever assembled to put an end to the growing power of England. Of the 130 ships that set sail, 26 were lost on, or just off, the coast of Ireland. In 1968 a fabulous hoard of gold and silver coins, heavy gold chains, a beautiful gold salamander pendant set with rubies, rings, ornamented crosses and a filigree brooch were all recovered off the coast of Antrim.

St Anne's Cathedral in Donegall Street was built in 1899 in Romanesque style, of the Basilican type. It is very imposing inside with some fine stained-glass windows. In the nave is the tomb of Lord Carson, the Northern Unionist leader, who died in 1935.

If you want to see the **Republican enclaves**, which are brightened by gaudy wall paintings and political slogans, take a black taxi. These run like miniature buses and serve areas such as the **Falls**, where public buses do not venture. These areas are a depressing sight as the housing is so awful, and visitors should exercise a certain amount of caution, as they might in parts of London or New York. The communities are closed to strangers and it would be wise not to go drinking in the pubs or illegal clubs. Nor would it be wise to walk about these parts at night.

Shopping

Crafts: The National Trust Shop, 86 Botanic Avenue. The Craftworks Gallery, 13 Linenhall, ✆ (01232) 236334.

Jewellery: Janice Gilmore, 28 Cyprus Park, ✆ (01232) 654867 for imaginative costume jewellery and accessories.

Woven/embroidered goods: Alice Clarke, 49 Eglantine Avenue, ✆ (01232) 662485, for colourful rugs and woven clothing. Karen Fleming, 29 Hillsborough Parade, ✆ (01232) 456991 for textile furnishings and embroidered wall hangings.

Cheap Irish linen: linen and towels at the Lamont Factory Shop, Stranmillis Embankment, ✆ (01232) 668285.

Sports equipment: for sale or hire. The Deep Concern, 70 High Street, Belfast 1, ✆ (01232) 238572. Surf Mountain, 12 Brunswick Street, ✆ (01232) 248877. Extremes Outdoors, 5/7 Pottingers Entry, High Street, Belfast, ✆ (01232) 328856.

Foodstuffs: June's Bakeshop, 376 Lisburn Road, ✆ (01232) 668886. Soda wedges, potato cakes for that great Ulster fry and lovely fresh cakes beside. Eatwell, 413 Lisburn Road. Good wholefood shop. Cargoes Delicatessen, 613 Lisburn Road, ✆ (01232) 665451. Stocks delicious salami, virgin olive oil etc.

The Suburbs of Belfast

Parliament House, Stormont, can be seen from the Newtownards Road (A20) about 2½ miles (4km) from the city centre. It is a very imposing Portland stone building in English Palladian style, with a floor space covering 5 acres (2ha) and standing in a park of 300 acres (121ha). Next door is **Stormont Castle**, built in Scottish baronial style, which houses Government departments. It is possible to tour these buildings if you organise it in advance.

There are many attractive parks around Belfast. In south Belfast, in the upper Malone Road (B103) area is **Barnett's Park**. Within the attractive parkland is an early 19th-century house with a permanent exhibition on Belfast parks (*open all year, 10–4; adm free*). Nearby is **Dixon Park**, where rose-fanciers will get a chance to view the **Belfast International Rose Trials**, the finals of which take place in the third week of July. The park borders the River Lagan, and all summer about 100,000 roses are in bloom (*open daily to dusk; adm free*). Continuing up the Malone Road, those of you interested in Neolithic sites should visit the **Giant's Ring**, near Ballylesson, and about a mile (1.6km) south of Shaw's Bridge. The Giant's Ring is a circular grassy embanked enclosure over 600ft (187m) in diameter with a chambered grave in the centre. The dolmen in the centre is called Druid's Dolmen. The original purpose of the site is disputed but it was probably ritualistic; its date is unknown. The giant it is named after is possibly Fionn MacCumhail, who is a favourite hero to tag on to such places (*see* **Old Gods and Heroes**, p.578). In the olden days, farmers used to stage horse-races in this huge circle. It is always accessible and free. **Shaw's Bridge**, just mentioned, is very picturesque and spans the River Lagan. It was originally built *c.* 1650.

On the B23 you can walk for 10 miles (16km) along the tow path of the River Lagan, past the public parks. Start at the Belfast Boat Club, Loughview Road, Stranmillis, and end at Moore's Bridge, Hillsborough Road. On the northern side of the city, on the Antrim road (A6), the baronial-style **Belfast Castle** appears unexpectedly from the wooded slopes of Cave Hill. It was built by the third Marquess of Donegall in 1870. His family, the Chichesters, were granted the forfeited lands of Belfast and the surrounding area in 1603; the Gaelic lords of the area, the O'Neills, lost everything and fled to the Continent. The planted grounds of the castle are open to the public, and always accessible. An easy climb to the summit of Cave Hill (1182ft/368m) gives stunning views over the city and Belfast Lough. There are five caves and the earthwork of MacArts Fort, named after a local Gaelic chieftain of the Iron Age. It was here that the United Irishmen, Wolfe Tone and his followers, took their oaths of fidelity in 1798 (*see* **History**, p.92).

There are several interesting places within easy reach of Belfast which are worth a visit. Northeast of the city, follow the A2 past the huge cranes (among the world's largest) of the shipyards and the aircraft works at Sydenham until you arrive at the wooded suburb of **Cultra**, about 6 miles (9km) from the city centre. Here in a parkland of nearly 200 acres (80ha), the **Ulster Folk and Transport Museum** (*open July and Aug, 10.30–6, Sun 12–6; April–June and Sept, 9.30–5, during the week; closed at 4pm for the rest of the year; adm*) provides a unique opportunity for visitors to explore the past of the province. The best museum of its type in Ireland, it gives a wonderful insight into what life in the countryside was like all over Ireland until 60 years ago. It is an open-air museum with representative buildings of rural Ulster: a linen scutch mill, a blacksmith's forge, a spade mill and farm houses of different regional styles. These are all furnished appropriately. Real fires burn in the grates and visitors are able to immerse themselves in the atmosphere of Ulster's agricultural communities. Those of you interested in the history of everyday objects—kitchen equipment, furniture, patchwork and agricultural equipment (remember Ferguson invented the tractor in Belfast)—will find this a rich storehouse. For those early-vehicle enthusiasts amongst you, an instructive collection of carriages and railway engines will be found across the Belfast–Bangor road on the opposite side of the museum, housed in a great building by the architect Ian Campbell. At **Helen's Bay**, a couple of miles (3.2km) north of Cultra, two lovely beaches joined by a path flank **Crawfordsburn Country Park**, with a stream flowing through the woods to the sea. The wooded demesne of Clandeboye Estate has protected this area from the work of the housing developer. In the distance can be seen the delightful **Helen's Tower**, erected in Victorian times by the first Marquess of Dufferin and Ava to the memory of his mother. The 19th-century English poet Alfred Lord Tennyson's lines are inscribed in the tower:

> *Helen's Tower, here I stand*
> *Dominant over sea and land.*
> *Son's love built me and I hold*
> *Mother's love in letter'd gold...*

It was erected at a time of destitution caused by the famine of 1845, and gave employment to many. It has become a symbol of Ulster; another Helen's Tower was raised in northern France near Albert to commemorate the appalling losses suffered by the men of Ulster in the First World War. The Somme Heritage Centre on the A21 Newtownards–Bangor road, ✆ (01247) 823202 carries on the theme. Clandeboye Estate is opened from time to time for charitable purposes, but it is not possible to see inside the tower.

Activities

Golf: nine-hole golf course about 5 miles (8km) outside Belfast on the A6 at 614 Antrim Road, Newtown Abbey, ✆ (01232) 843799. 18-hole course at Carrickfergus Golf Club, 7½ miles (12km) northeast of Belfast on the A2, ✆ (019603) 63713. Blackwood Golf Centre, Crawfordsburn Road, Claneboye, ✆ (01247) 852706.

Leisure centres: The Maysfield Leisure Centre, East Bridge Street, is very central and has a pool, gym, squash and sauna, ✆ (01232) 241633. Similar facilities are available at The Robinson Centre, Montgomery Road, ✆ (01232) 703948. General contact: Belfast City Council, Leisure Services Dept, ✆ (01232) 320202.

Belfast ✆ (01232–)

Where to Stay

luxury

Europa Hotel, Great Victoria Street, ✆ 327000. Very central, modern hotel which has been bombed so many times everybody has lost count. The **Culloden Hotel**, 142 Bangor Road, Holywood, ✆ 425223. This hotel, in the suburbs on the northeast of Belfast Lough, is very plush with lovely grounds and luxurious old-style furnishings. One of the nicest hotels in Belfast. Cheaper deals are also available at weekends when journalists and film crews have gone home. This is true of all the hotels. **Dukes Hotel**, 65 University Street, ✆ 236666. Quiet and central, close to good restaurants. **Claneboye Lodge Hotel**, Estate Road, Claneboye, Bangor, ✆ (01247) 853311. Luxurious hotlel adjoining Blackwood Colf Course.

expensive

The **Stormont Hotel**, 587 Upper Newtownards Road, ✆ 658621, is luxurious and comfortable, though it was bombed recently. The **Wellington Park Hotel**, 21 Malone Road, ✆ 381111, is modern and comfortable, close to the Botanic Gardens, with secure car parking.

moderate

Balmoral Hotel, Black's Road, ✆ 301234. Very reasonable. **Malone Lodge**, Eglantine Avenue, ✆ 382409. A small hotel with a pleasant atmosphere. **Ash Rowan Town-House**, 12 Windsor Avenue, ✆ 661758. 10 minutes from the city centre; cosy and attractive. Breakfasts only.

All the top-grade hotels are very expensive and without much style. The following B&B's are very reasonable and in the University area, close to the Ulster Museum and Botanical Gardens. Mrs Elsie McClure, **Malone House**, 79 Malone Road, BT9, ℗ 669565. Friendly and popular top-of-the-range guesthouse. **Malone Lodge**, Eglantine Ave, ℗ 382409. Small hotel with a pleasant atmosphere. **Ash Rowan Town House**, 12 Windsor Ave, ℗ 661758. 10 minutes from the city centre; cosy and attractive. Breakfast only. **Queen's University Common Room**, College Gardens, University Road, BT9, ℗ 665938. **Queen's Elms**, Queen's University, 78 Malone Road, BT9, ℗ 381608. Rooms are mainly singles with access to cooking facilities. **YWCA Hostel**, Queen Mary Hall, 70 Fitzwilliam Street, Lisburn Road, ℗ 240439, good and central.

self-catering

Belfast International Youth Hostel, 22 Donegall Road, Central Belfast, ℗ (01232) 324733. 126 beds and family rooms. Very clean.

Belfast ℗ (01232–)   ***Eating Out***

expensive

La Belle Epoque, 61 Dublin Road, ℗ 323244. This is considered by the locals to be one of the best restaurants in town and although there is a good atmosphere, the food is a little disappointing. . **Restaurant 44**, 44 Bedford Street, ℗ 244844. This restaurant has had a good reputation for game and fish dishes for years. It has recently changed hands and the reputation may or may not still hold. **Belfast Castle Restaurant**, Antrim Road, ℗ 776925. It has won an award for its skilfully prepared food. Decor is over the top but the views of the city are lovely. **Le Restaurant**, Europa Hotel, Great Victoria Street, ℗ 327000. Very good. **Roscoffs**, 7 Lesley House, Shaftesbury Square, ℗ 331532. Assured and unique cooking using imaginative and unusual ingredients. Michelin star. One of the best places to eat in Ireland. The chefs have just made a successful TV series called *Gourmet Ireland*. **Shanks Restaurant**, Blackwood Golf Centre, Claneboye, ℗ (01247) 852706. Creative chef trying to challenge Roscoff's

moderate

The **Strand**, 12 Stranmillis Road, ℗ 682266. An evening place with adventurous cooking and an old fashioned ambience. **Deane's on the Square**, Station Square, Helen's Bay, ℗ (01247) 852841. Excellent cooking in converted station waiting room. **Manor House**, 47 Donegall Pass, ℗ 238755. The best of many Chinese restaurants in the Botanic Avenue area. **Antica Roma**, 67/69 Botanic Avenue, ℗ 311121. Lively decor and ambience. Imaginatively cooked pastas, such as spaghetti with squid. **Nick's Warehouse**, 35/39 Hill Street, ℗ 439690. Slick modern interior. Simply cooked but really delicious fresh food. Currently very fashionable and it is easy to see why. **La Boheme**, 103 Great Victoria Street, ℗ 240666. Fine cooking, try the salmon with basil sauce.

Morrison's, 21 Bedford Street, ✆ 248458. Brilliant salads, salmon and chicken. The **Morning Star Pub**, 17 Pottingers Entry, off Anne Street. Great pub grub and a slice of Belfast life.

inexpensive

The **Crown Liquor Saloon**, 56 Great Victoria Street, ✆ 249476. Delicious Irish stew and oysters. Very conveniently placed for the Opera House. **Ashoka Indian Restaurant**, 363 Lisburn Road, ✆ 660362. Good Indian restaurant. **Archana**, 53 Dublin Road, ✆ 323713. Another good Indian restaurant. **C. Harveys**, 95 Great Victoria Street, ✆ 233433. Good for hamburgers. **Saints and Scholars**, 3 University Street, ✆ 325137. Simple and filling food with imaginative seasonings. Try the stir-fry vegetables or cassoulet. **Long's Fish and Chips**, 39 Athol Street, ✆ 321848. Great fish and chips. **Bewleys**, Donegall Arcade, ✆ 234955. A branch of the famous coffee shop from Dublin. **Scarletts**, 351–3 Lisburn Road, ✆ 683102. French bistro with good value cooking. **Chalet d'Or**, 48 Fountain Street, ✆ 324810. Traditional haunt of the Belfast literati. Old fashioned café—fish & chips etc. **Pierre Victoire**, 30 University Road, ✆ 315151. Part of a very successful chain. Good fun and good value. **Cargoes Café**, 613 Lisburn Road, ✆ 665451. This café/delicatessen is a hot favourite with Italian-food-lovers. Delicious and simple meals; take-out service also. **Bittles Bar**, 70 Upper Church Lane, ✆ 311088. City Centre pub. Irish stew and soup.

Belfast ✆ (01232–)   **Entertainment and Nightlife**

theatre

The **Grand Opera House**, Great Victorian Street, puts on shows as well as opera, ✆ 240411/241919.

The **Lyric Players Theatre**, off Strandmillis Road, ✆ 381081; the **Civic Arts Theatre**, Botanic Avenue, ✆ 224936. These always have well-produced and lively shows and plays. For details, pick up a free copy of *Artslink* from the tourist information centre, or the Arts Council Gallery at 59 Dublin Road, ✆ 321402. The newsletter lists cultural and recreational events throughout the province on a month-by-month basis.

film

The more avant-garde and art house films are shown at the **Queen's University Film Theatre** in a narrow lane off Botanic Avenue. Then there is the more commercial **Cannon** cinema just beside the Opera House, on College Square East which runs into Great Victoria Street. The biggest cinema complex is **MGM** at the north end of the Dublin Road, ✆ 245700.

art galleries

The **Arts Council Gallery** (address above) is worth visiting for information, and for the shows which are usually by Irish and Ulster artists. Other galleries are the **Bell Gallery**, 13 Adelaide Park, ✆ 662998; **Crescent Arts Centre**, 2–4 University Road, Belfast, ✆ 242338; **Emer Gallery**, Great Victoria Street, Belfast,

✆ 231377; the **Tom Caldwell Gallery**, Bradbury Place, ✆ 323226; and, of course, the **Ulster Museum**, Botanic Gardens (off Stranmillis Road), ✆ 381251.

The 'Troubles' seem to have generated a creative urge amongst Ulster artists which is both exploratory and introspective. Ulster Artists such as Tom Carr, T. P. Flanagan, Brian Ferran, Basil Blackshaw and Brian Ballard are producing excellent works. They paint various subjects, often Ulster scenery, in highly personal but understandable interpretations; nudes, and interpretations of ancient and modern Irish myths.

poetry readings

Ulster has also produced poets of international renown. Seamus Heaney started writing here when he was at Queen's University in the 1960s, as did Paul Muldoon at a later date. During the Belfast Arts Festival in November each year you could be lucky and hear them reading their work.

music

Classical music concerts take place in the **Whitla Hall**, Queen's University, off University Road, ✆ 245133. In the summer, the Ulster Orchestra plays a series of subscription concerts in the **Ulster Hall**, Linenhall Street, ✆ 323900.

Folk and traditional music is played mainly in the public houses. The best place in town is the **Rotterdam Bar** in Pilot Street, Belfast Docks. Also there is folk during the summer at **Queen's University Folk Music Society**, 29 University Square. There is only one session a fortnight, so check at the Union across the square.

Live rock takes place at night at the **Errigal Inn**, 320 Ormeau Road, ✆ 641410. You can have a relaxed and convivial drink with live music and food at the **Linenhall Bar**, 9 Clarence Street, ✆ 248458. Rock concerts tend to take place in the Ulster Hall. There is jazz in the **Guinness Spot**, Queen's University.

The best source of information for music events is the local *Belfast Telegraph*.

County Down

Sea-bordered and close to mainland Britain, this county has excited the envy and lust of waves of invaders and plunderers. Its farmlands are amongst the richest in Ireland. Scenically, it has the most attractive coastline, the famous Mourne Mountains, and a wealth of interesting historical buildings. For sailing enthusiasts there is the beautiful and sheltered water of Strangford Lough; for sea anglers, exciting sea fishing off Ardglass and Portavogie. And there are plenty of opportunities for hill-walking, golfing, bird-watching and sea-bathing. The climate has a reputation for being sunnier than other parts of Ulster. The people are mostly farmers and fisherfolk, although, being near to the city of Belfast, there are quite a few dormitory towns and light industries.

The county is rich in monuments from pre-history: there are cairns, standing stones, and dolmens dating from 3000 BC, scattered around the Strangford Lough and Lecale district, and evidence of man in the form of kitchen middens and flint tools dating from 6000 BC.

History

St Patrick is associated strongly with this county. After spending his boyhood as a slave in County Antrim, he spent 21 years in France preparing himself for his mission to bring Christianity to Ireland. In AD 432 he was on his way back to County Antrim, but was forced by bad weather conditions to land at the Slaney River between Strangford and the River Quoile. He founded an abbey nearby, at Saul near Downpatrick, where he died on 17 March AD 461. He is buried in the vicinity of Down Cathedral in Downpatrick. From St Patrick's work, and that of his missionaries in the following century, Christianity flourished and Ireland became a centre of great learning. In fact, during the Dark Ages in Europe, when the Roman Empire was in ruins, the monasteries of Ireland kept the light of Christianity and learning alive. The monastery founded by St Comgall in Bangor in the middle of the 6th century boasted three thousand students, but this famous place, like so many others in Ireland, was destroyed by the Norsemen (Vikings) in AD 824.

In the 17th and 18th centuries, County Down was planted with Scottish and English settlers, and the native Irish retreated into the hilly country around the Mourne mountains. Now County Down remains, like Antrim, a cornerstone of Ulster: loyalist, flying the Ulster flag with its red hand against a white background, except in the mountain areas where there is a Republican tradition—thus the killings around Newry and the shared hilly borderlands of County Louth.

Getting There and Around

By air: to Belfast International Airport.

By boat: to Larne Ferry port from Stranraer and Cairnryan in Scotland. By Seacat, Hoverspeed run 4 crossings daily from Stranraer to Belfast.

By rail: Northern Irish Railways run a suburban service to Holywood and Bangor.

By bus: Ulsterbus runs an excellent network of services to all parts of County Down, ✆ (01232) 320011/232356.

By car: car hire from Lyle Motors, Portaferry Road, Newtownards, ✆ (01247) 813376.

By bike: The Raleigh Rent-a-Bike network operates throughout County Down. Your local dealer is Ross Cycles, 44 Clarkhill Road, ✆ (013967) 78029.

Tourist Information

Bangor, ✆ (01247) 270069.

Newry, ✆ (01693) 668877.

Warrenpoint, ✆ (016937) 72950.

Newcastle, ✆ (013967) 22222.

Festivals

Local tourist offices will give you further details on all the following:

17 March: St Patrick's Day Celebrations at Downpatrick, Newry and Cultra.

June: Castleward Opera. Contact Castleward, Strangford, ✆ (0139686) 204.

Early/mid July: Booley Fair, Hilltown. Demonstrations of vanishing skills such as weaving, stone-carving, shoeing horses and other smithy work. Traditional music and dancing, street stalls and sheep fair.

July (usually): Scarva hosts a sham fight in a traditional pageant which has gone on for over 200 years. It is a symbolic enactment of the Battle of the Boyne between two horsemen in period costume—William of Orange and James II.

July: Orange marches all over County Down.

July: Ulster Harp Derby at the Down Royal Race Course.

July: Kingdom of Mourne Festival in Kilkeel, Cranfield and Annalong.

July/August: Portaferry Regatta.

August: Fiddlers Green Festival, Rostrevor. Five day festival.

September: Dromore Horse Fair, Dromore.

October: Newry and Mourne Arts festival.

The Ards Peninsula

The Ards Peninsula, which runs along the length of the east shore of Strangford Lough, takes its name from rocky coast (*ard*: rock). This finger of land curving round the Down mainland contains some of the most charming villages and towns created by the Scottish and English settlers. In between these towns are earlier sites: raths, holy wells and monastic ruins. You are never more than 3 or 4 miles (6.4km) from the sea. Prepare yourself for an exhilarating climate, unusual in Ireland, for this is the sunniest, dryest and breeziest bit of Ulster. A tour of the Ards is a good way to take in all the beauties.

Start from **Bangor**, a seaside resort popular with the Edwardians, as you will see from the architecture. It was a famous centre of learning in the 6th and 7th centuries, and from here Saints Columbanus and Gall set off to found Luxeuil Monastery in Burgundy, and St Gall Monastery in Switzerland. St Comgall, who founded this monastery in the middle of the 6th century, trained men like Columbanus and Gall to spread the word of Christ. They set off from Bangor in frail coracles and made their way to Europe. The plundering Norsemen in the 9th century ravaged the town. All that remains from these times is the tower of the **abbey church** opposite Bangor railway station. The church has a pretty painted ceiling and ancient settler grave-stones (*open to* *the public*). A very interesting interlude can be spent in the **Victorian Castle** (*open all year during normal working hours*), used as the town hall, which has a permanent display on Bangor and its great importance as an ancient place of learning. There is a tea room and car park. Apart from the Edwardian seafront, which has a great many B&Bs and small hotels, and a very fine marina for visiting yachtsmen, there is not much to attract one to Bangor. The beach has an over-used look, and the shops are tacky. It has turned into a dormitory town of Belfast.

Donaghadee, a pretty seaside town with a free harbour and a good number of pubs, used to be linked with Portpatrick in Scotland by a regular sailing boat. It has the feeling of an old port where generations of men and women have waited for the wind and the tide to change. The poet John Keats stayed at Grace Neill's Bar on the High Street, as did Peter the Great of Russia. (Gracie's is still one of the most attractive pubs in the town.) You can go out stream fishing at night in the summer with a white feather as a lure. Or at weekends go out to the **Copeland Islands**—long, low islands covered with spring turf and rabbit's trails, enchanting in spring and summer. The islands are very small and are sheep-farmed by one owner. It is possible to reach them and to go out stream fishing on a regular boat.

Following the coast road through **Millisle** down to **Ballyhalbert** you will pass some golden strands. There are pebbly beaches further on at Cloughy Bay. Notice the Scottish influence: snug, unpretentious houses and carefully worked fields. Many of the road names are intriguing: they are taken from the townlands, early units of land-holding, and are called such things as Ballydrain, Ringboy, Balloo, Bright, and Scollogs Town.

The most picturesque town on the Ards is **Portaferry**, situated where the tip of the Ards forms a narrow strait with the mainland of Down. On the waterfront you look across to Strangford village. The street here is wide, and the brightly painted old houses are attractive to look at. In Castle Street is the **Aquarium Exploris** (*open April–Aug daily, 10–6, Sun 1–6; rest of the year, 10.30–5; closed Mon, Sun 1–5; adm; © (012477) 28062*), where in spacious tanks you can see many of the sea animals that inhabit Strangford Lough; and there is plenty of interesting background information on the geology and plant life of the lough. In the summer you might be lucky and hear some open-air music, often played here in the evenings. A ferry runs between Portaferry and Strangford every half-hour, and the journey of 5 minutes is well worth it for the view up Strangford Lough. If you are an artist, you may be so won over by the charms of this part of the peninsula that you will want to enrol in one of the painting courses held here in the summer (*see* **Practical A–Z**).

The Strangford Shore

Sam Hanna Bell, the Belfast novelist, has described this area with great truth and beauty in his book, *December Bride*, which has been praised for going straight to the heart of the Ulster experience.

On the A20, which hugs the Strangford Shore, you can enjoy the beauty of this nearly landlocked water. Scattered with small islands, this area is of special interest to naturalists. The National Trust have a wildlife scheme operating which covers the entire foreshore of the lough, totalling about 5400 acres (2000ha). Vast flocks of wildfowl gather here as well

as seals and other marine animals. There are birdwatching facilities at Castle Espie, Mount Stewart Gashouse, and Island Reagh (*see* 'Activities', below). Strangford was named by the Viking invaders (*strang* means strong) after the strong tides at the mouth of the Lough. Here, in Norman times, the wealthy knights encouraged the monks to build amongst the lovely scenery. At **Greyabbey** (*An Mhainistir Liath*: the grey monastery), you can visit one of the most complete Cistercian abbeys in Ireland (*open April–Sept, Tues–Sat, 10–7 and Sun 2–7; adm; ℗ (01232) 230560*). Built in the 12th century by the wife of John de Courcy, Affreca, it represents the new monastic orders introduced to counteract Irish traditions. The Pope was determined to stop the independence shown by the Irish abbot-prince who combined temporal and spiritual power, and often ignored the pronouncements from Rome.

Approximately 15 miles (24km) east of Belfast on the A20 to Newtownards, following the lough, the demesne wall of **Mount Stewart**, the home of the Londonderry family, appears. The 18th-century house and grounds are now in the hands of the National Trust (*open May–Sept, daily (except Tues), 1–6; April–Oct at weekends. The temple hours are 2–5. The gardens are open April to Sept, daily, 10.30–6; April and Oct during weekends; adm for house, garden and temple; ℗ Greyabbey (012477) 88387*). Edith, Lady Londonderry, 7th Marchioness and one of the foremost political hostesses of her generation, created the wonderful gardens over 60 years ago for her children. There are some lovely topiary animals, colourful parterres and wonderful trees. If you ever come across her children's story *The Magic Inkpot*, you will recognize some of the place names from round here. Also in the grounds is the **Temple of the Winds**, inspired by the building in

Athens and built in 1780 for picnicking in style. From Arcadian pursuits of the 18th century to craft-wares of the 20th century: in the Mount Stewart school house you can buy patchworks and handmade cottage furniture. The tearoom in the house itself is painted very beautifully with the animals from the Ark. Edith, Lady Londonderry nick-named all the famous men and women of the day who were her friends after animals in Noah's Ark. It is fun to guess who is who.

To complete the tour of the Ards, a quick visit to **Newtownards** will be rewarding, partic-ularly for medievalists. The town square is also impressive and worth a visit. On the outskirts of the town on the road to Millisle is **Movilla Abbey**, built between the 13th and 15th centuries. There was an earlier establishment here founded in the 6th century by St Finian, a contemporary of that great Irish saint, Columba, also known as Colmcille. Unfortunately the two men did not get on. The story goes that it was St Finian's psalter that St Columba copied so stealthily, and they had a battle over it which caused many deaths. Columba was an O'Donnell prince as well as a cleric, and he was so dismayed at the bloodshed he had caused that he exiled himself and founded the famous church at Iona, an island off the coast of Scotland. From here Christianity spread to most of Scotland. The psalter he had copied became the warrior *Book of the O'Donnells* and was borne before them into battle. It is now in the National Museum, Dublin. It is always possible to see the Abbey. Newtownards has a 17th-century market cross and a fine town hall. You won't fail to notice the prominent tower on **Scrabo Hill**, a memorial to one of the Londonderry Stewarts and a good lookout point. It is always accessible, although the tower itself is not open. Close to the little village of Saintfield is another wonderful garden in National Trust care. This is **Rowallane**, famous throughout the horticultural and botan-ical world for its shrubs and trees (*open April–Oct, Mon–Fri, 10.30–6; Sat–Sun 2–6; Nov–Mar, Mon–Fri 10.30–5; adm; ✆ (01238) 510131*). The best time to see it is early spring when the azaleas and rhododendrons are a riot of colour.

Mid-Down

Mid-Down is drumlin country until you reach Slieve Croob, around Ballinahinch. Harris, a local historian who described Down in the 18th century, had a rather droll phrase for the countryside contours: they are like 'eggs set in salt'. Cap this with C. S. Lewis' recipe for his native county: 'earth-covered potatoes'! (Lewis, the Belfast-born novelist and critic, who died in 1963, was most famous for his children's stories, *The Chronicles of Narnia*.)

To explore mid-Down you might start from **Comber**, a pleasant town with a prominent statue of Robert Gillespie, one of the Ulster's military heroes in the Indian campaigns. Near here, off the A22 to Killyleagh, you can visit **Nendrum** (*open April–Sept, 10–7; always accessible; adm free*). This is one of the most romantic of the monastic sites, founded by a pupil of St Patrick on Mahee Island, and reached by a causeway through Island Reagh. It consists of a hill-top crowned with three circular stone walls, a church, a round tower stump, a sundial and cross slabs. There is an Interpretative Centre. If you have time it is worth taking a little detour at Balloo to **Ardmullan**. Whiterock yacht club is always a hive of activity and it looks out onto the islands of Strangford Lough; including Braddock Island where there is a lovely bungalow designed by T. W .Henry, brother of the better known painter Paul Henry. The little village of **Killyleagh** has a lovely-looking castle which is still lived in by its original family, who came from Ayrshire in the mid-17th century. It is not open to the public. Going west on the B7 you come to the **Ulster Wildlife Centre** at **Crossgar** (*open 17 April to 11 Sept; adm; ✆ (01396) 830282*). Here you can learn about wetland raised bog and meadowland flora and fauna.

If you continue down the west side of Strangford, you cross the River Quoile and arrive at **Downpatrick**, an attractive Georgian town built on an old hill-fort which reputedly belonged to one of the Red Branch Knights (*see **Old Gods and Heroes**, p.580*). It is sited at the natural meeting point of several river valleys, and therefore has been occupied for a long time, both suffering and benefiting from the waves of settlers and invaders—missionaries, monks, Norsemen, Normans and Scots (the army of Edward Bruce). **St Patrick's gravestone**, a large bit of granite, may be seen in the Church of Ireland Cathedral graveyard, although this is not the reason why the town carries his name. The association was made by the Norman John de Courcy, a Cheshire knight who was granted the counties of Antrim and Down by Henry II in 1176, and who established himself here at this centre of St Patrick's veneration by promoting the Irish saint. De Courcy donated some relics of Saints Patrick, Columba and Brigid to his Foundation; and gave the town its name, adding Patrick to Dundalethglas, as it was previously called. During the Middle Ages Downpatrick suffered at the hands of the Scots: in 1316 it was burnt by Edward Bruce; and, later, it was destroyed by the English during the Tudor wars. In the early 18th century stability returned to the town under the influence of an English family called Southwell who acquired the Manor of Downpatrick through marriage. They built a quay on the River Quoile and encouraged markets and building. The cathedral lay in ruins between 1538 and 1790 and reopened for use in 1818. It is very fine inside, with pleasant stained-glass windows. The **Southwell Charity School and Almshouse** in English Street near Down Cathedral is a handsome early-Georgian building in the Irish Palladian style. Nearby, in the old county jail in the Mall, is the **St Patrick Heritage Centre and Down Museum** (*open all year, Tues–Fri, 11–5, Sat 2–5; July and Aug, Mon 11–5 and Sun 2–5; ✆ (0396) 65218; adm free*). There are very interesting exhibits of Stone Age artefacts and local history, as well as a rewarding survey of St Patrick's life and work.

To the east of the town, some 2 miles (3.2km) outside, are the **Struell Wells** (*always accessible, adm free*). There must have been worshippers at this pagan shrine long before the arrival of St Patrick, and the waters were long known for their curative properties. To the east of Downpatrick on the A24 is the little village of **Seaforde**. In the grounds of the big house here is an attractive **butterfly garden**, which you can visit in the summer (*✆ (039687) 225*). It also has a hornbeam maze and specialist nursery. The area is rich in bird and plant life.

Cloughy Rocks Nature Reserve on the coast, south of Strangford village, is particularly rich in inter-tidal plants, and has an ever-changing variety of seabirds and wildfowl. Common seals can often be seen basking on the rocks at low tide. Near Downpatrick, just off the A25 and guarded by Castle Ward at its southeastern end, is the **Quoile Pondage Nature Reserve**. This was formed as the result of a barrage at Castle Island to prevent flooding caused by the tidal inrush of the sea from Strangford Lough into the river. The freshwater vegetation which has established itself here as a result is of great interest to the botanist. And for the ornithologist, a great variety of indigenous and immigrant birds feed and nest here. In springtime you can see great crested grebes displaying. **Inch Abbey** (*open April–Sept, daily, 10–7, Sun, 2–7 and closed on Monday; it closes at 4pm in the winter time; adm*) is a very beautiful ruined Cistercian abbey on an island in the Quoile Marshes. It was founded in the 1180s by John de Courcy.

Going on the A25 in an easterly direction, 1½ miles (2km) west of Strangford village, you will pass by **Castleward** (*open May–Aug, daily (except Thurs) 1–6; April and Sept–Oct, weekends 1–6; grounds open all year round until dusk; adm, car park fee*). The character and aspect of this house are worth a detour: it is a compromise between husband and wife, expressed in architecture. Built in the 1760s by Bernard Ward, afterwards Lord Bangor, and his wife Lady Anne, a great heiress, it has a neoclassical façade, and a Gothic castellated garden front. The interior echoes this curious divergence of tastes: the reception rooms are gracefully classical, following his Lordship, and the library and her Ladyship's rooms are elaborately neo-Gothic in the Strawberry Hill manner conceived by Horace Walpole. The ceiling in the boudoir caused the poet, John Betjeman, to exclaim that it was like 'standing beneath a cow'. The property is in the hands of the National Trust and there are a number of other attractions: a Palladian-style temple which overlooks an early 18th-century lake, an early tower house and lovely grounds. A goldsmith's studio provides souvenirs for those who are looking for more valuable mementoes than snapshots. In June the rooms of this gracious house are full of music during the **Castleward Opera Festival**. Close by and just off the A25 is **Loughmoney Dolmen**, which is probably over four thousand years old. It is typical of others scattered round this district.

Strangford village, which can be reached by a coastal footpath, is a few miles on. This is where you can catch the ferry across to the Ards village of Portaferry. No less than five small castles are within reach of Strangford, testifying to its strategic importance: Strangford Castle, Old Castle Ward, Audley's Castle, Walshestown and Kilclief. The nicest way to see them is from the lough, when the ferry is in mid-stream. **Kilclief Castle** (*always accessible, adm free*), which is easy to find on the A2 between Strangford and Ardglass, is very well preserved and in State care. It was built before 1440 and is a stately grey-stone tower house. More castles can be seen round the fishing village of **Ardglass**, an important port in medieval times and now a centre for herring fleets. The best-preserved castle is Jordan's Castle, a 15th-century tower house with four storeys (*open June–Sept 10–7 Tues–Sat, 2–7 Sun; closed Mondays and lunchtimes 1–1.30; adm*).

Also in the Strangford area is an 18-hole golf course. And there is good sea-angling off the coast here. The tree-lined village of **Killough**, about 1 mile (1.6km) from Ardglass, was developed as a grain port by the Ward family in the 18th century. There is a good beach and, further down, at St Johns Point, an old ruined church. There are also some very good **strands**, notably Tyrella on the Dundrum Bay. Interesting prehistoric monuments in this area are **Ballynoe Stone Circle** and **Rathmullen Mote**. They are both within easy reach of Downpatrick, situated amongst the maze of little roads in the triangle between A25, A2 and B176.

South Down

South Down is a mainly mountainous area, and extends across to the south Armagh border, girded to the south and east by a beautiful coastline. The rather splendid fjord-like inlet, Carlingford Lough (a name of Scandinavian origin), cuts through the middle of the upland area. It follows a fault line forming the Gap of the North and this has been the main north–south throughfare since ancient times. In this trough, astride the ancient road from Armagh to Tara, lies the town of Newry.

Within a 25-mile (40km) circle, some 48 peaks rise in a purple mass of rounded summits. The **Mourne Mountains** do not form a harsh, wild, rugged scenery (Bignian and Bearnagh are the only two with craggy tops), but one that suggests peace and solitude. Few roads cross the Mournes, so this is a walker's paradise: endless paths up and down through bracken and heather, peaceful unspoilt lakes and tumbling streams, the wild flowers of moor and heath, birds and birdsong, all to be enjoyed under an ever-changing sky.

Of the many walks possible, perhaps the loveliest are up to **Silent Valley** and to **Lough Shannagh** from above Kilkeel, to the glittering crystals of **Diamond Rocks**, to the summits above Spelga Dam, and of course **Slieve Donard** itself, where on a fine, clear day you can see across the water to England. For the benefit of the more hearty, it is worth mentioning the 20-mile (32km) boundary wall that links the main peaks. Quite a constructional feat in itself, it used to be followed on the Annual Mourne Wall Walk until erosion by thousands of pairs of feet caused the event to be cancelled a few years ago.

Perhaps the best place to start from when visiting this area is **Newcastle**, one of Ulster's most attractive and lively seaside resorts, though its popularity has sadly destroyed some of its charm. It has a lovely long sandy beach for bathing, and behind it there is the **Royal County Down Golf Course**, a fine championship course. Near Newcastle lies the magnificent forest park of **Tullymore**. It has many lovely, though rather well-trodden, forest trails and nature walks on the lower wooded slopes and along the River Shimna.

Before following the coast round, it is well worth heading northwards to visit one or two places. **Castlewellan**, which appeared on the map as recently as the end of last century, has two large marketplaces: one oval, one square. This neatly laid out town is surrounded by well-wooded demesnes, one of which is now a forest park, and is renowned for its arboretum and lovely gardens. Due north of Newcastle, about 2 miles (3.2km) away, is **Murlough Nature Reserve**, where you can explore the sand dunes. Exposed to the wind, the dunes are a wonderfully peaceful heaven for waders, waterbirds and shorebirds. Sweet-smelling wild flowers grow unhindered and in the summer delicious wild strawberries lie woven over the sand dunes. **Dundrum** is not far beyond. On the outskirts of this once flourishing fishing port, now more of a coal quay, ¾ mile (1km) northwest of Dundrum on a wooded hill, are the extensive ruins of a Norman motte and bailey **castle**, enclosing a magnificent partly ruined stone castle with a circular keep of the tower type (*grounds accessible at all times; adm free. The keep is open April–Sept, Tues–Sat, 10–7; Sun, 2–7; from Oct to Mar closes at 4pm. Closes Mon and lunch 1–1.30; adm*). Staircases, parapets, towers and a massive gatehouse make this an ideal picnic spot and adventure playground for children. It was built in about 1177 as one of John de Courcy's coastal castles.

Newcastle to Rostrevor

Now travel along the coast from Newcastle to Rostrevor on the A2. From here there's a fine view of the Mournes, with Slieve Donard rising majestically up as the centrepiece. Heading south out of Newcastle, past the old disused swimming pool and the now quiet harbour, you come to the National Trust **Mourne Coastal Path**, which runs for 4 miles (6.4km) from the very popular Bloody Bridge picnic site. A network of by-roads runs deep into the foothills behind Annalong and Kilkeel. Here is the unspoilt, undisturbed Mourne way of life: the stone cottages, the men and women at work in their pocket-handkerchief fields; the elderly, pipe or knitting in hand, passing the time of day; the children playing. It is not hard to imagine it all in the days before roads were made. Then, the prosperous economy was based on granite quarries and fishing, and the intensively farmed land was enriched from the wrack beds of Killowen. It has changed little since then.

Back again on the coast road: round the corner lies the little village of **Annalong**, set against a backcloth of mountains. The little old harbour still flourishes: boats are being repainted, nets repaired: everyone is doing something, no one hurries. **Kilkeel** is a surprisingly busy, prosperous town, home of the coast's main fishing fleet. It is on the site of an ancient rath, and the ruins of a 14th-century church still stand in the square. Just to the northeast of the town is a fine **dolmen** whose capstone measures over 10ft by 8ft (3m by 2.5m). Then the road climbs up and across the Spelga Pass towards Hilltown. It has many vantage points for viewing both the mountains and the coastal scenery.

Continuing on round the coast, the land levels out quite a bit. Down to the left lies the long strand that is **Cranfield**. Greencastle (*times and adm as for Dundrum Castle, see p.390*), the ancient capital of the Kingdom of Mourne, which existed in the 9th century, is visible on the horizon strategically sited at the entrance of Carlingford Lough. The tall, rectangular, turreted keep and some of the out-works are all that remain of this impressive 13th-century stronghold . From the topmost turret of the castle are splendid views across the lough to the Republic.

The road swings round still more, ever twisting and turning as it makes its way along the indented coast. The houses are larger, their gardens bigger and better kept. Clearly this was, and still is, a prosperous area. Sheltered by high hills and set against a purple and green backcloth of pine forests, the town of **Rostrevor** enjoys a mild and sunny climate, hence the profusion of brightly coloured flowers in the gardens, many of them of Mediterranean origin. It has a lovely long seafront and superb views across the lough, but sadly no sandy beach. It is a quiet place to use as a base for walking in the Mourne Mountains or in the pine-scented Rostrevor Forest. A mountain road climbs up northwards, passing the little old church of Kilbroney with its ancient cross, and levelling out to follow along the valley of the Bann to emerge at Hilltown. The many tumbling little streams, stony paths and patches of woodland make for excellent picnic sites en route.

Not far from Rostrevor is **Warrenpoint**, a lively and popular resort. It is spacious in layout and well planned, with a very big square and a promenade over half a mile (800m) long, the town being bounded by the sea on two sides. There is a new, well-equipped marina, golf and tennis facilities, and lots of live music in the pubs. Prior to the mid-18th century there was little here save a rabbit warren—hence its name. The Heritage Centre in Bridge Road (*open April–Oct, daily exc Mon*) has items of local historical interest. A little to the north, on a spur of rock jutting out into the estuary lies the square, battlemented tower house of **Narrow Water Castle** which is still privately owned. It was built in the 17th century on the site of a much earlier fortification.

From here the road improves dramatically and before long you reach **Newry**, an old and prosperous town sited where St Patrick planted a yew at the head of the strand—hence its name, which in Gaelic is *An Hir*: yew. It enjoys a strategic site astride the Clanrye River. Newry has been a busy mercantile town for centuries, and trade was accelerated in 1741 when the Newry Canal—believed to be the oldest canal constructed in the British Isles— connected Newry to Lough Neagh and Carlingford Lough. Today, the canal is stocked with fish. The long prosperity of this old town is clearly reflected in its large and imposing town houses and public buildings, though many are now rather dilapidated.

St Patrick's Parish Church is possibly the earliest Protestant church in Ireland. The 19th-century **Cathedral of St Colman** boasts some beautiful stained-glass windows. The town hall is impressively sited astride the Clanrye River, which forms the county boundary. There is much Georgian architecture, and many shops with small-paned windows and slate-hung gables. Some of Newry's oldest houses are to be found in Market Street. Remnants of far earlier centuries are the monastery, the castle and the Cistercian abbey. In the **Art Centre**, Bank Parade, is a small museum (*open all year, daily, except Sun*) with many varied and intereesting exhibits.

Two miles (3.2km) north of the town, near Crown Bridge, there is a very fine motte and bailey, giving rise to a crown-shaped mound. And at **Donaghmore** 3 miles (4.8km) on, in the parish graveyard, there is a fine 10th-century carved cross on the site of an earlier monastery under which lies a souterain. **Slieve Gullion Forest Park**, 4 miles (6.4km) west of Newry in County Armagh has a lovely 7-mile (11km) drive with wonderful views of lakes, which takes you nearly to the top of Slieve Gullion Mountain. A path continues upwards to 1900ft (580m), and you can explore two Stone Age cairns.

Inland around Hilltown

Heading from Newry back across to Newcastle you pass just north of the Mournes. The view across to the mountains is superb, ever-changing. The road is very twisty so it is nice to stop and appreciate the many panoramic vantage points. There are two towns worth visiting. The first, **Hilltown**, the more southerly where the mountain roads from Kilkeel and Rostrevor converge, is a small angling village located at a crossroads on top of a hill. The views are breathtaking. Just over 2 miles (3.2km) northeast of Hilltown, in Cloughmore on Goward Hill, is a huge dolmen known as **Cloughmore Cromlech**. Underneath its three massive upright supports and 50-ton granite capstone, there is a double burial chamber in which traces of bones were found. The road to Kilkeel (B27) passes close to Eagle Mountain and the Silent Valley reservoir—a deep valley between the peaks of the Mournes. The road, known as the Spelga Pass, demands careful driving as it rises and twists amongst the spectacular scenery.

Easily spotted in the distance by its distinctive mushroom-shaped water tower lies **Rathfriland**—a flourishing market town set high on a hill, and commanding a wide view of the Mournes and the surrounding countryside. This area from Loughbrickland to Rathfriland is called Brontë country because here lived the aunts, uncles and, when he was a boy, the father of novelists Charlotte, Emily and Anne. Emily is supposed to have modelled Heathcliff in *Wuthering Heights* on her wild great-uncle Welsh, who travelled to London with a big stick to silence the critics of his nieces' books! **Drumballyroney school** and **church** in Rathfriland houses a small **interpretative centre** on the Brontes. The family homestead is at Emdale.

Further north again, heading back for Belfast on the A25/A1, is the town of **Hillsborough**. It has become famous recently because the Anglo–Irish Agreement was reached here. It is one of the most English-looking villages in Ulster, with tasteful craft shops and numerous restaurants. 'Ulster says No' is painted on posters and flags, and a multitude of Union Jacks decorate the streets. Watch where you park your car because, with the Government house there, the security forces are very sensitive. To the south of the town in parkland is a massive fort built by Sir Arthur Hill, an English settler, in the 17th century (*open all year, Tues–Sat, 10–7; Sun 2–7 closed at 4 in the winter; adm; ✆ (01846) 683285*). **Government House**, which was the official residence of the Governor and is now the residence of the Secretary of State for Northern Ireland, stands in the parkland too. The wrought-iron gates which bar one's approach from the town are exquisite. The Church of Ireland parish church is in handsome Planter's-style Gothic, and was built by the Hill family in 1774.

Shopping

Crafts: The National Trust shops at Castleward, Strangford and Mount Stewart, Newtownards. The Bay Tree, Audley Court, Holywood. Iona, 27 Church Road, Holywood. Lovely craft shop which also sells organic vegetables. Also, several shops in the Main Street, Hillsborough.

Pottery: Parrot Lodge Pottery, 131 Ballyward Road, Castlewellan, ✆ (0182064) 314. Fish, birds of paradise, objects functional and surreal.

Antiques: shops in the Main Street, Greyabbey; at Balloo House, Killinchy; and in Killinchy Street, Comber. Also, The Gallery, Gilford Castle, Gilford.

Delicacies: excellent bread and cake shops throughout the county. In particular try Adelboden Lodge, Groomsport, ✆ (01247) 464288. For delicious wholemeal loaf and barmbrack, go to the Victoria Bakery, Castle Street, Newry, ✆ (01693) 2076. For excellent wines in an elegant shop. James Nicholson, 27a Killyleagh Street, ✆ (01396) 830091. Italian Delicatessen, Panini, at 25 Church Road, Holywood for the makings of a picnic.

Fresh oysters: sold in small amounts from Cuan Sea Fisheries Ltd, Sketrick Island, Killinchy.

Activities

Sea-angling: in Strangford Lough for tope, skate, haddock, conger eel. Fishing trips arranged from Portaferry. For local knowledge of Carlingford Lough, contact Mr Peter Wright, 152 Portaferry Road, Newtownards, ✆ (01247) 812081.

Shore-angling: off Ardglass and Portavogie. Contact Peter Wright, 152 Portaferry Road, Newtownards, ✆ (01247) 812081. And, for the Ardglass area, contact Captain R. Fitzsimons, Harbour-Master, ✆ (01396) 841291 or (01396) 841464 (home).

Game fishing: for brown trout and salmon on the River Bann near Hilltown, Spelga Dam, and Shimna River in Tullymore Forest Park.

Coarse fishing: in the River Quoile basin. Contact the local tourist office.

Sailing: in Strangford Lough. There is a sailing school on Sketrick Island in Strangford Lough where there are residential or day-long courses on all aspects of sailing. Contact Bangor and Strangford Sailing School, 13 Gray's Hill, Bangor, ✆ (01247) 455967 or (01238) 541592. Sailing boat charter from Terry Anderson, Down Yachts, 37 Bayview Road, Killinchy, ✆ (01238) 542210.

Pleasure cruises: weather permitting, cruise boats leave from Bangor and Donaghadee in summer at 10.30, 2.30 and 7.30pm for short cruises. Information is posted at piers or ✆ (01247) 270069 or (01247) 812215. Trips to Copeland Islands, ✆ (01247) 883403.

Sub-aqua: Mr Wright, 152 Portaferry Road, Newtownards, ✆ (01247) 812081.

Pony-trekking: Mount Pleasant Trekking Centre, Castlewellan, ✆ (013967) 78651 and Mourne Riding School, 98 Castlewellan Road, Newcastle, ✆ (013967) 24351.

Golf: at Ardglass, ✆ (01396) 841219; Bangor, ✆ (01247) 270922; Downpatrick, ✆ (01396) 615947; Donaghadee, ✆ (01247) 883624; The Royal County Down (Links) Course at Newcastle, ✆ (013967) 23314.

Walking: in the Mourne Mountains. The Ulster Way goes through Comber and along the shores of Strangford Lough, around the coast through Ardglass and Newcastle into the Mournes. Contact The Field Officer, Sports Council for Northern Ireland, House of Sport, Upper Malone Road, Belfast, ✆ (01232) 381222 for more details. Lovely walks on National Trust property in the Murlough Nature Reserve, near Newcastle, in the arboreteum of Castlewellan, at Castleward, Rowallane and Tullymore Park, Newcastle.

Bathing: Tyrella Strand, Dundrum Bay, Millisle.

Bird-watching: at the Castle Espie hide, ✆ (01247) 872517 and at Salt and Green Islands, Mount Stewart Gas House and Island Reagh—all on Strangford Lough, ✆ Saintfield (01247) 874146 or Strangford Wildlife Centre, ✆ (01396) 881411 for details. Ballymacormick Point, near Bangor. Lighthouse Island (part of the Copeland Islands) contact Mr N. McKee, ✆ (018494) 33068.

Open farm: Ark Open Farm, 296 Bangor Road, Newtownards. Rare breeds including Irish Moiled Cattle, ✆ (01247) 812672.

Where to Stay

See also Belfast, 'Where to Stay'.

expensive

Glassdrumman Lodge, 85 Mill Road, Annalong, ✆ (013967) 68451. A super place to spend the night, though on the pricey side. Next door at the Glassdrumman House Restaurant you can have a delicious meal made from vegetables from the garden and organic meat. You can tour the farm where the produce is grown so make sure you have got your wellies. **Slieve Donard Hotel**, Downs Road, Newcastle, ✆ (013967) 23681. Close to golf links. **Clandeboye Lodge**, Clandeboye, near Bangor, ✆ (01247) 853777 Brand new luxury hotel on the Clandeboye Estate with 18-hole golf course.

moderate

Burrendale Hotel, 51 Castlewellan Road, Newcastle, ✆ (013967) 22599. Modern, popular with bus tours. Mrs Maginn, **Rathglen Villas**, 7 Hilltown Road, ✆ (018206) 38090.

Portaferry Hotel, 10 The Strand, Portaferry, ✆ (012477) 28231. Old-fashioned with lovely situation. Mr & Mrs Corbett, **Tyrella House**, Downpatrick, ✆ (01396) 85422. Georgian country house with private sandy beach. Riding and grass tennis.

inexpensive

Mrs Coburn, **Sylvan Hill House**, Dromore, ✆ (01846) 692321. 18th-century house and delicious food. Mrs Muldoon, **The Cottage**, 377 Comber Road, Dundonald, ✆ (01247) 878189. This two-hundred-year-old cottage is very cosy, with turf fires, and is near to the National Trust properties of Rowallane and Mount Stewart. **Mr and Mrs Adair**, 22 The Square, Portaferry, ✆ (012477)

28412. A very simple and clean place to stay. Mrs Mabel Hall, **Abbey Farm**, 17 Ballywalter Road, Greyabbey, ✆ (012477) 88207. Old-fashioned farmhouse near to National Trust properties.

Mrs Macauley, **Havine Farm**, 51 Ballydonnell Road, Downpatrick, ✆ (01396) 85242. Comfortable farmhouse with pretty beamed ceilings in the bedrooms. Great home-made cakes. Mrs McCabe, **Still Waters**, 14 Killowen Road, Rostrevor, ✆ (06937) 38743. Gorgeous location and a lovely sun porch with garden. Mrs W. Mark, **The Maggimin**, 11 Bishopswell Road, Dromore, ✆ (01846) 693520. Delicious Ulster fry for breakfast.

self-catering

The following are all attractive old buildings: **Potter's Cottage**, Castleward, Strangford. Sleeps four, from £220 a week in the high season, ✆ (01225) 704545. **Castleward**: 2 flats, each sleeping eight, from £360 in the high season. Bookings through the National Trust, ✆ (01396) 881204.

Eating Out

See also Belfast, "Eating Out'.

expensive

Portaferry Hotel, 10 The Strand, ✆ (012477) 28231. Excellent seafood delivered straight from the fishing boats of Portavogie. **Woodlands**, 9 Spa Road, Ballynahinch, ✆ (01238) 562650. Delicious Strangford scallops. **Glassdrumman House**, 224 Glassdrumman Road, ✆ (013967) 68585. Memorable food, especially the steak and fish dishes. The family who run it grow their own vegetables and keep their animals in free-range conditions.

moderate

The Lobster Pot, 11 The Square, Strangford, ✆ (0139) 688 1288. Very good set meals and pub grub. Oysters and other shellfish a speciality. **Iona Bistro**, 27 Church Road, ✆ (01232) 425655. Bistro atmosphere and tasty food. Good for vegetarians. The **Back Street Café**, 14 Queens Parade, Bangor, ✆ (01247) 453990. Good atmosphere and imaginative food down a little backstreet lane. **Old School House**, 100 Ballydrain Road, Killinchy, ✆ (01238) 541182. Delicious rack of lamb and a consistently good menu. **The Grange**, Mill Hill, Main Street, Waringstown, ✆ (01762) 881989. Delicious baked salmon.

inexpensive

Mount Stewart House, Ark Club Tearooms, ✆ (012477) 88387. On the Strangford Shore, a place for light lunch and high tea in June, July, August. Light snacks at other times. Good soups, quiche and lasagne. **The Cabin**, 32 New Street, Donaghadee. Creamy home-made ice-cream in an old fashioned ice cream parlour. **The Baytree**, Audley Ct, Holywood, ✆ (01232) 426414. Sweet, friendly place; light lunches and cakes. **Hillside Bar**, 21 Main Street, Hillsborough,

✆ (01846) 682765. Salad bar and good homemade pâtés and soups. **Plough Inn,** The Square, Hillsborough, ✆ (01846) 682985. Pub grub. **O'Reilly's,** 7 Rathfriland Rd, Dromara, ✆ (01238) 532209. Excellent seafood. **The Gourmet,** The Square, Warrenpoint, ✆ (016937) 74089. Deli and tea shop with good cheese counter.

The **Red Pepper,** 28 Main Street, Groomsport, ✆ (01266) 270097. Good lamb and fondue. The **Bridewell Restaurant,** 19 High Street, Donaghadee, ✆ (01247) 882568. Italian restaurant in Georgian town house. Very good fish and spaghetti. Excellent value. **Daft Eddys,** Sketrick Island, Whiterock, Killinchy, ✆ (01238) 541615. Pub on island reached by a causeway. Good soups and steaks.

County Armagh

The smallest county in Ulster, Armagh's scenery is nevertheless varied: from the gentle southern drumlins, to wild open moorland, and the grander mountains and rocky glens further east. The Gaelic tradition of splitting land between all the family gives a familar pattern to the landscape. Here, an intricate network of dry-stone walls gather what fertility may be had into fields with barely enough room for a cow to turn in. As you travel north towards the reclaimed wetlands on the shore of Lough Neagh, the orchards and dairy pastures become more extensive, and are dotted with small lakes and the rivers that once turned the wheels of the flax mills.

In general, the people are fairly prosperous farmers, although the 'Troubles' of the last twenty years have taken their toll of misery and death. People here feel very strongly about politics, and there is very little middle ground, so you may find it easier to avoid political discussions.

Highlights of the county include Ardress House and The Argory, both National Trust properties which give great insight into more settled times of the 18th and 19th centuries. For the fisherman there are tremendous catches of bream in the Blackwater River, and walkers can enjoy the quiet tranquillity of Clare Glen. You might be lucky and see a game of road bowls, an old Irish sport that is played here and in County Cork. The area has the reputation for being very rainy. Ulsterbus transport is excellent throughout the county, and the main Belfast to Dublin railway line passes along its eastern border, stopping along the way.

History

One of the most fascinating aspects of County Armagh is its history. On the outskirts of Armagh City is the legendary *Emain Macha*, also known as Navan Fort. This was the crowning place of the Sovereigns of Ulster (350 BC to AD 332), and it was from here that the legendary Red Branch Knights sallied out to display their prowess and do great deeds of chivalry. The greatest of these knights was Cú Chulainn, who is supposed to have received his training at the fort (*see* **'Old Gods and Heroes'**, p.576). Of course, this ancient history is clouded with mystery and legend; it is part of Ulster's mythology and identity, just as Fionn MacCumhail and the *Fianna* are part of that of the rest of Ireland. Legends aside, we do know that when Fergus was King of Ulster in the 4th century *Emain*

Macha was burned and pillaged by forces from Tara, County Meath, and was never restored. After the decline of *Emain Macha*, the then small city of Armagh established itself as the ecclesiastical capital of Ireland. Here, in the 5th century, St Patrick built his first stone church. Around the church of St Patrick there grew up other churches, colleges and schools, as the city developed into a great centre of religion and learning until the 9th and 10th centuries with the incursion of the Vikings. Today, it is full of attractive 18th-century buildings, built in settled, prosperous days.

Getting There and Around

By air: Dublin International Airport is approximately 78 miles (124km) away. Belfast International airport is approximately 39 miles (62km) away.

By car: Avis, Lurgan, (01762) 321322.

By taxi: 127 Railways Street, Armagh, ✆ (01861) 527222.

By bus: Eight Ulsterbus expresses run daily from Belfast. Local buses from Armagh City Bus Station, ✆ (01861) 522266.

By bike: Brown's Bikes, 32 Cromeen Road, Killylea, ✆ (01861) 522782. Also, Raleigh Rent-a-Bike Centre at Raymonds, 65 Bridge Street, Portadown, ✆ (01762) 338128.

Tourist Information

Portadown, The Library, Edward Street, ✆ (01762) 353260, all year.

Belfast, River House, High Street, ✆ (01232) 246609, all year.

Armagh, Council Offices, Palace Domain, ✆ (01861) 524052.

Armagh, English Street, ✆ (01861) 527808, all year.

Festivals

Early August: All Ireland Intermediate Road Bowls Festival, on roads around Armagh City, ✆ (01861) 522437.

All year: Planetarium Star Shows every day at 2pm and 3pm, and every day except Saturday in July and August. Entry costs £2.50, ✆ (01861) 52389.

Armagh City and Environs

The city of **Armagh**, now sprawled over seven hills, used to be a centre of learning and tranquillity when Rome was in ruins and London glowed with endless fires started by the Barbarians. Today, there is little to show of the ancient city; its appearance is distinctly Georgian, especially in the Mall, yet it is still the ecclesiastical centre of Ireland. A visit to the **County Museum** in the Mall (*open Mon–Sat, 10–5; adm free*) helps to fill in the city's background. Here, a 17th-century painting shows the old wide streets, space for markets and the prominence of the early hill-top Cathedral of St Patrick. There is also a wide range of regional exhibits, a local natural history section, and an art gallery which has works by the Irish mystic poet George Russell (1867–1935), better known as A. E. The **Royal Fusiliers Museum** is also in the Mall (*open 10–12.30, 2–4; ℗ (01861) 522911*).

The two cathedral churches are unmistakable features of the city's skyline, for they each crown neighbouring hills. Founded by St Patrick, the ancient **Church of Ireland cathedral** is in the perpendicular style with a massive central tower. Its present appearance dates mainly from the 18th century, but its core is medieval. Before medieval times the city suffered terribly from the Viking raids, and the cathedral and town were sacked at least 20 times in five hundred years. Inside the cathedral is a memorial to Brian Boru, the most famous high king of all Ireland, who visited Armagh in 1004 and was received with great state. The precious *Book of Armagh* (*c.* AD 807), which is now in Trinity College, Dublin, was placed in his hands and his visit noted in the book. He presented 20 ounces of pure gold to the church. Ten years later he shattered the Vikings at the battle of Clontarf in 1014, which put a stop to their encroachment into inland areas (*see* **History**, p.95), but Brian Boru was killed in his tent after the battle was won. His body and that of his son were brought back to be buried here and the memorial to them is in the west wall.

The other heirloom of those ancient days is St Patrick's Bell, which is enclosed in a cover dating from the 12th century. It can be seen at the National Museum in Dublin. The moulding on the west door is very fine, and there is a good stained-glass window in the choir. Notice the carved medieval stone heads high up on the cathedral's exterior and the mysterious statues in the crypt. The surrounding streets run true to the rings of the Celtic rath or fort in which St Patrick (directed, so it is said, by a flight of angels), built his church. An **exhibition and historical centre** has opened in English Street. It is known as **St Patrick's Trian** (*open all year; ℗ (01861) 527808*) and derives this name from an ancient division of the city. The Armagh Story is illustrated through the ages by an audio visual show, and The Land of Lilliput is a child-orientated exhibition. The Centre also has art exhibitions, snacks, genealogical research and tourist information.

Across the valley are the twin spires of the Catholic **Cathedral of St Patrick**. This is a complete contrast, with its profusion of magnificent internal gilding, marbles, mosaics and stained glass. The building was finished in 1873, the passing of the years marked by a collection of cardinals' red hats suspended in the Lady Chapel!

Another feature of 18th-century Armagh is the **Observatory**, close to the more recent **Planetarium** and **Hall of Astronomy** (*Hall open Mon–Fri, 11.30–5, Sat and Sun 1.30–5; ℗ (01861) 523689*). Armagh has the most advanced facilities for astronomical studies in the British Isles. Exhibits include a mock-up of a *Gemini* spacecraft, *Space Shuttle* and *Voyager* from the American space programme. The institution owes its pre-eminence to Primate Robinson, who founded and endowed the observatory in 1790, and it is now one of the most established and oldest in the British Isles. It was designed by Francis Johnston, who is also responsible for the **Court House** and the Georgian terrace on the east side of the Mall. The **Palace Stables Heritage Centre** (*open all year; ℗ (01861) 522722*) is a restored 18th-century building in the parkland of the Bishop's

Palace. The 'Day in the Life' exhibition features typical scenes of life here in 1776. It holds craft exhibitions, fairs, lectures, art shows, music, dance and storytelling.

The ancient fort of **Emain Macha**, now called Navan Fort, dates from 600 BC and is about 2 miles (3.2km) west of Armagh City. The fort was a centre of ancient pagan power and culture, and is famous for its association with the Red Branch Knights. Today, the grassy rath extends over about 12 acres (5ha). It is easy to walk there from town, and you are rewarded with a pleasant view over the city when you arrive. It is fun to think of the feasting that went on in the richly painted halls of the palace that once graced this spot. More prosaically, the site once in danger of being destroyed to make way for a quarry has its preservation assured and a really excellent **Interpretative Centre** has opened close by (*open all year;* ✆ *(01861) 525550*). Definitely worth a detour.

To the northeast is the industrial part of County Armagh, with the old linen town of **Portadown** and the new town of **Craigavon**. Though lacking in beauty they do benefit from their proximity to Lough Neagh and the River Bann with man-made lakes, boating ponds and a dry ski slope. Craigavon's two large artificial lakes are used for water sports and trout fishing. There are two golf courses. It is possible to participate in a variety of courses run by the Craigavon Borough Council. They prefer you to come as a group of up to 28. Book by writing to the Craigavon Outdoor Recreation Office (details in 'Activities', below). Near Portadown a network of little roads runs through a charming district covered with fruit trees and bushes, and in May and June the gentle little hills are a mass of pink and white apple and damson flowers. You might time your visit here to coincide with the apple blossom in April and May. The orchards were a part of the old Irish agricultural economy long before the English settlers came here, though many of the fruit farmers are descended from Kent and Somerset families, well used to growing fruit. The retreating glaciers many millions of years ago left behind deposits of clay and gravel which form little hills known as drumlins, of which there are many in this part. The teardrop drumlin country is intersected by trout-filled lakes and streams, high hedges and twisting lanes. In **Richhill** you will find some furniture workshops and a fine **Jacobean manor** with curling Dutch gables. It is not open to the public but the sight it makes within the pretty well-kept village is worth stopping for.

The village of **Kilmore** has what is probably the oldest church in Ireland. In the heart of the present little parish church stands the lower half of a round tower dating from the first half of the 3rd century. Right in the centre of this fertile district is the quaint village of **Loughgall**, which is strung out along the main road, many of its little houses painted in the soft shades of blossom and their gardens bursting with colour. The little **museum** in the main street contains mementoes commemorating the founding of the Orange Order here in 1795 (*open in the summer; the caretaker lives beside the museum or you can contact Mr Walker;* ✆ *Loughgall (01762) 891524*).

Not far away is **Ardress House** (*open April–June and Sept, 2–6 on Sat, Sun and bank holidays; July–Aug, open daily except Thurs; adm for house and farmyard;* ✆ *(01762) 851236*). This is a 17th-century manor much altered by George Ensor who married the owner of this once simple farmhouse, so that it is now Georgian in character. It is on the

Portadown–May road (B28), 3 miles (4.8km) from Loughgall. Its elegant drawing room has one of the most beautiful decorative plasterwork ceilings in Ireland. The work is Adam in style and both the ceiling and the mural medallions have been carefully restored and sympathetically painted. Set in lovely parkland, it is now in the care of the National Trust. There is a farmyard display, picnic area, woodland walks and a small formal garden.

Coney Island, one of the few islands in Lough Neagh, is also a National Trust property. It lies to the north, not far from the mouth of the Blackwater, and can be reached by boat from Maghery. Apart from the excellent fishing, this thickly wooded, reedy island of 8½ acres (3.5ha) is also worth visiting for its huge and varied birdlife. St Patrick used the island as a retreat and there is also a rather overgrown holy well. Be prepared for the Lough Neagh flies which are food for the pollan, a fish unique to these waters and absolutely delicious fried in butter. The swarms of flies settle everywhere—in your car, your cup of tea, your mouth! Contact the National Trust about ways to get out there, ✆ (01238) 510721.

Peatlands Park with its narrow gauge railway is close by on the Lough Neagh basin. Educational video and outdoor exhibits on peat ecology, ✆ (01762) 851162. Further east again is the **Lough Neagh Discovery Centre**, which explains the geology and natural history of the area, ✆ (01762) 322205. Exit 10 off the M1 at Oxford Island.

Returning southwards along the Blackwater, which forms the county boundary, 2½ miles (4km) from Charlemont on a tiny little road off the B28 is **The Argory** (*opening times same as for Ardress House (above), except that it is closed on Thursdays; adm; ✆ (018687) 84753 for more details*). Standing in woodland and parkland, this rather lovely early 19th-century

neoclassical house overlooks the river. It is of particular interest in that its contents have remained almost completely undisturbed since the turn of the century. It is much more of a home than a museum, full of treasures gathered over the years from all corners of the earth. The large cabinet organ at the top of the grand cantilevered staircase is quite unique. So is the acetylene gas plant which still lights the house; every room has its own ingenious old light-fittings. Outside you can wander through the stable buildings, semi-formal gardens and woodland, and river walks.

The village of **Charlemont**, once an important parliamentary borough, is 2½ miles (4km) upstream. It has an 18th-century cut-stone bridge and ruins of a 17th-century fort, with star-shaped walls typical of that period, which was built by Lord Mountjoy, Lord Deputy of Ireland in 1602.

Flax-milling has ceased but flour milling still thrives in nearby **Tandragee**, a pretty well-kept town with brightly painted houses. It is of considerable age and was founded by the O'Hanlons, chieftains of these parts before the plantations of James I. The old castle and the town were destroyed in the Civil War of 1641. The present castle is barely more than a century old and now houses the factory of Ulster's foremost crisp, Tayto! It is possible to go on an intriguing tour of the crisp factory (*open all year, daily, adm free; © (0762) 840249 for more details*).

Clare Glen, one of the prettiest in the country, is 4 miles (6.4km) away to the east of Armagh City. A fine trout-stream winds under old bridges and past a now-silent mill. There are lovely walks around here and it ison such country lanes as these that you might come across a game of 'bullets' or road bowls. This game is played with 28oz (795g) balls made of iron, which are thrown along a quiet winding road. The aim is to cover several miles in the fewest shots. Little children are stationed along the course to warn motorists, and the betting and excitement amongst the watchers is infectious.

On the Newry road (A28) you pass the village of **Markethill** on the right, and **Gosford Castle**—a huge early 19th century mock-Norman castle, on the left (*open all year from 10am to dusk; pedestrians adm, car park fee*). The magnificent grounds are now open to the public and owned by the Forestry Commission . The walled cherry garden, the arboretum, nature trails and forest parks, make it an enjoyable place to while away some time. Further south and keeping to the more attractive minor roads, you come across the village of **Bessbrook**. This is a model linen manufacturing town, neatly laid out in the 19th century by a Quaker; it still has neither pub nor pawn house. The design of the model town of Bournville near Birmingham, famous for its chocolate industry, is based entirely on Bessbrook. Remains of the huge old mill, dams, weirs and sluices stand deserted, and nearby the impressive cut-stone Craigmore Viaduct still carries the main railway line to Dublin.

Just outside Bessbrook is **Derrymore House**. It is closed to the public, but you can get a glimpse of the small, thatched manor house set in parkland. Built in 1776, it was witness to the signing of the Act of Union in 1801, and is now in the care of the National Trust.

Travelling south from Bessbrook, the land becomes poorer, the fields smaller, the hedges higher and the roads have more of a twist to them. Soon the hills of south Armagh appear in the distance dominated by the peak of **Slieve Gullion**. This rugged group of hills is steeped in history and legend. Described as the mountains of mystery, the average tourist never hears of them, which is a pity as the whole region has magnificent scenery, beautiful lakes, streams and unspoilt little villages. There have been quite a few bloody incidents in this area since the recent troubles begun.

Crossmaglen has had a dicey reputation, but with the present ceasefire (February 1995) still holding it can only be hoped that the situation will improve. In general, however, although the present borderland reputation cannot be ignored, you can enjoy exploring this delightfully unkept area, so different from the tamer country in the north. Caught between Camlough Mountain and Slieve Gullion lies the beautiful ribbon-like Lough Cam. The surrounding hedges and shorelines are the homes of many flowers and birds and there is good fishing on the Fane River, Lough Cam and Lough Ross.

From the other side of Lough Cam, the road climbs up through the trees to the extensive, recently developed **Slieve Gullion Forest Park**. From the top of Slieve Gullion, wonderful panoramic views of the encircling mountains that make up the Ring of Gullion, and the distant hills of Belfast and Dublin, spread before you. Slieve Gullion (*Sliabh gCuillin*: Mountain of the Steep Slope), is often shrouded in mist, and according to local folklore it is magical. Legend tells us that Chulainn was a chief who owned a fierce watchdog which was slain by a boy of 15. The young hero was afterwards called *Cú Chulainn* ('Hound of Chulainn'). On the southern slopes there is an ancient church known as Killevy Church, which dates back to AD 450; a holy well and prehistoric passage grave. Close to the County Louth border, just off the N1, about 1.5 miles (2.4km) south of Jonesborough east of the bridge, is one of the earliest datable Christian monuments in Ireland. The inscribed **Kilnasaggart Pillar Stone** is early 8th century, and carved with crosses. It commemorates a local dignatory, and the inscription is in Gaelic. **Moyry Castle**, a three-storey ruin nearby, dates from 1601. It was built by Lord Mountjoy, and was ruined in the struggle between the English forces under Mountjoy and the Irish forces under Hugh O'Neill, during the Elizabethan wars.

Both the villages of **Forkhill**, with its trout stream, and **Mullaghbawn**, with its tiny museum furnished as a south Armagh farmhouse (*open by appointment with the care-taker, Mrs Nora McCoy; ✆ Forkhill (01693) 888278*), are picturesquely situated in their own valleys between the hills.

If you have time, it is worth going further southwest towards Monaghan to visit the town of **Crossmaglen**, with its staggeringly large market square, the largest in Europe. It is the centre of the recently revived cottage industry of lacemaking. Again, there are earthen works to explore: a superb example of a treble-ringed fort, remains of stone cairns, and a crannog (artificial island) on Lough Ross. You are now actually following the old coach road from Dublin to Armagh, itself the ancient link between Emain Macha and Tara (another ancient centre of power), in County Meath. At Dorsey to the east of the town there is the largest entrenched enclosure of its kind in Ireland. Constructed as a defensive outpost for Emain Macha, this huge earthwork encloses over 300 acres (121ha) and lies astride the route. Some of the earth ramparts still remain. It is part of the ancient earth dyke known as the **Black Pig's Dyke**, which extends over most of the borders of Ulster.

Leaving behind the mountains of south Armagh, you enter the attractive upland country known as the **Fews**. The isolated village of **Newtownhamilton** was founded in 1770, but the neighbourhood is associated with the legendary story of Lir, for it was here that the ocean god King Lir had his palace. Do not go straight back to Armagh, but branch off to the west and climb **Carrigatuke Hill**. From the top an outstanding view of the area as far as Meath to the south, and even Roscommon to the southwest, lies before you. This small area across and down to the border is a miniature Lake District with lots of little irregular lakes caught between tiny hills, vestiges of glacial movement and deposition. Many of the lakes are studded with islands. **Lake Tullnawood** is particularly picturesque. Just north of boot-shaped Clay Lake is the small market town of **Keady**. It was once a very important linen centre, hence the number of derelict watermills in the district. Nearby at **Nassagh Glen** there is a mill, and a huge viaduct that spans the wide valley. Under the viaduct's arches you can picnic among wild flowers, rose briars and red-berried rowan. Today it is noted chiefly for its tiny trout-lakes. From here it is only about 6 miles (9.6km) back to the city of Armagh.

To the west of the city, beyond the little hill-top village of Killylea, lies the pretty village of **Tynan**. In the middle of the main street stands a fine sculptured stone cross, over 13ft (4m) high and dating from the 10th century. There are other ancient crosses in the nearby extensive demesne of **Tynan Abbey**. It is worth enquiring at the estate if you wish to see the crosses.

Shopping

Antiques: Quinn's Antiques, 27 Dobbin Street, Armagh. Huey's Antique Shop, 45 Main Street, Loughgall. Charles Gardiner, 48 High Street, Lurgan, ℰ (01762) 323934. Antique Shop, 19 Thomas Street, Portadown.

Crafts: The National Trust Shop, The Argory, Moy. Gazette Arcade, Scotch Street, Armagh. Cloud Cuckoo, Ogle Street, Armagh.

Cheese: Boley Hill Cheddar, Mountnorris, ℰ (01861) 57209. The only farmhouse cheddar sold in the north, marketed and distributed by the owners.

Delicacies: Fine Foods Deli, Scott Street, Armagh. Good ingredients for a picnic available here.

Activities

Fishing: Between Benburb and Blackwater town an extensive river park makes fishing and water sports of all kinds possible. Contact the Armagh Tourist Office, ℰ (01861) 527808. Fishing on the Cusher and Callan Rivers, which are tributaries of the

Blackwater River. The local representative for angling, who knows all the rivers hereabouts, is Mr T. Toner, ☎ (01861) 526998.

Water sports: of all types through Craigavon Water Sports Centre, ☎ (01762) 342669.

Walking: Carnagh and Slieve Gullion Forest Park planned walks. Open from 10am to dusk. The Ulster Way, a signposted trail which traverses the mountains and coastline of Ulster, goes through Armagh. Details from the Tourist Office in Armagh. For more information phone the Sports Council for Northern Ireland to get details on the Ulster Way, ☎ (01232) 381222. Information on walks is also available from the Northern Ireland Tourist Board.

Garden and open farm: Tannaghmore Gardens and Farm, Silverwood, Craigavon, ☎ (01762) 343244. Victorian Rose garden and rare breeds.

Golf: 18-hole golf course in Palace Demesne, ☎ (01861) 525861. Craigavon Golf and Ski centre, ☎ Lurgan (01762) 326606. Tandragee Golf Club, Markethill Road, 18-hole course, ☎ (01762) 841272.

Coney Island: for birdlife and fishing. There is no ferry service: you have to hire a boat. Call the National Trust, ☎ (01238) 510721.

Oxford Island: Lough Neagh Discovery Centre, birdwatching and walks, ☎ (01762) 322205.

Where to Stay

moderate

The **Charlemont Arms Hotel**, 63 English Street, Armagh, ☎ (01861) 522008. **Drumshill House**, Moy Road, Armagh, ☎ (01861) 522009. Modern and bland but comfortable. **Gosford House Hotel**, Main Street, Markethill, ☎ (01861) 551676. Close to Gosford Forest Park. Unpretentious mid-range hotel.

inexpensive

Waterside House, Oxford Island, Lurgan, Craigavon, ☎ (01762) 327573. This house is located in the conservation area of Oxford Island, overlooking Lough Neagh. Mrs Kee, **Ballinahinch House**, 47 Ballygroobany Road, Richhill, ☎ (01762) 870081. Victorian famhouse with spacious rooms, old world ambience. **Mrs Joy Bingham**, 69 Sleepy Valley, Richhill, ☎ (01762) 871387. Pleasant country house with one double bedroom.

Mrs McKenna, **College Hill**, Armagh, ☎ (01861) 522693. Comfortable 1930s house in pretty garden. Within walking distance of the sights. Mrs Armstrong, **Deanshill**, Armagh, ☎ (01861) 524923. Pretty 18th-century house with lovely gardens, close to the Observatory. 2 en suite rooms (1 four poster). Also short lets for self-catering accommodation. Sleeps 4.

Waterside House, Oxford Island, Lurgan, ✆ (0762) 327573. Lough Neagh trout, eels and pollan. Booking essential. The **Famous Grouse**, 6 Ballyhagan Road, Loughgall, ✆ (0762) 891778. Reasonably priced and cosy restaurant. Try the pub grub at lunchtime or *à la carte* menu in the evening. **Gosford House Hotel**, Main Street, Markethill, ✆ (01861) 551676. Good beef stroganoff. **Seagoe Hotel**, Upper Church Lane, Portadown, ✆ (0762) 333076. Delicious beef and Irish stews.

Calvert Tavern, 3 Scotch Street, Armagh, ✆ (01861) 524186. Good open sandwiches and grills. **Doyles**, 22 Main Street, Camlough, ✆ (0693) 830269. Pub grub. **Ardress House**, 64 Ardress Road, Portadown, ✆ (0762) 851236. Picnic teas are available on Sundays in summer. **The Argory**, Moy. A good tearoom from June to August. **Hearty's Folk Cottage**, Glassdrummond, near Crossmaglen, ✆ (0693) 861916. *Sunday afternoons only.* Good home-baked scones and snacks. **Huntsman**, 65 Market Street, Tandragee, ✆ (0762) 841115. Good set lunches. **Palace Stables**, Palace Demesne, ✆ (01861) 522722. Snacks and lasagne. **Old Thatch**, 3 Keady Street, Markethill. Good cakes and coffee. **Archway**, 5 Hartford Place, The Mall, Armagh, ✆ (01861) 522532. Home-made apple pie.

County Donegal

Donegal (*Dun na nGall*: fort of the foreigner) is a microcosm of all Ireland and the second largest county. In the west is the Gaeltacht, with its mountains, heathery moors and boglands, home of the dispossessed Celt. In the east, there are rich pasturelands, plantation towns, and long-settled families which were originally Scottish or English. Set northwest against the Atlantic, much of its beauty comes from its promixity to the sea: from the sweep of Donegal Bay, the maritime cliffs around Slieve League, the intricate indentations of the coast up to Bloody Foreland, and the northern peninsulas formed by long sea loughs. Donegal is a county of beautiful countryside; the ancient mountain ranges are older than any others in Ireland, and the light of Donegal brings alive the subtle greens and browns of the landscape, and the strength of blue in the sky and sea. Although there are some exciting walks for the experienced (the area round the Poisoned Glen was used as practice ground by members of one expedition to Everest), there is also plenty of unexacting terrain. However, if you are going off on a hike be sure to leave some indication of your route, since there are no mountain rescue teams. Because of the mountains in central Donegal, the weather is often quite different in the southwest quarter.

Some people say that Donegal is the 26th county in a 25-county state, meaning that there is an individuality and independence up here which Dublin likes to ignore. This Ulster county has the largest number of Irish native speakers of any county in Ireland, though, curiously enough, 'Official Irish' is based on the Leinster dialect. The Ulster dialect has more in common with Highland Gaelic than with the southern strain. There are great links with Scotland. Many districts of Glasgow are reputed to be like parishes of west Donegal, and you will see buses going from places like Annagary all the way to Glasgow.

Politicians from here have a reputation for being independent. Neil Blaney, independent Fianna Fail, was the character on which one student of politics based his analysis of the 'Donegal Mafia'. The baby boom in Ireland has been experienced in this county more than anywhere else, which makes up for the rural depopulation which has scourged the countryside since the famine of 1845–49. Of course, the new generation are not being brought up on the old homesteads in lonely picturesque valleys, but in the numerous bungalows and housing estates which line the roads near the factories that the Irish Government has enticed in with substantial financial assistance.

History

The county has a large proportion of Neolithic and Early Bronze Age remains. The main monument which survives from prehistoric times is Grianan of Aileach, near Burt, a superb structure dating in parts back to the Iron Age and perhaps earlier. The Northern Ui Neill Kings occupied it as their royal seat c. AD 700 and in Donegal the two important branches of this clan were the O'Neills and the O'Donnells, who became great rivals. The chief of the O'Donnells was known as the Prince of Tyrconnell. The wars between them continued for centuries, but towards the end of the 16th century two chiefs, Red Hugh O'Donnell and Hugh O'Neill, combined their powers in an effort to prevent the English from taking over. They were defeated at the battle of Kinsale in 1601 and made their way to the Continent in what is known as the 'flight of the Earls'. This took place from the shores of Lough Swilly, near Rathmullen.

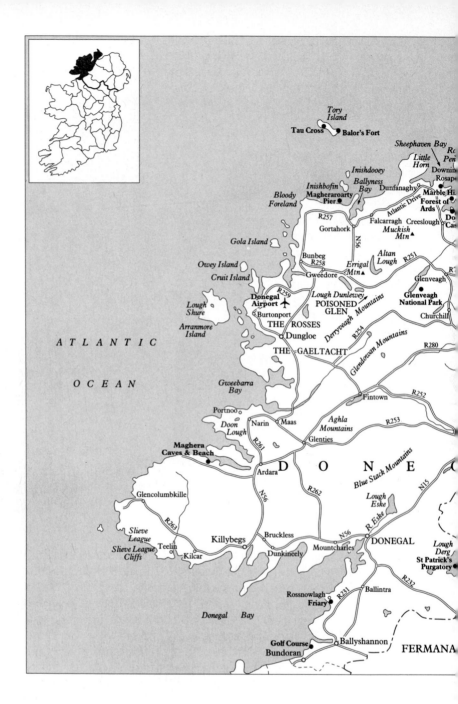

Tory
Island
Tau Cross • Balor's Fort

Sheephaven Bay
Little \ Pen
Horn
Inishdooey
Inishbofin Ballyness
Bay Dunfanaghy
Bloody Magheraroarty
Foreland Pier •
R257
Falcarragh Creeslough
Gortahork Muckish
Mtn ▲
Gola Island
Bunbeg Altan
R258 Lough
Owey Island Errigal
Cruit Island Mtn ▲
Gweedore Glenveagh
Lough Dunlewey Glenveagh
Donegal POISONED National Park
Lough Airport ✈ GLEN
Shure Burtonport Churchill
Arranmore THE ROSSES
Island Dungloe
THE GAELTACHT R280

A T L A N T I C

O C E A N Gweebarra
Bay Fintown R252
Portnoo
Doon Narin Maas Aghla R253
Lough Mountains
Glenties
Maghera
Caves & Beach D O N E
Ardara
Blue Stack Mountains N15
Glencolumbkille R262
Lough
Eske
Slieve
League R Eske
Slieve League Teelin Killybegs Bruckless DONEGAL Lough
Cliffs Kilcar Dunkineely Mountcharies Derg
St Patrick's
Purgatory •
R332
Rossnowlagh Ballintra
Friary •

Donegal Bay

Golf Course Ballyshannon
Bundoran FERMANA

County Donegal

20 km
15 miles

N

Getting There and Around

By air: daily services from Dublin, Glasgow and Manchester to Eglinton Airport, near Londonderry, about 40 minutes' drive from Letterkenny. Daily flights from Dublin to Sligo Airport, about 40 minutes' drive from Bundoran. Daily flights from Glasgow to Donegal Airport, Carrickfinn, ✆ (075) 48232/48284.

By rail: daily services from Belfast to Derry, and Dublin to Sligo.

By bus: express bus services from Dublin to Letterkenny. Local buses: the Lough Swilly Railway Company and CIE. link the various towns such as Ballyshannon, Burdoran, Donegal, Killybegs and Letterkenny, ✆ (074) 21309. O'Donnell Coaches daily to Galway, ✆ (075) 48114.

By car: local car hire at Hegarty's Autoservice, Lower Main Street, Letterkenny, ✆ (074) 21095.

By bike: the Raleigh Rent-a-Bike network operates here. Your local dealers are C. J. Doherty, Main Street, Donegal Town, ✆ (073) 21119; Vincent Carton, Falcarragh, ✆ (074) 35150.

getting to Tory Island

Tory Island Ferry Company operates daily between Tory and Bunbeg, Magheraroarty (and Portnablagh Wednesday only), ✆ (075) 31320/31340/31991. Sailing subject to the weather and tide. Approximately 75 minutes from Bunbeg and 40 minutes from Magheraroarty.

getting to Arranmore Island

By boat: There is a regular ferry that takes approximately 25 minutes. Contact Cornelius Bonner, ✆ (075) 21532.

Tourist Information

Bundoran, ✆ (072) 41350, June to September.

Donegal Town, ✆ (073) 21148, May to September.

Letterkenny, Derry Road, ✆ (074) 21160, all year.

Sligo, Temple Street, ✆ (071) 61201, all year.

Inishowen, Cardonagh, ✆ (077) 74933.

Festivals

All festival dates vary from year to year.

Early June: Lough Swilly Angling Festival, Rathmullen, ✆ (074) 21160.

June: St Columcille's Festival, Glencolumbkille. Also, a folk and traditional music festival at the beginning of June, Mary from Dungloe Festival, described as a family festival of music and song. For details of all these contact the Letterkenny tourist office, ✆ (074) 21160. For details of festivals in the Inishowen district, ✆ (077) 74933.

Late June: Rossnowlagh Open Surfing Championship, ✆ (074) 21160. Donegal International Motor Rally, Letterkenny, ✆ (074) 21221. Buncrana Folk Festival, Inishowen.
July: Ramelton Festival
Mid July: Folk Festival, Glencolumbkille, ✆ (074) 21160.
12 July: Orange Procession, Rossnowlagh.
Late July: Glencolumbkille Wild Walks, hill- and cliff-walking week, ✆ (071) 61201.
August: Letterkenny Folk Festival, ✆ (074) 21160.

Bundoran to Donegal Town

If you come up from Sligo along the superb sweep of Donegal Bay you will encounter one of Ireland's older seaside resorts, **Bundoran**. On the long main street there is a typical hodge-podge of hotels, amusements and souvenir shops. Nearby are wonderful beaches and the Bundoran Golf Course, one of the best-known golf courses in Ireland.

For those who are avoiding populous resorts, Ballyshannon, 2½ miles (4km) up the coast from Bundoran, is ideal. It is said to have been founded in 1500 BC when the Scythians settled a colony on a little island in the Erne estuary. The Scythians were an off-shoot of the Phoenician peoples who were supposed, in one version of the early history of Ireland (there are many!), to have colonized areas of the North. It has its own poet, the bard of Ballyshannon, William Allingham, whose lines,

> *Up the airy mountain,*
> *Down the rushy glen,*
> *We daren't go a hunting*
> *For fear of little men.*

must have been chanted by many generations of children. **The Lakeside Centre**, Belleek Road on the shore of Assaroe Lough provides lots of watersports and during the summer months a waterbus plies its way up and down the lough, the trip lasts about one hour. ✆ (072) 52555. The **Abbey Mill** just outside the town by the Abbey River was built by the Cistercians many centuries ago, and has now been restored by local enthusiasts and houses a local craft, gallery and a coffee shop.

Nearby are the sands of **Rossnowlagh**. If you are here around 12 July you may witness the last-remaining Orange procession this side of the border from Northern Ireland. Otherwise, Rossnowlagh is known for its surfing. At the **Franciscan friary**, before you reach the pretty little town of Ballintra, you will find the diminutive **Donegal Museum** (*open all summer;* ✆ *(072) 65342*), which has a few interesting items, including a piece of Muckish glass made from mica mined in the Muckish Mountains, which you will see as you go further north.

Donegal Town is the meeting point of roads which travel into the heart of Donegal, to the north and to the west. Situated on the River Eske, with a long history of habitation for its strategic site, it is a crowded busy place even without the tourist buses which tend to

congregate near the hotels on the Diamond. (A diamond—or square to most visitors—is an area where fairs and gatherings were held, and in the plantation period it was placed in the shadow of the castle so as to guard against the fighting that was the accompanying feature of these occasions.) **Donegal Castle** (*open all year round; adm free*), once a stronghold of the O'Donnells, the Princes of Tyrconnell, and then taken over by the planter Brooke family, is a handsome stone ruin built in 1474. It incorporates a square tower and turrets built by the O'Donnells in 1505, and the Jacobean house built by Sir Basil Brooke in 1610. Also of interest is the monument in the Diamond to the Four Masters. *The Annals of the Four Masters* is the history of old Ireland, written by three brothers called O'Clery and O'Mulconry, scholars and monks. The brothers were tutors to the O'Donnells and stayed for a while at the nearby abbey, situated where the River Eske and the sea meet. They wrote this great work between 1623 and 1626. It records an Irish society which was fast disappearing as the English and Scottish were settled in Ireland. Nowadays, Donegal Town is one of the best places to buy tweed. Try Magee's shop in the Diamond and the craft village on the Ballyshannon Road.

Further inland lies the pilgrim's shrine of Lough Derg. Although most holy tradition in Donegal is associated with St Columba (or *Colmcille*), this is known as St Patrick's Purgatory, and between June and August is the scene of one of the most rigorous Christian pilgrimages. People come here from all over the world to do penance, just as they did hundreds of years ago. The pilgrims stay on a small island on Lough Derg for 36 hours. They eat and drink only bread and water, they stay up all night praying, and wear no shoes whilst making the Stations of the Cross. Information can be obtained from the Priory, St Patrick's Purgatory, Lough Derg, Pettigo. Closer at hand is the lovely Lough Eske which gives good fishing for trout.

Donegal Town is a few miles away from the *Gaeltacht*, which begins after Killybegs. The *Gaeltacht* forms the officially recognized Irish-speaking area where government grants encourage the local people to stay put. Here you can walk into a shop or bar and catch fragments of true Irish, the oldest recorded Aryan language. It is strange language: rich, almost soft, but shot through with harsher, guttural tones. It is like folk music; poignant, moving but not melodious. The spoken English of Gaelic-speakers is, on the other hand, soft and poetic, as though through translation they have made a second language of it.

Killybegs to Portnoo and Ardara

Follow the N56 through **Mountcharles**, with its splendid view of Donegal Bay, Bruckless and Dunkineely. These were all centres of the now-defunct lace industry, and are still good places to buy hand-embroidered linen and the subtle patterned Donegal jumpers and rugs. There is a fine collection of early Irish portraits at Ballyloughan House, Bruckless. (*contact Mrs Tindal; © (073) 31507*). The narrow, winding and climbing road leads you to **Killybegs**. In the summer, bordering hedgerows bloom with honeysuckle and fuchsia, and as you get further west the sweet acrid peat smell on the damp soft air becomes all pervading. At Killybegs you reach an important fishing port; the progressive features of this harbour town are the modernized aluminium and glass shop-fronts which are slightly at odds with the old-worldliness of the neighbouring villages. There is very good fishing here, as you might expect, especially salmon. The highly paid fishing and processing industry has brought great prosperity. It is quite a sight to watch the catches of haddock, plaice and sole being unloaded. Beyond this town you encounter some of the grandest scenery in Donegal; the great cliffs of Bunglass, Scregeither and Slieve League are amongst the highest in Europe, rising to 1972ft (601m). If you walk along the cliffs from Bunglass along One Man's Pass, a jaggedy ridge, you will see on a clear day fantastic views right down to County Mayo. The determined bird-watcher should be able to see puffins and cormorants, and the botantist should be able to find alpine Arctic species on the back slopes of Slieve League. The village of **Teelin**, under Slieve League, is popular with students on Irish language courses, whilst **Kilcar** is the site of the *Gaelterra Eireann* factory of fabrics and yarns. The wools are hard-wearing and flecked with soft colours. You can buy them here and in craftshops all over County Donegal. This is also a centre for handwoven tweed.

Glencolumbkille should be visited next. A local priest called Father McDyer established a rural co-operative here to try to combat the flight of youth from the village through emigration. He helped the local economy greatly and there is a craftshop where you can buy handmade products such as jams, soaps and wines made from gorse and bluebells. A walk along the valley here is a 3¾-mile (5km) pilgrimage around 15 cross slabs and pillars known as the Stations of the Cross. It is interesting to follow it as it includes many of the ancient sites of the area, starting off with a Stone Age court-grave in the churchyard of the Church of Ireland. There are some attractively carved grave stones here too. The Stations of the Cross are still performed on 9 June, the saint day of Columba. Notice the beautifully built stone and turf sheds with their thatched roofs which abound in this area. Glencolumbkille also has a **folk village**: three cottages representing three different periods of Irish life (*open during the summer months; © (073) 30017*). The countryside is full of prehistoric antiquities, dolmens, cairns (including a famous horned cairn called Clochanmore), and ruins of churches connected with St Columba. On the other side of the mountain, through the spectacular Glengesh Pass, you arrive at **Ardara**, another centre of Donegal hand-woven tweed. Try Kennedy's of Ardara on Main Street. The new **heritage centre** on the Main Street tells the history of tweed in the area. Nancy's Bar, also on Main Street, is famous for its atmosphere and oysters.

If you follow the road to Maghera Caves signposted just outside Ardara on the road to Donegal Town (N56) you will come to one of the most beautiful **beaches** in Ireland; the single-track road from here unfolds a series of wonderful views of mountain, sea inlets, traditional farms, and near the end a waterfall. The walk to the caves and beach takes you through someone's farm and over sand-dunes so don't overload the picnic baskets.

If you travel a few miles on to the next little peninsula, you will come to **Portnoo** and **Narin**, two popular places for holidaymakers from Northern Ireland. At Narin, you can park or hire caravans. There is a fascinating fort near here, built on an island in Doon Lough (beside Narin). It is over two thousand years old and is a very impressive sight—a circular stone fort which spreads over most of the island. It can be seen easily from the lough shore. At the neck of this peninsula you go from **Maas**, a small fishing resort, to **Glenties** (*Na Gleannta*: the valley—so called because of its position at the junction of glens), which is a good place for knitwear. There is a striking **church** designed by the innovative contemporary Irish architect, Liam McCormick, who is responsible for many fine churches in County Donegal. This one was built in the 1970s.

Fintown to Gortahork

All along the northwest coast you will see mountain ranges broken by long river valleys which reach into the hinterland. Any route along these valleys brings you across the harsh mountainous areas where beauty is bleak and the cost of wresting a living from the poor soil is no longer acceptable. One such town, **Fintown**, situated on a lough, has become the centre of controversy because of the uranium deposits in its rocky fields. Exploitation of these rich deposits may bring untold wealth or untold disaster to the area.

There is a rather zig-zag road from Fintown to Doochary called 'the Corkscrew', which brings you into the **Gweebarra Glen**. Northeast of this, between the Derryveagh and Glendowan Mountains, the valley extends into Glenveagh, which is now part of a National Park. However, you should keep heading out towards the sea on the road to Dungloe (do not pronounce the 'g') if you want to see 'The Rosses', as this area is called. The Irish name is *naRosa*, meaning 'headlands', and is a good clue to the landscape. Although this area is going through a housing boom, it is still one of the most charming routes you can take to the north coast; loughs and loughlets are scattered through hilly country and the beaches are lovely. If you make your way to **Burtonport**, an attractive unspoilt fishing port, there is a regular ferry to **Arranmore Island**. You can have a good day's tramp around the island, there is good cliff scenery in the northwest. Arranmore Island has the only rainbow trout lake in Ireland, Lough Shure. **Cruit Island** can be reached from the mainland by a connecting bridge. From here you can look out at Owey Island, and across at Gola Island with their deserted cottages. Despite difficulties the islanders had to face, such as hard weather, no services and bureaucratic indifference to their needs, most of them did not want to leave their homes, and many return for the summer or for fishing. Boat hire must be negotiated with the local fishermen; none of them like to be tied down to taking people out on a regular basis. Try the pubs and ask around. **Bunbeg** has an attractive harbour and closeby at **Carrickfinn** is a small airport with flights to Glasgow. The locals speak Irish and it is a favourite area for Irish summer schools. Further north past Bloody Foreland in the heart of *Gaeltacht* is **Gortahork** (meaning 'garden of oats'), a small town on one arm of Ballyness Bay. It has a great strand which curves out into the sea nearly locking the shallow bay in from the ocean. If you are here in the evening you can see cattle fording the waters back to the home farms.

Tory Island

There's a regular ferry to **Tory Island** from the pier at Magheraroarty and from Downings. Bad weather often makes the 7-mile (11km) journey impossible, but if you make it, this windswept and barren island is endlessly fascinating. The island has two villages, called East Town and West Town. **East Town** is laid out in the traditional clochan or family grouping pattern of settlement. Close to the shore in **West Town** is the remanants of St Columbkille's **early-Christian monastery**. Here you can see a decapitated round tower, and a T-shaped cross known as a **Tau Cross**. There is only one other in Ireland, which is displayed in the Burren Centre, County Clare. On a sunny day it feels rather like a Greek island with its whitewashed cottages and bright blue and red doors. At the eastern end of the island is **Balor's Fort**, a great rock sticking out into the sea. Balor is the god of darkness with one eye in the middle of his forehead. Mythology says he was one of the Formorii leaders (*see* pp.575 and 578). In the summer you can buy snacks at a tea-room and the café close to the Island's only public bar. A small hotel has opened recently and there is a hostel and several B&Bs. The population is about 130 and thriving with a school and simple Catholic church. The island has become well-known for its fishermen artists who mostly use house paints to create their naive-style paintings of seascapes and birds. They have been promoted by the landscape artist and portrait painter Derek Hill, whose house and collection of pictures is open to the public at the Glebe Gallery, Churchill. You can buy their work at a small exhibition gallery on the island, although some of the more famous of the island painters exhibit and sell in Belfast and London.

The Mountains Errigal to Muckish

Looking inland from Gortahork you cannot help but notice the glorious outlines of the mountains. Errigal is cone-shaped, and Aghla More and Aghla Beg form a spaced double peak. Muckish means 'pig's back' in Irish, and you will see it is aptly named. You can approach these mountains from this angle, or you could take the road from Bunbeg, past the secret **Dunlewey Lough**, overlooked by a roofless white church. The **Lakeside**

Centre at Dunlewey (*open Easter to end October;* ℂ *(075) 31699*) has a fine craft shop and tea room, a farm museum, animals and demonstrations in carding, spinning and weaving wool. You can go on a storytelling trip on the lough surrounded by its beautiful glens. Traditional music sessions are held in June, July and August. Hidden behind this is the **Poisoned Glen**, so called either because the water in the lough is unfit to drink because of certain poisonous plants at the water's edge, or, so another story goes, because of the name some French travellers gave it, having caught some fish there! The hill and mountain climbs in this part are quite strenuous, although a fit pensioner could tackle them.

Climb Errigal from the roadside, and after about an hour's climb you will reach a narrow ridge of 2400ft (731m), from which you will see Dunlewey Lough on one side and Altan Lough on the other side. Climb Muckish from the Gap or western end. If you go straight for it from the Falcarragh side you may find yourself going up by the old mine-works, for the mountain was worked for its mica to be used in glass-making; this is quite a dangerous but interesting ascent. The people who lived in the cottages in these lonely sheep glens used to weave Donegal tweed in the evenings, and pass the time singing and composing poetry. The old weaver poets had a good phrase for Muckish, calling it 'an oul turf stack'. And so it is: flat-topped with its flat outline broken only by the remains of a cross. Looking across to Tory, you will see a huge hole, which is supposed to have been made when St Columba threw his staff from the top of Muckish.

Falcarragh to Doe Castle

Back to the coast between Falcarragh and Dunfanaghy is the great granite promontory of **Horn Head**. From a Falcarragh viewpoint it does indeed look like a horn or rock. You can do a complete circuit taking the little road signposted 'Horn Head Coastal Drive' at the top of the main street in **Dunfanaghy**, an attractive village overlooking Sheep Haven Bay. The road leads you past old Hornhead House (*not open to the public*), which was drowned by sand when the bent grass was cut. The road climbs round the rocky farms giving you dazzling views across Sheephaven Bay to Melmore Head to the east and back towards Bloody Foreland. The road passes a 1940s military lookout post, and from here it is possible to walk to the **Little Horn**, which plunges down into the sea with magnificent cliff scenery. From here there is a good walk ahead of you to an old tower. It will take about 40 minutes and you need wellington boots or heavy shoes. You can peer over the 300ft (91m) cliff heights to see if the puffin population is in residence; there are some caves and blow holes.

Sheephaven Bay is a complicated indentation with beautiful golden sands and a wooded shore. **Marblehill**, with its special provision for caravans, is a favourite place for holiday-makers. The mystic poet-politician George Russell (A. E.) used to stay here in **Marblehill House**. It is possible to rent apartments in the house and stableyard which overlooks the marvellous long curving beach. Further on, the **Forest of Ards** provides some scenic walks and splendid views. At **Creeslough** you can admire another modern church designed by Liam McCormick. Its shape echoes the view of Muckish that you have from there. Otherwise it's a busy town with good shopping and pubs. On the road to **Carrigart** is one of the most romantic castles in Ireland, set on the water's edge—**Doe Castle**. It belonged to the MacSwineys who came over from Scotland in the 15th century at the invitation of the O'Donnells. They came to help the O'Donnells fight against the encroaching Normans, and in the constant small battles which took place with the O'Neill clan. They were part of the influx of mercenary soldiers known as gallowglasses (*see* p.86). The castle was used right up until 1890. It had been taken by the English in 1650, and changed hands several times. In 1798 General George Vaughan Harte purchased it; he had been a hero in the Indian Wars, and his initials are carved over the main door. It is great fun scrambling up the defensive walls, and the view is superb, on one side looking over Sheephaven Bay and on the other the pretty bridge and waterfall of Duntally.

Downings to Portsalon

To get to the **Rosguill Peninsula** you cross a neck of sand similar to the causeway at Horn Head, and arrive at the fishing village of **Downings**, which is in the 'holidaymakers' zone' of **Rosapenna**, a long-established resort, with a good golf course and harbour. You can sail out to the islands of Tory or Inishbofin from Downings, to . Ask about boats in the local post office down by the harbour. Very good tweed is made in this area. Try McNutt's shop above the harbour, and also follow the sign for tweed going off to the right as you approach Downings village. The sign is approximately opposite the entrance to the Rosapenna Hotel. The beach beside the golf course is huge and unspoilt, ideal for a long walk and a swim, if you are hardy! The coastal ciruit (R245) leads to the spectacular **Atlantic Drive**. A branch road off this takes you past the Tra Na Rossen Youth Hostel, the only house designed by Lutyens in Ulster, and up to the wilder beaches of **Melmore Head**.

Leaving Carrigart, the loughside road takes you down to **Mulroy Bay**, a narrow-necked lough bordered by the Fanad Peninsula on the opposite side and strewn with wooded islands. Behind Carrigart rises the Salt Mountain. A little moor-bound road crosses this range and comes out near Cranford. High in these mountains is the deepest lough in Ireland, **Lough Salt**. To take advantage of the panorama you should go up to the lough from the Letterkenny–Creeslough road (N56) and look out to the bays stretching from Horn Head to Fanad.

Down the road is **Milford**, a pretty town on a hill near some good fishing at Lough Fern. From Milford you can explore the **Fanad Peninsula** on the old road, which takes you past the Knockalla range by Kerrykeel and into the hidden reaches of Mulroy by Tamney. In this secluded land there survives a very idiosyncratic Gaelic; although it was not untouched by the settlements of the 17th century; even in their isolation the Irish and the Scottish settlers remained distinct. At the far eastern point you can see Fanad Lighthouse which guards the entrance of Lough Swilly and looks across to the hills of Inishowen.

Portsalon is beautifully situated over **Ballymastocker Bay**, an immense curve of strand, and, like all the towns on the Swilly, rather than being separated it is curiously linked by the water in its landscape to the opposite view on Inishowen, . It's a little like the Greek idea of the sea being a bridge. Rita's Bar with a blazing fire is a famous place to retire to after a long walk along the beach. The golf course here is full of surprises, and the views are wonderful. Unfortunately the village of Portsalon is being spoilt by a profusion of holiday houses and ugly service buildings.

Knockalla Hills to Letterkenny

A terrific coastal drive, the R247, has been built with fabulous views over the Knockalla hills. This brings you to Rathmullen, nestling in a sheltered plain which borders the Swilly as far as Letterkenny. The whole of **Lough Swilly** has played an important role in many of history's famous episodes. It is deep enough to accommodate modern fleets of war, and indeed it did in the First World War. It has also been the departure route for the Gaelic aristocracy: in 1607 the Earls of Tyrconnell and Tyrone took their leave for France from here. Lough Swilly has been called 'the Lake of the Shadows', an apt enough description, although from the Irish it means Lake of Eyes or Eddies (*Loch Suilagh*).

Rathmullen (meaning: *Rath Maolin's* ring-fort) is a charming town with lots of tourist attractions like sandy beaches and hotels, and it is unspoiled. There used to be a ferry that operated between Fahan and the harbour here which, as you will see, is quite large.

The ruined **Carmelite friary** in the town has a romantic air, borne out by the story behind it. In 1587 the MacSwiney clan from Fanad had a castle here where Red Hugh O'Donnell was staying. An ordinary wine merchant's ship was lying in the bay and the reputation of its cargo enticed the young reveller onto the ship. Treachery was soon apparent, as the ship slipped its mooring and carried young O'Donnell off to Dublin Castle as a prisoner of Queen Elizabeth I. He was a great hostage to have captured, for his father was the Lord of Tyrconnell, the powerful Sir Hugh O'Donnell, and the son could be used to keep the father loyal to the English rulers. More information is available from the heritage centre in the Martello tower by the pier.

One of the most lovely routes in Ireland is on the road between Rathmullen and its neighbour, **Ramelton**. The place name translates as Mealtan's Fort, but the town you will see is a relatively unspoilt plantation town built by the Stewart family, one of the so-called undertakers of the plantation, meaning that they undertook to supply fighting men and build fortified dwellings to subdue and keep the wild Irish at bay. It developed as a prosperous market town with goods coming up the Lennon estuary from as far away as Tory Island. Ramelton was nearly self-sufficient in those 18th-century days, with locally made whiskey, linen and leather goods, and other small industries. The Ramelton merchants built themselves fine houses in the Mall. However, Letterkenny stole a march on the town fathers when the railway came. Now it is the boom town. Ramelton is famous for its annual **festival** in July, with its cheerful floats and Queen of the Lennon competition, and for its **pantomime** in February. It is also famous for its thriving bottling industry, and a soft drink whose sweetness cloys, called McDaid's Football Special. **The House on the Brae** on the Tank road has been restored by the local Georgian society. There is generally some sort of coffee room set up in the house in the summer. American Presbyterians will be interested in the old **meeting house** in the Back Lane which is early 18th century. It is here that the Reverend Francis Makemie (1658–1708) used to worship. He was ordained in 1682 and emigrated to America where he founded the first Presbytery in 1706. It has been restored and houses temporary exhibitions and a library. **Letterkenny** is a thriving town, with its new factories on the outskirts and new housing enclaves; yet it still manages to maintain its country town appearance, with one, long main street that loops round into the Swilly Valley. You can use this town as a centre for expeditions east and west. Folk music-lovers might time their visit for the **Letterkenny Folk Festival**, which hosts folk dance and music groups from all over Europe in the middle of August. The **Donegal County Museum** on the High Road (*© (074) 26402*) has a very interesting permanent collection of artefacts from early history and folk life, as well as travelling exhibitions.

The Swilly Valley to Doon Well

If you go through Letterkenny up the Swilly Valley you reach the countryside where St Columba spent his first years. (St Columba or Colmcille was the great Irish missionary who founded a church at Iona.) He was born about AD 521 on a height overlooking the two Gartan Loughs. A large cross just on Glenveagh Estate marks the spot. Gartan Clay (which can only be lifted by a family who claim descent from the followers of Columba), has powerful protective properties; soldiers fighting in the First World War carried it. You should follow the road around the lough; if you take one of the forest trails on the Churchill side a glorious prospect awaits you. The long glen which begins at Doochary on the southwest coast penetrates this far along the Derryveagh Mountains and into the scenic Glenveagh, parallel to the Valley of Gartan.

Glenveagh (meaning: the valley of the birch), is beautiful and isolated with a 19th-century fairytale castle (*open to the public from Easter to early Nov, daily 10am–6pm; adm for castle and grounds; restaurant, castle tearooms and visitor centre; adm; © (074) 37088 for more details*) figured against the mountains on the loughside. The gardens here have been developed by Henry McIlhenny, a millionaire whose grandparents came from these parts, and a visit is recommended . It would be difficult to find another such garden which combines the exotic and natural with such ease. Henry McIlhenny gave the wild, heathery acres of Glenveagh to be used as a National Park. Deer roam the glen and peregrine falcon's nest in the rocky ledges.

Close by in **Churchill**, the artist Derek Hill has given his house and art possessions to the nation. It is signposted from the village and is known as **St Columb's** (*open all summer; © (074) 37071*). This plain Georgian house is packed with exquisite and curious *objets d'art*; it also has a fine gallery, the Glebe Gallery, with a collection of Irish interest, besides paintings by Basil Blackshaw, Annigoni, and Victor Pasmore. The gardens are beautifully laid out with shrubs and trees down to the lough's edge . It would be a great pity to miss Glenveagh, and St Columb's and the Glebe Gallery, so make it a full day's outing. If you feel that a surfeit of castles, galleries and gardens may ensue, just make sure you tour the gardens of Gleaveagh and miss out the castle. Close to Churchill is the Gartan Heritage Centre which has a very informative display of days gone by. (Beside the Youth Hostel.)

On the way back from Glenveagh to Letterkenny you pass through **Kilmacrenan** (meaning: church of the son of Enan), called after one of St Columba's nephews. There are some ruins of a 15th-century friary, but the fame of the place rests on the claim that it was here Columba received his education. You can have tea at the traditional thatched cottage with its displays of old rural implements. Near here, at **Doon Rock** about 2 miles (3.2km) on the road to Creeslough, the Princes of Tyrconnell were inaugurated. At the curious **Doon Well**, the grateful cured have left tokens of their illness, rags mostly, although there is a story that a visiting film star left her lipstick.

Raphoe to Fahan

If you are travelling east from Letterkenny bound for the North, you will pass through the more prosperous midlands of Donegal whose centre is **Raphoe**, an ancient town with a venerable cathedral and a pretty village green. Your fellow passengers on the road will probably be bound for the mart, the key of most Irish farmers' lives, and another indication of the importance of Raphoe. St Adomnan who lived in the 7th century founded an early monastery here. He was an O'Donnell like his ancestor St Colmcille. He wrote a life of Colmcille which reveals a lot about the early Christian society; at one synod they passed a law exempting women from regular military service. At **Beltany,** between Raphoe and Lifford, just beyond the River Deele, is a stone circle which has some mystic alignment. Archaeologists who examined the site in 1921 suggested the building had an astronomical purpose because the standing stone in the southwest is an almost perfect equilateral triangle. Its circumference measures 450ft (140m). There are 64 out of a possible 80 stones still standing. There is a pleasant view from the top.

Lifford is the administrative centre of the county. The 18th-century courthouse is attractive. It is open to the public and houses a genealogical centre as well as a country kitchen where you can have a meal, and a clan centre which traces the importance of Lifford in the history of the county (*open Mon–Sat, 10am–6pm, Sun 2–6pm;* © *(074) 41228)*. If you find it open, go inside the **Clonleigh Parish Church** in the middle of the town. Here in an attitude of prayer, are the Jacobean stone figures of Sir Richard Hansard and his wife, who gave money for the church to be built.

Outside Lifford, just off the Letterkenny Road is **Cavanacor Historic House and Craft Centre** at **Ballindrait** (*open Easter to September, other times by appointment; ℗ (074) 41143*). This 17th-century house with a fortified yard was the ancestral home of James Knox Polte, the 11th President of America. You can have a splendid homemade tea and browse among the attractive crafts, pottery and watercolour paintings—all for sale.

The Inishowen Peninsula

Inishowen (*Inis Eoghain*: Eoghain's island) reaches out to the Atlantic between Loughs Swilly and Foyle, a kingdom of its own. Indeed, as its name conveys, it forms a different territory to the rest of Donegal which is part of Tyrconnell. This is O'Doherty country. After leaving Letterkenny you pass through the rolling plains round Manor and Newtowncunningham to the neck of the peninsula at **Burt**. An unforgettable sight of this unexplored almost islanded land can be obtained from the **Grianan of Aileach**, an ancient stone hill-fort. Turn right by an unusually roofed modern Catholic church, another of Liam McCormick's, and climb the unclassified mountain road which gives you views onto the Swilly. Why the Grianan of Aileach is not as well known as Tara in County Meath, considering its spectacular position and its associations, must be one of the curious twists in the recording of history. Besides the circular stone fort and its terraces there are three stone and earth ramparts, and underneath the Hill of Aileach there are said to be underground passages connecting the hill-top with Scalp Mountain which overlooks the village of Fahan, about 6 miles (7.6km) further down the peninsula. I have even heard the story that sleeping heroes of the past lie within the hill, to be wakened at Ireland's hour of need. The fort dates from about 1700 BC, and according to the *Annals of the Four Masters* it was the seat of power for the Northern O'Neill kings from the 5th to the 12th centuries. It was destroyed by their enemies in AD 675 and 1101. You can understand why this site was chosen, for here they and their property were secure against the onslaughts of any enemy. The fort guards all approaches, which is why it affords such good views over the Foyle, and the Swilly.

Inch Island, signposted off the main Buncrana–Londonderry Road is a beautiful, untouched place. At the crossroads by the local shop, take the right turn to **Inch Fort** and **Brown's Bay** and look across the limpid water to Fahan, or go for a swim. Mr Brown (ask in the only shop on the island), will hire you a boat or take you out fishing. There is an O'Doherty Clan Centre here (℗ *(077) 30017*).

Fahan is famous for its St Mura's Cross in the Church of Ireland graveyard. This 7th-century two-faced cross with mythological birds and ecclesiastical figures is all that remains of the rich Abbey of St Mura. Here in the rectory, looking across to Inch Top Hill, Mrs Alexander wrote 'There is a Green Hill Far Away', in 1848. There is a beautiful beach with lovely views all around, which stretches up to **Buncrana**, a rather jaded seaside resort. You might stop at the **Vintage Car and Carriage Museum** (*open every day 10am–10pm in summer; ℗ (077) 61130*). Just outside Buncrana, at Lisfannen, on the Derry road, is the **World Knitting Centre** which traces the history of traditional patterns, ℗ (077) 62365. Also of interest is the **textile exhibition** and **wildlife display** at **Tullyarvan Mill** (℗ *(077) 61613*). Close by at **Dunree** is **Fort Dunree Military**

Museum (*open daily 10am–6pm in summer; adm*), a restored coastal defence battery depicting 200 years of coastal and military history.

Buncrana to Muff

Near the River Cranagh you can see one of the O'Doherty's castles. Take the R238 through the mountains to the spectacular **Mamore Gap**, and gaze at the return view of the Fanad Peninsula. There are plenty of good beaches on the way, such as **Linsfort** and **Dunree**; and on the other side of the Gap, past Clonmany and the beaches around Isle of Doagh. This is an unspoiled country, full of fuchsia hedges and little whitewashed cottages. In the Church of Ireland graveyard in **Carndonagh** are some interesting monuments, including the Marigold Stone which has the same ornamentations as St Mura's Cross, and by the road-side opposite the church is one of the most far-famed crosses in Ireland, said to be the oldest low-relief cross in the country (AD 650). This richly decorated and well preserved cross must have been erected by a prosperous and settled community in those far off times. The most northerly village in Ireland, **Malin**, has a pretty green and a tidy look. It is a good example of a well preserved 17th-century plantation village, with a fine church. Nearby is the lovely **Five Fingers Strand**.

If you want to see the most northerly tip of Ireland, **Malin Head**, familiar to all of you who listen to radio shipping forecasts, take a road passing extensive sand dunes, after which you come to pebbly coves where you can pick up semi-precious stones. From Malin Head you can see lighthouse islands. From here to Glengad Head are cliffs rising to over 800ft (246m). To the east of **Culdaff** are some fine sandy beaches.

All this area is fine walking country; the cliff scenery is interspersed with great stretches of sandhills. You can choose whether to walk around Malin Head itself, or southwards towards **Inishowen Head**. Or visit yet another cross, 2 miles (3.2km) to the south of Culdaff in Clonca. This impressive shaft called St Boden's Cross is almost 12ft (4m) in height and is carved with a scene depicting the miracle of the loaves and the fishes. On the road from Culdaff to Moville, in **Carrowblagh**, is an example of an ancient sweathouse— the Irish form of a sauna. The almost enclosed room was heated like an oven, and having heated yourself thoroughly, you were immersed in cold water. This was said to be the cure for aching bones and temporary madness. **Greencastle** is a beach resort with the remains of a 14th-century castle built by Richard de Burgh, the Red Earl of Ulster in 1305, who needed it as a strategic base from which to try and dominate the O'Donnells of Tyrconnell (most of Donegal) and the O'Doherty's of Inishowen.

Further down the coast you come to **Moville**, formerly a point of departure for many emigrants to the New World. It is now a leisure resort with a well-planted green lined with seats from which you can comfortably gaze at the sea, or have a picnic. At Cooley, 1¾ miles (3km) to the northwest, is a 9ft (3m) high cross and the remains of a chapel with a corbelled stone roof. The area between Moville and Muff was a coastal foothold for many Planter castles. They are known as castles, but are actually big houses, and you get glimpses of them through the trees as you pass by. One of them, Redcastle, is now a luxury hotel; some would consider it ruined with all its modern embellishment. Behind them rise rather forbidding mountains, though if you venture on the mountain roads you come across lost clochans and megalithic monuments. What is more unique, you will find yellow raspberries in the hedges lining the lanes.

Shopping

Tweeds and knitwear: McNutts of Downings, ✆ (074) 55324. Magees of Donegal Town, ✆ (073) 21100. Gillespie Bros. Tweed Shop, Mountcharles. Jean's craft shop, Mountcharles. James Boyle, Front Street, Ardara, for tweed collages. John Molloy, Ardara. Studio Donegal Handwoven Tweed, Kilcar. Connemara Fabrics, Kilcar. Gaeltarra Yarns and Wools, Kilcar. World Knitting Centre, Lisfannon, ✆ (077) 62355. Traces the history of traditional patterns. Kennedy's of Ardara. Teresa's cottage industries, Church View, Bruckless, for scarves, shawls and Aran jumpers, ✆ (073) 37080. J. F. Hernon, Ardara for fine handknit sweaters. Falcarragh Knitwear, Falcarragh, ✆ (074) 35172.

Crafts: Donegal Craft Shop. Donegal table linens and handkerchiefs, Bruckless, ✆ (073) 37013. Mary Barr, Main Street, Buncrana ✆ (077) 61375. Hand embroidery from Jack Furey, Mountcharles. Donegal tweed, crafts, woodwork and batik pottery at the Donegal Town Craft Village (just outside the town on the road to Sligo). The Gallery, Dunfanaghy, for paintings, antiques and knitwear. Glencolumbkille Folk Village Shop for soaps, flower wines, St Brigid's crosses and honey. McCauslands Craft Shop, Milford. The Cottage Craft Shop, Malin. Lakeside Centre, Dunlewey; The Fish House, Ramelton; Tullyarvan Mill, Buncrana.

Willow baskets: turf, flower and fruit baskets; route signposted from Falcarragh at Upper Moyra.

Pottery: Cavanacor Studios, Cavanacor House, Ballindrait, Lifford, ✆ (074) 41143. Joanna O'Kane creates delicate off-white bowls and plates often decorated with red fuchsia flowers; also wonderful selection of crafts and pictures. Letterkenny Pottery, Mountain Top, Letterkenny, ✆ (074) 22738.

Activities

Walking: hill-walking on Slieve League, Muckish, Errigal, Scalp. Details about walking the Ulster Way, a signposted route, can be obtained from the Planning Department, DCC, Lifford, or the Long-distance Walking Route Committee, Cospair, 11th floor, Hawkings House, Dublin 2.

Sea and game fishing: in most parts of County Donegal, especially in the Killybegs region, Rathmullen and Inishowen. For deep-sea fishing boat hire in Killybegs, ✆ (073) 31288; in Rathmullen, ✆ (074) 58178; and in Moville, ✆ (077) 82010. Boats are also available for hire in Falcarragh, Ardara, Dungloe and Portnoo. For more information contact The Northern Regional Fisheries Board, Ballyshannon, ✆ (072) 51435.

Pony-trekking: Stracomer Riding School, Bundoran. Trail-riding holidays arranged, ✆ (072)41787. The Village Stables, Malin, ✆ (077) 70606. Residential Riding Holidays in the Gaeltacht, Ard na Scapall, Strawabroney, Derrybeg, Letterkenny, ✆ (075) 31587.

Golf: at Bundoran, Portsalon, Rosapenna, and Fahan. The course at Bundoran is a hundred years old, and is one of the best in the country. It runs along the high cliffs above Bundoran beach, ✆ (072) 41360. Portsalon is a very relaxed golf course: you leave your green fee in a box. The course runs above the beautiful Ballymastocker Bay. At Rosapenna the best part of the links runs in a low valley along the ocean, ✆ (074) 55301. Fahan is a gently rolling, sandy course over-looking the Swilly, ✆ (074) 61027.

Greyhound racing: Lifford, every Thursday and Saturday night, ✆ (074) 41083.

Pottery and art weekends: Mrs O'Kane, Cavanacor House, Ballindrait, Lifford, ✆ (074) 41143.

Swimming: Leisureland, Redcastle, ✆ (077) 82306; Waterworld, Bundoran, ✆ (072) 41172.

Where to Stay

expensive

Rathmullen House, Rathmullen, ✆ (074) 58188. This top country-house hotel is a lovely 18th-century house set on the edge of Lough Swilly. There are beautiful gardens, and there is excellent food to be had either in the dining room, or the charcoal grill. It has a very cosy bar with a turf fire in the old cellars, a very attractive indoor heated swimming pool and a sauna. **Redcastle County Hotel**, Redcastle, ✆ (072) 82073. Heavy, bad-taste décor has rather ruined the charm of this old Plantation house. Lovely setting, however, and popular with the Northern Irish. **St Ernans House Hotel**, St Ernans Island, Donegal Town, ✆ (073) 21065. Charming situation on a wooded tidal island. The décor is rather too tightly colour co-ordinated, but it is a lovely place to stay.

moderate

The Sand House, Rossnowlagh, ✆ (072) 51777. Excellent modern hotel, friendly, comfortable, with delicious food and lots of sports available, especially surfing. **Arnold's Hotel**, Dunfanaghy, ✆ (074) 36208. This is a fine, old-fashioned hotel, set in a pretty village overlooking Sheephaven Bay. Nearby is the splendid scenery of Horn Head. **Fort Royal Hotel**, Rathmullen, ✆ (074) 58100. It is another fine period house, with more of a 'family atmosphere' than Rathmullen House. **Castle Murray House Hotel**, St John's Point, Dunkineely, ✆ (073) 37022. Comfortable small hotel with fine French food and lovely views. Mr & Mrs Kieran Clark, **Ardnamona House**, Lough Eske, near Donegal Town, ✆ (073) 22650. Magical views, wonderful food and hospitality. Famous for its rhododendrons. **Viking House Hotel**, Belcruit, Kincasslagh, ✆ (075) 43295. Modern, family run hotel owned by Daniel O'Donnell, the famous country singer. **Malin**

Hotel, Malin, ✆ (077) 70606. Comfortable, small, family run hotel. **Castlegrove House**, Castlegrove, Letterkenny, ✆ (074) 51118. Marvellous Georgian house in wooded grounds overlooking Lough Swilly.

inexpensive

Mr and Mrs Evans, **Bruckless House**, Bruckless, ✆ (073) 37071. Charming 18th-century house overlooking Donegal Bay, run by a couple who will head you in the right direction whether your interest is walking, prehistoric monuments or just exploring the beaches and countryside. There are simple but comfortable rooms and a mature garden in which to wander about. An ideal place for a long stay. Mrs Scott, **The Manse**, Ramelton, ✆ (074) 51047. This house is caught in a time-warp of old-fashioned hospitality. You can be sure of stimulating conversation at dinner with your hostess, who is well-informed on local knowledge and history. Mrs Grier, **Crofton Farmhouse**, Aughnish, Ramelton, ✆ (074) 51048. You will get a fine Northern welcome in this homely farmhouse, which is set on the edge of Lough Swilly. Mrs Campbell, **Magheraclogher**, Derrybeg, ✆ (075) 31545. In the middle of the Gaelic-speaking area, this modern house is set on the edge of the pounding Atlantic. You can get excellent homemade food here and there is one bed with bath; three bedrooms in all.

Mrs Borland, **Avalon**, Tamney, ✆ (074) 59031. The Fanad Peninsula is a very beautiful and untouched rural area. This traditional-style house in the centre of the village has good home-cooked meals and four bedrooms. **Mrs S. Sweeney**, Tamney, ✆ (074) 59011. Delightful old-fashioned farmhouse on the shores of Mulroy Bay. Five bedrooms. Mrs Taylor, **Gortfad**, Castlefinn, Lifford, ✆ (074) 46135. Very old farmhouse full of antique furniture. Lovely food. Two beds with bath. Six bedrooms in all. The **Pier Hotel**, Rathmullen, ✆ (074) 58115. A favourite with the locals and foreign fishermen. Plenty of atmosphere to make up for the lack of luxury. **Glen Hote**, Arranmore Island, ✆ (075) 21505. Family-run and friendly. Mrs Doyle, **Barraicin**, Malin Head, ✆ (077) 70184. On the untouched and beautiful Inishowen Peninsula, about 4 miles (6.4km) from Malin village, this modern bungalow overlooks the sea. There are lots of country pursuits, and your hostess produces excellent home-cooked food. Three bedrooms.

Mrs Grant, **Pollin House**, Cardonagh Road, Ballyliffen, Clonmany, ✆ (077) 76203. Also near Malin, here you will find equally good food and a friendly welcome. Four bedrooms. Evening meal negotiable. Mrs Campbell, **Ardeen**, Ramelton, ✆ (074) 51243. Comfortable, friendly house in charming riverside town. **Ostan Thoraighe Hotel**, Tory Island, ✆ (074) 35920. Newly opened cosy hotel on this wonderful island. **Franciscan Friary**, Rossnowlagh—guesthouse accommodation, ✆ (072) 51342. Opened as a centre for peace and reconciliation, a quiet reflective place where you can join in a retreat if you want to.

self-catering

Mrs Clarke, **Ardnamona**, Lough Eske, ✆ (073) 22650. Pretty cottage in traditional yard, surrounded by lovely arboretum and scenery. Mrs Temple, **Salthill**

House, Mountcharles, ✆ (073) 35014. 18th-century lodge gate, sleeps 8. **Mr McFadden**, The Mall, Ramelton, ✆ (074) 51026. Georgian house in quiet town. Sleeps 12. **Tra na Rosann Youth Hostel**, Downings, ✆ (074) 55374.**Errigal Hostel**, Dunlewy, ✆ (075) 31180

Eating Out
expensive

Rathmullen House Hotel, Rathmullen, ✆ (074) 58188. Fresh, original cooking with vegetables from their walled garden. Sunday lunch is good value. **Castle Murray House Hotel**, St John's Point, Dunkineely, ✆ (073) 37022. Superb French cooking in lovely hotel.

moderate

Danby Restaurant, Rossnowlagh Road, Ballyshannon, ✆ (072) 51138. In an old house, delicious and reasonably priced dinner menu. **Jackson's Hotel**, Ballybofey, ✆ (074) 31021. Excellent salmon and ham. Also good bar lunch.

Kee's Hotel, Stanorlar, ✆ (074) 31018. Wholesome food, good service and cheaper bar food. **Mirabeau Steak House**, Ramelton, ✆ (074) 51138. Georgian town house with unpretentious cooking. **Mount Errigal**, Ballyraine, Letterkenny, ✆ (074) 22700. Better-than-average hotel food in modern setting.

Bunbeg House, The Harbour, Bunbeg, ✆ (075) 31305. Cosy family-run restaurant, where you can also stay. Healthy snacks and simple vegetarian meals, as well as heartier food. **St John's Restaurant**, Fahan, ✆ (077) 60289. You can be sure of a feeling of well-being in this comfortable Georgian house. Seafood and vegetables are very well-cooked and the owner is urbane and welcoming.

Danann's Restaurant, Main Street, Dunfanaghy, ✆ (074) 36150. Seafood a speciality. The **Fish House Bistro**, Ramelton, ✆ (074) 51316. Simple lunches, more elaborate in the evenings. **Castle Grove**, Ramelton Road, Letterkenny, ✆ (074) 51118. About 3 miles outside Letterkenny. Beautiful setting and good value. **Harvey's Point**, Lough Eske, Donelgal Town, ✆ (073) 22208. Continental food in beautiful surroundings.

inexpensive

Glencolumkille Folk Village Tearoom, ✆ (073) 30017. Home-made scones and bread, salads and soups. **Teach Killendarragh**, Annagary, ✆ (075) 48201. A welcome spot in the middle of the mountain wildness. Famous for its seafood pancakes. The **Village Restaurant**, Kerrykeel, ✆ (074) 50062. Good-value, home-cooked meals.

McGroarty's Pub, The Diamond, Donegal Town. Good pub food. The **Tearoom** at Glenveagh Castle. Homemade cakes. **Nancy's Bar**, Ardara, ✆ (075) 41187. Delicious oysters. **Lurgyvale Thatched Cottage**, Kilmacrenan. Homemade bread and scones for tea.

Music: in Nancy's Bar and Oliver's in Ardara. *Ceili* (traditional) music in Falcarragh. Look in the local newspapers for traditional and popular music sessions, which change venue all the time. Teach Ceoil, a house of music and traditional entertainment, at Ballyliffen during July and August on Tuesday and Thursday evenings, ✆ (077) 317522 for details. Leo's Bar, Crolly, is famous for its traditional music. Various members of Clannad, the popular folk group, learnt their skills here. Lurgyvale Thatched Cottage, Kilmacrenan, Thursday evenings. The Bridge Bar, Ramelton. The Irish Music Hostel, Finn Farm, Cappry, Ballybofey, ✆ (074) 32261; Lakeside Centre, Dunlewey. Seanos pub, Ballyshannon. Mount Errigal Hotel, Ballyraine, Letterkenny, ✆ (074) 22700. Venue for dances and music.

County Cavan

Cavan is a dreamy, unspoilt county. It is completely landlocked, yet there are attractive stretches of water everywhere, scattered as it is with lakes and rivers abounding in fish. It is a favourite county for coarse fishermen, many of whom come over from England every year for the huge catches. And for the city-dweller in search of peace and quiet, it is a perfect holiday place.

The countryside is pretty and interspersed with woods. The hills or drumlins left behind by a glacier in earlier times offer plenty in the way of wild glens. The highest mountain in the county is Cuilcagh, which is 2100ft (640m) high. On its southern slopes is the source of the great Shannon River which flows out to the sea as far away as County Clare. Along the winding roads you will hardly meet a soul, for the population is only 4000, mostly farmers. Many of them offer bed and breakfast accommodation.

Cavan is an undiscovered county to those who are not in the angling league, and this is undeserved. The ancient history of the county lingers on in the form of charming ruined castles and abbeys, and mysterious stone monuments from the Bronze and Iron Ages. Being in the lakelands, there are a number of crannog sites (early lakeland dwellings), and figures left over from pagan times. One of the most curious finds from west Cavan is the three-faced Corleck Head, now in the National Museum, Dublin. It is a rare example of a pagan Trinity figure. Christianity percolated slowly through this lake maze and even up to the 17th century some recorded devotions to saints had a pagan flavour. A principal shrine of the Celtic gods in Ireland was at Magh Sleacht near Ballyconnell, but there is nothing left of it now.

The opening up of the Victorian Ballinamore and Ballyconnell canal (now known as the Shannon Erne waterway) which links the Shannon water system with the Erne, has been a great impetus for tourism and no doubt new restaurants and bars will appear in the next few years to cater for the canal traffic.

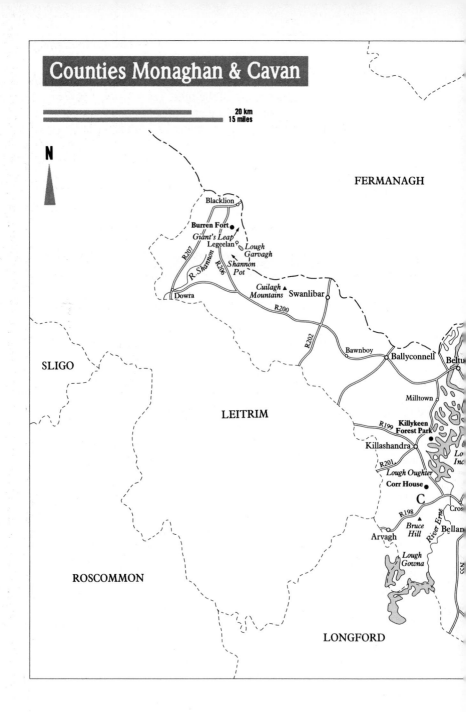

Counties Monaghan & Cavan

20 km
15 miles

N

FERMANAGH

Blacklion

Burren Fort
Giant's Leap
Legeelan
Lough Garvagh
R207
R.Shannon
R206
Shannon Pot
Dowra
Cuilagh Mountains
Swanlibar
R200

Bawnboy
Ballyconnell
Beltu
R202

SLIGO

Milltown

LEITRIM

R199 Killykeen Forest Park
Killashandra
R201
Lough Oughter
Corr House
Lo Inc

C
Cros

R198
Bruce Hill
Arvagh
River Erne
Bellan

Lough Gowna

N55

ROSCOMMON

LONGFORD

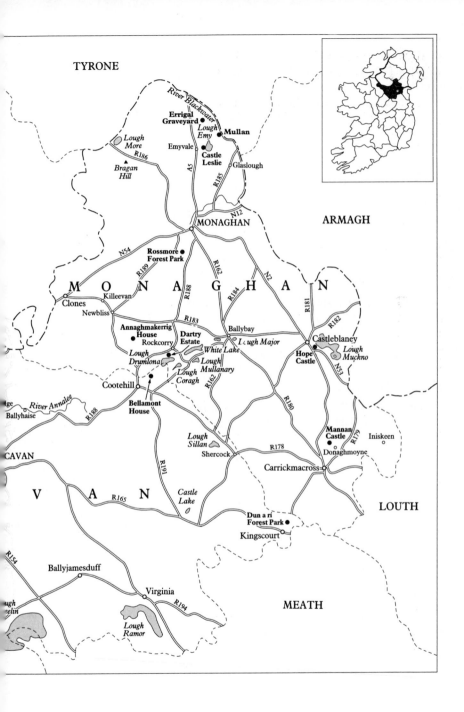

History

Cavan as it is defined today is a fairly recent county, made in 1584 by the British Lord Deputy. Previously, it was part of the ancient Kingdom of Breffni, and its Gaelic rulers were the O'Reillys. The O'Reillys managed to hold on to power until the division of the county amongst Scottish and English settlers in the 1600s.

In the 19th century the county suffered greatly from the famine, and the haemorrhage of emigration. It did have a small linen industry, now defunct, as it is elsewhere in the North. Along with County Donegal and County Monaghan it is separated politically from the rest of Ulster. This happened in 1921 with the division of Ireland into the 26-county state and the continuing allegiance of the other six Ulster counties to British Government.

Getting There and Around

By air: Sligo Airport is approximately 80 miles (128km) from Cavan Town. Dublin Airport is approximately 170 miles (272km) from Cavan Town.

By rail: no train service in County Cavan.

By bus: excellent express buses stop in Cavan en route between Belfast, Enniskillen, Galway and Dublin. The small towns are served by local buses. Contact Cavan Bus Depot, ✆ (049) 31353.

By car: you can hire a car from Michael Clarke, Main Street, Cavan.

By bike: Bike Alley Set Printers, Farnham Street, ✆ (049) 31932. On yer bike tours, ✆ (049) 31932, for cycling tours of area.

Public transport: is provided by the Provincial Bus Service, and express buses on their way from Dublin to Enniskillen in Belfast to Galway. Cavan Bus Depot, ✆ (049) 31353.

Tourist Information

Cavan, Town Hall, ✆ (049) 31942, April to December.

Festivals

Feb/March: Cavan International Song Contest, ✆ Anne Lennon, (049) 31444 or (049) 32237.

March: Cavan Drama Festival at the end of the month, ✆ (049) 31063.

Early June: Festival of the Lakes, Killeshandra. Music, dance, children's entertainment, powerboat racing and angling competitions.

Late July/early August: Belturbet Festival of The Erne, ✆ (049) 22595.

August: Cootehill Arts Festival, ✆ (049) 52321.

Around Cavan Town

Cavan (*An Cabhan*: the hollow), the county town, is an inconspicuous place. Once it was important as an O'Reilly stronghold in the ancient kingdom of East Breffni. Their castle,

Clough Oughter (pronounced 'ooter') is a well-preserved example of an Irish circular tower castle and is situated about 3 miles (4.8km) outside Cavan on an island in Lough Oughter. You approach it from the Crossdoney–Killeshandra road, and the wooded splendour of Killykeen Forest Park. It is possible to get out to the island if you hire a boat. This 13th-century tower is built over a crannog and looks very romantic, viewed from the lakeside. Its history is more sinister. It was used as a prison by the Confederates in the 1641 rebellion, and Eoghan Roe O'Neill, the great leader of the Confederates died here in 1649, poisoned, it is thought, by his Cromwellian opponents.

North of Cavan Town the **Lough Oughter System** of small- to medium-sized lakes is really an offshoot of the River Erne complex. This is a well known coarse fishing area. **Lough Inchin,** on the eastern side of the Oughter water system, is noted for pike fishing, though recently roach have been introduced. The **Killykeen Forest Park** is a good access point to the loughs.

There are some worthwhile diversions around Cavan, including a private Folk Museum called the **Pighouse Collection** (*open at the whim of the owner; adm; © (049) 37248*), named after the original pighouse in which it was preserved. It is located in Corr House, Cornafean, near Crossdoney (take the R198 west out of Cavan Town). On the road to Arvagh continuing along the R198 is **Bruce Hill** (755ft/260m), which is worth climbing for the view. During the times of the Penal Laws, when Catholics were forbidden to build churches, Mass was celebrated here in the open air. If you like ornate cut-glass you might take the opportunity to buy a bit of Cavan Crystal from the factory shop on the Dublin Road (N3) on the outskirts of Cavan. For those interested in prehistoric sites, a few miles out of Cavan on the R188 northwest to Blacklion on Shantemon Hill, off the Cootehill Road, are **Finn MacCool's Fingers,** standing stones within which the princes of Breffni, the O'Reillys, were crowned. (Many prehistoric standing stones are called after the heroes of Ireland's legendary past.) **Ballyhaise** is a pretty,

neat village on the Annalee river, reached by an unclassified road off the R198 going north out of Cavan Town. It has a rather grand arcaded market hall. Nearby is **Ballyhaise House**, built in 1733 and designed by Richard Cassels, who also designed Leinster House in Dublin. It is worth asking to go around it (it is now an agricultural college) to see the lovely oval saloon and plasterwork. It is also worth stopping in **Butlersbridge**, another pleasant village on the River Annalee, to lunch at Derragara Inn. The fishing is reputed to be good here too.

North Cavan

Another lakeland town is **Belturbet** on the N3 north of Cavan. It is now a thriving angling and boating centre, and was once a thriving depot for the traffic on the Ulster Canal, which might be somewhat revived now the canal has been reopened. A boat trip along here is like driving on Irish roads fifty years ago, it is so unspoilt, you will barely even see a house. Nearby, at **Milltown** is a Columban site called Drumlane with the remains of a later church and tower. Look out for the faint carving, on the north side, of a cock and a hen. The church has a lovely Romanesque doorway. Going northwest along the R200 you reach **Ballyconnell** which is now a stopping place on the Shannon Erne waterway, set on Woodford River. The 17th-century Protestant church here has a carved stone with a human head which came from a medieval monastery. In the grounds of the church are the outlines of two diamond-shaped fortifications dating from the Williamite Wars. The village is a pleasant base for fishing or hill-walking. Three miles (4.8km) southwest at **Killycluggin** is a stone circle with the remnant of an ornamental phallic stone.

For walkers, 5 miles (8km) to the west on the R200 is the tiny hamlet of **Bawnboy**, which is on the way to some pretty glens and mountains. You can climb 1148ft (350m) to **Glen Gap** between the peaks of Cuilcagh and Benbrack. For a panoramic view of the neighbouring counties, take the R200 to Glangevlin (also known as Glengevlin), and go through Glen Gap to the summit of the Cuilcagh Mountains. **Blacklion**, a small village on the Fermanagh border, sits between Upper and Lower Lough MacNean, and in the limestone foothills of the Cuilcagh Mountains, in a most attractive situation. It has a frontier post into Northern Ireland but, more importantly for walkers, from here you can walk up to **Lough Garvagh** and the **Giant's Cave** and **Giant's Leap**. These names refer to legendary figures whose origins are lost in the mists of time. For instance, nobody knows who built the fine ring-fort or cashel 3 miles (4.8km) south of Blacklion in **Burren**. It consists of three beautifully built stone walls. The central cashel is 82ft (25m) in circumference and has a rampart 10ft (3m) thick, with internal and external stairways. Inside the south cashel is a beehive-shaped sweat-house, an ancient type of Turkish bath. **The Cavan Way**, a signposted trail, passes on the way prehistoric monuments, a sweat-house near Legeelan, and wonderful views. It also goes close to the **Shannon Pot** (350yds/300m south of the trail), the reputed source of the mighty River Shannon. Just over the border from Blacklion in County Fermanagh are the famous **Marble Arch Caves**, which have been developed so the inexperienced can explore them without fear (*see* 'County Fermanagh', p.326). **Swanlinbar**, further to the southeast of this hilly country, is another frontier village. It was once known as the Harrogate of Ireland because of its sulphur baths.

Cootehill to Ballyjamesduff

Cootehill, on the county border about 15 miles (24km) northeast of Cavan Town, is a market town named after the Coote family who 'planted' the area with their followers in the 17th century. The Church of Ireland church at the end of its long main street is in the attractive Planters' Gothic style. Nearby, to the north of the town in Bellamont Forest, is **Bellamont House**, built by Thomas Coote and designed by the famous Irish architect Sir Edward Lovett Pearce in 1730. It is a beautiful Palladian mansion which fell into decay and was lovingly restored by an Englishman. It has been reserved by an Australian Coote but at the moment its future is uncertain and it is not open to the public, a great pity as the interiors are spectacular. The village next-door, **Sherlock**, is rather pretty, with a fine plain Presbyterian meeting house set on the shores of **Lough Sillan**—a good lake for coarse fishing. This is wooded and lake-studded country. Seven and a half miles (12km) away to the southeast is **Kingscourt**. Look in the Catholic church for the delightful stained-glass windows designed by the Dublin artist Evie Hone (1894–1955). Just over a mile (2km) away is **Dún a Ró Forest Park**, where you can picnic by the pretty Cabra River. There are planned walks here, and nature trails. You might see a wild deer amongst the trees. It was the former demesne of the Pratts of Cabra—their castle home is now a hotel. Beautifully situated on the edge of Lough Ramor is **Virginia**, a village founded in the reign of King James I but named after his aunt, Queen Elizabeth I. It is the most southerly of the Ulster Plantation villages. Although the Protestant population has dwindled since Elizabethan times, the centrepiece of the village is still the Protestant church, which is approached down a straight avenue of clipped yews. There are some pretty rusticated cottages in the main street. It is very attractive and well-planned town, with some pretty trees and traditional painted shop-signs. The lough is beautiful, and full of little islands. To the northwest is **Ballyjamesduff**, made famous by the jolly and nostalgic song written by the humorous writer and singer Percy French in the early years of this century. At one time French worked as Inspector of Drains with the Cavan County Council. His songs are still sung by Irish emigrant communities all over the world. For example:

> *There are tones that are tender, and tones that are gruff,*
> *And whispering over the sea*
> *Come back, Paddy Reilly, to Ballyjamesduff,*
> *Come back, Paddy Reilly to me.*

Shopping

Crafts: Carraig Crafts, Mountnugent, ✆ (049) 40179.

Crystal: Cavan Crystal, Dublin Road, Cavan, ✆ (049) 31800. Tours available.

Cheese: goats' cheese from Corleggy Farmhouse, Belturbet, ✆ (049) 22219. Besides buying this delicious cheese flavoured with herbs and peppers, you will also enjoy seeing this old-style farm with pigs that can wander in the yard, unlike the majority of porkers in this country. The factory-farming of pigs is big-money in Cavan. Another farmhouse cheese is Dun a Ró, a Gouda-type cheese found in the Main Street, Kingscourt.

Picnics: good materials available from Back to Nature Health Food Shop, Cavan, or the supermarket in Belturbet.

Coarse fishing: in most of the loughs, of which there are hundreds. Particularly good are Loughs Gowna, Bunn, Inchin and Oughter. The Annalee and Woodford Rivers are excellent fisheries: you can catch all species except dace. Local tackle shops are the best source of information on hire boats, bait and course and pike fishing licences. Try Mr J. McMahon, Supply Stores, Bridge Street, Belturbet; Mr Brian Mulligan, Main Street, Cavan; John Donoghue, 22 Bridge Street, Cavan; and Magnet Sports, Town Hall Street, Cavan. Bait stockists include Mrs Dunne, Hilltop Farm, Kilduff, ✆ (049) 22114; and Mrs I. Neill, Lisnamandra Farm, Crossdoney, ✆ (049) 37196. An excellent book to look out for on coarse fishing in County Cavan is the tome by Hugh Cough. Available in book-shops all over the country.

Walking: the Cavan Way is a 15-mile (24km) marked trail which runs from Blacklion to Dowra, roughly northeast to southwest through hills, forest and lime-stone scenery, passing on the way prehistoric monuments, a sweat-house near Legeelan, and wonderful views. It also goes close to the Shannon Pot (350yds/ 300m south of the trail), the reputed source of the Shannon. Information and leaflets from West Cavan Community Council, Blacklion, and Bord Fáilte. There are less strenuous walks in Dún a Rí Forest Park; in Killykeen Forest Park, 2 miles (3.2km) north of Killashandra on the R201; at Mulrick, 1½ miles (2.4km) south-west of Lough Gowna village on the edge of the lough; and at Castle Lake, a mile (1.6km) north of Bailiesborough on the R178.

Pony-trekking: Cavan Equestrian Centre, Shalom Stables, Lath, Cavan, ✆ (049) 32017.

Golf: Slieve Russell Hotel championship golf course, Ballyconnell, ✆ (049) 26444. Virginia Golf Club, ✆ (042) 65766. County Cavan Golf Club, Cavan Town, specializes in golf tuition, ✆ (049) 31283

Boat trips: Turbet Tours, Belturbet, ✆ (049) 22360, for boat trips on Lough Erne.

 Slieve Russell Hotel, Ballyconnell, ✆ (049) 26444. Big new hotel built by local millionaire, it boasts marble columns, fountains and jacuzzi bath tubs as well as a championship golf course.

The **Park Hotel**, Virginia, ✆ (049) 47235. Attractive old hunting lodge beside Lough Ramor with a nine-hole golf course. **Cabra Castle Hotel**, Kingscourt, ✆ (042) 87030. 15th-century pile, with landscaped gardens. Self-catering units available.

inexpensive

Mrs B. Neill, **Lisnamandra**, Crossdoney, ✆ (049) 37196. Ten minutes' drive from Lough Oughter, this traditional-style farmhouse with its comfortable rooms and home-cooking, has a very restful atmosphere. Four rooms with private bath, six bedrooms altogether. It has won many awards. Joe and Una Smith, **Riverside House**, Cootehill, ✆ (049) 52150. This old farmhouse which overlooks the tree-lined River Annalee is under a mile (1.6km) from the market town of Cootehill. It has elegant high ceilings and plasterwork, and open fires in the main rooms. Your host is an expert on all fishing matters, and there is a boat with engine available. Mrs Smith cooks delicious five-course meals in the evenings. There are two rooms with bath, eight bedrooms altogether. Mrs Maureen Campbell, **Ard Glas Farmhouse**, Corlea, Kingscourt, ✆ (042) 67316. Set in hilly landscape, this modern farmhouse is a place to grow content and fat on homemade delicacies. The vegetables are organic, the eggs free-range, and all the meat is from the farm. You can also have some soothing reflexology practised on you by your hostess. **Sandville House Hostel**, ✆ (049) 26297. IR£4.50 a night. Includes a couple of double rooms for same price per person.

self-catering

All the following are set in attractive locations.

Wooden chalets in Killykeen Forest Park. Contact the Manager, **Killykeen Forest Chalets**, Killykeen Forest Park, ✆ (049) 32541. From IR£220 per week. **Stone coach house** on loughside. 2 bedrooms. From IR£190 per week, ✆ (026) 42321.

Eating Out

expensive

Fred Muller's, Tiriliffin, Milltown, ✆ (049) 34260. An unusual experience. Fred will cook exotic and delicious food for you in his own house. Book in advance.

moderate

The **Old Post Inn**, Cloverhill, ✆ (047) 55266. Renovated old post-house with atmospheric gas lamps. The pork is always good; the pigs are fed on the whey of Corleggy cheese. **Macnean Bistro**, Blacklion, ✆ (072) 53022. Imaginative cooking such as fillet of ostrich with rosti. The desserts are much lauded. The **Olde Priory**, Main Street, Cavan, ✆ (049) 61898. Good atmosphere and plentiful flavoursome helpings. The **Park Hotel**, Virginia, ✆ (049) 47235. Imaginative and ambitious cooking. **Casey's Steak House**, Ballinagh, ✆ (049) 37105. 'The best steaks in Ireland' according to some.

inexpensive

Derragarra Inn, Butlersbridge, ✆ (049) 31003. Attractive pub by the river. Lots of seafood and traditional music on Fridays during the summer.

Entertainment and Nightlife

Music: McGinty's Corner Bar, Dublin Road, Cavan for traditional music. Also a winner of the Regional Pub of the Year Award. Try Louis Blessing's pub which sometimes has jazz.

County Monaghan

This pleasant, sheltered county is caught at the top betweeen the counties of Armagh and Fermanagh. There are no really high hills, just lots of little ones forming a gently rolling countryside. To the north lies a small fringe of mountains. The central area is hillocky with fairly rich farming land, in many ways reminiscent of County Down. Set among the hills to the south, at almost every bend of the road, lie small well-wooded lakes and sedgy bogholes. The little cultivated fields, trim hedges, tiny lakes, the profusion of wild flowers and the hordes of dragonflies, green and red, make it a land of satisfying detail. In contrast to the smallness of scale, there still remain a few large estates, with their landscaped parks, lakes, formal gardens and age-old trees. You get glimpses of these 'big houses', and the forgotten ones which are crumbling into ruins. Copper beech trees seem to have gone wild everywhere in Monaghan, quite a rarity in Ireland. A native of the place swore that this was the last retreat of the Fir Bolgs, who were squeezed out of the rest of Ireland by the Dé Danaan and the Celts.

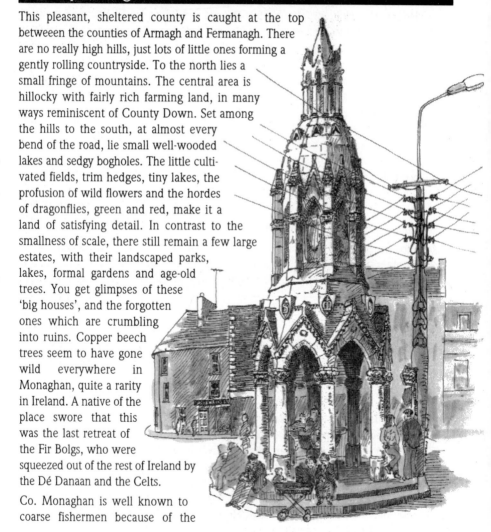

Co. Monaghan is well known to coarse fishermen because of the wealth of lakes; otherwise it has been little visited by tourists. The locals are hoping to change this, and quite a few attractions have been developed. Lough Muckno, near Castleblaney, offers many sporting activities and accommodation. In the southwest the Rural and Literary Resource Centre in Innishkeen is a magnet for admirers of the poet Patrick Kavanagh. To the northeast of the county, the pretty village of Glaslough has an excellent equestrian centre. Close by is Castle Leslie, a Victorian pile overlooking the lough and surrounded by beautiful trees. The castle is open for tours and elaborate dinners. After dinner, the cloaked mistress of the house will guide you by candlelight around its haunted rooms, a performance of fun and drama. This north eastern corner of Co. Monaghan is bounded by the Blackwater River and the N2, known as the Parish of Truagh, is one of the most untouched areas in the county. The roads are so unused that the grass grows up the middle; many of these little roads would have led into Co. Tyrone or Co. Armagh before the Troubles began, and it is hoped that the area will now begin to open up. You will find some pretty mountain scenery and views which stretch over Ulster and beyond.

The Ulster Way, a signposted track for walkers, joins up here. Certainly Co. Monaghan is a peaceful place for a fishing or walking holiday. Hilton Park near Scotshouse is the perfect place to stay in style and comfort, and for those on tighter budgets there are plenty of hospitable bed-and-breakfast establishments.

History

County Monaghan as it is now is a 16th-century creation. As the English conquered terri-tory, they shired it, hoping to make it easier to manage and more anglicized. By shiring it, they joined the territories of the two ruling families, the MacMahons and the McKennas. Other powerful families were the Duffys, O'Carrolls and the Connollys, whose power was finally broken after the 1642 rebellion, when the lands of the Irish chieftains were divided between the English and Scottish undertakers. (They were named this because in return for a grant of land they 'undertook' certain duties to keep Monaghan loyal to the English crown.) The descendants of those Gaelic families still live in the region today, whilst the undertaker families have disappeared or married into the local population. For over two hundred years, a smouldering resentment over land ownership made the relationship of peasants and landlord very uneasy, but this largely disappeared with the land acts of 1881 when the British government put up money for tenants to buy their own holdings.

In the 19th century County Monaghan benefited from the linen industry, and it was famous for its trade in horses, many of which were exported to Russia for the use of the Imperial army. Now both the linen and the horse trade have gone, along with the old rail and canal links. However, the county is well served by express buses going to and from Dublin and County Donegal, there is a good local bus network, and Monaghan is now noted for its furniture-making, poultry and mushroom production. The locals are mostly involved in farming activities. Many of the country's chickens, ducks and even the rather exotic quail are produced for the table in County Monaghan. The people are fairly pros-perous, and agriculture has been boosted tremendously by membership of the EU. The moist and mild climate produces good grass for cattle rearing, and there are many small mixed farms. The population is about 51,000.

By air: Belfast and Dublin Airports are approximately 60 and 70 miles (96 and 112km) from Monaghan Town, respectively.

By rail: no rail service in County Monaghan.

By bus: frequent express buses from Dublin and County Donegal. Monaghan Bus Station, ✆ (047) 82377. Try also the private operators such as McConnors, ✆ (047) 82020. There are excellent local bus services to the smaller villages.

By car: local car hire from Monaghan Self-drive, Monaghan, ✆(047) 82865.

By bike: Clerkin Cycles, Park Street, Monaghan, ✆ (047) 81434

Tourist Information

Monaghan (Market House), ✆ (047) 81122, April to December.

Festivals

Late June/early July: Monaghan Town Festival. Contact the tourist tffice.

August: Welcome Home Festival, Carrickroe. Contact the tourist tffice.

September: Jazz and Blues Festival, Monaghan.

Monaghan Town

Monaghan Town is a good place from which to start one's tour of the county. Built on an old monastic site, this market town has some very fine urban architecture, especially round the market square, called the Diamond. The large **Market House** dates from 1792. There is also a surprising amount of red brick in the smaller streets off the square. It is a very busy, prosperous town with lots of shops and a good restaurant in the square. The small county **Museum and Gallery** (✆ *(047) 82928; adm free*) on Hill Street, on the west side of Market Street, founded in 1974, won the EEC museum award in 1980. The museum has amongst its treasure the Clogher Cross, a fine example of Early-Christian metalwork, with its highly decorative detail. There are objects collected from the nearby lake dwellings, including sandals and glass beads. There are also displays dealing with everything from lace-making to railways. The pedimented Market House holds the tourist office and a gallery with varying exhibitions. Monaghan Town becomes very crowded during the **festival** every year in July (the actual dates vary each year), which is all about Irish music, pipe and brass bands, and dance. The 1860s **Roman Catholic cathedral**, on the N2 to Dundalk, is very fine. It was designed by J. J. McCarthy, whose work is in the style of Pugin—though sadly a modern improvement has been to remove the original altarpiece.

The **Heritage Centre** in the St Louis Convent (*open every day except Wed, ✆ (047) 83529*) traces the fascinating history of the order throughout the world. The building itself is a fine example of convent architecture.

Three miles (4.2km) to the south, on the R189 to Newbliss, is Rossmore Park, a beautiful estate, with grounds that are open to the public; picnic sites, forest and lakeshore walks to be enjoyed (*car park fee*). Beyond, the roads radiate out across the country.

Castleblaney to Carrickmacross

To the southeast lies **Castleblaney,** on a narrow strip of land at the head of Lough Muckno. This is the county's largest stretch of water with perhaps the best coarse fishing there is, though all the lakes around here vie for that award. Founded in the reign of James I, Castleblaney is now a prosperous town. The plain Georgian Court House is rather fine, and in the wooded demesne of **Hope Castle**, there are nature trails and picnic site (*car park fee*). The castle once belonged to the 17th-century Blayneys, who developed the town, but was bought in the 1870s by Henry Hope, who is remembered as the owner of the Hope diamond—the largest blue diamond in the world, but reputed to bring ill-luck to its owner. The Hopes sold up in 1916.

Heading west from Castleblaney on the R183, meandering between the hills and fish-filled lakes, you come down to the town of **Ballybay**, on the shore of Lough Major. It is attractive with the Catholic and Church of Ireland church rising up, each on its own hill overlooking the grassy lakes and farmland. Ballybay was noted for its horse fair but sadly this horse fair, like many, has become defunct with the age of the tractor. Flax-growing and tanning used to be very important industries here, but now they too have virtually disappeared.

Fifteen miles (24km) south of Ballybay is **Carrickmacross**, a market town famous for its handmade lace, a cottage industry which was established at the beginning of the century. The very fine lace, applique work on tulle, is much sought after. Examples can be seen in the Lace Co-operative, in Market Place (✆ *(042) 62506*) and in the Clones Lace Gallery, the Diamond (✆ *(047) 51051*). The **Roman Catholic church** here has 10 splendid windows by the stained-glass artist Harry Clarke, whose work was inspired by the Pre-Raphaelite style. About 3 miles (4.8km) north on the Castleblaney Road at Donaghmoyne is **Mannan Castle**, a great hilltop moat and bailey (*free access*). It was constructed in the 12th century, and in 1224 it was encased in stone, some of which can still be seen. Southwest of here, close to Kingscourt is Dun a Ró Forest Park (*see* p.433), a great place for walks. The hill top car park gives good views towards the Mourne Mountains.

Inishkeen to Newbliss

About 5 miles (8km) to the southeast of Carrickmacross, near the border with County Louth, is the small village of **Inishkeen**. St Dega founded a monastery here in the 6th century, and you can see the remains of the old abbey and its 40ft (12m) high round tower with a raised doorway. The **Folk Museum** (*open May–Sept on Sun afternoons, 3–6*) deals with local history, folklife, and the old Great Northern Railway which ran through the village. Patrick Kavanagh was born here in 1904 and the museum devotes a section to their famous son. His masterly poem 'The Great Hunger' is a very sad and ironic evocation of rural life in Ireland.

To the west of the county there are hundreds of small roads and lanes to explore, with lakes caught between, like a spider's web in the morning dew. Quite near the County Cavan border on the R188 lies the small village of **Rockcorry** which has some fine 19th-century stone dwellings built for destitute widows. Here too, on the southwestern edge of the village, is the **Dartry Estate** with its open parkland, little lakes and much woodland, now all in the care of the Forestry Commission. It was once a beautiful estate but is less attractive now with massive scars from tree-felling and an air of neglect. There are picnic sites and forest walks, but the big house is a ruin. Nearby, lakes with names like Coragh, Mullanary and Drumlona are full of fish. Further west is the pretty riverside village of Newbliss, and 5 miles (8km) to the northeast again is the town of Clones. Between the two towns, near Kileevan, lies the country church of **Drumswords**. Dating from AD 750 it has now sadly fallen into disrepair, but one window still has the remains of fine basket tracery. South of Newbliss, just off the R189, is **Annaghmakerrigh House**, which was once the home of Sir Tyrone Guthrie (1900–71). Sir Tyrone, a famous theatre, television and radio producer, left his estate to the nation on condition it be used as a house for those who lived by the arts. Many artists and writers come to spend some time in such a congenial place. You may walk through the forest near the house, and down to the lake. It is very peaceful with pretty parkland and trees.

Clones was once linked to Monaghan by the old Ulster railway and Ulster canal. In the days before the First World War it was a thriving town, but it is now rather run-down, although it is still an important agricultural centre. Built on an ancient site, it has some fine remains, many of which have been whisked away to the National Museum. However, it retains an overgrown rath with three concentric earthworks, an abbey, a well-preserved 75ft (23m) round tower, and a finely carved Early-Christian sarcophagus, which is probably a MacMahon family tomb. In the graveyard are some fine 18th-century gravestones carved with skulls and cross bones. The key is available from Pattons pub nearby. Presiding over the triangular marketplace, perversely called the Diamond, stands an ancient, much-inscribed cross. It is carved with scenes from the Bible, and is probably 12th century. There are many fine old houses, particularly the imposing market house, now the library. Clones is the main centre of traditional hand-crocheted lace; you will be able to buy some in the local shops, although the lace-making is very much on the decline. Charles Gavan Duffy (1816–1903), one of the leaders of the Young Ireland movement of the 1840s and, later, Prime Minister of Victoria in Australia, was born here. So too was Barry McGuigan, the famous lightweight boxer.

Around Glaslough

Only a small part of the county lies to the north of Monaghan town. It gently rises up from the flood plain of the Blackwater, to the high moorland of Slieve Beagh. Near the village of Glaslough, on the shores of a small grey lake, is the **Castle Leslie** demesne. Sir Shane Leslie wrote superb ghost stories in the early decades of this century. The house, which is still lived in by the Leslie family, is Italianate and full of art treasures. It is possible to tour the house (*open June–Sept, Tues–Sun, 11–8; adm*). Nice tearoom in the conservatory. You can also go riding at the Castle Leslie Equestrian Centre (✆ *(047) 88109*).

To explore the tangle of little roads in this area known as Truagh Parish you will need a detailed and local map. To the west of Emyvale is the pretty **Lough More** with good stocks of brown trout, and the mountain scenery of Bragan where the local people go to cut their turf. Northeast of here is the townland of **Mullanacross**, and in the graveyard of the ruined and ancient Errigal church are some superbly carved 18th-century gravestones. They depict the stag, emblem of the McKennas, and biblical animals. Just across the road is a holy well, sacred to St Mellan, the patron saint of these parts. Further to the southeast you come across the deserted village of Mullan which has some fine stone-built houses.

Shopping

Lace: Crochet lace in Clones, at McDonalds Drapery, Fermanagh Street and at Clones Lace, ✆ (047) 51051. Carrickmacross lace from the Lace Co-operative, Carrickmacross, ✆ (042) 62085.

Delicacies: quail from Emyvale, County Monaghan, ✆ (047) 87578. Delicious vegetables and fruit in season from Hilton Biodynamic gardens, Scotshouse. Clones, ✆ (047) 51611. Will also deliver boxes of the best of their produce that day.

Activities

Fishing: good coarse fishing in the numerous lakes especially Lough Ooney, Muckno, and the lakes beside Ballybay. Game fishing on the Finn, Fane and Monaghan Blackwater Rivers. Contact Mr McMahon, Carrick Sports Shop, Carrickmacross, ✆ (042) 61714, for advice and bait. Also available from Clones Development Company, ✆ (074) 51718. Talbot Duffy (Ballybay area), ✆ (042) 41692.

Cross-country riding instruction: Greystones Equestrian Centre, Castle Leslie, Glaslough, ✆ (047) 88100.

Golf: Nuremore Golf Club, Carrickmacross, ✆ (042) 61438. Rossmore Park, ✆ (047) 81316 for 18 holes, and at Hilton Park for a nine-hole course.

Leisure park: Lough Muckno Leisure Park, Castleblaney is open to day visitors. Sailing, canoeing, tennis, swimming, fishing, and windsurfing, ✆ (042) 46356.

Where to Stay

expensive

Mr and Mrs Madden, **Hilton Park Country House**, Scotshouse, Clones, ✆ (047) 56007. This stately house set in the middle of luxuriant parkland is a superb place to stay if you are feeling extravagant. The rooms are furnished in keeping with the period of the house, and the food has a reputation for quality. Particularly notable are the fruit and vegetables from the biodynamic farm on the estate, which operates within its own eco-system. There are plans afoot to open this and the gardens to the public. Fishing and shooting in season, golf and lake-swimming are all available to the guests. **Nuremore Hotel**, Carrickmacross, ✆ (042) 61438. One of the best places to stop for the night when travelling from Donegal to Dublin. Well equipped and clean.

The **Hillgrove**, Monaghan, ✆ (047) 82780. Has recently undergone a major facelift. Of the same stable as the Slieve Russell in Cavan. **Shirley Arms**, Main Street, Carrickmacross, ✆ (042) 61209. Hotel in the town centre.

inexpensive

Pillar House, Glaslough, ✆ (047) 88125. Simple hotel. **Ashleigh House**, 37 Dublin Street, Monaghan, ✆ (047) 82298. 2★ hotel. Mrs O'Grady, **Glynch House**, Newbliss, Clones, ✆ (047) 54045. **Creighton Hotel**, Clones, ✆ (047) 51055. Family-run traditional-style hotel.

self catering

Youth hostel: Lough Muckno Adventure Centre, Castleblaney, ✆ (042) 46356.

Eating Out

expensive

Hilton Park Country House (*see* above) The Nuremore Hotel, Carrickmacross, ✆ (042) 61438. Showy food.

moderate

The **Four Seasons Hotel**, Coolshannagh, ✆ (047) 81888. Comfortable and friendly. **Westenra Hotel**, The Diamond, Monaghan, ✆ (047) 81517. Popular locally.

inexpensive

Andy's Restaurant, Market Street, Monaghan, ✆ (047) 82277. All manner of foods cooked well. **Beaghbarton Manor**, Country Guest House, Ballybay, ✆ (047) 81008. Good menu. **Mamo's Tea Shop**, Clones Lace Gallery, The Diamond, Clones.

The Province of Leinster

Leinster (*Cuíge Laighean*) has always had a reputation for wealth, because of its fertile land. Over the centuries, aristocrats lived on estates which were within a day's ride from Dublin; the city, which is the symbolic centre of the province, grew larger as industry and people were attracted to it. The province includes the ancient Kingdom of Meath, and its pre-Christian kings were the most powerful in the land. Each successive wave of invaders since the Vikings have founded towns and built themselves strong castles in this beautiful and varied region.

It has a long sea coast, stretching from Dundalk Bay in County Louth to Hook Head in County Wexford. Important ports and trading places grew up along it, but Dublin, which became the centre of British rule, has always maintained its position as the most important. Today, the population of Dublin and its swelling suburbs is one million and a half, so the farms of the province are engaged in supplying the huge city market with milk, vegetables, cattle and poultry. Brewing, food processing and other industrial ventures have grown up in the Greater Dublin area, but the rest of Leinster is comparatively rural, and the locals are either farmers or white-collar workers who commute to town. The transport network between the main towns is very efficient but, even so, the most southeasterly tip of Leinster, Hook Head, is at least three hours' drive from Dublin.

The southeast coast has a reputation for being sunny, although the climate is fairly similar all over Ireland. Dublin is considered very cold and damp in winter! Tourist facilities are generally very good, because restaurants and lodgings have responded to the sophisticated tastes of the Dubliners. In fact, most travellers who come to Leinster head straight for Dublin City—the magnet which promises the most fun, history, culture and comfort. They might make a few sallies out into the countryside, perhaps to the beautiful Glendalough in County Wicklow; or tour the fascinating Boyne Valley burial grounds, or visit Tara in County Meath, the seat of the high kings. But Dublin City draws them all back, and the rest of Leinster pales into insignificance.

If you arrive at Rosslare in County Wexford, the province gets a fairer chance of being explored. There are many beautiful places in Counties Wexford, Wicklow, Kilkenny and Carlow. The centuries of history are marked by castles, monasteries and the more mysterious landmarks left behind by the Celts and those who went before. Also very charming are the lordly mansions built by the Anglo-Irish. Leinster has more than its fair share of them and many are open to the public. Castletown in County Kildare and Russborough in County Wicklow are the most impressive. The Bog of Allen, which takes up most of County Kildare and

County Offaly, is counterbalanced by the gentle rolling hills of the Blackstairs. The highest peak in the range, Mount Leinster (2610ft/ 796m), gives you a wonderful view and some exciting ridge-climbing. The spiky mountains and rounded summits of the Wicklow range, the bogland and mountain pools make a happy contrast to the noise and crowds of Dublin. On a clear, blustery day it is not difficult to imagine yourself a million miles from civilization, though the city is only an hour's drive away.

County Meath and County Louth

These two counties share many characteristics. Both are made up of rich farming land; both have some very exciting Neolithic, Celtic and Early-Christian remains. Both were extensively settled by the Anglo-Normans, who built some fascinating castles and monasteries.

County Meath is drained by the River Boyne and its tributary, the Blackwater, and is planted with fine deciduous trees. Cattle and horses move about the fields of well-kept estates, and there are many big houses, built during the 18th century. The River Boyne is wide and slow and very beautiful. It is famous for the great Battle of Boyne in 1690, when James II, relying on French and Irish forces to help him regain his English throne, was outnumbered and outflanked by the Protestant William of Orange. The low hills of Slane and Tara give lovely views over the countryside, and are vibrant with the memories of an ancient Ireland. Both figure in the mythology of the country and have been important since the Bronze Age.

County Louth shares part of the Boyne Valley, and enters the sea at Drogheda. It too has its well-planted estates, especially on the grassy plain around Ardee. But it has a wilder side, too. Going north are the heathery slopes of the Cooley or Carlingford peninsula; and the rocky coastline of Clogherhead lies to the east.

Both counties have experienced a huge rise in population in the last few decades, as they are within commuting distance of Dublin. Luckily, you can almost avoid the traffic on the major roads as there are lots of tiny country routes with hardly a soul on them.

History

The ancient history of this area is rich and colourful; it has Tara and the passage graves of Newgrange. Since the Anglo-Norman invasion in the 13th century, events have followed a similar pattern to that of the rest of Leinster. The Normans built themselves well-fortified castles, and later English settlers made themselves pleasant estates and farms amongst the rich agricultural land. The most famous confrontation between the Jacobite and Williamite armies took place along the Boyne river in 1690. Louth and Meath suffered marginally less than others during the famine years of the 1840s, although as was the case all over Ireland, the fate of the peasants depended to a great extent on whether or not they had a 'good' landlord. Today this area is prosperous with industry in the towns, whilst many of the locals in the countryside work in the horse-breeding industry.

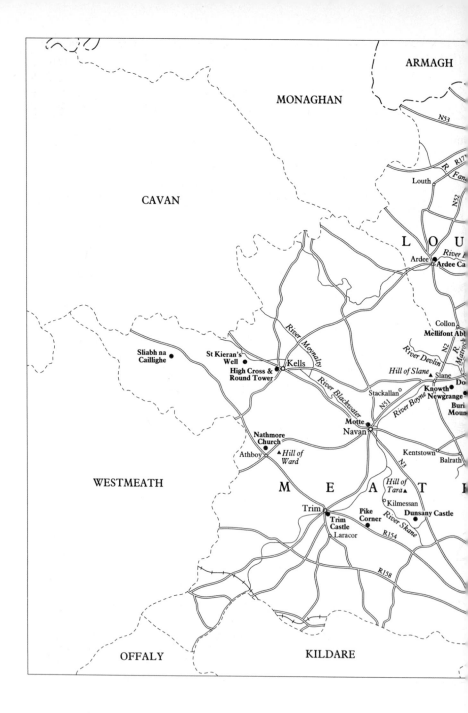

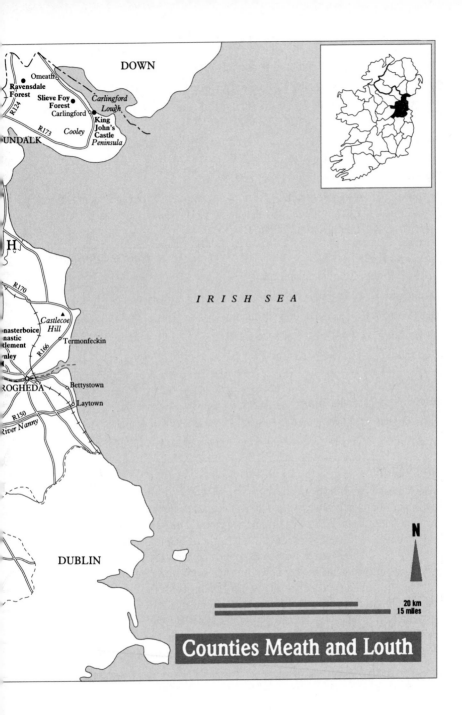

DOWN

Omeath
Ravensdale
Forest
Slieve Foy
Forest
Carlingford
R124
R173
Cooley
DUNDALK

Carlingford
Lough
King
John's
Castle
Peninsula

IRISH SEA

R170

Castlecoe
Hill
monasterboice
monastic
settlement
monley
R166
Termonfeckin

DROGHEDA
Bettystown
Laytown
R150
River Nanny

DUBLIN

N

20 km
15 miles

Counties Meath and Louth

By air: to Dublin International Airport.

By sea: Dun Laoghaire, Dublin and Larne ferry ports.

By rail: The main Dublin to Belfast railway line runs through Drogheda, (041) 38749.

By bus: Expressway buses run hourly to Navan, Drogheda and Slane. For local bus details ring Drogheda, ✆ (041) 35023; and Dundalk, ✆ (042) 34075.

By car: Practical Car Rental, ✆ (041) 36018.

By bike: The Raleigh Rent-a-Bike network operates here. Your local contacts are P. J. Carolan, 77 Trinity Street, Drogheda, ✆ (041) 38242; and Clarke's Sports Den, Trimgate Street, Navan, ✆ (046) 21130.

Trim, ✆ (046) 37111, summer only.

Mullingar, ✆ (044) 48650, all year.

Drogheda, ✆ (041) 37070, June to August.

Newgrange, ✆ (041) 24274, May to October.

Dundalk, ✆ (042) 35484, all year.

July: Vintage car rally, Trim.

Late August: Carlingford Oyster Festival, ✆ (042) 73259 for details.

Mid August: Moynalty Steam Threshing Festival, ✆ (046) 44390 for details.

The Boyne Valley

The Boyne Valley is gloriously green, with a crumbling estate at every corner of the road, and ancient tumuli at every curve of the river. The valley was the centre of power in Ireland for thousands of years. The wealthy and organized farmers of Neolithic times built their burial chambers at Newgrange, Dowth, and Tara long before the Egyptians built the pyramids. When the Celts arrived in waves, approximately between 500 and 100 BC, they recognized these burial mounds as very powerful and assimilated them into their culture. The Hill of Tara became a royal enclosure, whilst the burial chambers along the Boyne became the dwelling places of the Celtic god of love, Aonoenghus. It would be fun to plan your tour of the Boyne Valley as a bicycle tour. You can easily cover all the ancient places and monasteries in a few days at a leisurely pace on a bicycle. In the summer it is the most enjoyable way to travel along the country lanes laced with cow parsley.

Kells and Trim

Kells is not actually in the Boyne Valley, but in the wooded valley of the Blackwater. The village is extremely pretty, and has a vast wealth of history behind it. Most people who come to Ireland go to see *The Book of Kells*, now in Trinity College, Dublin. The beauty and richness of this illuminated 8th-century manuscript never cease to amaze. **Kells Monastery** in which it was so beautifully made is no more, but there are many fine ruins to contemplate. The High King of Ireland, Dermot (or *Diarmuid*) granted this defensive fort to St Columba in AD 550. (It is said to have been the residence of Cormac MacArt, a high king during the 3rd century AD.) St Columba (or *Colmcille* in Gaelic) was the princely monk who founded the first monastery in Iona in AD 563, and whose missionary zeal subsequently converted most of Scotland to Christianity. The religious centre he established became very important, and in AD 807 the Columba monks moved back here from Iona after being repeatedly pillaged by the Vikings. Today, in the graveyard of the Church of Ireland church, you can see a 9th-century round tower, which is in a good state of preservation; and the wonderful scriptural stone cross of St Patrick and St Columba, opposite the tower. St Columba's house is nearby. The circular ditch around the now-ruined monastery is reflected in the modern-day street patterns. The round tower was built as a belfry and to store precious things; most probably as a safeguard against the Vikings. Round towers are a uniquely Irish form of architecture: built of stone, tall and slender, with a conical top. The door is usually about 12ft (3.5m) from the ground. The tower at Kells has some dark associations as a claimant to the high kingship of Ireland was murdered in it in 1076. In the town is a 10th-century **market cross** which was removed from the graveyard; in the 1798 Rising it was used as a gallows. Its top has been broken off, but the fine carving of the scriptural scenes makes it well worth studying. On the head and shaft are scenes representing the Crucifixion, the Resurrection, Daniel in the lions' den, and the Fall of Man. The **high cross** of St Patrick and Columba in the graveyard is probably older. This has a wealth of decoration and another Crucifixion scene. St Columba's house is a high-roofed oratory with very early barrel-vaulting, and is similar to St Kevin's house at Glendalough in County Wicklow. It was probably built in the 9th century and is roofed with stone, the walls being at least 3ft (90cm) thick. Beside it is a well. A key may be obtained from Miss Carpenter, Church Lane. There is a replica of *The Book of Kells* in the modern Church of Ireland church, the tower of which dates from 1578. There is an information centre in the gallery of the church, which is open from March to November. It is worth making the extra effort to go to **St Ciaran's**, 3 miles (4.8km) away on the south bank of the Blackwater, where there is a very attractive holy well. You may only drink from it, for if you wash in it the well would lose its holy properties—a rather sane law of hygiene!

Trim is the usual starting point for a tour of the Boyne Valley. It was the capital of the Kingdom of Meath, which was granted to Hugh de Lacy by Henry II at the Norman Conquest. You should approach it from the Dublin road (R154) if you can, for suddenly all the ruins, towers and moats through which the River Boyne winds burst upon you. **King John's Castle**, built in 1172 by Hugh de Lacy, is the largest Anglo-Norman castle in Ireland. This imposing, well-preserved ruin dominates the town, covers 2 acres (0.8ha) and includes a massive square keep, with side turrets in the middle of each face, and a huge curtain wall with circular towers at regular intervals. There are two gateways, one of which still has a drawbridge, portcullis and barbican. The castle was at the centre of every battle during the Middle Ages and at one time the future King of England, afterwards Henry V, and the Duke of Gloucester were imprisoned here by Richard II. The first Duke of Wellington went to school in Talbot Castle, off High Street. His father, the 1st Earl of Mornington, built a castle nearby which is now completely ruined, and there is a handsome 15th-century tower attached to the 19th-century **Church of Ireland cathedral**. The tourist information, a Genealogical Centre, ✆ (064) 36633 and an audio visual presentation on Medieval Trim, ✆ (064) 31238, are all in Mill Street. Also on the outskirts of Trim, on the Kildalkey road, is **Butterstream Garden** (*open May–Sept, daily except Monday, 2–6pm; adm; ✆ (046) 36017*). It has been described as the Sissinghurst of Ireland. Structured and imaginative, it is planned as a series of rooms with a wonderful display of colour through spring and summer.

About two miles (3.2km) away is the small village of **Laracor**, where Jonathan Swift and Stella lived for a while; he must have been a curious rector, at least not the sort the local gentry felt at ease with!

Tara

The **Hill of Tara** is to be found on a small road off the R154, just south of Trim. The turn for it is known as Pike's Corner and you pass through the hamlet of Kilmessan. All that is left of **Tara**, the ancient palace of the high kings of Ireland, is a series of earthworks on a green hill in green fields, so do not be disappointed; the wooden buildings have long disappeared. It seems to have been abandoned sometime after Christianity came to Ireland in about the 6th century AD. According to tradition, Tara was, from the beginning of history, the seat of kings who controlled at least the northern half of the county. It is central to many legends and mentioned in early annals, sagas and genealogies such as the 12th-century *Book of Leinster*. One of the characters frequently mentioned in them is Cormac MacArt, a semi-mythical high king who is associated with the legendary time of Tara's greatest fame in the 3rd century AD. Shut your eyes and imagine the pagan rites which were enacted, and later the great triennial *feis*, where tribal disputes were settled and laws were made. The *Book of Leinster* describes Tara in its heyday as being full of warriors who combined fierceness with elegance; the great wooden buildings resounded with the clamour of people going about their business, with music, feasting and the whinnying of the Fianna's sleek horses. The pastures around would have been thick with herds of cattle representing the wealth and importance of the high king. (So many of the legendary battles seem to have centred round a bull or a prize cow.) The Great Assembly Hall was built by the Irish 'King Solomon', Cormac, who presided over the massive banquets and laid down lists of protocol—even meat was portioned out according to rank: the king, queen and nobles of the first rank ate ribs of beef, buffoons got shoulder fat, and chess-players shins; harpers and drummers got pigs' shoulders as their portion, whilst historians were entitled to the haunches!

The most important of the earthworks that remain are the Mound of the Hostages, Cormac's House, the Banquet Hall, and the *Lialh Fáil* (the coronation stone of the ancient kings). Daniel O'Connell, 'the Great Liberator' (1775–1847), who won Catholic emancipation through peaceful means, held one of his monster meetings here in 1845 when he was campaigning for the repeal of the Union with Britain. About a million people turned up to hear him speak. The legendary Fianna, who formed an élite band of fighting men in the service of the high king, must have been stirring in their graves in sympathy. There is an awful modern statue of St Patrick. Sixty-odd years ago, the whole place was dug up by enthusiastic but misled British Israelites, who believed that the Ark of the Covenant was buried in one of the large mounds. They got this information from a second-hand bookshop in the Charing Cross Road, and in those days no one did anything to stop them.

Navan District

Nearby on the N3 is the busy town of **Navan**, which is Norman in origin. In **St Mary's Catholic Church** there is a good wooden carving of Christ crucified dating from the 18th century. The sculptor, Edward Smyth, would have been at some risk carving such a subject during those penal times. The **Motte of Navan** dominates the town and the crossing on the River Blackwater. It is probably a natural mound of gravel deposited in an Ice Age, though legend says it was the burial tomb of a queen. The Norman baron of Navan built a bailey on top of it. There is a very pretty walk to Slane on the towpath of the old Navan to Drogheda Canal. It can be walked very easily to Stackallen where there is a youth hostel. The entrance to the walk is through a gateway on the left side of the Boyne road which leads from the market square. In this area are the pretty country roads leading to Balrath, Black Lion and the attractive Church of Ireland church at Kentstown, just off the R153.

Athboy, to the west of Navan, was founded by the Plunketts, a Norman family who produced St Oliver Plunkett (1625–81), a wise and brave Archbishop of Armagh who was hanged, drawn and quartered at Tyburn, after being falsely accused of complicity in the popish plot of Titus Oates in England in 1678. About 2½ miles (4km) outside Athboy is **Rathmore Church**, which was built in the 15th century by a Plunkett. It has fine stone carvings and monuments, and a fragmentary 16th-century cross. **Dunsany**, near the Hill of Tara, is the family house of the Catholic branch of the Plunketts. They are an example of a Catholic Norman family, Barons of the Pale, who survived the vicissitudes of Irish political life because one branch of the family was Protestant and protected their interests. The **Church of St Nicholas** in the demesne of **Dunsany Castle** is a 15th-century ruin (*open to the public in the summer months, mornings only, ℃ (046) 31845*). It has a beautifully sculptured fort with the figures of angels, apostles and saints on the basin and shafts. The castle, a 19th-century neo-Gothic mansion, is still lived in by the Lords Dunsany. Lord Dunsany (1878–1957) wrote some very fine novels in which he explores his love for Ireland, its vanishing ways, and the beauty of its countryside. Try to get hold of *The Curse of the Wise Woman* and *My Ireland*, both now out of print. He was a patron of the arts and discovered Francis Ledwidge, the soldier poet from Slane, and encouraged Anne Crone, who wrote a magnificent novel about the Fermanagh countryside and the tragedy of a mixed marriage, called *Bridie Steen*.

Slane, just northeast of Navan on the N2 and the River Boyne, once belonged to other Barons of the Pale, the Flemings. The Flemings lost out when they supported James II in the Williamite wars of the 1690s; their lands were forfeited, and a County Donegal family, the Conynghams, were awarded them in their stead. Burton Conyngham built a picture-book Gothic castle with fine gates in the 1780s, which when seen from the Navan–Slane road as you cross the River Boyne looks dreamlike. The present Marquis of Conyngham traditionally opened up **Slane Castle** for tours, wedding receptions and major rock concerts by stars such as Bowie, Springstein and The Rolling Stones although this has tailed off somewhat due to local complaints. It was designed by James Watt and Francis Johnston and has some magnificent rooms and a splendid circular library. Unfortunately, the castle and grounds are closed at the time of writing due to extensive fire damage in 1991. They will re-open after restoration; check the tourist office for details.

Look out for the the four Georgian houses in the village arranged in a square. They were built for the four spinster sisters of one of the Conynghams who could no longer stand their inquisitive chattering and quarrelling. They detested each other but could not bear to be parted, so he thought of that perfect solution; you can imagine them watching each

other through lace curtains. A few hundred yards outside Slane, on the Ardee road (N2), is a very ancient site known as the **Hill of Slane**, famous in legend and as a site of early Christianity. St Patrick is said to have kindled a fire here in the 5th century AD. The Druids forbade any but themselves to light a fire there, and by doing so St Patrick brought himself to the notice of the High King of Tara and converted him! The present monastic remains date from the 15th and 16th centuries. Some of the Flemings, Barons of Slane, are buried there. On the Drogheda road (N51) just outside Slane is the **Francis Ledwidge Cottage and Museum** [*open Mon–Sat, 10–6, Sun 10–5; ✆ (041) 24285*]. Ledwidge was a labourer who wrote fine poetry, and although he was a Nationalist he joined up to fight in the First World War—'neither for principle nor a people nor a law, but for the fields along the Boyne, for the birds and the blue skies over them'. He was killed in Belgium in 1917. If you take the Slane–Drogheda Road (N51), and about 2½ miles (4km) from Dowth turn left off the main road, you will pass **Townley Hall**, a fine Georgian house, now attached to Trinity College, Dublin. There is a lovely forest trail and walk in the grounds. Further on at the bridge at **Oldbridge**, you can follow the signposted route of the Battle of the Boyne, 1690; a pleasant riverside drive.

Newgrange

On the other side of the river, along a twisting road, you will come to the burial sites known as *Brugh na Boinne*, the Palace of the Boyne. (This piece of land is enclosed by the Boyne on three sides.) There are at least 15 passage graves from Neolithic times, some of them unexcavated. The three main sites are at Newgrange, Knowth and Dowth, and they are very well-signposted. It is fascinating to go to **Newgrange** [*open mid-Mar–May, 10–5; June–Sept, 10–7; mid-Sept–Oct, Mon–Sat, 2–5; more limited times during rest of the year; adm; ✆ (041) 24488*], its mound sparkling with white quartz pebbles like a beacon in the landscape. In the tourist shop at the car park there is an exhibition of the *Brugh na Boinne*; try to see it after your tour of the grave because it has most of the answers you will be provoked into asking by the sophistication of the building. And try to avoid going at the weekend in midsummer when the place is crowded: you cannot appreciate the age or the impressive atmosphere when you are squashed up sideways against a sacred stone—decorated with a lozenge or not! The guide gives you a very polished talk. Two of the most impressive facts amongst all the conjecturing that goes on about this site is that the corbelled roof of the chamber has kept the place dry for 45 centuries; and that it was designed so that the sun casts its rays inside the mound over the winter solstice.

Dowth [*organised tours between May and October, ✆ (041) 24824*] has not yet been tamed to satisfy the curiosity of the inactive, it is on private land and not open to the public. If you do get permission to explore it from the OPW, (Office of Public Works) ✆ (041) 24488, be prepared for a certain amount of scrambling if you want to see the two tombs inside and the early Christian souterrain at the entrance.

Knowth [*open May to October, 10–5; mid-June–mid Sept, 10–6.30*] has wonderfully lavish kerbstones placed round the mound. They are decorated with spirals and lozenges. Only part of the site is open to the public whilst archaeological excavations are carried out.

Close by at the Newgrange Open Farm, ✆ (041) 24119, you can get a good cuppa and a fascinating tractor-trailer ride around the 333-acre farm. It has some satellite tombs of Newgrange itself.

Laytown to Monasterboice

Between Drogheda and Dublin are numerous beach resorts. The only really noteworthy one is Laytown/Bettystown where the **Strand Races** are held one day a year, either in June, July or August. There is some speculation at the time of writing whether they will be run again in 1995 as there was an accident in 1994 and two horses were killed. Ring the Drogheda Tourist Office to confirm dates and times. If you want to find a quiet, undiscovered village along the coast make for **Termonfeckin** with its own 10th-century high cross. From here you can easily visit Mellifont and Monasterboice, two ancient ecclesiastical centres.

Mellifont Abbey (*open mid-June–mid-Sept, daily, 9.30–6.30; mid-Sept–Oct, daily, 10–5; 1 May–mid-June, Tues–Sat, 9.30–5.30, Sun, 2–5; adm, free during winter*) is a gracious ruin 6 miles (9.6km) west of Drogheda. It was built in 1142 by the first Cistercians to come to Ireland from Clairvaux in France. Their arrival and the new ideas in architecture and church organization introduced here were the result of the efforts of St Malachy, who as Archbishop of Armagh did much to bring the Irish Church more in line with Rome. There is an interesting lavabo, a few arches of a Romanesque cloister, and a 14th-century chapter house. The Cistercians are still in the area at New Mellifont. **Monasterboice**, a 5th-century monastic settlement, contains the most perfect high cross, the **Cross of Muireadach**, made in the early 10th century. Nearly every inch of the cross is covered in scenes from the Bible—the only way the poor and illiterate could 'read' the scriptures. The West Cross is almost as handsome and less squat. You can climb the damaged round tower that must have been the tallest in the country in its time. One of the best things about Irish ruins is that you are not accompanied everywhere by officious guides or directed by smart painted notices to 'keep off the grass' or 'away from the edge', so you still feel the spirit of adventure.

Drogheda to Ardee

Drogheda conjures up images of the cruelty of Cromwell, for which he is notorious in Ireland, but it has been a famous place in Ireland since the Normans settled there in around 1180, and today it is bustling with energy. The old Drogheda Society have adapted some of the buildings of **The Millmount**, an 18th-century military barracks on a motte, as a museum (*open all year, Tues–Sun, 2–6 in the summer and weekend afternoons in the winter; adm; ✆ (041) 33097*). It has many interesting exhibits including 18th-century guild banners, a 1912–22 room, information on the old industries of spinning, weaving, brewing, shoe and rope making. **St Lawrence's Gate**, a twin-towered, four-storey gate stands on the road going to Baltray. It is the best preserved of all the remaining gates of this once-walled town. Off West Street in the **Church of St Peter** is the preserved head of St Oliver Plunkett, Archbishop of Armagh, who, sadly, became caught up in the panic of 'the Popish Plot' fabricated by Titus Oates in 1678. The 'Plot' was a smoke-screen manufactured by powerful men in England to discomfit Charles II and his Catholic heir, James II. Plunkett was drawn into it because his fearless pursuit of his duties in a country full of treachery and unease, where Catholicism was basically outlawed. He was canonized in 1975, the first new Irish saint since St Lawrence O'Toole more than seven hundred years ago. Legal history in relation to Irish historic buildings was made here in 1989. Two of the finest 18th-century buildings in Drogheda were tumbled in spite of a court injunction to prevent the demolition; it took place early on a Sunday morning. The judge then issued a High Court order preventing any further demolition, and requiring the owners to rebuild and restore the buildings using any materials that could be salvaged. The developers who were responsible for such senseless destruction desperately tried to get around the law, but were impelled to start salvage work. You can see the site on Lawrence Street, where these magnificent buildings stood—one the town house of Lord Justice Singleton, the other Dr Clarke's Free School. Both were probably designed by Sir Edward Lovett Pearce in the 1730s. Perhaps the firm stance taken by the judge against this blatant disregard for the law may help preserve other historic buildings in Ireland, although the trade in beautiful carved fireplaces, staircases and mouldings, taken from old buildings to be sold in England or America, is allowed to flourish, as there are few conservation laws.

Collon, a small place on the N2 south of Ardee, has a Church of Ireland church which is a miniature pastiche of King's College Chapel, Cambridge. It was at **Ardee**, now a very attractive market town, that Cú Chulainn slew his friend Ferdia in a four-day combat to stop the raiding party stealing the Bull of Cooley for Queen Maeve. Ardee was an outpost of the Pale, and often used by the English as a base for attacking Ulster; that is why you will find two old castles along the main street. One of which, Ardee Castle, is under restoration to house a new museum and gift shop.

The Cooley Peninsula

The Cooley Peninsula in the extreme north of County Louth is one of the most beautiful, untouched places in Ireland. First, go to **Carlingford** which looks across its lough to the Mourne Mountains. This town is full of castellated buildings; it is said to have possessed 32 'castles' in the days of the Pale, when almost every house on the border was fortified in some way. The ruins of the Anglo-Norman **King John's Castle**, with arrow slits in the outer walls, is impressive. It was built in 1210 by John de Courcy and is similar to Carrickfergus Castle in County Antrim. The Norsemen founded this town, and it was a place of great strategic importance in medieval times. Nowadays, it is nothing more than a little village with a 16th-century arched **Tholsel**, a **mint**, and **Taaffe's Castle**, which is multi-storied and attached to a modern house. The Holy Trinity Centre in a restored medieval church provides more local history.

You can have a marvellous walk across the **Cooley Mountains** along the slopes of Slieve Foye and Ravensdale Forest. You will find Slieve Foye 2 miles (3.2km) northeast of Carlingford, on the R173 to Omeath. Omeath has a ferry to Warrenpoint in County Down and fishermen sell delicious shellfish in stalls by the boat. This is an area associated with the great story of the Bull of Cooley known as the *Tain Saga*, which is the oldest vernacular epic in western literature, and was written down by monks in various versions from Early-Christian times to the medieval period (*see* **Old Gods and Heroes**, p.579). Queen Maeve or Medb of Connacht wanted to outdo her husband, who had a fine bull, and decided to raid Ulster for the prize Bull of Cooley. Her rivalry bought about great grief and division, though the stories contained in the *Tain Saga* are full of fantastic heroism and impossible deeds. Cú Chulainn defends Ulster, and through his 'warp spasm' is able to change from a beardless youth to a warrior whose fury and blood-lust knows no barrier.

Seek out **Faughart Hill** which is just north of Dundalk, signposted a few miles off the Dundalk to Newry Road on the left. This is where Edward Bruce was killed in battle in 1318. He had been sent by his brother, Robert Bruce, King of Scotland, to make trouble for the Anglo-Normans in Ireland to take the pressure off him. From here, the whole of Leinster spreads out below you. You can see the Wicklow Hills rippling across the plain to join the Slieve Bloom and the Cooley Hills behind. This part too is touched by the splendour of myth—Cú Chulainn was born in these heather-coloured hills. In Faughart Graveyard, there is a **shrine to St Brigid**, patroness of Ireland. St Brigid is a semi-mythical figure who has pagan associations; she was a powerful Celtic goddess who was responsible for sacred wells, livestock, the home, poetry and learning. When the Christian missionaries arrived, they christianized Brigid, made her a saint, and her feast day was put on 1 February, which was the pagan Celtic Festival of **Imbolc** (Lactation of Ewes). It was in such a way that the Christian monks were able to make themselves and their religion acceptable in Ireland. Her shrine is very garish and consists of a well, St Brigid's Pillar and a stone surrounding a bank. People still come here to do stations—prayers centring around devotion to the saint.

Shopping

Flour: White River Mill, Dunleen, ✆ (041) 51141. Excellent freshly ground wholemeal flour.

Butter/cheese: Tara Cheese, Dunbin, Knockbridge, ✆ (042) 35654. The wares include lovely rich and creamy butter and cheese.

Woollens: Boinn Knits, Balgarthern.

Furniture:John McGrane, Delvin Farm Antique Galleries, Gormanstown, ✆ (01) 412285.

Crafts: Mary McDonnell, Slane, ✆ (041) 24722 and Elaine Hanrahan for jewellery at the Millmount Craft Centre, Drogheda, ✆ (041) 38385.

Wooden items: David Cornford, Enfield, ✆ (0405) 41306.

Charcuterie: The Continental Meat Centre, 20 Clanbrassil Street, Dundalk, ✆ (042) 32829.

Activities

Fishing: For salmon fishing on the river Glyde, contact Bellingham Castle, Castlebellingham, ✆ (042) 72176. For

salmon and brown trout fishing on the River Blackwater and River Boyne, contact Clarke's Sports Shop. Boat hire for Carlingford Loch contact Peadar Elmore, North Commons, Carlingford, ✆ (042) 73237. Beach fishing for bass and flounder at Laytown.

Pony-trekking: Bachelor's Lodge Riding Centre, Kells Rd, Navan, ✆ (046) 21736. For beach rides on Laytown Strand, try Briarleas School of Equitation, Mosney House, Mosney, ✆ (043) 29333. The school also arranges six-day trails through the Boyne Valley, stopping at all the major sights. These operate April to September.

Hunting: in Meath, over deep ditches and banks with the Ballymacad Hunt, near Oldcastle, ✆ (049) 41573; or with the Meath Hunt, ✆ (0405) 55210; or the Tara Harriers, ✆ (046) 21474. There is also the Louth Hunt, ✆ (041) 53348.

Golf: at Laytown, ✆ (041) 27170; and the Royal Tara Golf Club, Ballinter, ✆ (046) 25244.

Walking: the Tain trail, an 18-mile (30km) circular signposted route through the Cooley Mountains. Ask for Bord Fáilte information leaflet no.26 at any tourist office.

Where to Stay

expensive

Ballymascanlon Hotel, Dundalk, ✆ (042) 71124. Country-house mansion, much favoured by the clergy for ecumenical conferences. In the grounds is a fine example of a portal dolmen. Jim and Linda Connolly, **Red House**, Ardee, County Louth, ✆ (041) 53523. Attractive Georgian house in lovely parkland. Very well-run with comfortable rooms. Indoor heated swimming pool and sauna.

Mountainstown, Castletown, Kilpatrick, Navan, ✆ (046) 54154. Beautiful 17th-century house on wooded estate; peacocks on the lawn. Delicious food. Minimum stay 2 nights.

moderate

Old Mill House, Julianstown, ✆ (041) 29133. Converted flour mill on the River Nanny. Pleasing atmosphere and private fishing for residents. **Ardboyne Hotel**, Dublin Road, Navan, ✆ (046) 23119. Modern and friendly. **Conyngham Arms**, Slane, ✆ (041) 24155. Snug, friendly hotel right in the middle of the village. **The Gables**, Dundalk Rd, Ardee, ✆ (041) 53789. Simple accommodation with a fine restaurant serving good hearty cooking. The **Station House Hotel**, Killmessan, ✆ (046) 25239. A converted 1850 railway station. Very pleasant. Mrs Naper, **Loughcrew House**, Old Castle, ✆ (049) 41356. Delightful country house with woodland walks, tennis, fishing and riding all on hand. Good food. Minimum stay 2 nights.

Carlingford Centre and Holiday Hostel, Carlingford, ✆ (042) 73100. Cheap and basic. Mrs Mullin, **Lennoxbrook House**, Carnaross, Kells, ✆ (046) 45902. Nice old farmhouse, welcoming family, rooms full of pretty antique furniture, and good food. Trout fishing locally.

self-catering

Kells Hostel, **Carrick House**, Kells, ✆ (046) 40100; **Carlingford Adventure Centre and Hostel**, Tholsel Street, Carlingford, ✆ (042) 73100. For cottages to rent near Laytown contact **Liz Lyons**, ✆ (041) 28104.

Eating Out

There are a few excellent eating places in this region but also a mass of vile hotel menus and take-aways.

luxury

Dunderry Lodge Restaurant, Dunderry, Navan, ✆ (046) 31671. This little restaurant has acquired a tremendous reputation, and Dubliners think nothing of driving out to it for a meal. The restaurant is in converted farm buildings, and everything is just right with good décor, Mediterranean-influenced food and wine.

expensive

Ballymascanlon Hotel, Dundalk, ✆ (042) 71124. Irish and French cooking. **The Gables**, Dundalk Road, Ardee, ✆ (041) 53789. Small restaurant with an imaginative menu with large country portions.

moderate

Old Mill Hotel, Julianstown, ✆ (041) 29133. Irish cooking.

The **Buttergate Restaurant and Wine Bar**, Millmount, Drogheda, ✆ (041) 34759. Good plain food made more sophisticated by imaginative sauces. Open for lunch and dinner. **Forge Gallery Restaurant**, Collon, ✆ (041) 26272. Delightful little restaurant which combines with an antique shop. Dinner only and particularly good for vegetarians. The **Station House Hotel**, Kilmessan, ✆ (046) 25239. Dinner and Sunday lunch. Good tasty food. Fish, lamb, and beef cooked with herbs and sauces in this former train station. **Hudson's**, Railway Street, Navan, ✆ (046) 29231. Casual place with spicy chicken wings, burgers and pasta topping the menu. Open for dinner only. The **Wasteground** restaurant, Bettystown, ✆ (041) 28251. Offering seafood and soups at dinner time only. **Jordan's Pub and Bistro**, Newry Street, Carlingford, (042) 73223. Good simple cooking using the best of local ingredients including pig's trotters. There is also an early bird menu available. The **Coastguard Restaurant**, Bettystown, ✆ (041) 28251. Right on the beach with pleasantly simple food. Seafood, fowl and pork. A very good value supper and, later, a more sophisticated and expensive menu. *Evenings only: between 4.30 and 7.30pm.*

Newgrange Farm and Coffee Shop, ✆ (041) 24119. Homemade soups and sandwiches. **Bounty Pub**, Bridge Street, Trim. The oldest pub serving snacks in the county. **Kieran's Deli and Restaurant**, 15 West Street, Drogheda, ✆ (041) 38728. Delicious ham, and smoked salmon.

County Longford

For the coarse fisherman, this flat watery county has a particular attraction. It is right in the middle of Ireland, and lies in the basin of the Shannon River. Many small streams make their way westwards through the county to join the Shannon, and the place is resplendent with lakes: Lough Gowna in the north and Lough Kinale near Granard. Both have some pretty islands, and the county is well planted with trees.

The county also has strong associations for the literary. Oliver Goldsmith (1728–24) was born in Pallas. He wrote 'The Deserted Village', the classic poem so beloved of anthologies, and the play *She Stoops to Conquer*, which took the London stage by storm in 1773 and is constantly revived. Maria Edgeworth (1767–1849) was a well-educated and thoughtful woman whose work was read with respect by Sir Walter Scott and Jane Austen. Her novels on Irish life in the 19th century are superb. She administered a large estate and did much in her area of Longford to help during the famine years of the 1840s. Patraic Colum (1881–1972), a poet and dramatist who worked for the revival of Gaelic literature, was born in Longford Town.

In the past Longford was known as Annaly, after a 9th-century prince who ruled over it. His tribe were the O'Farrells. In 1547, the greater part of Annaly was formed into the new county of Longford. Today, the people of County Longford are mainly farmers or work in agriculture-related industries.

Getting Around

By air: to Dublin Airport.

By sea: Dun Laoghaire or Dublin ferry ports.

By rail: the main Dublin–Sligo line passes through Edgeworthstown (Mostim) and Longford Town.

By bus: Expressway services from Dublin to Longford Town, Granard and Ballymahom. Local bus services, ✆ (043) 45208.

By car: Hamill's, Dublin Rd, Mullingar, ✆ (0902) 72626.

Tourist Information

Longford, Main Street, ✆ (043) 46566, June to August.

Mullingar, ✆ (044) 48761, all year.

Festivals

July: The Longford Festival. Contact the tourist office, ✆ (043) 46566.

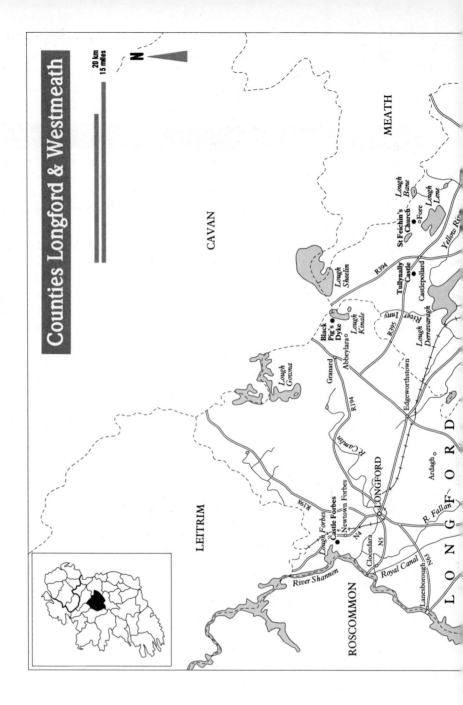

Counties Longford & Westmeath

20 km
15 miles

N

MEATH

CAVAN

Lough
Bane

Lough
Lene

St Feichin's
Church

Fore

Yellow River

Lough
Sheelin

R394

Tullynally
Castle

Castlepollard

River Inny

Lough
Derravaragh

R395

Black
Pig's
Dyke

Lough
Kinale

Abbeylara

Lough
Gowna

Granard

R194

R.Camlin

Edgeworthstown

LEITRIM

R198

LONGFORD

Ardagh

Lough Forbes

Castle Forbes

Newtown Forbes

N4

R. Fallan

Cloondara

N5

LONGFORD

ROSCOMMON

River Shannon

Lanesborough

Royal Canal

N63

460

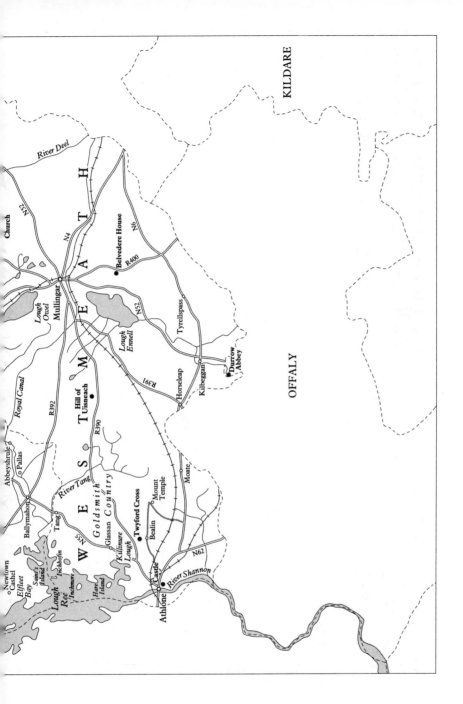

Longford is set on the River Camlin. It is a pleasant if somewhat run-down town, which grew up around a fortress of the O'Farrells which has long since disappeared. You cannot fail to notice the dominating 19th-century limestone **Cathedral of St Mel**, with its lofty towers. There is a modern **public library** in the Annaly car park, with a good local studies section and a comprehensive collection of titles by Oliver Goldsmith, Maria Edgeworth and Patraic Colum. The town is the administrative centre of the county, and has quite good shops, particularly for picnics.

Five miles (8km) to the west is **Cloondara**, a pretty village on the Royal Canal. It was formerly the Royal Canal terminal and the link with the River Shannon, and there is a fine cut-stone canal harbour. Cloondara has a *teach cheoil*, (Irish music house), where traditional Irish music, song and dance are performed in kitchen surroundings during the summer. **Newtownforbes**, 3 miles (4.8km) northwest of Longford, boasts a fine 17th-century mansion, **Castleforbes**, the seat of the Earls of Granard. It overlooks Lough Forbes and it is possible to view the grounds if you write to the Estate Office. **Carrigglas Manor** (*open mid-June–mid-Sept daily except Tuesdays and Wednesdays, 2–6.30. The stableyard and museum, tea rooms and gardens are open every day*

except Monday; adm; ℂ (043) 45165), 3 miles (4.8km) from Longford Town on the R194 (Longford to Granard road), is a romantic Tudor-Gothic mansion with castellated turrets. It was built by the Lefroys, a French Huguenot family, in the 1830s. The ceilings in the main rooms are beautifully corniced and moulded. The stable yard was built in 1790 by James Gandon, the architect of the Dublin Four Courts. The Lefroys still live in the house and it contains most of its original furniture. In a museum in the stable yard, antique costumes are on display. It is not only possible to tour the mansion, but to stay there as well.

Lough Gowra to the southeast of the county is a coarse fishing centre. **Granard**, on the R194 near Lough Gowra, is a bustling market town and angling centre for the River Inny, and Loughs Gowra and Sheelin, with a Harp Festival at the beginning of each August. Its name, *Grian-ard*, suggests that it was once a place of sun worship. There is a motte to the southwest of the town, crowned by a statue of St Patrick. Nearby, at Abbeylara is part of that intriguing prehistoric earthworks known as **Black Pig's Dyke** which once stretched from Donegal Bay to County Louth.

The Rest of County Longford

Ballymahon, south of Longford Town, is Oliver Goldsmith country, and his connection with these parts is proudly remembered. Ballymahon itself is a good place from which to explore the River Inny and the Shannon. **Pallas**, 5 miles (8km) to the east, is Goldsmith's birthplace. All this countryside is charming, with soft green fields and hedges of hawthorn, sloe and holly. This area is said to have had a seminal influence on Goldsmith's work. This is an extract from 'The Deserted Village':

> *Sweet was the sound, when oft at evening's close*
> *Up yonder hill the village murmur rose;*
> *There, as I passed with careless steps and slow,*
> *The mingling notes came soften'd from below:*
> *The swain responsive as the milkmaid sung,*
> *The sober herd that low'd to meet their young;*
> *The noisy geese that gabbled o'er the pool,*
> *The playful children just let loose from school;*
> *The watchdog's voice that bay'd the whisp'ring wind,*
> *And the loud laugh that spoke the vacant mind;*
> *These all in sweet confusion sought the shade,*
> *And fill'd each pause the nightingale had made.*
> *But now the sounds of population fail,*
> *No cheerful murmurs fluctuate in the gale,*
> *No busy steps the grass-grown footway tread,*
> *For all the bloomy flush of life is fled.*

Ardagh is a lovely village surrounded by woods where it is said that St Patrick founded a church, which can still be visited. **Abbeyshrule** on the banks of the Inny has the sad remains of a Cistercian abbey.

Edgeworthstown (Mostrim), just outside Longford on the N4 running south, is not a very noteworthy place, except that Maria Edgeworth and her innovative father lived here. Richard Edgeworth reclaimed bogs and improved roads on his large estate, had four wives and 22 children, advocated Catholic emancipation and educated his daughters. Maria, the novelist, was his second child. The quality of life for the peasant living in Ireland 150 years ago was miserable, and she cleverly showed the cause of this through the thoughts of the faithful servant Thady Quirk in *Castle Rackrent*. Uncaring greed, absenteeism and the exploitative methods of the middlemen are exposed in this great tale of moral fiction. She and her father are buried in the churchyard of St John's, as is Isolda Wilde, Oscar's sister. The Edgeworths' family home is now a nursing home and has been terribly altered.

Lanesborough is famous for its coarse fishing and is on the northern tip of Lough Ree. You may tour the power station which is fuelled by turf—one fossil fuel Ireland has a lot of! **Newtown Cashel**, a few miles south, is a pleasant town with a village green and stone walls. There is a lovely view of Lough Ree from the outskirts of the village, with the sympathetically restored **Abbey of Saint's Island** to the left. The Augustinian monastery on Saint's Island flourished in the 14th century. You can get to it by boat from Elfleet Bay, Lanesborough, in the summer. There is a variety of marsh birds around the lough and good fishing. Another attractive island on the loch is **Inchcleraun** (also known as Inisclothran), which has the remains of a monastery founded at the beginning of the 6th century by St Diarmuid. On the highest point of the island is the Belfry Church, a Romanesque church with a square tower at the west end. There are the remains of several other churches grouped together and some Early-Christian graves. The island is associated with Queen Maeve or *Medb*, who was killed by a stone fired from the sling of Fergus whilst she was bathing off the shore (*see* **Old Gods and Heroes**, p.579). It is easy to hire a boat out here during the summer from Coosan point, Athlone or from Elfleet, Lanesborough.

Shopping

Crafts: crafts and sweaters from Tom McGuiness, Main Street, Longford, ✆ (043) 46034. Mullingar Pewter Craft Shop, 46 Dominick Street, Mullingar (Co. Westmeath), ✆ (044) 48791. Craft shop attached to Prince of Wales Hotel, Church Street, Athlone. (Co. Westmeath).

Activities

Trout and coarse fishing: The Cut in Lough Ree near Lanesborough is famous for its big bream, rudd, perch and pike: Contact Michael Wyse, Pricewyse, Lanesborough, ✆ (043) 21503. An expedition may easily be made from here to Strokestown House, County Roscommon (*see* p.288), call ✆ (078) 33013 for times of opening.

Cruising: on the Shannon and Lough Ree. Contact Athlone Cruisers at the Jolly Mariner, Athone, ✆ (0902) 72892. Ballykeeran Cruises, Athlone, ✆ (043) 85163.

Pony-trekking: Chez Nous Riding Centre, Arva Rd, Drumlish, ✆ (043) 24368.

Golf: at Longford Club, ✆ (043) 46310.

luxury

Jeffry and Tessa Lefroy, **Carrigglas Manor**, Longford, ✆ (043) 45165. Lovely Tudor-Gothic mansion set in a woodland garden. You are treated with great friendliness and dine in great style. The bedrooms are large, comfortable and elegantly furnished.

moderate

The **Longford Arms**, Main Street, Longford, ✆ (043) 46296.Reasonable hotel in the centre of town.

inexpensive

The **Keenan family**, Shannon Side, Tarmonbarry, ✆ (043) 26052. Comfortable house on the edge of the Shannon. Your host is an expert on fishing matters and his boat is available. The Smyth family, **Toberphelim House**, Granard, ✆ (043) 86568. Pleasant old farmhouse, friendly family. En suite bedrooms.

Eating Out

expensive

Crookedwood House, Mullingar, (Co. Westmeath), ✆ (044) 72165. Cellar restaurant which has won awards for its excellent plain cooking. *Dinner only and Sunday lunch and closed on Mondays.*

moderate

The **Longford Arms**, Main Street, Longford, ✆ (043) 46296. Pub lunches and *à la carte* menu. The **Glassan Village Restaurant**, Glassan (Co. Westmeath), ✆ (0902) 85001. Excellent plain cooking with lots of seafood options. *Open for dinner and Sunday lunch.*

inexpensive/cheap

The **Rustic Inn**, Abbeyshrule, ✆ (044) 57424. Good value family-run restaurant. Plain food, steaks. **Café au Lait**, Main Street, Longford. Excellent salads, quiches and soups. Open 9am to 6. **Market Bar**, Market Square, Longford, ✆ (043) 41806. Pub lunches.

Entertainment and Nightlife

Traditional music: in the Camlin Lounge, Clondra, during the summer, ✆ (043) 26039.

County Westmeath

Westmeath (*Iarmhidh*) is one of the most fascinating counties for those who enjoy Irish history, fishing, and exploring the wooded lake country through which magnificent old-fashioned pubs and ruins are scattered; it has a quiet beauty.

The land is fairly level with four large, spreading lakes: Loughs Owel, Ennell, Derravaragh and Lene. It shares the beautiful Lough Sheelin in the north with County Cavan. The many other tiny lakes are humming with insect, bird and fish life, and are set amongst gorse and hazel-covered countryside. Totally unspoilt bogland makes up quite a section of the county and it has its own, unique bog-flora and fauna. Coarse fishermen catch bream, rudd, pike, eels and tench, and where the Shannon River expands into the islet-scattered Lough Ree, cruise boats can be hired. Many of the locals are cattle-farmers, although there is some light industry around Athlone and Mullingar.

History

In pre-Norman times the county was part of the Gaelic territory of Teffia and of the Province of Meath, and the Irish names which were recorded then are still common in the locality. These are the O'Flanagans, MacAuleys, MacGeoghegans, O'Dalys, O'Melaghlins and O'Fenelons. These tribes or septs were often at odds with each other, raiding cattle and encroaching on each others' territory. In approximately AD 300, the palace of the *ard rí* (high king) was at Uisneach, a small hill in the centre of the county from which you can see a long distance over the surrounding countryside. Nothing remains of the palace. The *ard rí* moved back to Tara in County Meath about AD 350. Yet this area was the chosen home of the high king again in the early 11th century, when Malachy II lived on the eastern shore of Lough Ennell. A large earthen mound marks the site of his fort, known as *Dun-na-Sgiath*.

Christianity came in the 5th century, and monasteries were founded by disciples of St Patrick in the following two centuries at Killare and Fore, and on Hare Island in Lough Ree. The Vikings raided up the Shannon and fought with the local Gaelic rulers. There is a story of how King Malachy slew the Viking chieftain, Turgesius, by throwing him into Lough Owel. When the Normans arrived after their successes in Waterford and Dublin in about AD 1170, they built themselves strongholds, and some of these can be seen today in the shape of mottes and baileys. Later they built stone castles and, from the 15th century onwards, tower houses. The Gaelic tribes of the region did not allow the Normans to settle in peacefully: there were constant skirmishes, and the usual muddle of complicated alliances between Norman and Gaelic lords. Under the rule of the Plantagenet kings it had been administered as part of Meath, but in 1542 the part known as Westmeath was split off from Meath because it was so difficult to control.

The 17th century bought great difficulties and much bitterness to the Gaels in the region. The Cromwellian wars of the 1640s resulted in huge amounts of land being confiscated, and today the local people still remember who the land once belonged to. (This is the same all over Ireland.) The new landowners soon settled in and built themselves fine houses. But the last decade of the 17th century was fraught with the Jacobean/Williamite war. The war was a disaster for the Jacobites and the Catholic peasantry who fought with them: more land was confiscated and given to those who had supported William III, and the Penal Laws to control the Catholic population were passed (*see* **History**, pp.90–1). There is a poem called *The Battle of the Aughrim*, written in 1927 by Richard Murphy, an excellent narrative poet from County Galway, which you should certainly try to read. It succinctly sums up the situation on the eve of the Battle of Aughrim in July 1691 by entering into the imagined thoughts and emotions of a Cromwellian landowner. Aughrim was one of the most decisive battles fought in the history of Ireland. William III's army of 18,000 men, under the command of Ginkel, met the Jacobite army of 24,000 men, under the command of a French General, St Ruth.

Getting Around

By air: Mullingar is about 1½ hours' drive from Dublin Airport.

By rail: The county is served by two rail routes: the Dublin–Sligo line which stops at Mullingar, and the Dublin–Galway line which stops at Athlone. Mullingar Station, ✆ (044) 48274.

By bus: Frequent express bus services stop at Kinnegad, Mullingar, Moate and Athlone. The local bus service stops at Killucan, Multyfarnham, Glasson and Kilbeggan, Mullingar Bus Depot, ✆ (044) 48274.

By bike: Buckley Cycles, Main Street, Moate, ✆ (0902) 81606.

Tourist Information

Mullingar, Dublin Road, ✆ (044) 48761/48650, all year.

Athlone, ✆ (0902) 94630, Easter to mid-October.

Festivals

Late April/early May: All Ireland Amateur Drama Festival, Deane Hall, Athlone, ✆ (0902) 72333 for details.

July: The Mullingar Bachelor's Festival, ✆ (044) 44044 for details.

Athlone

Athlone, half of which is in County Roscommon but is dealt with here, is a good touring centre on the River Shannon, which immediately spreads into the lovely Lough Ree. From here you can head for either Connemara or Dublin. Westmeath is rather flat, but the little hillocks, never more than 850ft (259m) high, are well-placed and attractive.

Athlone (*Ath Luain*: the ford of Luain), has always been important as the crossing place on the Shannon between the kingdoms of Leinster and Connacht; many raids were launched from here by the fierce Connacht men who wanted the fat cattle of Meath. Later, when the Anglo-Normans had established themselves in Leinster, Athlone became the last strong outpost of that civilization, for behind it and around it stretched the world of the Gaels. The castle was built by King John and from it the English attempted to govern Connacht. Over the centuries, the castle and walls had to be rebuilt many times, but the most memorable stories concern the siege of Athlone when the town was held for James II against the Williamite forces. Sergeant Custume (after whom the present barracks is named), and 10 volunteers gave their lives in hacking down the temporary wooden bridge over which the enemy was about to swarm into the breach in the walls. Unluckily for the Irish, their leader, a French general called St Ruth, was a prize idiot, and having secured what he thought was victory, decided to throw a grand party, even though Patrick Sarsfield, our Limerick hero, begged him to take the rumours of further attack seriously. Thus the Williamite forces were able to take the city whilst the Irish troops were drunkenly sleeping over their cups.

Today, Athlone is a thriving market town, a major rail and road terminus, and has a harbour on the inland navigation system. It is full of good food shops, and places where you can have a good jar and listen to traditional or jazz music. One of the most striking buildings in the town is the enormous Roman Catholic **Church of St Peter and St Paul**, off Grace Road, built in the Roman Renaissance style. It was erected in the grounds of the old military barracks and opened for worship in 1937. On the west bank overlooking the bridge, almost opposite the church, is **King John's Castle** (*open June–Oct, 11–4.30 daily except Sundays, 12–4.30; adm; Ⓒ (0902) 94630*). It was built in the 13th century and has always been a strong military post. Although it has been strengthened over the centuries it retains its classic Norman design. It was used as a military post up until 1969, when it was declared a national monument and a museumx was established in the central keep. The museum has interesting exhibits on the folklife and the archaeology of the area. If you want to immerse yourself further in times past, wander into **St Mary's Church** in Church Street where, frozen into stone statues, Tudor squires kneel with their ladies in perpetual prayer. The atmosphere is like that of a village church in England. (You get the same atmosphere in the Church of Ireland church in Raphoe, County Donegal.) The tower bell is one of those removed at the despoiling of Clonmacnoise.

Lough Ree

If you are staying in Athlone, you may find time to explore the many islands in Lough Ree. Ask down at the marina about hiring a boat to Hare Island, Inchmore, Inchbofin, Iniscleraun and Saint's Island, all of which in ancient times were the homes of saints. **Hare Island** is very attractive, and contains the ruins of a church founded by St Ciaran in the 6th century before he moved to Clonmacnoise in County Offaly. **Saints Island**, in the eastern part of the lake, has the ruins of a well-preserved monastery and church (*see* **County Longford**.) If you follow the N55 to **Glassan** a few miles outside Athlone, you get a lovely view of inner Lough Ree and its wooded islands and shoreline. Glasson is a pretty little place where the artisans' cottages are smothered with roses and clematis in summer. All the little country roads from here down to the left lead to Lough Ree, and little coves such as Killinure and Killeenmore. Scholars and the tourist board have claimed the area between Glassan and Tang as Oliver Goldsmith Country. Goldsmith (1729–74) was the son of a clergyman, and was actually born over the border at Pallas in County Longford. He attained great fame for his plays, most notably *She Stoops to Conquer*, and for his long verse 'The Deserted Village'. At Tang you can have a relaxing drink in the Three Jolly Pigeons, the old house which features in 'The Deserted Village'. For one week in late April/early May, Athlone is brimming with people who come for the **All-Ireland Amateur Drama Festival** and the side-shows.

Moate to Mullingar

If you follow the N6 east, you enter rich cattle-raising and dairy country. **Moate** is an important market town, traditionally supposed to be named after the mound of **Mota Grainne Oige**, which rises beside it. Mota was the wife of O'Melaghlin, an early Celtic chief of the district. The mound was definitely used as a defensive site by the Normans when they arrived in the 12th century. At **Bealin**, on a little road between Athlone and Mount Temple, is a sculptured cross from the 8th century called the **Twyford Cross**. It is almost 7ft (2m) high and was found in a nearby bog. Close by is an esker—a long, winding ridge formed during the Ice Age. There are many small commercial sand pits in the esker near Moate. Along the ridge runs one of the ancient roads of Ireland, going to Tara in County Meath; the surface of it is covered in hazel, hornbeam, bracken and gorse. If you are on your way to Dublin, you might stop in **Horseleap** on the N6. The place gets its name from the tradition that the Norman Baron de Lacy was being chased by a party of native Gaels—the MacGeoghegans—and jumped his horse over the castle drawbridge. In the village is a partly damaged Norman motte and bailey which dates from 1192. Also, a well-preserved 16th-century tower house which was built by the MacGeohegans, a ruling Gaelic family whose lands remained fairly intact up to the time of Cromwell in the 1640s.

The little country roads around here are really rural and very enticing, with many fine demesnes and ruins set in wooded fields. The roads are also nearly empty of cars, so you can really enjoy motoring or, even better, cycling. The next village along the N6 is **Kilbeggan**. It has an old distillery, founded in 1757, which has been restored as an **industrial museum and craft centre** by an enthusiastic local committee (*open May–Oct, 9–6; Nov–Mar, 10–4; © (0506) 32134*). The huge water wheel is back in operation. On the Tullamore road a few miles out is the ruined **Durrow Abbey**, a famous monastery founded in the 6th century by St Columba. Amongst its attractions are a holy well and, in the disused graveyard, the **Durrow High Cross** (*see* **County Offaly**). Back on the N6 to Dublin is **Tyrrellspass**, a very pretty village, laid out as a crescent around the central green in the 18th century by the Countess of Belvedere. The area was ruled by an Anglo-Norman family, the Tyrells, until Cromwellian times. The castle, a private residence, was built by them in the 15th century. Richard Tyrell was a late-16th-century hero who annihilated a large Elizabethan force near here with the help of a small band of men. **Belvedere House** (*open June–Oct daily, 12–6; adm; © (044) 40861*) lies between Tyrellspass and Mullingar on the shores of Lough Ennell. It was built for Robert Rochfort, Lord Belfield, afterwards 1st Earl of Belvedere, in about 1740. It was probably built by Richard Cassels, also known as Castle, Ireland's foremost Palladian architect. The house is small and comprises a three-bay recessed centre between projecting bay ends. The plasterwork on the ground floor is superb, with cherubs and classical figures amidst fruit, flowers, clouds and stars. The 1st Earl was a vindictive man who kept his young wife a prisoner in a nearby house for 31 years after her supposed adultery with his younger brother. The gardens are superb with many old-fashioned shrubs. Also 18th-century follies and ruins make it a delight to walk in.Twelve miles (19km) west of Mullingar on the Ballymore Road is **Uisneach Hill**, from where you can see a vast expanse of country. In ancient times, before Christianity, it was an important meeting place and the seat of kings, but now there is little left but a field with a broken wall around it.

Mullingar was a garrison town and has now become a noted angling centre with a busy, brightly painted main street, several excellent pubs, and grocery shops that sell Brie and salami! It is one of the nicest market towns in Ireland, and has a feeling of energy which is often lacking in the dreary towns scattered through the middle of the country. The area around Mullingar is great shooting, fishing and hunting country, and the new squires who lead the way are German and French (which explains the Brie!). There is a very interesting little **museum** depicting local history of the War of Independence in the Column Barracks. You must seek permission to view from the officer in charge, ✆ (044) 48391 for an appointment. There is also a fine local history and folklore museum in the **Market House** (*open June–Sept; adm; ✆ (044) 48152*). There is a lovely anonymous rhyme which relates an episode in Mullingar. It goes like this:

There was an elopement down in Mullingar
But sad to relate the pair didn't get far,
'Oh fly!' said he, 'darling, and see how it feels'.
But the Mullingar heifer was beef to the heels.

Around Mullingar

Five and a half miles (8.9km) from Mullingar on the R394, east of Crookedwood village, is **St Munna's Church**. This fairytale church was built in the 15th century and has a castle-like tower and battlements. The key is kept in the house opposite the graveyard. In **Crookedwood**, at the southern tip of Lough Derravaragh, the scenery is really charming, for it looks over the glittering lake. Now, take the little road through Collinstown to **Fore**, once an important ecclesiastical centre, situated between Loughs Lene and Bane and freely accessible. Fore has the same magical atmosphere as Glendalough in County Wicklow, but has not really been looked after. Seek out **St Feichin's Church** in the western graveyard, which dates from the 10th century and is remarkable for its huge doorway; a cross in a circle marks the massive lintel. The Benedictine priory is very well-preserved. It was built by Walter de Lacy, a powerful Anglo-Norman, in the beginning of the 13th century on the remains of an earlier abbey founded by St Feichin in AD 630. An ancient anchorite cell on the hillside was occupied by a hermit as late at 1764, and was later turned into a family vault for the Grenville-Nugents of Delvin. From the hills around Fore there are some lovely views of Meath, Cavan and Longford.

Castlepollard is an attractive 19th-century town with a triangular green. Close by, on the Granard Road (R395), are the beautiful grounds of **Tullynally Castle** (which used to be Pakenham Hall), the seat of the Earls of Longford (*open April–Oct, 10–6; adm; ✆ (044) 61259*). Seen from a distance, in a romantic setting, Tullynally makes you think of a castle

in an illustrated medieval manuscript. The hall became a Gothick Castle in the 1790s; the new castellated additions were designed by Francis Johnston for the 2nd Lord Longford whose family, the Pakenhams, had bought the property in 1655. Inside the castle is a fine collection of family portraits and furniture, and there is a fascinating collection of family memorabilia in the museum, kitchen and tower. Maria Edgeworth, the novelist, was an enthusiastic visitor here and described it as, 'the seat of hospitality and the resort of fine society'. The present family are extremely literary: Lady Antonia Fraser is of this family and her brother, the present Viscount, is a respected historian. The grounds are beautiful and the castle looks down to Lough Derravaragh, which is one of the loughs associated with the story of the Children of Lir. It was here that their jealous stepmother transformed the children into swans.

Shopping

Venison: Clonhugh, Durfarm, Multyfarnham, ✆ (044) 71117.

Goats' milk: Ardnurcher Farm, Horseleap, Moate, ✆ (0506) 35112.

Wool: Tom Berminghams Menswear, 37 Oliver Plunkett Street, Mullingar, ✆ (044) 40760. Good for tweeds and knits. Mostly tweed, but also pewter and crafts, from Mullingar Weavers, The Weaver's Loft, 46 Dominick Street, Mullingar, ✆ (044) 48791.

Antiques: Locke's Distillery, Kilbeggan, ✆ (0506) 32134.

Fishing: Brown trout fishing on Lough Sheelin. Coarse fishing on Loughs Owel, Ennell and Derravaragh. For tackle and advice, contact O'Malley's, 33 Dominick Street, Mullingar, ✆ (044) 48300; Sam's tackle shop, Castle Street, Mullingar. Also very good pike fishing all over Lough Ree.

Boating: cruiser and rowing boat hire from Athlone Cruisers, the Jolly Mariner, Athlone, ✆ (0902) 72892; Ballykeeran cruises, Athlone, ✆ (0902) 85163; and Greville Arms Hotel, Mullingar, ✆ (044) 48563.

Pony trekking: Ladestown House, Mullingar, ✆ (044) 48218. Trail rides along the lake.

Hunting: with the Streamstone Harriers, ✆ (044) 26470; and with the Westmeath Hunt, ✆ (044) 42244.

Golf: Athlone Golf Club; ✆ (0902) 92073. Mullingar Golf Club, Belvedere, ✆ (044) 48366.

Horseleap

Temple Farmhouse, Horseleap, ✆ (0506) 35118 (*moderate*). Charming Georgian farmhouse, with lovely bright rooms, and elegant dining room. Much of the wholesome food cooked in the house comes from the farm or vegetable garden. Relaxation therapies are also available.

Mullingar

The **Greville Arms Hotel**, Pearse Street, Mullingar, ✆ (044) 48563 (*moderate*). Traditional hotel. **Mornington House**, Mullingar, ✆ (044) 72191 (*moderate*). This fine manor house overlooks Lough Derravaragh. Period beds, large pretty rooms and delicious fresh food, particularly on the dessert front. The O'Haras can help you organise some fox hunting or fishing also. Mrs Maxwell, **Woodlands Farm**, Streamstown, Mullingar, ✆ (044) 26414 (*inexpensive*). Not a pretty house, but very typical of Irish farmhouses—crammed with holy pictures, full of welcome and delicious food. The Pendred family, **Mearescourt House**, Rathconrath, Mullingar, ✆ (044) 55112 (*inexpensive*). Mansion house set in pretty parkland. Good home cooking, comfortable rooms.

Tyrellspass

The **Village Inn**, Tyrellspass, ✆ (044) 23171 (*moderate*). This cosy period townhouse hotel is in an elegant crescent around a village green. Service and food are excellent.

Kinnegad

The **Old Glebe**, Kinnegad, Killucan, ✆ (044) 74263 (*moderate*). Regency country-house hotel in mature parkland. Has recently been transformed into a kind of health farm.

Moate

Mrs Galvin, **Coolatore House**, Rosemount, Moate, ✆ (090) 236102. Comfortable Victorian house, good food. Close to Hill of Uisneach and Knockastia Hill (*inexpensive*).

Eating Out

Athlone

Le Château, ✆ (0902) 94517 (*moderate*). Good-value and friendly. **Conlon's Restaurant**, 5–9 Dublingate Street (*moderate*). The **Jolly Mariner**, Abbey Road, ✆ (0902) 72892 (*inexpensive*). Riverside restaurant and bar. The

Glassan

Glassan Village Restaurant, ✆ (0902) 85001 (*moderate*). Straightforward but tasty Irish cooking. The **Wineport Restaurant**, ✆ (0902) 85466 (*moderate*). Very popular locally. Open for lunch and dinner.

Mullingar

Crookedwood House, ✆ 044 72165 (*expensive*). Country house cellar restaurant. Good value. **Danny Byrne's**, 27 Pearse Street, ✆ (044) 43792 (*inexpensive*). Victorian-style pub and restaurant, good for pub lunches.

Tyrellspass

Tyrrellspass Castle, ✆ (044) 23105 (*expensive*). Medieval banquets and excellent Sunday lunches. **Village Inn**, ✆ (044) 23171 (*inexpensive*). Good pub-style lunches.

Fore

The **Thatched Cottage**, ✆ (0410) 66306 (*inexpensive*). 400-year-old cottage. Light lunches and excellent home baking. Call in advance for opening hours.

Kinnegad

The **Cottage**, ✆ (044) 75284 (*inexpensive*). Snack lunches and good fresh scones.

Entertainment and Nightlife

Traditional music and jazz: in the Green Olive and Sean's Bar, Athlone, and the Three Jolly Pigeons, Tang. Occasional shows in County Hall, Mullingar.

To many travellers the only significance of these two counties is that you travel through them on your way to Tipperary or Cork. They lie in the centre of Ireland's saucer-shape, in the flat plains and boglands, separated from Galway and Roscommon on the west by the Shannon. Both counties are delightfully untouched by organized tourism, there are no bus tours to speak of; even travellers to the famous monastic site of Clonmacnoise will find it as quiet and tranquil as did the 6th-century monks who sought out this island of fertility along the river.

Most of County Offaly is bogland, which is alive with its own special flora and fauna. It is bordered in the west by the River Shannon, and there is plenty of scope for cruising along its beautiful waters, and through the Grand Canal which divides the county in two. In the southwest, Offaly shares with County Laois the glens of the Slieve Bloom Mountains. They are not a great height—2000ft (610m) at their highest point—but they have a grandeur of their own, amongst the flat watery boglands around them. Both counties have a great wealth of Early-Christian sites, and some superb examples of 18th-century big houses. The villages grew up around such landlord properties and are still, on the whole, very attractive. Birr is a gem of a planned 18th-century town, and the Parsons family who laid it out still own the magnificent gardens and arboretum their ancestors planted. You can spend hours in it, marvelling at the exotic species and grand design.

County Laois is bordered on its east by the Grand Canal which runs alongside the River Barrow at Monasterevin, finally merging into the Barrow at Athy in County Carlow. The River Nore flows through Laois on its western side, so there is plenty of scope for the coarse fisherman.

History

Perhaps because of the bogland, our knowledge of Stone Age man in these parts is scarce. However, at Lough Boora near Kilcormac excavations in 1977 discovered traces of nomadic activity of some 7000 years BC. There is plenty of evidence that man was around in these parts during the Bronze Age (2000 BC), as weapons and ornaments have been found, those at Banagher being particularly famous. The Iron Age and the arrival of the Celts is marked by numerous hill forts; such as Aghancon, near Leap Castle. The septs which eventually emerged were the O'Connors, O'Molloys, O'Dempseys, MacCoghlans, Foxes and O'Carrolls in County Offaly; and the O'Moores, Fitzpatricks, and O'Dunnes in County Laois.

When the Anglo-Normans arrived in 1169 they could never establish themselves securely here, and gradually retreated back to the Pale, a small area of land around Dublin, Meath and Louth. In the 16th century, the English started their experiment of planting disloyal parts of Ireland with loyal English. The boundaries of County Offaly and County Laois began to take shape with bits taken from the older Kingdoms of Ossory (now Kilkenny), Meath, Thormond and Munster. When plantation did not work well enough, the Crown ordered the transplantation of the chief tribes and their followers to County Kerry, around

Tarbert. By the 1620s families such as the Parsons, now the Earls of Rosse, had taken over the strongholds of the native Gaelic chiefs; in this case, the O'Carrolls of Ely in County Offaly.

Today, the people living in these counties work mainly in small industries such as the manufacture of vitrified clay pipes, or for Bord na Mona, the Irish turf development authority, which employs over five thousand people. Most of them have small farms which they work on a part-time basis.

Getting Around

By air: Dublin and Shannon International Airport.

By sea: Dun Laoghaire and Rosslare ferry ports.

By rail: to Tullamore, Portarlington, Portlaoise and Ballybrophy.

By bus: Expressway services from Dublin to all the major towns. Good provincial network, Tullamore Depot, ✆ (0506) 21431.

By car: car hire from Deverells, Ballymorris Road, Portarlington, ✆ (0502) 23284.

By bike: The Raleigh Rent-a-Bike network operates here. Your local contact is M. Kavanagh, Railway Street, Portlaoise, ✆ (0502) 21357. P. L. Dolan and Sons, Main Street, Birr, ✆ (0509) 20006.

Tourist Information

Clonmacnoise, ✆ (0905) 74134, April to October.

Birr, ✆ (0509) 20110, May to Sept.

Portlaoise, ✆ (0502) 21178, all year round.

Tullamore, ✆ (0506) 52617, June to August.

Festivals

Mid-July French festival of Portarlington to celebrate the French Huguenot influence on the town, ✆ (0502) 23985.

Early August: Steam Rally in Stradbally; ✆ (0502) 25444.

Mid August: Birr Vintage Car Week, and singing competitions, ✆ (0509) 20433.

County Offaly

Clonmacnoise *(open June–Sept daily, 9–7; rest of the year, ✆ (0905) 74195 for opening times; guided tours; adm)*, near the Shannon, is one of Ireland's most celebrated holy places. In AD 548 St Kiaran founded a monastery here which became one of the most famous of all the monastic settlements in Ireland. T. W. Rolleston (1857–1920) adapted an early Gaelic poem entitled 'Clonmacnoise' which suggests what a great centre of worship and learning it was, and the place it holds in the romantic Celtic twilight view of history:

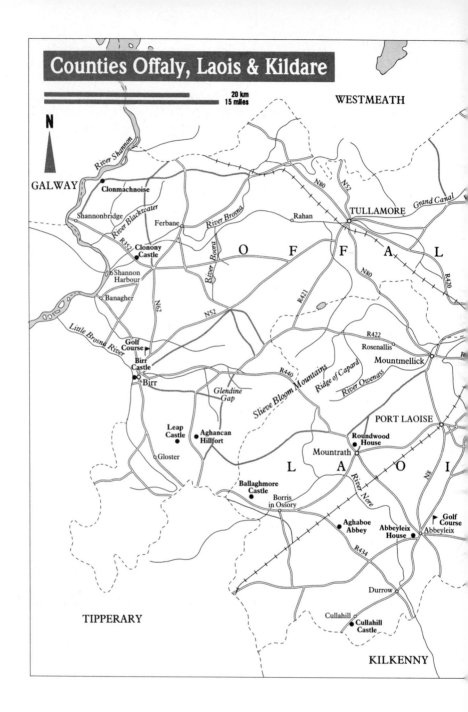

Counties Offaly, Laois & Kildare

20 km
15 miles

N

WESTMEATH

GALWAY

River Shannon

Clonmacnoise

Shannonbridge

River Blackwater

Ferbane

River Brosna

Rahan

TULLAMORE

Grand Canal

N80

N52

R352

Clonony
Castle

O   F   F   A   L

River Boora

N80

R420

Shannon
Harbour

Banagher

N62

N52

R421

Little Brosna River

Golf
Course

Birr
Castle

Birr

Glendine
Gap

R440

Slieve Bloom Mountains

Ridge of Capard

River Owenass

R422

Rosenallis

Mountmellick

R

PORT LAOISE

Leap
Castle

Aghancan
Hillfort

Gloster

Mountrath

Roundwood
House

L   A   O   I

N8

Ballaghmore
Castle

Borris
in Ossory

River Nore

Aghaboe
Abbey

Abbeyleix
House

Golf
Course
Abbeyleix

R434

Durrow

TIPPERARY

Cullahill

Cullahill
Castle

KILKENNY

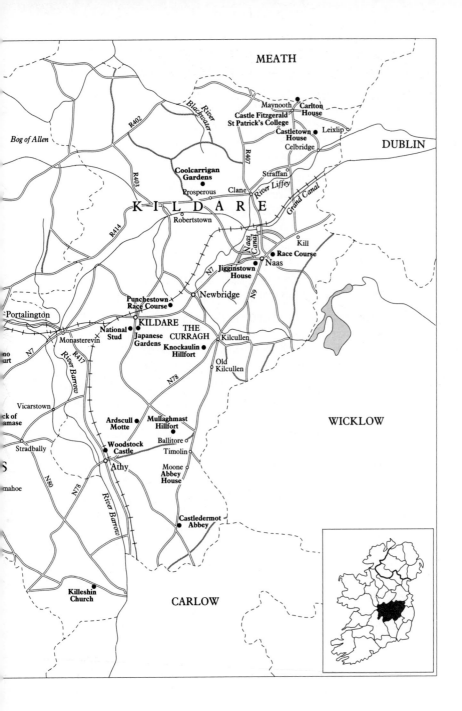

MEATH

River Blackwater
R402
Maynooth • Carlton House
Castle Fitzgerald
St Patrick's College
Castletown • Leixlip o
House
Bog of Allen
Celbridge

DUBLIN

R403
Coolcarrigan Gardens
Straffan
River Liffey
Grand Canal
Prosperous
Clane

K I L D A R E
Robertstown o

R414

Naas Canal

Kill
• Race Course
Jigginstown House • Naas
N7

Punchestown Race Course •
Newbridge
N9

:Portalington
KILDARE THE
National • Japanese CURRAGH
Monasterevin Stud Gardens Knockaulin • Kilcullen
Hillfort
N7 R417
River Barrow
Old Kilcullen

WICKLOW

N78

Vicarstown
ck of
amase
Ardscull • Mullaghmast
Motte Hillfort
Stradbally
Woodstock Ballitore o
Castle Timolin o
Athy Moone
Abbey House
mahoe
N80 N78
River Barrow
Castledermot •
Abbey

Killeshin • Church
CARLOW

477

In a quiet water'd land, a land of roses,
Stands Saint Kieran's city fair;
And the warriors of Erin in their famous generations
Slumber there.

There beneath the dewy hillside sleep the noblest
Of the clan of Conn,
Each below his stone with name in branching Ogham
And the sacred knot thereon.

There they laid to rest the seven Kings of Tara,
There the sons of Cairbre sleep–
Battle-banners of the Gael that in Kieran's plain of crosses
Now their final hosting keep.

And in Clonmacnoise they laid the men of Teffia,
And right many a lord of Breagh;
Deep the sod above Clan Creide and Clan Conaill,
Kind in hall and fierce in fray.

Many and many a son of Conn the Hundred-fighte
In the red earth lies at rest;
Many a blue eye of Clan Colman the turf covers,
Many a swan-white breast.

The monastery was well sited on a major ford on the Shannon, on a huge Esker ridge which stands well above the boggy plain. It became a centre of great learning in medieval times and was patronized by the O'Connor Kings. Turlough and Rory were buried there. The monastery suffered terribly from Viking raids and inter-dynastic wars between different septs. The coming of the Normans spelt the decline of Clonmacnoise, for they built a fort by the river, and an English garrison was built at Athlone. It further fell into a decline after the Reformation, and was sacked in 1552 by the English garrison at Athlone. Today, the remains are extensive and include a number of churches, two fine high crosses, two round towers, and some decorated early grave slabs—they date from the 8th, 9th and 10th centuries. Many of the names on them are found in the annals, the ancient manuscripts of Ireland. A few of them are displayed in the reception area as you enter the monastery. The ruins are dispersed in a large grassy enclosure, and each building is well described. It takes at least an hour to walk around them. Of particular note is the 10th-century West Cross with its decorative panels of figure-carving. The lowest panel on the east face of the shaft shows two figures clasping a post on which a bird perches. These have been interpreted as St Ciaran, the founder, and the local king, Diarmuid, who granted the land for the monastery. It is said that Diarmuid helped to build the first wooden church with his own hands, and was rewarded for his piety by the high kingship of Ireland! The largest church, the Cathedral, has a fine north doorway (*c.* 1460) of lime-stone with foliate carvings and figure-sculpture. All the churches have Romanesque features; Teampul Finghin on the northern border of the site has a beautiful chancel arch in three orders decorated with chevrons and animal heads. It dates from the second half of the 12th century. A small round tower rises from the chancel.

There is a small Bord Fáilte office in the car park, a coffee shop and some picnic benches are arranged around the entrance to the reception area. A pilgrimage is held here on 12 September, the feast of St Ciaran.

If you travel south towards Birr from Clonmacnoise and Shannonbridge on the R357, you will pass a lovely little castle at **Clonony** (*always accessible*), built in Henry VIII's time. It is a four-storey tower house with a 19th-century reconstructed bawn. Gravestones uncovered here belonged to the Ormonde Butlers. **Shannonbridge** has a power station, artillery fortifications dating from the Napoleonic period, and a superb reputation for coarse fishing. It also has an excellent pub, and supermarkets to supply the cruiser trade.

Nearby is **Shannon Harbour**, where the Grand Canal and the Shannon River meet. You moor your boat underneath the ruins of an old hotel. Many an emigrant said goodbye here, before sailing to America. The boglands around **Ferbane** and **Boher**, just south of the river, are fascinating in their way, and the medieval church remains in these tiny places are very interesting. You can go by rail on a fascinating and informative bog tour on the Blackwater Bog, near Shannonbridge (*see* 'Activities'). At **Banagher**, you will see a Martello tower guarding the western side of the river. It was built as a lookout to warn against a possible Napoleonic invasion. The town is attractive, and has a link with the novelist Anthony Trollope, who was stationed here as Post Office Surveyor in 1841.

Birr is a must on any tour of Ireland: the **castle gardens** are superb, and the town itself is beautifully laid out with wide, Georgian streets and squares. The hand of the Parsons family is obvious in this; it is the planned, landlord towns which have grown old gracefully. Birr stands on land granted to Laurence Parsons in 1620 and used to be called Parsonstown. In Emmet Square is Dooley's Hotel, a very old coaching inn. The Galway Hunt were tagged the Galway Blazers after setting fire to the hotel during a night of celebration in 1809. West of Emmet Square is **John's Mall** with its Georgian houses. Notice the fine fanlights above the doors. There is a pleasant walk downstream following the river, and to the right of Oxmanton Bridge is St Brendan's Church, and the Convent of

Mercy designed by Pugin. The entrance to Birr Castle (*open daily, 9–1 and 2–6, or until dusk in the winter; exhibitions open daily, May–Sept, 2.30–5.30; adm*) is in William Street, and there are over 100acres (40ha) of pleasure grounds laid out by Laurence Parsons, the 2nd Earl of Rosse (1757–1841). The castle itself is not open to the public. Various exhibitions are held in the gallery, in the grounds during the summer, and you can see the remains of a gigantic reflecting telescope built in 1845. The 3rd Earl of Rosse planned and constructed it himself. The gardens are famous for their elegant shrubs, magnolias and box hedges which are as tall as trees, and the park for its variety of trees. There is a proper kitchen garden, which is a rarity nowadays. A scientific centre is planned for the near future.

In the southern corner of Offaly near Gloster is **Leap Castle**, which guards the valley from Leinster into Munster. A large tower house, altered and restored in about 1750 by the Darby family, it is rather a spooky place now, but before its destruction in 1922 it was actually famous for its smelly ghost. The present owner hopes to restore it (the house). **Tullamore** is the county town of Offaly; a prosperous place which has grown up on the banks of a small river. The Grand Canal also passes through it, and it is a major cruiser base. Irish Mist and Tullamore Dew whiskey are manufactured here, and there are good shops and restaurants. Six and three-quarter miles (11km) west at **Rahan** is a lovely old canalside pub called The Thatch. Take the N52 out of Tullamore for 5 miles (8km) and take the second turning on the right. You can combine a drink here with a visit to the ancient churches of Rahan. Two of them are 12th century and in Romanesque style. One of them is very well-preserved, and joined to a later church built in 1732. The chancel arch has elaborate piers carved into human heads with flowing hair. Always accessible. About 5 miles (8km) north of Tullamore, off the N52, is **Durrow Monastery**, which was founded by St Colmcille (Columba) in the 6th century. It is most famous for the *Book of Durrow*, a 7th-century illuminated maunuscript, now at Trinity College, Dublin, and for the Crozier of Durrow, now in the National Museum, Dublin. Nothing remains of the monastery except a 10th-century high cross and some fine early tombstones. It is always accessible.

County Laois

County Offaly used to be known as King's County after Phillip II, Spanish Consort of Mary Tudor. County Laois was Queen's County after Mary herself. She was responsible for 'planting' this area with loyal supporters in 1556, but this policy did not bring peace, and early in the 17th century many of the rebellious Irish septs were banished to County Kerry. The new colonists built lovely houses and attractive villages. Houses of note include Abbeyleix, Roundwood House and Emo Court (*see* below).

The county town is **Portlaoise**, which has nothing much to recommend it, except that it is an important rail junction. It has a certain notoriety, as there is a well known prison in the neighbourhood. Of great interest is the **Rock of Dunamase**, just outside the town on the Stradbally road (N80). This is an ancient defensive fort, and the annals record that it was plundered by the Vikings in AD 845. It came into Anglo-Norman hands through the marriage of Aoife, daughter of the King of Leinster, to the warlord Strongbow. It was blown sky-high by Cromwellian artillery in 1650. The climb to the top is easy and the views are wonderful. At **Stradbally** there is a **Steam Traction Museum** (*by appointment or on Sundays, 2–6; contact the Irish Steam Preservation Society, ✆ (0502) 25236*). There is a steam rally every August bank holiday weekend. **Vicarstown** and **Monasterevin**, both on the River Barrow section of the Grand Canal, are peaceful cruiser harbours.

North of Portlaoise is the canal town of **Portarlington**. The town was founded at the end of the 17th century and became an important centre for Dutch and French Protestant refugees. In 1696 Henri de Massue, Marquis de Ruvigny, also the Earl of Galway, was granted title to the lands round here; he was one of William III's foreign favourites who excited much jealousy among English courtiers. The connection is commemorated by the so-called French style of the old town houses; their gardens stretch down to the river rather than into the street.

Mountmellick, Mountrath and the Slieve Bloom Mountains

To the western side of the county are the Slieve Bloom Mountains. Before exploring their wooded glens, waterfalls, boglands and magnificent views which are very well signposted, it is worth stopping at the magnificent **Emo Court Demesne** (*grounds open all year round, 10.30–5.30; adm; house open April–Oct on Mondays, 2–6, adm; ✆ (0502) 26110*), designed in 1795 by Gandon. The domed rotunda room is very impressive, and Siena marble and gilded capitals add to its richness. It was rescued and restored by its present owner, Mr Cholmeley Harrison. The gardens are laid out between a large lough and the house, and grassy paths lead you to a series of vistas. It is a mixture of old and new planting. Emo is on the Dublin to Cork Road (N8) between Monasterevin and Portlaoise.

Nearby **Mountmellick** was founded in the 17th century by Quakers and grew prosperous on cotton, linen and woollen-manufacturing industries. The town is curled into a bend of the River Owenass and today still retains an 18th-century feeling. **Mountrath**, further to the south, is another attractive town which was founded in the 1600s by Charles Coote, an active entrepreneur, whose family built houses all over Ireland. He established charcoal-burning ironworks which ate up the natural forests. Today the Irish State has planted thousands of acres of sitka spruce and pine in Laois which, although rather monotonous, will be a good cash crop for the future. Close to Mountrath is **Roundwood House**, a fine Palladian mansion which has won many awards as a first-class guest house. The owners would be delighted to show you around. The house is to be found by following the N7 from Dublin to Mountrath, and then following signs for the Slieve Bloom Mountains. It is about 3 miles (4.8km) out of town. The Irish Georgian Society rescued Roundwood House from ruin in the 1970s, and the Kennan family continue the good work. Notice the unusual staircase carved in Chinese chippendale style. Beyond Borris in Ossory, following the N7 to Roscrea, is **Ballaghmore Castle**, which was a Fitzgerald outpost on the borders of old Ossory, and has a *sheila-na-Gig* (*see* p.590) high up on its walls. In the Slieve Bloom Mountains, the **Ridge of Capard** has outstanding views. It is reached from Rosenallis Village. **Glendine Gap** is also spectacular; from here you look over the four provinces of Ireland. One of the ancient highways of Ireland, the Munster Road, crosses the area from north to south through Glenlitter, Glynsk and the Tulla Gap. The pine marten, Ireland's rarest mammal, is found in these glens.

Durrow to Abbeyleix

In the southern tip of County Laois is the attractive town of **Durrow** (on the N8), which was owned at one time by the Duke of Ormonde. **Castle Durrow**, now a convent, was built in 1716. You can ask to look around it. To the south is the pretty village of **Cullahill**. In the village is a fine old gabled castle (*not open to the public*) built by the Fitzpatricks, lords of the area before the Normans arrived. Going back north again, following the N8, is the town of **Abbeyleix**. Nothing remains of the Cistercian monastery, founded here by Conor O'Moore in the 12th century, which became part of the Earl of Ormonde's vast possessions in Elizabeth I's reign. The town is well laid-out, and in the south is the beautiful Adam House built by Viscount de Vesci after a design by William Chambers. Sadly, it is not open to the public. There is a lovely pub called Morisseys on Main Street, a good stop for a sandwich and a glass of stout. It has a lovely old-fashioned stove used in the wintertime.

Another place of great interest in the area is **Timahoe**, on the R426 between Portlaois and Swan. Here there is a 12th-century round tower over 100ft (30m) high, with a double door decorated with stone heads in a Romanesque style. It is always accessible.

Shopping

Sheep fleeces: slippers, jackets from Mrs Stanley, Woodville Farm, Shinorne, Birr, ✆ (0505) 47278.

Brass: Banagher Brass and Copper, Banagher, ✆ (0902) 51381.

Cheese: Abbey Blue Brie, Ballacollon, ✆ (0502) 38599.

Charcuterie: homemade sausages, traditional smoked bacon from Rudds, Busherstown House, Moneygall, ✆ (0505) 45206.

Activities

Coarse fishing: Contact Moody's Tackle Shop, 29 Main Street, Birr, ✆ (0509) 20560; J. Hiney's Pub & Tackle, Main Street, Ferbane, ✆ (0902) 54344. Brosna Hotel, Banagher, ✆ (0902) 51350.

Cruising: cruiser hire from Celtic Canal Cruisers, Tullamore, Co. Offaly, ✆ (0506) 21861; Carrick Craft (based in Banagher), P.O. Box 14, Reading RG3 6TA, England, ✆ (01734) 422975.

Bog Tour: Blackwater Bog. Starting point the Bord na Mona Blackwater Works, Shannonbridge. 8km circular tour aboard the Clonmacnois and West Offaly Railway. Open April–Oct. The train runs every hour, on the hour 10–5.

Birdwatching: in the flood meadows on either side of the Little Basna River, for golden plover, wigeon, whooper swans, curlews, lapwings and black-tailed godwits.

Walking: The Slieve Bloom Way, a signposted circular route of 31 miles (50km) starting at Glenmonicknew Forest car park. Ask for Bord Fáilte information sheet 67 at any tourist office.

Orienteering: in the Slieve Blooms. Contact the Outdoor Pursuit Centre, Birr, County Offaly, ✆ (0509) 20029.

Golf: at Birr; ✆ (0509) 20082. Pitch & Putt, Banagher, ✆ (0509) 51458.

Where to Stay

County Offaly

George Gossip, **Tullanisk**, Birr, ✆ (0509) 20572 (*moderate*). Lovely Georgian dower house on the Birr Castle estate. Delightful atmosphere, delicious food. **Moorhill House**, Tullamore (*see below; moderate*). Charming Victorian house, with comfortable, heated rooms.

Shepherd's Wood, Screggan, Tullamore, ✆ (0506) 21499 (*moderate*). 1930s house surrounded by woods. Mrs Keyes, **Canal View**, Killina, Rahan, ✆ (0506) 55868 (*moderate*). En suite rooms on the Grand Canal.

Mrs N. O'Hara, The **Old Rectory**, Deerpark, Shannon Harbour, ✆ (0902) 57293 (*inexpensive*). Cosy country house near the lively cruising port.

County Laois

Frank and Rosemarie Kennan, **Roundwood House**, Mountrath, ✆ (0502) 32120 (*moderate*). A 1740s Palladian mansion run by a delightful family who will instantly make you welcome. The atmosphere is relaxed and comfortable. Children are welcome, and have part of the top floor to amuse themselves in. The food is delicious and all six bedrooms have central heating and private bathrooms.

Glebe House, Ballinakill, ✆ (0562) 33368 (*moderate*). Friendly country house. The owners are delighted to share their local knowledge.

Mrs P. Carroll, **River House**, Errill, near Rathdowney, ✆ (0505) 44120 (*inexpensive*). Charming old-fashioned farmhouse, good cooking and comfortable rooms. There is a chance to ride on the farm, and much to see in the area. At Skirke is an ancient ring-fort, and nearby are the Timoney Stones, a mysterious collection of 300 stones of uncertain origin.

County Offaly

Dooley's Hotel, Emmet Square, Birr, ✆ (0509) 20032 (*moderate*). Adequate, rather pretentious food in the restaurant and a good coffee shop. **County Arms**, Birr, ✆ (0509) 20791 (*moderate*). Georgian country-house hotel. Reasonable food. The **Stables Restaurant**, Oxmantown Street, Birr, ✆ (0509) 20263 (*moderate*). Basic menu, steaks, etc. **Moorhill House Restaurant**, Clara Road, Tullamore, ✆ (0506) 21395 (*moderate*). Restaurant in the converted stables of a Victorian country house. Dinner only. Imaginative food and excellent breakfasts. The **Cottage Coffee House**, Castle Street, Birr (*inexpensive*). Excellent for a home cooked lunch and coffee and also open for dinner from Wed–Sat. Bring your own wine. Opposite the gates to Birr Castle, ✆ (0509) 20985. **Brosna Lodge Hotel**, Banagher, ✆ (0902) 51350 (*moderate*). Bland but good-value cooking. The **Vine House**, Banagher, ✆ (0902) 51463 (*moderate*). Good-value, simple cooking.

County Laois

Morrissey's, Abbeyleix, ✆ (0502) 31233 (*inexpensive*). Charming pub and grocery shop with old cake tins and a stove. Good for stout and sandwiches.

County Kildare

Kildare is a county of bog and plain, divided by the Liffey in the northeast, and the basin of the Barrow in the south. The Bog of Allen, a huge raised bog formed over five thousand years ago, spreads to the northwest. The county is crossed by the Grand Canal that links Dublin and the Shannon River at Banagher; its towpath provides lovely walks away from the traffic and fumes of the roads, and excellent coarse fishing. Being so near to Dublin, Kildare is one of the most populated counties, yet it is possible to explore the canal villages, and its many castles, stately houses, and gardens, and still feel you are in the heart of the country. Do not linger too long in the towns, many of which tend to get jammed with traffic during the rush-hours as they are situated on major through-routes to Dublin.

Most people have heard of The Curragh, a plain of over 5000 acres (2000ha) situated just east of Kildare Town, where some of the fastest horses in the world are bred and exercised. It was formed in the Ice Ages, when the ice ground the surface of the limestone plain to a powder which mixed with vegetable remains to produce a rich pasture, famed for making the bones of horses grazed on it very strong. You may wish to visit the National Stud and Irish Horse Museum at Tully near Kildare Town. Or there is great fun to be had attending the races, both at The Curragh and Punchestown where, besides having a flutter, you can admire a Bronze Age standing stone, 23ft (7m) in height, which is in the grounds of the racecourse.

This county also contains two of the grandest houses in the country: Carton House, seat of the Earls of Kildare; and the next-door estate of Castletown House, a fine Palladian mansion.

History

The history of the county is fascinating, for its fertile river plains have attracted many invaders. The first recorded inhabitants are a Celtic people, the Ui Dunlainge, who may have originated from Cornwall. They built great hill-forts, the remains of which can be seen at Mullaghmast in the south, Knockaulin in the centre, and the Hill of Allen in the west. Knockaulin, near Kilcullen, dates from the late Bronze Age, and shares with Tara in Meath and Emain Macha in Armagh a legendary importance in the folk memories of the Irish people. Christianity came in the 5th century and the monks built their churches near these centres of Celtic pagan power. Moone, near the fort of Mullaghmast, has an 8th-century stone cross which is wonderfully carved with scenes from the Bible. The Ui Dunlainge split off into branches, becoming rivals and fighting for territory. The Norsemen arrived in early AD 900 and established their power in Dublin and the northeast of Kildare. The Anglo-Normans under the leadership of Richard de Clare, called Strongbow, came in the 12th century. They had been invited over by Dermot (Diarmuid) MacMurragh, King of Leinster, to help him regain his kingdom. Strongbow did indeed help him to capture Dublin and defeat his enemies but, as the *Book of Leinster* records, 'he died after the victory of unction and penance; thence forward is the miserable reign of the Saxons, amen, amen' (*see* **History**, p.85). The Normans soon squeezed out the Celtic tribes, who took to the Wicklow Mountains, where they became the O'Tooles and mounted attacks on the Norman colony.

By 1300 Kildare was dominated by the Norman Fitzgerald Earls of Kildare, known as the Geraldines. For a time in the late 15th century, they were so powerful and wealthy that they were the uncrowned kings of Ireland. Gerald, the 8th Earl, known as the Great Earl, was made Deputy of Ireland in 1481 by Edward IV, who reasoned that if all Ireland could not rule this man, he would let him rule all Ireland. Inevitably, however, the Tudor kings viewed the power of the Fitzgeralds with increasing resentment. By 1534 they had completely fallen out with the English government, and the 9th Earl died in the Tower of London. His son Thomas renounced his allegiance to Henry VII and attacked Dublin Castle. He is known as 'Silken Thomas' because his followers had silken fringes on their helmets. His army was routed and he retreated to his stronghold at Maynooth. But in March 1535 Sir William Skeffington took it and the garrison was given the 'Maynooth pardon'; that is, they were executed. Thomas had escaped the bloodshed, but he eventually submitted and was given a guarantee of personal safety. This was not fulfilled and he too was sent to the Tower, and was hanged, drawn and quartered with his five uncles in 1537. The Kildares lost much of their power again with the Cromwellian wars and plantation, although their estates were restored by Charles II. They survived the Williamite wars of 1689–91 and built Carton House. Many of the old Norman families did not fare so well, and were replaced by new loyal 'colonists' known as planters. They were Protestant, and built themselves fine houses of beautiful craftsmanship. The great famine of 1845–49 and the various uprisings put an end to all of this. Dublin has grown hugely in this century, especially in the last 20 years, so that many villages like Leixlip and Celbridge have become dormitory suburbs of Dublin.

By air: Dublin International Airport is within 30 minutes' drive of Kildare.

By boat: Dun Laoghaire and Dublin ferry ports.

By rail: Sallins and Kildare Town are on the main line from Dublin to Cork, ✆ (01) 836 3333.

By bus: Dublin, ✆ (01) 836 6111 for details.

By car: car hire available in Dublin, and from Dublin Airport e.g. Avis.

By bike: The Raleigh Rent-a-Bike network operates in Kildare. Your local contact is John Cahill and Son, Sallins Road, Naas, ✆ (045) 79655.

Tourist Information

Newbridge, ✆ (045) 33835, 20 June–27 Aug.

Kildare Town, ✆ (045) 22696, May–Sept.

Mullingar, ✆ (044) 48650, all year.

Festivals

Early May: Prosperous Coarse Fishing Festival, ✆ (045) 68150.

Northeast Kildare

Naas, only 21 miles (33.8km) from Dublin, is a busy industrial town, a good shopping town, with a mixture of old-fashioned and modern stores; and a hunting and horse-racing centre, on the edge of the Wicklow Mountains. In Irish it is known as *Nas na Riogh*, 'meeting place of the kings'. It used to be one of the seats of the kings of Leinster, and was the centre of the Irish kingdom of Ui Dunlainge. All that remains of their fort is a motte, a large hill in the middle of the town. At **Kill**, 1½ miles (3km) away off the N7 to Dublin, is Goffs, the old established horse auctioneers which sell 50 per cent of all Irish-bred horses. John Devoy (1842–1928), the Irish-American newspaper man and Fenian, was born here. He was influential in organizing publicity in America, and worked in the early 20th century to help the Irish Freedom Movement with money and propaganda, through such organizations as *Clan na Gael*. **Jigginstown House**, just a mile (1.6km) southwest on the Kildare Road (N7), is now a massive ruin. It was built by Thomas Wentworth, Earl of Strafford, when Charles I proposed to visit him. The visit never came off and 'Black Tom', one of the most unpopular men in Ireland, was executed in 1641 by the Roundheads before it was finished. If it had been completed it would have been the largest unfortified house ever built in Ireland. The cellars are the only part in complete form now. It is possible to drive up to it.

If you are in need of a little refreshment, an old-fashioned pub called Fletcher's with cosy snugs and wooden floors should fill that gap nicely.

Punchestown is famous for its standing stone, and its races. The stone is 3 miles (4.8km) southeast of Naas, off the Woolpack Road, and is 23 ft high (7 m) with a Bronze Age burial chamber at its base. To the northwest are the quiet canal villages of Prosperous and Robertstown. (The Grand Canal was built in the 1760s and carried agricultural produce between Dublin and the River Barrow at Athy.) The railways destroyed the villages' passenger and commercial trade, but today the Grand Canal and the Naas Canal, a branch of the Grand, have been restored. The canal side has some very attractive walks and drives, and cruisers are for hire at Tullamore (*see* 'Activities').

Robertstown, on the banks of the Grand Canal, is ideal for a quiet and leisurely visit. The locals are very proud of the town's 18th-century associations, and the waterfront has been restored to look as it did in the days when travellers used to alight from their boats for an overnight stop. Some of the barges have been restored, and you can go for short trips on the canal. Eighteenth-century banquets are re-created in the Grand Canal Hotel, which no longer functions as a hotel, but is used for all sorts of entertainments. The evening begins with a horse-drawn barge cruise, and then there is the meal. During weekends in July and August, there are concerts, lectures on the Georgian and canal eras, and lots of festivities. Between Clane and Prosperous is a Victorian garden at **Coolcarrigan** (*open by appointment only, © (045) 63512/63524; adm for house and gardens*). It is best seen in spring and autumn, as there are some magnificent trees.

Celbridge, 8 miles (5km) north of Naas, is a must for all lovers of Georgian country houses: within a few miles are both Castletown and **Carton**. Sadly, the future of the latter is at the moment rather precarious and it is difficult to view it. It was the seat of the Earls of Kildare, a powerful Norman family who became more Irish than the Irish, and the grounds were laid out by Capability Brown in a park where 'art and nature in just union reign'. The house was designed in the 1730s by Richard Castle or Cassels, a French Huguenot who did a lot of work in Ireland. There is a **Shell House** in the grounds. Mrs Delaney, who is still remembered for her diaries which recorded the privileged life of the Protestant ascendency, helped to decorate the house when she stayed at one of the many house parties held at Carton during the mid-18th century.

Castletown (*open Apr–Oct, daily (except Sats in Oct), Nov–Mar, Sundays and bank holidays, © 628 8252*) at the eastern end of Celbridge village, is approached through a fine avenue of lime trees. This splendid Palladian mansion was built for William Connelly, speaker of the Irish House of Commons from 1715 to 1719, and contains some elaborate plasterwork by the Francini Brothers. (They taught Irish craftsmen the art of stucco.) It has the only 18th-century print room in Ireland, and some superb 18th-century furnishings. One of the hunt balls held during the week of the Dublin Horse Show takes place in its gracious rooms. From the windows of the Long Gallery you can see the extraordinary Connelly Folly, an obelisk supported on arches, built by the widow of Speaker Connelly to provide relief work after a particularly hard winter. In 1994 Castletown became the property of the state and is now run by the Office of Public Works. It is one of the venues for the Music Festival in Great Irish Houses, held in June (*see* **Practical A–Z**, p.18).

A few miles south west of Celbridge between the N7 and the R403 is the pretty village of Straffan which has a wonderful steam museum (*open all year, Sundays and public holidays; in June, July and August open daily, © (01) 627 3155; adm on a 'live' steam day*), with rare examples of industrial steam engines and locomotives. Good teahouse too!

Maynooth, a couple of miles north of Celbridge, has ancient associations with the great Geraldine family, the Fitzgeralds, later Earls of Kildare and Dukes of Leinster. The fine ruins of the 12th-century **Castle Fitzgerald** may be explored if you get the key from Castleview House, across the road from the castle. A gate house, a massive keep and a great hall survive. This is where Sir William Skeffington, acting for Henry VII, presided over the killing of the Geraldine followers when he took the castle in 1535. Today, Maynooth is more closely associated with **St Patrick's College**, which has been turning out catholic priests since 1795, although it is now a lay university as well. Funnily enough, it was established by the British, who did not like the idea of the Irish priests studying abroad where they might pick up revolutionary ideas. The buildings are late-Georgian in style; with a Gothic Revival addition by J. J. McCarthy, a pupil of Pugin, the famous British Gothic Revival architect who rebuilt the British Houses of Parliament. Call ✆ (01) 628 5499 for an appointment to view the **Ecclesiastical Museum** which includes vestments made by Marie Antoinette for an Irish chaplain.

Leixlip is on the banks of the Liffey; its name comes from the Danish *Lax-laup*, which means 'salmon leap'. Before the falls were utilized for hydroelectric power, it was a wonderful sight to see the salmon do just that. The 12th-century Norman castle is owned by Desmond Guinness, the force behind the Irish Georgian Society, which has done so much to preserve the rich treasury of 18th-century buildings in Ireland. It is not open to view. Leixlip has grown enormously as Dublin spreads ever outwards. The swift waters of the Liffey in this area are a great challenge to sportsmen, and canoeists come from all over the world.

The Curragh

Kildare Town is on the edge of the Curragh, and is now an important centre for horse-breeding. It is said that St Brigid spread her handkerchief over enough land on which to build a convent and the ruling king had to grant it to her. Her nunnery thrived during the 6th century, although by the 7th century it had become a monastery. **The Church of Ireland cathedral** on the hill in the middle of the town dates in parts from the 13th century, and stands on the site of a 6th-century church. This venerable pile of stones has been pillaged and burnt many times, and lay in ruins between 1641 and 1875. (A roof-restoration appeal is now being run.) The cathedral has some fine monuments, and a three-light west window with scenes from the lives of Brigid, Patrick and Colmcille, the three Patron Saints of Ireland. Beside it there is a 10th-century round tower with an 18th-century top which you can climb. The **National Stud** at **Tully** (*open Easter Sun–end Oct, weekdays 10.30–5; Sat and public holidays 10.30–6; Sun 2–6; adm for stud and gardens; ✆ (045) 21617*), just outside Kildare Town on the R415, was started by Colonel Hall-Walker (later Lord Wavertree). He bred the famous Derby winner Minoru, and many others. In 1915 he presented the estate and horses to the Crown, and it was handed over to the Irish state in 1943. Its importance in the bloodstock and racing world is without parallel. The National Stud is open for guided tours in the summer, and there is a **Horse Museum** there. The Japanese gardens in the grounds are perfectly maintained: they symbolize the life of man, from cradle to the grave. They were planted by the Japanese gardener of Colonel Hall-Walker between 1906 and 1910.

The green spring grass of the **Curragh** stretches for miles, with the blue hills of Dublin on the horizon. The land is said to be so good for rearing horses because the pasture that grows on its limestone plain is the best in the world for building bone. But it is the skill of the breeders in choosing the sires which has made Curragh bloodstock so successful, and the excitement at the races when their skill is put to test is phenomenal: the chat is fast and furious, porter is downed in the tents; and the horses are splendid, thundering along in the green distance. Numerous meetings are held between March and November. The most famous are the Irish Sweep Derby in mid-summer, the Irish 2000 Guineas, the Irish Oaks and the Irish St Leger. The Curragh is also famous as the largest army camp in the country.

The Hill of Allen (676ft/206m), south east of Rathangan, is famous in Irish legend as the other world seat of Fionn MacCumhail (*see* p.578). The summit is 15 minutes' walk from the road, and at the top is a 19th-century folly built by a Sir George Aylmer, 'in thankful remembrance of God'. The hill, together with Naas, and *Dun Aillinne* (Knockaulin), which is just northwest of Kilcullen on the N9, was a residence of the kings of Leinster. Straight lines joining them form an equilateral triangle, with sides 9 miles (14.5km) long. At Lullymore, **Rathangan** (℃ *(045) 60133 for opening hours*) is an information centre devoted to bogland, and its flora and fauna. **Newbridge** (*Droichead Nua*) to the east is an industrial centre on the Liffey. Outside it, near the Dominican College is an ancient motte.

Athy, south of Kildare Town on the R417, has developed from a 13th-century Norman settlement at a fording point on the River Barrow. In Irish, *Athy* means 'ford of Ae'. Ae was the king of Munster who was killed trying to take control of the ford in the 11th century. A 16th-century castle looks over Crom-a-boo bridge. (The name refers to the war-cry of the Desmond branch of the Fitzgerald family.) It is privately owned. There is a lovely old market house in the town. It can be viewed from the outside only, as it is now a fire station. The modern Dominican church is worth looking at—pentagon-shaped and built of massed concrete, with attractive stained-glass windows.

Half a mile (0.8km) out of town on the R417, the 13th-century **Woodstock Castle** still survives in the form of a rectangular tower. A short expedition can be made to another historical spot, the **Ardscull Motte**, some 4 miles (6.4km) north of Athy, off the N78. It was used by Edward Bruce in 1315 to defeat an English army. **Moone High Cross** (*always accessible*), one of the most famous and beautiful of all the high crosses, is 8 miles (12.9km) from Athy, in the demesne of Moone Abbey House, beside the little village of Timolin on the N9. The cross is 17½ft (5.3m) high and has 51 sculptured panels depicting scenes from the Bible. It is also known as St Colmcille's Cross.

At **Timolin**, the art of pewter has been restored (*you can visit the workshop between 11am and 5pm, ℃ (0507) 24164*). The neighbouring village of **Ballitore** was once a flourishing Quaker settlement. The old meeting house is now a library and museum (*can be visited free of charge, although the opening times are irregular, ℃ (0450) 31109*). Ballitore School was famous for its high standard of education. Edmund Burke, the 18th-century political writer and orator; Napper Tandy (1740–1803), the United Irishman; and Cardinal Cullen (1803–1878), who was instrumental in setting up a Catholic University in Dublin, were all pupils. The **corn mill** (*open April–Sept, daily, 10–7; rest of the year, Sundays only 10–4; adm*) by the river has been restored and there is a collection of industrial archaeology and exhibitions on milling and the life of the community in the 19th century. Nearby, west of the village, is the **Rath of Mullaghmast**, an earthern Stone Age fort, rich with folklore. It is said that Garret Og Fitzgerald, the 11th Earl of Kildare, sleeps here, emerging once every seven years. A grisly massacre took place on this spot in 1597; and it was the setting for one of Daniel O'Connell's mass meetings in 1843, when he was campaigning for the repeal of the Act of Union which had taken place between England and Ireland in 1801.

Close to the River Liffey and just southeast of the Curragh Camp are the tiny villages of Old Kilcullen and Knockaulin. **Old Kilcullen**, just off the N9, is the site of an Early-Christian monastery, with fragmentary 8th-century crosses like those at Moone. There is also a ruined round tower. West of the tower, across the N78, is the Iron Age **Hill Fort of Knockaulin** (also called *Dun Ailinne*). From both these sites you can get a wonderful view of the Barrow Valley. The petty chieftains of this area who had ambitions to become kings of Leinster, associated themselves with the power and royal connections of the fort long after it had been abandoned as a royal centre in the first centuries AD. They referred to themselves as Kings of Dun Ailinne. The monks were doing the same thing by building Kilcullen monastery so close!

Castledermot, south of Moone on the N9, is famous for the remains of its **Franciscan abbey**, high crosses and round tower. The tower is tall and slender, and facing it is a lovely 12th-century Romanesque doorway. A modern copy of it in the church is in use. There are two attractive sculptured granite high crosses in the graveyard. Castledermot was a place of great importance, once upon a time: a walled town in which Hugh de Lacy built an Anglo-Norman fortress. Edward Bruce fought for it in the 14th century, but was defeated; and Cromwell sacked it in 1649. There are some remains of the stone walls, and Carlow Gate still stands. A few miles outside the town is **Kilkea Castle**, once the home of the Earls of Kildare, now a luxury hotel and health farm.

Shopping

Pottery: Brenda O'Brien, Dun Buain Lodge, Kill, Naas, ✆ (045) 77502.

Wooden items: Peter Sweetman, Ashgrove Park, Naas, ✆ (045) 79385. Beautiful wooden bowls. Kate Beaumont, Harristown Estate, Brannockstown, Naas, ✆ (045) 83614, for timber toys. Michael Hughes, Leixlip Park, Leixlip, for woodturning.

Pewter: from the workshop at Timolin.

Textiles Hans Smits, Straffan, ✆ (01) 627 2256, for printed textiles. Eager's Couturier Fabrics, Henry Street, Newbridge, ✆ (045) 32442.

Food market: Friday Country Market, Town Hall, Naas, between 10.45 and 12 noon. Fresh vegetables and herb cheeses.

Activities

Racing: at Punchestown and the Curragh. Look for details in the national newspapers, and in the back of the Bord Fáilte *Calendar of Events* which is published every year.

Coarse fishing: in Prosperous and all along the Grand Canal. Contact Mrs Travers, Curryhills House, Prosperous, Naas, ✆ (045) 68150 or Ned O'Farrell, Curryhills, Prosperous, ✆ (045) 68092. For coarse trout and salmon fishing information, call Kane's Pub, Athy, ✆ (0507) 31729/31434.

Cruiser hire: Celtic Cruisers, Tullamore, Co. Offaly, ✆ 0506 21861.

Canoeing: Kilcullen Canoe and outdoor pursuits club, Kilcullen, ✆ (045) 81240.

Barge buffets: in Robertstown, for groups only, ✆ (045) 60808.

Hunting: Kildare Hunt, ✆ (045) 79098. Ward Union Hunt, ✆ (01) 272671.

Pony-trekking: Kilkea Dressage Centre, Castledermot, ✆ (0503) 45112. Also organise holidays and trekking trips.

Where to Stay
expensive

Moyglare Manor, Maynooth, ✆ (01) 628 6351. An elegant Georgian house built in 1775, it is supposed to be the dower house to the Carton Estate. Expect immaculately kept bedrooms, comfortable antiques and a friendly, clubby bar, delicious food and fresh flowers everywhere. Garden suite available.

Kilkea Castle, Castledermot, ✆ (0503) 45156. Built by Hugh de Lacy in 1180, it is the oldest inhabited castle in Ireland and has with nice views over the gardens. Good health and sporting facilities. **Barberstown Castle**, Straffan, ✆ (01) 6288157/6288206. An attractive jumble of Norman, Elizabethan and Edwardian building. The **Kildare Hotel and Country Club**, Straffan, ✆ (01) 627 3333. Starrated Michelin restaurant.

moderate

Kilkea Lodge Farm, Castledermot, ✆ (0503) 45112. Charming 18th century farmhouse, comfortable and well furnished, riding holidays arranged. **Doyles Schoolhouse Restaurant and B&B**, Castledermot, ✆ (0503) 44282. Delightful eating place with a high standard of cuisine and some very comfortable rooms, run as a country inn. **Curryhills House Hotel**, Prosperous, Naas, ✆ (045) 68150. Georgian farmhouse with a lovely atmosphere and good food.

inexpensive

Mrs Donoghue, **Woodcourte**, Moone, Timolin, ✆ (0507) 24167. Modern bungalow in quiet countryside. Situated near a nice bar called the Moone High Cross Inn, there is also a tennis court available. Arts and Crafts weekends are also organised.

expensive

Moyglare Manor Hotel, Maynooth, ✆ (01) 6286351. There is a romantic ambience and the menu includes lots of seafood for dinner and Sunday lunch (*see* above). **Kildare Hotel and Country Club**, Straffan, ✆ (01) 627 3333. Very sophisticated with superb food; Michelin-starred restaurant.

moderate

Tonlegee House, Athy, Co. Kildare, ✆ (0507) 31473. Imaginative and delicious cooking. **Doyles School House Restaurant**, Castledermot, ✆ (0503) 44282. A small friendly restaurant with a simple and delicious *table d'hôte*. **Michaelangelo Restaurant**, Main Street, Celbridge, ✆ (01) 624 2086. Irish/Italian food. *Evenings only*. The **Red House Inn**, Newbridge, ✆ (045) 31516. French food, home-grown vegetables. *Evenings only*. **Curryhills House**, Prosperous, Naas, ✆ (045) 68150. Predictable but good-value menu. **The Hideout**, Kilcullen, ✆ (045) 81232. Large cavernous bar with a restaurant. **Moone High Cross Inn**, Moone. Friendly, old fashioned pub. Better than average pub food including home-cooked roasts, brown bread sandwiches and scrumptious apple pie. Open for lunch and dinner.

County Dublin

Ireland's capital city sprawls over a large part of this county and threatens to dominate it completely, but if you wish to be guided by the example of the fun-loving Dubliner you will follow him to the jaunty sea resorts along the coast, to the lavish gardens of Howth Castle, or to the unique collection of Irish furniture and portraits at Malahide Castle. When you are in the National Gallery, search out Nathaniel Hone's picture, *Cattle at Malahide*, for he has caught the glancing light of the east coast perfectly. Those James Joyce disciples who are travelling by themselves around the *Ulysses* landmarks in Dublin should not neglect the museum of Joyceana in the Martello tower, and Sandymount where Gertie McDowell showed Mr Bloom her garters! Further to the south sweeps the lovely Killiney Bay, whilst to the north of Dublin, the flat, tidy fields of the Skerries and Rush slope down to the sea, and the wide arm of Dublin Bay ends at the beautiful penin-sula of Howth Head. Most of the population of the county commute to Dublin City to work, although there is a certain amount of vegetable-growing and dairy farming. Many of the little villages described are fast becoming dormitory towns of Dublin. Some of the new developments are not particularly attractive: the poorer housing is traditionally badly built but this has improved enormously. Dublin City has its beggars, housing ghettos, and prob-lems with theft and drugs just like any other capital city. But it also has a wealth of Georgian architecture, a lively, youthful atmosphere and a charm that is particular to the city itself. Its beautiful setting beside the sea within such easy reach of beaches and moun-tains gives its people a great escape route out when they need it, even if it is only for a few

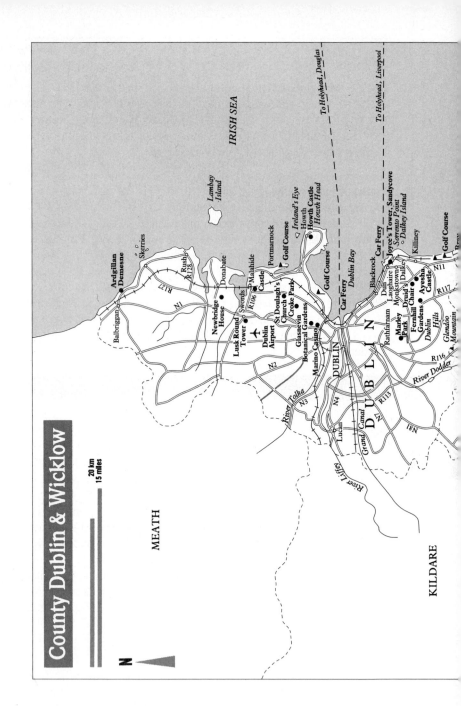

County Dublin & Wicklow

20 km
15 miles

N

MEATH

KILDARE

IRISH SEA

Lambay Island

To Holyhead, Douglas

To Holyhead, Liverpool

Ireland's Eye

Howth
Howth Castle
Howth Head

Golf Course

Portmarnock

Golf Course

Dublin Bay

Ardgillan Demesne

Skerries

Balbriggan

Rush
R128

R127

Donabate

Malahide
Castle

R106

R1N

Newbridge House

Swords

Lusk Round Tower

St Doulagh's Church

Croke Park

Dublin Airport

Glasnevin Botanical Gardens

Marino Casino

N2

River Tolka

N3

N4

Lucan

Grand Canal

River Liffey

DUBLIN

DUBLIN

Car Ferry

Golf Course

Blackrock Car Ferry

Dun Laoghaire

Joyce's Tower, Sandycove
Sorrento Point
Dalkey Island

Monkstown
Dalkey

Killiney

Golf Course

Bray

N11

R117

Marley Park

Fernhill Gardens

Druid's Chair

Ayesha Castle

Dublin Hills

Rathfarnham

Glendlo Mountain

R116

River Dodder

R113

N7

N81

KILDARE

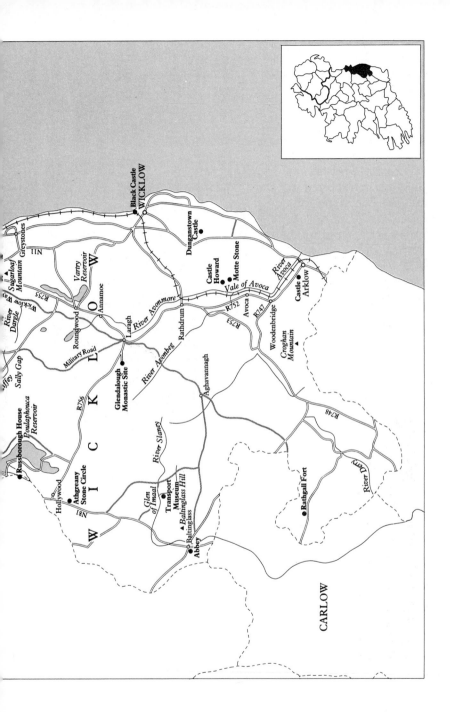

WICKLOW

Black Castle
WICKLOW

Dunganstown Castle

Greystones

N11

Sugarloaf Mountain

Vartry Reservoir

Castle Howard
Motte Stone

River Dargle

R755

Wicklow Way

Annamoe

Vale of Avoca

River Avonmore

Rathdrum

River Avoca

Castle
Arklow

Roundwood

Military Road

Laragh

R752

R753

Avoca

R747

Woodenbridge

Croghan Mountain

Liffey

Sally Gap

River Avonbeg

Glendalough Monastic Site

Aghavannagh

R756

Russborough House

Poulaphouca Reservoir

R748

River Slaney

River Derry

Athgreany Stone Circle

Hollywood

Glen of Imaal

Transport Museum

Rathgall Fort

N81

Baltinglass Hill

Baltinglass

W

Abbey

CARLOW

hours. Many Dublin writers, Flann O'Brien, James Joyce and Samuel Beckett to name just three, drew great inspiration from the countryside around them.

History

The history of the county is closely bound up with Dublin City and the Norman Conquest. The area was settled with Christian Celts living in and around monastic settlements. The marauding Vikings arrived in AD 840 and established a fortress and a settlement along the banks of the Liffey estuary. From a simple base for raiding expeditions, Dublin grew to a prosperous trading port with Europe. The local Gaelic rulers were very keen to grab it for themselves, but it was not until the Battle of Clontarf in 1014 that the dominance of the Danes was severely curtailed. They were finally driven out in 1169 by the Anglo-Normans under Strongbow (Richard de Clare), who took Dublin by storm and executed the Viking leader. The arrival of

the Anglo-Norman foreigners began the occupation of Ireland by the English, which lasted for seven hundred years. Dermot MacMurragh, King of Leinster, invited the invasion by asking Henry II of England for the help of Anglo-Norman mercenaries in his battle for the high kingship of Ireland. They came, and their military campaigns were so successful that they soon controlled not only Wexford and Waterford but most of Leinster and, of course, Dublin. Once here, the Normans had no intention of leaving. In 1172 Henry II came to Dublin to look over his kingdom, and to curb the powers of his warlike vassal lords. Between the 11th and 17th centuries the power of the English crown ran within the Pale, a small area of fortified land around Dublin. The Anglo-Normans did not always manage to break the power of the Gaelic septs outside it, and sometimes became independent of the Crown themselves. County Dublin is rich in Anglo-Norman castles and monastic settlements dating from these times, such as Malahide Castle.

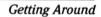

Getting Around

By air: Dublin and Belfast International Airports.
By boat: Dublin and Dun Laoghaire ferry ports.

By boat to the islands: boats to Ireland's Eye are operated by Mr Doyle from May to October and leave daily from Howth Pier, as required, ✆ (01) 831 4200 for more details. Boats to Dalkey Island leave frequently from Coliemore Harbour during the summer.

By rail: mainline rail and suburban services (DART) link most of the suburbs and towns, ✆ (01) 836 6222 for details. DART (Dublin Area Rapid Transit) trains run from 6.30–11.30 along a north–south line around Dublin Bay, from Howth to Bray. At IR£1.10 this is a good way to get an inexpensive tour of the coastline.

By bus: frequent services to all suburbs and county Dublin villages, ✆ (01) 830 2222 for information on schedules, day and week-long return tickets, and trips. For intercity services, ✆ (01) 873 4222.

Tourist Information

Dublin, ✆ (01) 284 4768, all year.

Dun Laoghaire, St Michael's Wharf, ✆ (01) 284 4768, all year.

Festivals

July: Dun Laoghaire Festival (music), ✆ (01) 284 1888.

North County Dublin

On the east coast, **Skerries** and **Balbriggan** are noted for their dry, sunny climate and their safe, sandy beaches. The locals are involved in the fishing industry. The Ardgillan Demesne (*✆ (01) 849 2212 for more details*) between Balbriggan and Skerries is a lush public park of 194 acres of pasture, woods and gardens, amidst which is a Victorian castle, the main rooms are open to the public, and furnished in Victorian style. Closed December and January. **Rush** is another attractive fishing village, which overlooks **Lambay Island** with its 500ft (152m) cliffs rising out of the sea. You have to get permission to land there from the owner, for it is the sanctuary of many rare birds, but the beauty of the island can be seen by sailing around it. About 3 miles (5km) west of Rush is **Lusk Round Tower**, and a Church of Ireland church built in 1839 which contains some fine medieval tombs. The key to the round tower and a second, square, 16th-century tower attached to it is available from Joe Carton, The Square, Lusk. There is a small **museum** (*open on Sundays and public holidays, April to October,* ✆ *(01) 843 7276*) with exhibits portraying rural life here between 60 and 100 years ago. It is named in honour of Willie Monks, a famous antiquarian. At **Donabate** off the N1 is the splendid **Newbridge House** (*open April–Oct, Tues–Fri, 10–5; Sat 11–6, Sun 2–6; Nov–Mar, Sat and Sun only 2–5; adm;* ✆ *(01) 843 6534*), with its Robert West plasterwork. This is early 18th century and was built for Charles Cobbe, later Archbishop of Dublin. The drawing room and its early-Georgian furniture and curios are unique; as is the collection of antique dolls and a dolls' house with 14 rooms. There is also a small museum, made up of curiosities brought from all over the world and displayed in specially designed cabinets.

Malahide, a few miles further south, is another seaside resort, with a wonderful old castle which was the seat of the Talbots of Malahide from 1185 to 1976. Today, **Malahide Castle** (*open April–Oct, Mon–Fri, 10–5, Sat, 11–6, Sun, 2–6; Nov–Mar, Sat–Sun, 2–5; adm grounds only or combined with castle; ℗ (01) 846 2184*) is publicly owned and a part of the National Portrait Collection is housed there. *The Boswell Papers*, which give us such an insight into 18th-century travel, were found here in a croquet box. The castle is made up of three different periods, the earliest being a three-storey tower house dating from the 12th century. The façade of the house is flanked by two slender towers built in about 1765. Inside is the only surviving original medieval great hall in Ireland, hung with Talbot family portraits. The display of Irish 18th-century furniture is fascinating and shows the sophistication of the craftsmanship and artistry existing in Ireland at the time. The grounds are superb, laid out with thousands of clearly labelled species by Lord Talbot de Malahide between 1948 and 1973. There is also a model railway museum in the grounds, ℗ (01) 845 2758. The handmade models were built by Cyril Fry, a railway engineer and draughtsman in the 1930s. They are laid out on a track which includes stations, bridges, trams, barges, boats and the River Liffey.

Swords, just inland from Malahide, has a very interesting monastic settlement found by St Columba in AD 563. The monastery flourished, although raided by the Norsemen, and became so rich that it was known as 'The Golden Prebend'. To protect their precious manuscripts and jewelled croziers, the monks built a **round tower**, 74ft (22.5m) high, the remains of which you can see in the Church of Ireland grounds. The church is 14th century with a square tower. They can be viewed from the outside only. The archbishops of the 12th and 13th centuries were often as well-armed as any baron, and the Archbishop of Dublin built the strongly fortified castle at Swords for himself. The 12th-century **Archbishop's Castle** is five-sided and has been shored up against further ruin; its court-yard is enclosed by strong walls flanked by square towers. **Portmarnock**, 5 miles (8km) further south along the coast, has a beach 3 miles (4.8km) long nicknamed 'velvet strand'. Two miles (3.2km) inland at Balgriffin, just off the R107, is **St Doulagh's Church** (*contact Canon Cooper in advance to make arrangements about the key if you wish to go inside, ℗ (01) 845 0239*), which incorporates a 12th-century anchorite cell and a small subterranean chamber covering a sunken bath, known as St Catherine's Well. The stone-roofed chancel dates from the 12th century. A square tower was added in the 15th century. The Velvet Strand stretches up the neck of the Howth Peninsula, whilst a mile (1.6km) out to sea is **Ireland's Eye**, a great place for a picnic; you can take a boat out there from Howth Harbour during the summer months. Its name comes from the corruption of *Inis Eireann*, which means 'island of Eire', a Gaelic goddess. The old stone church on the island is all that is left of a 6th-century monastery.

Howth comes from the Danish word *hoved*, meaning 'head'. Before the Anglo-Norman family of St Lawrence muscled their way into the area, Howth was a Danish settlement. The castle still remains in the hands of the St Lawrence family. The public are allowed to walk around tropically bright gardens (*open 8am–sunset, adm free*); in late spring they are gloriously coloured by rhododendrons. There is a lovely story attached to the castle which concerns Grace O'Malley, the famous 16th-century pirate-queen from County Mayo. She stopped in at Howth to replenish her supplies of food and water, and decided to visit the St Lawrences. The family were eating however, and she was refused admittance. Enraged by this rudeness, she snatched Lord Howth's infant son and heir and sailed away with him to Mayo. She returned the child only on condition that the gates of the castle were always left open at mealtimes, and a place set at the table for the head of the O'Malley clan—a custom which is still kept. The village of Howth has plenty of charm, it used to be an important mailboat port until superseded by Dun Laoghaire. Today, its harbour is full of pleasure craft.

In the northern suburbs of Dublin, in Malahide Road, is the **Casino at Marino** (*open mid-June–30 Sept, daily, 9.30–6.30; Oct–early-June, Sat, 10–5, Sun, 2–5; adm; ✆ (01) 833 1618*), an 18th-century miniature classical temple of three storeys designed by Sir William Chambers, between 1762 and 1771, for Lord Charlemont. It is one of Ireland's architectural gems. The public park nearby was part of Lord Charlemont's estate, the main house being demolished in 1921. It was exceedingly fortunate that this beautiful building did not go the same way. It has recently been restored and opened to the public. So ingenious was the architect that from the outside it only appears to be one storey high. The basement is actually below street level, whilst the ground and first floor are not distinguished in the façade. Inside are splendid inlaid floors, delicate plasterwork ceilings and silk-covered walls. Close by is **Croke Park**, the famous hurling ground. Further west at Glasnevin are the **National Botanical Gardens** (*open summer Mon–Sat, 9–6, Sun, 11–6; winter Mon–Sat, 10–4.30, Sun, 11–4.30, ✆ (01) 837 7596*), which were founded in 1795 by the Royal Dublin Society. The range of beautiful plants and mature trees here make it a wonderful place to walk. There is a magnificent curvilinear glasshouse over 400ft (122m) in length, built and designed by the Dublin ironmaster Richard Turner between 1843 and 1869. Funds have been raised for its restoration.

South County Dublin and the Coast

Blackrock is a pleasant middle-class suburb south of Dublin, with a pretty public park overlooking the sea. In the 19th century, Martello towers were built all along this wharf to warn of a possible invasion by Napoleon. At **Monkstown**, about ½ mile (0.3km) south is the headquarters of *Comhaltas Ceoltóirí Eireann*, the cultural movement set up in 1951 to preserve and nurture traditional Irish entertainment. In the summer a variety of shows of traditional music, singing and dancing is held here every week. The building also includes a music library (*see* 'Activities').

Dun Laoghaire, pronounced *Dun Lay-reh*, is a terminus for car ferry services from Britain. This Victorian town, with its bright terraced houses, was traditionally a holiday resort which is pleasant to stroll around before exploring the wilder delights of the Wicklow Mountains. Dun Laoghaire is called after Laoghaire, who was high king of Ireland when St Patrick converted him in the 5th century. For a time this busy port was called Kingstown, after George IV visited Ireland in 1821, but the name was dropped at the establishment of the Free State. The houses along the Marine Parade are very handsome, painted different colours, and with intricate ironwork and Regency detail. The two great granite piers were built between 1817 and 1859. Both make for an invigorating walk, especially on a Sunday for people-watching. It is an important **yachting centre**, and the Royal Saint George and Royal Irish Clubs are situated here. **The National Maritime Museum of Ireland** is in the Mariner's Church, Haigh Terrace (*open May–Sept, Tue–Sun, 2–5; adm;* ☎ *(01) 280 0969*). The Sacred Heart Oratory, Dominican Convent, George's Street is a little gem of the Celtic Revival style, decorated by Sister Concepta Lynch in a combination of Celtic and Art Nouveau style. Access by appointment only. **Marine Parade**, laid out with trees and flowers, takes you to **James Joyce's Tower** in Sandycove (*open May–Sept, Mon–Fri, 10–5, Sat, 10–5, Sun, 2–6; April and Oct on workdays only; Nov–April by appointment only; adm;* ☎ *(01) 280 8571*). In fact the Martello tower was rented by Oliver St John Gogarty, whose witty book *As I Walked Down Sackville Street* is a must for all true Hibernian enthusiasts. Joyce stayed with him for the weekend, and used the visit in the opening scene of *Ulysses*. Gogarty ('stately plump Buck Mulligan'), and James Joyce later quarrelled. Now their names are perpetually linked. Few people have actually read *Ulysses*, and for a long time it was banned by the heavy-handed Irish censor for revealing too much of the earthy Dublin character. But the tower is a shrine where foreigners, especially Americans, can worship and ponder over the collection of Joyceana. Just beside the tower is a forty-foot bathing place. In *Ulysses*, Buck Mulligan had a morning dip here. It is traditionally a men-only bathing spot, but women do break the barriers. Aficionados swim here all year round, even on Christmas Day.

Dalkey, adjoining, is a small fishing village where Bernard Shaw used to stay and admire the skies from Dalkey Hill. In the 15th and 16th centuries it used to be the main landing place for passengers from England. In the main street are the remains of fortified mansions from that time. A boat may be hired from Coliemore Harbour to Dalkey Island where there is a Martello tower and the remains of an ancient church (*see* 'Activities'). The Vico road runs along the coast, unfolding beautiful views of Killiney Bay. From the village centre you can walk to Sorrento Point where you get a panoramic view of the distant coastline, the Sugar Loaf Mountains and the sweep of Killiney Bay itself. If you climb Killiney Hill you will have an even clearer view of the bay, the mountains and the Liffey Valley. Overlooking the crescent bay is **Ayesha Castle** (*open April and May, Tues–Thurs, 2–5, June and July weekends 11–3; other times by appointment; adm, extra with tea;* ☎ *(01) 285 2323*), a neo-Gothic granite pile which has a small formal garden, and steep paths which lead through woods down towards the sea. On the south side of the hill is an old church and a collection of stones known as the 'Druid's Chair'. The obelisk here was put up as a famine-relief project in the 1840s.

You pass through the little village of Glencullen on the R117 if you wish to go higher into the Dublin Hills, which merge into the Wicklow Mountains at Enniskerry. You can take the old 'Military Road' up into the Wicklow glens, or go back towards Dublin on the R116 through forest and hill. On the way to Rathfarnham, a pleasant suburb about 25 minutes from the city centre, is **Marlay Park** (*gardens open all year, 10–5, with longer hours in* *the summer; adm free; ✆ (01) 493 4059).* Formerly the estate of David La Touche, an 18th-century banker, it was left to the county for public use. Dublin County Council has developed it, with a **crafts centre** in the converted stables, where you can buy some lovely things. The craft workers include a bookbinder, harpmaker, woodcarver, antique restorer and potter.the parkland is laid out with lakes, woods, a golf course and miniature railway. The house itself is still being restored. The **Wicklow Way**, a long-distance, sign-posted walking trail over the mountains, starts in Marlay Park. **Sandyford**, a neighbouring suburb, contains the green shades of **Fernhill Garden**, at Lamb's Cross (*open Mar–Nov, Tues–Sat, 11–5; Sun 2–6, bank holidays 11–5; adm; ✆ (01) 295 6000*). Giant Wellingtonia redwood trees form a sheltered walk, the front field is a wild meadow where cowslips grow, and in the walled garden is a Victorian vegetable and flower garden. There is also a rare example of a Victorian level garden and a fine rhododendron collection.

Lucan, a suburb to the west of the city, used to be a minor Bath, and is placed on a beautiful stretch of the Liffey. James Gandon (1743–1823), Ireland's most famous architect, lived here and is buried in Drumcondra graveyard. The village is now very built-up.

Shopping

Crafts: Malahide Castle craft shop. Marlay Park Craft Centre, Rathfarnham, ✆ (01) 494 2083, for pottery, musical instruments, woven cloth. Open Mon–Sat 11–5.30, Sun 11–6. Coach-house designs, The Crescent, Monkstown, for dried flowers and baskets. Sweet snackbar attached.

Delicacies: Hick's Pork Butchers, Woodpark, Sallynoggin, ✆ (01) 285 4430. Frequently referred to as the best pork butcher in Dublin selling wonders such as garlic or orange and fennel seed sausages. Cavistons Delicatessen, 59 Glasthule Road, Sandycove, ✆ (01) 280 9120. Old-fashioned-style deli with fresh fish, Irish cheeses, smoked salmon. Boswell's, Sydney terrace, Blackrock, ✆ (01) 288 2287, for more gourmet sausages and breads. Superquinn, Blackrock Shopping Centre, stocks Irish cheese, honey, chocolate and organic produce.

Fresh fish: Nicky's Plaice, Howth Harbour, Monday to Friday, ✆ (01) 832 3557.

Activities

Golf: at Portmarnock, a premier tournament course, ✆ (01) 846 2601. The Open Golf Centre, Newtown House, St Margaret's, ✆ (01) 864 0324, off main Ashbourne to Slane road, adjacent to the airport; 27 holes; open to visitors 7 days a week on a pay and play basis. Also has driving range and tuition. The Royal Dublin Golf Course, North Bull Island, Dollymount, ✆ (01) 833 7153. Luttrelstown Golf Course, Clonsilla, Co. Dublin, ✆ (01) 821 3237.

Pony-trekking: Calliaghstown Riding Centre, Calliaghstown, Rathcoole, ✆ (01) 458 9236. Malahide Riding School, Ivy Grange, Malahide, ✆ (01) 846 3622.

Hunting: with the Fingal Harriers, ✆ (01) 849 1467.

Walking: The Wicklow Way starts in Marlay Park. The signposted trail goes over the Dublin Hills into the glens of the Wicklow Mountains, and down to Clonegal in County Carlow. The Way is marked on Ordinance Survey maps, 1/50000.

Fishing: Trout fishing on the River Dodder and Bohernabrenna Reservoir, contact Redmond O'Hanlon, ✆ (01) 298 2112. Sea fishing all along Dublin coastline, contact Hugh O'Rourke, IFSA, ✆ (01) 280 6873.

Sailing: junior, youth and adult courses in sail training and windsailing from Fingall Sailing School, Upper Strand Road, Broadmeadow Estuary, Malahide, ✆ (01) 845 3689. Dun Laoghaire Sailing School, 115 Lower George Street, Dun Laoghaire, ✆ (01) 280 6654.

Windsurfing: Wind and Wave Windsurfing School, 16a The Crescent, Monkstown, County Dublin, ✆ (01) 284 4177.

Beaches: Balscadden Beach, Howth, is sandy but shallow. Portmarnock and Malahide are long and sandy. Portmarnock has donkey rides in summer. Portrane and Donabate are famous for their dunes. Portrane has a bird sanctuary at the north end. Killiney is stony, and good for long walks.

Racing: at Leopardstown. See the *Irish Field* or *Racing Post* for dates.

Where to Stay

expensive

The **Royal Marine Hotel**, Dun Laoghaire, ✆ (01) 280 1911. Old-fashioned, comfortable and friendly. The best rooms are situated in the old building.

moderate

Chestnut Lodge, 2 Vesey Place, Monkstown, ✆ (01) 280 7860. Gracious Georgian house with lovely comfortable rooms, good breakfasts and a very friendly atmosphere where nothing is too much trouble. It is situated close to Dun Laoghaire Ferry. Mrs Carroll, **Avondale House**, Scribblestown, Castleknock, ✆ (01) 838 6545. Great food, comfortable rooms, stunning décor; close to the airport.

inexpensive

Mrs A. Dalton, **Annesgrove**, 28 Rosmeen Gardens, Dun Laoghaire, ✆ (01) 280 9801. Clean and cosy. Mrs M. Treanor, **Seaglade House**, Coast Road, Portmarnock, ✆ (01) 846 0179. Also clean and cosy.

Eating Out

There is a wealth of good restaurants in County Dublin.

King Sitric, East Pier, Howth, ✆ (01) 832 5235. Famous for its seafood.

Ayumi-Ya, Japanese Restaurant, New Park Centre, Newtown Park Avenue, Blackrock, ✆ (01) 831767. Excellent seafood, vegetarian stir-fry, noodles and tempura. **Restaurant na Mara**, Dun Laoghaire, ✆ (01) 280 0509. Classical seafood place over the elegant DART station. A touch formal. **Claret's**, 63 Main Street, Blackrock, ✆ (01) 288 2008. Modern French cooking and excellent service. Try the marinated wild salmon and the crème brulée. The **Red Bank Restaurant**, 7 Church Street, Skerries, ✆ (01) 849 1005. Superb fish.

Saffron, 62 Lower George Street, Dun Laoghaire. High-class take-away, mainly southern Indian. **China Sichaun Restaurant**, 4 Lower Kilmacud Road, Stillorgan, ✆ (01) 288 0882. Authentic Sichuan food. The **Old Schoolhouse**, Coolbanagher, Swords, ✆ (01) 840 2846. Informal bistro with pretty Victorian conservatory. **La Tavola**, 114 Rock Road, Booterstown, ✆ (01) 283 5101. Good crunchy pizzas and pasta in a cheerful little bistro. **Torula's**, 21 Railway Road, Dalkey, ✆ (01) 284 0756. Light snacks during the day and more substantial food in the evenings in the pretty village of Dalkey. **Roches Bistro**, New Street, Malahide, ✆ (01) 854 2777. Cheerful local restaurant with chequered tablecloths and good country-style French food. Nice atmosphere. **Old Street Wine Bar**, Old Street, Malahide, ✆ (01) 845 1882. Hearty soups, vegetarian options and fruit pies. Good for lunch as well as dinner. Full of *craic*. **Mr Hung's**, 5a, The Crescent, Monkstown, ✆ (01) 284 3982. Cantonese Cooking. **P.D's Woodhouse**, 1 Coliemore Road, Dalkey, ✆ (01) 284 9399. Nice friendly atmosphere and tasty oak wood-barbequed food.

Outlaws, 62 Upper George Street, Dun Laoghaire, ✆ (01) 384 2817. Cheerful spot serving good steaks, chicken and burgers. **Krishna Indian Restaurant**, 1st Floor, 47 Lower George Street, Dun Laoghaire, ✆ (01) 280 1855. Good food and big meals, above a butcher's shop. **Malahide Castle**, Malahide, ✆ (01) 845 2655. Good daytime soups and snacks. **Purty Kitchen**, Old Dun Laoghaire Road, ✆ (01) 284 3576. Good food with a strong emphasis on seafood and tempting salads. *Open for lunch only.* **The Queens**, Castle Street, Dalkey, ✆ (01) 285 4569. Pub serving good sandwiches and seafood chowder. Pleasant on a sunny day. **Foxes Pub**, Glencullen, ✆ (01) 295 8714. Good seafood pub on Wicklow border.

... The Dublin girl that's born an' bred,
Above all Ireland holds her head,
Still upper lip's her beauty.
No holy poke, she likes a joke,
She shies at nayther drink nor smoke,
An' at cards she knows her duty

The Dublin boy that's born and bred,
Above 'em all high holds his head
For swagger, sport, an' cunning!
He's neither North, South, East, nor West,
But a blend of all that each holds best,
An' the tips he gets are stunning...

Here's Granua Aile, boys! Drink her down!
Quick end to all her troublin'!
May beauty, wit, and wisdom crown
Her Parliament in Dublin!

Dublin doggerel

Dublin has a worldwide reputation for culture, wit, friendliness and beauty, and this image perpetuates itself as the casual Dublin charm works its way into the heart of every visitor. Irish people themselves call it, 'dear dirty Dublin', and at first glance you may think that they are right and discount the affection in their voices when they talk about it. For there is no doubt that Dublin can be a bit of a disappointment and you may ask yourself what on earth all the fuss is about: the rosy-coloured Georgian squares and delicate, perfectly proportioned doorways are jumbled up together with some grotesque adventures into

DUBLIN

1 Abbey Theatre
2 Airport
3 Bank of Ireland in old Parliament building
4 Botanic Gardens
5 Christ Church Cathedral 11th-c Strongbow's tomb
6 City Hall 18th-c
7 Civic Museum Record of Dublin's history
8 Connolly Station
9 Croke Park hurling and Gaelic football
10 Dublin Castle
11 Eblana Theatre Busarus main Bus Station
12 Four Courts

13 Gate Theatre
14 Government Buildings
15 Heuston Station
16 Hugh Lane Municipal Gallery of Modern Art
17 Lansdowne Road Rugby Ground
18 Leinster House: Dail National Library
19 Mansion House
20 Olympia Theatre
21 Pearse Station
22 Phoenix Park and Zoo
23 Pro Cathedral
24 Royal Dublin Society Showgrounds
25

26 St Michan's Church remarkable vaults
27 St Patrick's Cathedral, Swift's tomb
28 St Stephen's Green
29 Tourist Information Centre
30 Trinity College and Library Book of Kells
31 Powerscourt Shopping Centre, S. William Quay
32 Custom House, Custom Quay
33 Rotunda Hospital, Parnell Square
34 Guiness Brewery
35 St Catherine's Church
36 Nat. Museum, Kildare St.
37 Marshes' Library, St Patrick's Close
38 St Werburgh's Church, Werburgh St.

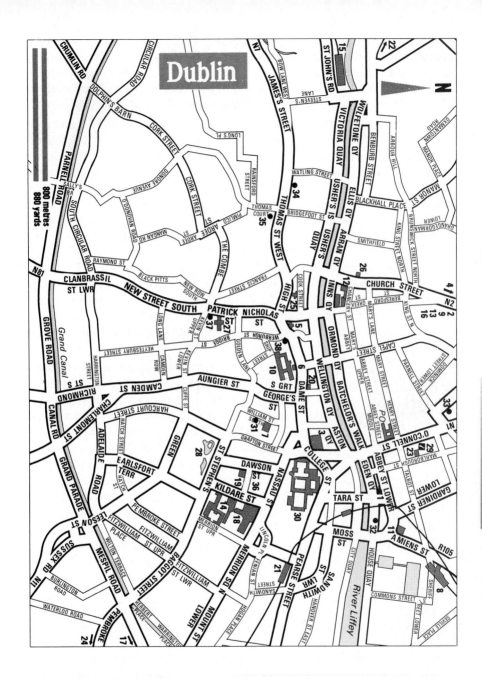

505

modern architecture. Fast-food signs and partially demolished buildings mingle with expensive and tacky shops, and the housing estates through which you pass on the way into the centre can be depressing. The tall houses north of the Liffey were divided into run-down flats, although many are now being done up and through the doors and windows you catch glimpses of their former glory—elegant staircases and marvellous plasterwork.

Modern Dublin was bent on tumbling the past or ignoring it so that it crumbled away on its own, especially during the seventies. Should you ask about Wood Quay, official indifference reveals itself. Wood Quay was the complete 9th- to 11th-century Danish settlement of houses, walls and quays which was recently excavated, giving great insight into the lives of those first Dubliners. The Dublin City Corporation actually built their ugly modern office block on top of it, despite sustained protests from those who felt the old city should be preserved. On the positive side, the Custom House Quay development is a fine attempt at regeneration of the docklands area; it houses a financial centre. And the last few years have seen a quickening of interest in preserving the lovely old buildings of the past. The Dublin Millennium Celebrations in 1988 caused a great sprucing up, and Dubliners took great pride in their city's history and heritage. In 1991 Dublin was the European City of Culture, which encouraged more refurbishment. Sadly, there is still a certain amount of uncoordinated planning. Dublin is threatened with plans for road-widening, and what amounts to a motorway has been built cutting through the city centre.

Nevertheless, you will find that gradually the charm and atmosphere of Dublin—and atmosphere is what it is all about—begins to filter through that first, negative impression. Get up early and explore the ancient medieval streets around Dublin Castle in the morning sunshine, and breakfast at Bewley's Café. Walk down Grafton Street, where noisy, laughing shoppers mingle with some genuine eccentrics. Have a few drinks in one of its atmospheric pubs; the city is about rhythm and the ability to let go, to enjoy oneself (something the Dubliners excel at). Relax, go with the flow and notice the pleasant things about Dublin which have been staring you in the face all along.

History

The Greek philosopher Ptolemy mentioned Dublin in AD 140, when it was called Eblana, but it really came to prominence under the Danes during the 9th century because of its importance as a fording place and as a base for maritime expeditions. They established themselves on a section of ground between the River Liffey and Christ Church. The name Dublin comes from the Irish *Dubhlinn* (dark pool), although the Irish form in official use at the moment is *Baile Atha Cliath*: the town of the hurdle ford. This refers to a river crossing near the present Heuston Station, made before the Vikings arrived.

After the Norman invasion in 1169 Dublin began to play a dominant role as the centre of English power. The Anglo-Normans fortified themselves with strong castles, and the area surrounding Dublin where they settled, was known as the Pale; anything outside was dangerous and barbaric—hence the expression, 'beyond the Pale'! For a short and glorious period in the late 18th century Ireland had its own parliament here; the élite who sat in it had many liberal ideas such as the introduction of Catholic emancipation. It is interesting to speculate whether the course of Ireland's history might have been happier if this independent parliament had been allowed to develop. A great surge of urban building took place during 'Grattan's Parliament' (1782–1800). Grattan was typical of the liberal landowners who wanted legislative reform, and is remembered for his powers of oratory. Unfortunately, the influence of the French Revolution, and the growth of the United Irishmen frightened the British Government. The 1798 Rising was a realization of their worst fears, and the English Parliament resumed direct control of Irish affairs in 1800. This meant that the resident and educated ruling class left Dublin, and with them some of its dynamism and cultural expansion. The struggle for independence from English rule manifested itself in violent episodes and street clashes in the 19th century, with violence becoming more common in the early 20th century. During the 1916 Rising, buildings and lives were shattered by Nationalists fighting with British troops, and later during the Civil War that followed the peace with England. Many of those buildings such as the Customs House, the masterpiece of James Gandon (1743–1823) have been restored to their former grandeur.

It was under the rule of the so-called Anglo-Irish Ascendency that Dublin acquired her gracious streets and squares, which amaze one with their variety. Many of the houses were built in small groups by speculators when Dublin was the fashionable place to be— hence the variety. Each door is slightly different and the patterns of the wrought-iron balconies and railings change from house to house. You will not see ironwork like this in London, as most railings were ripped up and melted down during the First World War.

The size of Dublin increased very slowly during the 19th and early 20th centuries, due in part to the lack of industrialization countrywide and to the famine and emigration. The population started to grow in the 1950s with a shift from rural to urban areas; and today Dubliners suffer from a lack of housing and jobs, facilities for sewage, and cars and heavy trucks. The population of young people in Ireland, and in Dublin particularly, is high. Greater Dublin has a population of nearly one million, and plenty of families are living on the dole. Unfortunately, lack of opportunities is syphoning off the most educated, and they are leaving for America or England after going through university; although Dublin has recently been successful in attracting a number of good-size high technology projects. Whilst income per person is about 70 per cent that of Britain, the cost of living is higher. Car theft and joyriding have become as common here as in other European capitals, so make sure you lock your car and don't leave anything of value visible.

Throughout the centuries Dublin has produced great writers: Swift (who suggested in his frighteningly plausible essay *A Modest Proposal* that the ruling class in Ireland should eat all newborn babies to cure the problems of poverty and overpopulation!), Bishop Berkeley, Edmund Burke, Thomas Moore, Sheridan, Le Fanu, Wilde and Goldsmith to name but a few. Towards the end of the 19th century Dublin became the centre of the Cultural Movement, which resulted in the formation of the Gaelic League, which became entangled with the Nationalists' aspirations of the time. How much influence this movement had on the next flurry of great writers it is hard to say, but George Bernard Shaw, George Moore, James Stephens, Yeats, James Joyce and later Samuel Beckett drew much of their inspiration from the streets of Dublin. This is an extract from *No Mean City* by Oliver St John Gogarty (1878–1957), a writer, wit and surgeon who details Dublin's famous men:

> *Dublin, Dublin of the vistas! What names come to mind, names filling more than two centuries from the days of the gloomy Dean Swift, who left his money to found a lunatic asylum 'to show by one sarcastic touch no nation needed it so much', to Mrs Bernard Shaw, who left her money to teach manners to Irishmen; and some say (they would in Dublin) that, in spite of all his acumen, the man for whom it was principally intended failed to see the sarcastic touch; Oliver Goldsmith; Bishop Berkeley, who wrote 'Westward the course of Empire takes it way' and went his way to Rhode Island and gave his name to Berkeley, California; Hamilton, who discovered proleptically the Quaternion Theory by the banks of the Royal Canal; Burke, who thundered in defence of American liberation; Molyneaux, whose nationalism caused his books to be burned by the common hangman; Fitzgerald, who anticipated Marconi in the discovery of aetherial waves; Mahaffy, who was the greatest Humanist of his time as well as the expeller from Trinity College of Oscar Wilde to Oxford; down to Yeats, A. E., and lastly James Joyce, in whose Anna Livia Plurabelle the whole history of Dublin may be discerned by thought, this time cataleptic. All these men lived in Dublin, but most of them died elsewhere. Dublin, that stick of a rocket which remains on the ground while its stars shoot off to light the darkness and die enskied.*

Getting There

By air: a variety of airlines fly into Dublin Airport, which is 8 miles (10km) from the city. Aer Lingus handles the most traffic, ✆ (01) 844 4777.

By airport bus: a bus service runs between the Central Bus Station, Busarus in Store Street and Dublin Airport. Buses run every 20 minutes from early morning to 11.20pm. IR£2.50 each way; children under 16 pay half. You can also get the cheaper 41A and 41C buses, which run to and from the airport and the city's Central Bus Station.

By taxi: to the city from the airport costs IR£10–12.

By car: reliable car hire firms with a base at the airport include Avis, ✆ (01) 844 4466; Murray's, ✆ (01) 668 1777; and Hertz, ✆ (01) 666 2255.

By boat: to Dun Laoghaire or Dublin ferry ports. Buses 7,7A and 8 run from Dun Laoghaire to O'Connell bridge, which is in the centre of Dublin. If you arrive at Dun Laoghaire a train from the pier will take you to Pearse station on Westland Row, and then continue on to Connolly Station. Single fare, IR£1.10. If you arrive at the Dublin ferry port, there is no trouble finding buses to the city centre on the Alexandra Road. All buses with An Lar labels are going there.

By bus: all intercity Expressway buses run by Bus Eireann end up in Busarus, Store Street. Dublin Bus controls all public bus services in the Greater Dublin Area (which includes parts of Wicklow, Kildare and Meath), including the DART feeder system and commuter services, ✆ (01) 836 6222. A Dublin District Bus and Train timetable is available from CIE (Coras Iompair Eireann), Ireland's national internal transport authority, at 59 Upper O'Connell Street, D1. All information regarding rail and bus services may be obtained from the CIE Information Bureau, ✆ (01) 836 6222.

By rail: there are two main train stations. Heuston serves the south, southwest and west; ✆ (01) 677 1871. Connolly serves Wexford, Sligo, Derry and Belfast, and DART stations north of Dublin including Howth, Skerries and Balbriggan, ✆ (01) 874 2941. DART (Dublin Area Rapid Transit) electric trains serve 25 suburban stations from Howth to Bray.

Left luggage: Connolly Station, Mon–Sat 7.40–9.30, Sun 9–9.40. Heuston Station, Mon–Sat 7.15–9, Sun 8–2 and 5–9. Busarus Station, Mon–Sat 8–8, Sun 10–6.

Getting Around

Look back to the section entitled 'Getting Around Ireland' (**Travel**, pp.10–12) for details of concession tickets, etc. The best and cheapest way of getting around Dublin is by walking, because most of the museums, shops and galleries are fairly near to each other. The tourist office should give you a free street map, or you can buy one at countless stationers.

By bus: a guide is available from CIE, 59 Upper O'Connell Street, and any of the tourist offices will help you with your route. You should try and have the correct change, although it's not a disaster if you don't.

By taxi: found outside hotels and railway stations, and in special taxi parking areas in Central Dublin. There are 24-hour ranks at St Stephen's Green and O'Connell Street. Taxis should always have meters. They charge extra per piece of luggage, per person and at night.

By car: parking is difficult in the centre, but there is a new computerised system with strategically placed screens telling you which car parks have spaces. The main car parks are in Frederick Street and the St Stephen's Green Shopping Centre, and there is metered parking around St Stephen's Green and Merrion Square. On the north side you might find a parking place in the Irish Life Shopping Centre, entrance off Lower Abbey Street. Driving in Dublin is delightfully disordered, so be on your guard. It is mostly a matter of nerve and panache! Using your horn is the worst insult, so keep it as a last resort.

Dublin is a compact city; the central area clusters around the River Liffey and occupies about one square mile. Most of the museums, galleries, theatres, architectural sights and restaurants are within this small area. The Liffey separates the north side from the south. It is spanned by several bridges, the most central being O'Connell

Bridge. The streets along the River Liffey are called quays, and they change names between bridges. St Stephen's Green, Trinity College, Grafton Street and the Castle area are south of the river. O'Connell Street, Henry Street and Parnell Square are north. Grafton Street and Henry Street are pedestrianized. Phoenix Park (1760acres/712ha) is under 2 miles (3km) from the city centre, to the north-west. The Grand Canal crosses the city and joins the River Liffey, enclosing the southern part of the city centre in a gentle curve.

Dublin ✆ (01–)   ***Tourist Information***

13/14 Upper O'Connell Street, ✆ 284 4768, all year. July and August: Mon–Sat, 8.30–8; Sun,10.30–2; Sept–May, Mon–Sat, 9–5; June, Mon–Sat 9–3.30.

Baggot Street Bridge, ✆ 676 5871, Feb–30 Oct, Mon–Fri, 9.15–5.15 (small information office).

Dublin Airport: ✆ 844 5387, daily, Oct to beginning of May, 8–6; May, 8am–8pm; June to first half of Sept 8–10.30; second half of Sept 8–8.

Dublin ✆ (01–)   ***Practical A–Z***

Airlines: Aer Lingus, 41 Upper O'Connell Street, D1 and 42 Grafton Street, D2, ✆ 844 4777 for UK enquiries, ✆ 844 4747 for European and Trans-Atlantic flights. Ryanair, 3 Dawson Street, D2; ✆ 677 4422. British Midland, Merrion Centre, Merrion Rd, ✆ 704 4259.

Banks: open Mon–Fri, 10–4, open until 5pm Thurs.

Bureaux de Change: Dublin and East Tourism, 14 Upper O'Connell Street, D1, ✆ 874 7733. Thomas Cook, 118 Grafton Street, D2, ✆ 677 1307. American Express, 116 Grafton Street, D2, ✆ 677 2874.

Car hire: Avis Rent-a-Car, 1 Hanover Street East, D2, ✆ 677 4010; Murray's Europcar, Baggot Street Bridge, D4, ✆ 668 1777.

Chemist, late-night: 55 Lower O'Connell Street, D1, ✆ 873 0427.

Embassies: *see* pp.21–22.

Emergency services: dial 999.

Hospitals: The Meath Hospital, Heytsbury Street, ✆ 453 6555.

St Vincent Hospital, Elm Park, D4, ✆ 269 4533.

St James' Hospital, James' Street, D8, ✆ 453 7941.

Rotunda Maternity Hospital, Parnell Square, D1, ✆ 873 0700.

The Dublin Dental Hospital, 20 Lincoln Place, Dublin 2, ✆ 662 0766.

Irish Student Travel Agency (USIT): 19 Aston Quay, ✆ 679 8833. Open Mon–Fri 9.30–5.30, Sat 10–1.

An Oíge (Irish Youth Hostel Assoc.): 61 Mountjoy Street, D1, ✆ 830 1766.

Passenger car ferries: Stena Sealink, 15 Westmoreland Street, D2, ✆ 280 8844. B&I, 10 Westmoreland Street, D2, ✆ 679 7977. Irish Continental Line, 2/4 Merrion Row, D2, ✆ 661 0511.

Police (*Garda Siochana*): Dublin Metropolitan Area HQ, Harcourt Terrace, ✆ 676 3481.

Taxis: Try calling VIP Radio Taxi, ✆ 478 3333; National Radio Cabs, ✆ 677 2222; Blue Cabs, ✆ 676 1111/676 1320; Metro Cabs, ✆ 668 1777.

Telephones: local calls cost 20p for three minutes. Payphone centres are located in the General Post Office, O'Connell Street, and beside the Gaiety Theatre on South King Street. More and more of these are cardphones. The cards may be bought in the post office and selected newsagents. The big hotels are other reliable sources for public telephones.

Dublin ✆ (01–)   ***Books and Publications***

Listings: *In Dublin* magazine was started by a group of students and was so successful that you can now buy it at every news-stand. Bord Fáilte publish a guide to *What's On In Dublin*, which is very useful as well. Also, check *Hot Press* for concert and cinema listings. The *Evening Press and Herald* also cinema listings. Read the *Irish Times* for reviews of plays, concerts, films. Every Saturday it also lists special happenings in Dublin and the provinces. Comhaltas Ceoltoiri Eireann at 32 Belgrave Square, Monkstown (take bus 8 from O'Connell Street), have a booklet on what's on in the traditional music scene, ✆ 280 0295.

Maps: Free 'In Dublin' street map from tourist offices, USIT and big hotels. Bord Fáilte sell a good map, and Geographia publish a colour street atlas for IR£4.

For books of Irish interest: Cathach Books, 10 Duke Street, ✆ 671 8676; Fred Hanna, Nassau Street, D2, ✆ 677 1255; Waterstone's, Dawson Street, D2, ✆ 679 1415; Eason & Son, Lower O'Connell Street, D1, ✆ 873 3811. Greene's Bookshop Ltd, 16 Clare Street, D2, ✆ 676 2554, for scarce and out-of-print books. Another bookshop with many books of Irish interest, in a tranquil, learned atmosphere is Parsons, Bridge House, Baggot Street, Bridge, ✆ 660 3616. Winding Stair Books, 40 Lower Ormond Quay, ✆ 873 3292, has an excellent café and three floors of second hand books and a lovely view. The bookshop in the Dublin Writers' Museum, 18 Parnell Square provides an out-of-print and antiquarian book search service, ✆ 872 2077.

Museums, Galleries and Libraries

The **National Museum** in Kildare Street, and 7–9 Merrion Row (*open Tues–Fri, 10–5, Sun, 2–5; adm free;* ✆ *661 8811*) is absolutely vital for anyone who has not yet realized that Ireland between AD 600 and 900 was the most civilized part of Europe. It has the finest collection of Celtic ornaments and artefacts in the world, and items recently excavated from the Danish settlement in Wood Quay. The Historical Collection traces the history of Ireland from the 18th to the mid-20th century. In the Antiquities Department you can see the beautiful filigree gold whorl enamelling and design which reached perfection in the Tara brooch and the Ardagh Chalice. The many beautiful torcs, croziers, and decorated shrines on display will leave you amazed at the sophistication and skill of the craftsmen in those days. Also very interesting are the findings of the Stone and Early-Bronze Ages. Besides the Antiquities Department, you will find the Art and Industry Departments fascinating.

Linked to the museum is the **National Library**, which is also in Kildare Street. It has over half a million books and a fascinating collection of Irish-interest source material. There is usually an exhibition on in the entrance hall. The staff are very helpful to visitors. **The Genealogical Office** is also housed here (*open Mon–Fri, half-day on Sat; adm free; ✆ 661 8811*). Incidentally, the impressive building next door is Leinster House, the Irish Parliament Building where the Dail sits. If you are in search of natural history (the museum seems to have thousands of stuffed birds, fish and animals, and some fascinating elk skeletons) approach the **National History Museum** from Merrion Street (*open Tues–Sat 10–5, Sun 4–5; closed Mon; adm free; ✆ 661 8811*). It has barely changed in decades and has a charming musty atmosphere.

The National Gallery is in Merrion Square just opposite the fountain (*open weekdays 10–6, except Thurs 10–9; Sun 2–5. Tours on Saturday at 3pm and Sunday at 2.30, 3.15 and 4pm; adm free; ✆ 661 5133*). A statue of George Bernard Shaw greets you in the forecourt. He bequeathed one third of his estate to the gallery because he learnt so much from the pictures. Certainly this is one of the most enjoyable, top-class small galleries in the world. It has just been very sympathetically redecorated and many pictures rehung. There are over two thousand works on view, including a small collection of superb work by Renaissance painters; Spanish, French and Italian 16th- and 17th-century painters; and Dutch Masters. The Irish Room includes work by J. B. Yeats (the father of the poet W. B. Yeats). Also on show are works by Jack Yeats (the brother of W. B. Yeats), his son, who produced wild and colourful oils which are very well regarded; and some elegant portraits by Lavery, Orpen and many others. Gainsborough is well represented with 10 major works. Upstairs in the Arts Reference Library there is a good collection of Irish water-colours. The gallery restaurant is a good place for lunch or early supper, and the shop selling postcards and art books is also excellent.

The Irish Architectural Archive at 73 Merrion Square (south side), a wonderful example of a Georgian town house, opens its reading room to the public (*Mon–Fri 10–5. adm free; ✆ 676 3430*). **The Royal Irish Academy** in Dawson Street has one of the largest collections of ancient Irish manuscripts, one of which is on view (*open Tues–Fri 9.30–5; closed Mondays; adm free; ✆ 676 2570*).

The Dublin Civic Museum, in a fine 18th-century Assembly House in South William Street (*open Tues–Sat, 10–6, Sun 11–2; closed Mondays; adm free*), has a collection of old newspapers, cuttings, prints, pictures and coins which build up a very clear picture of old Dublin. Artefacts include the head of Lord Nelson's statue blown up by the IRA in the 1960's.

Dublinia is an interpretative centre in Christ Church Synod Hall (*open April to mid-September daily 10am–5pm; adm; ✆ 679 4611*). It recreates the period between 1170 and 1540 with life-like displays and audio-visual aids.

Marsh's Library, close to St Patrick's Cathedral in St Patrick's Close (*open weekdays except Tues, 10–5, Sat, 10.30–12.30; adm free although donations are appreciated; ✆ 454 3511*), is the oldest public library in the country and was founded in 1707. Dean Swift once owned the copy of Clarendon's *History of the Great Rebellion*, and you can look at his pencilled notes. The entrance is very welcoming with herbaceous plants softening the stone steps up, and a feeling of hallowed learning inside. The library is classical in proportion and has a superb collection of Latin and Greek literature.

The Municipal Gallery of Modern Art is at 1 Parnell Square (*open Tues–Sat, 9.30–5, Sun 11–5; adm free; ✆ 874 1903*). The bulk of the collection was formed by Sir Hugh Lane in the early 20th century (W. B. Yeats wrote a poem about his bequests), and the gallery has a small but wonderful collection of works by well-known artists; portraits of W. B. Yeats, Synge and other famous Irish figures; and a bust of Lady Gregory by Epstein. Because of a disputed codicil in Lane's will, his pictures alternate between London and Dublin. The stained-glass window by Harry Clarke is magical. It portrays the story of 'St Agnes' Eve' by John Keats.

The Writers' Museum, No.18 Parnell Square (*adm ; ✆ 872 2077*) is a fine 18th-century building. The permanent displays introduce you to centuries of Irish literature, illustrated by letters, photographs, first editions and memorabilia. The Irish Writers Centre within the museum has a varied programme of lectures, readings, workshops and courses. The museum also has a very good bookshop and restaurant.

The Chester Beatty Library (*open Tues–Fri, 10–5; conducted tours Wed and Sat 2.30, closed Mon; adm free; ✆ 269 2386*) is one of the gems of Dublin and is tucked away in Dublin's most fashionable residential area, at 20 Shrewsbury Road, Ballsbridge. To get there, you can catch either a no.6, 7, 7a or 8 bus from Eden Quay, north side, all of which go through the centre of the city and will drop you just by the entrance to Shrewsbury Road. The library has one of the finest private collections of oriental manuscripts and miniatures in the world, as well as albums, picture scrolls, and jades from the Far East. The highlights are the *Korans*, the Persian and Turkish paintings, the Chinese jade books, and Japanese and European woodblock prints. The collection is due to move to Dublin Castle, but no dates have been decided. Do check in advance. It would be a great pity to miss this wonderful exhibition. Sir Alfred Chester Beatty (1875–1968) was an American mining millionaire and collector who decided to make Dublin his home. It is indeed fortunate for Dublin that he left his collection here.

Newman House, 85–6 St Stephen's Green (*open to the public, ✆ 475 7255 for exact details of times as restoration work is still in progress*). These two buildings contain some of the finest late Baroque and Rococo plasterwork in Ireland. No.85 was built in 1738, designed by Richard Cassels, and it contains the ravishing Apollo room, a masterpiece of stucco decoration by the Francini brothers. No.86 was built in 1765 for the MP Richard Chapell Whaley, father of the notorious Buck Whaley whose memoirs of 18th-century

Dublin are still a good read. The house has very good plasterwork by Robert West; the stairhall is decorated with motifs of musical instruments. The two houses were connected and used in the late 19th century for Newman's Catholic University. The extensive and carefully done restoration work has been undertaken by University College, Dublin.

Royal Hospital and Irish Museum of Modern Art, Kilmainham, is situated to the west of the city, close to Heuston Station (*open Tues–Sat, 10–5.30, Sun 12–5.30; © 671 8666*). A 79 bus will drop you close by. The restoration of this wonderful classical building, which is now used as the National Centre for Culture and Arts, is one of the most exciting things to happen to Dublin recently. The Government footed the enormous bill, and has earned much prestige through its role in saving it. The hospital was founded by James Butler, Duke of Ormonde, a very able statesman who survived the turbulent times of the Great Rebellion of 1640, and Cromwell's campaigns. He remained loyal to the Stuart kings, and was well rewarded by Charles II on his succession in 1660. The duke was a pragmatist, and was responsible for securing the passing of the Act of Explanation in 1665, which largely approved the Cromwellian land confiscations. But he also did some very charitable works, amongst them the building of this hospital for pensioner soldiers, similar in style to that of *Les Invalides* in Paris. The Royal Hospital is the largest surviving 17th-century building in Ireland and the most fully classical. Arranged around a quadrangle, it includes a Great Hall hung with rich and splendid royal portraits. The chapel has a magnificent baroque ceiling of plasterwork designs of fruit, flowers and vegetables. Different and sometimes excellent modern art exhibitions are held in the long galleries which were only reopened in 1991, so check out what is on. There are excellent car-parking facilities and a snack restaurant.

Kilmainham Jail (*open July–Sept, daily, 11–6; Oct–May, Mon–Fri, 1–4, Sun, 1–6; adm; © 453 5984*) is now a historical museum. It is rather a grim building where countless patriots were imprisoned, but, nevertheless, it is exceptionally interesting and quite moving. It was used as the prison in the film *In The Name of The Father*, starring Daniel Day Lewis.

At the **Gallery of Photography**, 33 East Essex Street, Temple Bar, you can expect well-presented and interesting exhibitions. Check newspapers and *What's On* for details, or © 671 4654.

The Museum of Childhood, 20 Palmerston Park, Rathmines (*open Sundays only, 2–5.30, © 497 3223*) has a charming private collection of antique dolls and toys.

Fernhill Garden, Sandyford, County Dublin (described under South County Dublin, p.501) has a modern sculpture exhibition every summer. **The James Joyce Museum**, Sandycove, is also described under South County Dublin (p.500). **Malahide Castle** is described in North County Dublin (p.498), as is **Newbridge House**, Donabate (p.497).

Churches and Cathedrals

Christchurch Cathedral is at the western end of Lord Edward Street (*open Oct–April, Tues–Fri, 9.30–4.30, Sat, 10–1; May–Sept, Mon–Sat, 10–5, and Sun, 10–4; adm*). The present building was founded by King Sitric and Bishop Donatus in 1038, expanded by

Strongbow in the 12th century, and heavily restored in the 19th century. The magnificent stonework and graceful pointed arches are well worth a visit, as is the effigy representing Strongbow, who was buried in the church. The crypt is the oldest surviving portion of the building. The arch which joins the cathedral to the Synod Hall delicately frames a view of Winetavern Street and the River Liffey. The Synod Hall contains a medieval exhibition, **Dublinia**, a multi-media exhibition of Dublin life in medieval times for which the opening hours are the same as above (*see* p.513).

St Patrick's Cathedral, a short distance south in Patrick's Street (*open Mon–Fri, 9–6, Sat, 9–5; on Sundays, between services; minimum visitors' contribution*), was founded in 1190 and is Early-English in style. It was built outside the city walls on what was marshy ground by a powerful Norman bishop who was also a baron, in order to outshine Christchurch. In the 14th century it was almost completely rebuilt after a fire and during the 17th century it suffered terribly from the fighting during the Cromwellian campaign, and was not restored until the 1860s. Benjamin Guinness, the drink magnate, provided the initiative and funds for this great undertaking. It is an inspiring experience to attend a choir recital here, for its huge dimensions make a perfect auditorium for the song of red-frocked choir boys. It is here that Dean Swift preached his forceful sermons in an effort to rouse some unselfish thoughts in the minds of his wealthy parishioners; over the door of the robing room is his oft-quoted epitaph, 'He lies where furious indignation can no longer rend his heart.' Swift's death mask, chair and pulpit are displayed in Swift Corner. Nearby is the grave of Stella, Swift's pupil and great love. Notice the monument to Richard Boyle, first Earl of Cork, and the monument to the last of the Irish bards, O'Carolan.

St Werburgh's Church in Werburgh Street, off Christ Church Place (*open to the public by arrangement Mon–Fri, 10–4; entrance by the north door, 7/8 Castle Street; © (01) 478 3710; visitors are invited to give a contribution to its upkeep*), is worth visiting for the massive Geraldine monument and the pulpit, a fine piece of carving, possibly by Grinling Gibbons. Lord Edward Fitzgerald of the United Irishmen and the leader of the 1798 rebellion, is interred in the vault here. This church was for a long time the parish church of Dublin, and before the Chapel Royal in the Dublin Castle complex was built in the 18th century (it is now known as the Church of the Most Holy Trinity), British viceroys were sworn in here.

St Audoen's Church, Cornmarket, off the High Street, is Dublin's only surviving medieval church. The bell tower (restored in the 19th century) has three 15th-century bells. Notice the beautiful Norman font and make a wish at the 'lucky stone'.

St Catherine's Church in Thomas Street. This fine 18th-century church has a lovely Roman Doric façade. It is occasionally used for concerts and owned by the Dublin Corporation. No access inside. The **Rococo Chapel** in the Rotunda Hospital is very sumptuous with large scale allegorical figures, and curving plasterwork decorated with cherubs and putti. This was the first maternity hospital founded in Europe in the 1740s. Arrangements to view it must be made in writing to the Hospital Secretary, Rotunda Hospital, Parnell Square, D1. **St Anne's Church** in Dawson Street is one of the finest 18th-century churches in Dublin (*open for worship during the week and on Sundays*).

Pro Cathedral, Metropolitan Church of St Mary, Marlborough Street. Greek Revival Doric temple built between 1815 and 1825. Lovely sung mass at 11am on Sundays.

The Chapel Royal, Dublin Castle. Designed by Francis Johnston in 1807. Fine exhuberant plasterwork and oak wood carving.

St Michan's on Church Street, west of the Four Courts (*open Mon–Fri, 10–12.45 and 2–4.45; vaults closed Sundays; adm; guided tours by special arrangement Nov–Mar © (01) 672 4154*), is a 17th-century structure on the site of an 11th-century Danish church. Most people are interested in getting to the ghoulish vaults where bodies have lain for centuries without decomposing. Here the air is very dry due to the absorbant nature of the limestone foundations. The skin of the corpses remains as soft as in life and even their joints still work! Layers of coffins have collapsed into each other, exposing arms and legs; you can even see a crusader from the Holy Land. The body of Robert Emmet is said to be buried here. The only things that live down in this curiously warm and fresh atmosphere are spiders who feed on each other and there are so many types that people come from afar to study them. It is said that a Dublin lad has honourable intentions if he takes his girl there! The interior of the church itself is very fine and plain. A superb wooden carving of a violin intermingled with flowers and fruits decorates the choir gallery, and is supposed to be by Grinling Gibbons. Whoever carved it was a genius, and it is sad that so many people go only to the vaults. The guide is an idiosyncratic old man, the warden and odd-job man about the place, who responds enthusiastically to any questions.

Famous Buildings

Many of the great buildings of Dublin were designed by James Gandon (1743–1823). The son of a French man, who was self-educated and studied later under the Scotsman William Chambers, he came to Dublin at the request of John Beresford, a statesman of the time.

Parliament House is now the Bank of Ireland in College Green (*open during banking hours*). The brainchild of Lovat Pearce, who designed it in 1729, it was finished in 1785 by James Gandon. It was between these walls that Grattan stunned everybody with his oratory when he demanded constitutional independence from the English Parliament. Later, in 1800, a well-bribed House voted for the Union and Parliament House became redundant. It is an imposing classical building with Ionic porticos. Inside you may see the coffered ceiling of the old House of Lords, a Waterford chandelier dating from 1765; and two fine 18th-century tapestries depicting the Battle of the Boyne and the Siege of Derry and the Golden Mace. **College Green** itself is a bustling thoroughfare usually jam-packed with cars, pedestrians and bicyclists.

Just opposite Parliament House is the entrance to **Trinity College**, and during term-time the students are clustered around it, joking, chatting, or handing out political leaflets. As you enter through the imposing 1759 façade, you leave bustling Dublin far behind, and come upon a giant square laid out with green lawn and cobbled stone, and surrounded by gracious buildings. Stop to look at the Museum Building which has stone carving by the O'Shea brothers, who also created the amusing monkeys which play round what used to be the Kildare Street Club, the brick palazzo on the northeast corner of Kildare Street. The other buildings in the quadrangle are 18th century and are described below, but first pass through the peaceful grounds into the second quadrangle, as your main objective will probably be to visit **Trinity College Library** to take a look at the priceless *Book of Kells* (*students offer amusing tours around the college for a small fee which includes access to the library*). The library is on the right of the second quadrangle and dates from 1712. It has been a copyright library since 1801 and contains an enormous amount of manuscripts including the diaries of Wolfe Tone and the manuscripts of John Millington Synge. The Library is a fine building and contains the Long Room, which has a barrel-vaulted ceiling and gallery bookcases. The area underneath the Long Room known as the Colonnades, has been remodelled and the *Book of Kells* is permanently displayed there. Every day one of the thick vellum pages of the book is turned to present more fantastic and intricate designs. Someone once said that the book was made up of imaginative doodles! The man who copied out the gospels and enlivened them with such 'doodles' was able to draw so perfectly that sections as small as a postage stamp reveal no flaws when magnified. The book is probably 8th-century and comes from an abbey in Kells, County Meath. Have a look too at the *Book of Durrow*, the *Book of Armagh* and the *Book of Dimma*, which are also beautifully illuminated (*viewing times Mon—Fri, 9.30–5, Sun, 12–5; adm*). Next door is the **Berkely Library** which contains over two million books. It was built in 1967 to designs by Paul Koralek, as was the skilfully designed **Arts Building**, erected in 1978. An audio-visual show, 'The Dublin Experience' (*open late May–Oct; adm*), is held in the Arts building. It tells the story of the city from its Viking beginnings to the present day. The exit through the Arts Building takes you into Nassau Street.

Trinity College was founded in 1592 in the reign of Elizabeth I. The land on which it was erected had once been occupied by the Augustinian monastery of All Hallows, founded by Dermot MacMurragh in the 12th century. The squares are made up of a mixture of buildings, ranging from early 18th century to present-day. The red-brick Rubrics beyond the campanile (detached bell-tower) in the middle of the quad is the oldest bit still standing and dates from *c.* 1700. Oliver Goldsmith had his chambers here, as do present-day students and professors. Trinity College has a long and venerable history; so many famous scholars, wits and well-known men of Ireland were educated here. It was freed from its Protestant-only restrictions in 1873, and Catholics were allowed to study there, but Paul Cullen, the Catholic Archbishop of the day, threatened excommunication to any that did! The university remained the preserve of the Protestant gentry for some time (although that is far from the case now), but distinguished itself by admitting women students as early as 1903, as well as non-Christians. The Provost's House (on the left of the main entrance) is a fine 18th-century mansion. One of its most famous occupants was John Mahaffy (1839–1919) a great scholar and clergyman, as was essential for the fellowship of the college. He was also, in the last year of his life, a knight! His witty dinner talk was legendary, but he could also be very wounding. The story goes that he impressed on Oscar Wilde the importance of good social contacts and brilliant conversation! And he declared that James Joyce's *Ulysses* was 'the inevitable result of extending university to the wrong sort of people'. On the right as you enter the first cobbled quadrangle is the Theatre, or Examination Hall, which was built between 1779 and 1791 with an Adam-style ceiling, and a gilt oak chandelier. On the left is the chapel, built in 1798. Both buildings were designed by William Chambers, the Scottish architect who never actually set foot in Dublin! (*The Theatre and Chapel can be seen on request; ask at the Porter's Lodge*). Beyond the Chapel is the Dining Hall, designed by Richard Cassels (or Castle) in 1743. It was nearly destroyed by fire in 1984 and has now been restored. The quick responses of the staff and students ensured the survival of the portraits and other works of art which now grace its walls again: they formed a human chain to get them safely out. Quite often there is music of some sort in the Junior Common Room, and the **Douglas Hyde Gallery** in the Arts Building often mounts mid-career and retrospective exhibitions of major Irish artists (*for information, © 670 2116*).

The Custom House is on the north bank of the River Liffey, near Butt Bridge, and is the most impressive building in Dublin. A quadrangular building with four decorated faces, it houses the Customs and Excise and Department of Local Government. It was designed by Gandon and completed in 1791. Unfortunately, its impact on the waterfront is lessened by a railway bridge which passes in front of it and the new development behind. Gutted by fire in 1921 during the civil war, by the Republican side, it has been perfectly restored so that the graceful dome, crowned by the figure of commerce, still rises from the central Doric portico.

The General Post Office in O'Connell Street is memorable not for its beauty but for the events of 1916 when a free republic was proclaimed from here. Later it was shelled from the Liffey by an English gunboat, and completely gutted by fire. Inside is a memorial to the 1916 heroes in the form of a bronze statue of the dying Cú Chulainn (see **Old Gods and Heroes**, p.576). Its historical role in the struggle for an independent Ireland rendered it a site for all manner of protest meetings. It is quite useful to remember that the GPO keeps very long hours and you can buy stamps here until late in the evening.

Dublin Castle (*open Mon–Fri, 10–12.15 and 2–5, Sat, Sun and bank holidays, 2–5; adm; © 679 3713*) is well worth a visit, not only because of the place it has in Irish history, but for the **State Apartments** which are beautifully decorated, and for the Church of the Most Holy Trinity, designed by Francis Johnston, in the Lower Castle Yard. The various buildings which make up the castle complex are still reminiscent of a fortified city within its own walls. The original medieval walls and towers are gone but the squares of faded red-brick houses with their elegant Georgian façades are a unity still. The place buzzes with history: there were so many executions, attempted seizures, fires. The present buildings date from 1688, with most of the upper yard being built in the mid 18th century. From the 18th century onwards a vice-regal court grew up around the Lord deputy and his administrators, and there were receptions, balls and levees for the gentry and Dublin merchants. It was far removed from the lives of the ordinary people of Ireland. At that time Dublin Castle was the seat of an alien power, and to the young Republican activists of the 19th and early 20th century it was understandably a symbol of tyranny. It was handed over to the provisional government of Ireland in 1922, and is used today for rituals such as the inauguration of the President. A guided tour of the State Apartments is very enjoyable. The lavish decoration, fine proportions, grand chimney pieces and beautiful antique furniture are a feast to the eye. Particularly attractive is the Bermingham

Tower Room with its Gothic windows. It was from here that, in 1592, Red Hugh O'Donnell, one of the last great Gaelic leaders, managed to escape to the Wicklow Hills (see his story under Rathmullen). The other blocks in the quadrangle have been refurbished inside and out but, sadly, the proportions and original woodwork have been mucked about.

Temple Bar is sold as Dublin's left-bank in the brochures. The area is named after Sir William Temple, a provost of Trinity College in the 17th century. It was neglected for a long time and was nearly raised by town planners to build a bus depot. While they were deliberating, artists moved in and rented out studio spaces very cheaply, although now there is a continual battle with property developers, who want to oust the low-rent artistic element, even though the desirability of the area is mainly due to its so-called bohemian atmosphere. The area is home to various alternative book stores, the Gallery of Photography, a Hare Krishna Centre, the Irish Film Centre and some good shops as well as lots of little restaurants. The temple bar information centre at 18 Eustace Street can provide information but the best way to get the feel of the place is to take a walk around at a leisurely pace and have a drink somewhere like the Temple Bar.

At the **Four Courts** down by Ormond Quay (*open Mon–Fri, 10.30–4.30 except Aug and Sept, © 872 5555*) you get one of the most characteristic views of Dublin. The Four Courts was designed by Gandon and completed by Thomas Cooley (1776–84). It was almost completely destroyed in the Civil War of 1921 but it has since been restored. The Law Courts were reinstalled here in 1931. The central block has a Corinthian portico and a copper green dome. It is flanked by two wings enclosing quadrangles. You may look inside the circular waiting hall under the beautiful dome. **The Public Record Office** next door was burnt down completely in 1921, with an irredeemable loss of legal and historical documents.

Powerscourt Town House in South William Street, built in 1771, is typical of Georgian town houses of the Ascendency. It has fine Rococo and Adamesque plasterwork. The **shopping centre** behind it is a triumph of enlightened development and is a pleasure to visit. It has a variety of restaurants including a very good vegetarian one right at the top. It also houses the largest crafts co-operative in Europe. Here you can see Ireland's finest boutiques (including the Irish Designers' Centre) and speciality shops, enclosed under a great glass-roofed courtyard (see 'Shopping', p.523).

Leinster House was finished in 1745, built to the design of Richard Cassels (or Castle), who was reponsible for so many lovely houses in Ireland—Russborough House in Wicklow, for instance. Leinster House has two different faces, one looking out over Kildare Street, and the other on to the pleasant garden of Merrion Square. It was the town house of the Dukes of Leinster and was originally known as Kildare House. Leinster House is now the seat of the Irish Parliament, which consists of the Dail (lower house) and the Seanad (upper house or senate). Dail deputies are elected by proportional representation. Gardai officers keep watch on its gates.

The Marino Casino, Fairview Park, near Glasnevin, is described under the section North County Dublin (p.499).

Other Places of Interest

The Guinness Brewery is in Crane Street off St James's Gate (*open Mon–Fri, 10–3.30, ℂ 453 6700*). Not only can you try some of the delicious, creamy porter for free in a cosy bar, but there is a video of the processes that go into making it, and a museum in the newly renovated hop store. The top two floors are used for temporary art exhibitions. The shop sells all sorts of 'black gold' souvenirs to take home with you.

The Liberties. An old residential area close to the Guinness Brewery, and many of the brewery workers come from this self-sufficient part of town. It was called 'The Liberties' because it stood outside the jurisdiction of the medieval town, and had its own shops and markets. In the late 17th century, French Huguenots set up a poplin and silk-weaving industry along the river valley (known as the Coombe) of the Poddle, a now-defunct river which used to flow through the Liberties, and joined the Liffey at Wood Quay. The area still has great character; it's very much a working class district, the people who live in it are the Dubliners of ballad and songs. Some families have lived here for many generations. In the late 18th century, faction-fighting was commonplace between the Liberty Boys, or tailors and weavers of the Coombe, and the Ormond Boys, butchers who lived in Ormond Market. Sometimes the fighting would involve up to a thousand men. Wallet-snatching has occurred in this area so be on your guard.

At **Irish Whiskey Corner**, Bow Street Distillery, Smithfield (*tours Mon–Fri, 3.30; adm ; ℂ 872 5566*), a visitors' centre is housed in what was once a warehouse. It features an exhibition on the history of Irish whiskey, a 15-minute film and, most important, a generous tasting of all the different Irish whiskeys.

The beautiful Georgian **Merrion Square** is one of the best-preserved in Dublin, and was the home of many famous literary people and politicians. Sir William and Lady 'Speranza' Wilde (Oscar's parents) lived at No. 1; Daniel O'Connell at No.58; W. B. Yeats at Nos.52 and 82; George Russell, known as A. E., at No.84; and Sheridan Le Fanu at No.70. The square contains the **National Art Gallery of Ireland**. Some of the houses need a lick of paint, and are inhabited by such organizations as the Irish Potato Board. **Fitzwilliam Square** is another well preserved example of 18th-century architecture with pretty doors and fanlights above. 29 Fitzwilliam Street is furnished in the style of a middle class family of the period 1790–1820 (*ℂ 676 5831 for details of opening hours*).

Ely Place is more melancholy and just a stone's throw away, between Merrion Row and Baggot Street. It was once very grand, but is now wrapped in a gloom which strip-lighting glimpsed through the elegant windows does nothing to dispel. **Ely House** is now owned by the Knights of Colombanus, a charity organization, and they will let you in to see the magnificent staircase. Many of the ceilings and panellings were sold off, adding to the urban decay. Although the grandeur which enveloped them can still be sensed. There are few restrictions to control the activities of building developers and architectural salvage firms, although this is beginning to change. If you want to depress yourself further, go north to Henrietta Street and Mountjoy Square. Parallel to Henrietta Street is **St Saviour's Orphanage** at 20 Lower Dominick Street. It has wonderful 18th-century plasterwork, and the inhabitants very kindly allow visitors to look at it.

The Huguenot Graveyard is a secret place. If you are passing the famous Shelbourne Hotel on St Stephen's Green, you may notice a shuttered garden, just to the left of it. Even Dubliners hardly know it is there. You can peer through the gates and see the mellow gravestones which mark the names of French Huguenots who successfully merged into the Irish way of life after a couple of generations. Ten thousand Huguenots arrived in Ireland to escape persecution for their religous beliefs, between the 1650s and 1700s. They had a great civilizing influence on early 18th-century Dublin, which was then very small and only just beginning to develop its own cultural activities after the turbulence of the 17th century. The Huguenots expanded the wine trade, started silk and poplin indus-tries, and introduced a Horticultural Society where they used to toast their favourite flowers! Ring the Secretary of the Huguenot Society if you want to know more about the graveyard, ✆ (01) 669 2852. The surviving Anglo-Norman aristocracy, Cromwellian adventurers and the new gentry (mainly composed of those who had profited from the seizure of forfeited lands), then built their grand houses and squares. Science and Art Societies were founded, amongst them the Royal Dublin Society, in 1731.

The Grand Canal Visitor Centre, Office of Public Works, St Stephens Green, ✆ 661 3111 x 2597. This exhibition tells the story of the construction and architecture of the waterways, their role in the history of Ireland, and their flora and fauna. The Grand Canal marks the extent of the Georgian city south of the Liffey; and the towpath which runs alongside it is a lovely walk which takes you past wild fowl and over humpbacked bridges.

The broad thoroughfare of **O'Connell Street** is now choked with traffic, and nothing like as elegant as it used to be in the 18th century. Tatty shop fronts, fast-food signs, and empty, untidy building sites also diminish its charm. When it was widened in the 18th century, it was intended that it should be purely residential with a stately mall running up its centre to the Rotunda Hospital. The construction of the Carlisle (now O'Connell) Bridge over the Liffey, changed it into a main street, for vehicle traffic and people. The monuments lining the centre of the street are rather fine, and still add glory to it, as do the variety of architectural styles, which you notice if you lift your eyes above shop-level. The (mainly Victorian) statues you see are: Daniel O'Connell (1745–1833), the lawyer who won Catholic emancipation (the street was named after him in 1927; before that it was called Sackville Street); William Smith O'Brien (1803–64), the Nationalist leader; Sir John Gray (1816–75), owner of *The Freeman's Journal* and a Nationalist, who was knighted for organizing Dublin's water supply; James Larkin (1867–1943), the trade union leader; Father Theobald Mathew (1790–1856), who advocated and set up temperance clubs; and Charles Parnell (1846–91), a great parliamentary leader whose career was destroyed by the scandal of his affair with a married woman, Kitty O'Shea.

Lord Nelson, who defeated the French at Trafalgar, used to grace the pedestal outside the GPO but was damaged by an IRA explosion and subsequently demolished.

Parks and Gardens

St Stephen's Green (*open at 8am, closes when it is dark*) at the top of Grafton Street, in the south part of the city centre, is a major landmark. It was once ancient commonage, and was laid out in formalized design by the munificence of the Guinness family in the 1880s. In the middle is a romantic landscaped park with a lake and waterfall, ducks and weeping willows. Every age and type of Dubliner uses it to dander in, and enjoy the trees and flowers. Its cool, green gardens make a perfect setting for a picnic. At the western edge of the green is Henry Moore's graceful monument to W. B. Yeats.

The National Botanical Gardens on the north side of the city in Glasnevin consist of 50 acres (8ha) of plants and trees, many of them rare, a sunken garden, a rock garden and a lily pond. The gardens are superb by any standards, and are described fully under North County Dublin. Parnell and O'Connell are buried in the Glasnevin Cemetery nearby.

Phoenix Park is huge, the largest park in a city in Europe. It is actually within walking distance of central Dublin. (Cross the river northwards and walk west along the quays to Conyngham Road.) The Dubliners are very proud of the park—with good reason. There are sports fields, woodland, small lakes, duck ponds and the **Dublin Zoo**, and it finds room in its 1760 acres (712ha) to house **Aras an Uachtarain** (the residence of the President), the residence of the American Ambassador and a hospital. The name of the park comes from a corruption of the Gaelic *Fionn Uisce*, which means 'bright water', from a spring which rises near the Phoenix Column near the Knockmaroon Gate. To English ears the pronunciation of the Gaelic sounded rather like Phoenix. The column was put up in 1747 by Lord Chesterfield, who was the viceroy of the time, and who had the impetus and foresight to plant this part of the park with trees. The land was offered by Charles II to one of his mistresses, which illustrates to what degree Dublin, and indeed the whole of Ireland, was up for grabs in the 17th century. Luckily, the Duke of Ormonde (who built Kilmainham Hospital), suggested it should be granted to the City of Dublin itself. Two hundred years later, in 1882, the Chief Secretary, Lord Frederick Cavendish, and the Under Secretary were stabbed to death in the park. History aside, the park is memorable as a place where cattle still graze and deer can be glimpsed through the trees. It is open to the public at all times. At the northern end is the old **Phoenix Park Race Course**. At the southern end, near the Parkgate Street entrance, are the **People's Flower Gardens** (*open daily, winter 10.30–5; summer 10.30–8; adm free*). Between the two lie the **Zoological Gardens** (*open Mon–Sat, 9.30–6, Sun,11–6; winter, shut at sunset; adm*), one of the oldest in Europe.

The Garden of Remembrance (*always accessible*) is behind the Gate Theatre, off Parnell Square. The cause it commemorates is Irish freedom. The central, watery feature of the garden is dominated by a sculpture of the legendary Children of Lir, by Oísín Kelly.

At **45 Sandford Road**, Ranelagh, Dublin 6, is a lovely city garden with secret areas of light and shade, pool and fountain, clematis-draped arches, borders filled with flowers, tubs of sweet-smelling lilies, wild flowers and roses (*open Sun only; group visits by written appointment; adm; ⓒ (01) 497 1308*).

The War Memorial Gardens, Island Bridge. Designed by Edwin Lutyens in 1931, this is a very architectural garden. You approach it by formal avenues which centre on the warstone at the heart of the garden. Circles and ovals commemorate the 49,400 Irish soldiers who died in World War I. There are two sunken gardens, surrounded by terraces, roses, flowers and shrubs. Off the south circular road (just before Islandbridge, the gardens are signposted to the left).

The smartest and best shopping is to be found in a small area around Grafton Street and the little streets leading off it, just northeast of the river. **Brown Thomas** and **Switzers** in Grafton Street (soon to be merged in one building) are first-class department stores. Brown Thomas, in particular, always carries Irish designer labels such as Paul Costelloe, Louise Kennedy, John Rocha and Michaelina Stacpoole. The designer room is excellent as is the Wardrobe department for less expensive options. **Firenze** in Balfe Street stocks a well-chosen selection of international designers such as Dolce & Gabbana and Dries Van Noten. For inexpensive clubby gear, **Makullas** in Suffolk Street is worth a visit as is **Se Si Progressive** in Temple Bar, which seeks out new young designer talent. Also in Temple Bar is the **Design Yard** for contemporary Irish jewellery, mostly silver. **A-Wear** on Grafton and Henry Streets is inexpensive and stocks diffusion ranges by Richard Lewis and the excellent John Rocha as well as Quin and Donnelly; the prices here are very keen and will appeal to all ages. **Boutiques** to visit for older ladies in search of a smart dress are **Pat Crowley**, in Molesworth Place, **Richard Lewis**, 26 South Fredrick Street and **Richard Alan** on Grafton Street. And, of course, you should go to the **Powerscourt Town House Centre** in Clarendon Street. This is an innovative shopping centre which is generally regarded as a showpiece marriage between conservation and commerce. The building is elegant Georgian, constructed over two hundred years ago as a town residence for Lord Powerscourt, an 18th-century nobleman. A glass dome over the old courtyard makes a wonderful space for **cafés and restaurants**. Small craft shops, fashion shops, antique shops and jewellers have spaces in the old house. Names to look out for include Emma Stewart Liberty and Patrick Flood (silversmiths), the Collective for hats and jewellery, and the Irish Design Centre, which sells clothes by up-and-coming as well as established designers including Mariad Whisker and Louise Kennedy as well as Lainey Keogh and Deirdre Fitzgerald who design gorgeous and luxurious knitwear. The Crafts Council upstairs also sell crafts.

The Westbury Centre round the corner has an Aladdin's cave of a lingerie shop, a leather studio and good coffee shop called Costa. The huge glass **St Stephen's Green Shopping Centre** on the corner of St Stephen's Green and Grafton Street has a wide variety of small shops and a huge Dunnes store (somewhat like Marks & Spencer). Sybil Connolly, the doyenne of **Irish designers**, has her shop in Merrion Square. Many of the **English companies**—Next, Principles, Knickerbox, Marks & Spencer—have set up in Dawson Street. For something in Irish tweed, and for high-quality craft design, head for **Nassau Street**, at the College Green end of Dawson Street. The **Blarney Woollen Mills**, 21–3 Nassau Street, sell tailored skirts and jackets, soft jersey dresses and jumpers, scarves and luxurious woollen coats, in a good range of colours—from the clear primaries to tweeds full of subtle shades, like the Irish countryside, although some of the designs are a little staid. **The Kilkenny Design Shop** next door sells excellent glass, pottery, rugs and sweaters. **Cleo's** in Kildare Street is a good designer-tweed shop. For men **Kevin and Howlin** sell lovely tweed caps and scarves. **Kennedy McSharry** also on Nassau Street will make beautifully tailored suits from Donegal tweed. For men's designer clothes, try **FX Kelly**, Grafton Street, **Alias Tom**, Duke Lane or **A-Wear** for John Rocha's diffusion range.

The **antique shops** in Molesworth, South Anne Street and Kildare Street are well thought of, and sell top-quality furniture, silver and ornaments. For more junky stuff and bargains try Francis Street, in the Liberties, where there are individual antique shops and an antiques arcade. Just across the road from the Tivoli Theatre is the **Iveagh Market**, a fine 19th-century covered market, now very shabby and occupied by second-hand clothes dealers. For good second-hand clothes, Jenny Vander in the George's Street Arcade has lovely antique pieces of clothing and **costume jewellery**; A Star is Born on Clarendon Street, which is only open on a Saturday, or Se Si in Temple bar for funkier and cheaper stuff. **Irish Crafts** can be bought in the Tower Design Centre, Pearse Street, where craft-workers produce glass, jewellery, woodcarving, pottery, weaving and other lovely things, ✆ 677 5655 for details. For more pottery, Anthony O'Brien at 14a Ailsbury Road, D4, supplies President Robinson with dinner sets, ✆ 269 8618. Visit the Irish Georgian Society, 74 Merrion Square, ✆ 676 7653, for historical placemats, books etc.

For **edible Irish goodies,** you can really indulge yourself with fabulous cakes and breads, as well as cheese at Cookes Bakery either in Francis Street or at 32 Dawson Street. Magill's in Clarendon Street is a wonderful old fashioned place smelling of Charcuterie and sourdough breads. Across the road in the Powerscourt is the Ow Valley Farm shop for all manner of olives, nuts, dried and fresh fruit. For smoked salmon, McConnell's at 38 Grafton Street will even post fish to your pals back home. For Belgian chocolates, Leonidas in the Hibernian way are sadly yummier than their Irish counterparts, Butler's on Grafton Street. For exotic ingredients, the Asia Market at 30 Drury Street is very good. A cheerful wholefood grocer's, Fitzpatricks, can be found up on Camden Street at number 40. Just up from here near the canal, is the famous Bretzel Kosher Bakery, which doles out treats such as ginger-bread men, walnut loaves and lovely shiny twisted plaits of bread.

commercial art galleries

The following galleries put on shows by Irish artists. You may wish to invest and take a painting home.

Kerlin Gallery, Anne's Lane, off South Anne Street; ✆ 677 9179. Established and new talent. Lovely gallery space.

Rubicon, 11 Upper Mount Street; ✆ 676 2331. Mostly contemporary.

Taylor Galleries, 34 Kildare Street; ✆ 676 6055. Established artists.

Anya Von Gosseln, inside Makullas, 13 Suffolk Street; ✆ 671 4079. For contemporary objects, drawings and furniture.

City Arts Centre, Moss Street; ✆ 677 0643. Young emerging artists. The centre also has a pleasant café.

Green on Red, 58 Fitzwilliam Square, ✆ 661 3881. Contemporary paintings and sculpture.

Solomon Gallery, Powerscourt Centre, ✆ (01) 679 4237. Pretty pictures. Occasionally verges on the twee.

Oriel Gallery, Clare Street, ✆ (01) 676 3410. Mostly traditional and figurative early twentieth century.

For auctions **James Adams and Sons** for silver, paintings and furniture. **Stephen's Green**, ✆ (01) 676 0261 and **Taylor de Vere's** for mostly Irish paintings, 35 Kildare Street, ✆ (01) 676 8300.

street markets

Moore Street is the place for fruit and vegetables, although some of the produce is rather suspect, so watch for the rotten ones. It is also a good place to observe Dublin life. Here the warmly wrapped pram people wait with their wares: in place of a gurgling infant, veteran market-traders, usually women, use prams to carry jewellery, fish, turf, concrete blocks, flowers, evening newspapers. You can buy their vegetables, fruit and the most gaudy of Taiwanese toys. The 'perambulators' are not strictly allowed, as they do not pay rent, unlike the properly established stands; and if the boys in blue do appear, they melt away into the crowds. Some of the prams are as old as 70 years, and still going strong. **Henry Street** nearby sometimes has a few market stores and is the busiest shopping street in Dublin— and generally cheaper than the upmarket Grafton Street area. Mother Redcap's open air market near Christchurch sells pottery, books and bric-a-brac. Check out The Gallic Kitchen for delicious pies and cakes and Ryefield Foods for farmhouse cheeses. The Dublin Food Co-op at St Andrew's hall, in the middle of Pearse Street every second Saturday, has the best Irish produce from surrounding counties.

Dublin ✆ (01–)

Sports and Activities
spectator sports

Greyhound racing: Shelbourne Park and Harold's Cross.

Hurling/Gaelic football: Parnell Park, Phoenix Park, Croke Park.

Polo: Polo Grounds, Phoenix Park.

Rugby/football: Landsdowne Road.

Horse-racing: Leopardstown and Fairyhouse.

Check *In Dublin* and evening newspapers for details.

To join the daily Historical Walking Tour of Dublin, assemble at the front gate of Trinity College, call for times, ✆ 845 0241. Cost IR£3.50. For guided tours of Old Dublin, assemble at Bewley's, Grafton Street or Dublin Writer's Museum, Parnell Square; call ✆ 679 4291 for times. Cost IR£4.00. The Dublin Literary Pub Crawl (see under 'pubs') meets at the Bailey bar on Duke Street, ✆ 454 0228. Cost IR£5, although you'll need more money for the Guinness.

Signposts have been erected around the city to guide you; there's the Georgian Trail, the Cultural Trail, the Old City Trail and the Rock'n' Stroll Trail. Contact the tourist office for more details, ✆ 284 4768.

For Bicycle tours, call Citycycle, 1a Temple Lane, ✆ 671 5606. Cost IR£10. including bike and helmet.

Dublin ✆ *(01–)*   **Festivals and Fairs**

Early March: Dublin International Film Festival, ✆ 679 2937. Highly recommended.

March 17th: St Patrick's Day. Celebrations and parades starting on O'Connell Street.

Late March/early April: Dublin Grand Opera Season. Gaiety Theatre, ✆ 677 1717.

Early May: Spring Show (agricultural). Contact Royal Dublin Society, Ballsbridge, D4, ✆ 668 3070.

Mid August: Antique and Collectors Fair, Mansion House, Dawson Street, ✆ 676 2852. Timed to coincide with the Dublin Horse Show. Contact Royal Dublin Society, Ballsbridge, D4, ✆ 668 3070.

September: The All-Ireland Hurling Final.

Late September/early October: Dublin Theatre Festival. ✆ 677 8439. Dublin City Marathon, ✆ 677 1717.

October Theatre festival in Dublin.

December: Dublin Grand Opera Winter Season, Gaiety Theatre, ✆ 660 8488.

Dublin ✆ *(01–)*   **Summer Schools**

These consist of courses on Irish literature, theatre, fine arts, folklore, Gaelic language and politics.

Irish Theatre Summer School at the Gaiety School of Acting.

Ireland in Europe at Trinity College. Contact USIT, 19 Aston Quay, D2, ✆ 677 8117.

Institute of Irish Studies, 6 Holyrood Park, D4; ✆ 269 2491. Lectures on Irish civilization, based at Trinity College, Dublin.

University College, International Summer School for Irish Studies, based at Belfield Campus.

James Joyce Summer School based Stephen's Green, Contact UCD International Summer School Office, Newman House, 86 St Stephen's Green, D2, ✆ 475 2004.

Dublin ✆ (01–)

luxury

Westbury, off Grafton Street, D2, ✆ 679 1122. Modern hotel, top of the range and very central for shopping.

Shelbourne Hotel, St Stephens's Green, D2, ✆ 676 6471. Lovely old-fashioned hotel in which the Irish Constitution was drafted. An elegant drawing room and gem of a bar. Favoured resting place of visiting celebrities, although the staff can be a bit stuffy.

Jury's, Ballsbridge, D4, ✆ 660 5000. Large, modern hotel with executive wing.

Hotel Conrad, Earlsfort Terrace, D2, ✆ 676 5555. Top-of-the-range modern Hilton hotel with excellent facilities and a pleasant atmosphere.

expensive

Longfields Hotel, Fitzwilliam Street, D2, ✆ 676 1542. Georgian town house, quiet and intimate with period furnishings, and an excellent restaurant.

Gresham, Upper O'Connell Street, D1, ✆ 874 6881. Built in the days when a first-class hotel had big bedrooms and huge baths, this still has the atmosphere of the 20s and 30s, even if O'Connell Street itself is now a bit seedy. Best bedrooms are at the front. Car parking for residents.

Georgian House, 20 Lower Baggott Street, D2, ✆ 661 8832. Own phone, TV, telephone, in a Georgian house which has been internally altered to create snug, pastel-coloured rooms. Very central, so you can walk everywhere. Private car park in back garden.

Buswell's Hotel, Molesworth Street, D2, ✆ 676 4013. An old-fashioned, cheerful family hotel. Very central.

Clarence Hotel, 6 Wellington Quay, ✆ 677 6178. Traditional, U2-owned 30s hotel with lovely wood-panelling, a fashionable bar and friendly staff. Recently refurbished and well situated at the edge of the Temple Bar area.

Sachs Hotel, 19 Morehampton Road, Donnybrook, D4, ✆ 668 0995. Small, traditional hotel in Georgian terrace. Ample parking.

moderate

Anglesea Guesthouse, 63 Anglesea Road, Ballsbridge, D4, ✆ 668 3877. No sign outside to guide you to this comfortable haven in a smart residential area of Dublin, about ten minutes from the city centre by car. Deep carpets, clean rooms, with TV, bathroom and phone. Fabulous breakfasts with a huge variety of home-baked breads, delicious baked cereal, kippers, etc. Car parking on street.

Mr and Mrs Doyle, **Hilton House**, 23 Highfield Road, Rathgar, D6, ✆ 497 6837. Large Victorian house in a quiet secluded area.

Mrs Egan, **Haddington Lodge**, 49 Haddington Road, Ballsbridge, D4, ✆ 660 0974. Elegant Georgian house.

Merrion Hall, 56 Merrion Road, Ballsbridge, D4, ✆ 668 1426. Family-run guest-house with pretty bedrooms, a friendly atmosphere and a delicious breakfast which includes home-made yoghurt.

Ariel House, 52 Lansdowne Road, Ballsbridge, D4, ✆ 668 5512. A charming Victorian house with lots of antiques. The bedrooms in the older part of the house are more individual. Breakfast in served in the conservatory.

Brian & Mary Bennett, 31 Leeson Close, D2 ✆ 676 5011. Stylish modern décor, comfortable with a secure car park.

For more, moderately priced accommodation in the suburbs of Dublin, look under County Dublin.

inexpensive

Avalon House, 55 Aungier Street, ✆ 475 0001. Old building converted into modern hostel with twin, family and dormitory rooms. Central, clean and efficiently run.

Mountjoy Square, Youth Hostel, 39 Mountjoy Square, D1, ✆ 836 3111/836 4750. Central, clean and friendly. From IR£9.

Isaacs Hostel, The Dublin Tourist Hostel, 2–5 Frenchman's Lane, D1 (beside Busarus), ✆ 874 9321/836 3877. Built as a wine warehouse on the Liffey in the 1700s, this is a very clean, central, friendly place, with excellent restaurant facilities and a patio garden. Basic dormitory from IR£5.50 per night, double rooms IR£11.25 per person, single rooms IR£15.25. The restaurant is good value.

Kinlay House Hostel, Lord Edward Street, ✆ 679 6644, Near Christ Church. Big and well-equipped, currently undergoing refurbishment. IR£8.50 for four bed dorms and IR£17 for a single. Prices include continental breakfast.

self-catering

Campus-type apartments, UCD village, Belfield. University apartments, 4 miles from city centre. 3 & 4 bedrooms during summer only. From IR£250 per week. Contact Robin Hickey, ✆ 269 7111.

Dublin ✆ (01–)   ***Eating Out***

The following restaurants are open for lunch and dinner, although you should always check before turning up. (See also 'Eating Out' in County Dublin, p.503.)

luxury

Le Coq Hardi, 35 Pembroke Road, Ballsbridge, D4, ✆ 668 9070. Superb traditional French cooking based around the seasons, in the middle of a smart residential area. **Patrick Guilbaud**, 46, James Place, Baggot Street Lower, D4, ✆ 676 4192. Excellent classic French cuisine in a modern interior. Could benefit from being a little less formal.

expensive

Cooke's Café, 14 South William Street, D2, ✆ 679 0536. One of the nicest intimate little restaurants in Dublin. Lovely Italiante interior and superb modern Italian/Californian cooking. Home-baked focaccia breads with olive oil dips and patisseries to die for—try the Calvados tart. A very good value early evening set menu. **Les Frères Jacques**, 74 Dame Street, D2, ✆ 679 4555. Atmospheric and romantic restaurant. French food and friendly staff. Try the lobster ravioli. The **Old Dublin Restaurant**, 91 Francis Street, D8, ✆ 454 2028. A very appealing and well-presented menu which inclines towards the Oriental and east-European—mainly Scandinavian and Russian. Lovely kasha barley or savoury rice; and vegetarian *satsiv*, a crispy version of curried fresh vegetables. The **Barley Mow Pub**, next door, has no connection with the restaurant but you can have a drink there whilst the waiter from the Old Dublin takes your orders. **Locks Restaurant**, 1 Windsor Terrace, Portobello, D8, ✆ 453 8352. This cosy place overlooks the Grand Canal, and has an assured and friendly feel to it. Some of the dishes are adventurous, yet wholesome, with extensive use of organic produce from Co. Wicklow.

L'Ecrivain, 112 Lower Baggot Street, D2, ✆ 661 1919. Friendly little basement restaurant serving imaginative French food. Popular with local business people and particularly buzzy at lunchtime. **La Stampa**, 35 Dawson Street, D2, ✆ 677 8611. Fashionable and graceful brasserie, often frequented by film stars and rock musicians. **Le Mistral**, 16 Harcourt Street, D2, ✆ 478 1662. One of the few Dublin restaurants with a star. Excellent Provençal-inspired food and the best tarte tatin this side of Paris. Good value set lunch and dinner menus.

moderate

Roly's Bistro, 7 Ballsbridge Terrace, Ballsbridge, D4, ✆ 668 2611. Lovely interior, fun and fashionable café atmosphere, with food to match. Very popular, so book in advance. **Marrakesh**, 11 Ballsbridge Terrace, D4 ✆ 660 5539. Small, authentic Moroccan restaurant. Traditional dishes include delicious soups, generous helpings of couscous and a choice of tagines. The **Grey Door**, 22/23 Upper Pembroke Street, D4, ✆ 676 3287. Russian and Scandinavian food. **Tosca**, 20 Suffolk Street, ✆ 679 6744. Stylish southern European food. **Ayumi-Ya Steakhouse**, 132 Lower Baggot Street, D2 ✆ 622 0233. Teppanyaki chicken and meats cooked over a hot griddle. Good value early-bird menu. The **Chili Club**, 1 Anne's Lane, South Anne Street, D2 ✆ 677 3721. Proper Thai cooking by a Thai chef—the lemongrass soups have a real kick, whilst the curries vary in terms of spiciness. **Nico's Restaurant**, 53 Dame Street, D2, ✆ 677 3062. Busy and friendly Italian restaurant with a theatrical atmosphere. **Il Primo**, 16 Montague Street, D2, ✆ 478 3373. Cheerful flavoursome Italian food. **Oísíns**, 31 Upper Camden Street, D2, ✆ 475 3433. Serves indigenous food very well. You can choose from cockle soup, ham and cabbage, and real Dublin coddle (a dish of sausage, onions and potatoes). **Little Caesar's Pizza**, 5 Chatham House, Balfe Street, D2, ✆ 671 8714. **The Kapriol**, 45 Campden Street, D2, ✆ 475 1235. Homely Italian food in a cosy little spot.

inexpensive

Pasta Fresca, Chatham Street, D2, ✆ 679 2402. Crowded fresh-pasta shop which serves its own produce at a limited number of tables. Simple pasta with a good variety of sauces. **Gotham Café**, 8 South Anne Street, D2, ✆ 679 5266. Pizza/pasta and more. Open quite late. **101 Talbot**, 101 Talbot Street, D1, ✆ 874 5011. Cheerful atmosphere, mediterranean and eastern-inspired cooking. Good for vegetarians and popular with theatre-going folk. **Irish Film Centre**, 6 Eustace Street, D2, ✆ 677 8788. Continental-style café filled, unsurprisingly, with film buffs. Good hamburgers and vegetarian food, pitta bread sandwiches and salads. **Pizzeria Italia**, 23 Temple Bar, D2, ✆ 677 8528. Tiny cheerful restaurant with counters. Really good classic pastas and pizzas cooked by real Italians. Don't miss the garlic mussels. **The Old Stand**, 37 Exchequer Street, D2 ✆ 677 7220. Bar food, famous for its steaks. **Pierre Victoire's**, Crow Street (and Fade Street), D2. Tasty French food and a lively atmosphere at very keen prices. Cheap lunchtime menus too. Book in advance at weekends. **Chez Jules**, D'Olier Street, D2, ✆ 677 0499. Another Parisian-style bistro, very informal with chequered tablecloths and scrubbed wooden floor. **Tosca**, 20 Suffolk Street, D2, ✆ 679 6744. Nice modern interior. Quite popular, although the quality of the food can vary. The **Stag's Head**, Dame Court, ✆ 679 3701. Boiled bacon and cabbage, Irish stew.

Dublin ✆ (01–)   *Restaurants for Lunch*

moderate

Fitzer's Café, 24 Upper Baggot Street (also on Dawson Street), D4, ✆ 660 0644. Sassy food from the Pacific rim & Mediterranean. *Open all day.* **Elephant and Castle**, 18 Temple Bar, D2, ✆ 679 3121. Burgers, omelettes and really good bumper sandwiches. Although always busy, good for brunch on Sundays. **Ryan's**, Parkgate Street, D8, ✆ 677 6097. Cosy Victorian pub serving fine bar fare, especially the salad plates. **Kitty O'Shea's Restaurant**, 23/25 Upper Canal Street, D4, ✆ 660 8050. Also good for brunch on Sundays. **Good World Chinese Restaurant**, 18 South Great Georges Street, D2, ✆ 677 5373. Nice any time, but great for dim sum on a Sunday. **The Periwinkle**, Powerscourt Town House Centre, South William Street, ✆ 679 4203. Hot and cold seafood dishes. **Imperial**, 13 Wicklow Street, D2. Smart Chinese restaurant with good value set lunches and dim sum. **Pizza Italia** (*see* above).

inexpensive

Pasta Fresca (*see* above). **Blazing Salads**, Powerscourt Centre, D2, ✆ 671 9552. Imaginative and streets ahead of the average, vegetarian cooking. Excellent soups, salads and home-made desserts. Caters for yeast/gluten/sugar-free diets. Organic wine and fresh-pressed vegetable juices. **Fitzers** in the National Gallery of Art, Merrion Square, ✆ 668 6481. Tempting salads and pasta dishes. Just the place to relax after exploring the gallery. **National Museum Café**, Kildare Street, ✆ 602 1269. Simple and tasty. Coddle, salads and cakes. The **Winding Stair**, 40 Lower Ormond Quay, ✆ 873 3292. Soup and sandwiches in a charming café cum bookshop with a lovely view over the Liffey. **Burdocks**, 2 Werburgh Street, D6, ✆ 454 0306. Excellent take-away fish and chips to eat in the park around the corner. **Bewley's Café**, 78–79 Grafton Street, D2 (also at Westmoreland Street), ✆ 677 6761. Where Dubliners have met, talked and enjoyed delicious coffee and cakes (especially the brack or almond buns) for generations. A real slice of Dublin life. **Cornucopia**, Wicklow Street, D2, ✆ 677 7583. Vegetarian restaurant serving wholesome bakes and soups. Caters for restricted diets, although the staff can be a bit grumpy. **Captain America**, 1st floor, Grafton Court, Grafton Street, ✆ 671 5266. For those who miss burgers and milkshakes. Loud music. **Kilkenny Kitchen**, Nassau Street, ✆ 667 7066. Does good imaginative salads and fresh breads in their self-service lunch bar.

Dublin ✆ (01–)   ***Entertainment and Nightlife***

theatre

It is worth spending money on the theatre in Dublin. The most convenient place to book tickets is at the stall in Brown Thomas's in Grafton Street. You can also get them at the tourist office at 14 Upper O'Connell Street, or the theatres themselves.

The Abbey Theatre, Lower Abbey Street, ✆ 878 7222, was founded by the indomitable Lady Gregory and W. B. Yeats. The old building was burned down; the new one also houses **The Peacock Theatre** which concentrates on contemporary playwrights whereas the Abbey sticks predominantly to the old Irish classics. The new theatre house is functional and modern in design with a great array of portraits of Dublin literati. The Abbey has made the Irish turn of phrase famous throughout the world with plays such as *Playboy of the Western World* by J. M. Synge and *Juno and the Paycock* by Sean O'Casey.

The Gate Theatre, 1 Cavendish Row, Parnell Square, ✆ 677 4085, stages productions of international and classic dramas. **The Gaiety**, South King Street, ✆ 677 1717, is a splendid, tiered Victorian theatre, showing more traditional plays, and it provides a venue for opera, musicals and pantomime. **The Olympia**, Dame Street, ✆ 677 7741, has drama, ballet, musical as well as late night concerts.

The Project Arts Theatre, 39 East Essex Street, ✆ (01) 6712321, is perhaps some of the most experimental and stimulating theatre in Dublin, with art exhibitions as well as plays as does the City Centre Arts Centre, Moss Street, ✆ 677

0643. Other fringe theatres include **Focus Theatre**, Pembroke Place, Pembroke Street, ✆ 676 3071; **Andrew's Lane Theatre** Andrews Lane, ✆ 670 5720, **Samuel Beckett Centre**, Trinity College, ✆ 702 1239, which often has exciting lunchtime theatre; **SFX Centre**, Upper Sherrard Street, ✆ 674 1775; **Tivoli**, Francis Street, ✆ 453 5998, which stages musicals and plays, usually excellent productions; **The International Bar,** Wicklow Street, ✆ 779250, also has a cellar area devoted to comedy.

Theatre really takes off in Dublin during the festival in October, with new plays by Irish authors, some of which have become Broadway hits! Most theatres are not open on Sundays. Performances in the evening usually begin around 8. If you have a student card or receive an old age pension you get a discount off tickets for the Abbey, Peacock, Project and Focus Theatres.

cinema

Film is extremely popular in Dublin, indeed the Irish attend the cinema more frequently than any other European. All cinemas are listed in the papers.

Adelphi Cinema, 98 Abbey Street (middle), ✆ 873 1161.

Ambassador Cinema, O'Connell Street (upper), ✆ 872 7000. Recently refurbished grand old cinema.

Irish Film Centre, 6 Eustace Street, Temple Bar, ✆ 679 5744. Foreign and art house releases. The film festival in March is organised from here. There is also a nice café with good snacks.

Lighthouse, Abbey Street (middle), ✆ 873 0438. Art house and foreign films.

Savoy Cinema, 19 O'Connell Street (upper), ✆ 874 8487.

Screen at College, College Street, ✆ 671 4988. Independent, less commercial films.

classical music

The National Concert Hall, Earlsfort Terrace, ✆ 671 1533. The National Symphony Orchestra is based here.

Point Theatre, East Link Bridge, ✆ 836 3633. For hotshots as diverse as Pavarotti and Joe Cocker.

Hugh Lane Municipal Gallery, Parnell Square, ✆ 874 1903. Lunchtime concerts.

Gaiety Theatre, South King Street, ✆ 677 1717. For opera.

bars

Dublin's bars are famous for their convivial atmosphere, their snugs (enclosed spaces within a pub), whiskey mirrors and pub food; and of course, their Guinness. If you have not experienced Dublin pubs, then you have not experienced Dublin. The following are recommended.

Ryan's Bar, Parkgate Street. Well-preserved Victoriana, cosy snugs and very good pub food, especially at lunch.

Mulligans, Poolbeg Street. A reputation for high-quality Guinness. Popular with journalists.

Doheny and Nesbitt's, Lower Baggot Street. Victorian decor. Frequented by lawyers and politicians.

Toner's, Baggot Street. Victorian fittings and a mixed crowd. Nice toasted cheese sandwiches.

Neary's, Chatham Street, off Grafton Street. Good sandwiches and a theatrical atmosphere.

Palace Bar, Fleet Street. A writers' haunt in the 50s.

Stag's Head, Dame Court. Cosy interior snug. Friendly staff and good for sausages, chips and guinness at teatime.

McDaids, Harry Street. Traditionally a literary haunt.

The Bailey, Duke Street. Another literary stop-off.

The Shelbourne Hotel, Horseshoe Bar, St Stephen's Green. Elegant and popular with lawyers, politians and journalists.

Davy Byrnes, Duke Street. Busy with tourists on the literary trail. But they do make good sandwiches.

Long Hall, South Great George's Street. Crammed with knick-knacks and lovely mirrors. Nice barmen.

Dawson Lounge, Dawson Street. Quirky basement bar.

Grogan's, 15 South William Street. Aspiring writers, artists etc.

The International, Wicklow Street. Nice in the afternoon.

Kehoe's, South Anne Street. Authentic and quirky. A good snug.

Cafe En Seine, Dawson Street. Generally known as Café Insane. French-style brasserie for cappuccinos and after-work drinkies.

The Temple Bar, Temple Bar. Hip and cosy little boozer.

The Chocolate Bar, Harcourt Street. Glamorous cocktail bar against the Poo nightclub. Extended late-night licence.

The Globe, South Great Georges Street. Café. Popular with the young and beautiful—good sandwiches and cappuccinos at lunchtime.

Hogans, South Great Georges Street. Best during the day.

Clarence Hotel Bar, Essex Street. U2-owned. Friendly staff and fashionable with theatre/film people.

Traditional Music

Traditional music can be heard on different nights at each venue. Sessions are free, unless a big name is playing. Check in the local newspaper or with the bar.

Hughes, Chancery Street, ℗ 872 6540. One of the best.

Kitty O'Sheas, 23 Upper Grand Canal Street, ℗ 660 9965.

Piper's Club, *Na Piobairi Uillean*, 15 Henrietta Street, D2, ℗ 873 0093.

Wexford Inn, Wexford Street, ℗ 478 0391. Trad and folk.

Mother Redcaps, Black Lane (beside Tailors' Guildhall, Christchurch, ℗ 453 8306. Folk also.

John M Keating's, 14 Mary Street. Nice comfortable atmosphere.

An Beal Bocht, 58 Charlemont Street, ℗ 475 5614. Named after Myles Na gCopaleen's play which is also performed here.

Slattery's, Capel Street, ℗ 872 7971. Very popular.

Brazen Head, Bridge Street, ℗ 677 9549. Oldest bar in Dublin.

The Merchant, Lower Bridge Street. Also do set dancing.

O'Donoghues, Merrion Row, ℗ 661 4303.

The Continental Ceili is run by a small company called Discover Dublin. It is an evening of traditional Irish music and dance, with ballads and set dancing (with instruction). The venue is O'Sheas Old Moran's Hotel on the corner of Talbot Street and Gardiner Street. For bookings, ℗ 478 0191.

Some enterprising fellows have started a literary pub crawl through Dublin, which is great fun and hugely entertaining. The starting point is the Bailey in Duke Street, and you combine drinking in atmospheric pubs with learning about the cultural religious and political past and present of the city. Bookings can be made through the tourist office, ℗ 284 4768.

Folk, Jazz and Rock

McDaid's. Harry Street, ℗ 679 4395. Blues upstairs.

Baggot Inn, Baggot Street, ℗ 676 1430. Music seven nights a week.

Whelans, 25 Wexford Street, ℗ 478 0766. Excellent line-up.

O'Dwyers, Lower Mount Street, ℗ 676 2887.

Harry's Bar, Point Depot, East Link Bridge, ℗ 836 6764. Also the Point Depot itself for big rock concerts like U2.

The Rockgarden, Crown Alley, ℗ 679 9114. Studeny.

An Beal Bocht, Charlemont Street, ℗ 475 5614.

J. J. Smyth's, Aungier Street, ℗ 675 2565. Mostly jazz.

Bad Bob's, East Essex Street, ℗ 677 5482. Country.

The nightclub scene in Dublin has come on in leaps and bounds over the past couple of years; indeed it has been voted 'hippest city in Europe' by several fashion magazines. Whether it deserves that reputation or not, there is no doubt that Dublin at night can be fun. That said, most of the clubs that have sprung up over the past few years are aimed at the under thirty bracket. They are also by their very nature fairly transient, so do check in advance. The cabaret scene is more established as it caters to a different kind of clientèle.

cabaret

Jury's Hotel, Ballsbridge, D4, ✆ 660 5000. A bit touristy during the summer months.

Clontarf Castle, Clontarf, ✆ 833 2271.

Braemor Rooms, Churchtown, ✆ 498 8664.

Abbey Tavern, Howth, ✆ 839 0282.

nightclubs

Lillie's Bordello, off Grafton Street, ✆ 679 9204. The longest established of Dublin's currently fashionable clubs. Frequented by models and visiting rock stars. Wide-ranging in age.

The POD, Harcourt Terrace, ✆ 478 0166, Great-looking interior, young and hip, popular with a fashion/model crowd. Techno/funk music.

The Kitchen, Clarence Hotel, East Essex Street, ✆ 677 6178. U2-owned. Currently popular on a Friday night.

RiRa, Dame Lane, ✆ 677 4835. Studenty, unpretentious and good for late-night drinking upstairs.

Temple of Sound, Ormond Hotel, Ormond Quay, ✆ 872 1811, lots of techno dance music.

Shaft, Ely Place. Mixed/gay crowd. Its days might be numbered as the Knights of Columbanus charity next door are kicking up a rumpus.

Annabel's, Burlington Hotel, Upper Leeson Street, ✆ 660 5222. Mainstream professional clientele.

Joy's, Lower Baggot Street, ✆ 676 6729. Mixed age-group. Old timers mix with golden youth late when all the other clubs have closed.

Club M, at Bloom's Hotel, Anglesea Street, ✆ 671 5622. A let-your-hair-down kind of place for people who wear suits rather than club kid gear.

Le Cirque, 16 Merrion Road, D4, ✆ 660 2236. Been around for years, popular with over-40s. Has something of a 'singles' reputation.

County Wicklow

County Wicklow has everything that is thought Irish in its landscape: wild heather-covered glens and forests, high mountain peaks, deep loughs, ancient churches, stately houses and silvery beaches. Yet it is within half an hour's drive of Dublin City. Dubliners call it 'the garden of Ireland'. Certainly it is their playground, and many come out to walk in the hills and picnic in the many beautiful places. Nothing could be more in contrast to the hustle and bustle of Dublin life.

In the winter the Wicklow hills are severe and savage, their bare conical shapes softened by snow. In the summer these same hills are clothed in verdant oak, beech and fir; the loughs are blue, and the little streams which tumble from the hills make delightful music. Pubs and restaurants are of a high standard, and if you want to be organized into rock-climbing, canoeing or orienteering, there are two adventure centres hidden away in the glens. The coastline has great charm. The Victorian resort towns of Bray and Greystones have many amenities, and it is possible to walk for miles from Dalkey to Wicklow Town between the railway and the sea, with nothing to interrupt the peace, except the occasional train. The rugs made in the Avoca Woollen Mills are wonderful, a perfect combination of the colours you see around you in the countryside, and something to cherish when you go home. The monastic remains of Glendalough are amongst the best in Ireland, as are the gardens at Powerscourt, and the magnificent furniture and pictures at Russborough House. So, if you do not have much time in Ireland, County Wicklow might give you a taste for it, and bring you back again.

The county has a growing population of well over 100,000, many of whom work in Dublin. Greystones and Blessington are the main commuter towns. The towns of Bray and Arklow have a wide range of industries, including the Arklow pottery. In the mountains, hill-farming with sheep is practised, whilst the eastern coastal strip and the land in the southwest supports richer farms.

History

Historically, County Wicklow was part of the kingdom of the Leinster kings, the MacMurraghs, whilst the Vikings established towns at Arklow and Wicklow. The modern boundary lines were drawn up by the English during the reign of Elizabeth Tudor. The Mountain septs of Wicklow earned themselves a reputation for guerilla warfare when the Anglo-Normans arrived in 1167: they wore the Normans down with constant skirmishes, and contained them within the Pale—a small fortified area around Dublin where the English king had control. O'Byrne and O'Toole were the two clans who made life so awkward for the Normans, and they continued to do so for centuries. In the reign of Elizabeth Tudor, in the 1570s, Fiach MacHugh O'Byrne constantly harried the English forces, and won some small victories that rallied the Gaelic cause in these parts for 20 years. The next great revolt was in 1798, and in Wicklow the Irish folk armed themselves with pikes to fight the English forces. They were led by Michael Dwyer (1771–1826). The uprising was suppressed, and Michael Dwyer surrendered in 1803. He was spared execution because of the humanity he had shown in various engagements, and was sentenced instead to transportation to New South Wales, where he later became High Constable of Sydney. (You can go round his cottage home in the Glen of Imaal.) The English government then built the Military Road which runs through the mountains from north to south, and is still in use today. It helped them to flush out the rebels. The Great Famine of the 1840s reduced the population from 126,000 to 100,000, and it further declined with emigration to America and Australia. Charles Stuart Parnell (1846–91) was a vigorous and effective voice of the Irish in the British parliament. His estate and house at Avondale is now a museum. The political campaigns he fought bore fruit in the Wyndham Land Acts, which made government loans available to tenant farmers to buy the land they had leased. Sadly, his career was bought down by his affair with Kitty O'Shea, a married women, for the scandal rocked Catholic Ireland, and he lost support.

Getting Around

By air: Dublin Airport.

By boat: Dublin, Dun Laoghaire and Rosslare ferry ports.

By rail: The main line from Dublin to Wexford runs through Wicklow via Bray, Wicklow, Rathdrum and Arklow. DART to Dublin run from Bray.

By bus: express buses and provincial bus services serve the major towns and minor villages regularly, ℘ (01) 873 4222. A privately run bus service, (St Kevin's Bus, ℘ (01) 281 8110) leaves daily at 11.30 from St Stephen's Green in Dublin to Glendalough.

By car: car hire in Dublin and Wexford Town.

By bike: the Raleigh Rent-a-Bike network operates here. J. Caulfield, King's Hill, Arklow, ℘ 0402 32284; and E. R. Harris, 87 Green Park Road, Bray, ℘ (01) 286 3357.

Tourist Information

Dun Laoghaire, ℘ (01) 284 4768, all year.

Wicklow Town, ℘ (0402) 6911, all year.

Bray, ℘ (01) 286 7128, all year.

Arklow, ℘ (0402) 32484, July and August.

Festivals

March: Marching Band Festival, Arklow, ℘ (0402) 32484 for details.

June: Garden of Ireland Festival, with events in famous gardens, ℘ (0404) 69117 for details. Synge Summer School, Rathdrum. The International Cartoon Festival, Rathdrum.

July: The Bray Seaside Festival and the Horticultural Rose Show, Delgany; telephone the local tourist office for details.

August: Parnell International Summer School.

Bray is one of Ireland's principal coastal resorts and has golf, horse riding, swimming and cinema—all sorts of amenities, although it seems a bit run-down and seedy at the moment. The **Bray Heritage Centre** in the old court house (*open every day, 10–4; Ⓒ (01) 286 6796*) contains a fine array of photographs, records, maps and artefacts relating to the area. The town has a safe beach of shingle and sand. There are good walks to Bray Head, and a cliff walk to Greystones of about 3 miles (5km). The Glen of Dargle to the west of Bray off the N11 is another lovely place to walk. A narrow pathway runs beside the Dargle River, and a road follows the glen to the south. A huge rock, known as the 'lover's leap' juts out over the wooded gorge through which the river runs. **Kilruddery Gardens**, between the N11 and R761 south of Bray (*open May, June and Sep, daily, 1–5; adm*), were laid out in the 17th century. Here, a pair of long canals reflect the sky, and a high beech hedge encircles a pool and fountains. There is also a fine parterre edged with box and filled with pink moss roses. The house, which opens to the public at the same time as the gardens, is an 1820 Elizabethan Revival mansion built for the 10th Earl of Meath. It has fine plasterwork.

Three miles (4.8km) west of Bray on the N11 is **Powerscourt Estate** and the gardens at Enniskerry. (*The Italianate and Japanese-style gardens, and the Monkey Puzzle Avenue, are all open every day from 17 Mar–31 Oct, 9–5.30; adm; Ⓒ (01) 286 7676*). Tragically, the house—one of the most beautiful in Ireland, was gutted by fire in 1976, after being carefully restored by the Slazenger family of tennis-racket fame. However, the gardens remain and the setting of the house, facing the Sugar Loaf Mountain, makes it an unforgettable sight: you walk towards the house thinking it is still intact, but it is a mere shell, though the Slazenger family have not given up and are planning further restoration. On the Powerscourt Estate there is a breathtakingly beautiful waterfall, the highest in Ireland. The water falls from 400ft (122m) into a fine stream which winds its way through numerous walks. **Enniskerry** itself is a fine estate village with good food, shops and clothes boutiques. It is an excellent base for excursions into the surrounding hills. Within the sound of the Powerscourt waterfall is a lovely garden at the foot of Long Hill. **Valclusa Gardens** (*open June–Sept daily; adm;* ✆ *(01) 286 9485*) has a rockery, a pool garden and beds of old roses, geraniums and hostas, and an area is devoted to attracting butterflies and other insects. Follow signs for Powerscourt Waterfall on the Roundwood Waterfall Road.

From Enniskerry, follow the road through the Scalp, a glacier-formed gap. The forests surrounding the Scalp have some lovely trails. If you want to glut yourself on forest scenery, take the Military Road which runs through the mountains from Rathfarnham to Aghavannagh. This road bisects the county and takes you through mysterious glens and remote valleys; you see turf-cutting country and some stupendous mountain scenery. One of the most spectacular glens is **Glencree**, which curves from near the base of the Sugarloaf Mountain to the foot of the Glendoo Mountain. Through it flows the Glencree River, which later joins the Dargle. The wild and beautiful **Sally Gap** is a cross-roads, from which you can follow the old Military Road to Laragh, the road to Roundwood or the valley road to Manor Kilbridge and Blessington. Dubliners come at weekends to cut their turf at Sally Gap.

Laragh is a pleasant little village where roads from the north, south, east and west meet. Near here, northeast on the R755 is the village of **Roundwood**, which is reputedly the highest village in Ireland, being 780ft (238m) above sea level. It is close to Varty Reservoir which supplies water to Dublin City, and to the wild scenery around Lough Dan. The high ground in these mountainous areas was the realm of the 'mountainy men'—the Irish who had been deprived of their lands on the plain by the English settlers. Up here in the hills, the rule of Dublin Castle had little influence.

Glendalough to Avondale

The important Early-Christian site of **Glendalough**, 'the glen of two lakes', has overwhelmed people with its peace and isolation for many centuries, an enclave of holiness amongst the wilderness. Its setting is unforgettable, and uniquely Irish: high in the hills, with two small lakes cupped in a hollow, a tall round tower and a grey stone church. There are the remains of a famous monastic school, founded by St Kevin in AD 520; and remains of churches spread between the upper and lower lakes, and the little river. An nformation centre (*open all year, daily; free adm to the churches*) has been built beside the car park as you enter. There are very interesting exhibits, and an audio-visual show to inform you before you explore the remains yourself. The seven churches and a round tower are clustered together by the little Glenealo River. On the southeast corner to the upper lake, by Poulanass Waterfall, is **Reefert Church** where the O'Toole rulers were buried. On the southern shore is the **Church of the Rock**, which you can get to by boat. The trip across takes 15 minutes, and the information centre provides details on boats. Between Reefert Church and the lower lake are five crosses which marked the boundaries of the monastic land and later became station crosses in the Pilgrims' Way. The story goes that St Kevin came here to recover from the effort involved in rejecting the advances of a beautiful girl named Kathleen. However, she chased him to the monastery, and he had to hit her with stinging nettles to lessen her ardour. Another version of the tale, recounted by Thomas (Tom) Moore, is that he cooled her off by pushing her into the lake. Despite Kevin's wish to be a hermit, his refuge became a centre of learning and later a place of pilgrimage. You can see **St Kevin's Kitchen**, the church with its corbelled roof, and the ruins of the cathedral with its 12th-century chancel. More intrepid visitors can walk up to **St Kevin's Bed**, on the southern cliff-face of the upper lake, although it is easier to view it from the lake. This is the cell where St Kevin stayed before the seven churches of the settlement were built. The views of the lakes are remarkable. **St Saviour's Monastery**, about 430yds (400m) northeast of the cathedral, is also very handsome. It is said to have been founded in the 12th century by St Lawrence O'Toole. The chancel arch is a lovely bit of Romanesque architecture: three orders resting on large clustered piers, decorated with dog-tooth, chevron and floral ornament. Human heads and animals decorate the capitals and bases.

Continuing south for 5 miles (8km) on the Military Road, you go through **Rathdrum** which has some good untouched pubs, such as P. Cullen's Bar in the Main Street, and enchanting woodland in the Avondale Valley. The big house here belonged to that great Irishman, Charles Stewart Parnell, who fought for the land rights of the peasants in the mid-19th century. The house is now used as a forestry school, and the estate is a **forest park** (*open all year, Mon–Fri, 10–6, Sat–Sun, 12–6; car park fee*). through which two **nature trails** have been signposted. Three rooms in the late 18th century house (*open daily, 11–6; adm; © (0404) 46111*) are devoted to displays of Parnell memorabilia.

The Vale of Avoca to Arklow

The scenery continues to be delightful as you travel south through the **Vale of Avoca**, immortalized in the Romantic poetry of Thomas Moore's 'The Meeting of the Waters', where the Avonmore and Avonbeg Rivers meet. Copper is mined in the valley still. 'The Meeting' is marked by a very ugly pub with a glassy ballroom tacked on to its back wall. But the atmosphere inside is difficult to beat; everybody is there to have some fun. Traditional bands play here at the weekends, and some of them are excellent.

You can understand the appeal of such scenery to the Romantic poets of the late 19th century, amongst them William Wordsworth, who did an Irish tour. About 2½ miles (4km) northeast of Avoca village and the rivers, and high above them, is the **Motte Stone**, a glacial boulder of granite perched on the summit of the 800ft (244m) Croneblane Ridge. It commands a spectacular view. It used to be used by travellers as a milestone because it is halfway between Dublin and Wexford. Along the valley road are shops selling the well-known Avoca-weave rugs, which make lovely presents. You can visit the **weaving centre** in Avoca village (*open every day from late May to October*).

Woodenbridge, at the end of this 'sweet vale', was the site of a gold rush in 1796, and supplied much gold for Ireland's earliest goldsmiths. Nearby, the Croghan Mountain was the scene of another 18th-century gold rush.

Blessington to Baltinglass

West Wicklow is relatively unexplored, and ruggedly attractive. Travelling southwest out of Dublin on the N81 you come to **Blessington**, a small town on the northern arm of the **Poulaphouca Reservoir**. This huge reservoir, formed by the damming of the River Liffey, is picturesque enough to warrant a visit. Other attractions are **Russborough House** and its art collection (*open Easter–end Oct on Sundays, public holidays, and every day during June, July and Aug, 10.30–5.30; adm; there is a picnic area, tea room, shop and children's playground; ℂ (045) 65239*). The house was designed by Richard Cassels (Castle) in the 1740s for the Earl of Milltown, and its silvery Wicklow granite has aged magnificently. It is Palladian in style, with a central block and two semi-circular loggias which link the wings. The main rooms are decorated with elaborate plasterwork. The house was purchased by Sir Alfred and Lady Beit in 1951, and their art collection is one of the chief attractions of Ireland. It includes paintings by Rubens, Gainsborough, Murillo, Reynolds, Vernet, Velasquez and Guardi. Unfortunately the house has been burgled on a couple of occasions and some treasures have been lost.

South from Blessington, you will come to Poulaphouca Lake, which forms the Wicklow Gap, and the lovely Hollywood Glen, before you arrive at Laragh. The nearby Glen of Imaal is also beautiful. The **Michael Dwyer McAllister cottage-museum** is open to the public here. The key is available all year round from Mr Hoxey, Derrynamuck, who lives on the farm there. Part of the glen is used as a military firing range: look out for the signs.

Baltinglass, which lies 19 miles (30km) south of Blessington on the N81, is in the Slaney Valley. The remains of a 12th-century **Cistercian abbey** lie to the north of the town. Six Gothic arches on either side of the nave remain to delight the eye. Baltinglass Hill rises above the town to the east. On the top of the hill are the remains of a large cairn containing a group of Bronze Age burial chambers. It is an easy climb and there is a splendid view over the countryside.

Wicklow Town to Arklow

The county town, **Wicklow**, overlooks a crescent-shaped shingle bay. The English name is a corruption of the Danish *Wyking alo*, 'Viking meadow'. Maurice Fitzgerald, a Norman warlord, built the ruined **Black Castle** on the promontory overlooking the sea at the eastern end of the town. He was granted the lands here by Henry II in the 12th century, but he did not have a very comfortable existence, for the castle was constantly raided by the O'Tooles and O'Byrnes. The ruined **Dunganstown Castle**, about six miles (9.6km) south on an unclassified road, is far more spectacular. Back in town, the 18th-century Church of Ireland Church in Wicklow, off the main street, has a fine carved Romanesque doorway in the south porch.

At **Ashford**, a couple of miles north of Wicklow Town on the main Dublin to Wexford road, is **Mount Usher Garden** (*open 17 Mar–31 Oct, daily except Sundays; adm; ✆ (0404) 40116*). A wonderful example of a naturalised garden; it is on the river Vartry, and is famous for its eucalyptus and encryphia. The woodland walks here provide beautiful vistas of azalea, rhododendrons, and spring bulbs.

By taking the R750, it is possible to stay close to the coast all the way from Wicklow to Arklow, passing lovely sandy beaches which are sheltered by sand-dunes. **Arklow** was another Danish settlement in the 9th and 10th centuries, and it grew up at the mouth of the River Avoca. It is now a popular resort town, as the beaches surrounding it are safe for bathing. There is a golf course and a sports centre, and boat rides on the river start from behind the car park off the main street during the summer. The remains of a 12th-century castle stand on the Bluff overlooking the river. It was built by Theobald Butler, and became one of the four strongest fortresses of the Ormonde family. Later it was sacked by the Irish, then ruined by Cromwell in 1649. Father Murphy, the leader of the insurgents in the 1798 Rising, was repulsed in Arklow with heavy losses, and there is a monument to his memory marking the site where he died. The **Arklow Maritime Museum** in the Old Technical School, St Mary's Road is well worth a visit (*open daily, 10–1 and 2–5, exc Sun during summer and Sat during winter; adm; ✆ (0402) 32868*).

Shopping

Cloth and wool: Avoca Handweavers Mill Shop, Kilmacanogue, for tweeds, rugs and sweaters, ✆ (01) 286 7466. Nice café too.

Pottery: Arklow Pottery Factory, Arklow. Open Mon–Fri 10–4.30, for tours and shopping, ✆ (0402) 32401. This is the largest pottery factory in the country. Mount Usher Craft Centre Courtyard, Ashford, ✆ (0404) 840205. A collection of pottery.

Crafts: Wicklow Willows, Roundwood, ✆ (01) 281 8217. Glendalough Craft Centre, Glendalough, ✆ (0404) 45156.

Markets: Roundwood Sunday Market, Parish Hall, Roundwood. Home-baking, country butter, flowers. March to December, 3–5. North Wicklow County Market, St Patrick's Hall, Kilcoole. 10.30am every Saturday.

Delicacies: Boswell's, The Mall, Wicklow Town. Fabulous sausages flavoured with all kinds of herbs and a superb fennel and tomato bread.

Activities

Adventure sports: The Tiglin Adventure Centre, Ashford, runs field courses in mountaineering, orienteering, canoeing, surfing and skiing, ✆ (0404) 40169 for further information. Blessington Lakes Leisure, Blessington, ✆ (045) 65092 with similar activities to Tiglin. Adventure Park: Waterslides and boats for children. Clara-Lara Funpark, Rathdrum, ✆ (0404) 46161.

Pony-trekking: Bel-Air Hotel Riding School, Ashford, ✆ (0404) 40109. Brennanstown Riding School, Hollybrook, Kilmacanogue, Bray, ✆ (01) 286 3778. Scenic rides through forest trails and mountain lands.

Horse-drawn caravans: Dieter and Mary Clissman, Clissman Horse-drawn Caravans, Carrigmore Farm, Wicklow, ✆ (0404) 48188.

Hunting: Bray Harriers, ✆ (01) 269 4403. Shillelagh and District Hunt, ✆ (01) 497 2266. Wicklow Hunt, ✆ (0404) 41745. Hunting lessons: Broomfield Riding School, Broomfield, Tinahely, ✆ (0402) 38117.

Angling: for brown trout at Blessington. Contact Ray Dineen, Tara House, Redcross, ✆ (0404) 41645 or J. Byrne, ✆ (0404) 67716 for advice on fishing matters.

Golf: Woodbrook Golf Club, Bray, ✆ (01) 282 1838. Charlesland Golf and Country Club, (01) 287 6764. Greystones Golf Club (01) 287 4136.

Walking: A signposted trail, the Wicklow Way, starts in County Dublin at Marley Park and climbs rapidly into the Wicklow Mountains, switching from glen to glen. After Aghavannagh, the way passes through lower ground and village areas. O.S. 1/50000 maps mark the route. For local walking trips contact Damien Cashin, Tomdarragh, Roundwood, ✆ (01) 281 8212, and Barry Dalby, 155 Beachdale, Kilcoole, ✆ (01) 287 5990.

Where to Stay

expensive

Rathsallagh House, Dunlavin, ✆ (045) 53112. A large, comfortable old farmhouse, run by a master of fox hounds. Very good food and chat. The bedrooms are large with en suite bathrooms, and the sporting facilities include hunting, billiards, croquet, swimming and sauna.

Tinakilly House, Rathnew, ✆ (0404) 69274. Very stylish Victorian house and furnishings. Delicious food, in particular the brown bread. Luxurious bedrooms in peaceful surroundings. (No children under seven). **Old Rectory**, Wicklow Town. ✆ (0404) 67048. Cosy rooms, delicious breakfasts and dinners using organic produce when possible.

moderate

Enniscree Lodge Inn, Enniskerry, ✆ (01) 286 3542. Small country hotel in lovely mountain surroundings. **Hunter's Hotel**, Rathnew, ✆ (0404) 40106. Attractive old coaching inn run by the same friendly family for five generations. Lovely garden sitting room with an old world atmosphere. The **Powerscourt Arms Hotel**, Enniskerry, ✆ (01) 286 3507. Attractive town hotel where they serve extra specially delicious Guinness in the bar. **Downshire House**, Blessington, ✆ (045) 65199, small and central. **The Manor**, Manor Kilbride, near Blessington, ✆ (01) 582105. Large Victorian mansion with lovely grounds. Outdoor heated swimming pool.

inexpensive

Mrs Byrne, **Ballynocken House**, Glenealy, near Ashford, ✆ (0404) 44627. Pretty farmhouse set between the Wicklow mountains and the sea. Advice on local walks, pony on the farm. Children welcome. Mrs Klaue, **Lissadell House**, Ashdown Lane, Wicklow, ✆ (0404) 67458. Friendly Irish-German couple with a comfortable modern house. Mrs McDowell, **Plattenstown House**, Arklow ✆ (0402) 32582. Peaceful and comfortable country house.

self-catering

Restored traditional cottage in Glen of Imaal. Two bedrooms. Contact **Michael Henry**, Glendhu, 10 South Park, Foxrock, Dublin 18, ✆ (01) 289 3661.

Eating Out

expensive

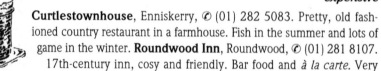

Curtlestownhouse, Enniskerry, ✆ (01) 282 5083. Pretty, old fashioned country restaurant in a farmhouse. Fish in the summer and lots of game in the winter. **Roundwood Inn**, Roundwood, ✆ (01) 281 8107. 17th-century inn, cosy and friendly. Bar food and *à la carte*. Very large helpings! **The Tree of Idleness**, Seafront, Bray, ✆ (01) 286 3498. Run by a Greek-Cypriot, so lots of fetta cheese, olive oil and herbs. Has had a good reputation for years.

The **Old Rectory**, Wicklow Town, ✆ (0404) 67048. The couple who run this country house and restaurant produce original food using herbs and flowers to decorate it, and they try to use only organic vegetables. During the Wicklow gardens festival, they do a ten course 'floral dinner' on Wednesdays. *Dinner only*. **Tinakilly House**, Rathnew, ✆ (0404) 69274. Ambitious and delicious *cuisine française*, in elegant dining room. *Dinner only, reservations essential.*

moderate

Hunter's Hotel, Rathnew, ✆ (0404) 40106. Famous for its cream teas, and excellent plain Irish cooking. This place has an old world atmosphere and a lovely garden. **The Hungry Monk**, Greystones, ✆ (01) 287 5759. A family-run restaurant specialising in fish. Good spot for Sunday lunch. **Harvey's Bistro**, Newtownmount Kennedy, ✆ (01) 281 9203. Homely cooking. **Mitchell's**, Laragh, ✆ (0404) 45302. A nice old restored schoolhouse. Comfy dining room and excellent food serving local produce such as Wicklow lamb and lovely home-baked cakes. *Open for afternoon tea.*

inexpensive

Armstrong's Bar, Annamoe. Run by an Irish Italian. Very good snack lunches. **Poppies Restaurant**, Enniskerry. Salad lunches and home-baking. Nice and lively at the weekends. Pleasant little shop next door. **Avoca Handweavers**, Kilmacanogue, ✆ (01) 286 7466. Excellent café serving home-made soups, vegetable bakes and cakes. The **Stone Oven**, Arklow, ✆ (0402) 39418. Bakery and coffee shop. Specialists in German breads. **Laragh Inn**, Glendalough. **Foxes Pub**, Glencullen.

Entertainment and Nightlife

Music: country music and folk singing during the summer months on Friday and Saturday nights at the Esplanade (Doona Lawn) Hotel, the Strand Hotel, the Mayfair Hotel and the Cois Farraige Hotel, all in Bray.

County Wexford

If you are invading Ireland from the south, as the Normans did, you will land at Rosslare Harbour—the warmest, driest part of the whole country. The countryside of Wexford is said to be similar to that of Normandy, with low hills, rich valleys and extremely tidy farms. Some of the thatched cottages have upper floors, which is something you do not find elsewhere in Ireland. Perhaps it is a sign of the relative prosperity of the peasants, and the influence of the English settlers in the 16th century. Vegetables and fruit are grown in the light, sandy soil. Farm implements are manufactured and bacon is cured. The population is approximately 100,000.

Along the coast there are gloriously sandy beaches, and some old resort towns. Many Irish families still take their holidays here, rather than southern Spain. Tower houses dating from the 14th century are a common feature; some are ivy-clad, but others blend into the farmhouses and yards which have grown up around them. Happily, these centuries-old buildings have been treated with a bit more care than is usual in Ireland. There are some magnificent monastic remains and old castles to explore; as well as Kennedy Park, planted with shrubs and trees from all over the world to honour John F. Kennedy. This arboretum is still very immature; for the garden lover there are several small and beautiful gardens open by arrangement with their owners.

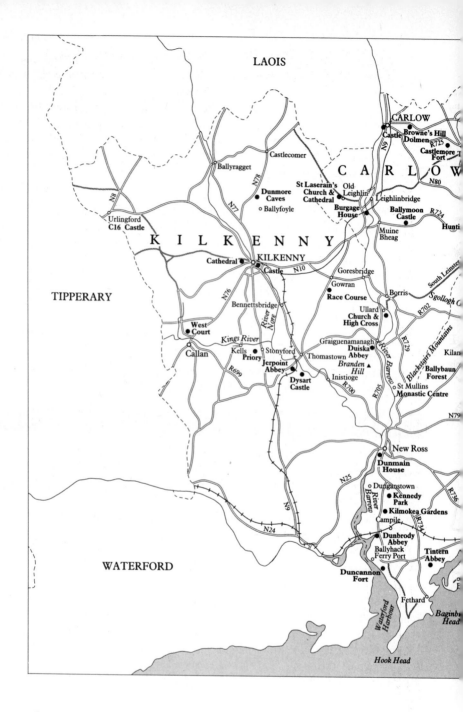

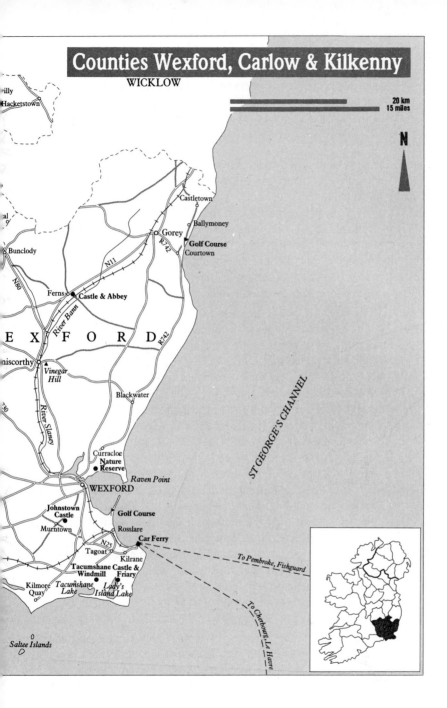

Counties Wexford, Carlow & Kilkenny

WICKLOW

20 km
15 miles

N

...illy
Hacketstown

...al

Bunclody

Ferns ⊙ ● Castle & Abbey

N11

N80

River Barn

E X F O R D

R742

...niscorthy ⊙

Vinegar Hill

...30

River Slaney

Blackwater

Castletown

Ballymoney

Gorey

R742

Golf Course
Courtown

Curracloe
● Nature Reserve

Raven Point

⊙ WEXFORD

Johnstown Castle ●

Murntown

Golf Course

Rosslare
Car Ferry

N25

Tagoat

Kilrane

ST GEORGE'S CHANNEL

To Pembroke, Fishguard

To Cherbourg, Le Havre

Tacumshane Castle & Windmill Friary

Kilmore Quay

Tacumshane Lake

Lady's Island Lake

Saltee Islands

547

Bird-lovers will find herring gulls, kittiwakes, razorbills, puffin colonies, petrels, gannets, Greenland white-faced geese and terns in the numerous bird sanctuaries which have been established around the coast.

Wexford is internationally famous for its Opera Festival, which was established in 1951 and specializes in rarely produced works. This week of first-class music and performers takes place in the autumn, and Wexford town buzzes with fun.

History

County Wexford has a full history, due to its closeness to mainland Britain and Europe. It has been the landing place of many; and in past centuries trade across the sea was constant. This brief sketch starts about 350 BC, when the Celts arrived from Europe in waves. They absorbed many of the existing customs, but they also imposed their own legal, religious and cultural beliefs. Their ruling élite divided into hereditary royal families who ruled over small politically defined areas, and were often at odds with their neighbours. Thus, what is now Wexford had a hereditary enmity with the kingdom of Ossory, which roughly corresponds to County Kilkenny. The monks arrived about the 5th century and, with ease it seems, took over the mantle of respect and power from their pagan predecessors.

The family or sept which seemed to produce the most dynamic leaders was that of the MacMurraghs. They played a great part in Ireland's history, and made alliances with Norsemen, Welsh and Anglo-Norman mercenaries when it suited them. The arrival of the Norsemen or Vikings in AD 819 was a blow to the rich monasteries, which were plundered and sacked. The Norsemen liked it here and stayed, establishing a settlement called *Waesfjord*, now known as Wexford Town. All over Ireland, the story is the same: it is the Norsemen and the Anglo-Normans who founded the towns, never the Celts. Surnames did not exist in Ireland until the 12th century, but it was a MacMurragh king who in 1068 laid siege to Bristol—the only Irish monarch to threaten an English city! His descendant, Diarmuid or Dermot MacMurragh (1110–71), is reviled in Irish history for having invited the Anglo-Normans over to help him in his territorial struggles. In fact, Diarmuid was following a well-used practice in hiring Flemish, Norman and Welsh mercenaries; but these ones stayed on, and laid claim to the whole of Ireland. The names of Fleming, Prendergast, Fitzhenry and Roche are still a reminder of these people, and can be seen around the county on shop signs and pubs. The MacMurraghs produced another great leader in the late 14th century. Art MacMurragh Kavanagh became king of what is now Carlow, Wexford and the old kingdom of Leinster. He was so powerful that Richard II was forced into leaving his precarious throne in England to lead two campaigns against him in 1394 and 1399. Both were failures, and he lost his own throne into the bargain.

The Normans were gradually absorbed into Gaelic way of life. Up until the beginning of this century, in the ancient Norman Baronies of Forth and Bargy in the southeast corner, the locals spoke in the Flemish-sounding Yola dialect. Some words are still in everyday use; for example, *stour*, meaning a truculent woman! Later settlers were brought in over the centuries by the British government, and given land in payment for military services. Wexford is perhaps the most 'planted' of all the Irish counties; but the 'foreigners' moved in gradually, and not with the systematic force with which the Scots moved into the north. The Rebellion of 1798 is remembered in the many memorials placed around the countryside and towns. There is great emotive value placed on it still, for it was such a brave and pathetic struggle: thousands of peasants armed with pitch forks held off the well-trained forces of the English for six weeks, until they were defeated at Vinegar Hill with huge losses (*see* **History**, p.93).

Getting Around

By air: to Dublin Airport.

By boat: Rosslare Harbour handles passenger and car ferry boats from Fishguard, Pembroke and the French ports of Le Havre and Cherbourg. The car ferry between Ballyhack and Passage East in County Waterford runs nonstop.

By rail: mainline services from Dublin to Wexford and Rosslare, stopping at smaller places en route.

By bus: Expressway buses from Dublin go to Wexford Town hourly. For details of local services, ✆ Waterford (053) 22522.

By car: Hertz (car hire), Ferrybank, Wexford, ✆ (053) 23511; and at Rosslare (053) 33511.

By bike: the Raleigh Rent-a-Bike network operates here. Your local contacts are 'Hayes', 108 South Main Street, Wexford, ✆ (053) 22462; and the Bike Shop, 9 Selskar Street, Wexford, ✆ (053) 22514. Bridge Cycles, 6 Bridge Street, New Ross, ✆ (051) 25348.

Tourist Information

Wexford, Crescent Quay, ✆ (053) 23111, May to September.

Rosslare Harbour, ✆ (053) 33622, all year.

Gorey, Lower Main Street, ✆ (055) 21248, July and August.

Wexford Heritage Park, ✆ (053) 41733, March to October.

New Ross, ✆ (051) 21857, July and August.

Festivals

June–July: Strawberry Fair, Enniscorthy, ✆ (064) 34623.

October–November:The Wexford Festival Opera. Contact the Wexford Festival Office, Theatre Royal, Wexford Town. Details of all fringe events can be found in *What's On* magazine, and in the local press during the festival or from Jerome Hynes, ✆ (053) 22400.

Wexford and Environs

Wexford Town is one of the most atmospheric of all Irish places with a past. It was originally settled by a Celtic Belgic tribe called the Manapii, about 350 BC, and later by the

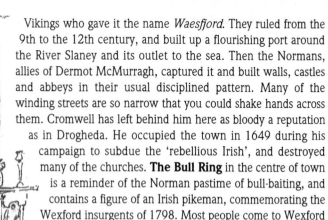

Vikings who gave it the name *Waesfjord.* They ruled from the 9th to the 12th century, and built up a flourishing port around the River Slaney and its outlet to the sea. Then the Normans, allies of Dermot McMurragh, captured it and built walls, castles and abbeys in their usual disciplined pattern. Many of the winding streets are so narrow that you could shake hands across them. Cromwell has left behind him here as bloody a reputation as in Drogheda. He occupied the town in 1649 during his campaign to subdue the 'rebellious Irish', and destroyed many of the churches. **The Bull Ring** in the centre of town is a reminder of the Norman pastime of bull-baiting, and contains a figure of an Irish pikeman, commemorating the Wexford insurgents of 1798. Most people come to Wexford for the **Opera Festival** held every year in October. Programmes of lesser-known operas are produced with world-famous soloists, an excellent local chorus and the RTE Symphony Orchestra. Its reputation for originality and quality is held worldwide. Many fringe events, exhibitions, revues, and plays take place at the same time (*see* 'Festivals', above). Near Westgate Tower, off Abbey Street, the only remaining fortified gateway of the original five, is **Selskar Abbey**. It was built in the late 12th century, and the remains consist of a square, battlemented tower, and a church with a double nave and part of its west gable. The 19th-century church stands on the spot where the first treaty between the Anglo-Normans and the Irish was ratified, in 1169. Always accessible. **The Maritime Museum** (*open in summer, ℗ (053) 23111*) on the quay is also of interest. In 1172, Henry II spent Lent in the town, doing penance for the murder of Thomas à Becket. Notice the **Commodore John Barry Memorial** on Crescent Quay. He was born 10 miles (16km) away at Ballysampson and is remembered as the father of the American navy. Lady Wilde (1826–96), mother of Oscar, and known as 'Speranza', was born in the Old Rectory, Main Street. Sir Robert McClure (1807–73), who discovered the Northwest Passage, is another famous Wexford son. Westgate Heritage Centre is in the Westgate Tower, a remnant of the Norman City walls. Here you can see an audio-visual presentation of the history of Wexford. There are mud flats close to the town at Ferrybank, which were reclaimed from the sea in the 1840s. The **Wexford Wild Life Reserve** provides over 2500 acres (1000ha) of mud flats, or 'slobs' for a huge variety of bird life in winter. Vast numbers of Greenland white-fronted geese rest and feed here. There is a lecture hall, library and observation tower in the public area of the reserve. About 2½ miles (4km) north of Wexford Town is **Ferrycarrig Folk Park** (*open Mar–Oct, daily, 10–7; Nov–Feb 10–5; adm; ℗ (053) 41911*). Here you will find reconstructions of life as it was in the past from 7000 BC to the medieval period, including a Viking boat. It is a scholarly and exciting Heritage Park with full-scale replicas of the dwellings, places of worship, forts, and burial grounds built by these ancient people.

Three miles (4.8km) south of Wexford, near Murntown, is **Johnstown Castle** (*open daily, 9–5; weekends 2–5; adm; ℗ (053) 42888*). Built in 19th-century Gothic style, it is now a State Agricultural College and visitors can tour round the landscaped gardens, lakes and the folk museum. There are three lakes and a walled garden. The museum has excellent displays on the history of farming and Irish rural life.

Rosslare to Hook Head

Five miles (8km) north of Rosslare Harbour, the ferry port, is the resort of **Rosslare**, with 6 miles (9.7km) of curving strand. The coastline beyond, approached from the R736, is well worth travelling around. On **Lady's Island** there are ruins of an Augustinian priory, and a Norman castle built in 1237. The rare roseate tern can be heard, if not seen, and the woolly cottonweed plant still grows on the sea bar, even though it died out on the English south coast a couple of centuries ago. The island is sacred to the Blessed Virgin and is still a favourite place of pilgrimage. In **Tacumshane**, a tiny village of a few houses and a petrol station-cum-shop, is an example of a working windmill with an attractive thatched top. This is part of the ancient Barony of Forth, and the technology for the windmill was brought here by the families of Flemish and Norman mercenaries. Mr Michael Meyler of the petrol station has the key to the mill, and will let you see round it. At Tagoat is a restored Yola farmstead with a craft centre and great tea shop (*open June–Sept, daily, 10am–6pm, © (053) 31177*).

Kilmore Quay is an attractive thatched fishing village where you can get a boat, weather permitting, to the **Saltee Islands**. You will have to persuade a local fisherman to take you out. Nobody lives on the islands, which are verdant with waist-high bracken. The puffins are magnificent. There is a curious coronation place erected by the self-styled king of the Saltees. The view from **Kilmore Quay Harbour** along the headlands looks rather like the 19th-century Dutch-influenced landscapes of the Norwich School of Painters. There is a small maritime museum on a lightship (*open May–Oct, daily, 12 noon–6pm; adm*).

Keeping close to the sea, the R736 passes through Carrick, and you can visit historic **Bannow**, the first corporate town established by the Normans. The town is now buried deep under the shifting sands, a process which began in the 17th century, though the benighted steeple and a couple of chimneys still returned MPs to the Irish Parliament until 1798! All that is left today of this proud Norman town is the ruin of St Mary's Church and an old graveyard. On the way to Hook Head, at the crossroads of the R733 and R734 you pass **Tintern Abbey**, said to have been founded in AD 1200 by William the Marshall, Earl of Pembroke, in gratitude for surviving a terrible storm in St George's Channel. 'Mastless, a wreck unhelmed', he and his wife vowed that if they were saved they would found an abbey wherever they landed. The vessel beached itself in this lovely creek. The Office of Public Works is in the process of restoring this magnificent Cistercian ruin, although it is still accessible to the public. Nearby **Fethard** is a quiet resort, and there is a lovely walk over the sea pinks and grass to the ruined ramparts at **Baginburn**, which the Normans hastily built to repel the Norsemen and the Gaels. The Normans won the day by driving a herd of cattle into the advancing army. It is claimed that at the Creek of Baginburn, Ireland was lost and won. Certainly, the Norsemen of Waterford and MacMurragh's Ossory enemies were slaughtered, and the captured thrown over the cliffs into the sea. Raymond le Gros held the earthworks until he joined Strongbow before the siege of

Waterford in 1170. The road continues down to the tip of Hook Head where the 700-year-old lighthouse still keeps the light burning. The colourful and lively village of **Ballyhack** has a car ferry to Passage East in County Waterford and a large tower house which is open to the public in the summer. At Duncannon there is star-shaped fort built in 1588 as a defence against the Spanish (*open May–Sept*).

Campile to New Ross

Near to **Campile**, on the R733, is **Dunbrody Abbey** beside the winding River Barrow. This is is one of the most underestimated ruins in Ireland. It was built by the monks of St Mary's Dublin in 1182. A vast pile of weathered, grey stone, it was suppressed in 1539. The west door is magnificent, and so are the lancet windows over the high altar. A small visitor centre has opened opposite the abbey. It has a tearoom, a small museum, picnic site and a fully grown maze. Close by is **Dunmain House** (*open to view; adm; ✆ (051) 62122*), a 17th-century building, slate-covered, quite a common sight as you move further south in Ireland. **Kilmokea** (*adm by arrangement; ✆ (051) 388109*), near Campile, is a Georgian rectory with superb grounds. There is a rock garden, an Italian garden, a traditional herbaceous border, a lupin border, wide lawns with topiary hedges, and a water garden set in woodland.

The Kennedy ancestral home is in **Dunganstown**. In 1848 Jack Kennedy left his family homestead for a new life in America after the dreadful years of the famine. From there the Kennedy success story needs no further telling: suffice to say, his great-grandson is remembered all over the world, and especially in Ireland! The homestead is now a ruin. **New Ross** on the River Barrow has some ancient gabled houses and a medieval feel to it. It was built by Isobel, Strongbow's daughter, and has seen fighting against Cromwell and during the 1798 rebellion. Although there was much brutality on both sides, the massacre of Scullabogue during the 1798 rebellion is still not forgotten. Hundreds of British prisoners were burnt alive by the frightened rebels after they had fled from the fight in New Ross. It is possible to cruise for two or three hours on the rivers Nore and Barrow, with or without a meal. For details *see* 'Eating Out'. The Kennedy Centre at the Quay in New Ross, ✆ (051) 25239 provides a genealogical centre for those compiling family records in the area. Visit the **John F. Kennedy Park and Arboretum** (*open all year, ✆ (051) 88171; adm*), with marvellous young trees and shrubs laid out in a scientific manner. A really worthwhile trip can be made to **Berkeley Forest Garden**, New Ross (*open by appointment, ✆ (051) 21361; adm*). It is an Italian garden, planted with mainly blues and greens. Also here is the **Berkeley Costume and Toy Museum** (*open May–Oct, Thurs–Sun, from about 11.30 till 4 or 5; ring in advance for exact times; adm*), which has a collection of rare and delicate dolls and costumes—the lady who runs it makes tiny exquisite dolls' hats, and for these alone it is worth stopping here.

Killann to Enniscorthy

Along the side of the Blackstairs Mountains you sometimes meet a lone deer making its way between these hills and the Wicklow Mountains; the tiny farms on these slopes are more reminiscent of the West than the neat prosperity of the rest of Wexford. Stop in **Killann** on the R731 from New Ross, at Rackards Pub, one of the friendliest traditional pubs in Ireland; a local dive, with no hint of 'the singing pubs for tourists' style. The Rackard family are famous for their skill at hurling. Four of them were in the team that won the Leinster Trophy in 1951. Killann was an important ecclesiastical centre in medieval times, though nothing much remains.

Enniscorthy is the most attractive town in County Wexford. It is a thriving market town on the River Slaney, presided over by Vinegar Hill from which there is a great view of the river and rich farming land around. You might time your arrival for the **Strawberry Fair** in early July. **The County Museum** (*open all year, summer 10–6; winter 2–5; adm; Ⓒ (054) 35926*) is in the castle, built by Raymond le Gros and later owned by the Roche family. It has an interesting folk section. All around County Wexford it is traditional for the mummers or rhymers to act out in dance the characters of Irish heroes to the rhythm of Irish reels. The mummers dress themselves in strawsuits and tinsel and act out the perpetual struggle of Good over Evil. This tradition actually originated in England. In other parts of Ireland, custom differs. Like all country customs, mumming is in decline, but the mummers still 'visit' the houses of local people at Christmas time, and you might be lucky and see them perform at the Wexford Opera Festival. **Bunclody** (N80), on the borders with County Carlow in the northwest of the county, is a very pretty mountainside town. Many people stay here to go walking on the Blackstairs Mountains. It has a very attractive Church of Ireland church.

Nearer to Enniscorthy, on the N11, is Ferns. **Ferns** is rather like Swords in County Dublin—full of memories and former glory. In the 12th century the King of Leinster, Dermot MacMurragh (the one who invited the Normans to invade), made it his capital and founded a rich abbey there, but after the Norman conquest the town declined. It has been pillaged and burnt so often that there is little left of it. Yet it is a fascinating place with a vast, **ruined cathedral**, a segment of which is now the Church of Ireland Cathedral. A 13th-century Anglo-Norman **castle** built by William de Valence, which has a fine chapel in its southeast tower, was built on the site of the ancient fortress of the kings of Leinster. It was destroyed by the O'Connor and O'Rourke forces in their conflict with Dermot MacMurragh, and it was here that he waited for his allies, the Normans, sending guides to Baginburn to show them the way. Dermot is buried here in the ruins of the **Augustinian priory** that he founded. The High Cross covered in a fretwork pattern marks his grave. An interesting quirk of fate links Ferns with another man who may have changed the course of history! In the graveyard of the modern Catholic church is the grave of Father Ned Redmond, who as a young priest in France saved Napoleon Bonaparte from drowning during his student days.

The East Coast from Castletown to Curracloe

Along the coast is the pretty village of **Castletown** and the family resort of **Ballymoney**. There are numerous sandy coves here, perfect for bathing. **Courtown** on the R742 is a harbour resort on the Ounavarra River with two miles of sandy beach. **Blackwater** is a very pleasant coastal village which has won numerous 'tidy town' competitions. This national award, run by the Tourist Board, inspires proud villagers to spruce up their paint-work and tidy their gardens each year. Courtown is said to be the *Ardladhru* frequently mentioned in the Gaelic sagas: that is, the fort of Ladhru, one of the principal Celtic leaders at the time of their first landings. There is a fine hill-top earthworks just outside the village. **Curracloe Strand** on the way back to Wexford is super for walking or bathing. It has 6 miles (9.7km) of golden beach and attractive white-washed houses. The **Raven Point Peninsula**, stretching from Curracloe to Wexford Harbour-mouth, is 3 miles (5km) of forest, bird and plant life, and sand dunes, and is a protected nature reserve.

Shopping

Cheese: Carrigbyrne Cheese, Adamstown, Enniscorthy, ✆ (054) 40500. Delicious hexagonal Brie-type cheese. Widely available. Croghan Farmhouse Cheese, Ballynadishogue, Blackwater, ✆ (053) 29331. Fine cheese made from goat's milk.

Delicacies: Greenacres, Main Street, Wexford, ✆ (053) 22975. Good vegetables, wholefoods and a small, but good meat counter.

Fish: Atlantis, Redmond Road. Freshly caught fish sold from a caravan.

Pottery: Kiltrea Bridge Pottery Ltd, Kiltrea Bridge, Cairn, Enniscorthy, ✆ (054) 35107 and Hillview Potteries, Enniscorthy, ✆ (054) 35443.

Handwoven rugs: Tapestry Weavers, Pollmounty Mill, New Ross, ✆ (051) 24735.

Crafts: good shops in Wexford Town and the John F. Kennedy Park. Shirna Craft Studio, Ferns, ✆ (054) 66186. Leather and Patchwork. The Honey Pot, 4 Main Street, Gorey, for home-baked breads as well as crafts.

Activities

Walking: Wexford coastal path from Kilmichael Point to Ballyhack 138 miles (221kms)—ask for details from tourist office. Walking tour of Wexford Town led by local historical society member. Summer evenings only, departing Whites and Talbot Hotel. Confirm with tourist office.

Golf: Courtown Golf Course at Kiltennel, near Gorey, ✆ (055) 25166. Rosslare Golf Club, Rosslare Strand, ✆ (053) 32113. St Helen's Bay, ✆ (053) 33234; Enniscorthy, ✆ (054) 34519.

Deep-sea fishing: boat hire from Nick Bowie, 143 The Faythe, Wexford, ✆ (053) 45888; or Richard Hayes, Ballytigue, Kilmore Quay, ✆ (053) 29704.

Cruising: cruiser hire at New Ross, ✆ (051) 21703; for cruises up the River Barrow with Celtic Canal Cruisers, Tullamore, County Offaly, ✆ (0502) 21861.

Day trips: to the Saltee Islands. Ask local fishermen on the harbour of Kilmore Quay. If nobody is around, try the hotel.

Pony-trekking: Horetown Equestrian Centre, Foulksmills, ✆ (051) 63786/ 63633. Combine a hunting course, picnic rides, hacking and beginners' courses with staying in a lovely 17th-century manor house. Boro Hill Equestrian Centre, Clonroche, ✆ (054) 44117, offers unaccompanied children's riding holidays and trekking.

Hunting: with the Island Hunt, ✆ (054) 77125; and The Wexford Hunt, ✆ (051) 21225.

Farm Tours: Ballylane Farm, New Ross (off N25), ✆ (051) 21315.

Where to Stay

expensive

Whites Hotel, George Street, Wexford Town, ✆ (053) 22311. Central and comfortable; it was the smartest hotel in town for years. It is now largely modern but incorporates part of an old coaching inn.

Ferrycarrig Hotel, Ferrycarrig Bridge, Wexford, ✆ (033) 22999. This is a brand new hotel built on the Slaney Estuary. Nice views and good leisure facilities.

moderate

Mrs Pim, **Furziestown House**, Tacumshane, ✆ (053) 31376. Nice farmhouse serving wholesome food. Also caters imaginatively for vegetarians and vegans.

Mrs V. Young, **Horetown House**, Foulksmills, ✆ (051) 63771. Old fashioned 17th-century manor house in beautiful parkland setting. Good plain food in the Cellar Restaurant. Equestrian centre in the courtyard.

Sir Richard and Lady Levinge, **Clohamon House**, Bunclody, ✆ (054) 77253. This charming 18th-century house is set in an estate of 180 acres (40ha) in the lovely Slaney Valley, on a hill with a view of Mount Leinster. Private fishing for salmon or trout on the Slaney River, and a Connemara pony stud. Delicious food, and comfortable period rooms with four-poster beds. Maria Levinge is a charming hostess with a good knowledge of local goings-on.

Paul and Min Drumm, **Newbay House**, Wexford, ✆ (053) 42779. Log fires, excellent meals and pine/period furnishings in this 1820s house only 2 miles (3.2km) from Wexford Town and 20 minutes from Rosslare. Lovely gardens to stroll in and friendly owners. Take the N25 out of Wexford past the racecourse. Just before the roundabout on the new ring-road take the first left. Go to the first crossroads, turn right under a new bridge. Newbay is 220yds (200m) on the right.

inexpensive

Josephine Flood, **Creacon Lodge**, New Ross, ✆ (051) 21897. Situated close to the John F. Kennedy Park, this cosy house has tiny mullioned windows and creeper climbing up the walls.

Betty and Tom Breen, **Clonehouse**, Ferns, ✆ (054) 66113. Pretty farmhouse, well-prepared simple food, clean and attractive rooms. Kathleen Hayes, **Clonard House**, Clonard Great, Wexford, ✆ (053) 43141. Lovely late-Georgian house with a staircase that curves into the ceiling because the money ran out for the top floor. Delicious plain food. Perfect views and farmland to the sea.

Mr and Mrs Parker, **Salville House**, Enniscorthy, ✆ (054) 35252. Simple, large bedrooms overlooking a pretty wood. Mr & Mrs O'Flaherty, **Glenfarne**, 5 Richmond Terrace, Spawell Road, Wexford, ✆ (035) 45290. Spacious en suite rooms. Mrs S. Whitehead, **Kilrane House**, Kilrane, Rosslare Harbour, ✆ (053) 33135. Comfortable house, only 2 minutes from Rosslare Harbour.

self catering

The Granary at **Clohamon House**, Bunclody. ✆ (054) 77253. From IR£300. Very nicely converted farm grain store. Will sleep 4–6. West wing of 18th-century house on River Barrow. **Killowen House**, Dunganstown, New Ross, ✆ (051) 88105. Contact Mrs Ryan; from IR£125 a week.

Eating Out

expensive

Galley Cruising Restaurant, The Quay, New Ross, ✆ (051) 21723/21705. Six-course meals whilst you cruise on the River Barrow. **Marlfield House**, Gorey, ✆ (055) 21124. Top-cuisine modern restaurant in fine Regency country house. Lobster from a tank, oysters and scallops, veal, delicious seafood, and local fresh ingredients. Booking essential.

moderate

The Granary, Westgate, Wexford, (053) 23935. Delicious classic cooking with exceptionally friendly service. **Talbot Hotel**, Trinity Street, Wexford, ✆ (053) 22666. Renowned for its tripe. **Eugene's**, Ballyedmond, ✆ (054) 89288. Pub, chipper and restaurant, all cooked for by top chef Eugene Callaghan, winner of the Roux Brothers chef of the year award. Wholesome and enterprising cooking using lots of locally-produced goodies. **Lobster Pot**, Carne, ✆ (053) 31110. Locally popular cosy bar and restaurant. Great seafood and pub grub served all day. **Neptune**, Ballyhack, New Ross, ✆ (051) 89284. Overlooking the harbour. Good value dinner menus. Seafood a speciality and you can bring your own wine. **Oyster Restaurant**, Strand Road, Rosslare Strand, ✆ (053) 32439. Scallops and black sole are a speciality.

inexpensive

The **Cellar Restaurant**, Wexford Arts Centre, ✆ (051) 63771. Good salad lunches. **Bohemian Girl**, North Main Street, Wexford, ✆ (053) 24419. Tudor-style pub serving good stews, salads, steaks. **Kingsbay Inn**, Arthurstown, ✆ (051) 89173. Good bar food. **Cedar Lodge Restaurant and Hotel**, Carrigbyrne, Newbawn, New Ross, ✆ (051) 28386. On the main Wexford–New Ross road.

Good-quality food. **Tim's Tavern**, 51 South Main Street, Wexford, ℗ (053) 23861. Good lunchtime food.

Entertainment and Nightlife

Music: many pubs in the New Ross area have a good reputation for traditional music.

County Carlow

County Carlow is the second-smallest county in Ireland, lying between Counties Wicklow, Wexford and Kilkenny. It is flat, with undulating plains of rich farmland, although its borders to the south, east and west touch the hilly uplands of mountainous areas. To the southeast are the Blackstairs Mountains on the Wexford Border; in the west, the River Barrow threads through a limestone region which forms the boundary with Kilkenny; in the northeast the River Slaney flows through the granite fringe shared with the Wicklow Mountains.

The rich river valleys contain many remains from the Anglo-Norman past in the form of castles and tower houses. There are Early-Christian monastic ruins as well. The wide, twisting rivers provide opportunities for salmon and trout fishing, and you can cruise on the River Barrow. There is unstrenuous walking in the Slievemargey Hills above Carlow Town; and the South Leinster Way, a signposted long-distance walk, starts in Kildavin and passes through some fine mountain countryside in the Blackstairs range, before dropping down to follow the towpath of the River Barrow, with the all different bird life and tranquillity that the river world offers.

Travelling through the sleepy villages and the verdant countryside, one is struck by how unspoilt it is. The farms look old-fashioned, hedges and trees have been left to decorate the fields and side roads. If you come from a highly industrialized country such as England, where farming is big business and almost every inch of land has been ploughed up, it is very appealing. Carlow seems to have escaped the indiscriminate building of bungalows, which so often mar the wild beauty of Connacht and the counties along the western seaboard. It is also still far enough away from Dublin to be ignored by commuters. Most people who live here work in agriculture, or at the big sugar beet factory in Carlow Town.

History

In the 7th century Saint Moling founded a great monastic centre at St Mullins on the River Barrow, and later many of the towns were Anglo-Norman strongholds held for the king of England. In the 14th century, their position of power was challenged by a great chieftain, Art MacMurragh Kavanagh, who became King of Leinster and waged many successful battles against Richard II of England. MacMurragh was initially put down by a huge expeditionary force led by Richard, but as soon as he had submitted and a treaty been agreed, he mounted another attack. He joined with the O'Neills of Ulster and the Earl of Desmond, and at the Battle of Kellistown in 1399 King Richard's cousin and heir, Roger Mortimer, was routed and killed. Richard's preoccupation with Ireland, and his extensive losses there, gave his enemies in England a chance to organize against him, and Bolinbroke usurped his throne. Richard returned to imprisonment and death, and MacMurragh got his kingdom back.

For the next 135 years the authority of the English crown was reduced to the narrow 'Pale' around Dublin. Carlow Town was for a time its most southern outpost, and heavily fortified. The Cromwellian confiscations of the 1650s, the Williamite wars of the 1690s and the penal laws had their dire effect on the Gaelic culture and society of Carlow, as they did elsewhere in Ireland. The 1798 rebellion against English rule claimed may lives, for the rebel army consisted of peasant mobs who were no match for the trained and well-armed British forces. Most of the leaders of this uprising are still remembered locally, amongst them Father John Murphy, who was executed in the Market Square of Tullow, a small place east of Carlow Town. There is a monument to him there, and he still lives on in folk memories. Famines during the 1840s hit hard, and the lives of the county's inhabitants followed the usual pattern of death, and emigration.

Getting Around

By air: to Dublin airport.

By rail: mainline trains to Waterford from Dublin pass through Carlow.

By bus: express bus service from Dublin and good local bus services. For details, Waterford Bus Depot, ✆ (051) 73401; or (01) 873 4222.

By car: car hire from Pratt's, Pollerton Road, Carlow, ✆ (0503) 32333

By bike: the Raleigh Rent-a-Bike network operates throughout the county. Your local dealer is A. E. Coleman, Dublin Street, Carlow, ✆ (0503) 31273.

Tourist Information

Kilkenny, ✆ (056) 51500, all year.

Carlow, ✆ (0503) 31554, June to September.

Festivals

May/June: Carlow Arts Festival. Music exhibitions, recitals, dances, ✆ (0503) 40491.

Carlow Town

Carlow Town is at the crossing of the River Barrow in the northwest of the county and is steeped in history. It was an Anglo-Norman stronghold, and much later it was the scene of a bloody scrimmage in the 1798 rebellion (*see* **History**). Nowadays it is involved in the manufacturing of sugar beet, which was introduced in 1926 as part of the Irish self-sufficiency programme. Sights include the **Norman castle**, probably early-13th century, with its two drum towers. Its ruins were further reduced by a Dr Middleton, who built a lunatic asylum here in 1814. It is in private hands, but permission to look around it is readily given. Ask at the house near the castle, which is right in the centre of the town near the east bank of the River Barrow. There is a prominent **Gothic Revival Catholic church**, completed in 1833, off College Street; and a handsome **courthouse** with a Doric portico, after the Parthenon, at the junction of Dublin Street and Dublin road. You are welcome to visit it during working hours. You may like to visit **Carlow Museum** in the Town Hall on Centaur Street (*times of opening chop and change but generally open 2.30–5.30*), which has displays on folklife, archaeology and local history.

Outside Carlow, 2 miles (3.2km) to the east, is the largest capstoned dolmen in Ireland, the **Browne's Hill Dolmen** (*always accessible*). This is very impressive and is estimated to weigh over a hundred tonnes. **Killeshin**, 3 miles (4.8km) west of Carlow town, off the R430, is a ruined 12th-century church with an exceptionally fine Romanesque doorway. In the graveyard you will find the oldest decorated font in Ireland.

Moving southwards following the river Barrow, you come to Leighlinbridge and Old Leighlin on the N9. They are both pleasant spots. **Leighlinbridge** has a superb stone bridge with a Norman castle on its eastern side which was built in 1181. It is always open. On the unclassified road leading to Old Leighlin is **St Laserain's Church**, which has a very attractive bell-tower. **Old Leighlin** has the remains of a 7th-century monastery and fine cathedral. It was the centre of a bishopric from the 12th century until the diocese was joined with Ferns in County Wexford in 1600. The 12th-century **Cathedral of St Laserain** has some fine 13th- and 15th-century architectural details, and in the grave-

yard are St Laserain's stone cross and a holy well. In the grounds of **Burgage House** near Leighlinbridge is a large rath, known as **Dinn Righ**, an ancient residence of the kings of Leinster. You can ask to visit it.

If you want to do some inland water cruising, all Ireland's rivers are beautiful and unspoilt. In Carlow, it is possible to cruise through Carlow Town, St Mullins and Muine Bheag, having hired a boat in Tullamore, County Offaly (*see* 'Activities', below). The river Barrow connects with the Grand Canal to Dublin, and links up with the Shannon. **Muine Bheag**, formally Bagenalstown, was destined by Walter Bagenal to become an Irish Versailles—a plan which never came off (perhaps he ran out of money?). About 2 miles (3km) away on the R724 is the impressive ruin of **Ballymoon Castle** (*always accessible*), built in the 14th century, and one of the earliest Anglo-Norman strongholds built in Ireland. Legend says that it has never been occupied. It has two square towers of great strength, for the cut-granite walls are over 8ft (2.5m) thick.

Borris is another pretty river town surrounded by the woods of Borris Castle. This is where the descendants of Art MacMurragh Kavanagh—14th-century ruler of Leinster and scourge of Richard II, once lived. One of the famous members of his family, Arthur, who lived in the 19th century, was born without limbs; yet he was a great sportsman and could ride, fish, shoot and sail. He was also M.P. for Carlow, and was married and had children. The MacMurragh Kavanaghs are still well-remembered. Arthur's daughter died in 1930 in The Step House, which is opposite the gates of the castle.

The kings of Leinster are supposed to have been buried at **St Mullins**, a very pretty village off the R729 on the way to New Ross. It is beautifully situated on the River Barrow, and was once a site of great ecclesiastical importance. St Moling, Bishop of Ferns, founded a monastery here in the 7th century and there are the remains of several ancient churches and an abbey. His little stone cell, the stump of a round tower, a holy well, the remains of a small nave and chancel church, and an old weathered stone cross are grouped together around the abbey.

The Blackstairs Mountains to the southeast of the county are gently rolling, and there is a pretty pass through the Sgollogh Gap (R702). The R746 leads to Bunclody in County Wexford at the northeast end of the mountain range. On an unclassified road to the north of Bunclody is **Clonegal**, a small village situated on the River Derry. In the centre is a fine Elizabethan building, **Huntingdon Castle** (*open Sun 2–4*), which has belonged to the Robertson family for centuries. The courtyard is rather fine, and it has a modern sculpture museum. In the basement is a temple to the Goddess Isis, a rich medley of eastern statues and colour and there's a magnificent yew walk in the grounds. You can write or ring for an appointment to see it, ℰ (054) 77552. Following the N80/81 and the River Slaney northwards you come to **Tullow**, the biggest town in the county and an angling centre for those fishing the Slaney for salmon and trout. If you are interested in archaeology, the raths ringing the town are worth a visit. **Castlemore**, the most important, lies a mile (1.6km) to the west. Three miles (4.8km) east of the town, just off the R725, there is the ancient stone fort of **Rathgall**. This has four ramparts; the outer ring is 1000ft (300m) in diameter. Both sites are always accessible. **Altamont Gardens**, 5½ miles (9km) off the

Tullow–Bunclody Road (*open Easter Sun until last Sun of Oct, 2–6; or by appointment; adm; ℗ (0503) 59128*), is a superb place to spend a few hours, with a formal garden, herbacious borders, a water garden, and good teas. In autumn there are masses of naturalized cyclamen.

A short drive northeast of Tullow lies **Hacketstown**, situated in the Wicklow foothills. This was the scene of a desperate engagement between the insurgents and the yeomanry in 1798 (*see* **History**). The tiny village of **Rathvilly** on the N81 to the west has a spreading view of the distant mountain ranges—the Blackstairs and the Slieve Blooms. It has a reputation to keep up, as winner of the All-Ireland title for the tidiest town three times over.

Shopping

Crafts: Kilkenny Design Workshops, Castleyard, Kilkenny, ℗ (056) 22118. (*See* 'Shopping' in County Kilkenny.)

Shamrock seed: Honeysuckle Products, The Watermill, Hacketstown, ℗ (0508) 71375.

Activities

River cruising: hire at Tullamore through Celtic Canal Cruisers, ℗ (0502) 21861.

Pony-trekking: Carrigbeg Stables, Bagenalstown, ℗ (0503) 21962.

Golf: Carlow Golf Club, Carlow Town, ℗ (0503) 31695.

Walking: The South Leinster Way. Contact the tourist office for detailed maps. At Bahana, 3 miles (4.8km) south of Barrow Bridge, Graignamanagh, on an unclassified road to St Mullins, is a forest walk by a canal.

Fishing: on the River Barrow for brown trout. Also, coarse fishing. Angling centres in *Muine Bheag* (Bagenalstown) and Tullow. For details of fishing waters, contact Irwin Hutchinson, Fishy Business, Carlow, ℗ (0503) 40877 and the tourist office in Carlow Town.

Where to Stay

expensive

Lord Rathdonnell, **Lisnavagh**, Rathvilly, Co. Carlow, ℗ (0503) 61104. Victorian Gothic country house on a huge estate with an outdoor, heated swimming pool.

moderate

Royal Hotel, Dublin Street, Carlow, ℗ (0503) 31621. Old, established hotel in the middle of Carlow Town. Quiet and comfortable with an attractive garden. Mrs B. Smith, **Lorum Old Rectory**, Kilgreaney, *Muine Bheag* (Bagenalstown), ℗ (0503) 75282. The ideal place for those with children. You are all made to feel very welcome and there is plenty to do on the farm, as well as outdoor toys, dogs, pet sheep and croquet in the garden. Delicious meals and pretty, old-fashioned rooms. It is next to a riding school.

inexpensive

Mrs Owens, **Sherwood Park House**, Kilbride, ✆ (0503) 59117. Peaceful Georgian house with brass end canopy beds.

self-catering

Old farmhouse in lovely wooded setting by a river. Accommodates seven. Contact **Mrs Smyth**, Garryhill, *Muine Bheag* (Bagenalstown), ✆ (0503) 57652. From IR£130 a week. Apartment in Elizabethan castle. Contact Mrs Moira Robertson, **Huntingdon Castle**, Clonegal, ✆ (054) 77552. Also in Clonegal, a 2-bedroomed stone cottage from IR£120 a week. Contact **Mrs Kirwan**, Kilcarry, Clonegal, ✆ (054) 77742.

Eating Out

moderate

The **Lord Bagenal Inn**, Leighlinbridge, ✆ (0503) 21668. Extremely popular restaurant serving a very varied and good menu and an excellent wine list. The **Beams Restaurant**, 59 Dublin Street, Carlow Town, ✆ (0503) 31824. Three-hundred-year-old coaching inn with bistro. Attached to the restaurant is an excellent wine and cheese shop. **Ballykealey House**, Ballon, Near Carlow, ✆ (0503) 57278. Country-house-style restaurant, which has just changed hands, check in advance. **Royal Hotel**, Dublin Street, Carlow, ✆ (0503) 31621. Good food in the centre of town.

inexpensive

The **Green Drake Inn**, Main Street, Borris, ✆ (0503) 73209. Simple meals made of local produce.

County Kilkenny

The countryside round Kilkenny is lush and well cultivated, reminiscent of England; so, too, are the villages with their neatness and mellowed cottages. History colours the land-scape wherever you are in Ireland, but in this county there is more visible evidence than in most others of the interaction of Norman and Gael, and later of English landlords and Welsh miners. The Anglo-Normans invaded Ireland in 1169, and quickly established themselves as the ruling power. These lords of conquest built themselves motte and bailey castles to hold their new territory, and as the centuries advanced and they grew more confident and wealthy, large and fine castles proclaimed their success. In Kilkenny, their dramatic castles along the river valleys of the Nore and the Barrow, the splendid remains of Jerpoint Abbey and, above all, the old city of Kilkenny itself make an exploration of the county a fascinating and rewarding occupation.

Apart from the ancient and stately buildings of Kilkenny, its wooded and well-tended countryside offers fishing, golf, horse-racing and riding. In Kilkenny City itself there is an arts festival, and good design and craft shops. The county's prowess also extends to hurling, a very ancient game recorded in Irish sagas. One of the most exciting things you can do is go to Nowlan Park, the hurling stadium in Kilkenny City, to watch a match.

Today County Kilkenny is a thriving agricultural county, with many craftsmen working in Kilkenny City, and in small studios in the heart of the countryside such as the Nicholas Mosse pottery at Bennettsbridge. Here there is a small pottery museum, and you can buy a good value 'second' of lovely spongeware decorated with farmyard animals and flowers.

History

A brief survey of the history of Kilkenny inevitably centres on the Anglo-Normans, but before they arrived, the county formed part of the old Gaelic kingdom of Ossory, an independent buffer state which sometimes joined with Leinster and sometimes with Munster. The old kingdom is remembered still in the diocese of Ossory, which stretches from near Waterford City in the south to the Slieve Bloom Mountains in the north. Its ruling family was called MacGiolla Phadruig, anglicized as Fitzpatrick. The kingdom of Ossory is said to date back to the 2nd century AD and it was a stable force in the 11th century; so much so that the king of the time decided to try for the kingship of Leinster.

The arrival of the Anglo-Normans, and the ease with which they triumphed over the ill-prepared Irish, eclipsed the Fitzpatricks. Soon the new name of Butler became all-powerful, and continued so for centuries. Theobald Fitzwalter was the first to carry the name. He came with Henry II on his great expedition in 1171, and in 1177 he was appointed Chief Butler in Ireland. Henceforth, his descendants were known as Butler, and by 1328 the head of the family was made Earl of Ormonde by Edward III. Confusingly, in many of the places you will visit, the names Butler and Ormonde are interchangeable! By 1391 the Butler family seat was in Kilkenny Castle, and many other castles in County Tipperary and Kilkenny became theirs as their clan grew in strength and numbers.

The Norman adventurers who first came to Ireland were brought to acknowledge the authority of the English crown by military expeditions staged by the monarch. But they frequently chafed at the restraint, and as time wore on they intermarried with the native Irish and became thoroughly Irish themselves. During the 14th century the colony went into a decline. There was the devastation of the Black Death, the native Irish began to reassert themselves, and the Norman families identified more and more with Gaelic Ireland. The effect of this was that royal authority was confined, apart from in a few walled towns, to an enclave on the east coast around Dublin—the Pale. In 1366 London reacted by calling a parliament in Kilkenny City which passed the Statutes of Kilkenny. These laws made it high treason for a Norman to marry an Irish woman, or for an Irish man to live in Kilkenny City. Normans were not allowed to wear Irish dress (the long cloak), or to adopt the customs, legal arrangements or language of the Irish. (If you go to Cahir Castle in County Tipperary, close to Kilkenny, there is an excellent permanent exhibition on the Brehon (Gaelic) laws and customs.) The statutes were rigidly enforced for a while, but they came too late and soon fell into decline.

A mutual antagonism between the Butlers and the Fitzgeralds, another powerful Norman family, created many a betrayal and pitched battle in the following two centuries. The Fitzgeralds in Leinster were the Earls of Kildare, and the Fitzgeralds in Munster were the Earls of Desmond. Both branches are often referred to as the Geraldines. The ramifications of the Butler dynasty and their feud with the Fitzgeralds spread far and wide. Anne Boleyn, the second wife of Henry VIII was the grand-daughter of Thomas Butler, the seventh earl. Elizabeth I's cousin, Black Tom Butler, put down the late 16th century revolt of the Earl of Desmond, on behalf of the crown. The Bishop of Cloyne, a brave man, said at a requiem Mass for the wife of the 4th Earl of Desmond in 1391: 'Eternal God, there are two in Munster who destroy us and our property, namely the Earl of Ormonde, and the Earl of Desmond with their followers, who at length, the lord will destroy, through Christ our Lord, Amen.' This prayer so incensed Butler and Geraldine, that the bishop was compelled to pay Ormonde damages, and was deprived of his see. The feud was finally healed by the marriage of James Butler, first Duke of Ormonde, to his cousin Elizabeth Preston, heiress of the Earl of Desmond in 1629.

Kilkenny City played a very important part in the Great Rebellion of 1641, which broke out in Ulster. The Norman and Gaelic families made an alliance, united in resentment against the new settlers—Protestants 'planted' by James I, and the decades of economic, political and religious oppression. In May 1642 the city became the seat of the Confederate Parliament of the Catholics, with representatives from all the counties and main towns. Government was taken into their hands, taxes levied, armies raised, weapons and powder manufactured. Owen Roe O'Neill commanded for Ulster, Preston for Leinster; Munster was under Barry, and Connacht under Burke. The Confederation lasted until 1648. But the alliance between the 'Old Foreigners' and the 'Old Irish' was complicated by their different loyalties, as the Civil War in England between Charles I and Parliament spilled over into Ireland. The Butlers of Kilkenny were loyal to the Stuarts; the old Gaelic families felt nothing for him and turned to France and Spain the traditional enemies of England. But this split was overshadowed in its turn by the rise of Cromwell. The ruthless campaign of Cromwell began in Ireland, and in March 1650, after five days' defence, Kilkenny City capitulated to him and his forces. James, Duke of Ormonde, at this time was deeply involved in the internal hostilities between the Confederates. He had supported Charles I, and after his execution, proclaimed Charles II. The successes of Cromwell forced him to retreat to France, but he was later restored to his estates, and given an English dukedom and peerage by Charles II. The Butler family was in any case probably destined to survive, for, as with many of the aristocratic families in Ireland, there were Protestant Butlers and Catholic Butlers, so they managed to keep a foot in each camp. In the more recent history of Ireland, the Butlers have ceased to play any part.

Getting Around

By air: Dublin Airport is 71 miles (114km) from Kilkenny.

By sea: Rosslare ferry port.

By rail: Kilkenny City is on the main line from Dublin to Waterford.

By bus: Expressway bus service links Kilkenny with all the major towns. Local bus routes are well-served. Contact McDonagh Station in Kilkenny for details, ✆ (056) 22024.

By car: car hire from Barry Pender Motors, Dublin Road, ✆ (056) 63839.

By bike: the Raleigh Rent-a-Bike network operates here. Your local contact is J. J. Wall, 88 Maudlin Street, Kilkenny, ✆ (056) 21236.

Tourist Information

Kilkenny, Shee Alms House, Rose Inn Street, ✆ (056) 51500, all year.

Festivals

June: Murphy's Irish Open Golf Championship, Mount Juliet, Thomastown. Country's premier international golf event, ✆ (056) 24455.

Late August: Arts Festival, Kilkenny, in the last week of the month. One of the most important arts festivals in Ireland—opera, art exhibitions, music of all sorts, ✆ (056) 63663 for details, or contact the tourist office in Kilkenny.

North Kilkenny

Places to visit, from west to east, include **Urlingford** on the border with Tipperary. There is a ruined 16th-century castle and the remains of a pre-Reformation church. The town itself dates only from 1755; the site was established after the bog had been cut away. **Ballyragget** on the River Nore has more to recommend it to historians, besides being a pretty little place. It was the scene of a dramatic trial of strength between Black Tom, Earl of Ormonde and Lord Lieutenant of Ireland in Elizabeth I's time, and Owen MacRory O'More, head of the ruling Laois family. The battle ended in the capture of the Earl in April 1600. Further east, about 7 miles (11km) north of Kilkenny, just off the N78 near Ballyfoyle, is the dramatic **Dunmore Cave** (*open mid-June–30 Sept daily, 10–7, and at more limited times throughout the rest of the year; there are guided tours; adm; ✆ (056) 67726*). During the Viking raids people took refuge here, but the Vikings found them and killed nearly a thousand. However, it continued to be used as a shelter by local people. It is a fantasy world of coloured caverns, and you can spend a good hour down there. The Office of Public Works runs the cave, which is notable for its huge chambers and 'market cross' stalagmite column. Nearby **Castlecomer** was laid out in Italian village-style by Sir Christopher Wandersforde in 1635. The area was once prosperous because of the coal field in this region, which skilled Welshmen were imported to mine. The mines finally closed in the 1970s.

East of Kilkenny

Gowran deserves your attention if you love horse-racing, for it has an excellent course. The town was an important fortress of the kings of Ossory until Theobald Fitzwalter, the first Butler and ancestor of the Dukes of Ormonde, was granted it by Strongbow. Sadly, nothing remains of the castle he built, as Cromwell's troops burned it down in 1650.

However, the Church of Ireland church has some interesting monuments, and is a mixture of 12th- and 13th-century architectural details. There is an effigy in armour of the first Earl of Ormonde (1327). On one of the grave stones is rather a witty couplet erected to a man and his two wives:

Both wives at once alive he could not have
Both to enjoy at once he made this grave.

Goresbridge is another attractive river village, which joins County Carlow to County Kilkenny across the River Barrow. Many people come and fish for brown trout and a variety of coarse fish here. At Goresbridge you can also buy ornaments and other objects made out of a speciality of the county—the highly polished black limestone which has been used as paving in Kilkenny City itself. Sadly, this 'marble' is no longer mined, although you may find Kilkenny marble chimneys pointed out to you in many big houses. Off the N9, 2kms from Kilfane is a lovely glen and waterfall further adorned by a romantic garden laid out in the 18th century. It has a cottage ornee. (*Open summer afternoons; ✆ (056) 27491*).

Going south, you reach lovely **Thomastown** (on the Waterford road), with its mellowed grey-stone buildings. Near here, on an unmarked road to the south of the town is the ruin of **Dysart Castle** (*open May–mid-Sept, Tues–Sun, 2–5.30 or by appointment; adm; ✆ (056) 24558*), the home of the famous idealist philosopher George Berkeley (1685–1753), who gave his name to the city and university of Berkeley, California. The castle can be viewed from the road. To the west of Thomastown, near Stonyford, is one of the best-kept estates in Ireland, **Mount Juliet**, where the Kilkenny Hunt Kennels are located. The house is an hotel, and the gardens are beautiful, especially the delphiniums in the walled garden. Part of the grounds have become a Jack Nicklaus champion golf course. But the jewel of the area must be the fine monastic ruin of **Jerpoint Abbey**, just off the N9, which dates from the late 12th century (*open only in the summer*). It follows a typical Cistercian plan with two chapels in each transept. The ancient parts of the chancel and the transepts are in Irish Romanesque style, and appear to have been built by the same masons who raised Baltinglass in Wicklow. The abbey was founded in 1158 by Donal MacGiolla Phadruig, King of Ossory, and suppressed in 1540. Restoration work has been sympathetic and it is an impressive ruin. You should take a look at the cloisters with their sculptured lords and ladies.

Due east rises the hill of Brandon which gives you a clear view of this well-worked countryside, with the Blackstairs Mountains to the east on the Carlow-Wexford border. On your way here you will pass the charming town of **Inistioge**, home of the Tighes. This family was connected with a pair of remarkable ladies who exercised a great influence on taste in the 18th century. The ladies of Llangollen, Lady Eleanor Butler and Sarah Ponsonby, exemplified the Romantic and the Gothick by running away together to live in a Welsh cottage. Inistioge square is planted with lime trees, and there are wooded stretches surrounding the town through which the River Nore runs. A Norman motte overlooks the river and there are the fine ruins of an Augustinian priory, founded in 1210. Always accessible. North of Inistioge is **Graignamanagh**, right on the Carlow border. It is picturesquely sited on a mountainous ravine and has a splendid early Cistercian abbey called **Duiske**, which survived the suppression of the monasteries in the 16th century, as did the Catholic church which has some 9th-century crosses in the graveyard. Both are always accessible to the public. Notice the effigy of a knight, crosslegged in 13th-century armour, in the church. At **Ullard**, 3 miles (4.8km) north on the R705, there are remains of another foundation: a high cross and the remains of an old church, with granite carvings on the Romanesque doorway. St Fiachre set off for France from Ullard. He is one of the saints that chose the isolation of a foreign land in preference to a lonely island hermitage. He is the patron saint of Parisian taxi-drivers, because the first carriage conveyances in Paris used to congregate round the Hôtel de St Fiachre. About 3 miles (4.8km) southeast of Kilkenny City at **Sheastown**, on the way to Bennettsbridge, is a well dedicated to St Fiachre. Patterns are held here in late August around the time of the Arts Festival in Kilkenny. (Patterns are ritualized prayers and a procession held in honour of a particular Saint.) Before leaving the Graignamanagh district, take the opportunity to investigate the woolcrafts. Cushendale Mills produce very finely woven goods.

West of Kilkenny

West of Kilkenny City is the ancient town of **Callan** which seems to have nourished a fair number of Ireland's great men. One of them, Edmund Ignatius Rice (1762–1844), a candidate for canonization, founded the influential teaching order of the Christian Brothers who now not only educate most of Ireland's politicians, but also some of the Third World's. He was born in a thatched cottage (marked by a plaque) at Westcourt, just outside Callan. Robert Fulton (b.1765), who designed the world's first steam engine, and James Hoban (1762–1831), architect of the White House, came from near here.

Nearby on the Kings River is the complete, fortified, turreted and walled enclosure of **Kells** (*always accessible*). Since the early history of the Kingdom of Ossory, Kells has heard the murmur of prayer and the clash of warfare. Now it is a supremely peaceful place, and the impressive collection of early ecclesiastical buildings must make it a highlight of any Kilkenny tour. It was founded in the late 12th century by Geoffrey Fitzrobert de Marisco, who built a stong castle and an Augustinian priory. But it had been a centre of importance in the early history of Ossory, and most probably a mystical pagan site. St Kieran of Seer founded a monastery here in the 5th century, but it is the remains of the 12th-century priory which still impress. Its ruins cover 5 acres (2ha) and are divided into two courts by a moat and a wall. The north court is surrounded by a tall wall, and fortified with towers, and contains the church, cloisters and other monastic buildings. The south court is fortified, turreted and walled, but contains no buildings and was an enclosure for cattle in times of trouble.

Kilkenny City

Kilkenny City (*Cill Chainnigh*: St Canice's church) was the focal point of the Anglo-Norman and Irish resistance to the Cromwellians in 1642, and where they formed their Confederate Parliament. Before that it was the seat of power for the 'old English', the first foreign war-lords. The city (really a large town), takes its name from St Canice, who established a monastery here in the 6th century. The cathedral called **St Canice's** now occupies that site off Vicar Street, and here you can see the finest collection of medieval sepulchral monuments in Ireland. The 100ft (30m) round tower beside the church also dates from this earlier time. The Cathedral was much restored in the 19th century; the nearby library houses some 3000 books dating from the 16th and 17th century. This grouping of ecclesiastical buildings with the Church of Ireland vicarage is curious but charming, and represents the strength of the anglicizing influence in its best aspects. In the town centre, the great fortress of the Ormondes, **Kilkenny Castle** (*open mid-June to mid-Sept daily, 10–7; Oct to mid-June, Tues–Sat, 10.30–5.30, Sun, 11–5; adm; ℗ (056) 21450*), remains a dominant feature. Kilkenny Castle acts as an exhibition centre during the Arts Festival and there is a nice restaurant for snacks in the old kitchen. William the Marshall, a Norman commander who married Strongbow's daughter, built the castle between 1195 and 1207. The building today is a mixture of Gothic, Classical and Tudor styles and is very dramatic, set as it is above the River Nore. The hall is hung with superb Butler portraits, some of them 14th century. The sixth Marquess of Ormonde presented the castle and a portion of its grounds to the people of Kilkenny in 1967. Until 1935 it was the principal residence of the Butlers. Now you can go round it and enjoy the lovely gardens sheltered behind the castle walls. It has an art gallery with temporary exhibitions. Opposite the castle, on the parade, is the Castle Yard and the **Kilkenny Design Centre** which promotes Irish goods; their label is almost a guarantee of good taste and quality workmanship. In the shop you will find china, glass, hand-knitted jerseys, tweed coats and jackets, kitchen ware, ornaments, linen and jewellery. The Crafts Council based in the Yard aims to develop and encourage designers through travelling scholarships. Their workshops are behind the Design Centre, in the converted stables of the castle.

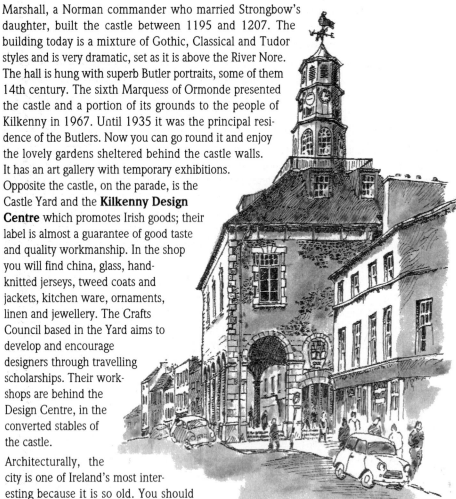

Architecturally, the city is one of Ireland's most interesting because it is so old. You should try to visit **Rothe House**, on Irish Parliament Street, a unique example of an Irish Tudor merchant's house, built in 1594. It has an arcaded shop front and consists of three buildings, parallel to each other but separated by two inner courtyards and joined on one side by a linking passageway. Inside is the City and County Museum, a costume collection and a geneological centre. The **Kilkenny Archaeological Society** (*open every Sat and Sun, all year, 3–5; 1 April–31 Oct, Mon–Sat, 10.30–5; other times on request; adm; ℗ (056) 22893*), a pioneer of its kind in Ireland and forerunner of the Royal Society of Antiquities in Ireland, houses its collection there. Further into the town, in the High Street, you can see the **Tholsel**, formerly the Toll House or Exchange and now the City Hall, which was built in 1761. It is built of black Kilkenny marble, and extends over the pavement to form an arcade made up of Tuscan pillars. It is possible to look inside if you ask. The **Shee Alms House**, Rose Inn Street (*open May–Sept, Mon–Sat, 9–6, Sun 11–5; Oct–April, Tues–Sat, 9–5; closed for lunch; adm*) dates from 1594, and contains an interesting Cityscope exhibition with a model of the medieval city.

Nearby in Abbey Street is the **Black Abbey** that gives the street its name. It has been restored and is once more an active place of prayer. The **Black Abbey Gate**, known also as the Black Freyre (Friar's) Gate, is the only gate remaining from the former town walls.

Across the River Nore, in Lower John Street, is **Kilkenny College**, a handsome Georgian building where some of Ireland's greatest writers were educated, including the satirist Dean Swift, the philosopher Berkeley and the dramatist Congreve. It is not possible to visit.

The city acts as host to one of the finest cultural festivals in Ireland, the Kilkenny Festival. It takes place at the end of August and includes all the arts: visual, performing and gustatory (if you go by the number of people in the smarter pubs drinking the homebrew, Smithwick's, a beer which is as popular as Guinness). The castle and many other historic buildings are used as venues. For a quiet jar after all this sightseeing try **Tynan's Bridge House Bar**, close to John's Bridge, an unspoilt Victorian pub with all the original fittings. Incidentally, many of the pubs in Kilkenny have hand-painted signs, which makes them much more attractive to look at.

Shopping

Crafts: Nicholas Mosse Pottery, Bennettsbridge; ℗ (056) 27105/ 27126, possibly the nicest pottery in Ireland, slight seconds are available here. Stoneware Jackson Pottery, Bennettsbridge, ℗ (056) 27175. Lots of swirley bright patterns. Jerpoint Glass Studios, Stoneyford; ℗ (056) 24350. Thickly-blown glass. Potters' Inistioge, Inistioge, ℗ (056) 58522. Pretty handmade pottery from a pretty little cottage. The Kilkenny Design Centre and Yard, Castleyard, Kilkenny, ℗ (056) 22118. An excellent selection of Irish crafts.

Fabric: Cushendale Woollen Mills, Graignamanagh, ℗ (0503) 24118, for tweed and woollen goods.

Silver jewellery: Liam Costigan, Collierslane, Off High Street, Kilkenny, ℗ (056) 62408. Rudolf Heltzel, 10 Patrick Street, Kilkenny, ℗ (056) 21497.

Leather: Chesneau Leather, Bennettsbridge, ✆ (056) 27456. Mostly handbags and knapsacks.

Delicacies: Shortis Wong, 74 John Street, Kilkenny, ✆ (056) 61305. Excellent deli. Lavistown Foods, Lavistown, ✆ (056) 65145. Cheese, homemade sausages. Will also organise organic farming courses and mushroom hunts. Mileeven Ltd, Owning Hill, Pilltown, ✆ (051) 43368. Honey, cider, beeswax polish.

Activities

Hurling: Kilkenny is famous for the quality and artistry of its hurling matches at Nowlan Park. See local newspapers for league and championship matches.

Fishing: at Graignamanagh and along the Lower River Barrow for brown trout, tench, rudd and bream. Contact O'Leary's (tackle shop), Lower Main Street, Graignamanagh, ✆ (0503) 21405 or Mr McCabe, Ballyogan, Graignamanagh, ✆ (056) 24191. Michael McGrath, Lower Patrick Street, Kilkenny, ✆ (056) 21388. Sports Shop, High Street, Kilkenny, ✆ (056) 21532. John Mealy, Carlow Road, ✆ (056) 21532.

Golf: at Mount Juliet, a Jack Nicklaus designed course amidst mature woodland, used for top notch international competitions, ✆ (056) 24455.

Pony-trekking: at Mount Juliet Equitation Centre, Thomastown, ✆ (056) 24455.

Horse-racing: at Gowran Park throughout the year. Check the local newspapers and at the back of Bord Fáilte's *Calender of Events*.

Hunting: Kilkenny Hunt, ✆ (056) 26143. North Kilkenny Hunt, ✆ (056) 33206.

Walking: Guided walks in Kilkenny, depart from the tourist office several times a day in the summer.

Where to Stay

luxury

Mount Juliet Estate Hotel, Thomastown, ✆ (056) 24455. This is a lovely stately house, recently converted into a swish hotel and country club, with beautiful grounds, friendly staff and good sporting facilities such as golf, riding and fishing.

expensive

Newpark Hotel, Castlecomer Road, Kilkenny, ✆ (056) 22122. Country house-style. Sporting facilities. **Butler House**, Patrick Street, Kilkenny, ✆ (056) 22828. Smart guest house. Central and comfortable. Sally & Richard St George, **Kilrush House**, Freshford, ✆ (051) 32236. Pretty, 18th-century country house, comfortable en suite rooms, good simple cooking, tennis court.

Lacken House, Dublin Road, Kilkenny, ℘ (056) 61085. A family-run guest house in attractive grounds, with eight bedrooms en suite, and well-cooked food elegantly produced by the chef-owner. **The Club House**, Patrick Street, Kilkenny, ℘ (056) 21994. Originally the headquarters of the Foxhounds Club, this old hotel has many gracious features of another age. It is very central for all the sights of Kilkenny City.

inexpensive

Mrs J. Prendergast, **Garranavabby House**, The Rower, ℘ (051) 23613. Ivy-covered old farmhouse in a lovely setting near Graignamanagh and charming Inistioge. **Cullintra House**, the Rower, Inistioge, ℘ (051) 23614. Very relaxed place with delicious meals, breakfast until mid-day.

Eating Out
expensive

Newpark Hotel, Castlecomer Road, Kilkenny, ℘ (056) 22122. Plush restaurant serving Irish and Continental food. **Lacken House**, Dublin Road, Kilkenny, ℘ (056) 62435. Popular family-run restaurant serving imaginative perfectly-cooked food. **Mount Juliet**, Thomastown, ℘ (056) 24455. A grand setting for any meal, the lofty restaurant is grandly decorated in white and Wedgwood blue and the lovely food makes use of lots of local produce. You might also spot celebrity golfers.

moderate

The Motte, Inistioge, ℘ (056) 58655. A charming cosy little restaurant in this most picturesque of villages, the food is adventurous yet fun and the atmosphere just right. **Edward Langton Restaurant/Bar**, 69 John Street, Kilkenny, ℘ (056) 21728. Good pub lunches and dinners, including vegetarian dishes. It has won the Pub of the Year award three times. **The Club House** Hotel, Patrick Street, Kilkenny, ℘ (056) 21994. Good for steaks. **The Loft**, the Hunters Yard, Mount Juliet, Thomastown, ℘ (056) 24455. Traditional Irish food.

inexpensive

Good teas served on the terrace of a lovely little water garden on the Bennettsbridge road in Thomastown. It is beautifully planted with aquatic plants. Open May to September, ℘ (056) 25578 for details. There is an entrance fee of 50p.

The Millstone, Bennettsbridge, ℘ (056) 27644. A craft and coffee shop—the latter run by two Ballymaloe-trained cooks. Good for soup, scones and cakes. **Kilkenny Design Centre**, Coffee Shop, Castleyard, Kilkenny, ℘ (056) 22118. Good soups, cooked meats and salads for lunch. The restaurant in the old kitchen of Kilkenny Castle, ℘ (056) 21450. Delicious lunches and teas during the summer only. **Rinuccini Restaurant**, 1 The Parade, Kilkenny ℘ (056) 61575. Home-made pasta.

The Old Gods and Heroes

The first Celts arrived in Ireland before 1000 BC; the last around the 3rd century BC. The Greek chroniclers were the first to name these people, calling them Keltori. Celt means 'act of concealment', and it has been suggested that they were called 'hidden people' because of their reluctance to commit their great store of scholarship and knowledge to written records. Kilt, the short male skirt of traditional Celtic dress may also come from this word!

The Celtic civilization was quite sophisticated, and much of the road-building attributed to the Romans has been found to have been started by the Celts. The Romans built on their foundations. In Ireland, ancient roads are quite often discovered when bog is being cleared.

The Irish language, and its ancient and rich epic stories, is predated only by Greek and Latin. But the tradition was strictly oral until the Christian era. Even then, it was well into the 7th century before the bulk of it was written down by scribes, who often added to or changed the story to make some moral Christian interpretation. The reluctance of the Celts to commit their knowledge to writing is directly related to the Druids and their power, for the Druidic religion was the cornerstone of the Celtic world, which stretched from Ireland to the Continent and as far south as Turkey. Irish mythology is therefore concerned with the rest of that Celtic world: there are relationships with the gods and heroes of Wales, Scotland, Spain and middle Europe.

The *Book of the Dun Cow* and the *Book of Leinster*, the main surviving manuscript sources, date from the late 11th century. Many earlier books were destroyed by the Viking raids and entire libraries lost. The various sagas and romances which survived have been categorized by scholars into four cycles. First, the **mythological cycle**: the stories which tell of the various invasions of Ireland, from Cesair to the Sons of Milesius. These are largely concerned with the activities of the Tuatha Dé Danaan, the pagan gods of Ireland. Next there is the **Ulster Cycle**, or deeds of the Red Branch Knights, which include the tales of Cú Chulainn. Then there is the **Cycle of Kings**, mainly stories about semi-mythical rulers. And finally, the **Fenian Cycle** which relates the adventures of Fionn MacCumhail (Finn MacCool) and the warriors of the Fianna. Only qualified story-tellers could relate these sagas and tales under Brehon (Celtic) laws, and they were held in great respect. Several qualities emerge from these sagas and tell us a great deal about the society of Iron Age Ireland, and indeed Europe. The stories are always optimistic, and the Celts had evolved a doctrine of immortality of the soul.

The heroes and gods were interchangeable—there were no hard and fast divisions between gods and mortals. Both had the ability to shape change, and often reappear after the most gruesome deaths. The gods of the Dé Danaan were tall, beautiful and fair, although, later, in the popular imagination, they became fairies or the 'little people'. They were intellectual as well as beautiful, and as gullible as mortals with all our virtues and vices. They loved pleasure, art, nature, games, feasting and heroic single combat. It is difficult to know whether they are heroes and heroines made into gods by their ancestors. In the 11th century, Cú Chulainn was the most admired hero, particularily by the élite of society. Then Fionn MacCumhail took over. He and his band of warriors became very popular with the ordinary people right up to the early 20th century. The English conquests in the 17th century and the resulting destruction and exile of the Irish intelligentsia meant that much knowledge was lost, though the peasantry kept it alive in folklore recited by the *seanachie* or village story-teller. Then, with the famines and vast emigration of the 19th century, the Irish language came under great threat and, with it, the folklore.

It was anglicized by antiquarians and scholars at the end of the 18th century, and later in the 19th century, who did much to record and translate the Irish epic stories into English, and to preserve the Gaelic; many were Ulster Presbyterians. Other names which should be remembered with honour are William Carleton, Lady Wylde, T. Crofton-Croker, Standish James O'Grady, Lady Gregory and Douglas Hyde. Their writings and records of Irish peasant culture have become standard works.

The question of where Irish myth ends and history begins is impossible to define. Historical accounts are shot through with allegory, supernatural happenings and fantasy. Nothing has changed, for a similar mythical process is applied to modern history.

Directory of the Gods

Amergin: a Son of Milesius. The first Druid of Ireland. There are three poems credited to him in *The Book of Invasions*.

Aonghus Óg: the God of Love. His palace was by the River Boyne at Newgrange.

Ard Rí: the title of High King.

Badhbha: goddess of battles.

Balor: a god of death, and one of the most formidable Fomorii. His one eye destroyed everything it gazed on. Destroyed by his own grandson, Lugh.

Banba, Fotla and Eire Dé Danaan: sister goddesses who represent the spirit of Ireland, particularly in Irish literature and poetry. It is from the goddess Eire that Ireland takes its modern name.

Bilé: god of life and death. He appears as Cymbeline in Shakespeare's play.

Bran: 'Voyage of Bran'. The earliest voyage poem, which describes through beautiful imagery the Island of Joy and the Island of Women. Also, the hound of Fionn MacCumhail.

Brigid: goddess of healing, fertility and poetry. Her festival is one of the four great festivals of the Celtic world. Also a Christian saint who has become confused in popular folklore with the goddess.

Caílte: cousin of Fionn MacCumhail. One of the chief Warriors of the Fianna, and a poet. A Christian addition to his story has returned him from the Otherworld to recount to St Patrick the adventures of the Fianna.

Conall Cearnach: son of Amergin, a warrior of the Red Branch, and foster brother and blood cousin of Cú Chulainn. He avenged Cú Chulainn's death by slaying his killers.

Conchobhar MacNessa: king of Ulster during the Red Branch Cycle. He fell in love with Deidre (*see* below) and died from a magic 'brain ball' which had been lodged in his head seven years before by the Connacht warrior, Cet.

Conn: one of the Sons of Lir, the ocean god, changed into a swan by his jealous step-mother, Aoife. Also, Conn of the hundred battles, High King from AD 177 to 212.

Cormac MacArt: High King from AD 254 to 277 and patron of the Fianna, who reigned during the period of Fionn MacCumhail and his adventures. His daughter was betrothed to Fionn MacCumhail but eloped with one of Fionn's warriors, Diarmuid. His son succeeded him and destroyed the Fianna.

Cú Chulainn: the hound of Culainn, also called the Hound of Ulster. He has similarities with the Greek hero, Achilles. He was actually called Sétanta until he killed the hound belonging to Culann, a smith god from the Otherworld. He promised to take its place and guarded his fortress at night. He became a great warrior whose battle frenzy was incredible. Women were always falling in love with him, but Emer, his wife, managed to keep him. He is chiefly famous for his single-handed defence of Ulster during the War of the Tain (Bull of Cuailgne) when Ailill and Medb of Connacht invaded (*see* Medb). He was acknowledged as champion of all Ireland, and forced to slay his best friend, Ferdia, during a combat at a crucial ford. Later Cú Chulainn rejected the love of the goddess of battles, Mórrigań, and his doom was sealed; his enemies finally slew him. During the fatal fight he strapped his body to a pillar stone because he was too weak to stand. But such was his reputation that no one dared to come near him until Mórrigań, in the form of a crow, perched on his shoulder, and finally an otter drank his blood.

Dagha: father of the Gods and patron god of the Druids.

Diarmuid: foster son of the love god, Aonghas Óg, and a member of the Fianna. The goddess of youth put her love spot on him, so that no woman could resist loving him. He eloped with Grainne, who was betrothed to Fionn MacCumhail, and the Fianna pursued them for 16 years. Eventually the couple made an uneasy peace with Fionn, who went out hunting with Diarmuid on Ben Bulben, where Diarmuid was gored by an enchanted boar who was also his own stepbrother. Fionn had the power to heal him with some enchanted water, but he let it slip through his fingers. Aoughas Óg, the god of love, took Diarmuid's body to his palace and, although he did not restore him to life, sent a soul into his body so that he could talk to him each day.

Deidre: Deidre of the Sorrows was the daughter of an Ulster chieftain. When she was born it was forecast by a Druid that she would be the most beautiful woman in the land, but that, because of her, Ulster would suffer great ruin and death. Her father wanted to put her to death at once but Conchobhar, the Ulster King, took pity on her and said he would marry her when she grew up. When the time came she did not want to marry such an old man, particularly as she had fallen in love with Naoise, a hero of the Red Branch. They eloped to Scotland. Conchohbar lured them back with false promises, and Naoise and his brothers were killed by Eoghan MacDuracht. Deidre was forced to become Conchobhar's wife. She did not smile for a year, which infuriated her husband. When he asked her who she hated most in the world, she replied, 'you and Eoghan MacDuracht'. The furious Conchobhar then said she must be Eoghan's wife for a year. When she was put in Eoghan's chariot with her hands bound, she somehow mangaged to fling herself out and dash her head against a rock. A pine tree grew from her grave and touched another pine growing from Naoise's grave, and the two intertwined.

Emain Macha: the capital of the kings of Ulster for six centuries, which attained great glory during the time of King Conchobhar and the Red Branch Knights.

Emer: wife of Cú Chulainn. She had the six gifts of womanhood: beauty, chastity, eloquence, needlework, sweet voice and wisdom.

Female champions: in ancient Irish society women had equal rights with men. They could be elected to any office, inherit wealth and hold full ownership under law. Cú Chulainn was instructed in the martial arts by Scáthach, and there was another female warrior in the Fianna called Creidue. Battlefields were always presided over by goddesses of war. Nessa, Queen of Ulster, and Queen Medb of Connacht were great warriors and leaders. Boadicea of Britain was a Celtic warrior queen who died in AD 62, and this tradition survived with Grace O'Malley of County Mayo into the 16th century.

Ferdia: the best friend of Cú Chulainn, killed by him in a great and tragic combat in the battle over the Brown Bull of Cuailgne (or Cooley).

Fergus MacRoth: Stepfather of Conchobhar, used by him to deceive Deidre and Naoise and his brothers. He went into voluntary exile to Connacht in a great fury with the King, and fought against Conchobhar and the Red Branch. But he refused to fight against Cú Chulainn, which meant the ultimate defeat of Queen Medb and her armies.

The Fianna: known as the Fenians. A band of warriors guarding the high king of Ireland. Said to have been founded in about 300 BC, they were perhaps a caste of the military élite. Fionn MacCumhail was their greatest leader. In the time of Oscar, his grandson, they destroyed themselves through a conflict between the clans Bascna and Morna. In the 19th century the term was revived as a synonym for Irish Republican Brotherhood, and today it is used as the title for one of the main Irish political parties, Fianna Fail, which means 'Soldiers of Destiny'.

Fintan: the husband of Cesair, the first invader of Ireland. He abandoned her and survived the Great Deluge of the Bible story by turning into a salmon. Also, the Salmon of

Knowledge who ate the Nuts of Knowledge before swimming to a pool in the River Boyne, where he was caught by the Druid Finegas. He was given to Fionn MacCumhail to cook. Fionn burnt his finger on the flesh of the fish as he was turning the spit, sucked his thumb, and acquired the knowledge for himself.

Fionn MacCumhail: anglicized as Finn MacCool. He was brought up by two wise women, then sent to study under Finegas, the Druid. After acquiring the Knowledge of the salmon, Fintan, he became known as Fionn, the Fair One. He was appointed head of the Fianna by Cormac MacArt, the High King at the time, in place of Goll MacMorna who had killed his father. His exploits are many and magical. His two famous hunting hounds were Bran and Sceolan, who were actually his own nephews, the children of his bewitched sister. His son, Oísín, was the child of the goddess Sadb, but he suffered unrequited love for Grainne. In the story of the Battle of Ventry, Fionn overcomes Daire Donn, the King of the World. He is said not to be dead, but sleeping in a cave, waiting for the call to help Ireland in her hour of need.

Dé Fionnbharr and Oonagh: gods of the Dé Danaan who have degenerated into the King and Queen of the Fairies in folklore.

Fionnuala: the daughter of Lir. She and her brothers were transformed into swans by her jealous stepmother, Aoife. The spell was broken with the coming of Christianity, but they were old and senile by then.

Fir Bolg: 'Bagmen'. A race who came to Ireland before the Dé Danaan. They do not take much part in the myths.

Fomorii: a misshapen and violent people, the evil gods of Irish myth. Their headquarters seems to have been Tory Island, off the coast of County Donegal. Their leaders include Balor of the Evil Eye, and their power was broken for ever by the Dé Danaan at the second Battle of Moytura, in County Sligo.

Gaul: Celt: Gaulish territory extended over France, Belgium, parts of Switzerland, Bohemia, parts of modern Turkey and parts of Spain.

Geis: a taboo or bond which was usually used by Druids and placed on someone to compel them to obey. Grainne put one on Diarmuid.

Goibhnin: smith god, and god of handicraft and artistry.

Goll MacMorna: leader of the Fianna before Fionn MacCumhail.

Grainne: anglicized as Grania. Daughter of Cormac MacArt, the high king. She was betrothed to Fionn MacCumhail but thought him very old, so she put a *geis* on Diarmuid to compel him to elope with her. Eventually he fell in love with her (see Diarmuid). After Diarmuid's death, although she had sworn vengeance on Fionn, she allowed herself to be wooed by him and became his wife. The Fianna despised her for this.

Laeg: charioteer to Cú Chulainn.

Lir: ocean god.

Lugh: sun god who slew his grandfather, Balor, and the father of Cú Chulainn by a mortal woman. His godly status was diminished into that of a fairy craftsman, Lugh Chromain, a leprechaun.

Macha: a mysterious woman who put a curse called *nioden* on all Ulstermen, so that they would suffer from the pangs of childbirth for five days and four nights in times of Ulster's greatest need. This curse would last nine times nine generations. She did this because her husband boasted to King Conchobhar that she could race and win against the king's horses, even though she was pregnant. She died in agony as a result.

Medb: anglicized as Maeve. Queen of Connacht, and wife of Ailill. She was famous for her role in the epic tale of the cattle raid of Cuailgne (Cooley), which she started when she found that her possessions were not as great as her husband's. She wanted the Brown Bull of Cuailgne which was in Ulster, to outdo her husband's bull, the White-Horned Bull of Connacht. This had actually started off as a calf in her herd, but had declined to stay in the herd of a woman! She persuaded her husband to join her in the great battle that resulted. The men of the Red Branch were hit by the curse of the *nioden* (*see* Macha), and none could fight except Cú Chulainn, who was free of the weakness the curse induced and single-handedly fought the Connacht champions. Mebh was killed by Forbai, son of Conchobhar, whilst bathing in a lake. The bulls over which the great battle had been fought eventually tore each other to pieces.

Milesians: the last group of invaders of Ireland before the historical period. Milesius was their leader, a Spanish soldier, but his sons actually carried out the Conquest of Ireland.

Nessa: mother of Conchobhar. A strong-minded and powerful woman who secured the throne of Ulster for her son.

Niall of the Nine Hostages: High King from AD 379 to 405, and progenitor of the Uí Neill dynasty. There is a confusion of myth and history surrounding him.

Niamh: of the golden hair. A daughter of the sea god Manannán Maclir. She asked Oísín to accompany her to the Land of Promise and live there as her lover. After three weeks, he discovered three hundred years had passed.

Nuada of the Silver Hand: the leader of the Dé Danaan gods, who had his hand cut off in the great battle with the Fomorii. It was replaced by the god of healing.

Ogma: god of eloquence and literature, from whom Ogham Stones were named. These are upright pillars carved with incised lines which read as an alphabet from the bottom upwards. They probably date from AD 300.

Oísín: son of Fionn and Sadh, the daughter of a god, and leading champion of the Fianna. He refused to help his father exact vengeance on Grainne (to whom Fionn was betrothed) and Diarmuid (with whom Grainne eloped), and went with Niamh of the Golden Hair to the Land of Promise. Oísín longed to go back to Ireland, so Niamh gave him a magic horse on which to return, but warned him not to set foot on land, as three hundred years had passed since he was there. He fell from his horse by accident and turned into an old, blind man. A Christian embellishment is that he met St Patrick, and Oísín told him the stories of the Fianna, and they had long debates about the merits of Christianity. Oísín refused to agree that his Ireland was better off for it. The spirit of his mood comes through in this anonymous verse from a 16th-century poem translated by Frank O'Connor.

> *Patrick you chatter too loud*
> *And lift your crozier too high*
> *Your stick would be kindling soon*
> *If my son Osgar stood by.*

Oscar or Osgar: son of Oísín. He also refused to help Fionn, his grandfather, against Diarmuid and Grainne. The high king of the time wished to weaken the Fianna and allowed the two clans in it, Morna and Bascna, to quarrel. They fought at the battle of Gabhra. Oscar was killed and the Fianna destroyed.

Partholón: the leader of the third mythical invasion of Ireland. He is supposed to have introduced agriculture to Ireland.

Red Branch: a body of warriors who were the guardians of Ulster during the reign of Conchobhar MacNessa. Their headquarters were at Emain Macha. The Red Branch cycle of tales has been compared to the *Iliad* in theme. The main stories are made up of the Tain Bo Cuailgne (the Brown Bull of Cuailgne or Cooley). Scholars accept that the cycle of stories must have been transmitted orally for nearly a thousand years, providing wonderfully accurate descriptions of the remote past.

From Stone Circles to Castles

Ireland is fascinatingly rich in monuments, and you cannot fail to be struck by the number and variety of archaeological remains all over the country. They crown the tops of hills or stand out, grey and mysterious, in the green fields. Myths and stories surround them, handed down by word of mouth. Archaeologists too have their theories, and they are as varied and unprovable as the myths!

Man is known to have lived in this country since Middle Stone Age times (roughly from about 6000 BC). There are no structures left from these times but, after the coming of Neolithic or New Stone Age peoples, some of the most spectacular of the Irish monuments were built.

Here is a brief description of the types to be seen in order of age.

Stone Circles

The stone circles served as prehistoric temples and go back to Early Bronze Age times. Impressive examples may be seen at Lough Gur, County Limerick, and on Beltany Hill, near Lifford, County Donegal. Earthen circles probably served a similar purpose. For example, the Giant's Ring at Drumbo near Belfast, which surrounds a megalith. They have been variously interpreted as ritual sites and astronomical calenders. They are mainly found in the southwest and north. Associated with them are standing stones.

Megalithic Tombs

Neolithic colonisers came with a knowledge of agriculture to Ireland between 3000 and 2000 BC and erected the earliest megalithic chambered tombs. They are called the court cairns, because the tombs are made up of a covered gallery for burial with one or more unroofed courts or forecourts for ritual. Pottery has been found in these tombs. Court cairns are mainly found in the northern part of the country—north of a line between Clew Bay in the west and Dundalk Bay in the east. Good examples are the full-court cairns at Creevykeel, County Sligo, and Ballyglass, County Mayo (one of a group on the west shores of Killala Bay).

Linked to the court cairns is the simple and imposing type of megalith—the dolmen or portal dolmen. This consists of a large, sometimes enormous, capstone and three or more supporting uprights. The distribution of the dolmen is more widespread but tends to be eastern. There is one with a huge capstone at Browne's Hill, just outside Carlow Town. Another variety of megalith is the wedge-shaped gallery. There are numbers of such tombs in the Burren area in County Clare, where they are built from the limestone slabs so common in the region. Most excavated wedges belong to the Early Bronze Age—2000 to 1500 BC. They are now largely bare of the cairns or mounds which covered them. The people who built them advanced from being hunters to growing crops and keeping domestic animals.

The most spectacular of the great stone tombs are the passage-graves. The best known is Newgrange, one of a group on the River Boyne, west of Drogheda, County Louth, which by its construction and by the carvings on the stones puts it amongst the most important megalithic tombs in Europe. The graves belong to a great family of structures found from eastern Spain to southern Scandinavia. The decorative carving which covers many of the stones consists of spirals, lozenges and other motifs, and it is thought to have some religious significance. Unchambered burial mounds also occur throughout the country. They date largely from the Bronze Age, but earlier and later examples are known.

Standing Stones

Also known as gallauns. Single pillar stones which also have a ritual significance, and occasionally mark grave sites. Others carry inscriptions in ogham characters.

Ring-forts

The most numerous type of monument to be seen in Ireland is the ring-fort, known also as rath, lios, dun, caher, and cashel. There are about 30,000 in the country. These originated as early as the Bronze Age and continued to be built until the Norman invasion. The circular ramparts, varying in number from one to four, enclosed a homestead with houses of wood, wattle-and-daub or partly stone construction. Well-preserved examples of stone forts are those at Staigue, County Kerry, the royal site at Grianan of Aileach, near Derry, and the cashels of the Aran Islands. Collections of earthworks identify the royal seats at Tara, County Meath, and Emain Macha, County Armagh, where earthen banks are now the only reminders of the timber halls of kings. They, like Tara in County Meath, lie at the centre of a complex tangle of myth and tradition in the ancient Celtic sagas.

Hill-forts

Larger and more defensive in purpose are the hill-forts, whose ramparts follow contour lines to encircle hill-tops. To this class belongs the large green enclosure at Emain Macha known as Navan Fort, County Armagh.

Crannogs

Crannogs, or artificial islands, found in lakes and marshy places, are defensive dwelling sites used by farmers, with even earlier origins than the forts, which continued in use sometimes until the 17th century. The Craggaunowen Centre in County Clare has a very good example, and many were found at Lough Gara, near Boyle, County Roscommon.

Early Irish Architecture

Before the Norman invasion most buildings in Ireland were of wood. None of these has survived. In the treeless west, however, tiny corbelled stone buildings shaped like beehives and called **clochans** were constructed. They were used as oratories by holy men. Some, possibly dating from the 7th century, still exist. Clochans are particularly common in County Kerry: there are many in the Dingle Peninsula and some very well preserved examples in the early monastic settlement on the Skellig Rock, off the Kerry coast. Also in Kerry is the best-preserved example of an early boat-shaped oratory, at Gallarus.

Most of the early mortared churches were modelled on wooden prototypes. They were very small, and already were built with stylistic features which are characteristic of Irish buildings: steeply pitched roofs, inclined jambs to door and window-openings. Many of these small churches would have been roofed with wood, tiled or thatched, but some were roofed with stone. The problem of providing a pitched roof of stone over a rectangular structure was solved by inserting a relieving semi-circular arch below the roof. The small space over the arch forms a croft. A fine example is Glendalough, St Kevin's Church, County Wicklow. These buildings lack features by which they can be accurately dated; a conservative dating would be from the beginning of the 9th century onwards.

Round Towers

Contemporary with these early Irish churches and very characteristically Irish, are round towers, of which about 120 are known to have existed in Ireland. They are tall, gracefully tapering buildings of stone, with conical stone roofs, which were built as monastic belfries, with the door approximately 12ft (3.5m) from the ground. This is a clue to their use as places of refuge or watch towers during the period of Viking raids between the 9th and 11th centuries. Food, precious objects and manuscripts were stored in them. The ladder could then be drawn up. There are about seventy surviving examples in varying degrees of preservation. A good example is the one on the Rock of Cashel, County Tipperary.

The monk who wrote these beautiful lines expresses the tensions of those days:

> Bitter the wind tonight,
> Combing the sea's hair white:
> From the North, no need to fear
> the proud sea coursing warrior.

version by John Montague

High Crosses

These carved stone crosses, usually in the typical 'Celtic' ringed form, contain a great variety of Biblical scenes and ornament. They are found in most parts of the country in early monastic sites. The earliest type are simple crosses carved on standing stones. They are most common in the west and in the Dingle Peninsula, County Kerry. The development of low-relief carving began in the 7th century, gradually becoming more complex, for example the cruciform slab at Carndonagh, County Donegal. It is carved with scenes of the Crucifixion, and interlaced ornament. The ringed high cross first appears at a later date; the earliest group of high crosses, dating from the 8th century, and are in southern Kilkenny and Tipperary. Good examples are at Ahenny, County Tipperary, and at Kilkieran, County Kilkenny. In this group the cross-shafts and heads are magnificently carved in sandstone with spirals and other decorative forms derived from metalwork, with figure-carvings on the bases. To the north, in the Barrow valley, is another group, later in date and more roughly carved—in granite. The Barrow group has an interesting innovation: the faces of the shafts and heads are divided into panels, in which a scene, usually biblical, is portrayed. The best of these crosses is at Moone, County Kildare.

Sandstone was used again for these crosses in the 10th century; they still grace monastic ruins scattered across the Central Plain. The West Cross and Muiredach's Cross at Monasterboice in County Louth are the best examples. In each case the east and west faces are carved with scriptural scenes while the north and south faces have spirals, vine-scrolls, and other decorations. Favourite subjects for the carver were the Crucifixion; the Last Judgment; Adam and Eve; Cain and Abel; and the arrest of Christ. Later elaborate crosses may be seen at Clones, County Monaghan, Drumcliff, County Sligo, Ardboe, County Tyrone, and Donaghmore, County Down.

By the end of the 11th century the cross was changed; the ring was often left off, and the whole length of the shaft was taken up with a single figure of the crucified Christ. Ecclesiastical figures often appear on the opposite face and on the base, and the decoration of the north and south faces usually consists of animal-interlacing. Crosses of this style were carved up until the mid-12th century. A good 11th-century cross exists at Roscrea, County Tipperary, and a good 12th-century cross at Tuam, County Galway.

Romanesque Architecture

Characteristics of this decorative style appear in Irish buildings of the 12th century. While remaining structurally simple, the Irish churches of the period have carved doorways, chancel-arches or windows, with ornament in an Irish variation of the style. The most impressive example of the style is the arcaded and richly carved Cormac's Chapel on the Rock of Cashel, County Tipperary, consecrated in 1134. The use of rib-vaulting over the chancel here is very early, not only for Ireland, but for the rest of Europe. Many of the characteristic features of the early churches, such as antae and sloping jambs, were kept throughout the Romanesque period. The use of the chevron, an ornamental moulding, is common in Irish-Romanesque work, and it is nearly always combined with rows of beading. The use of carved human heads as capitals to the shafts in the orders of the doorway may be seen in the doorway at Clonfert, County Galway which has some of the most richly carved Irish-Romanesque decoration. Also referred to as Hibernio-Romanesque.

Transitional Architecture

At the same time as the Romanesque style was so popular, another plainer type of church building was being introduced by the Cistercian order, whose first church in Ireland, Mellifont Abbey in County Louth, was designed after churches of the Continental type and carved decoration was simple. Examples of the 12th-century churches of their transitional order may be seen at Baltinglass, County Wicklow; Boyle, County Roscommon; and Jerpoint, County Kilkenny.

Gothic Architecture

With the coming of the Normans and changes they wrought, the native tradition in building declined, and Gothic architecture was introduced in the 13th century. The Irish Gothic cathedrals were on a smaller scale than their English and Continental counterparts and the grouping of lancets in the east window and south choir wall are typical of the Irish buildings, such as those in the ruined cathedral of Cashel, County Tipperary. The restored Cathedrals of St Canice, Kilkenny, and St Patrick, Dublin, are good examples. Gothic parish churches in the plain Early-English style were built only in the anglicized parts of the country, for example at Gowran, County Kilkenny.

Because of the turbulent times during the 14th century there was very little building done in Ireland, but this changed in the 15th and 16th centuries and a native Gothic style began to emerge, particularly in the west. It is best seen in the Franciscan friaries and the rebuilt Cistercian abbeys of the period. A good example of the Franciscan style, with narrow church, a tall tapering tower, carved cloister and small window openings can be seen at the well-preserved ruin at Quin, County Clare. The Cistercian style, with a larger church, a huge square tower topped by stepped battlements, and a large carved cloister, can be seen at Kilcooly and Holycross, County Tipperary.

Castles

Although the Normans had built many castles before they came to Ireland, in the first years of the invasion they built fortifications of wood, usually taking over the sites of ancient Irish forts. The remains of these can be seen all over the eastern half of the country in the form of mottes and baileys. At the end of the 12th century the construction of stone fortifications on a large scale began. An early example of Norman building skill is at Trim, County Meath. It has a great square keep in a large bailey, defended by a high embattled wall, with turrets and barbicans. Other examples of this type are at Carlingford, County Louth, and Carrickfergus, County Antrim. A very attractive feature of the Irish countryside is the ruined 15th- or 16th-century tower house. From about 1420 these buildings became common fortified farms consisting of a tall, square tower which usually had a small walled bawn or courtyard. In most cases the bawn has disappeared, but well-preserved examples can be seen at Doe Castle near Creeslough, County Donegal, Pallas, County Galway, and Dunguire (Dungory), near Kinvara, County Galway.

Glossary of Archaeological, Architectural and Associated Terms

Anglo-Norman: the name commonly given to the 12th-century invaders of Ireland, who came in the main from southwest Britain, and also their descendants, because they were of Norman origin.

Bailey: the space enclosed by the walls of a castle, or the outer defences of a motte (*see* Motte-and-bailey).

Barrel-vaulting: simple vaulting of semi-circular form, such as in the nave of Cormac's Chapel, Cashel, County Tipperary, where the vault is strengthened with transverse arches.

Bastion: a projecting feature of the outer parts of a fortification, designed to command the approaches to the main wall.

Battlement: a parapet pierced with gaps to enable the defenders to discharge missiles.

Bawn: a walled enclosure forming the outer defences of a castle or tower-house. Besides being an outer defence it provided a safe enclosure for cattle. There is a good example at Dungory Castle, Kinvara, County Galway.

Beehive hut: a prehistoric circular building, of wood or stone, with a dome-shaped roof, called a clochan.

Bronze Age: the earliest metal-using period from the end of the Stone Age until the coming of the Iron Age in Ireland, 2500 BC.

Caher: a stone fort.

Cairn: a mound of stones over a prehistoric grave; they frequently cover chambered tombs.

Cashel: a stone fort, surrounded by a rampart of dry stone walling, usually of late Iron Age date (*see* Ring-fort).

Chancel or choir: the east end of a church, reserved for the clergy and choir, and containing the high altar.

Chapter house: the chamber in which the chapter, or governing body of a cathedral or monastery met. One of the finest Irish examples is the 14th-century chapter house at Mellifont, County Louth.

Chevaux-de-frise: a stone or stake defence work set upright and spaced. It occurs at Dun Aengus, Inishmore, Aran Islands, County Galway.

Cist: A box-like grave of stone slabs to contain an inhumed or cremated burial, often accompanied by pottery. Usually Bronze Age or Iron Age in date.

Clochans (I): little groups of cottages, too small to be villages, grouped in straggly clusters according to land tenure and the ties of kinship between families. The land around the clochan forms the district known as a townland. A familiar sight is deserted or ruined clochans in mountain and moorland areas where huge numbers of people left with the land-clearances and famine during the 19th century.

Clochan (clochaun) (II): a small stone building, circular in plan, with its roof corbelled inwards in the form of a beehive. There are many examples in the west, especially in County Kerry. The word clochan is from the Irish *cloch*, a stone. The structures were early monks' cells. Nowadays they are used for storing things.

Cloisters: a square or rectangular open space, surrounded by a covered passage, which gives access to the various parts of a monastery. Many medieval cloisters survive in Ireland, e.g. at Quin, County Clare.

Columbarium: a dovecote, as seen at Kilcooly Abbey, County Tipperary.

Corbel: a projecting stone in a building, usually intended to carry a beam or other structural member.

Corbelled vault: a 'false dome', constructed by laying horizontal rings of stones which overlap on each course until finally a single stone can close the gap at the centre. It is a feature of prehistoric tombs.

Corinthian: the third order of Greek and Roman architecture, a development of the Ionic. The capital has acanthus-leaf ornamentation.

Court cairn: a variety of megalithic tomb consisting of a covered gallery for burials and one or more open courts or forecourts for ritual purposes. Very common in the North of Ireland.

Crannog: an artificial island constructed in a lake or marsh to provide a dwelling-place in an easily defended position for isolated farming families. Large numbers of crannogs (from *crann*: a tree) have been discovered as a result of drainage operations at Lough Gara, near Boyle, County Roscommon. They would have been in use until the 17th century.

Curragh or currach: a light canoe consisting of skins, or in more recent times tarred canvas, stretched over a wickerwork frame.

Curtain wall: the high wall constructed around a castle and its bailey, usually provided at intervals with towers.

Demesne: land/estate surrounding a house which the owner has retained for his own use.

Dolmen: the simplest form of megalithic tomb, consisting of a large capstone and three or more supporting uprights. Some appear to have had forecourts.

Doric: the first order of Greek and Roman architecture, simple and robust in style. The column had no base and the capital was quite plain.

Dun: a fort, usually of stone and often with formidable defences, e.g. Dun Aengus, Inishmore on the Aran Islands, County Galway.

Early English: the earliest Gothic architecture of England and Ireland, where it flourished in the 13th century. It is characterized by narrow lancet windows, high pointed arches and the use of rib-vaulting.

Esker: a bank or ridge of gravel and sand, formed by sub-glacial streams. The most notable esker in Ireland stretches from the neighbourhood of Dublin to Galway Bay: Clonmacnoise and Athlone stand on off-shoots of it.

Folly: a structure set up by a landlord to provide work for needy tenants in the 19th century, and to amuse himself.

Fosse: a defensive ditch or moat around a castle or fort.

Gallaun: *see* Standing Stone.

Gallowglass: Scottish mercenary soldier hired by Irish clan leaders to fight their enemies.

Hill-fort: a large fort whose defences follow a contour round a hill to enclose the hilltop. Hill-forts are usually Early Iron Age.

Hospital: in medieval times, an alms-house or house of hospitality with provision for spiritual as well as bodily welfare, usually established to cater for a specific class of people. The foundation of the Royal Hospital, Kilmainham, at Dublin for aged soldiers, was in the medieval tradition.

Ionic: the second order of Greek and Roman architecture. The fluted column was tall and graceful in proportion and the capital had volutes (spiral scrolls in stone) at the top.

Irish-Romanesque: the Irish variety of the Romanesque style in architecture. (See Romanesque). Cormac's Chapel, Cashel, County Tipperary; and Clonfert, County Galway, provide examples.

Iron Age: the Early Iron Age is the term applied to the earliest iron-using period: in Ireland, from the end of the Bronze Age, *c.* 500 BC, to the coming of Christianity in the 5th century.

Jamb: the side of a doorway, window or fireplace. Early Irish churches have characteristic jambs inclined inwards towards the top. The incline is called the batter.

Keep: the main tower of a castle, serving as the innermost stronghold. There is a fine rectangular one at Carrickfergus, County Antrim, and at Trim, County Meath. Round keeps are rare in Ireland, but occur at Nenagh, County Tipperary. Castles with keeps date from the late 12th century until about 1260.

Kerne: an Irish foot-soldier of Tudor times.

Kitchen-midden: a prehistoric refuse-heap, in which articles of bronze, iron, flint and stone have been found; also shellfish debris, which indicate what our ancestors ate.

Lancet: a tall, narrow window ending in a pointed arch, characteristic of the Early-English style. Lancets often occur in groups of three, five or seven, as in Cashel Cathedral, County Tipperary.

La Tène: a pre-Christian Irish classic ornamental style, which is linked to ornamental designs found in France.

Lunula: a crescent-shaped, thin, beaten gold ornament, of Early Bronze Age date—an Irish speciality.

Megalithic tomb: a tomb built of large stones for collective burial, Neolithic or Early Bronze Age in date.

Misericord or miserere: a carved projection on the underside of a hinged folding seat which, when the seat was raised, gave support to the infirm during the parts of a church service when they had to stand. Good examples in St Mary's Cathedral, Limerick.

Motte-and-bailey: the first Norman fortresses which were made of earth. The motte was a flat-topped mound, shaped like a truncated cone, surrounded by a fosse and surmounted by a wooden keep. An enclosure, the bailey, bounded by ditch, bank and palisade, adjoined it. The bailey served as a refuge for cattle and in it were the sheds and huts of the retainers. This type of stronghold continued to be built until the early 13th century.

Nave: the main body of the church, sometimes seperated from the choir by a screen.

Neolithic: applied to objects from the New Stone Age which was characterized by the practice of agriculture, in Ireland, between 3000 and 2000 BC.

Ogham stones: early Irish writing, usually cut on stone. The characters consist of strokes above, below or across a stem-line. The key to the alphabet may be seen in the *Book of Ballymote*, now in the library of the Royal Irish Academy, Dublin. Ogham inscriptions occur mainly on standing stones. The inscription is usually commemorative in character. They probably date from AD 300.

Pale: the district around Dublin, of varying extent at different periods, where English rule was effective for some four centuries after the Norman invasion of 1169.

Passage grave: a type of megalithic tomb consisting of a burial-chamber approached by a long passage, and covered by a round mound or cairn.

Pattern: the festival of a saint, held on the traditional day of his death.

Plantation castles: a name given to defensive buildings erected by English and Scottish settlers under the plantation scheme between 1610 and 1620, which were very common in Ulster.

Portcullis: a heavy grating in a gateway, sliding up and down in slots in the jambs, which could be used to close the entrance quickly. There is a good example at Cahir Castle, County Tipperary.

Rath: the rampart of an earthen ring-fort. The name is often used for the whole structure.

Rib-vaulting: roofing or ceiling in which the weight of the superstructure is carried on comparatively slender intersecting 'ribs' or arches of stone, the spaces between the ribs being a light stone filling without structural function.

Ring-fort, rath or lis: one or more banks and ditches enclosing an area, usually circular, within which were dwellings. It was the typical homestead of Early-Christian Ireland, but examples are known from c. 1000 BC to c. AD 1000. The bank sometimes had a timber palisade. Some elaborate examples were defensive in purpose.

Romanesque: the style of architecture, based on late Classical forms, with round arches and vaulting, which prevailed in Europe until the emergence of Gothic in the 12th century. See Irish-Romanesque.

Round towers: slender stone belfries, also used as refuges. Built between the 9th and 12th centuries.

Rundale: a system of holding land in strips or detached portions. The system has survived in parts of County Donegal.

Sedilia: seats recessed in the south wall of the chancel, near the altar, for the use of the clergy. A richly carved example may be seen in Holycross Abbey, County Tipperary.

Sept: in the old Irish system, those ruling families who traced their descent from a common ancestor.

Sheila-na-Gig: a cult symbol or female fertility figure, carved in stone on churches or castles. No one is sure of their origin.

Souterrain: artificial underground chambers of wood, stone, earth, or cut into rock. They served as refuges or stores and in some cases even as dwellings. They occur commonly in ring-forts and, like these, date from the Bronze Age to at least Early-Christian times.

Standing stone: an upright stone set in the ground These may be of various dates and served various purposes, marking burial places or boundaries, or serving as cult objects.

Stone fort: a ring-fort built of dry-stone walling.

Sweat houses: an ancient form of sauna. Sometimes the mentally ill were incarcerated in them for a while in an attempt to cure them.

Teampull: a church.

Torc: a gold ornament from the Middle to Late Bronze Age, made of a ribbon or bar of gold twisted like a rope and bent around to form a complete loop. They are of Middle to Late Bronze Age date. Two very large examples were found at Tara, County Meath.

Tracery: the open-work pattern formed by the stone in the upper part of Middle- or Late-Gothic window.

Transepts: the 'arms' of a church, extending at right-angles to the north and south from the junction of nave and choir.

Tumulus: a mound of earth over a grave; usually the mound over an earth-covered passage grave, e.g. Tara, County Meath.

Undertaker: one of the English or Scottish planters who were given confiscated land in Ireland in the 16th century. They 'undertook' certain obligations designed to prevent the dispossessed owners from reacquiring their land.

Vaulting: a roof or ceiling formed by arching over a space. Among the many methods, three main types were used: barrel-vaulting, groin-vaulting and rib-vaulting. Rib-vaulting lent itself to great elaboration of ornament.

Zoomorphic: describing decoration based on the forms of animals.

The Irish language is the purest of all the Celtic languages, and Ireland is one of the last homes of the oral tradition of prehistoric and medieval Europe. Preserved by the isolated farming communities, there are also many expressions from the dialects of early English settlers. Irish was spoken by the Norman aristocracy and they patronized the Gaelic poets and bards. But with the establishment of an English system of land tenure and an English-speaking nobility Gaelic became scarce, except in the poorer farming areas. The potato famine in the 1840s hit the people who lived in such areas, thousands died and emigrated, and Gaelic speaking was severely reduced.

Language

The Gaelic League, founded in 1870, initiated a new interest and pride in the language and became identified with the rise of nationalism. In 1921 its survival became part of the the new State's policy. It was decided that the only way to preserve Gaelic was to protect and stimulate it where it was still a living language. The areas where it is spoken today are mostly in the west, and around the mountainous coast and islands. They form the Gaeltacht. Here everything is done to promote Irish-speaking in industry and at home. Centres have been set up for students to learn amongst these native speakers. There are special grants for people living in Irish-speaking areas but the boundaries are rather arbitrary. In Galway there's a boundary line through a built-up area so there's a certain amount of animosity towards those living on one side of the line, Irish speakers or no! There is also the problem of standardizing Irish, for the different dialects are quite distinct. The modern media tend to iron out these with the adoption of one region's form of words in preference to others. County Donegal seems to get the worst deal, being so much further from the centre of administration, although it has the largest number of native speakers.

You can appreciate all the reasons for promoting Irish, but it is only in the last few generations that the language has become popular. Before, it was left to Douglas Hyde and Lady Gregory to demonstrate the richness of Irish language and myth, and they had the advantage of being far away from the grim realities of hunger and poverty that the Irish-speakers knew. Gaelic, like certain foods (usually vegetables), had associations with hunger and poverty, and belonged to a hard past. Even now, people prefer to use English rather than stay in the Gaeltacht existing on grants and other government hand-outs. Gaelic is a compulsory subject in schools in the Republic, and there is a certain amount in the newspapers, on television, signposts and street names (with English translations!). But on the whole it is only *just* a living language.

The carrying over of Irish idiom into English is very attractive and expressive. J. M. Synge captured this in his play *Riders to the Sea*. In fact, English as spoken by the Irish is in a class of its own. Joyce talked of 'the sacred eloquence of Ireland', and it is true that you could hardly find a more articulate people. Their poetry and prose is superb, and the emotions which their songs and ballads can release is legendary. Hardship and poverty, have not killed the instinctive desire within to explain life away with words. The monks who scribbled in the margin of their psalters wrote with oriental simplicity this poem entitled 'Winter'.

> *My tiding for you: The stag bells*
> *Winter snows, summer is gone.*
> *Wind is high and cold, low the sun,*
> *Short his course, sea running high.*
> *Deep red the bracken, its shape all gone,*
> *The wild goose has raised his wonted cry.*
> *Cold has caught the wings of birds;*
> *season of ice—these are my tidings.*

9th century, translation by Kuno Meyer

That hardship brings forth great poetry is a theory strengthened by the school of contemporary northern Irish poets who have become known all over the world: Seamus Heaney,

James Simmons, Derek Mahon, to name a few. The cutting criticisms of Brian O'Nolan (known as Flann O'Brien), the gentle irony of Frank O'Connor and the furious passion of Sean O'Casey, Patrick Kavanagh and Liam O'Flaherty to name only a few, have become part of our perception of the Irish spirit since Independence. The list of recent writers could go on and on. One can only urge you to read them. There is a particularly good anthology of short stories edited by Benedict Kiely and published by Penguin, and an anthology of Irish verse, edited by John Montague and published by Faber & Faber which you could get copies of.

Even though the disciplined cadences of the Gaelic bardic order was broken by the imposition of an English nobility in the 17th and 18th centuries, the Irish skill with words has survived, and is as strong as ever. As a visitor to Ireland you will notice this way with words when you have a conversation in a pub, or ask the way at a crossroads, or simply chat to the owners of the farmhouse where you spend the night.

The Meaning of Irish Place Names

The original Gaelic place names have been complicated by attempts to give them an English spelling. In the following examples, the Gaelic versions of the prefixes come first, followed by the English meaning.

Gaelic	English	Gaelic	English
agh, augh, achadh	a field	doo, du, duv, duf, dubh	black
aglish, eaglais	a church	dun, dún	a fort
ah, atha, áth	a ford	dysert, disert	hermitage
all, ail, aill	a cliff	glas, glen, gleann	a valley
anna, canna, éanarch	a marsh	illaun, oileán	an island
ard, ar, ard	a height	knock, cnoc	a hill
as, ess, eas	a waterfall	ken, kin, can, ceann	a headland
aw, ow, atha	a river	kil, kill, cill	a church
bal, bel, béal	the mouth (of a river or valley)	lis, liss, lios	a fort
		lough, loch	a lake or sea inlet
bal, balli, bally, baile	a town	ma, may, moy, magh	a plain
ballagh, balla bealach	a way or path	mone, mona, móna	turf or bog
bawn, bane, bán	white	monaster, mainistir	a monastery
barn, bearna	a gap	more, mór, mor	big or great
beg, beag	small	owen, avon, abhainn	a river
boola, booley, buaile, booleying	the movement of cattle from lowland to high pastures	rath	a ring-fort
		rinn, reen	a point
		roe, ruadh	red
		ross, ros	a peninsula, a wood
boy, buidhe	yellow	see, suidhe	a seat, e.g. Ossian's seat
bun	the foot (of a valley) or the mouth (of a river)		
		shan, shane, sean	old
caher, cahir, cathair, carraig	a rock	slieve, sliabh	a mountain
cashel, caiseal, caislean	a castle	tir, tyr, tír	country
clogh, cloich, cloch	a stone	tubber, tobrid, tubbrid, tobar	a well
clon, clun, cluain	a meadow	tra, traw, tráigh, trá	a strand or beach
derg, dearg	red		

an oul sceach	crosspatch	harp six	tumble
assay	calling attention, as in Hi!	he hasn't a titter of wit	no sense at all
auld flutter guts	fussy person	jar	a couple of drinks
balls of malt	whiskey	lashins	plenty
ballyhooley	a telling off (in Cork)	mended	improved in health
blow-in	stranger to the area	mizzlin	raining gently
boreen	country lane	mullarkey	man
brave	commendable, worthy, e.g. a brave wee sort of a girl	neb	nose
		nettle	drive someone barmy
		ni	now, this moment
bravely	could be worse, e.g. business is doing bravely	not the full shilling	half-witted
		oul or auld	not young, but can be used about something useful, e.g. my oul car
caution	(as in 'He's a caution'), a devil-may-care-type		
chawing the rag	bickering couple	owlip	verbal abuse
chick	child	palsie walsie	great friends
cleg	horsefly	paraletic	intoxicated
clever	neat, tight-fitting, usually refers to a garment	plamas	sweet words
		playboy	conceited fellow
coul	wintry, cold	poless	police
crack	fun, lively chat	put the caibosh on it	mess things up
cranky	bad-tempered	quare	memorable, unusual
craw thumper	a 'holy Mary' or hypocrite	qurrier or cowboy	bad type, rogue
cut	insulted, hurt	rare	to bring up, educate
dead on	exactly right	rightly	prospering, e.g. he's doing rightly now
deed	passed away, dead		
destroyed	exhausted	scalded	bothered, vexed, badly burned
dingle	dent, mark with an impression		
		she's like a corncrake	chatterbox
dip	bread fried in a pan	skedaddled	ran quickly
dither	slow	skiff	slight shower or rain
doley little fella	he's lovely	slainte	drinking toast
dulse	edible seaweed	soft	rainy, e.g. it's a grand soft day
eejit	fool		
fairly	excellent, e.g. that wee lad can fairly sing	spalpeen	agricultural labourer
		spittin'	starting to rain
feed	meal	terrible	same use as 'fierce'
fern	foreign	themins	those persons
in fiddler's green	you're in a big mess	thick as a ditch	stupid
fierce	unacceptable, extreme, e.g. it's fierce dear (expensive)	thundergub	loud-voiced person
		village bicycle	loose woman
		wean	pronounced wain, child
figuresome	good at sums	wee	little; also in the north means with, e.g. did I see you wee that man?
fog feed	lavish meal		
foostering around	fiddling about		
guff	impertinence, cheek	you could trot a mouse on it	strong tea
half sir	landlord's son		

Wise, and beautifully expressed with a delightful wry humour, these sayings and proverbs have passed into the English language. They highlight the usual Irish preoccupations with land, God, love, words and drinking, as well as every other subject under the sun. These are just a few examples; for a comprehensive collection read *Gems of Irish Wisdom*, by Padraic O'Farrell.

On God

It's a blessing to be in the Lord's hand as long as he doesn't close his fist.

Fear of God is the beginning of wisdom.

God never closes the door without opening another.

Man proposes, God disposes.

On the Irish Character

The wrath of God has nothing on the wrath of an Irishman outbid for land, or horse or woman.

The best way to get an Irishman to refuse to do something is by ordering it.

The Irish forgive their great men when they are safely buried.

Advice

No property—no friends, no rearing—no manners, no health—no hope!

Never give cherries to pigs, nor advice to a fool.

Bigots and begrudgers will never bid the past farewell.

When everybody else is running, that's the time for you to walk.

You won't be stepped on if you're a live wire.

Keep away from the fellow that was reared in his bare feet, for they will be hardened from walking on people.

If you get the name of an early riser you can sleep till dinner time.

There are finer fish in the sea than have ever been caught.

You'll never plough a field by turning it over in your mind.

Don't make a bid till you walk the land.

A man with humour will keep ten men working.

Do not visit too often or too long.

If you don't own a mount, don't hunt with the gentry.

You can take a man out of the bog but you cannot take the bog out of the man.

What is got badly, goes badly.

A watched pot never boils.

Enough is as good as plenty.

Beware of the horse's hoof, the bull's horn and the Saxon's smile.

Time is the best story-teller.

On Marriage and Love

Play with a woman that has looks, talk marriage with a woman that has property.

After the settlement comes love.

A lad's best friend is his mother until he's the best friend of a lassie.

A pot was never boiled by beauty.

There is no love sincerer than the love of food. (G. B. Shaw)

It's a great thing to turn up laughing having been turned down crying.

Though the marriage bed be rusty, the death bed is still colder.

On Argument and Fighting

Argument is the worst sort of conversation. (Dean Swift)

There is no war as bitter as a war amongst friends.

Whisper into the glass when ill is spoken.

If we fought temptation the way we fight each other we'd be a nation of saints again.

We fought every nation's battles, and the only ones we did not win were our own.

On Women

It takes a woman to outwit the Devil.

A cranky women, an infant, or a grievance, should never be nursed.

A women in the house is a treasure, a woman with humour in the house is a blessing.

She who kisses in public, often kicks in private.

If she is mean at the table, she will be mean in bed.

On Drinking

If Holy Water was porter he'd be at Mass every morning.

It's the first drop that destroys you; there's no harm at all in the last.

Thirst is a shameless disease, so here's to a shameless cure.

On the Family

Greed in a family is worse than need.

Poets write about their mothers, undertakers about their fathers.

A son's stool in his father's home is as steady as a gable; a father's in his son's, bad luck, is shaky and unstable.

On Old Age

The older the fiddle, the sweeter the tune.

There is no fool like an old fool.

On Loneliness

The loneliest man is the man who is lonely in a crowd.

On Bravery

A man who is not afraid of the sea will soon be drowned. (J. M. Synge)

On Flattery

Soft words butter no turnips, but they won't harden the heart of a cabbage either.

On Experience

Experience is the name everyone gives to their mistakes. (Oscar Wilde)

c. **8000** BC	Humans arrive in Ireland, travelling across the land bridge with Scotland.
c. **3000** BC	New Stone Age race build Newgrange in County Meath.
c. **2000** BC	Arrival of Beaker people.
c. **100** BC	Arrival of one wave of Gaelic (Celtic) peoples.
AD **200**	The Kingdom of Meath is founded, and the high kingship at Tara, County Meath begins.
AD **432**	St Patrick starts his Mission.
AD **C7–8**	Gaelic Christian Golden Age.
795	Viking raids begin.
1014	Battle of Clontarf and death of Brian Boru, the high king who won this decisive battle over the Vikings.
1170	Anglo-Norman conquest begins with the arrival of Richard, Earl of Pembroke, called 'Strongbow'.
1171	Henry II visits Ireland, and secures the submission of many Irish leaders and that of his own Norman barons.
1314	The Bruce Invasion, which failed, under Edward Bruce.
1366	Statutes of Kilkenny which forbade the English settler to speak the Gaelic language, adopt an Irish name, wear Irish apparel, or marry an Irishwoman.
1394–99	Irish leaders war with Richard II.
1534–35	Rebellion of Silken Thomas, known as the 'Kildare Rebellion'.
1541	Irish Parliament accepts Henry VIII as King of Ireland.
1558	Accession of Elizabeth I. The Reformation does not succeed in Ireland.
1562 on	Elizabethan Conquest and settlement of various counties.
1569–73	The first Desmond Revolt.
1579–83	Final Desmond Revolt and suppression.
1592–1603	Rebellion of the Northern Lords, known as the Tyrone War.
1601	Battle of Kinsale—a defeat for Hugh O'Neill, Earl of Tyrone and his Ulster chiefs.
1607	Flight of the Earls of Tyrone and Tyrconnell to the Continent.
1608	Plantation of Ulster with Scots begins in Derry and Down.
1641	Irish Rising begins. At this time, 59 per cent of land in Ireland is held by Catholics.
1642–49	Catholic Confederation of Kilkenny.
1649	Cromwell arrives in Ireland.

Chronology

1650	Catholic landowners exiled to Connacht.
1652	Cromwellian Act of Settlement.
1660	Restoration of Charles II.

1680	Accession of James II.
1689	April to July, Siege of Derry.
1690	July, The Battle of the Boyne. A great victory for William of Orange.
1691	September to October, Siege of Limerick.
1691	October, Treaty of Limerick.
1695	Beginning of Penal Laws. Catholics now own 14 per cent of land.
1699	Irish woollen industry destroyed by English trade laws.
1704	Protestant non-conformists excluded from public office by Test Act.
1714	Catholics own 7 per cent of land.
1772	Rise of the Patriot Party in parliament, known as Grattan's parliament.
1778	Organization of Irish Volunteers.
1778	Gardiner's Relief Act for Catholics eases the Penal Laws.
1779	English concessions on trade and the repeal of most of the restrictive laws.
1782	Establishment of Irish Parliamentary independence.
1791	The Society of United Irishmen founded.
1795	Orange Order founded.
1798	Rebellion of '98.
1801	Act of Union.
1829	Catholic Emancipation Bill passed.
1842–48	The Young Ireland Movement.
1845–49	The Great Famine which began with the blight of the potato harvest.
1840s on	Emigration of thousands to the New World.
1848	Abortive rising led by Smith O'Brien.
1867	Fenian Rising.
1869	Disestablishment of the Church of Ireland.
1875	Charles Parnell elected Member of Parliament for County Meath.
1877	Parnell becomes Chairman of the Home Rule Confederation.
1879–82	Land war.
1886	Gladstone's first Home Rule Bill for Ireland defeated.
1890	Parnell cited in divorce case and he loses the leadership of the Irish Party in the House of Commons.
1892	Gladstone's second Home Rule Bill defeated.
1893	Gaelic League founded.
1899	The beginning of the Sinn Fein movement.
1903	Wyndham's Land Act.
1912	The third Home Rule Bill introduced.
1913	Ulster Volunteer Force founded.
1914	The outbreak of the First World War. The third Home Rule Bill receives Royal assent, but is deferred until the end of the war.

1916	The Easter Uprising.
1918–21	The Anglo-Irish War.
1920	Amendment Act to the Home Rule Bill which allows the Six Counties in Ulster to vote themselves out and remain with the rest of Britain.
1920–21	Heavy fighting between the Auxiliaries (the Black and Tans) and the Irish Nationalist forces.
1921	July, King George V officially opens the Stormont Parliament in the Six Counties.
1921	December, the Anglo-Irish treaty signed.
1922	January, the treaty is ratified in Dail Eireann. The start of the Irish Civil War between pro-treaty majority and anti-treaty forces.
1922	November, executions of anti-treaty leaders by Free State in Dublin.
1923	End of Civil War.
1926	De Valera founds Fianna Fail.
1932	General Election. Fianna Fail win.
1937	Constitution of Eire.
1938	Agreement with Britain; economic disputes are ended. Britain gives up tributary and naval rights in 'Treaty' ports.
1939	IRA bombing campaign in Britain. Outbreak of Second World War; Eire is neutral.
1945	End of Second World War.
1948	General Election in Ireland. Defeat of Fianna Fail, and de Valera is out of office for first time in 16 years.
1952	Republic of Ireland declared and accepted by Britain, with a qualifying guarantee of support to the Six Counties.
1956–62	IRA campaign in the North.
1968	First Civil Rights march.
1969	January, people's democracy march from Belfast to Derry. Marchers attacked at Burntollet Bridge.
1969	August, British troops sent to Derry.
1971	February, first British soldier killed by IRA. August, internment of IRA suspects. Reforms to the RUC, and electoral system.
1972	Direct Rule imposed from Westminster. Stormont Government and Parliament suspended.
1973	The Sunningdale Agreement. An Assembly established with power-sharing between different political leaders.
1974	Ulster Worker's Strike brings down Assembly. Direct Rule reimposed.
1981	Bobby Sands dies after 60-day hunger strike.
1985	Anglo-Irish Agreement.
1993	Downing Street Initiative.
1994	August—IRA Ceasefire.

Brennan, M.: *Boyne Valley Vision* (Dolmen).

Craig, Maurice: *Dublin 1660–1860* (Allen Figgis).

Craig, Maurice: *Classical Irish Houses of the Middle Size: Lost Demesnes* (Architectural Press).

Crookshank, Anne and The Knight of Glin: *Painters of Ireland* c. *1660–1920* (Barrie & Jenkins).

de Breffny and Folliott: *Houses of Ireland* (Thames & Hudson).

de Breffny and Mott: *Castles of Ireland* (Thames & Hudson).

de Breffny and Mott: *Churches and Abbeys of Ireland* (Thames & Hudson).

Estyn Evans, E.: *Prehistoric Ireland* (Batsford).

Guinness, Desmond: *Georgian Dublin* (Batsford).

Further Reading

Guinness, Desmond: *Great Irish Houses and Castles* (Weidenfeld & Nicholson).

Guinness, Desmond: *Palladio* (Weidenfeld & Nicholson).

Harbison, P.; Potterton H. and Sheehy J.: *Irish Art and Architecture* (Thames & Hudson).

Henry, Françoise: *Early Christian Irish Art* (Mercier).

Maire de Paor: *Early Irish Art* (Aspect of Ireland Series).

O'Brien, Jacqueline and Guinness, Desmond: *A Grand Tour* (Weidenfeld & Nicholson).

O'Riordain, S. P. O.: *Antiquities of the Irish Countryside* (Methuen).

Sheehy, J.: *Discovery of Ireland's Past* (Thames & Hudson).

White: *John Butler Yeats and the Irish Renaissance* (Dolmen).

Burkes Guide to Country Houses: Ireland (Burkes).

Historic Monuments of Northern Ireland (HMSO 1983).

Guides and Topographical

Craig, Maurice and Knight of Glin: *Ireland Observed* (Mercier).

Harbison, Peter: *Guide to the National Monuments of Ireland* (Gill & Macmillan).

Mason, T. H.: *The Islands of Ireland* (Mercier).

Morton, H. V.: *In Search of Ireland* (Methuen).

Murphy, Dervla: *A Place Apart* (Penguin).

Praeger, R.: *The Way That I Went* (Figgins).

Robinson, Tim: *The Aran Islands* (The Author).

Synge, J. M.: *The Aran Islands* (Blackstaff).

AA Guide Book to Ireland (Hutchinson).

A Literary Map of Ireland (Wolfhound).

Irish Walk Guides

O'Suilleabhain, Sean: *No. 1 South West* (Gill & Macmillan).

Whilde, Tony: *No. 2 West* (Gill & Macmillan).

Simon, Patrick and Foley, Gerard: *No. 3 North West* (Gill & Macmillan).

Boidell, Jean; Casey, M. and Kennedy, Eithne: *No. 5 East* (Gill & Macmillan).

Martindale: *No. 6 South East* (Gill & Macmillan).

Maps

Historical Map (Bartholomew).

Ireland Map, by Bord Fáilte (Ordnance Survey).

Ireland Touring Map (Bartholomew).

Irish Family Names Map (Johnson & Bacon)—divided into North, East, South and West.

Ordnance Survey maps., 25 sheets—1:126720 (Half-Inch). (Sheet 5 covering Belfast is no longer available.)

Folklore, Music and Tradition

Cross, E.: *The Tailor and Ansty* (Mercier).

Danaher: *Folktales of the Irish Countryside* (Mercier).

Estyn Evans, E.: *Irish Folk Ways* (Routledge).

Feldman, Allan and O'Doherty: *The Northern Fiddler: Music and Musicians of Donegal and Tyrone* (Blackstaff).

Flower, R.: *The Irish Tradition* (Clarendon Press).

Gaffney S. and Cashman, S.: *Proverbs and Sayings of Ireland* (Wolfhound).

Gregory, Lady Isabella Augusta: *Gods and Fighting Men* (Smythe).

Healy, J. N.: *Love Songs of the Irish* (Mercier).

Healy, J. N.: *Percy French and his Songs* (Mercier).

Henry, S.: *Tales from the West of Ireland* (Mercier).

Hyde, Douglas: *Beside the Fire* (Irish Academic Press).

Hyde, Douglas: *The Stone of Truth and other Irish Folktales* (Irish Academic Press).

O'Boyle, Sean: *The Irish Song Tradition* (Gilbert Dalton).

O'Connell, James: *The Meaning of the Irish Coast* (Blackstaff).

O'Faolain, S.: *Short Stories* (Mercier).

O'Farrell, P.: *Folktales of the Irish Coast* (Mercier).

O'Flaherty, Gerald: *A Book of Slang, Idiom and Wit* (O'Brien).

O'Keeffe D. and Healy, J. N.: *Book of Irish Ballads* (Mercier).

O'Sullivan, Sean: *Folklore of Ireland* (Batsford).

Wilde, William: *Irish Popular Superstitions* (Irish Academic Press).

Photography

Daly, Leo: *The Aran Islands* (Albertine Kennedy).

Estyn Evans, E. and Turner, B. S.: *Ireland's Eye: The Photographs of Robert John Welch* (Blackstaff).

Johnstone and Kirk: *Images of Belfast* (Blackstaff).

Walker, B. M.; O'Brien, A. and McMahon, S.: *Faces of Ireland* (Appletree Press).

History and Literary History

Beckett, J. C.: *The Making of Modern Ireland* (Faber).

Corkery, Daniel: *Hidden Ireland* (Gill & Macmillan).

Cruise O'Brien, M. and C.: *Concise History of Ireland* (Thames & Hudson).

Cruise O'Brien, Conor: *States of Ireland* (Hutchinson).

Edwards, R. Dudley: *A New History of Ireland* (Gill & Macmillan).

Edwards, R. Dudley: *An Atlas of Irish History* (Methuen).

Foster, R. F. (ed): *The Oxford History of Ireland* (OUP)

Foster, R. F.: *Modern Ireland 1600, 1972* (OUP)

Kavanagh, P.: *The Irish Theatre* (The Kerryman).

Kee, Robert: *The Green Flag* (Sphere).

Lyons, F. S. L.: *Ireland Since the Famine* (Fontana).

MacLysaght, E.: *Surnames of Ireland* (Irish Academic Press).

MacLysaght, E.: *Irish Families: Their Names and Origins* (Figgins).

Maxwell, Constancia: *Country and Town under the Georges* (Dundalgan Press).

O'Farrell, P.: *How the Irish Speak English* (Mercier).

Stewart, A. T. Q.: *The Narrow Ground* (Faber).

Wallace, M.: *A Short History of Ireland* (David & Charles).

Burkes Irish Family Records (Burkes).

Burkes Landed Gentry (Burkes).

Biography and Memoirs

Bence Jones, Mark: *Twilight of the Ascendancy* (Constable).

Chambers, Anne: *Granuaile: The Life and Times of Grace O'Malley* (Wolfhound).

Hunt, Hugh: *The Abbey, Ireland's National Theatre 1904–79* (Gill & Macmillan).

Joyce, James: *Portrait of an Artist as a Young Man* (Longman).

Krause, David: *A Self Portrait of the Artist as a Man (Sean O'Casey through his letters)* (Dolmen).

Lyons, J. S.: *Oliver St John Gogarty*, A Biography (Blackwater Press).

Moore, George: *Hail and Farewell* (Smythe).

Murphy, William: *The Yeats Family and the Pollexfens of Sligo* (Dolmen).

O'Crohan, Thomas: *The Islandman* (OUP).

O'Sullivan, Maurice: *Twenty Years a-growing* (OUP).

Shuilleabhain, E. H.: *Letters from the Great Blasket* (Mercier).

Somerville-Large, P.: *Irish Eccentrics* (Lilliput Press).

Thomson, David: (*Woodbrook*, Penguin).

Yeats, John Butler: *Early Memories* (Irish Academic Press).

Yeats, W. B.: *Synge and the Ireland of his Time* (Irish Academic Press).

All the *Irish Heritage* Series (Eason).

Fiction

Berry, James (ed. Horgan, M. and Gertrude): *Tales of the West of Ireland* (Dolmen).

Bowen, Elizabeth: *Elizabeth Bowen's Irish Stories* (Poolbeg).

Carleton, William: *The Black Prophet* (Irish University Press).

Carpenter and Fallon (ed.): *The Writers, A Sense of Ireland* (O'Brien Press).

Crone, Anne: *Bridie Steen* (Blackstaff).

Durcan, Paul; Yeats, W. B.; Heaney, Seamus; Simmons, James and Clarke, Austin: *The Faber Book of Irish Verse* (Faber).

Edgeworth, Maria: *The Absentee* (OUP).

Farrell, J. G.: *Troubles* (Penguin).

Kickham, C.: *Knocknagow, Or the Homes of Tipperary* (Mercier).

O'Connor, Frank: *Guests of the Nation* (Poolbeg).

The Penguin Book of Irish Verse and *The Penguin Book of Irish Short Stories* (Penguin).

Novels by Edith Somerville and Martin Ross especially *The Great House at Inver* (Zodiac Press) and *The Real Charlotte* (Arrow Books).

All the plays by J. M. Synge.

Any stories by Mary Lavin (Penguin).

Any novels by George Birmingham (Blackstaff, BBC and others).

Any novels by Sam Hanna Bell (Blackstaff, BBC and others).

Any novels by Kate O'Brien (Blackstaff, BBC and others).

Any novels by William Trevor (Penguin and others).

Stories and plays, by Brian Friel (Penguin and others).

Cooking, Crafts, Flora, Fauna and Fishing

Anything by Theodora Fitzgibbon.

Allen, Myrtle: *Ballymaloe Cook Book* (Gill & MacMillan).

Heron, Marianne: *The Hidden Gardens of Ireland* (Gill & Macmillan).

Lewis, C. A.: *Hunting in Ireland* (J.A. Allen).

O'Brien, Louise: *Crafts of Ireland* (Gilbert Dillon).

O'Reilly, Peter: *Trout & Salmonn Loughs of Ireland* (Harper Collins).

O'Reilly, Peter: *Trout & Salmon Rivers of Ireland* (Merlin Unwin Books).

Reeves-Smyth, Terence: *Irish Gardens* (Appletree Press).

Webb, D. A.: *An Irish Flora* (Dundalgan).

Traditional Irish Recipes (Appletree Press).

Gill & Macmillan do a series of fishing guides on Game, Coarse and Sea Angling.

Bridgestones Guides to Where to Stay and Eat in Ireland (Estragon Press).

Major references to counties are printed in **bold**. Numbers in *italic* indicate maps.

Index

Ballycasey (Clare) 215
Ballycastle (Antrim) 361–2
Ballycastle (Mayo) 275
Ballyconneely (Galway) 244
Ballyconnell (Cavan) 427, 431
Ballycotton (Cork) 173
Ballydavid (Kerry) 153
Ballydehob (Cork) 178
Ballyduff (Waterford) 195
Ballyfarnon (Roscommon) 284
Ballyferriter (Kerry) 153
Ballygally (Antrim) 359
Ballyglass (Mayo) 582
Ballyhack (Wexford) 552
Ballyhaise (Cavan) 431
Ballyheige (Kerry) 154
Ballyjamesduff (Cavan) 433
Ballykelly (Londonderry) 341
Ballymacarberry (Waterford) 195
Ballymahon (Longford) 463
Ballymaloe House (Cork) 25, 173,
    182, 184
Ballymastocker Bay (Donegal) 417
Ballymena (Antrim) 365–6
Ballymoney (Wexford) 553
Ballymoon Castle (Carlow) 560
Ballymote (Sligo) 304
Ballynoe Stone Circle (Down) 389
Ballypatrick Forest (Antrim) 361
Ballyporeen (Tipperary) 204
Ballyragget (Kilkenny) 565
Ballyshannon (Donegal) 411
Ballyvaughan (Clare) 219
Balor 321, 575
Baltimore (Cork) 177–8
Baltinglass (Wicklow) 541
Baltray (Louth) 29
Banada (Sligo) 302
Banagher (Offaly) 475, 479
Bandon (Cork) 31, 176–7
Bangor (Down) 383, 384–5
Bangor Erris (Mayo) 274
banks 35
Banna (Kerry) 154
Bannow (Wexford) 551
Bann Valley (Londonderry/
    Antrim) 343, 351
banshee 65
Bantry (Cork) 31, 93, 178–9
Bantry Bay House (Cork) 178–9
Barleycove (Cork) 178
Barnaderg Castle (Galway) 239
Barna (Galway) 242
Baronscourt Estate (Tyrone) 331, 334
Barrow, River 484, 560
Barry, Commodore John 550

Barryscourt Castle (Cork) 172
bars and pubs 27–8, 62, 532–3
Bawnboy (Cavan) 432
beaches 32, 50
Beaghmore Stone Circles (Tyrone)
    335
Beagh's Forest (Antrim) 361
beagling 42
Beaker People 83, 147
Bealadangan (Galway) 242
Bealin (Westmeath) 469
Bear Island (Cork) 164
bed and breakfast 25, 59–60
beers 27
Beg, Lough (Londonderry) 343–4
Belcoo (Fermanagh) 325
Belfast 351, **371–82**, *374–5*
    activities 379
    centre 373–7
    eating out 380–81
    entertainment 373–4, 381–2
    festivals 373
    history 371–2
    shopping 377
    suburbs 377–9
    tourist information 373
    travel 10–11, 372–3
    where to stay 379–80
Bellaghy (Londonderry) 344
Bellamont Forest (Cavan) 76
Bellamont House (Cavan) 433
Bellanaleck (Fermanagh) 327
Bellarena (Londonderry) 342
Belleek (Fermanagh) 40, 324–5
Belle Isle (Fermanagh) 327
Belmullet (Mayo) 274
Beltany (Donegal) 420
Belturbet (Cavan) 431
Belvedere House (Westmeath)
    469–70
Benburb, Battle of 88
Berkeley Costume and Toy Museum
    (Wexford) 553
Bessbrook (Armagh) 402
Bettystown (Meath) 454
Bianconi, Charles 200
bicycle hire 15–16
Billy, King *see* William of Orange
bird-watching 42
Birr (Offaly) 479
Birr (Tipperary) 206
Black Bog (Tyrone) 334–5
Blacklion (Cavan) 432
Black Pig's Dyke 311, 316, 404,
    463
Blackrock (Dublin) 499

Blackstairs Mountains 552–3, 560
Black and Tan hounds 71
Black and Tans (Auxiliaries) 102
Black Tom *see* Ormonde, 10th Earl
    of; Strafford, Earl of
Blackwater (Wexford) 553
Blackwater Valley (Cork) 173
Blarney (Cork) 170–71
Blasket Islands (Kerry) 152–3
Blessington (Wicklow) 541
Boa Island (Fermanagh) 323
boating *see* cruising; sailing
Boggerach Mountains (Cork) 175–6
boglands 68–9, 273
Boher (Offaly) 479
Book of Armagh 65, 399
Book of Dimma 206
Book of the Dun Cow 574
Book of Durrow 480
Book of Invasions (*Lebor Gabala*)
    149, 186, 211,305, 317
Book of Kells 84, 449, 517
Book of Leinster 450, 485, 574
Book of the O'Donnells 387
booleying 221
Boolynagreana (Clare) 221
border crossings 14
Borris (Carlow) 560
Bowen, Elizabeth 174
Boycott, Captain 98, 265
Boyle family 194
Boyle (Roscommon) 284, 286
Boyne, Battle of the 89
Boyne Valley (Meath/Louth) 83, 89,
    186, 448–54
Bray (Wicklow) 538
Breen Wood (Antrim) 362
Breffni 309, 430
Breffni Castle (Leitrim) 311
Brendan, St 117–18, 153, 216, 274
Brian Boru 85, 211, 215, 317, 399
Brigid, St 115, 118, 456, 575
Bristol, Frederick Augustus Hervey,
    4th Earl of 342–3
Broadford (Clare) 216
Bronte country (Down) 393
Brooke family 104, 326, 412
Brooke, Sir Basil (Viscount
    Brookeborough) 104, 326
Brookeborough (Fermanagh) 326
Broughshane (Antrim) 366
Browne's Hill Dolmen (Carlow) 559
Bruce, Edward 86, 456
Bruce, Robert 85–6, 456
Bruce Hill (Cavan) 431
Bruckless (Donegal) 413

Newport (Mayo) 271
New Ross (Wexford) 552
Newry (Down) 392
Newry Canal 77, 392
newspapers 36
Newtownards (Down) 387
Newtown Cashel (Longford) 464
Newtown Castle (Clare) 219
Newtown-Crommelin (Antrim) 366
Newtownforbes (Longford) 462
Newtownhamilton (Armagh) 404
Newtownstewart (Tyrone) 334
Niall of the Nine Hostages 317, 579
Niamh 360–61, 579
Nire Valley (Waterford) 195
Noah 149, 323
non-conformists *see* dissenters
Norman invasion 85–6
  see also Anglo-Normans
Norsemen *see* Vikings
Northern Ireland
  Catholics in 103–6, 111–12
  cross-border cooperation 316–17
  government (Stormont) 104–6, 112
  history 100, 101–2, **103–12**,
    316–17
  peace process 107–9
  political parties 111
  religion in 114, 116, 354, 357
  see also Ulster

O'Brien family 211, 215, 217, 224
O'Brien, Flann (Brian O'Nolan) 333
O'Brien, William Smith 127
O'Brien's Tower (Clare) 220
O'Bruadair, David 142
O'Byrne family 536
O'Carolan, Turlough 285–6, 288,
  309
O'Conaire, Padraic 247
O'Connell, Daniel 94–5, 142, 148,
  217, 450–51
O'Connell, Eileen 125, 148
O'Connor family 284, 287–8, 478
O'Connor, Frank 126
O'Connor, Rory 85, 266, 478
O'Connor, Turlough 266–7, 478
O'Doherty family 421–2
O'Donnell family 271, 317, 387, 407,
  412, 418
O'Donnell, Red Hugh 86, 418
O'Dowd family 301
O'Dowd's Castle (Sligo) 301
Offaly 474–80, *476–7*, 482–4
  activities 482–3
  eating out 484

festivals 475, 479
history 474–5
shopping 482
tourist information 475
travel 475
where to stay 483
O'Flaherty family 230, 241, 246
O'Flaherty, Liam 256
ogham stones 139, 146–7, 579, 589
O'Hempsey, Denis 342
O'Higgins, Kevin 102
Oisín *see* MacCumhail, Oisín
Olderfleet Castle (Antrim) 357
Old Head of Kinsale (Cork) 172
Old Kilcullen (Kildare) 491
Old Leighlin (Carlow) 559–60
Oldtown (Meath/Louth) 453
Omagh (Tyrone) 334
O'Malley, Grace 229, 245, 270, 272,
  498–9
Omeath (Louth) 455
O'Neill family 317, 330–32, 335,
  336, 340, 421
O'Neill, Hugh 86
O'Neill, Owen Roe 88
O'Neill, Terence 105
opening hours 28, 35, 37, 38
opera 190–91, 548, 549
Orange marches 67, 112, 411
Orange Order 91, 104, 112
Oriel, kings of 337
Ormonde, James Butler, 1st Duke of
  514, 564
Ormonde, Thomas Butler, 10th Earl
  of (Black Tom) 200, 564
Ormonde Castle *see* Carrick on Suir
O'Rourke family 309, 310
O'Rourke, Tiernan 85, 187, 309,
  311–12
Ossian *see* MacCumhail, Oisín
Ossian's Grave (Antrim) 360
Ossory 563, 567
O'Toole family 120, 536, 539, 540
Oughter, Lough (Cavan) 431
Oughterard (Galway) 240
Owenahincha (Cork) 177
oyster festivals 234, 236, 248

packing 36–7
Pain brothers 76
Paisley, Rev. Ian 105, 107
Pakenham family 470–71
Palatine (Limerick) 133
Pale, the 86, 507
Pallas (Longford) 463
Pallas Castle (Galway) 236

Parke's Castle (Leitrim) 312
Parkes Castle (Sligo) 296
Parnell, Charles Stewart 97, 98,
  99–100, 537, 540
Parsons family (Earls of Rosse) 206,
  474–5, 479–80
partition of Ireland 98, 102–4
Passage East (Waterford) 191–2
passports 9
Patrick, St 84, 115, 121, 269, 275,
  580
  life of 121, 201, 382–3
Patterson's Spade Mill (Antrim) 367
Pearce, Sir Edward Lovett 76, 78
Pearse, Patrick 100, 101, 242
peat 68–9, 273
Peatlands Park (Armagh) 401
Peep-O'Day Boys 91, 93, 112
Penal Laws 90–92
pets 10, 48, 62
Pettigo (Donegal) 324
Pighouse Collection (Cavan) 431
Pillar Stone of Daithi (Roscommon)
  287
place names 593
'plantations' 87
plasterwork 77
Plunkett family 451
Plunkett, St Oliver 122, 451, 454–5
poetry *see* literature
Poisoned Glen (Donegal) 416
polo 46
Pomeroy (Tyrone) 335
ponies *see* horse fairs
Pontoon (Mayo) 276
pony-trekking *see* horse-riding
Pook 65
Portacloy (Mayo) 275
Portadown (Armagh) 400
Portaferry (Down) 385
Portarlington (Laois) 481
Portballintrae (Antrim) 364
Portbraddan (Antrim) 363
Portlaoise (Laois) 480
Portlaw (Waterford) 191
Portmarnock (Dublin) 498
Portnoo (Donegal) 414
Portora Royal School (Fermanagh)
  322
Portrush (Antrim) 30, 365
Portsalon (Donegal) 417–18
Portstewart (Londonderry) 30, 343,
  365
Portumna (Galway) 73, 236
post offices 37
potato blight 96 *see also* famine

poteen 28
pottery 40
Poulaphouca Reservoir (Wicklow) 541
Powerscourt Estate (Wicklow) 77,
  538–9
prehistoric Ireland 82–3, 114,
  316–17, 357, 485, 582–3
Presbyterians 116, 354
Preston, Thomas 88
prices 26, 36, 56–7
Prince Connell's Grave (Leitrim) 311
Prosperous (Kildare) 487
Protestant churches see Church of
  Ireland; dissenters;
  Methodists; Presbyterians
proverbs 595–6
Provisional IRA 105–9, 111
Provisional Sinn Fein 111
  see also Sinn Fein
public holidays 37
public houses see bars and pubs
Pugin, Augustus 76
Punchestown (Kildare) 484, 487

Qouile Pondage Nature Reserve
  (Down) 388–9
Quilty (Clare) 221
Quin (Clare) 216–17

Raghly (Sligo) 299
Rahan (Offaly) 480
rain 20
Raleigh, Sir Walter 133, 173
Ramelton (Donegal) 418
Ramore (Tyrone) 337
Randalstown (Antrim) 367
Raphoe (Donegal) 420
Rathangan (Kildare) 490
Rathcroghan (Roscommon) 287
Rathdrum (Wicklow) 540
Rathfarnham (Dublin) 500–501
Rathfran Abbey (Mayo) 276
Rathfriland (Down) 393
Rathgall (Carlow) 560–61
Rathgormack (Waterford) 195
Rathkeale 133
Rathlin Island (Antrim) 363–4
Rathmore (Meath) 451
Rathmullen (Donegal) 418
Rathmullen Mote (Down) 389
raths 65, 79, 589, 590
Rathvilly (Carlow) 561
Raven Point Peninsula (Wexford) 554
rebellions see risings
Recess (Galway) 243
Red Branch Knights 574, 580

Redcastle (Donegal) 423
Ree, Lough 464, 466, 468–9
religion 64, **114–22**
  history 82–4, 88–90, 99, 114–16,
    122
  see also Celts
restaurants see eating out
Restoration 88–9
Rice, Edward Ignatius 567
Richard II, King 557–8
Richhill (Armagh) 400
riding see horse-riding
Rindown, Castle of (Roscommon) 290
Ring (Waterford) 193
ring-forts 79, 583
Ring of Kerry 147–50
Rising of 1798 93–5
Rising of 1916 101
Riverside House (Cork) 170
road bowls 402
roads 12–13
Robertson, William 79
Robertstown (Kildare) 487
Robinson, Mary 110
Rockcorry (Monaghan) 439–40
Rockfleet Castle (Mayo) 272
Rockingham House (Roscommon)
  284, 286
Roman Catholics see Catholic
Roosky (Leitrim) 289, 313
Ros, Amanda McKittrick 357
Rosapenna (Donegal) 417
Roscommon 281–92, *282–3*
  activities 291
  eating out 292
  festivals 285–6
  history 284
  shopping 289, 290–91
  tourist information 285
  travel 285
  where to stay 291
Roscommon Town 289–90
Roscrea (Tipperary) 206
Rosguill Peninsula (Donegal) 417
Rosmuc (Galway) 242
Rossaveal (Galway) 242
Rossbeigh (Kerry) 149
Rossbrin (Cork) 178
Rosscarbery (Cork) 177
Ross Castle (Galway) 240
Ross Castle (Kerry) 145–6
Rossclogher Abbey and Castle
  (Leitrim) 311
Rosse, Earls of see Parsons family
Rosserk (Mayo) 276
Ross Errilly Abbey (Galway) 240

Rosses, The (Donegal) 414
Rosses Point (Sligo) 30, 297
Rossinver (Leitrim) 311
Rosslare (Wexford) 551
Rossnowlagh (Donegal) 411
Rostrevor (Down) 391
Roughan (Clare) 218
Roundstone (Galway) 40, 243–4
round towers 584
Roundwood (Wicklow) 539
Roundwood House (Laois) 481, 483
Rowallane (Down) 387
Royal Ulster Constabulary (RUC)
  105–6, 109, 111
RUC see Royal Ulster Constabulary
Rush (Dublin) 497
Russborough House (Wicklow) 541
Russell, George (A.E.) 416

safety 32–3
sailing 47–9, 51
  entry formalities 48
St Brendan's Shrine (Kerry) 153
St Brigid's crosses 115, 333
St Ciaran's Holy Well (Meath) 449
St Doulagh's Church (Dublin) 498
St Finbarr's Well (Cork) 176
St Laserain's Church (Carlow) 559
St MacDara's Island (Galway) 242–3
St Mary's Holy Well (Kerry) 144
St Mullins (Carlow) 560
St Patrick's Bed and Holy Well
  (Galway) 241
St Patrick's Day 120–21
St Patrick's Well (Tipperary) 200
St Ruth 89–90, 131, 238, 466–7
saints **117–22**
Saint's Island (Longford) 464
Sally Gap (Wicklow) 539
Salruck (Galway) 245
Salt, Lough (Donegal) 417
Saltee Islands (Wexford) 551
Salthill (Galway) 249
Sandycove (Dublin) 500
Sandyford (Dublin) 501
Sarsfield, General Patrick 89–90, 127,
  131, 468
Saul (Down) 382
Scarteen Hunt 71–2
Scarva (Down) 383
Scattery Island (Clare) 222
Scotshouse (Monaghan) 437, 441
Scotti 351–4
sea, safety 32
Seaforde (Down) 388
self-catering 60